THE LAMPLIGHTER

AMERICAN WOMEN WRITERS SERIES

Joanne Dobson, Judith Fetterley, and Elaine Showalter, series editors

The American Women Writers Series makes available for the first time in decades the work of the most significant, influential, and popular American women writers from the 1820s to the 1920s. Coming during a period of explosive growth in women's studies, this ongoing series challenges many assumptions about our twentieth-century objectivity, the sacred nature of the American literary canon, and nineteenth-century history and culture. Each volume in the series is edited by a major scholar in the field and has been entirely retypeset and redesigned.

ALTERNATIVE ALCOTT
Louisa May Alcott
Elaine Showalter, editor

STORIES FROM THE COUNTRY
OF LOST BORDERS
Mary Austin
Marjorie Pryse, editor

CLOVERNOOK SKETCHES
AND OTHER STORIES
Alice Cary
Judith Fetterley, editor

HOBOMOK AND OTHER WRITINGS
ON INDIANS
Lydia Maria Child
Carolyn L. Karcher, editor

"HOW CELIA CHANGED HER
MIND" AND SELECTED STORIES
Rose Terry Cooke
Elizabeth Ammons, editor

THE LAMPLIGHTER
Maria Susanna Cummins
Nina Baym, editor

RUTH HALL AND OTHER
WRITINGS
Fanny Fern
Joyce Warren, editor

QUICKSAND AND PASSING
Nella Larsen
Deborah E. McDowell, editor

OLDTOWN FOLKS
Harriet Beecher Stowe
Dorothy Berkson, editor

HOPE LESLIE
Catharine Maria Sedgwick
Mary Kelley, editor

THE HIDDEN HAND
E.D.E.N. Southworth
Joanne Dobson, editor

WOMEN ARTISTS, WOMEN
EXILES
"Miss Grief" and Other Stories
Constance Fenimore Woolson
Joan Myers Weimer, editor

THE LAMPLIGHTER

MARIA SUSANNA CUMMINS

Edited and with an Introduction by

NINA BAYM

RUTGERS UNIVERSITY PRESS

New Brunswick and London

Library of Congress Cataloging-in-Publication Data

Cummins, Maria S. (Maria Susanna), 1827–1866.

The lamplighter / Maria Susanna Cummins ; edited and with an
introduction by Nina Baym.

      p.   cm. — (The American women writers series)

      Bibliography: p.

    ISBN 0-8135-1332-4   ISBN 0-8135-1333-2 (pbk.)

      I. Baym, Nina. II. Title. III. Series.

PS1474.C5L3 1988

813'.3—dc19

CONTENTS

ACKNOWLEDGMENTS

I WANT TO THANK the University of Illinois Library for finding me a copy of the first edition of *The Lamplighter,* and for providing many other research amenities, without which preparation of this manuscript would have been immensely more difficult and time consuming. I owe a particular debt to my former student and research assistant, Ellen Brown, who spent the better part of a summer tracking down the sources of *The Lamplighter*'s epigraphs.

"*WHAT IS THE MYSTERY* of these innumerable editions of the Lamplighter?" Nathaniel Hawthorne grumbled in an irate letter to his publisher. And well might he complain. While *The Scarlet Letter* sold under 10,000 copies in Hawthorne's lifetime, *The Lamplighter* sold 40,000 copies in its first month alone and 60,000 more before it had been out for a year. Yet Hawthorne has had his revenge: the standard American Literature survey does not include *The Lamplighter,* or any book like it, in its syllabus. Our literary history defines the 1850s as the decade when the United States first produced a great national literature, but situates greatness in the work of Ralph Waldo Emerson, Henry David Thoreau, Nathaniel Hawthorne, Herman Melville, Walt Whitman, and Emily Dickinson. It has no place for—to quote the *Dictionary of American Biography*—"the story of a child lost in infancy, rescued from a cruel woman by an old lamplighter, adopted by a blind woman, and later discovered by her well-to-do father."

The very popularity of *The Lamplighter* has hurt its later reception. Many literary critics believe that popular literature is designed to reassure rather than stimulate its readers; it is therefore assumed to be aesthetically conventional and intellectually uncritical. The very essence of major writing, from this perspective, involves resistance to the popular. So, the argument goes, one finds the best literature of an era among its relatively eccentric and unread works (in the case of Dickinson, unpublished works)—such as *Walden, Leaves of Grass, Moby-Dick, The Scarlet Letter*—rather than among works that everybody was wild about at the time—

such as *Evangeline* (1847), *The Wide, Wide World* (1850), *Uncle Tom's Cabin* (1852), and *The Lamplighter* (1854).

Certainly no one can maintain that only popular books have lasting value. And, indeed, the persistence of "great" works beyond the age that produced them is often pointed to as proof of their superiority over the popular. Such proof, however, ignores the obvious fact that many great literary works are kept from oblivion only through the strenuous and continuing labor of critics and teachers who carry them forward from generation to generation. We could stand the elite approach on its head by arguing that to perpetuate the great tradition without examining it is a conventional and uncritical act.

We would do well to put aside the question of *The Lamplighter* as a great work, and emphasize rather that an attentive and sympathetic reading will connect us to another world and bring a perspective—whether by calling attention to similarity or difference—to our own. This other world is more than the world that *The Lamplighter* reflected; it is also world that *The Lamplighter* helped bring into being.

We begin, then, with the crucial fact that *The Lamplighter* tells a *woman*'s story, a story found with variations in many novels written in the middle of the nineteenth century. A young girl, without financial and emotional support, has to win her own way in the world. She has many trials; she triumphs. Although at the end she may be rewarded with money and dependable love, she succeeds along the way through her own powers. It is on the development and deployment of these powers that the plot centers.

On a psychological level, such a story comprises a tale of female growth and development. Like its male counterpart, and emerging historically at the same moment, this Bildungsroman shows awareness of the formative role of the early years and begins its story in childhood. It differs from the more widely studied male Bildungsroman in several fundamental ways, however. First, it is much more overtly concerned with gender, which circumscribes the heroine's options and determines her goal. Her growth and development must be carried out in a situation starkly delimited by her sex, and her success is judged according to whether she becomes a woman as well as an adult. Novels of this type register the problems of reconciling individuation with womanhood. But—and this is critical—these novels do not merely reflect a current ideology of womanhood; they participate vigorously in constructing and analyzing such an ideology. The woman's fiction attempts to show that women who cultivate dependency, passivity, or decorative uselessness—the very qualities extolled by the cult of true womanhood of the era—are dangerously unfit for real life. And in this respect these novels are anything but the intellectually uncritical documents that they have been dismissed as being. Rather, the issues with which they are engaged have not been deemed, by those in charge of our literary heritage, to be important or interesting.

Second, this women's version of the Bildungsroman is much concerned with the formation of character in the old-fashioned sense of strengthening within individuals particular traits that are deemed admirable. Chief among these are self-control and its near relation, self-discipline. This typically Victorian emphasis, which may not seem attractive to late twentieth-century readers, stems from a belief that only the firmly organized and self-controlled character can act effectively. Though character formation along these lines is essential for both men and women, it is more important for women because, first, they must compensate for starting out in a much less powerful position than men, and, second, they must struggle against a strong cultural preference for women who are weak and vulnerable.

Finally, the female Bildungsroman is much more concerned with the quality of those responsible for women's upbringing, because it was designed for an audience of women consisting equally of those who were in the process of development—young girls themselves—and those in charge of that development—mothers or mother surrogates. It follows that these fictions (although they do contain realistic elements) were not meant as accurate representations of a prior reality; facile criticism of their lack of realism is beside the point. The depictions of young women alone in the world invited women readers to scrutinize their own situations and attempted to influence their scrutiny. The form is engaged rather than contemplative; it intends to be useful. The perfect woman whom the typical female Bildungsroman features is neither a realistic character nor a role model. She is an imaginary construct who spurs, provokes, and inspires her audience.

In order for this heroine to do her work in the readers' world, that world must be made to invest its sympathy in her. The strategies of the woman's novel—characterization, story, setting, narrator intervention—focus narrowly on the central character, so that the reader has no choice but to take her part. The character must be made appealing *from the beginning*—which means, before she develops into a perfect woman. So, then, interest is created by endowing her character with serious yet endearing imperfections that mark the distance she must traverse. Almost always, the imperfections involve surplus energy: high-spiritedness, temper, passion, willfulness, impulsiveness, outspokenness. This unruly character, apt to make mistakes, is placed in a situation where the odds are against her.

Most American best sellers of the 1850s were women's novels of this type. Their popularity is tied to the emergence in this period of a vast number of women readers. And this emergence, in turn, evolved within the context of the growing urbanization of the country and the related development of an ever-larger middle class, two matters that *The Lamplighter* treats directly. *The Lamplighter*'s characters are, in the main, country folk who have come to Boston from the impoverished small towns and farms of New England. The influx depicted here corresponds with reality. Rural women—or the daughters of rural women—could not merely replicate the behavior of the uplands they had left behind. To be a woman in a new social setting was, in effect, to be a new kind of woman.

In the towns and cities, women were more likely to be literate, have time to read, and have access to books than their mothers and grandmothers on the farm. Women's historians sometimes maintain that the growth of the middle class—by separating women from the scene of production, transforming them into consumers, and confining them to the home—resulted in a decline in women's status compared to earlier times. If we think that literacy is an improvement in one's status, we must dissent from this judgment. Nineteenth-century American middle-class women themselves saw their lot as considerably better than that of earlier generations. Many women writers of the era put their disenchantment with farm life on the record. They celebrated a particularly modern type of female capability, often by contrast with an older generation of unskilled and long-suffering women.

As women became avid readers, they also became writers. In fact, for women, reading and writing were sides of the same coin. Self-styled men of letters were, in the main, slow to realize that the female audience existed and, when they discovered it, were most reluctant to write for it. Acute publishers, however, saw what was happening and opened the way—first through women's magazines and then through books—for women authors. As a result, authorship became one of the two earliest professions that American women entered in large numbers. The second profession was teaching, and many women thought of authorship as an extension of the teaching role.

In such a context, authorship might seem a natural choice to such a woman as Maria Susanna Cummins. Though relatively little is known of her life, what we do know makes clear that she was in no way a pioneer or a crusader. Born in 1827 in Salem, Massachusetts, she came from a family of high social standing and relative affluence. Both parents traced their ancestry to the settlers of Ipswich, Massachusetts. Her father, David Cummins, was a Dartmouth-educated (class of 1806) lawyer and judge. Her mother came from a family of physicians; she was David Cummins's third wife. Maria was their first child, but the twice widowed David already had four children; Maria was followed by three more children to make eight, a family size not uncommon for the time. This was a world in which almost half the children died by the age of five, in which women bore many children in hope that some would survive to adulthood, and in which death of the mother in childbirth was frequent. Therefore, men (less frequently, women) were likely to marry more than once, and families of stepbrothers and sisters were common. The ubiquitous fictional motifs of the orphan, the stepparent, and what we would call the reconstituted family today are, therefore, more realistic than we might think at first. In *The Lamplighter,* Emily Graham's father has three marriages, and Emily is the child of his first wife; his second wife has a son by an earlier marriage, while his third wife, though childless, has charge of two nieces, one an orphan and the other with only a father living.

When Maria Cummins was a young girl her family settled in Dorchester, Massachusetts, where her father became judge of the court of common pleas of Norfolk County. Dorchester, now incorporated into Boston, was then a pleasant rural suburb six miles from the city center. The Cummins family had a cultivated and comfortable life in a fine Colonial house with surrounding lawns and gardens. This home is the model for the country seat in the suburb of D—— in *The Lamplighter.*

Far from discouraging her intellectual growth, Maria's father directed her education for a time, and she was very much attached to him. The pattern of elite New England fathers supporting and supervising their daughters' educations is widespread during the period—among writers, one thinks of Margaret Fuller earlier, and of Sarah Orne Jewett later. In this situation daughters often surpassed the educational levels of their mothers and in some respects became closer to their fathers than their mothers. Maria Cummins was exposed to accomplished women as well, for as an adolescent she attended Mrs. Charles Sedgwick's Young Ladies' School in Lenox, Massachusetts. The Sedgwicks were among Massachusetts's first families, and Mrs. Sedgwick's school (located in her home, where the students also boarded) was a pioneering institution in the education of women. It became alma mater for the daughters of many prominent Massachusetts families, a large number of whom went on to become educators and writers in their turn.

As it happened, Mrs. Sedgwick's husband, Charles, was brother of the nation's foremost woman author, the much admired Catharine Maria Sedgwick, who lived a good part of the time in her brother's house and kept a sort of literary salon there. In 1822 she had published *A New-England Tale*, one of the earliest examples of women's fiction. Its heroine, Jane Elton, endures the bankruptcy and death of her once-rich father when she is twelve years old, the death of her pious, passive mother (who is unequal to the rigors of impoverished widowhood) a year later, the abuse of the aunt with whom she goes to live, and the humiliation of an impulsive and unwise engagement, undertaken mostly to get away from her aunt. But nineteenth-century Jane, in contrast to the typical eighteenth-century literary heroine, is not seduced and does not sink to an early grave. She breaks her engagement, gets a job as a teacher, rents lodgings in a boardinghouse, and in general takes control of her own life. Ultimately she marries a middle-aged widower with two daughters. They live in Jane's childhood home; becoming his wife and mother to his daughters, Jane creates for others the family that she never had. Certainly, Sedgwick meant this tale to make a historical statement about women's improving situation in the nineteenth century, and to urge women to use their new advantages.

The novel also referred to entrenched conflicts among New Englanders about religious beliefs and practice. Jane's devious aunt is an old-style Calvinist, obsessed with religious forms but neglectful of good works. Mr. Lloyd, Jane's husband, is a Quaker, for whom form means little and good works much. Thus the heroine's story of growth was placed in a construct that invoked community, family, and religion as historically specific matters impinging on female development and requiring women's attention. Moreover, this woman's story was implicitly critical of particular social and cultural practices. Therefore, Sedgwick showed not only how a woman's story might be written, but also the way women writers could use that story to comment on issues conventionally thought of as beyond their sphere.

Sedgwick would have been an inspiration to any student at her sister-in-law's school, and especially to one who thought about being a writer herself. Not the least lesson that she might have taught Maria Cummins is that a woman did not need to be ashamed of being unmarried; the single life as she exemplified it was neither wasted nor useless. Unmarried women were very much in evidence in America during Cummins's lifetime. In many families, one daughter chose—or was chosen—to live at home and take care of her parents when they grew old; this was the case, for example, with Ellen Tucker Emerson, older daughter of Ralph Waldo Emerson, as it was with Louisa May Alcott. Often, an unmarried aunt would take the mother's place in a bereaved family—the Warner sisters (Susan Warner wrote *The Wide, Wide World*) were raised by their father's unmarried sister. In still other close-knit families, no special pressure was put on the daughters to leave home if they chose not to—the family of Emily Dickinson is a case in point. Women who were sickly (as, for example, Alice James, sister of William and Henry) were also free not to marry. Catharine Sedgwick did not marry, nor did either Warner sister; the sisters Alice and Phoebe Cary, both poets, kept house together in New York City at the center of feminist and literary circles, happily single. While the married woman was supposed to be thoroughly content with her lot, the unmarried middle-class woman was virtually enjoined to seek some useful alternative to bearing and raising children; this in itself could be an incentive not to marry. Returning to Dorchester after her schooling was completed, Cummins remained single.

Without any doubt Cummins would have thought of her writing as a way of making a contribution to society. For both men and women in New England at this time, writing had to be justified in social and moral terms. Neither the romantic mode of self-expression, nor the Platonic ideal of an intellectual life above the fray, was appropriate for descendants of the Puritans. The gender difference—and certainly there is one—involved audience. It was not deemed appropriate for women to address men in a public manner. Women authors, therefore, had to limit their explicit aims to the improvement of their own sex and children. Men could and did read women's books, but the implied audience of *The Lamplighter* is exclusively female. Male characters in the book are seen almost entirely in their relations to, and contact with, the women characters. And the purpose of such representations is to consider the way women may use their contacts with men to exert influence upon them.

SUSAN WARNER'S *Wide, Wide World,* published in 1850, propelled the female Bildungsroman into the very center of the literary landscape. This novel established the category of the best seller as we know it today, and thus revolutionized the publishing industry. It went through fourteen printings in two years and for the first time made publishers aware of the potential size of the book-buying public. The runaway success of the novel made it clear, too, that this public was significantly composed of women, and from that moment to our own time book publishers, no matter how they might publicly denigrate women writers and readers, have known that publishing depends on such women.

In *The Wide, Wide World* the heroine, Ellen Montgomery, endures separation from, and then the death of, her beloved invalid mother when she is ten; abandonment by her irresponsible father, who drowns soon after; the exploitation and petty cruelty of her Aunt Fortune, on whose farm in rural New York she goes to live; and the assorted nastinesses of various minor characters among whom her lot is thrown. The resemblance to *A New-England Tale* is far from accidental. But unlike Sedgwick's Jane Elton, Ellen Montgomery is spoiled and "passionate," and much of her training for adulthood consists in learning to endure what she cannot cure. In such an education, she has the example and guidance of a young neighbor, Alice Humphreys, who advises Ellen to try to win over her aunt "by untiring gentleness, obedience, and meekness." The strength for such an effort will come by turning to God, who is found within oneself at the moment when all other support fails. In fact, Alice explains, God's strategy is precisely to remove all external aids so that one has no place else to turn.

There is less human goodness, and the good are less powerful, in Warner's world than in Sedgwick's. Though the novel preached triumph through submission, it presented such submission as a form of passive resistance and carried its point by appealing to the reader's defiant emotionality rather than, as Sedgwick had, to the reader's common sense. Warner's vision was also much less social than Sedgwick's, concerned with the inner life far more than the outer. What Ellen wins, she wins for herself alone. From Sedgwick's Unitarian vantage point, the Calvinist Warner would be insufficiently interested in her heroine's good works, and the goodness or badness of the other characters would be assessed too narrowly according to whether they were good or bad *to Ellen*.

The success of *The Wide, Wide World* inspired a host of imitations and derivatives and helped to create several successful authorial careers, including that of Maria Cummins. *The Lamplighter* was published when she was only twenty-seven. Considerably outselling even *The Wide, Wide World*, it became the second most popular book of the decade, surpassed only by *Uncle Tom's Cabin*. It was rapidly translated into French (*L'allumeur de réver-*

bères), German (*Der Lampenputzer*), Danish (*Lampenpudseren*), Italian (*Il lampionaio*), and other languages. And, like most American books, it was reprinted by several British publishers. After the copyright expired in the 1890s, many cheap reprint publishers issued it in a variety of formats; such reprintings appeared almost yearly until the 1920s.

Such similarities would have emphasized to contemporary readers Cummins's rewriting of Warner's story in a more benevolent and rationalist mode, a returning to the Sedgwick camp. There are many more good people in Cummins's novel, the sexes are less polarized, power is less concentrated. And the story is kinder to its characters: where Ellen's mentor Alice dies, Gerty's Emily is rewarded with earthly happiness. Where Ellen's eventual husband will be her master and superior, Gerty's will be a friend and equal. And, most significantly, *The Lamplighter* imagines social usefulness for its heroine; *The Wide, Wide World* does not. Each novel has a fairy-tale ending, but in one case (Ellen's) the heroine is rescued from society while in the other (Gerty's) she is firmly planted within it. (And the self-centered vision of *The Wide, Wide World* is even more clear in the recent Feminist Press edition, which includes a final chapter, never published before, where Ellen receives from her new husband the ultimate earthly gift of a beautifully furnished sitting room: a room of her own.) For Gerty, throughout *The Lamplighter*, the ideal room is shared with others: the key questions are all relational. In sum, while working closely with the materials of *The Wide, Wide World*, Cummins revises them in *The Lamplighter* by insisting that women and men alike had work to do in God's good world, that self-improvement was not a private matter.

The Lamplighter gripped its readers not only by its woman's story, but also by its urban setting and working-class characters, as well as its depiction of an emergent middle class. The phenomenal growth of American cities in the 1840s created a host of anxieties and interests to which fiction responded with a literary form known at the time in America as the metropolitan novel. This form originated in Europe, with the novels of such French authors as Honoré de Balzac, Victor Hugo, and above all Eugène Sue whose *Mysteries of Paris,* published serially in 1842 and 1843, created a storm in its several American translations. An even more important practitioner of the genre for Americans was the Englishman Charles Dickens.

Throughout his career, which began in 1836 with *The Pickwick Papers,* Dickens was the most popular author in the United States. His phenomenal combination of talent and success was almost single-handedly responsible for the common complaint that America lacked comparable literary talent to the Old World. Dickens usually set his novels in London, among the very poor, whom he treated with immense sympathy. The vision of urban life, articulated within the frame of the English class system, implied that the urban poor turned to antisocial and criminal activities only because they had no opportunity to rise in society. The criminal was interpreted as a comment on the criminality of the social structure that produced him. The possibility and even desirability of social revolution were strongly suggested in Dickens's pages.

With their own revolution not that far behind them, American critics and writers claimed that a Dickensian critique of society was irrelevant on this side of the Atlantic. But when, in the second quarter of the nineteenth century, American cities grew larger and wealth became more concentrated, this country seemed to be developing a class structure of its own. By 1850, questions concerning poverty and the character of the urban poor, wealth and the character of the urban rich, class rigidity and social mobility, responsibility for the cities and means of administering them—such questions had become intensely important and interesting to the American public. Conservative and liberal critics alike saw a new danger in the Dickensian glorification of outcasts. Granting that a rigid class structure might drive people to crime, they insisted that in the American republic class was based on merit. Nobody in this country had to remain poor, or become a criminal to get rich. With virtue and hard work, anybody could become middle-class, and to be middle-class was better than to be wealthy. In *The Lamplighter,* Cummins Americanized the Dickens story along these lines, concentrating on the virtuous, rather than the vicious poor and presenting them as essentially middle-class in their styles of life and values.

The Lamplighter thus was conversing not only with Susan Warner and women's fiction, but also with Charles Dickens and urban melodrama. This intertextuality is worth noting for at least two reasons. First, we must be careful not to think of women writers as sealed in a literary tradition inhabited only by other women. Especially where fiction and poetry are concerned, literate women had access to the writings of precursors and contemporaries who were men as well as women. They were free to follow and borrow as they chose. Second, writers do not—cannot—approach the real world directly, nor spin fantasies out of some pure, noncultural psychological core. Their work is always a discourse with other writing, through which their representations are mediated. Even diaries, journals, and letters—where we might seek raw experience—are composed ac-

cording to conventions. *The Lamplighter* is equally Cummins's attempt to
write about women's experience in a particular contemporary setting and
her deployment of the established conventions of women's fiction and
urban novels in a particular (and, from the point of view of her contemporaries, particularly successful) way. The search for writing that leads directly to women's experience, whether past, present, or future, cannot
succeed; even the most experimental women's writing will produce only
new conventions. We want to think about, then, not how *The Lamplighter* is
or is not true, but what its deployment of conventions might have contributed to the very construction of the truth that Cummins's contemporaries experienced.

THE LAMPLIGHTER introduces Gerty, our heroine—"but eight years old,
and all alone in the world." It is a chilly November evening and the orphan
child is out on the street, hiding from Nan Grant, the cruel woman with
whom she lives. Soon she is summoned indoors and locked in the dark
garret for the night. A situation in which the street must serve as a refuge
from home and a woman is a child abuser calls out for correction. And a
man—kindhearted Trueman Flint, the lamplighter—will soon come to
the rescue. As Nan is identified with the dark, so is Trueman Flint linked
with light. In Gerty's imagination the stars become lamps, lit by a more
distant lamplighter. This childish vision implies the possibility of religious
and ethical growth.
    The religious ideology within which the novel operates is made overt
at the end of the first chapter. "Poor little, untaught, benighted soul! Who
shall enlighten thee? Thou art God's child, little one! Christ died for thee.
Will he not send man or angel to light up the darkness within, to kindle a
light that shall never go out, the light that shall shine through all eternity!"
Aimed at an audience of Protestant Christians, *The Lamplighter* does not
argue for Christianity per se but for a particular kind of Protestantism.
Holding that the possibility of enlightenment exists in everyone, even an
abused and abandoned child, it rejects the Calvinism still strong in New
England; declaring that enlightenment is a gradual educative process, it
rejects the Evangelicalism increasingly prominent in American religious
life. Everyone has an inner light, but all need confirmation and strengthening through social relations.
    When an enraged Nan Grant throws Gerty out for good (ch. III),
Trueman takes her home with him. A native of New Hampshire who was
orphaned and came to Boston when he was fifteen, he is now "between

fifty and sixty years old, a stoutly-built man, with features cut in one of nature's rough moulds, but expressive of much good-nature." He is touched by Gerty's plight. "All alone in this big world, and so am I. Please God, we'll bide together." He lives by himself in one disorderly room in a poor but respectable tenement. His near neighbor, Mrs. Sullivan, makes new clothes for ragged Gerty and then undertakes to make his house into a home by tidying it up and showing Gerty how to keep it neat. Mrs. Sullivan is the widow of a country clergyman and living with her aged father, Mr. Cooper, Trueman's good friend. Her son Willie boards with the pharmacist who employs him, but comes home for weekends. Like Trueman, these people have been swept into Boston on the tide of migration from the poor farms and towns of New England. And, in Cummins's vision of city life, they form a network, a neighborhood.

For Mrs. Sullivan, cleanliness and order are identical with virtue and happiness, and although the narrator is gently humorous about her passion for neatness, the book supports her position. There is no such thing as a home without love or without order. The tangible space in which one lives literally forms the self; successful self-formation requires the organization and ordering of psychic space. A disorderly home will produce a disorderly person—it is as simple, and as profound, as that.

From the start, then, Gerty's development is linked to the home, and this word in turn becomes the key to understanding the right interrelations of human beings. The possibilities and liabilities of home come into play as soon as more than one person occupies a given space, and have little to do with whether people are actually kin. If, at the poor end of the social scale, Nan Grant fails to make a home, so (later in the novel) do Mr. Graham and this third wife, the widow Holbrook, at the wealthier end. While *The Lamplighter* implies that home may be anywhere that human beings are in right relation to each other, it also suggests that home has a better chance in some surroundings than in others. The middle range between poverty and fashion is best. Among the poor, women are too often overloaded with care; among the rich, they are too often diverted by social entertainments. What we are seeing here, in brief, is the campaign for the stable middle-class style of life as antidote to social turmoil in nineteenth-century America.

Now, ensconced in a home—albeit only one room—and aided by the extended network of friends and benefactors which radiates from Trueman, Gerty begins her transformation from wild thing into Christian lady. She flourishes in the loving atmosphere provided by True, Mrs.

Sullivan, and Willie (who is five years older than she and, of course, a natural for her eventual husband). Such good family traits as respect, love, support, aid, and instruction, are exercised; the bad—cruelty, competition, the urge to dominate—are nowhere to be found. These early chapters of the book create, with this odd assortment of characters, a true idyll of the family.

Trueman Flint's network also extends to the wealthy Emily Graham, the blind daughter of a former employer. While working for Graham, True suffered a serious accident that depleted his savings and reduced him to work at various odd jobs; yet True's attitude is only one of gratitude for whatever favors Graham now does for him. Relations between employer and employed in *The Lamplighter* smack of the feudal; thus Cummins avoids the fear of class unrest—or rather, puts that fear to rest—in her positive depiction of the city.

The devout Emily first subsidizes Gerty's education and then takes charge of it. For the child, and for her guardians, the chief obstacle to growth is interior—Gerty has a fierce temper. Temper, the unrestrained expression of passion and anger, is the novel's word for all that is most destructive in human relations. It also stands for that which destroys the self. In contrast to an ideology of romantic individualism, the view here is that temper not only represents the disintegration of an organized self but actually contributes to such disintegration. Cummins is hardly a Freudian—it would seem difficult to imagine anything less Freudian than her perspective here—but one could easily think of temper as the eruption of the id into the space of the ego, a form of insanity or pathology. Much later in the novel, when Emily tells Gertrude how she came to be blind, this vision is forcefully presented again.

Now, as a naturally good person, Gerty seldom feels temper unless she is being unjustly treated; yet, to become an enlightened adult, she has to understand why displays of temper even in the face of injustice are destructive to others and to self. And before she is adult enough for understanding, she has to be trained in self-control. Home here is the space where such training can be carried out with love, because only love will induce children to do what otherwise seems so contrary to their impulses. We understand that all of Nan Grant's threats and punishments only exacerbated Gerty's temper and would have led, over time, to her becoming another Nan Grant. Nan's ideological function in the novel is to justify the argument that temper must be controlled. And in case we are not prepared for the intellectual level of this representation, we are led by our strong emotional involvement with Gerty to detest everything that Nan stands for. Nan, on the one hand, and the third Mrs. Graham, on the other, represent the book's most serious examples of human failure.

These failures are women. Does this mean that Cummins is hostile to women? On the contrary, it is her high estimate of women's capabilities, along with her stern sense of their responsibilities, that leads her to feature these women who fall short. The home is their work place, and the business of creating human beings within it is their particular work. It is not that men lack home values—if well trained (for their childhood training is also women's work) they will have them. But these values include the allocation of the home's work to women, and thus the man with home values will value a woman who values home. So Willie—like all good men, a product of his mother's loving upbringing—announces near the end of the novel that what he has looked forward to during the years of separation from Gerty is a home, which he may share with her; and Gerty, in his mind, stands for the perfection of the home-loving woman (ch. XLIV).

This looks like a closed circle—training women *in* the home, *by* the home, and *for* the home, to assure the burden of creating characters whose highest value will be *of* the home. It *is* a closed circle. The moment that either the values of home begin to be questioned, or the gendered distribution of its workload is questioned, one steps outside the circle and sees it as an elaborate cultural construct rather than a natural fact of human life.

If Gerty has a temper that is stirred by injustice, then the example of Emily, who has been accidentally blinded for life, confronts her continuously with an injustice beyond anything she can comprehend, and also with a pious acceptance of it. At the end of Chapter I, the narrator has implored God to send "man or angel" to light the way for Gerty. Trueman Flint is the man, Emily Graham the angel, who answer the narrator's prayer. Emily is the "messenger" (the literal meaning of the word angel is messenger) "from whose closed eyes the world's paths were all shut out, but who had been so long treading the heavenly road, that it was now familiar ground. Who so fit to guide the little one as she, who with patience had learned the way?" (ch. XI). Emily's message is her Christlike example. The Christ whom she exemplified is, in many respects, a feminized or infantilized figure, submissive to the father's will. Christ's death is viewed, from this perspective, as an example that humanity can and should attempt to emulate. Christ is not the atoner, but the heavenly teacher, and his message had become entrusted to women.

The idea among devout women that they had been appointed to

convey the message of true religion formed, in this period, a tremendous source of self-esteem. At the same time, however, it implicated them in a power system from which they were institutionally estranged. For this reason religion is essentially informal in *The Lamplighter* and other women's fiction in which Christianity plays a significant role. Emily, not the Reverend Mr. Arnold, is Gertrude's religious instructor. "I know of no religion but that of the heart," Gertrude will instruct another in turn (ch. XXXIX). The religion of the heart allows women to play a role that the religion of formal observance does not.

By Chapter XII, Gerty has been educated. Now it is time for testing. The second quarter of the novel (chs. XIII–XXVI) shows her passing through several trials. First comes a moving sequence in which Trueman Flint suffers a stroke, sickens, and dies; the twelve-year-old Gerty, more often now called Gertrude in recognition of her maturity, becomes his nurse and stays at his side until the end. Then, when she moves to the Grahams' as the informal ward of Emily, she must endure the malice of the jealous housekeeper Mrs. Ellis. Willie, her dearest friend, departs for a clerkship in India (he is effectively out of the action from chapters XVII to XXXVIII). But by far the most important test involves Gertrude's decision to disobey Mrs. Graham by taking a teaching job and moving in with the ailing Mrs. Sullivan and her infirm father. What Gertrude does here is heroic on many counts: she drops down several notches on the social scale, she leaves a comfortable life for a difficult one, and above all she crosses Mr. Graham and thereby loses his protection. Once more, then, Gertrude is on her own in the world.

The chapters in which she comes to this decision and implements it (chs. XX–XXII) constitute a major crisis in the novel and represent an obligatory moment in the female Bildungsroman, the moment when the heroine defies unjust patriarchal authority. Graham maintains that he and Emily have rescued Gertrude from penury and that she owes him unquestioning obedience in exchange. Neither love nor pleasure are at issue here; it is a matter of principle, a conflict between duty as defined by Gertrude's inner sense of right and duty as defined by the outer law, the law of the father. In a long female antinomian tradition in America, one that goes back to Anne Hutchinson, Gertrude chooses and accepts exile, even though it means separation from Emily.

Following the deaths in rapid succession of Mrs. Sullivan's father and then Mrs. Sullivan herself, Gertrude moves into a boarding house and continues her teaching. For one brief chapter, she is an independent and happy woman. Now, however, comes another test. Mr. Graham unexpectedly marries a fashionable widow with a couple of dependent nieces. Emily now needs support. As one of Gertrude's friends expresses it, to return to the Graham household means "not merely giving up three hundred and fifty dollars a year of her own earning, and as pleasant a home as there is in Boston; it is relinquishing all the independence that she has been striving after, and which she was so anxious to maintain." Nevertheless, Gertrude chooses to return. In doing so, she completes the repayment in kind of all those who had helped her: Trueman Flint, Mrs. Sullivan, and now Emily. So, by the end of Chapter XXVI, when Gertrude returns to the Grahams', her testing period is over.

Or is it? In the Graham household as it has been revamped by the new Mrs. Graham and her entourage, Gertrude faces new unpleasantness. Her virtue is tested (very briefly) by the temptation to join the fashionable world, and (more protractedly) by the malice of that world when she declines to do so. To many readers of the book today, this third quarter of the novel (chs. XXVII–XLI) may seem disconnected from the earlier part of the story. But the struggle of Emily and Gertrude—Gertrude above all on *behalf* of Emily—to preserve "home" as they know it, within the space that has now been appropriated for worldly values, is very much of a piece with the larger story that *The Lamplighter* has been telling. And, in chronicling this struggle, the novel uses Gertrude to critique the emergent American moneyed aristocracy from the standpoint of liberal Protestant domesticity.

This critique focuses on two matters: the aristocratic style of life and aristocratic manners. The critique of the style of life centers, as suggested above, on the question of what the fashionable world does with "home." In the space of Graham's suburban retreat, the quarrel between Mrs. Graham and her niece Isabel (with the wavering complicity of the second niece, Kitty) on the one side, and Gertrude and Emily on the other, is expressed by the contrast of the downstairs parlor where guests are entertained with the upstairs sitting room where our two heroines pass their days. In one space are strangers, loud noise, late hours, rudeness, vapid conversation, continual coming and going; in the other, reading, writing, thinking, communing, wit, laughter, affection.

In Mrs. Graham's parlor, the home is becoming an outpost of the world and thereby losing all its moral force. The contrast between the insincerities of the downstairs parlor and the simplicities of the upstairs chamber is made many times. It is registered with particular intensity, for example, in Mr. Graham's awareness one night when he returns un-expectedly and unannounced from a long business trip (ch. XXXIII):

> The parlor was so brilliantly lighted that he at once suspected the truth that a large company was being entertained there. He felt vexed, for it was Saturday night, and in accordance with old New England customs, Mr. Graham loved to see his household quiet on that evening. He was, moreover, suffering from a violent headache, and, avoiding the parlor, he passed on to the library, and then to the dining-room; both were chilly and deserted. He then made his way upstairs, walked through several rooms, glanced indignantly at their disordered and slovenly appearance,—for he was excessively neat,—and finally gained Emily's chamber.

Here, upon opening the door noiselessly, he is treated with the sight of "fire-light reflected upon the white curtains, the fragrant perfume which proceeded from a basket of flowers upon the table, the perfect neatness and order of the apartment, the placid, peaceful face of Emily, and the radiant expression of Gertrude's countenance."

Although Gertrude and Emily have made themselves a home within their home, their effective banishment from those spaces where home mediates with the outer world signifies a decline in domestic power. It is no wonder, then, that the two are most happy when the new family goes to Europe for a season and leaves them to board in Boston. Returning to the very boardinghouse where Gertrude had lived independently, they pass a season of "undisturbed tranquillity" (ch. XXXIV). For a few hours each day, Gertrude works at the school where she had previously taught; other-wise the two friends attend lectures, concerts, art galleries, socialize with "a small but intelligent circle of friends," walk, and work among the poor. Although this is, for them, the season when they live "in a beautiful world of their own," the reader cannot fail to notice that they are living in exile. Could it be that at the moment of its most intense affirmation, domestic ideology is shown to lack the material foundation on which it must rest? To be, that is, a lost cause?

The critique of fashionable manners contrasts the sincerity of Gertrude's manner with the mannered artifice of society, and especially with the behavior of Gertrude's archrival, Isabel. Isabel, or Belle as she is called, would be a familiar figure to readers of fiction by women. She is the belle of the ball, the superficial and self-engrossed social butterfly, the heroine's foil. Numerous scenes in which Gertrude, the victim of Belle's petty malice, declines to respond in kind, serve to point up not only the falsity but the essential incivility of manners as they are practiced by the very group that defines itself as civilized. For they amount to nothing more than the repeated and self-conscious assertion of one's superiority to others; in *The Lamplighter,* the moment one lays claim to such superiority, one loses it. To assert superiority requires one to undermine the Other, while true manners consist always in sympathizing with the Other, putting oneself in the place of the Other, and when called upon to do so, putting the Other ahead of the self. The last thing in the world that Belle could do is put anybody ahead of herself—in fact she is always competing for pre-eminence—and therefore, despite all her advantages, she is essentially a savage.

The idea of good manners here is not simply a matter of correcting Belle's outward behavior, however. When at one point Kitty asks Gertrude how she can learn to be polite, Gertrude answers to the effect that she must cultivate her heart (ch. XXIX). The idea, again, is of a second nature: of sincere outward behavior that corresponds to learned principles and feelings. It is not the cult of the heart, but the *cultivation* of the heart, that is advised. Once more education is the key, and women are the educators. Thus, in the third section of the book, Gertrude functions as the teacher of proper behavior to elite women—both women characters *in* the book and women readers *of* the book.

A paradigm to others in this section, Gertrude still has her own problems. Willie, returned at last, appears to have defected to the glamorous Isabel. And Emily's health is clearly failing. Faced with the apparent loss of her dearest friend, and the imminent loss of another, Gertrude arrives at the low point of her adult life (ch. XXXIX). At just this point, a mysterious older man appears on the scene and takes an intense interest in her; and now, at last, Emily tells Gertrude the awful story of how she came to be blind (ch. XL). After this recitation, Gertrude feels her "heart penetrated with that deep love and trust which seldom come to us except in the hour of sorrow, and prove that it is through suffering only we are made perfect."

These words signal that Gertrude, through vicarious participation in Emily's agony, has at last become perfect, that is, Christlike. They mark the moment in *The Lamplighter* that probably makes the greatest demand on a late twentieth-century reader's capacity for imaginative historical projection. In the context of our radically different approach to human nature, we may miss completely the intended force of this transcendent moment in the novel. And likewise we may find Gertrude's exalted and consequent action simply incomprehensible: during a shipboard fire, she substitutes Isabel for herself so that Isabel is rescued, by the mysterious stranger, in her stead (ch. XLI).

This deed of inspired heroism moves Gertrude far beyond the gendered goodness that she has exemplified in the novel to this point. Nothing in her behavior previously has challenged the idea that women were the more physically timid, the weaker sex; she has been a paragon, but her heroism has been heroinism—the purely womanly activities of nursing, teaching, consoling. Even her defense of Mr. Graham had its womanly justification. Now, however, Gertrude does something that makes her a "hero." Emily's word for Gertrude, when she learn of the deed, is noble and that word has been carefully chosen for its masculine aura. Gertrude's best deed by far—in a novel devoted to expounding domestic ideology— shatters the constraints of domesticity.

From the depths of despair to the heights of heroism in two chapters: the novel has now exhausted its force and can only descend toward its resolution. For nine satisfying chapters, readers who have come to care about Gertrude, and Emily as well—readers who do not believe for an instant that noble Willie would prefer Isabel; readers who know, somehow, that the mysterious stranger augurs well for Gertrude—will enjoy the clearing up all mysteries, the righting of all misunderstandings, and the bestowal of appropriate rewards on both Gertrude and Emily. Religious as the book may be, and confident of heaven as the place where all earthly wrongs will be set right, The Lamplighter is a novel after all—a worldly form, and not prepared to postpone the happiness of its heroines to the afterlife.

WHEN SHE WAS thirty-seven, Cummins became seriously ill; she died two years later in 1866, from an "abdominal complaint." After The Lamplighter she was able to write only three novels: Mabel Vaughan (1857), El Fureidîs (1860), and Haunted Hearts (1864). These later works varied the woman's story and situated the variant within a different fictional and representational world. The vision of women and their potential seems quite different in each.

As The Lamplighter tells the story of the poor girl's rise, Mabel Vaughan (1857) tells that of the heiress's fortunate fall—fortunate, because she does not stay fallen and rises again. Both novels identify the fullest development

Introduction

of a woman's powers with upper middle-class existence. But unlike *The Lamplighter*, which accepts the presence of an urban American aristocracy and sets about improving that aristocracy, *Mabel Vaughan* is passionately hostile to the upper class. Mabel's situation as a rich girl is all sham. Reduced to objects of display in the world of wealth, women lack all power; trained as ornaments, they would be incapable of using power if they should have it. Conversely, the wealthy class is corrupt precisely because it is organized to exclude the particular kind of power that women might exercise—what is called in several didactic passages the power of love. In other words, and in contrast to *The Lamplighter*, *Mabel Vaughan* sees no possibility for middle-class values to take hold among the elite, and thus finds the group unredeemable.

The story proper begins when eighteen-year-old Mabel leaves her country home and joins her wealthy widower father and her brother in the city. With her married sister—the novel's belle—Mabel joyfully immerses herself in society, neglecting her father and brother while her sister neglects husband and children. Mabel gets involved with a sophisticated older man, whose attentions flatter her vanity. In short order, however, the sophisticate finds a more brilliant woman, the brother becomes an alcoholic, the sister's husband is killed in a train wreck and turns out to be bankrupt, the sister goes into shock and dies, the father loses all his money. The only possession left is a tract of Illinois land, and here the chastened family (including the dead sister's two young sons) makes a new life centering on hard work and on the woman—Mabel—who is its domestic core.

The novel tries to convince us that Mabel is not only busier, but happier, on the Illinois prairie than she was when triumphing as the belle of the ball. Thanks to her strength, energy, and the loving support that she gives her father, brother, and nephews—significantly, all males—the Vaughans do not stay poor for very long. Nor does the prairie long remain empty; within six years the Vaughan homestead becomes the hub of a community where everybody lives comfortably but nobody is rich. Mabel gets a husband, but the conclusion emphasizes romance less than the forging and maintaining—by women—of their families and of an extended, quasi-kinship system of friends and neighbors.

To situate Mabel in an all-male family is to address, more directly than *The Lamplighter*, the question of whether a male ideology (stressing competition, individualism, and materialism) or a female ideology (stressing cooperation, community, and love) was better: for women, for men, and for the nation. In *The Lamplighter*, there is certainly a conflict of values,

Introduction

but the exponents of the two systems do not divide along strict gender lines. Both Trueman Flint and Willie Sullivan are womanly men, while Gertrude, as we have seen is ultimately a manly woman. At the same time, *The Lamplighter* is replete with close friendships among women, of which that between Gertrude and Emily is the paradigm; in *Mabel Vaughan* the heroine is solitary. In this novel then, women are portrayed as both the victims of male ideology and those responsible for overcoming it. Despite victimization, women would appear to maintain an essential core that can provide the basis for their triumph.

More confrontational than *The Lamplighter* in its representation of gender conflict, *Mabel Vaughan* is also more utopian. To move the family from the corrupt old East to the promising young Midwest, under the tutelage of women, is to envision the national future as a matriarchy. The useless and destructive female type represented by Mabel's sister is left behind as an anachronism, like the city itself. Although *The Lamplighter* was perhaps naive in presenting a city inhabited entirely by rural New Englanders, it did acknowledge the city as the significant form of American life. In *Mabel Vaughan,* America is equated with the prairie.

Cummins's third novel, *El Fureidîs* (1860) was composed in the greatly popular oriental mode which blended exotic travel narrative with religious speculation. The story follows a romance between the Englishman Meredith—a world traveler visiting the holy lands of Lebanon, Syria, and Palestine—and Havilah, a beautiful Christian Arab, a child of nature. Havilah is perfect in a different way from the dutiful middle-class women of Cummins's two previous novels. She is brave, daring, dashing, untrammeled, expressively free; her Christianity includes no requirements for silent suffering or self-discipline. Although in time she comes to love the hero, he must wait passively for her choice. And when she loves him, she expresses sexual feelings—a trait omitted from the makeup of all other Cummins heroines.

El Fureidîs is one of the period's many novels featuring gypsy and outlaw heroines or heroines who, donning various disguises (for example, Capitola in E. D. E. N. Southworth's wildly popular *The Hidden Land,* serialized in 1859 and reprinted in this series), combine the purity and delicacy of traditional women with physical action and bold initiative, who are highly self-expressive, and who claim a right to pleasure and happiness without paying for them in advance by a long apprenticeship of suffering and self-sacrifice. Such novels react to the strenuous female ideology that such books as *The Lamplighter* and *Mabel Vaughan* expound. And, since they

Introduction

appeared during the same period, they remind us that the question of women was posed in many ways and was given many answers.

Cummins's last novel, *Haunted Hearts* (1864), was also her gloomiest. It is a piece of historical fiction set during the War of 1812, which somberly penalizes its heroine, Angeline Cousin, for nothing more serious than thoughtlessness. Instead of guiding and supporting men, Angeline flirts with them. When her suitor, Gordon Rawley, is thought to have killed someone and then committed suicide on account of Angeline's misbehavior, she is blamed for what has happened. The community does not formally punish her, as the Puritans punish Hawthorne's heroine Hester Prynne in *The Scarlet Letter* (the novel that *Haunted Hearts* is surely responding to), but they ostracize her.

Moreover (unlike Hawthorne's Hester), Angeline comes fully to share the community's judgment of her blameworthiness, and the narrator praises her for this. Yet, no good deed issues from Angeline's conversion; after five years of exemplary goodness, another mistake lands her in jail and leads to a public trial. Miraculously, Rawley returns to vindicate both himself and her.

One can only speculate about why, in the 1860s, Cummins's view of women's potential had contracted so markedly. The likeliest explanation is the Civil War then in progress; to one who took domestic ideology seriously, the war could only signal that female influence had been greatly overestimated. The wartime setting of *Haunted Hearts* would thus be a key to its contemporary purpose. The Civil War, so widely imaged as a fraternal conflict, meant that either the national family was shattered or the attempt to think of the nation in the image of family was ludicrous in the first place. The idea that family values—by which one meant women's values—could shape the body politic did, in fact, lose force after the Civil War. Middle-class women wanting to do something in the world now began to enter the world directly, in large numbers, and without apology, thereby creating the New Woman by the century's end.

If we suppose that Cummins, from first to last, addressed women not only on behalf of what they might make of themselves, but also for the good they might do in the world, we can take *Haunted Hearts* as evidence of a sense that her program had failed. If so, it is disheartening to realize that the failure is laid squarely at the doorstep of women themselves: it is Angeline's fatal frivolity, her lack of seriousness, her trifling—in short, her rejection of her moral mission—that creates all this woe. *Haunted Hearts* seems to say that women had an opportunity that they let pass; now it is gone forever.

ANALYZING THE CULTURAL codes articulated and organized in *The Lamplighter* cannot, of course, bring back its impact on nineteenth-century readers. Such a study can only give us the materials to imagine what reading it might have been like for a reader in its own time. That reader was thoroughly at ease with the symbol system that, as cultural archaeologists, we can come to understand intellectually but can never be at home with. The contemporary reader of *The Lamplighter* did not interpret the novel; she experienced it. If it worked for her, she put it down inspired— inspired, as our contemporary saying has it, to be all that she could be. But this is not all. She became, in the reading of *The Lamplighter,* a lover of reading. Or, if she already loved to read, she was confirmed in that love. Gertrude's first, and most important, service to her blind friend is to read to her. Throughout *The Lamplighter,* the two young women are constantly reading. The mysterious secret of those "innumerable editions of *The Lamplighter*" is nothing more or less than the joy of reading, the pleasure of the text. The proponents and practitioners of our serious elite literature have never succeeded as *The Lamplighter* and its sister books did in creating a huge audience that deeply loved to read.

SELECTED BIBLIOGRAPHY

NOTE: Biographical material on Maria Susanna Cummins is very sparse. The account of her life in the Introduction is based on entries in the *Dictionary of American Biography* and *Notable American Women.*

WORKS BY MARIA SUSANNA CUMMINS

Mabel Vaughan. Boston: John P. Jewett & Co.; Cleveland: Henry P. B. Jewett; London: Sampson Low, Son & Co., 1857.

El Fureidîs. Boston: Ticknor and Fields, 1860.

Haunted Hearts. Boston: J. E. Tilton and Co., 1864.

SECONDARY SOURCES

Baym, Nina. *Woman's Fiction: A Guide to Novels by and about Women in America, 1820–1870.* Ithaca: Cornell UP, 1976.

————. *Novels, Readers, and Reviewers: Responses to Fiction in Antebellum America.* Ithaca: Cornell UP, 1984.

Brown, Herbert Ross. *The Sentimental Novel in America.* Durham, N.C.: Duke UP, 1941.

Buell, Lawrence. *New England Literary Culture: From Revolution through Renaissance.* New York: Cambridge UP, 1986.

Selected Bibliography

Chambers-Schiller, Lee. *Liberty, A Better Husband: Single Women in America; The Generations of 1780–1840.* New Haven: Yale UP, 1984.

Cott, Nancy. *The Bonds of Womanhood: "Woman's Sphere" in New England, 1780–1835.* New Haven: Yale UP, 1977.

Davidson, Cathy N. *Revolution and the Word: The Rise of the Novel in America.* New York: Oxford UP, 1986.

Dobson, Joanne. "The Hidden Hand: Subversion of Cultural Ideology in Three Mid-Nineteenth-Century Women's Novels," *American Quarterly,* 38(1986):223–42.

Douglas, Ann. *The Feminization of American Culture.* New York: Knopf, 1977.

Fetterley, Judith, ed. *Provisions: A Reader from 19th-Century American Women.* Bloomington: Indiana UP, 1985.

Friebert, Lucy, and Barbara A. White. eds. *Hidden Hands: An Anthology of American Women Writers, 1790–1870.* New Brunswick, N.J.: Rutgers UP, 1985.

Halttunan, Karen. *Confidence Men and Painted Women: A Study of Middle-Class Culture in America, 1830–1870.* New Haven: Yale UP, 1982.

Kelley, Mary. *Private Woman, Public Stage: Literary Domesticity in Nineteenth-Century America.* New York: Oxford UP, 1984.

Kolodny, Annette. *The Land before Her: Fantasy and Experience of the American Frontiers, 1630–1860.* Chapel Hill: North Carolina UP, 1984.

Papashvily, Helen Waite. *All the Happy Endings.* New York: Harpers, 1956.

Reynolds, David S. *Faith in Fiction: The Emergence of Religious Literature in America.* Cambridge, Mass.: Harvard UP, 1981.

Ryan, Mary P. *Cradle of the Middle Class: The Family in Oneida County, New York, 1790–1865.* New York: Cambridge UP, 1981.

Tompkins, Jane. *Sensational Designs: The Cultural Work of American Fiction, 1790–1860.* New York: Oxford UP, 1985.

Warner, Susan. *The Wide, Wide World.* ed. Jane Tompkins. New York: Feminist, 1987.

Welter, Barbara. *Dimity Convictions: The American Woman in the Nineteenth Century.* Athens: Ohio UP, 1976.

A NOTE ON THE TEXT

THE TEXT OF *The Lamplighter* has been reset from the first edition, published in Boston by John P. Jewett & Company, and simultaneously in
Cleveland by Jewett, Proctor, and Worthington, in 1854. The original text
is remarkably clean, and has required little emendation—only a period or
semicolon here and there has been necessary for grammatical sense. There
has been no attempt to normalize or modernize what is, in any event, a
strong, plain style that wears well.

THE

LAMPLIGHTER

CHAPTER I

Good God! to think upon a child
That has no childish days,
No careless play, no frolics wild,
No words of prayer and praise!
                        —*Landon*

IT WAS GROWING dark in the city. Out in the open country it would be light for half an hour or more; but within the close streets where my story leads me it was already dusk. Upon the wooden door-step of a low-roofed, dark, and unwholesome-looking house, sat a little girl, who was gazing up the street with much earnestness. The house-door, which was open behind her, was close to the side-walk; and the step on which she sat was so low that her little unshod feet rested on the cold bricks. It was a chilly evening in November, and a light fall of snow, which had made everything look bright and clean in the pleasant open squares, near which the fine houses of the city were built, had only served to render the narrow streets and dark lanes dirtier and more cheerless than ever; for, mixed with the mud and filth which abound in those neighborhoods where the poor are crowded together, the beautiful snow had lost all its purity.

A great many people were passing to and fro, bent on their various errands of duty or of pleasure; but no one noticed the little girl, for there was no one in the world who cared for her. She was scantily clad, in garments of the poorest description. Her hair was long and very thick; uncombed and unbecoming, if anything could be said to be unbecoming to a set of features which, to a casual observer, had not a single attraction,— being thin and sharp, while her complexion was sallow, and her whole appearance unhealthy.

She had, to be sure, fine, dark eyes; but so unnaturally large did they seem, in contrast to her thin, puny face, that they only increased the

peculiarity of it, without enhancing its beauty. Had any one felt any interest in her (which nobody did), had she had a mother (which, alas! she had
not), those friendly and partial eyes would perhaps have found something
in her to praise. As it was, however, the poor little thing was told, a dozen
times a day, that she was the worst-looking child in the world; and, what
was more, the worst-behaved. No one loved her, and she loved no one; no
one treated her kindly; no one tried to make her happy, or cared whether
she were so. She was but eight years old, and all alone in the world.

There was one thing, and one only, which she found pleasure in. She
loved to watch for the coming of the old man who lit the street-lamp [1] in
front of the house where she lived; to see the bright torch he carried flicker
in the wind; and then, when he ran up his ladder, lit the lamp so quickly
and easily, and made the whole place seem cheerful, one gleam of joy was
shed on a little desolate heart, to which gladness was a stranger; and,
though he had never seemed to see, and certainly had never spoken to her,
she almost felt, as she watched for the old lamplighter, as if he were
a friend.

"Gerty," exclaimed a harsh voice within, "have you been for
the milk?"

The child made no answer, but, gliding off the door-step, ran quickly
round the corner of the house, and hid a little out of sight.

"What's become of that child?" said the woman from whom the
voice proceeded, and who now showed herself at the door.

A boy who was passing, and had seen Gerty run,—a boy who had
caught the tone of the whole neighborhood, and looked upon her as a sort
of imp, or spirit of evil,—laughed aloud, pointed to the corner which
concealed her, and, walking off with his head over his shoulder, to see what
would happen next, exclaimed to himself, as he went, "She'll catch it! Nan
Grant'll fix her!"

In a moment more, Gerty was dragged from her hiding-place, and,
with one blow for her ugliness and another for her impudence (for she was
making up faces at Nan Grant with all her might), she was despatched
down a neighboring alley with a kettle for the milk.

She ran fast, for she feared the lamplighter would come and go in her
absence, and was rejoiced, on her return, to catch sight of him, as she drew
near the house, just going up his ladder. She stationed herself at the foot of
it, and was so engaged in watching the bright flame, that she did not
observe when the man began to descend; and, as she was directly in his
way, he hit against her, as he sprang to the ground, and she fell upon the

pavement. "Hollo, my little one!" exclaimed he, "how's this?" as he stooped to lift her up.

She was upon her feet in an instant; for she was used to hard knocks, and did not much mind a few bruises. But the milk!—it was all spilt.

"Well! now, I declare!" said the man, "that's too bad!—what'll mammy say?" and, for the first time looking full in Gerty's face, he here interrupted himself with, "My! what an odd-faced child!—looks like a witch!" Then, seeing that she looked apprehensively at the spilt milk, and gave a sudden glance up at the house, he added, kindly, "She won't be hard on such a mite of a thing as you are, will she? Cheer up, my ducky! never mind if she does scold you a little. I'll bring you something, tomorrow, that I think you'll like, may be; you're such a lonesome sort of a looking thing. And, mind, if the old woman makes a row, tell her I did it.—But didn't I hurt you? What was you doing with my ladder?"

"I was seeing you light the lamp," said Gerty. "and I an't hurt a bit; but I wish I hadn't spilt the milk."

At this moment Nan Grant came to the door, saw what had happened, and commenced pulling the child into the house, amidst blows, threats, and profane and brutal language. The lamplighter tried to appease her; but she shut the door in his face. Gerty was scolded, beaten, deprived of the crust which she usually got for her supper, and shut up in her dark attic for the night. Poor little child! Her mother had died in Nan Grant's house, five years before; and she had been tolerated there since, not so much because when Ben Grant went to sea he bade his wife be sure and keep the child until his return (for he had been gone so long that no one thought he would ever come back), but because Nan had reasons of her own for doing so; and, though she considered Gerty a dead weight upon her hands, she did not care to excite inquiries by trying to dispose of her elsewhere.

When Gerty first found herself locked up for the night in the dark garret (Gerty hated and feared the dark), she stood for a minute perfectly still; then suddenly began to stamp and scream, tried to beat open the door, and shouted, "I hate you, Nan Grant! Old Nan Grant, I hate you!" But nobody came near her; and, after a while, she grew more quiet, went and threw herself down on her miserable bed, covered her face with her little thin hands, and sobbed and cried as if her heart would break. She wept until she was utterly exhausted; and then gradually, with only now and then a low sob and catching of the breath, she grew quite still. By and by she took away her hands from her face, clasped them together in a convulsive manner, and looked up at a little glazed window by the side of the bed. It was but three panes of glass unevenly stuck together, and was the only chance of light the room had. There was no moon; but, as Gerty looked up, she saw through the window shining down upon her *one* bright star. She thought she had never seen anything half so beautiful. She had often been out of doors when the sky was full of stars, and had not noticed them much; but this one, all alone, so large, so bright, and yet so soft and pleasant-looking, seemed to speak to her; it seemed to say, "Gerty! Gerty! *poor* little Gerty!" She thought it seemed like a kind face, such as she had a long time ago seen or dreamt about. Suddenly it flashed through her mind, "Who lit it? Somebody lit it! Some good person, I know! O! how could he get up so high!" And Gerty fell asleep, wondering who lit the star.

Poor little, untaught, benighted soul! Who shall enlighten thee? Thou art God's child, little one! Christ died for thee. Will he not send man or angel to light up the darkness within, to kindle a light that shall never go out, the light that shall shine through all eternity!

CHAPTER II

Who shall assuage thy griefs, "thou tempest-toss'd!"
And speak of comfort, "comfortless!" to thee?
—*Emily Taylor*

GERTY AWOKE the next morning, not as children wake who are roused by each other's merry voices, or by a parent's kiss, who have kind hands to help them dress, and know that a nice breakfast awaits them. But she heard harsh voices below; knew, from the sound, that the men who lived at Nan Grant's (her son and two or three boarders) had come in to breakfast, and that her only chance of obtaining any share of the meal was to be on the spot when they had finished, to take that portion of what remained which Nan might chance to throw or shove towards her. So she crept down stairs, waited a little out of sight until she smelt the smoke of the men's pipes as they passed through the passage, and, when they had all gone noisily out, she slid into the room, looking about her with a glance made up of fear and defiance. She met but a rough greeting from Nan, who told her she had better drop that ugly, sour look; eat some breakfast, if she wanted it, but take care and keep out of her way, and not come near the fire, plaguing round where she was at work, or she'd get another dressing, worse than she had last night.

Gerty had not looked for any other treatment, so there was no disappointment to bear; but, glad enough of the miserable food left for her on the table, swallowed it eagerly, and, waiting no second bidding to keep herself out of the way, took her little old hood, threw on a ragged shawl, which had belonged to her mother, and which had long been the child's best protection from the cold, and, though her hands and feet were chilled by the sharp air of the morning, ran out of the house.

Back of the building where Nan Grant lived, was a large wood and coal yard; and beyond that a wharf, and the thick muddy water of a dock. Gerty might have found playmates enough in the neighborhood of this place. She sometimes did mingle with the troops of boys and girls, equally ragged with herself, who played about in the yard; but not often,—there was a league against her among the children of the place. Poor, ragged and miserably cared for, as most of them were, they all knew that Gerty was still more neglected and abused. They had often seen her beaten, and daily heard her called an ugly, wicked child, told that she belonged to nobody, and had no business in any one's house. Children as they were, they felt their advantage, and scorned the little outcast. Perhaps this would not have been the case if Gerty had ever mingled freely with them, and tried to be on friendly terms. But, while her mother lived there with her, though it was but a short time, she did her best to keep her little girl away from the rude herd. Perhaps that habit of avoidance, but still more a something in the child's nature, kept her from joining in their rough sports, after her mother's death had left her to do as she liked. As it was, she seldom had any intercourse with them. Nor did they venture to abuse her, otherwise than in words; for, singly, they dared not cope with her;—spirited, sudden and violent, she had made herself feared, as well as disliked. Once a band of them had united in a plan to tease and vex her; but, Nan Grant coming up at the moment when one of the girls was throwing the shoes, which she had pulled from Gerty's feet, into the dock, had given the girl a sound whipping, and put them all to flight. Gerty had not a pair of shoes since; but Nan Grant, for once, had done her good service, and the children now left her in peace.

It was a sunshiny, though a cold day, when Gerty ran away from the house, to seek shelter in the wood-yard. There was an immense pile of timber in one corner of the yard, almost out of sight of any of the houses.

Of different lengths and unevenly placed, the planks formed, on one side, a series of irregular steps, by means of which it was easy to climb up. Near the top was a little sheltered recess, overhung by some long planks, and forming a miniature shed, protected by the wood on all sides but one, and from that looking out upon the water.

This was Gerty's haven of rest, her sanctum, and the only place from which she never was driven away. Here, through the long summer days, the little, lonesome child sat, brooding over her griefs, her wrongs and her ugliness; sometimes weeping for hours. Now and then, when the course of her life had been smooth for a few days (that is, when she had been so fortunate as to offend no one, and had escaped whipping, or being shut up in the dark), she would get a little more cheerful, and enjoy watching the sailors belonging to a schooner hard by, as they labored on board their vessel, or occasionally rowed to and fro in a little boat. The warm sunshine was so pleasant, and the men's voices at their work so lively, that the poor little thing would for a time forget her woes.

But summer had gone; the schooner, and the sailors, who had been such pleasant company, had gone too. The weather was now cold, and for a few days it had been so stormy, that Gerty had been obliged to stay in the house. Now, however, she made the best of her way to her little hiding-place; and, to her joy, the sunshine had reached the spot before her, dried up the boards, so that they felt warm to her bare feet, and was still shining so bright and pleasant, that Gerty forgot Nan Grant, forgot how cold she had been, and how much she dreaded the long winter. Her thoughts rambled about some time; but, at last, settled down upon the kind look and voice of the old lamplighter; and then, for the first time since the promise was made, it came into her mind, that he had engaged to bring her something the next time he came. She could not believe he would remember it; but still, he might, he seemed to be so good-natured, and sorry for her fall.

What could he mean to bring? Would it be something to eat? O, if it were only some shoes! But he would n't think of *that*. Perhaps he did not notice but she had some.

At any rate, Gerty resolved to go for her milk in season to be back before it was time to light the lamp, so that nothing should prevent her seeing him.

The day seemed unusually long, but darkness came at last; and with it came True—or rather Trueman—Flint, for that was the lamplighter's name.

Gerty was on the spot, though she took good care to elude Nan Grant's observation.

True was late about his work that night, and in a great hurry. He had only time to speak a few words in his rough way to Gerty; but they were words coming straight from as good and honest a heart as ever throbbed. He put his great, smutty hand on her head in the kindest way, told her how sorry he was she got hurt, and said "It was a plaguy shame she should have been whipped too, and all for a spill o' milk, that was a misfortin', and no crime."

"But here," added he, diving into one of his huge pockets, "here's the critter I promised you. Take good care on 't; don't 'buse it; and, I'm guessin', if it's like the mother that I've got at home, 't won't be a little ye'll be likin' it, 'fore you're done. Good-by, my little gal;" and he shouldered his ladder and went off, leaving in Gerty's hands a little gray-and-white kitten.

Gerty was so taken by surprise, on finding in her arms a live kitten, something so different from what she had anticipated, that she stood for a minute irresolute what to do with it. There were a great many cats, of all sizes and colors, inhabitants of the neighboring houses and yard; frightened-looking creatures, which, like Gerty herself, crept or scampered about, and often hid themselves among the wood and coal, seeming to feel, as she did, great doubts about their having a right to be anywhere. Gerty had often felt a sympathy for them, but never thought of trying to catch one, carry it home and tame it; for she knew that food and shelter were most grudgingly accorded to herself, and would not certainly be extended to her pets. Her first thought, therefore, was to throw the kitten down and let it run away.

But, while she was hesitating, the little animal pleaded for itself in a way she could not resist. Frightened by its long imprisonment and journey in True Flint's pocket, it crept from Gerty's arms up to her neck, clung there tight, and, with its low, feeble cries, seemed to ask her to take care of it. Its eloquence prevailed over all fear of Nan Grant's anger. She hugged pussy to her bosom, and made a childish resolve to love it, feed it, and, above all, keep it out of Nan's sight.

How much she came in time to love that kitten, no words can tell. Her little, fierce, untamed, impetuous nature had hitherto only expressed itself in angry passion, sullen obstinacy, and even hatred. But there were in her soul fountains of warm affection yet unstirred, a depth of tenderness never yet called out, and a warmth and devotion of nature that wanted only an object to expend themselves upon.

So she poured out such wealth of love on the little creature that clung to her for its support as only such a desolate little heart has to spare. She loved the kitten all the more for the care she was obliged to take of it, and the trouble and anxiety it gave her. She kept it, as much as possible, out among the boards, in her own favorite haunt. She found an old hat, in which she placed her own hood, to make a bed for pussy. She carried it a part of her own scanty meals; she braved for it what she would not have done for herself; for she almost every day abstracted from the kettle, when she was returning with the milk for Nan Grant, enough for pussy's supper; running the risk of being discovered and punished, the only risk or harm the poor ignorant child knew or thought of, in connection with the theft and deception; for her ideas of abstract right and wrong were utterly undeveloped. She would play with her kitten for hours among the boards, talk to it, and tell it how much she loved it. But, when the days were very cold, she was often puzzled to know how to keep herself warm out of doors, and the risk of bringing the kitten into the house was great. She would then hide it in her bosom, and run with it into the little garret-room where she slept; and, taking care to keep the door shut, usually eluded Nan's eyes and ears. Once or twice, when she had been off her guard, her little playful pet had escaped from her, and scampered through the lower room and passage. Once Nan drove it out with a broom; but in that thickly-peopled region, as we have said, cats and kittens were not so uncommon as to excite inquiry.

It may seem strange that Gerty had leisure to spend all her time at play. Most children living among the poorer class of people learn to be useful even while they are very young. Numbers of little creatures, only a few years old, may be seen in our streets, about the yards and doors of houses, bending under the weight of a large bundle of sticks, a basket of shavings, or, more frequently yet, a stout baby, nearly all the care of which devolves upon them. We have often pitied such little drudges, and thought their lot a hard one. But, after all, it was not the worst thing in the world; they were far better off than Gerty, who had nothing to do at all, and had never know the satisfaction of *helping* anybody. Nan Grant had no babies; and, being a very active woman, with but a poor opinion of children's services, at the best, she never tried to find employment for Gerty, much better satisfied if she would only keep out of her sight; so that, except her daily errand for the milk, Gerty was always idle,—a fruitful source of unhappiness and discontent, if she had suffered from no other.

Nan was a Scotchwoman, no longer young, and with a temper which, never good, became worse and worse as she grew older. She had seen life's roughest side, had always been a hard-working woman, and had the reputation of being very smart and a driver. Her husband was a carpenter by trade; but she had made his home so uncomfortable, that for years he had followed the sea. She took in washing, and had a few boarders; by means of which she earned what might have been an ample support for herself, had it not been for her son, an unruly, disorderly young man, spoilt in early life by his mother's uneven temper and management, and who, though a skilful workman when he chose to be industrious, always squandered his own and a large part of his mother's earnings. Nan, as we have said, had reasons of her own for keeping Gerty, though they were not so strong as to prevent her often having half a mind to rid herself of the encumbrance.

CHAPTER III

Mercy and Love have met thee on thy road,
Thou wretched outcast!
——*Wordsworth*

WHEN GERTY HAD had her kitten about a month, she took a violent cold from being out in the damp and rain; and Nan, fearing she should have trouble with her if she became seriously ill, bade her stay in the house, and keep in the warm room where she was at work. Gerty's cough was fearful; and it would have been a great comfort to sit by the stove all day and keep warm, had it not been for her anxiety about the kitten, lest it should get lost, or starve, before she was well enough to be out taking care of it; or, worst of all, come running into the house in search of her. The whole day passed away, however, and nothing was seen of pussy. Towards night, the men were heard coming in to supper. Just as they entered the door of the room where Nan and Gerty were, and where the coarse meal was prepared, one of them stumbled over the kitten, which had come in with them, unperceived.

"Cracky! what's this 'ere?" said the man, whom they all were accustomed to call Jemmy; "a cat, I vow! Why, Nan, I thought you kind o' hated cats!"

"Well, 't an't none o' mine; drive it out," said Nan.

Jemmy started to do so; but puss, suddenly drawing back, and making a circuit around his legs, sprang forward into the arms of Gerty, who was anxiously watching its fate.

"Whose kitten's that, Gerty?" said Nan.

"Mine!" said Gerty, bravely.

"Well, how long have you kept pets? I should like to know." said Nan. "Speak! how came you by this?"

The men were all looking on. Gerty was afraid of the men. They sometimes teased, and were always a source of alarm to her. She could not think of acknowledging to whom she was indebted for the gift of the kitten; she knew it would only make matters worse, for Nan had never forgiven True Flint's rough expostulation against her cruelty in beating the child for spilling the milk; and Gerty could not summon the presence of mind to think of any other source to which she could ascribe the kitten's presence, or she would not have hesitated to tell a falsehood; for her very limited education had not taught her a love or habit of truth where a lie would better serve her turn, and save her from punishment. She was silent, and burst into tears.

"Come," said Jemmy, "give us some supper, Nan, and let the gal alone till arterwards."

Nan complied, ominously muttering, however.

The supper was just finished, when an organ-grinder struck up a tune outside the door. The men stepped out to join the crowd, consisting chiefly of the inmates of the house, who were watching the motions of a monkey that danced in time to the music. Gerty ran to the window to look out. Delighted with the gambols of the creature, she gazed intently, until the man and monkey moved off; so intently, that she did not miss the kitten, which, in the mean time, crept down from her arms, and, springing upon the table, began to devour the remnants of the repast. The organ-grinder was not out of sight when Gerty's eyes fell upon the figure of the old lamplighter coming up the street. She thought she would stay and watch him light his lamp, when she was startled by a sharp and angry exclamation from Nan, and turned just in time to see her snatch her darling kitten from the table. Gerty sprang forward to the rescue, jumped into a chair, and caught Nan by the arm; but she firmly pushed her back with one hand, while with the other she threw the kitten half across the room. Gerty heard a sudden splash and a piercing cry. Nan had flung the poor creature into a large vessel of steaming-hot water, which stood ready for some household purpose. The little animal struggled and writhed for an instant, then died in torture.

All the fury of Gerty's nature was roused. Without hesitation, she lifted a stick of wood which lay near her, and flung it at Nan with all her strength. It was well aimed, and struck the woman on the head. The blood started from the wound the blow had given; but Nan hardly felt the blow, so greatly was she excited against the child. She sprang upon her, caught her by the shoulder, and opening the house-door, thrust her out upon the side-walk. "Ye'll never darken my doors again, yer imp of wickedness!" said she, as she rushed into the house, leaving the child alone in the cold, dark night.

When Gerty was angry or grieved, she always cried aloud,—not sobbing, as many children do, but uttering a succession of piercing shrieks, until she sometimes quite exhausted her strength. When she found herself in the street, she commenced screaming;—not from fear at being turned away from her only home, and left all alone at nightfall to wander about the city, and perhaps freeze before morning (for it was very cold),—she did not think of herself for a moment. Horror and grief at the dreadful fate of the only thing she loved in the world entirely filled her little soul. So she crouched down against the side of the house, her face hid in her hands, unconscious of the noise she was making, and unaware of the triumph of the girl who had once thrown away her shoes, and who was watching from the house-door opposite. Suddenly she found herself lifted up and placed on one of the rounds of Trueman Flint's ladder, which still leaned against the lamp-post. True held her firmly, just high enough on the ladder to bring her face opposite his, recognized her as his old acquaintance, and asked her, in the same kind way he had used on the former occasion, what was the matter.

But Gerty could only gasp and say, "O, my kitten! my kitten!"

"What! the kitten I gave you? Well, have you lost it? Don't cry! there—don't cry!"

"O, no! not lost! O, poor kitty!" and Gerty began to cry louder than ever, and coughed at the same time so dreadfully, that True was quite frightened for the child. Making every effort to soothe her, and having partially succeeded, he told her she would catch her death o' cold, and she must go into the house.

"O, she won't let me in!" said Gerty, "and I would n't go, if she would!"

"Who won't let you in?—your mother?"

"No! Nan Grant."

"Who's Nan Grant?"

"She's a horrid, wicked woman, that drowned my kitten in bilin' water!"

"But where's your mother?"

"I han't got none."

"Who do you belong to, you poor little thing!"

"Nobody; and I've no business anywhere!"

"But who do you live with, and who takes care of you?"

"O, I lived with Nan Grant; but I hate her. I threw a stick of wood at her head, and I wish I'd killed her!"

"Hush! hush! you must n't say that! I'll go and speak to her."

True moved towards the door, trying to draw Gerty in with him; but she resisted so forcibly that he left her outside, and, walking directly into the room, where Nan was binding up her head with an old handkerchief, told her she had better call her little girl in, for she would freeze to death out there.

"She's no child of mine," said Nan; "she's been here long enough; she's the worst little creature that ever lived; it's a wonder I've kept her so long; and now I hope I'll never lay eyes on her agin,—and, what's more, I don't mean to. She ought to be hung for breaking my head! I believe she's got an ill-spirit in her, if ever anybody did have in this world."

"But what'll become of her?" said True. "It's a fearful cold night. How'd you feel, marm, if she were found to-morrow morning all *friz* up just on your door-step?"

"How'd I feel?—That's your business, is it? S'posen you take care of her yourself! Yer make a mighty deal o' fuss about the brat. Carry her home, and try how yer like her. Yer've been here a talkin' to me about her once afore; and I tell you I won't hear a word more. Let other folks see to her, I say; I've had more'n my share; and, as to her freezin', or dyin' anyhow, I'll risk her. Them children that comes into the world nobody knows how, don't get out of it in a hurry. She's the city's property—let 'em look out for her; and you'd better go long, and not meddle with what don't consarn you."

True did not wait to hear more. He was not used to women; and an angry woman was the most formidable thing to him in the world. Nan's flashing eyes and menacing attitude were sufficient warning of the coming tempest, and he wisely hastened away before it should burst upon his head.

Gerty had ceased crying when he came out, and looked up into his face with the greatest interest.

"Well," said he, "she says you shan't come back."

"O, I'm so glad!" said Gerty.

"But where'll you go to?"

"I don't know; p'raps I'll go with you, and see you light the lamps."

"But where'll you sleep tonight?"

"I don't know where; I have n't got any house. I guess I'll sleep out, where I can see the stars. I don't like dark places. But it'll be cold, won't it?"

"My goodness! You'll freeze to death, child."

"Well, what'll become of me, then?"

"The Lord only knows!"

True looked at Gerty in perfect wonder and distress. He knew nothing about children, and was astonished at her simplicity. He could not leave her there, such a cold night; but he hardly knew what he could do with her if he took her home, for he lived alone, and was poor. But another violent coughing spell decided him at once to share with her his shelter, fire and food, for one night, at least. So he took her by the hand, saying, "Come with me;" and Gerty ran along confidently by his side, never asking whither.

True had about a dozen more lamps to light before they reached the end of the street, when his round of duty was finished. Gerty watched him light each one with as keen an interest as if that were the only object for which she was in his company, and it was only after they had reached the corner of the street, and walked on for some distance without stopping, that she inquired where they were going.

"Going home," said True.

"Am I going to your home?" said Gerty.

"Yes," said True, "and here it is."

He opened a little gate close to the side-walk. It led into a small and very narrow yard, which stretched along the whole length of a decent two-storied house. True lived in the back part of the house; so they went through the yard, passed by several windows and the main entrance, and, keeping on to a small door in the rear, opened it and went in. Gerty was by this time trembling with the cold; her little bare feet were quite blue with walking so far on the pavements. There was a stove in the room into which they had entered, but no fire in it. It was a large room, and looked as if it might be pretty comfortable, though it was very untidy. True made as much haste as he could to dispose of his ladder, torch, &c., in an adjoining shed; and then, bringing in a handful of wood, he lit a fire in the stove. In a few minutes there was a bright blaze, and the chilly atmosphere grew warm. Drawing an old wooden settle up to the fire, he threw his shaggy great-coat over it, and lifting little Gerty up, he placed her gently upon the comfortable seat. He then went to work to get supper; for True was an old bachelor, and accustomed to do everything for himself. He made tea; then, mixing a great mug full for Gerty, with plenty of sugar, and all his cent's worth of milk, he produced from a little cupboard a loaf of bread, cut her a huge slice, and pressed her to eat and drink as much as she could; for he judged well when he concluded, from her looks, that she had not always been well fed; and so much satisfaction did he feel in her evident enjoyment of the best meal she had ever had, that he forgot to partake of it himself, but sat watching her with a tenderness which proved that the unerring instinct of childhood had not been wanting in Gerty, when she felt, as she watched True about his work, so long before he ever spoke to her, that he was a friend to everybody, even to the most forlorn little girl in the world.

Trueman Flint was born and brought up in New Hampshire; but, when fifteen years old, being left an orphan, he had made his way to Boston, where he supported himself for many years by whatever employment he could obtain; having been, at different times, a newspaper carrier, a cab-driver, a porter, a wood-cutter, indeed, a jack-at-all-trades; and so honest, capable and good-tempered, had he always shown himself, that he everywhere won a good name, and had sometimes continued for years in the same employ. Previous to his entering upon the service in which we find him, he had been for some time a porter in a large store, owned by a wealthy and generous merchant. Being one day engaged in removing some heavy casks, he had the misfortune to be severely injured by one of them falling upon his chest. For a long time no hope was entertained of his recovering from the effects of the accident; and when he at last began to mend, his health returned so gradually that it was a year before he was able to work again. The sickness swallowed up the savings of years; but his late employer never allowed him to want for any comforts, provided an excellent physician, and saw that he was well taken care of.

True, however, had never been the same man since. He rose up from his sick bed ten years older in constitution, and his strength so much enfeebled that he was only fit for some comparatively light employment. It was then that his kind friend and former master obtained for him the situation he now held as lamplighter; in addition to which, he frequently earned considerable sums by sawing wood, shovelling snow, &c.

He was now between fifty and sixty years old, a stoutly-built man, with features cut in one of nature's rough moulds, but expressive of much good-nature. He was naturally silent and reserved, lived much by himself, was known to but few people in the city, and had only one crony, the sexton of a neighboring church, a very old man, and one usually considered very cross-grained and uncompanionable.

But we left Gerty finishing her supper; and now, when we return to her, she is stretched upon the wide settle, sound asleep covered up with a warm blanket, and her head resting upon a pillow. True sits beside her; her little thin hand lies in his great palm,—occasionally he draws the blanket closer round her. She breathes hard; suddenly she gives a nervous start, then speaks quickly; her dreams are evidently troubled. True listens intently to her words, as she exclaims, eagerly, "O, don't! don't drown my kitty!" and then again, in a voice of fear, "O, she'll catch me! she'll catch me!" once more; and now her tones are touchingly plaintive and earnest,— "Dear, dear, good old man! let me stay with you, *do* let me stay!"

Great tears are in Trueman Flint's eyes, and rolling down the furrows of his rough cheeks; he lays his great head on the pillow and draws Gerty's little face close to his; at the same time smoothing her long, uncombed hair with his hand. He too is thinking aloud—what does *he* say?

"Catch you!—no, she *shan't!* Stay with *me!*—so you shall, I promise you, poor little birdie! All alone in this big world and so am I. Please God, we'll bide together."

CHAPTER IV

In age, in infancy, from others' aid
Is all our hope; to teach us to be kind:
That Nature's first, last lesson to mankind.
   —*Young*

LITTLE GERTY HAD found a friend and a protector; and it was well she had, for suffering and neglect had well-nigh cut short her sad existence, and ended all her sorrows. The morning after True took her home, and she woke in a high fever, her head and limbs aching, and with every symptom of severe illness. She looked around, and found she was alone in the room; but there was a good fire, and preparation for some breakfast. For a moment or two she was puzzled to know where she was, and what had happened to her; for the room seemed quite strange, now that she first saw it by daylight. A look of happiness passed over her sick little face when she recalled the events of the previous night, and thought of kind old True, and the new home she had found with him. She got up and went to the window to look out, though her head was strangely giddy, and she tottered so that she could hardly walk. The ground was covered with snow, and it was still stormy without. It seemed as if the snow dazzled Gerty's eyes; for she suddenly found herself quite blinded, her head grew dizzy, she staggered and fell.

Trueman came in, a moment after, and was very much frightened at seeing Gerty stretched upon the floor; but soon found out the real state of the case, for he had made up his mind during the night that she was a very sick child, and was not surprised that she had fainted in endeavoring to walk. He placed her in bed, and soon succeeded in restoring her to consciousness; but, for three weeks from that time, she never sat up, except when True held her in his arms. True was a rough and clumsy man about most things; but not so in the care of his little charge. He knew a good deal about sickness; was something of a doctor and nurse in his simple way; and, though he had never had much to do with children, his warm heart was a trusty guide, and taught him all that was necessary for Gerty's comfort, and far, far more kindness than she had ever experienced before.

Gerty was very patient. She would sometimes lie awake whole nights, suffering from pain and extreme weariness at her long confinement to a sick bed, without uttering a groan, or making any noise, lest she might waken True, who slept on the floor beside her, when he could so far forget his anxiety about her as to sleep at all. Sometimes, when she was in great pain, True had carried her in his arms for hours; but even then Gerty would try to appear relieved before she really was so, and even feign sleep, that he might put her back to bed again, and take some rest himself. Her little heart was full of love and gratitude to her kind protector, and she spent much of her time in thinking what she could ever do for him when she got well, and wondering whether she were capable of ever learning to do any good thing at all. True was often obliged to leave her, to attend to his work; and, during the first week of her sickness, she was much alone, though everything she could possibly want was put within her reach, and many a caution given to her to keep still in bed until his return. At last, however, she grew delirious, and for some days had no knowledge how she was taken care of. One day, after a long and quiet sleep, she woke quite restored to sense and consciousness, and saw a woman sitting by her bedside sewing.

She sprang up in bed to look at the stranger, who had not observed her open her eyes, but who started the moment she heard her move, and exclaimed, "O, lie down, my child! lie down!" at the same time laying her hand gently upon her, to force the injunction.

"I don't know you," said Gerty; "where's my Uncle True?" for that was the name by which True had told her to call him.

"He's gone out, dear; he'll be home soon. How do you feel,—better?"

"O, yes! much better. Have I been asleep long?"

"Some time; lie down now, and I'll bring you some gruel; it will be good for you."

"Does Uncle True know you are here?"

"Yes. I came in to sit with you while he was away."

"Came in?—From where?"

"From my room. I live in the other part of the house."

"I think you're very good," said Gerty. "I like you. I wonder why I did not see you when you came in."

"You were too sick, dear, to notice; but I think you'll soon be better now."

The woman prepared the gruel, and after Gerty had taken it reseated herself at her work. Gerty laid down in her bed, with her face towards her new friend, and, fixing her large eyes upon her, watched her some time while she sat sewing. At last the woman looked up, and said, "Well, what do you think I'm making?"

"I don't know," said Gerty; "what are you?"

The woman held up her work, so that Gerty could see that it was a dark calico frock for a child.

"O! what a nice gown!" said Gerty. "Who is it for?—Your little girl?"

"No," said the woman, "I have n't got any little girl; I've only got one child, my boy, Willie."

"Willie; that's a pretty name," said Gerty. "Is he a good boy?"

"Good?—He's he best boy in the world, and the handsomest!." answered the woman, her pale, care-worn face lit up with all a mother's pride.

Gerty turned away, and a look so unnaturally sad for a child came over her countenance, that the woman, looking up, thought she was getting tired, and ought to be kept very quiet. She told her so, and bade her shut up her eyes and go to sleep again. Gerty obeyed the first injunction, and lay so still that the latter seemed in a fair way to be fulfilled, when the door opened gently, and True came in.

"O! Miss Sullivan," said he, "you're here still! I'm very much obleeged to you for stayin'; I had n't calkerlated to be gone so long. And how does the child seem to be, marm?"

"Much better, Mr. Flint. She's come to her reason, and I think, with care, will do very well now.—O! she's awake," she added, seeing Gerty open her eyes.

True came up to the bedside, stroked back her hair, now cut short and neatly arranged, felt of her pulse, and nodded his head satisfactorily. Gerty caught his great hand between both of hers and held it tight. He sat down on the side of the bed, and, glancing at Mrs. Sullivan's work, said, "I should n't be surprised if she needed her new clothes sooner than we thought for, marm. It's my 'pinion we'll have her up and about afore many days."

"So I was thinking," said Mrs. Sullivan; "but don't be in too great a hurry. She's had a very severe sickness, and her recovery must be gradual. Did you see Miss Graham to-day?"

"Yes, I did see her, poor thing! The Lord bless her sweet face! She axed a sight o' questions about little Gerty here, and gave this parcel of *arrer*root, I think she called it. She says it's excellent in sickness. Did you ever fix any, Miss Sullivan, so that you can jist show me how, if you'll be so good; for I declare I don't remember, though she took a deal o' pains to tell me."

"O, yes; it's very easy. I'll come in and prepare some, by and by. I don't think Gerty'll want any at present; she's just had some gruel. But father has come home, and I must be seeing about our tea. I'll come in again, this evening, Mr. Flint."

"Thank you, marm, thank you; you're very kind."

During the few following days Mrs. Sullivan came in and sat with Gerty several times. She was a gentle, subdued sort of woman, with a placid face, that was very refreshing to a child that had long lived in fear, and suffered a great deal of abuse. She always brought her work with her, which was usually some child's garment that she was making.

One evening, when Gerty had nearly recovered from her tedious fever, she was sitting in True's lap by the stove fire, carefully wrapped up in a blanket. She had been talking to him about her new acquaintance and friend; suddenly looking up in his face, she said, "Uncle True, do you know what little girl she's making a gown for?"

"For a little girl," said True, "that needs a gown, and a good many other things; for she has n't got any clothes, as I know on, except a few old rags. Do you know any such little girl, Gerty?"

"I guess I do," said Gerty, with her head a little on one side, and a very knowing look.

"Well, where is she?"

"An't she in your lap?"

"What, you!—Why, do you think Mrs. Sullivan would spend her time making clothes for you?"

"Well," said Gerty, hanging her head, "I should n't *think* she would; but then you *said*—"

"Well, what did I say?"

"Something about new clothes for me."

"So I did," said True, giving her a rough hug; "and they *are* for you;—two whole suits, and shoes and stockings into the bargain."

Gerty opened her large eyes in amazement, laughed and clapped her hands. True laughed too; they both seemed very happy.

"Did she buy them, Uncle True? Is she rich?" said Gerty.

"Miss Sullivan?—no, indeed!" said True. "Miss Graham bought 'em, and is going to pay Miss Sullivan for making them."

"Who is Miss Graham?"

"She's a lady too good for this world—that's sartain. I'll tell you about her some time; but I better not now, I guess; it's time you were abed and asleep."

One Sabbath, after Gerty was nearly well, she was so much fatigued with sitting up all day, that she went to bed before dark, and for two or three hours slept very soundly. On awakening, she saw that True had company. An old man, much older, she thought, than True, was sitting on the opposite side of the stove, smoking a pipe. His dress, though of ancient fashion, and homely in its materials, was very neat; and his hair, of which he had but little, and that perfectly white, growing in two long locks just behind his ears, was nicely combed up, and tied on the top of his head, which was elsewhere bald and shiny. He had sharp features, and Gerty thought, from his looks, it must be easy for him to say sharp things; indeed, rather hard for him to say anything pleasant. There was a sarcastic expression about the corners of his mouth, and a disappointed look in his whole face, which Gerty observed, though she could not have defined, and from which she drew her conclusions with regard to his temper. She rightly conjectured that he was Mrs. Sullivan's father, Mr. Cooper; and in the opinion she formed of him from her first observation she did not widely differ from most other people who knew the old church-sexton. But both his own face and public opinion somewhat wronged him. It was true his was not a genial nature. Domestic trials, and the unkindness and fickleness of fortune, had caused him to look upon the dark side of life,—to dwell upon its sorrows, and frown upon the bright hopes of the young and the gay, who, as he was wont to say, with a mysterious shake of his head, knew but little of the world. The occupation, too, which had of late years been his, was not calculated to counteract a disposition to melancholy; his duties in the church were mostly solitary, and, as he was much withdrawn in his old age from intercourse with the world at large, he had become severe towards its follies, and unforgiving towards its crimes. There was much that was good and benevolent in him, however; and True Flint knew it, and loved to draw it out. True liked the old man's sincerity and honesty; and many a Sabbath evening had they sat by that same fireside, and discussed all those questions of public policy, national institutions, and individual rights, which every American feels called upon to take under his especial consideration, besides many matters of private feeling and interest, without their friendly relations being once disturbed or endangered; and this was the more remarkable, inasmuch as Trueman Flint was the very reverse of old Paul Cooper in disposition and temper, being hopeful and sanguine, always disposed to look upon the bright side of things, and, however discouraging they might seem, ever averring that it was his opinion 't would all come out right at last. On the evening of which we are speaking, they had been talking on several of their usual topics; but when Gerty awoke she found herself the subject of conversation. Of course she soon became deeply interested.

"Where," said Mr. Cooper, "did you say you picked her up?"

"At Nan Grant's," said True. "Don't you remember her? she's the same woman whose son you were called up to witness against, at the time the church-windows were broken, the night afore the 4th of July. You can't have forgotten her at the trial, Cooper; for she blew you up with a vengeance, and did n't spare his honor the Judge, either. Well, 't was just such a rage she was in with this 'ere child, the first time I see her; and the *second* time she'd just turned her out o' doors."

"Ah, yes, I remember the she-bear. I should n't suppose she'd be any too gentle to her own child, much less a stranger's; but what are you going to do with the foundling, Flint?"

"Do with her?—Keep her, to be sure, and take care on her."

Cooper laughed rather sarcastically.

"Well, now, I s'pose, neighbor, you think its rather freakish in me to be adoptin' a child at my time o' life; and p'raps it is; but I'll explain to you just how 't was. She'd a died that night I tell yer on, if I had n't brought her home with me; and a good many times since, what's more, if I, with the help o' your darter, had n't took mighty good care on her. Well, she took on so in her sleep, the first night ever she came, and cried out to me all as if she never had a friend afore (and I doubt me she never had), that I made up my mind then she should stay, at any rate, and I'd take care on her, and share my last crust with the wee thing, come what might. The Lord's been very marciful to me, Mr. Cooper, very marciful. He's raised me up friends in my deep distress. I knew, when I was a little shaver, what a lonesome thing it was to be fatherless and motherless; and when I see this little sufferin' human bein', I felt as if, all friendless as she seemed, she was more partickerlerly the Lord's, and as if I could not sarve him more, and ought not to sarve him less, then to share with her the blessins he has bestowed on me. You look round, neighbor, as if you thought 't wan't much to share with any one; and 't an't much there is here, to be sure; but it's a *home,* — yes, a *home;* and that's a great thing to her that never had one. I've got my hands yet, and a stout heart, and a willin' mind. With God's help, I'll be a father to that child; and the time may come when she'll be God's embodied blessin' to me."

Mr. Cooper shook his head doubtfully, and muttered something about children, even one's own, not being apt to prove blessings.

But he had not power to shake Trueman's high faith in the wisdom, as well as righteousness, of his own proceedings. He had risen in the earnestness with which he had spoken, and, after pacing the room hastily and with excitement, he returned to his seat, and said: "Besides, neighbor Cooper, if I had not made up my mind the night Gerty came here, I would n't have sent her away after the next day; for the Lord, I think, spoke to me by the mouth of one of his holy angels, and bade me persevere in my resolution. You've seen Miss Graham. She goes to your church regular, with the fine old gentleman, her father. I was at their house shovelling snow, after the great storm three weeks since, and she sent for me to come into the kitchen. Well may I bless her angel face, poor thing!—if the world is dark to her, she makes it light to other folks. She cannot see Heaven's sunshine outside; but she's better off than most people, for she's got it in her, I do believe, and when she smiles it lets the glory out, and looks like God's rainbow in the clouds. She's done me many a kindness, since I got hurt so bad in her father's store, now some five years gone; and she sent for me that day, to ask how I did, and if there was anything I wanted that she could speak to the master about. So I told her all about little Gerty; and, I tell you, she and I both cried 'fore I'd done. She put some money into my hand, and told me to get Miss Sullivan to make some clothes for Gerty; more than that, she promised to help me if I got into trouble with the care of her; and when I was going away, she said, 'I'm sure you've done quite right, True; the Lord will bless and reward your kindness to that poor child.'"

True was so excited and animated by his subject, that he did not notice what the sexton had observed, but did not choose to interrupt. Gerty had risen from her bed and was standing beside True, her eyes fixed upon his face, breathless with the interest she felt in his words. She touched his shoulder; he looked round, saw her, and stretched out his arms. She sprang into them, buried her face in his bosom, and, bursting into a paroxysm of joyful tears, gasped out the words, "Shall I stay with you always?"

"Yes, just as long as I live," said True, "you shall be my child."

CHAPTER V

A light, busy foot astir
In her small housewifery; the blithest bee
That ever wrought in hive.
—*Mitford*

IT WAS A stormy evening. Gerty was standing at the window, watching for True's return from his lamplighting. She was neatly and comfortably dressed, her hair smooth, her face and hands clean. She was now quite well—better than for years before her sickness. Care and kindness had done wonders for her, and though still a pale and rather slender-looking child, with eyes and mouth disproportionately large to her other features, the painful look of suffering she had been wont to wear had given place to a happy though rather grave expression. On the wide window-sill in front of her sat a plump and venerable cat, parent to Gerty's lost darling, and for that reason very dear to her; she was quietly stroking its back, while the constant purring that the old veteran kept up proved her satisfaction at the arrangement.

Suddenly a rumbling, tumbling sound was heard in the wall. The house was old, and furnished with ample accommodations for rats, who seemed, from the noise, to have availed themselves of this fact to give a ball, such an excitement were they manifesting. One would almost have thought a chimney was falling down, brick by brick. It did not alarm Gerty, how-ever; she was used to old, rat-inhabited walls, and too much accustomed to hearing such sounds all around her, when she slept in the garret at Nan Grant's, to be disturbed by them. Not so, however, with the ancient gri-malkin, who pricked up her ears, and gave every sign of a disposition to rush into battle. No war-horse could have been more excited by the sound of the trumpet, then was puss at the rushing of her foes through the ceiling.

"Lie still, pussy," said Gerty, "lie still, I say; don't you be running off after rats. You must sit up straight, and be good, till you see Uncle True coming, so's to hear what he'll say when he sees the room and *me.*"

Here Gerty turned and glanced around the room with an air of in-finite satisfaction; then, clambering upon the wide, old-fashioned window-sill, where she could see up the yard, and have a full view of the lamplighter the moment he entered the gate, she took the cat in her arms, smoothed down her dress, gave a look of interest and pride at her shoes and stock-ings, and then composed herself, with a determined effort to be patient. It would not do, however; she could not be patient; it seemed to her that he never came so late before, and she was just beginning to think he never would come at all, when he turned into the gate. It was nearly dark, but Gerty could see that there was some person with him. He did not look tall enough to be Mr. Cooper, and did not step like him; but she concluded it must be he, for whoever it was stopped at his door further up the yard, and went in. Impatient as Gerty had been for True's arrival, she did not run to meet him as usual, but waited in a listening attitude, until she heard him come in through the shed, where he was in the habit of stopping to hang up his ladder and lantern, and remove the soiled frock and overalls which he wore outside his clothes when about his work. She then ran and hid behind the door by which he must enter the room. She evidently had some great surprise in store for him, and meant to enjoy it to the utmost. The cat, not being so full of the matter, whatever it was, was more mindful of her manners, and went to meet him, rubbing her head against his legs, which was her customary welcome.

"Hollo, whiskers!" said True; "where's my little gal?"

He shut the door behind him as he spoke, thus disclosing Gerty to view. She sprung forward with a bound, laughed, and looked first at her own clothes, and then in True's face, to see what he would think of her appearance.

"Well, I declare!" said he, lifting her up in his arms and carrying her nearer to the light; "little folks do look famous! New gown, apron, shoes!— got 'em all on! And who fixed your hair? My! you an't none too handsome, sartain, but you do look famous nice!"

"Mrs. Sullivan dressed me all up, and brushed my hair; and *more too*—don't you see what *else* she has done?"

True followed Gerty's eyes as they wandered around the room. He looked amazed enough to satisfy her anticipations, great as they had been; and no wonder. He had been gone since morning, and things had indeed undergone a transformation. Woman's hands had evidently been at work, clearing up and setting to rights.

Until Gerty came to live with True, his home had never been sub-jected to female intrusion. Living wholly by himself, and entertaining scarcely any visitors, it had been his habit to make himself comfortable in his own way, utterly regardless of appearances. In his humble apartment [1] sweeping-day came but seldom, and spring cleaning was unknown. Two large windows, facing the yard, were treated with great injustice, the cheerful light they were capable of affording being half obscured by dirt and smoke. The corners of the ceiling were festooned with cobwebs; the high, broad mantel-piece had accumulated a curious medley of things useful and useless; while there was no end to the rubbish that had collected under the stove. Then the furniture, some of which was very good, was adjusted in the most inconvenient manner, and in a way to turn the size of the room to the least possible advantage. During Gerty's illness, a bed made up on the floor for True's use, and the various articles which had been required in her sick-room, had increased the clutter to such an extent that one almost needed a pilot to conduct him in safety through the apartment.

Now, Mrs. Sullivan was the soul of neatness. Her rooms were like wax-work. Her own dress was almost quaker-like in its extreme simplicity, and freedom from the least speck or stain. No one could meet her old father, or her young son, even in their working dress, without perceiving at once the evidence of a careful daughter and mother's handiwork. It was to nurse Gerty, and take care of her in True's absence, that she first entered a room so much the reverse of her own; and it is not easy to appreciate the degree in which the virtue and charity of her so doing was enhanced, unless one can realize how painful the contrast was to her, and how excessively annoying she found it, to spend sometimes a whole afternoon in a room, which, as she expressed herself afterwards at home, it would have been a real pleasure to her to clear up and put to rights, if it were only to see how it would look, and whether anybody would recognize it. Mrs. Sullivan was a little bit of a woman, but had more capability and energy than could have been found in any one among twenty others twice her size. She really pitied those whose home was such a mass of confusion; felt sure that they could not be happy; and inwardly determined, as soon as Gerty got well, to exert herself in the cause of cleanliness and order, which was in her eyes the cause of virtue and happiness, so completely did she identify outward neatness and purity with inward peace. She pondered in her own mind how she could broach the subject of a renovation in his affairs to True himself, without wounding his feelings; for she was herself so sensitive on a point of neatness, that she imagined he must be somewhat the same,—and the little woman, being as tender-hearted as she was tidy, would not have mortified him for the world,—when a mode of action was suggested to her by Gerty herself.

On the day previous to that on which the great cleaning operations took place, Gerty was observed by Mrs. Sullivan standing in the passage near her door, looking shyly but wistfully in.

"Come in, Gerty," said the kind little woman; "come in and see me.—Here," added she, seeing how timid the child felt about intruding herself into a strange room; "you may sit up here by the table, and see me iron. This is your own little dress. I am smoothing it out, and then your things will be all done. You'll be glad of some new clothes, shan't you?"

"Very glad, marm," said Gerty. "Am I to take them away, and keep them all myself?"

"Yes, indeed," said Mrs. Sullivan.

"I don't know where I'll put 'em all; there an't no place in our room,—at least, no very nice place," said Gerty, glancing with admiration at the open drawer, in which Mrs. Sullivan was now placing the little dress, adding it to a pile of neatly-folded garments.

"Why, part of them, you know, you'll be wearing," said Mrs. Sullivan; "and we must find some good place for the rest."

"You've got good places for things," said Gerty, looking round the room; "this is a beautiful room, is n't it?"

"Why, it is n't very different from Mr. Flint's. It's just about the same size, and two front-windows like his. My cupboard is the best; yours is only a three-cornered one; but that's about all the difference."

"O, but then yours don't look one bit like ours. You have n't got any bed here, and all the chairs stand in a row, and the table shines, and the floor is so clean, and the stove is new, and the sun comes in so bright! O! I wish our room was like this! I should n't think ours was more than half as big, either. Why, Uncle True stumbled over the tongs, this morning, and he said there was n't room to swing a cat."

"Where were the tongs?" said Mrs. Sullivan.

"About in the middle of the floor, marm."

"Well, you see I don't keep things in the middle of the floor. I think, if your room were all cleaned up, and places found for everything, it would look almost as well as mine."

"I wish it could be fixed up nice," said Gerty; "but what could be done with those beds?"

"I've been thinking about that. There's that little pantry,—or bathing-room, I think it must have been once, when this house was new, and rich people lived in it; that's large enough to hold a small bedstead and a chair or two; 't would be quite a comfortable little chamber for you. There's nothing in it but rubbish that might just as well be thrown away, or, if it *were* good for anything, put in the shed."

"O, that'll be nice!" said Gerty; "then Uncle True can have his bed back again and I'll sleep on the floor in there."

"No," said Mrs. Sullivan; "it won't be necessary for you to sleep on the floor. I've got a very good little cross-legged bedstead, that my Willie slept on when he lived at home; and I will lend it to you, if you'll try to take good care of it and of everything else that is put into your room."

"O, I will," said Gerty.—"But can I?" added she, hesitating; "do you think I can? I don't know how to do anything."

"You never have been taught to do anything, my child; but a girl eight years old can do a great many things, if she is patient and tries hard to learn. I could teach you a great deal that would be useful, and that would help your Uncle True very much."

"What could I do?"

"You could sweep the room up every day; you could make the beds, after a fashion, with a little help in turning them; you could set the table, toast the bread, and wash the dishes. Perhaps you would not do these things in the best manner at first; but you would keep improving, and by and by get to be quite a nice little house-keeper."

"O, I wish I could do something for Uncle True!" said Gerty; "but how could I ever begin?"

"In the first place, you must have things cleaned up for you. If I thought Mr. Flint would like it, I'd get Kate McCarty to come in some day and help us; and I think we could make a great improvement in his home."

"O, I know he'd like it," said Gerty; "'t would be grand! May I help?"

"Yes, you may do what you can; but Kate'll be the best hand; she's strong, and knows how to do cleaning very well."

"Who's she?" said Gerty.

"Kate?—She's Mrs. McCarty's daughter, in the next house. Mr. Flint does them many a good turn,—saws wood, and so on. They do most of his washing; but they can't half pay him all the kindness he's done that family. Kate's a clever girl; she'll be glad to come and work for him, any day. I'll ask her."

"Will she come to-morrow?"

"Perhaps she will."

"Uncle True's going to be gone all day to-morrow," said Gerty; "he's going to get in Mr. Eustace's coal. Would n't it be a good time?"

"Very," said Mrs. Sullivan. "I'll try and get Kate to come to-morrow."

Kate came. The room was thoroughly cleaned, and put in complete order. Gerty's new clothes were delivered over to her own keeping; she was neatly dressed in one suit, the other placed in a little chest which was found in the pantry, and which accommodated her small wardrobe very well.

It was the result of all Mrs. Sullivan's, Kate's, and Gerty's combined labor which called forth True's astonishment on his return from his work; and the pleasure he manifested made the day a memorable one in Gerty's life, one to be marked in her memory as long as she lived, as being the first in which she had known *that* happiness—perhaps the highest earth affords—of feeling that she had been instrumental in giving joy to another. Not that Gerty's assistance had been of any great value; or that all could not have been done as well, or even better, if she had been where Nan Grant always put her,—out of the way. But the child did not realize that: she had been one of the laborers; she had entered heart and soul into every part of the work; wherever she had been allowed to lend a helping hand, she had exerted her whole strength. She could say, with truth, "*We* did it,—Mrs. Sullivan, Kate and *I.*"

None but a loving heart, like Mrs. Sullivan's, would have understood and sympathized in the feeling which made Gerty so eager to help. But *she* did, and allotted to her many little services, which the child felt herself more blessed in being permitted to perform than she would have done at almost any gift or favor that could have been bestowed upon her.

She led True about to show him how judiciously and ingeniously Mrs. Sullivan had contrived to make the most of the room and the furniture; how, by moving the bed into a deep recess, which was just wide enough for it, she had reserved the whole square area, and made, as True declared, a parlor of it. It was some time before he could be made to believe that half his property had not been spirited away, so incomprehensible was it to him that so much additional space and comfort could be acquired by a little system and order.

But his astonishment and Gerty's delight reached their climax, when she introduced him into the former lumber-closet, now transformed into a really snug and comfortable bed-room.

"Well, I declare! Well, I declare!" was all the old man could seem to say. He sat down beside the stove, now polished, and made, as Gerty declared, new, just like Mrs. Sullivan's; rubbed his hands together, for they were cold with being out in the frosty evening, and then, spreading them in front of the fire, took a general view of his reformed domicile, and of Gerty, who, according to Mrs. Sullivan's careful instructions, was preparing to set the table and toast the bread for supper. She was standing on a chair, taking down the cups and saucers from among the regular rows of dishes shining in the three-cornered cupboard, having already deposited on the lower shelf, where she could reach it from the floor, a plate containing some smoothly-cut slices of bread, which the thoughtful Mrs. Sullivan had prepared for her. True watched her motions for a minute or two, and then indulged in a short soliloquy. "Mrs. Sullivan's a clever woman, sartain, and they've made my old house here complete, and Gerty's gettin' to be like the apple of my eye, and I'm as happy a man as—"

CHAPTER VI

Some dream that they can silence, when they will,
The storm of passion, and say *peace, be still!*
    Cowper

HERE TRUE WAS interrupted. Quick, noisy footsteps in the passage were followed by a sudden and unceremonious opening of the door.

"Here, Uncle True," said the new comer; "here's your package. You forgot all about it, I guess; and I forgot it, too, till mother saw it on the table, where I'd laid it down. I was so taken up with just coming home, you know."

"Of course,—of course!" said True. "Much obliged to you, Willie, for fetchin' it for me. It's pretty brittle stuff it's made of, and most like I should a smashed it, 'fore I got it home."

"What is it?—I've been wondering."

"Why, it's a little knick-knack I've brought home for Gerty, here, that—"

"Willie! Willie!" called Mrs. Sullivan from the opposite room, "have you been to tea, dear?"

"No, indeed, mother;—have you?"

"Why, yes; but I'll get you some."

"No, no!" said True: "stay and take tea with us, Willie, take tea here, my boy. My little Gerty is makin' some famous toast, and I'll put the tea a steepin' presently."

"So I will," said Willie; "I should like to, first-rate. No matter about any supper for me, mother; I'm going to have my tea here, with Uncle True. Come, now, let's see what's in the bundle; but first I want to see little Gerty; mother's been telling me about her. Where is she?—has she got well? She's been very sick, has n't she?"

"O, yes, she's nicely now," said True. "Here, Gerty, look here! Why, where is she?"

"There she is, hiding up behind the settle," said Willie, laughing. "She an't afraid of me, is she?"

"Will, I did n't know as she was shy," said True. "You silly little girl," added he, going towards her, "come out here, and see Willie. This is Willie Sullivan."

"I don't want to see him," said Gerty.

"Don't want to see Willie!" said True; "why, you don't know what you're sayin'. Willie's the best boy that ever was; I 'spect you and he'll be great friends, by and by."

"He won't like me," said Gerty; "I know he won't!"

"Why shan't I like you?" said Willie, approaching the corner where Gerty had hid herself. Her face was covered with her hands, according to her usual fashion when anything distressed her. "I guess I shall like you first-rate, when I see you."

He stooped down as he spoke, for he was much taller than Gerty, and, taking her hands directly down from her face and holding them tight in his own, he fixed his eyes full upon her, and, nodding pleasantly, said,

"How do do, Cousin Gerty,—how do do?"

"I an't your cousin!" said Gerty.

"Yes you are," said Willie, decidedly; "Uncle True's your uncle, and mine too;—so we're cousins—don't you see?—and I want to get acquainted."

Gerty could not resist Willie's good-natured words and manner. She suffered him to draw her out of the corner, and towards the lighter end of the room. As she came near the lamp, she tried to free her hands, in order to cover her face up again; but Willie would not let her, and, attracting her attention to the unopened package, and exciting her curiosity as to what it might contain, he succeeded in diverting her thoughts from herself, so that in a few minutes she seemed quite at her ease.

"There, Uncle True says it's for you," said Willie; "and I can't think what't is, can you? Feel—it's hard as can be."

Gerty felt, and looked up wonderingly in True's face.

"Undo it, Willie," said True.

Willie produced a knife, cut the string, took off the paper, and disclosed one of those white plaster images, so familiar to everyone, representing the little Samuel[1] in an attitude of devotion.

"O, how pretty!" exclaimed Gerty, full of delight.

"Why did n't I think?" said Willie; "I might have known what't was, by the feeling."

"Why! did you ever see it before?" said Gerty.

"Not this same one: but I've seen lots just like it."

"Have you?" said Gerty. "I never did. I think it's the beautifullest thing that ever was. Uncle True, did you say it was for me? Where did you get it?"

"It was by an accident I got it. A few minutes before I met you, Willie, I was stoppin' at the corner to light my lamp, when I saw one of those *furren* [2] boys with a sight o' these sort of things, and some black ones too, all set up on a board, and he was walkin' with 'em a-top of his head. I was just a wonderin' how he kept 'em there, when he hit the board agin my lamp-post, and, the first thing I knew, whack they all went! He'd spilt 'em every one. Lucky enough for him, there was a great bank of soft snow close to the side-walk, and the most of 'em fell into that, and was n't hurt. Some few went on to the bricks, and were smashed. Well, I kind o' pitied the feller; for it was late, and I thought like enough he had n't had much luck sellin' of 'em, to have so many left on his hands—"

"On his head, you mean," said Willie.

"Yes, Master Willie, or on the snow," said True; "any way you're a mind to have it."

"And I know what you did, Uncle True, just as well as if I'd seen you," said Willie; "you set your ladder and lantern right down, and went to work helping him pick 'em all up,—that's just what you'd be sure to do for anybody. I hope, if ever you get into trouble, some of the folks you've helped will be by to make return."

"This feller, Willie, did n't wait for me to get into trouble; he made return right off. When they were all set right, he bowed, and scraped, and touched his hat to me, as if I'd been the biggest gentleman in the land; talkin', too, he was, all the time, though I could n't make out a word of his lingo; and then he insisted on my takin' one o' the figurs. I wan't agoin to, for I did n't want it; but I happened to think little Gerty might like it."

"O, I shall like it!" said Gerty. "I shall like it better than—no, not better, but almost *as well* as my kitten; not *quite* as well, because that was alive, and this is n't; but *almost*. O, an't he a cunning little boy?"

True, finding that Gerty was wholly taken up with the image, walked away and began to get the tea, leaving the two children to entertain each other.

"You must take care and not break it, Gerty," said Willie. "We had a Samuel once, just like it, in the shop; and I dropped it out of my hand on to the counter, and broke it into a million pieces."

"What did you call it?" said Gerty.

"A Samuel; they're all Samuels."

"What are *Sammles?*" said Gerty.

"Why, that's the name of the child they're taken for."

"What do you s'pose he's sittin' on his knee for?"

Willie laughed. "Why, don't you know?" said he.

"No," said Gerty; "what is he?"

"He's praying," said Willie.

"Is that what he's got his eyes turned up for, too?"

"Yes, of course; he looks up to heaven when he prays."

"Up to where?"

"To heaven."

Gerty looked up at the ceiling in the direction in which the eyes were turned, then at the figure. She seemed very much dissatisfied and puzzled.

"Why, Gerty," said Willie, "I should n't think you knew what praying was."

"I don't," said Gerty; "tell me."

"Don't you ever pray,—pray to God?"

"No, *I* don't.—Who is God? Where is God?"

Willie looked inexpressibly shocked at Gerty's ignorance, and answered, reverently, "God is in heaven, Gerty."

"I don't know where that is," said Gerty. "I believe I don't know nothin' about it."

"I should n't think you did," said Willie. "I *believe* heaven is up in the sky; but my Sunday-school teacher says, 'heaven is anywhere where goodness is,' or some such thing," he said.

"Are there stars in heaven?" said Gerty.

"They look so, don't they?" said Willie. "They're in the sky, where I always used to think heaven was."

"I should like to go to heaven," said Gerty.

"Perhaps, if you're good, you will go, some time."

"Can't any but good folks go?"

"No."

"Then I can't ever go," said Gerty, mournfully.

"Why not?" said Willie; "an't you good?"

"O, no! I'm very bad."

"What a queer child!" said Willie. "What makes you think yourself so very bad?"

"O! I *am,*" said Gerty, in a very sad tone; "I'm the worst of all. I'm the worst child in the world."

"Who told you so?"

"Everybody. Nan Grant says so, and she says everybody thinks so; I know it, too, myself."

"Is Nan Grant the cross old woman you used to live with?"

32

"Yes. How did you know she was cross?"

"O, my mother's been telling me about her. Well, I want to know if she did n't send you to school, or teach you anything?"

Gerty shook her head.

"Why, what lots you've got to learn! What did you used to do, when you lived there?"

"Nothing."

"Never did anything, and don't know anything; my gracious!"

"Yes, I do know one thing," said Gerty. "I know how to toast bread;—your mother taught me;—she let me toast some by her fire."

As she spoke she thought of her own neglected toast, and turned towards the stove; but she was too late,—the toast was made, the supper ready, and True was just putting it on the table.

"O, Uncle True," said she, "I meant to get the tea."

"I know it," said True, "but it's no matter; you can get it to-morrow."

The tears came into Gerty's eyes;—she looked very much disappointed, but said nothing. They all sat down to supper. Willie put the Samuel in the middle of the table for a centre ornament, and told so many funny stories, and said so many pleasant things, that Gerty laughed heartily, forgot that she did not make the toast herself, forgot her sadness, her shyness, even her ugliness and wickedness, and showed herself, for once, a merry child. After tea, she sat beside Willie on the great settle, and, in her peculiar way, and with many odd expressions and remarks, gave him a description of her life at Nan Grant's, winding up with a touching account of the death of her kitten.

The two children seemed in a fair way to become as good friends as True could possibly wish. True himself sat on the opposite side of the stove, smoking his pipe; his elbows on his knees, his eyes bent on the children, and his ears drinking in all their conversation. He was no restraint upon them. So simple-hearted and sympathizing a being, so ready to be amused and pleased, so slow to blame or disapprove, could never be any check upon the gayety or freedom of the youngest, most careless spirit. He laughed when they laughed; seemed soberly satisfied, and took long whiffs at his pipe, when they talked quietly and sedately; ceased smoking entirely, letting his pipe rest on his knee, and secretly wiping away a tear, when Gerty recounted her childish griefs. He had heard the story before, and he cried then. He often heard it afterwards, but never *without crying*.

After Gerty had closed her tale of sorrows, which was frequently interrupted by Willie's ejaculations of condolence or pity, she sat for a moment without speaking; then, becoming excited, as her ungoverned and easily roused nature dwelt upon its wrongs, she burst forth in a very different tone from that in which she had been speaking, and commenced uttering the most bitter invectives against Nan Grant; making use of many a rough and coarse term, such as she had been accustomed to hear used by the ill-bred people with whom she had lived. The child's language expressed unmitigated hatred, and even a hope of future revenge. True looked worried and troubled at hearing her talk so angrily. Since he brought her home he had never witnessed such a display of temper, and had fondly believed that she would always be as quiet and gentle as during her illness and the few weeks subsequent to it. True's own disposition was so placid, amiable, and forgiving, that he could not imagine that any one, and especially a little child, should long retain feelings of anger and bitterness. Gerty had shown herself so mild and patient since she had been with him, so submissive to his wishes, so anxious even to forestall them, that it had never occurred to him to dread any difficulty in the management of the child. Now, however, as he observed her flashing eyes, and noticed the doubling of her little fist, as she menaced Nan with her future wrath, he had an undefined, half-formed presentiment of coming trouble in the control of his little charge; a feeling almost of alarm, lest he had undertaken what he could never perform. For the moment, she ceased, in his eyes, to be the pet and plaything he had hitherto considered her. He saw in her something which needed a check, and felt himself unfit to apply it.

And no wonder. He *was* totally unfit to cope with a spirit like Gerty's. It was true he possessed over her one mighty influence,—her strong affection for him, which he could not doubt. It was that which made her so submissive and patient in her sickness, so grateful for his care and kindness, so anxious to do something in return. It was that deep love for her first friend, which, never wavering, and growing stronger to the last, proved, in after years, a noble motive for exertion, a worthy incentive to virtue. It was that love, fortified and illumined by a higher light, which came in time to sanctify it, that gave her, while yet a mere girl, a woman's strength of heart and self-denial. It was that which cheered the old man's latter years, and shed joy on his dying bed.

But for the present it was not enough. The kindness she had received for the few weeks past had completely softened Gerty's heart towards her benefactors; but the effect of eight years' mis-management, ill treatment, and want of all judicious discipline, could not be done away in that short time. Her unruly nature could not be so suddenly quelled, her better capabilities called into action.

The plant that for years has been growing distorted, and dwelling in a barren spot, deprived of light and nourishment, withered in its leaves and blighted in its fruit, cannot at once recover from so cruel a blast. Transplanted to another soil, it must be directed in the right course, nourished with care and warmed with Heaven's light, ere it can recover from the shock occasioned by its early neglect, and find strength to expand its flowers and ripen its fruit.

So with little Gerty;—a new direction must be given to her ideas, new nourishment to her mind, new light to her soul, ere the higher purposes for which she was created could be accomplished in her.

Something of this True felt, and it troubled him. He did not, however, attempt to check the child. He did not know what to do, and so did nothing.

Willie tried once or twice to stop the current of her abusive language; but soon desisted, for she did not pay the least attention to him. He could not help smiling at her childish wrath; nor could he resist sympathizing with her in a degree, and almost wishing he could have a brush with Nan himself, and express his opinion of her character in one or two hard knocks. But he had been well brought up by his gentle mother, was conscious that Gerty was exhibiting a very hot temper, and began to understand what made everybody think her so bad.

After Gerty had railed about Nan a little while, she stopped of her own accord; though an unpleasant look remained on her countenance, one of her old looks, that it was a pity should return, but which always did when she got into a passion. It soon passed away, however, and when, a little later in the evening, Mrs. Sullivan appeared at the door, Gerty looked bright and happy, listened with evident delight while True uttered warm expressions of thanks for the labor which had been undertaken in his behalf, and, when Willie went away with his mother, said her good-night and asked him to come again so pleasantly, and her eyes looked so bright as she stood holding on to True's hand in the doorway, that Willie said, as soon as they were out of hearing, "She's a queer little thing, an't she, mother? But I kind o' like her."

CHAPTER VII

Prayer is the burden of a sigh,
The falling of a tear,
The upward glancing of an eye,
When none but God is near.
——*Montgomery*

IT WOULD HAVE BEEN hard to find two children, both belonging to the poorer class, whose situations in life had, thus far, presented a more complete contrast than those of Gerty and Willie. With Gerty's experiences the reader is somewhat acquainted. A neglected orphan, she had received little of that care, and still less of that love, which Willie had always enjoyed. Mrs. Sullivan's husband was an intelligent country clergyman; but, as he died when Willie was a baby, leaving very little property for the support of his family, the widow went home to her father, taking her child with her. The old man needed his daughter; for death had made sad inroads in his household since she left it, and he was alone.

From that time the three had lived together in humble comfort; for, though poor, industry and frugality secured them from want. Willie was his mother's pride, her hope, her constant thought. She spared herself no toil or care to provide for his physical comfort, his happiness, and his growth in knowledge and virtue.

It would have been strange enough if she had not been proud of a boy whose uncommon beauty, winning disposition, and early evidence of a manly and noble nature, won him friends even among strangers. He had been a handsome child; but there was that observable in him, now that he had nearly reached his thirteenth year, far excelling the common boyish beauty, which consists merely in curly hair, dark eyes and rosy cheeks. It was his broad, open forehead, the clearness and calmness of his full gray eye, the expressive mouth, so determined and yet so mild, the well-developed figure and ruddy complexion, proclaiming high health, which gave promise of power to the future man. No one could have been in the boy's company half an hour, without loving and admiring him. He had naturally a warm-hearted, affectionate disposition, which his mother's love and the world's smiles had fostered; an unusual flow of animal spirits, tempered by a natural politeness towards his elders and superiors; a quick apprehension; a ready command of language; a sincere sympathy in others' pleasures and pains; in fine, one of those genial natures, that wins hearts one knows not how. He was fond of study, and until his twelfth year his mother kept him constantly at school. The sons of poor parents have, in our large cities, almost every educational advantage that can be obtained by wealth; and Willie, having an excellent capacity, and being constantly encouraged and exhorted by his mother to improve his opportunities to the utmost, had attained a degree of proficiency quite unusual at his age.

When he was twelve years old he had an excellent opportunity to enter into the service of an apothecary, who did an extensive business in the city, and wanted a boy to assist in his store. The wages that Mr. Bray offered were not great, but there was the hope of an increased salary; and, at any rate, situated as Willie was, it was not a chance to be overlooked. Fond as he was of his books, he had long been eager to be at work, helping to bear the burden of labor in the family. His mother and grandfather assented to the plan, and he gladly accepted Mr. Bray's proposals.

He was sadly missed at home; for, as he slept at the store during the week, he rarely had much leisure to make even a passing visit to his mother, except on Saturday, when he came home at night and passed Sunday. So Saturday night was Mrs. Sullivan's happy night, and the Sabbath became a more blessed day than ever.

When Willie reached his mother's room on the evening of which we have been speaking, he sat down with her and Mr. Cooper, and for an hour conversation was brisk with them. Willie never came home that he had not a great deal to relate concerning the occurrences of the week; many a little anecdote to tell; many a circumstance connected with the shop, the customers, his master the apothecary, and his master's family, with whom he took his meals. Mrs. Sullivan was interested in everything that interested Willie, and it was easy to see that the old grandfather was more entertained by the boy than he was willing to appear; for, though he sat with his eyes upon the floor, and did not seem to listen, he usually heard all that was said, as was often proved afterwards by some accidental reference he would make to the subject. He seldom asked questions, and indeed it was not necessary, for Mrs. Sullivan asked enough for them both. He seldom made comments, but would occasionally utter an impatient or contemptuous expression regarding individuals or the world in general; thereby evidencing that distrust of human nature, that want of confidence in men's honesty and virtue, which formed, as we have said, a marked trait in the old man's character. Willie's spirits would then receive a momentary check; for *he* loved and trusted *everybody,* and his grandfather's words, and the tone in which they were spoken, were a damper to his young soul; but, with the elasticity of youth and a gay heart, they would soon rebound, and he would go on as before. Willie did not fear his grandfather, who had never been severe to him, never having, indeed, interfered at all with Mrs. Sullivan's management; but he sometimes felt chilled, though he hardly knew why, by his want of sympathy with his own warm-heartedness. On the present occasion the conversation having turned at last upon True Flint and his adopted child, Mr. Cooper had been unusually bitter and satirical, and, as he took his lamp to go to bed, wound up with remarking that he knew very well Gerty would never be anything but a trouble to Flint, who was a fool not to send her to the alms-house at once.

There was a pause after the old man left the room; then Willie exclaimed, "Mother, what makes grandfather hate folks?"

"Why, he don't, Willie."

"I don't mean exactly *hate*—I don't suppose he does *that, quite,* but he don't seem to *think* a great deal of anybody—do you think he does?"

"O, yes; he don't show it much," said Mrs. Sullivan; "but he thinks a great deal of you, Willie, and he would n't have anything happen to me for the world; and he likes Mr. Flint, and—"

"O, yes, I know that, of course; I don't mean that; but he does n't think there's much goodness in folks, and he don't seem to think anybody's going to turn out well, and—"

"You're thinking of what he said about little Gerty."

"Well, she an't the only one. That's what made me speak of it now, but I've often noticed it before, particularly since I went away from home, and am only here once a week. Now, you know I think everything of Mr. Bray; and when I was telling to-night how much good he did, and how kind he was to old Mrs. Morris and her sick daughter, grandfather looked just as if he did n't believe it, or did n't *think* much of it, somehow."

"O, well, Willie," said Mrs. Sullivan, "you must n't wonder much at that. Grandpa's had a good many disappointments. You know he thought everything of Uncle Richard, and there was no end to the trouble he had with him; and there was Aunt Sarah's husband—he seemed to be such a fine fellow when Sally married him, but he cheated father dreadfully at last, so that he had to mortgage his house in High-street, and finally give it up entirely. He's dead now, and I don't want to say anything against him; but he did n't prove what we expected, and it broke Sally's heart, I think. That was a dreadful trial to father, for she was the youngest, and had always been his pet. And, just after that, mother was taken down with her death-stroke, and there was a quack doctor prescribed for her, that father always though did her more hurt than good. O, take it altogether, he's had a great deal to make him look on the dark side now; but you must n't mind it, Willie; you must take care and turn out well yourself, my son, and then he'll be proud enough; he's as pleased as he can be when he hears you praised, and expects great things of you, one of these days."

Here the conversation ended; but not until the boy had added an-other to the many resolves already made, that, if his health and strength were spared, he would prove to his grandfather that hopes were not always deceitful, and that fears were sometimes groundless.

O! what a glorious thing it is for a youth when he has ever present with him a high, a noble, an unselfish motive! What an incentive it is to exertion, perseverance and self-denial! What a force to urge him on to ever-increasing efforts! Fears that would otherwise appall, discourage-ments that would dishearten, labors that would weary, obstacles that would dismay, opposition that would crush, temptation that would over-come, all, all lie disarmed and powerless, when, with a single-hearted and worthy aim, he struggles for victory!

And so it is, that those born in honor, wealth and luxury, seldom achieve greatness. They were not *born* for labor; and, without labor, nothing that is worth having can be won. Why will they not make it their great and absorbing motive (a worthy one it certainly would be), to over-come the disadvantages of their position, and make themselves great, learned, wise and good, in spite of those riches, that honorable birth, that opportunity for luxurious sloth, which are, in reality, to the clear-judging eye of wise men and angels, their deadliest snare? A motive Willie had long had. His grandfather was old, his mother weak, and both poor. He must be the staff of their old age; he must labor for their support and comfort; he must do *more;*—they hoped great things of him; they *must* not be disap-pointed. He did not, however, while arming himself for future conflict with the world, forget the present, but sat down and learned his Sunday-school lessons. After which, according to custom, he read aloud in the Bible; and then Mrs. Sullivan, laying her hand on the head of her son, offered up a simple, heart-felt prayer for the boy,—one of those mother's prayers, which the child listens to with reverence and love, and remembers in the far-off years; one of those prayers which keep men from temptation, and deliver them from evil.

After Willie went home that evening, and Gerty was left alone with

True, she sat on a low stool beside him for some time, without speaking. Her eyes were intently fixed upon the white image which lay in her lap; that her little mind was very busy, there could be no doubt, for thought was plainly written on her face. True was not often the first to speak; but, finding Gerty unusually quiet, he lifted up her chin, looked inquiringly in her face, and then said:

"Well, Willie's a pretty clever sort of a boy, isn't he?"

Gerty answered, "Yes;" without, however, seeming to know what she was saying.

"You like him, don't you?" said True.

"Very much," said Gerty, in the same absent way. It was not Willie she was thinking of. True waited for Gerty to begin talking about her new acquaintance; but she did not speak for a minute or two. Then looking up suddenly, she said:

"Uncle True?"

"What say?"

"What does Samuel pray to God for?"

True stared. "Samuel!—pray!—I guess I don't know exactly what you're saying."

"Why," said Gerty, holding up the image, "Willie says this little boy's name is Samuel; and that he sits on his knee, and puts his hands together *so,* and looks up, because he's praying to God, that lives up in the sky. I don't know what he means,—*way* up in the sky,—do you?"

True took the image and looked at it attentively; he moved uneasily upon his chair, scratched his head, and finally said:

"Well, I s'pose he's about right. This 'ere child is prayin', sartain, though I did n't think on it afore. But I don't jist know what he calls it a Samuel for. We'll ask him, some time."

"Well, what does he pray for, Uncle True?"

"O! he prays to make him good; it makes folks good to pray to God."

"Can God make folks good?"

"Yes. God is very great; he can do anything."

"How can he *hear?*"

"He hears everything and sees everything in the world."

"And does he live in the sky?"

"Yes," said True, "in heaven."

Many more questions Gerty asked; many strange questions, that True could not answer; many questions that he wondered he had not oftener asked himself. True had a humble, loving heart, and a child-like

faith; he had enjoyed but little religious instruction, but he earnestly endeavored to live up to the light he had. Perhaps, in his faithful practice of
the Christian virtues, and especially in his obedience to the great law of
Christian charity, he more nearly approached to the spirit of his Divine
Master than many who, by daily reading and study, are far more familiar
with Christian doctrines. But he had never inquired deeply into the
sources of that belief which it had never occurred to him to doubt; and he
was not at all prepared for the questions suggested by the inquisitive, keen
and newly-excited mind of little Gerty. He answered her as well as he
could, however; and, where he was at fault, hesitated not to refer her to
Willie, who, he told her, went to Sunday-school, and knew a wonderful
sight about such things. All the information that Gerty could gain
amounted to the knowledge of these facts: that God was in heaven; that his
power was great; and that people were made better by prayer. Her little
eager brain was so intent upon the subject, however, that, as it grew late,
the thought even of sleeping in her new room could not efface it from her
mind. After she had gone to bed, with the white image hugged close to her
bosom, and True had taken away the lamp, she lay for a long time with
her eyes wide open. Just at the foot of the bed was the window. Gerty
could see out, as she had done before in her garret at Nan Grant's; but, the
window being larger, she had a much more extended view. The sky was
bright with stars; and the sight of them revived her old wonder and curiosity as to the author of such distant and brilliant lights. Now, however, as
she gazed, there darted through her mind the thought, "God lit them! O,
how great he must be! But a *child* might pray to him!" She rose from her
little bed, approached the window, and, falling on her knees and clasping
her hands precisely in the attitude of the little Samuel, she looked up to
heaven. She spoke no word, but her eyes glistened with the dew of a tear
that stood in each. Was not each tear a prayer? She breathed no petition,
but she longed for God and virtue. Was not that very wish a prayer? Her
little uplifted heart throbbed vehemently. Was not each throb a prayer?
And did not God in heaven, without whom not a sparrow falls to the
ground, hear and accept that first homage of a little, untaught child; and
did it not call a blessing down?

Many a petition did Gerty offer up in after years. In many a time of
trouble did she come to God for help; in many an hour of bitter sorrow did
she from the same source seek comfort and, when her strength and heart
failed her, God became the strength of her heart. But never did she approach his throne with a purer offering, a more acceptable sacrifice, than

when, in her first deep penitence, her first earnest faith, her first enkindled hope, she took the attitude, and her heart uttered, though her lips pronounced them not, the words of the prophet-child, "Here am I, Lord!"

CHAPTER VIII

"——Revenge, at first though sweet,
Bitter ere long back on itself recoils."
—*Milton*

THE NEXT DAY was Sunday. True was in the habit of going to church half the day at least, with the sexton's family; but Gerty, having no bonnet, could not go, and True would not leave her. So they spent the morning together, wandering round among the wharves and looking at the ships, Gerty wearing her old shawl pinned over her head. In the afternoon, True fell asleep by the fireside, and Gerty played with the cat.

Willie came in the evening; but it was only to say good-bye, before going back to Mr. Bray's. He was in a hurry, and could not stop at all; for his master had a sober household, and liked to have his doors closed early, especially Sunday night. Old Mr. Cooper, however, made his usual visit; and, when he had gone, True, finding Gerty sound asleep on the settle, thought it a pity to wake her, and laid her in bed with her clothes on.

She did not wake until morning; and then, much surprised and amused at finding herself dressed, sprang up and ran out to ask True how it happened. True was busy making a fire; and Gerty, having received satisfactory answers to her numerous inquiries,—when and where she fell asleep, and how she came in bed,—applied herself earnestly to help in every possible way about getting the breakfast, and putting the room in order. She followed Mrs. Sullivan's instructions, all of which she remembered, and showed a wonderful degree of capability in everything she undertook. In the course of the few following weeks, during which her perseverance held out surprisingly, she learned how to make herself useful in many ways, and, as Mrs. Sullivan had prophesied, gave promise of becoming, one day, quite a clever little housekeeper. Of course, the services she performed were trifling; but her active and willing feet saved True a great many steps, and she was of essential aid in keeping the rooms neat, that being her especial ambition. She felt that Mrs. Sullivan expected her, now that the dust and cobwebs were all cleared away, to take care that they should not accumulate again; and it was quite an amusing sight, every day, when True had gone out as usual to fill and clean the street-lamps, to see the little girl diligently laboring with an old broom, the handle of which was cut short to make it more suitable for her use. Mrs. Sullivan looked in occasionally, to praise and assist her; and nothing made Gerty happier than learning how to do some new thing. She met with a few trials and discouragements, to be sure. In two or three instances the toast got burned to a cinder; and, worse still, she one day broke a painted teacup, over which she shed many a tear; but, as True never thought of blaming her for anything, she forgot her misfortunes, and experience made her careful.

Kate McCarty thought her the smartest child in the world, and would sometimes come in and wash up the floor, or do some other work, which required more strength or skill than Gerty possessed.

Prompted by her ambition to equal Mrs. Sullivan's expectations, and still more by her desire to be useful to True, and in some degree manifest her love to him by her labors, Gerty was usually patient, good-natured and obliging. So very indulgent was True, that he rarely indeed laid a command upon the child, leaving her to take her own course, and have her own way; but, undisciplined as she was, she willingly yielded obedience to one who never thwarted her, and the old man seldom saw her exhibit in his presence that violent temper, which, when roused, knew no restraint. She had little to irritate her in the quiet home she now enjoyed; but instances sometimes occurred which proved that the fire of her spirit was not quenched, or its evil propensities extinguished.

One Sunday, Gerty, who had now a nice little hood which True had bought for her, was returning with Mr. Cooper, Mr. Flint and Willie, from the afternoon service at church. The two old men were engaged in one of their lengthy discussions, and the children, having fallen into the rear, had been talking earnestly about the church, the minister, the people and the music, all of which were new to Gerty, and greatly excited her wonder and astonishment.

As they drew near home, Willie remarked how dark it was growing in the streets; and then, looking down at Gerty, whom he held by the hand, he said, "Gerty, do you ever go out with Uncle True, and see him light the lamps?"

"No, I never did," said Gerty, "since the first night I came. I've wanted to, but it's been so cold Uncle True would not let me; he said I'd just catch the fever again."

"It won't be cold this evening," said Willie; "it'll be a beautiful night; and, if Uncle True's willing, let's you and I go with him. I've often been, and it's first rate; you can look into the windows and see folks drinking tea, and sitting all round the fire in the parlors."

"And I like to see him light those great lamps," interrupted Gerty; "they make it look so bright and beautiful all round. I hope he'll let us go; I'll ask him; come," said she, pulling him by the hand; "let's catch up with them and ask him now."

"No,—wait;" said Willie; "he's busy talking with grandpa; and we're almost home,—we can ask him then."

He could hardly restrain her impatience, however; and, as soon as they reached the gate, she suddenly broke away from him, and, rushing up to True, made known her request. The plan was willingly acceded to, and the three soon started on the rounds.

For some time Gerty's attention was so wholly engrossed by the lamplighting that she could see and enjoy nothing else. But, when they reached the corner of the street, and came in sight of a large apothecary's shop, her delight knew no bounds. The brilliant colors displayed in the windows, now for the first time seen by the evening light, completely captivated her fancy; and when Willie told her that his master's shop was very similar, she thought it must be a very fine place to spend one's life in. Then she wondered why this was open on Sunday, when all the other stores were closed; and Willie, stopping to explain the matter to her, and to gratify her curiosity on many other points, found, when they again started on their way, that True was some distance in advance of them. He hurried Gerty along, telling her that they were now in the finest street they should pass through, and that they must make haste, for they had nearly reached the house he most wanted her to see. When they came up with True, he was just placing his ladder against a post opposite a fine block of buildings. Many of the front windows were shaded, so that the children could not see in; some, however, either had no curtains, or they had not yet been drawn. In one parlor there was a pleasant wood-fire, around which a group were gathered; and here Gerty would fain have lingered. Again, in another, a brilliant chandelier was lit, and though the room was vacant, the furniture was so showy, and the whole so brilliant, that the child clapped her hands in delight, and Willie could not prevail upon her to leave the spot, until he told her that further down the street was another house, equally attractive, where she could perhaps see some beautiful children.

"How do you know there'll be children there?" said she, as they walked along.

"I don't know, certainly," said Willie; "but I think there will. They used always to be up at the window, when I came with Uncle True, last winter."

"How many?" asked Gerty.

"Three, I believe; there was one little girl with such beautiful curls, and such a sweet, cunning little face. She looked like a wax doll, only a great deal prettier."

"O, I hope we shall see her!" said Gerty, dancing along on the tops of her toes, so full was she of excitement and pleasure.

"There they are!" exclaimed Willie; "all three, I declare, just as they used to be!"

"Where?" said Gerty; "where?"

"Over opposite, in the great stone house. Here, let's cross over. It's muddy; I'll carry you."

Willie lifted Gerty carefully over the mud, and they stood in front of the house. True had not yet come up. It was he that the children were waiting for. Gerty was not the only child that loved to see the lamps lit.

It was now quite dark, so that persons in a light room could not see anyone out of doors; but Willie and Gerty had so much the better chance to look in. It was indeed a fine mansion, evidently the home of wealth. A clear coal-fire, and a bright lamp in the centre of the room, shed abroad their cheerful blaze. Rich carpets, deeply-tinted curtains, pictures in gilded frames, and huge mirrors, reflecting the whole on every side, gave Gerty her first impressions of luxurious life. There was an air of comfort combined with all this elegance, which made it still more fascinating to the child of poverty and want. A table was bountifully spread for tea; the cloth of snow-white damask, the shining plate, above all, the home-like hissing tea-kettle, had a most inviting look. A gentleman in gay slippers was in an easy-chair by the fire; a lady in a gay cap was superintending a servant-girl's arrangements at the tea-table, and the children of the household, smiling and happy, were crowded together on a window-seat, looking out, as we have said.

They were, as Willie had described them, sweet, lovely-looking little creatures; especially a girl, about the same age as Gerty, the eldest of the three. Her fair hair fell in long ringlets over a neck as white as snow; she had blue eyes, a cherub face, and a little round, plump figure. Gerty's admiration and rapture were such that she could find no expression for them, except in jumping up and down, shouting, laughing, and directing Willie's notice first to one thing and then another.

"O, Willie! is n't she a darling? and see what a beautiful fire,—what a splendid lady! And look! look at the father's shoes! What is that on the table? I guess it's good! There's a big looking-glass; and O, Willie! an't they dear little handsome children?"

In all her exclamations, she began and ended with her praises of the children. Willie was quite satisfied; Gerty was as much pleased as he had expected or wished.

True now came up, and, as his torch-light swept along the sidewalk, Gerty and Willie became, in their turn, the subjects of notice and conversation. The little curly-haired girl saw them, and pointed them out to the notice of the other two. Though Gerty could not know what they were saying, she did not like the idea of being stared at and talked about; and, hiding behind the post, she would not move or look up, though Willie laughed at her, and told her it was now *her* turn to be looked at. When True took up his ladder, however, and started to move off, she commenced following him at a run, so as to escape observation, but Willie calling to her, and saying that the children were gone from the window, she ran back as quickly to have one more look, and was just in time to see them taking their places at the tea-table. The next instant the servant-girl came and drew down the window-shades. Gerty then took Willie's hand again, and they hastened on once more to overtake True.

"Should n't you like to live in such a house as that, Gerty?" said Willie.

"Yes, indeed," said Gerty; "an't it splendid?"

"I wish I had just such a house." said Willie. "I mean to, one of these days."

"Where will you get it?" exclaimed Gerty, much amazed at so bold a declaration.

"O, I shall work, and grow rich, and buy it."

"You can't; it would take a lot o' money."

"I know it; but I can earn a lot, and I mean to. The gentleman that lives in that grand house was a poor boy when he first came to Boston; and why can't one poor boy get rich, as well as another?"

"How do you suppose he got so much money?"

"I don't know how *he* did; there are a good many ways. Some people think it's all luck, but I guess it's as much smartness as anything."

"Are you smart?"

Willie laughed. "An't I?" said he. "If I don't turn out a rich man, one of these days, you may say I an't."

"I know what I'd do, if I was rich, said Gerty.

"What?" asked Willie.

"First, I'd buy a great, nice chair, for Uncle True, with cushions all in the inside, and bright flowers on it,—just exactly like that one the gentleman was sitting in; and next, I'd have great big lamps, ever so many all in a bunch, so 's to make the room as *light*—as *light* as it could be!"

"Seems to me you're mighty fond of lights, Gerty," said Willie.

"I be," said the child. "I hate old, dark, black places; I like stars, and sunshine, and fires, and Uncle True's torch—"

"And I like bright eyes!" interrupted Willie; "yours look just like stars, they shine so to-night. An't we having a good time?"

"Yes, real."

And so they went on. Gerty jumping and dancing along the sidewalk, Willie sharing in her gayety and joy, and glorying in the responsibility of entertaining and at the same time protecting the wild little creature. They talked much of how they would spend that future wealth which, in their buoyant hopefulness, they both fully calculated upon one day possessing; for Gerty had caught Willie's spirit, and she, too, meant to work and grow rich. Willie told Gerty of the many plans he had for surrounding his mother and grandfather, and even herself and Uncle True, with every comfort and luxury he had ever heard or dreamt of. Among other things, his mother was to wear a gay cap, like that of the lady they had seen through the window; and at this Gerty had a great laugh. She had an innate perception of the fact that the quiet, demure little widow would be ridiculous in a flowered head-gear. Good taste is inborn, and Gerty had it in her. She felt that Mrs. Sullivan, attired in anything that was not simple, neat and sober-looking, would altogether lose her identity. Willie had no selfish schemes; the generous boy suggested nothing for his own gratification; it was for the rest he meant to labor, and in and through them that he looked for his reward. Happy children! happy as children only can be! What do they want of wealth? What of anything, material and tangible, more than they now possess? They have what is worth more than riches or fame. They

are full of childhood's faith and hope. With a fancy and imagination un-
checked by disappointment, they are building those same castles that so
many thousand children have built before,—that children always will be
building, to the end of time. Far off in the distance, they see bright things,
and know not what myths they are. High up they rise, and shine, and
glitter; and the little ones fix their eyes on them, overlook the rough, dark
places that lie between, see not the perils of the way, suspect not the gulfs
and snares into which many are destined to fall; but, confident of gaining
the glorious goal, they set forth on the way rejoicing. Blessings on that
childhood's delusion, if such it be. Undeceive not the little believers, ye
wise ones! Check not that God-given hopefulness, which will, perhaps, in
its airy flight, lift them in safety over many a rough spot in life's road.
It lasts not long, at the best; and check it not, for as it dies out the way
grows hard.

One source of the light-heartedness that Willie and Gerty experienced undoubtedly lay in the disinterestedness and generosity of the emotion which occupied them; for, in the plans they formed, neither seemed
actuated by selfish motives. They were both filled with the desire to con-
tribute to the comfort of their more aged friends. It was a beautiful spirit of
grateful love which each manifested,—a spirit in a great degree natural to
both. In Willie, however, it had been so fostered by pious training that it
partook of the nature of a principle; while in Gerty it was a mere impulse;
and, alas for poor human nature, when swayed by its own passions alone!
The poor little girl had—as who has not?—other less pleasing impulses;
and, if the former needed encouraging and strengthening, so did the latter
require to be uprooted and destroyed.

They had reached the last lamp-post in the street, and now turned
another corner; but scarcely had they gone a dozen steps, before Gerty
stopped short, and, positively refusing to proceed any further, pulled hard
at Willie's hand, and tried to induce him to retrace his steps.

"What's the matter, Gerty?" said he; "are you tired?"

"No, O no! but I can't go any further."

"Why not?"

"O because—because" and here Gerty lowered her voice, and, putting her mouth close to Willie's ear, whispered,—"there is Nan Grant's; I
see the house! I had forgot Uncle True went there; and I can't go—I'm
afraid!"

"Oho!" said Willie, drawing himself up with dignity, "I should like to
know what you're afraid of, when I'm with you! Let her touch you, if she

dares! And Uncle True, too!—I *should* laugh." Very kindly and pleasantly did Willie plead with the child, telling her that Nan would not be likely to see *them,* but that perhaps they should see *her;* and that was just what he wanted,—nothing he should like better. Gerty's fears were easily allayed. She was not naturally timid; it was only the suddenness of the shock she received, on recognizing her old home, that had revived, with full force, her dread and horror of Nan. It needed but little reasoning to assure her of the perfect safety of her present position; and her fears soon gave place to the desire to point out to Willie her former prosecutor. So, by the time they stood in front of the house, she was rather hoping, than otherwise, to catch sight of Nan. And never had any one a fairer chance to be looked at than Nan at that moment. She was standing opposite the window, engaged in an animated dispute with one of her neighbors. Her countenance ex-pressed angry excitement; and, an ill-looking woman at best, her face now was so sufficient an index to her character, that no one could see her thus and afterwards question her right to the title of vixen, virago, scold, or anything else that conveys the same idea.

"Which is she?" said Willie; "the tall one, swinging the coffee-pot in her hand? I guess she'll break the handle off, if she don't look out."

"Yes," said Gerty, "that's Nan."

"What's she doing?"

"O, she's fighting with Miss Birch; she does most always with some-body. She don't see us, does she?"

"No, she's too busy. Come, don't let's stop; she's an ugly-looking woman, just as I knew she was. I've seen enough of her, and I'm sure you have,—come."

But Gerty lingered. Courageous in the knowledge that she was safe and unseen, she was attentively gazing at Nan, and her eyes glistened, not, as a few minutes before, with the healthy and innocent excitement of a cheerful heart, but with the fire of a kindled passion,—a fire that Nan had kindled long ago, which had not yet gone out, and which the sight of Nan had now revived in full force. Willie, thinking it was time to be hurrying home, and perceiving once more that Mr. Flint and his torch were far down the street, now left Gerty, and started himself, as an expedient to draw her on, saying, at the same time, "Come, Gerty, I can't wait."

Gerty turned, saw that he was going, then, quick as lightning, stooped, and, picking up a stone from the side-walk, flung it at the win-dow. There was a crash of broken glass, and an exclamation in Nan's well-known voice; but Gerty was not there to see the result of her work. The instant the stone had left her hand, and she heard the crash, her fears all returned, and, flying past Willie, she paused not until she was safe by the side of True. Willie did not overtake them until they were nearly home, and then came running up, exclaiming, breathlessly, "Why, Gerty, do you know what you did?—You broke the window!"

Gerty jerked her shoulders from side to side to avoid Willie, pouted, and declared that was what she meant to do.

True now inquired what window; and Gerty unhesitatingly acknowledged what she had done, and avowed that she did it on purpose. True and Willie were shocked and silent. Gerty was silent, too, for the rest of the walk; there were clouds on her face, and she felt unhappy in her little heart. She did not understand herself, or her own sensations: we may not say how far she was responsible for them, but this much is certain, her face alone betrayed that, as evil took violent possession of her soul, peace and pleasantness fled away. Poor child! how much she needs to learn the truth! God grant that the inward may one day become as dear to her as now the outward light!

Willie bade them good-night at the house-door, and, as usual, they saw no more of him for a week.

CHAPTER IX

But peace! I must not quarrel with the will
Of highest dispensation, which herein
Haply had ends above my reach to know.
——*Milton*

"FATHER," SAID MRS. SULLIVAN, one afternoon, as he was preparing to go out and to take with him a number of articles which he wanted for his Saturday's work in the church, "why don't you get little Gerty to go with you, and carry some of your things? You can't take them all at once; and she'd like to go, I know."

"She'd only be in the way," said Mr. Cooper; "I can take them myself."

But when he had swung a lantern and an empty coal-hod on one arm, taken a little hatchet and a basket of kindlings in his hand, and hoisted a small ladder over his shoulder, he was fain to acknowledge that there was no accommodation for his hammer and a large paper of nails.

So Mrs. Sullivan called Gerty, and asked her to go to the church with Mr. Cooper, and help him carry his tools.

Gerty was very much pleased with the proposal, and, taking the hammer and nails, started off with great alacrity.

When they reached the church, the old sexton took them from her hands, and, telling her she could play about until he went home, but to be sure and do no mischief, left her and went down into the vestry-room to commence there his operation of sweeping, dusting, and building fires. Gerty was thus left to her own amusement; and ample amusement she found it, for some time, to wander around among the empty aisles and pews, and examine closely what, hitherto, she had only viewed from a corner of the gallery. Then she ascended the pulpit, and in imagination addressed a large audience. She was just beginning to grow weary and restless, however, when the organist, who had entered unperceived, commenced playing some low, sweet music; and Gerty, seating herself on the pulpit-stairs, listened with the greatest attention and pleasure. He had not played long before the door at the foot of the broad aisle opened, and a couple of visitors entered, in observing whom Gerty was soon wholly engrossed. One was an elderly man, dressed like a clergyman, short and spare, with hair thin and gray, forehead high, and features rather sharp; but, though a plain man, remarkable for his calm and benignant expression of countenance. A young lady, apparently about twenty-five years of age, was leaning on his arm. She was attired with great simplicity, wearing a dark-brown cloak, and a bonnet of the same color, relieved by some light-blue ribbon about the face. The only article of her dress which was either rich or elegant was some beautiful dark fur, fastened at her throat with a costly enamelled slide. She was somewhat below the middle size, but had a pleasing and well-rounded figure. Her features were small and regular; her complexion clear, though rather pale; and her light-brown hair was most neatly and carefully arranged. She never lifted her eyes as she walked slowly up the aisle, and the long lashes nearly swept her cheek.

The two approached the spot where Gerty sat, but without perceiving her. "I am glad you like the organ," said the gentleman; "I'm not much of a judge of music, myself, but they say it is a superior instrument, and that Hermann plays it remarkably well."

"Nor is my opinion of any value," said the lady; "for I have very little knowledge of music, much as I love it. But that symphony sounds very delightful to me; it is a long time since I have heard such touching strains; or, it may be, it is partly owing to their striking so sweetly on the solemn quiet of the church, this afternoon. I love to go into a large church on a week-day. It was very kind of you to call for me this afternoon. How came you to think of it?"

"I thought you would enjoy it, my dear. I knew Hermann would be playing about this time; and, besides, when I saw how pale you were looking, it seemed to me the walk would do you good."

"It has done me good. I was not feeling well, and the clear cold air was just what I needed; I knew it would refresh me; but Mrs. Ellis was busy, and I could not, you know, go out alone."

"I thought I should find Mr. Cooper, the sexton, here," said the gentleman. "I want to speak to him about the light; the afternoons are so short now, and it grows dark so early, I must ask him to open more of the blinds, or I cannot see to read my sermon to-morrow. Perhaps he is in the vestry-room; he is always somewhere about here on Saturday; I think I had better go and look for him."

Just then Mr. Cooper entered the church, and, seeing the clergyman, came up, and after receiving his directions about the light, seemed to request him to accompany him somewhere; for the gentleman hesitated, glanced at the young lady, and then said, "I suppose I ought to go to-day; and, as you say you are at leisure, it is a pity I should not; but I don't know—"

Then, turning to the lady, he said, "Emily, Mr. Cooper wants me to go to Mrs. Glass' with him; and I suppose I should have to be absent some time. Do you think you should mind waiting here until I return? She lives in the next street; but I may be detained, for it's about that matter of the library-books being so mischievously defaced, and I am very much afraid that oldest boy of hers had something to do with it. It ought to be inquired into before to-morrow, and I can hardly walk so far as this again to-night, or I would not think of leaving you."

"O! go, by all means," said Emily; "don't mind me; it will be a pleasure to sit here and listen to the music. Mr. Hermann's playing is a great treat to me, and I don't care how long I wait; so I beg you won't hurry on my account, Mr. Arnold."

Thus assured, Mr. Arnold concluded to go; and, having first led the lady to a chair beneath the pulpit, went away with Mr. Cooper.

All this time Gerty had been quite unnoticed, and had remained very quiet on the stair, a little secured from sight by the pulpit. Hardly had the doors closed, however, with a loud bang, when the child got up, and began to descend the stairs. The moment she moved, the lady, whose seat was very near, started, and exclaimed, rather suddenly, "Who's that?"

Gerty stood quite still, and made no reply. Strangely enough, the lady did not look up, though she must have perceived that the movement was above her head. There was a moment's pause, and then Gerty began again to run down the stairs. This time the lady sprung up, and, stretching out her hand, said, as quickly as before, "Who is it?"

"Me" said Gerty, looking up in the lady's face; "it's only me."

"Will you stop and speak to me?" said the lady.

Gerty not only stopped, but came close up to Emily's chair, irresistibly attracted by the music of the sweetest voice she had ever heard. The lady placed her hand on Gerty's head, drew her towards her, and said, "Who are you?"

"Gerty."

"Gerty who?"

"Nothing else but Gerty."

"Have you forgotten your other name?"

"I have n't got any other name."

"How came you here?"

"I came with Mr. Cooper, to help him bring his things."

"And he's left you here to wait for him, and I'm left too; so we must take care of each other, must n't we?"

Gerty laughed at this.

"Where were you?—On the stairs?"

"Yes."

"Suppose you sit down on this step by my chair, and talk with me a little while; I want to see if we can't find out what your other name is. Where do you say you live?"

"With Uncle True."

"True?"

"Yes. Mr. True Flint, I live with now. He took me home to his house, one night, when Nan Grant put me out on the side-walk."

"Why! are you that little girl? Then I've heard of you before. Mr. Flint told me all about you."

"Do you know my Uncle True?"

"Yes, very well."

"What's your name?"

"My name is Emily Graham."

"O! I know," said Gerty, springing suddenly up, and clapping her hands together; "I know. You asked him to keep me; he said so,—I *heard* him say so; and you gave me these clothes; and you're beautiful; and you're good; and I love you! O! I love you ever so much!"

As Gerty spoke with a voice full of excitement, a strange look passed over Miss Graham's face, a most inquiring and restless look, as if the tones of the voice had vibrated on a chord of her memory. She did not speak, but, passing her arm round the child's waist, drew her closer to her. As the peculiar expression passed away from her face, and her features assumed their usual calm composure, Gerty, as she gazed at her with a look of wonder (a look which the child had worn during the whole of the conversation), exclaimed, at last, "Are you going to sleep?"

"No.—why?"

"Because your eyes are shut."

"They are always shut, my child."

"Always shut!—What for?"

"I am blind, Gerty; I can see nothing."

"Not see!" said Gerty; "can't you see anything? Can't you see me now?"

"No," said Miss Graham.

"O!" exclaimed Gerty, drawing a long breath, "*I'm so glad.*"

"*Glad!*" said Miss Graham, in the saddest voice that ever was heard.

"O, yes!" said Gerty, "so glad you can't see me!—because now, perhaps, you'll love me."

"And shouldn't I love you if I saw you?" said Emily, passing her hand softly and slowly over the child's features.

"O, no!" answered Gerty; "I'm so ugly! I'm glad you can't see how ugly I am."

"But just think, Gerty," said Emily, in the same sad voice, "how would you feel if you could not see the light, could not see anything in the world?"

"Can't you see the sun, and the stars, and the sky, and the church we're in? Are you in the dark?"

"In the dark, all the time, day and night in the dark."

Gerty burst into a paroxysm of tears. "O!" exclaimed she, as soon as she could find voice amid her sobs, "it's too bad! it's too bad!"

The child's grief was contagious; and, for the first time for years, Emily wept bitterly for her blindness.

It was for but a few moments, however. Quickly recovering herself, she tried to compose the child also, saying, "Hush! hush! don't cry; and don't say it's too bad! It's not too bad; I can bear it very well. I'm used to it, and am quite happy."

"*I* should n't be happy in the dark; I should *hate* to be!" said Gerty. "I *an't* glad you're blind; I'm real *sorry*. I wish you could see me and everything. Can't your eyes be opened, anyway?"

"No," said Emily, "never; but we won't talk about that any more; we'll talk about you. I want to know what makes you think yourself so very ugly."

"Because folks say that I'm an ugly child, and that nobody loves ugly children."

"Yes, people do," said Emily, "love ugly children, if they are good."

"But I an't good," said Gerty; "I'm real bad!"

"But you *can be good,*" said Emily, "and then everybody will love you."

"Do you think I can be good?"

"Yes, if you try."

"I will try."

"I *hope* you will," said Emily. "Mr. Flint thinks a great deal of his little girl, and she must do all she can to please him."

She then went on to make inquiries concerning Gerty's former way of life, and became so much interested in the recital of the little girl's early sorrows and trials, that she was unconscious of the flight of time, and quite unobservant of the departure of the organist, who had ceased playing, closed his instrument, and gone away.

Gerty was very communicative. Always a little shy of strangers at first, she was nevertheless easily won by kind words; and, in the present case, the sweet voice and sympathetic tones of Emily went straight to her heart. Singularly enough, though her whole life had been passed among the poorer, and almost the whole of it among the lowest class of people, she seemed to feel none of that awe and constraint which might be supposed natural, on her encountering, for the first time, one who, born and bred amid affluence and luxury, showed herself, in every word and motion, a lady of polished mind and manners. On the contrary, Gerty clung to Emily as affectionately, and stroked her soft boa with as much freedom, as if she had herself been born in a palace, and cradled in sable fur. Once or twice she took Emily's nicely-gloved hand between both of her own, and held it tight; her favorite mode of expressing her enthusiastic warmth of gratitude and admiration. The excitable but interesting child took no less strong a hold upon Miss Graham's feelings. The latter saw at once how totally neglected the little one had been, and the importance of her being educated and trained with care, lest early abuse, acting upon an impetuous disposition, should prove destructive to a nature capable of the best attainments. The two were still entertaining each other, and, as we have said, unconscious of the lateness of the hour, when Mr. Arnold entered the church hastily, and somewhat out of breath. As he came up the aisle, when he was yet some way off he called to Emily, saying, "Emily, dear, I'm afraid you thought I had forgotten you, I have been gone so much longer than I intended. Were you not quite tired and discouraged?"

"Have you been gone long?" replied Emily. "I thought it was but a very little while; I have had company, you see."

"What, little folks!" said Mr. Arnold, good-naturedly. "Where did this little body come from?"

"She came to the church this afternoon, with Mr. Cooper. Is n't he here for her?"

"Cooper?—No: he went straight home, after her left me; he 's probably forgotten all about the child. What's to be done?"

"Can't we take her home? Is it far?"

"It is two or three streets from here, and directly out of our way; altogether too far for you to walk."

"O no, it won't tire me; I'm quite strong now, and I would n't but know she was safe home, on any account. I'd rather get a little fatigued."

If Emily could but have seen Gerty's grateful face that moment, she would indeed have felt repaid for almost any amount of weariness.

So they went home with Gerty, and Emily kissed Gerty at the gate, and Gerty was a happy child that night.

CHAPTER X

By the strong spirit's discipline,
  By the fierce wrong forgiven,
By all that wrings the heart of sin,
  Is woman won to Heaven.
    —N. P. Willis

AS MAY BE SUPPOSED, the blind girl did not forget our little Gerty. Emily Graham never forgot the sufferings, the wants, the necessities, of others. She could not see the world without, but there was a world of love and sympathy within her, which manifested itself in abundant benevolence and charity, both of heart and deed. She lived a life of love. She loved God with her whole heart, and her neighbor as herself. Her own great misfortunes and trials could not be helped, and were borne without repining; but the misfortunes and trials of others became her care, the alleviation of them her greatest delight. Emily was never weary of doing good. Many a blessing was called down upon her head, by young and old, for kindness past; many a call was made upon her for further aid; and to the call of none was she ever deaf. But never had she been so touched as now by any tale of sorrow. Ready listener, as she was, to the story of grief and trouble, she knew how many children were born into the world amid poverty and privation; how many were abused, neglected and forsaken; so that Gerty's experience was not new to her. But it was something in the child herself that excited and interested Emily in an unwonted degree. The tones of her voice, the earnestness and pathos with which she spoke, the confiding and affectionate manner in which she had clung to her, the sudden clasping of her hand, and, finally, her vehement outbreak of grief when she became conscious of Emily's great misfortune,—all these things so haunted Miss Graham's recollection, that she dreamt of the child at night, and thought much of her by day. She could not account to herself for the interest she felt in the little stranger; but the impulse to see and know more of her was irresistible, and, sending for True, she talked a long time with him about the child.

True was highly gratified by Miss Graham's account of the meeting in the church, and of the interest the little girl had inspired in one for whom he felt the greatest admiration and respect. Gerty had previously told him how she had seen Miss Graham, and had spoken in the most glowing terms of the dear lady, who was so kind to her, and brought her home when Mr. Cooper had forgotten her, but it had not occurred to the old man that the fancy was mutual.

Emily asked him if he did n't intend to send her to school.

"Well, I don't know," said he; "she's a little thing, and an't much used to being with other children. Besides, I don't exactly like to spare her; I like to see her round."

Emily suggested that it was time she was learning to read and write; and that the sooner she went among other children, the easier it would be to her.

"Very true, Miss Emily, very true," said Mr. Flint. "I dare say you're right; and, if you think she'd better go, I'll ask her, and see what she says."

"I would," said Emily. "I think she might enjoy it, besides improving very much; and, about her clothes, if there's any deficiency, I'll—"

"O, no, no, Miss Emily!" interrupted True; "there's no necessity; she's very well on 't now, thanks to your kindness."

"Well," said Emily, "if she should have any wants, you must apply to me. You know we adopted her jointly, and I agreed to do anything I could for her; so you must never hesitate,—it will be a pleasure to serve either of you. Father always feels under obligations to you, Mr. Flint, for faithful service, that cost you dear in the end."

"O, Miss Emily," said True, "Mr. Graham has always been my best friend; and as to that 'ere accident that happened when I was in his employ, it was nobody's fault but my own; it was my own carelessness, and nobody's else."

"I know you say so," said Emily, "but we regretted it very much; and you must n't forget what I tell you, that I shall delight in doing anything for Gerty. I should like to have her come and see me, some day, if she would like to, and you'll let her."

"Sartain, sartain," said True, "and thank you kindly; she'd admire to come."

A few days later, Gerty went with True to see Miss Graham; but the housekeeper, when they met in the hall, told them that she was ill and could see no one. So they went away full of disappointment and regret.

It proved afterwards that Emily took a severe cold the day she sat so long in the church, and was suffering with it when they called; but, though confined to her room, she would have been glad to have a visit from Gerty, and was sorry and grieved that Mrs. Ellis should have sent them away so abruptly.

The Lamplighter

One Saturday evening, when Willie was present, True broached the subject of Gerty's going to school. Gerty herself was very much disgusted with the idea; but it met with Willie's warm approbation, and when Gerty learned that Miss Graham also wished it, she consented, though rather reluctantly, to begin the next week, and try how she liked it. So, on the following Monday, Gerty accompanied True to one of the primary schools, was admitted, and her education commenced. When Willie came home the next Saturday, he rushed into True's room, full of eagerness to hear how Gerty liked going to school. He found her seated at the table, with her spelling-book; and as soon as he entered, she exclaimed, "O, Willie! Willie! come and hear me read!"

Her performance could not properly be called reading. She had not got beyond the alphabet, and a few syllables which she had learned to spell; but Willie bestowed upon her a much well-merited praise, for she had really been very diligent. He was astonished to hear that Gerty liked going to school, liked the teacher and the scholars, and had a fine time at recess. He had fully expected that she would dislike the whole business, and very probably go into tantrums about it,—which was the expression he used to denote her fits of ill-temper. On the contrary, everything, thus far, had gone well, and Gerty had never looked so animated and happy as she did this evening. Willie promised to assist her in her studies; and the two children's literary plans soon became as high-flown as if one had been a poet-laureate and the other a philosopher.

For two or three weeks all appeared to go on smoothly. Gerty went regularly to school, and continued to make rapid progress. Every Saturday Willie heard her read and spell, assisted, praised and encouraged her. He had, however, a shrewd suspicion that, on one or two occasions, she had come near having a brush with some large girls, for whom she began to show symptoms of dislike. Whatever the difficulty originated in, it soon reached a crisis.

One day, when the children were assembled in the schoolyard, during recess, Gerty caught sight of True in his working-dress, just passing down the street, with his ladder and lamp-filler. Shouting and laughing, she bounded out of the yard, pursued and overtook him. She came back in a few minutes, seeming much delighted at the unexpected encounter, and ran into the yard out of breath, and full of happy excitement. The troop of large girls, whom Gerty had already had some reason to distrust, had been observing her, and, as soon as she returned, one of them called out, saying,

"Who's that man?"

"That's my Uncle True," said Gerty.

"Your what?"

"My uncle, Mr. Flint, that I live with."

"So you belong to him, do you?" said the girl, in an insolent tone of voice. "Ha! ha! ha!"

"What are you laughing at?" said Gerty, fiercely.

"Ugh! Before I'd live with him!" said the girl, "old Smutty!"

The others caught it up, and the laugh and epithet Old Smutty circulated freely in the corner of the yard where Gerty was standing.

Gerty was furious. Her eyes glistened, she doubled her little fist, and, without hesitation, came down in battle upon the crowd. But they were too many for her, and, helpless as she was with passion, they drove her out of the yard. She started for home on a full run, screaming with all her might.

As she flew along the side-walk, she brushed roughly against a tall and rather stiff-looking lady, who was walking slowly in the same direction, with another and much smaller person leaning on her arm.

"Bless me!" said the tall lady, who had almost lost her equilibrium from her fright and the suddenness of the shock. "Why, you horrid little creature!" As she spoke, she grasped Gerty by the shoulder, and, before the child could break away, succeeded in giving her a slight shake. This served to increase Gerty's anger, and, her speed gaining in proportion, it was but a few minutes before she was at home, crouched in a corner of True's room behind the bed, her face to the wall, and, as usual, on such occasions, covered with both her hands. Here she was free to cry as loud as she pleased; for Mrs. Sullivan was gone out, and there was no one in the house to hear her,—a privilege, indeed, of which she fully availed herself.

But she had not had time to indulge long in her tantrum, when the gate at the end of the yard closed with a bang, and footsteps were heard coming towards Mr. Flint's door. Gerty's attention was arrested, for she knew by the sound that it was the step of a stranger who was approaching. With a strong effort, she succeeded, after one or two convulsive sobs, in so far controlling herself as to keep quiet. There was a knock at the door, but Gerty did not reply to it, remaining in her position concealed behind the bed. The knock was not repeated, but the stranger lifted the latch and walked in.

"There does n't seem to be any one at home," said a female voice; "what a pity!"

"Is n't there? I'm sorry," replied another, in the sweet, musical tones of Miss Graham.

Gerty knew the voice, at once.

"I thought you'd better not come here yourself," rejoined the first speaker, who was no other than Mrs. Ellis, the identical lady whom Gerty had so frightened and disconcerted.

"O, I don't regret coming," said Emily. "You can leave me here while you go to your sister's, and very likely Mr. Flint or the little girl will come home in the mean time."

"It don't become you, Miss Emily, to be carried round everywhere, and left, like an expressman's parcel, till called for. You caught a horrid cold, that you're hardly well of now, waiting there in the church for the minister; and Mr. Graham will be finding fault next."

"O, no, Mrs. Ellis; it's very comfortable here; the church must have been damp, I think. Come, put me in Mr. Flint's arm-chair, and I can make myself quite contented."

"Well, at any rate," said Mrs. Ellis, "I'll make up a good fire in the stove before I go."

As she spoke the energetic housekeeper seized the poker, and, after stirring up the coals, and making free with all True's kindling-wood, waited long enough to hear the roaring and see the blaze; and then, having laid aside Emily's cloak and boa, went away with the same firm, steady step with which she had come, and which had so overpowered Emily's noiseless tread, that Gerty had only anticipated the arrival of a single guest. As soon as Gerty knew, by the swinging of the gate, that Mrs. Ellis had really departed, she suspended her effort at self-control, and, with a deep-drawn sigh, gasped out, "O, dear! O, dear!"

"Why, Gerty!" exclaimed Emily, "is that you?"

"Yes," sobbed Gerty.

"Come here."

The child waited no second bidding, but, starting up, ran, threw herself on the floor by the side of Emily, buried her face in the blind girl's lap, and once more commenced crying aloud. By this time her whole frame was trembling with agitation.

"Why, Gerty!" said Emily; "what is the matter?"

But Gerty could not reply; and Emily, finding this to be the case, desisted from her inquiries until the little one should be somewhat composed. She lifted Gerty up into her lap, laid her head on her shoulder, and with her own handkerchief wiped the tears from her face.

Her soothing words and caresses soon quieted the child; and when she was calm, Emily, instead of recurring at once to the cause of her grief, very judiciously questioned her upon other topics. At last, however, she asked her if she went to school.

"I *have been*," said Gerty, raising her head suddenly from Emily's shoulder; "but I won't ever go again!"

"What!—Why not?"

"Because," said Gerty, angrily, "I hate those girls; yes, I hate 'em! ugly things!"

"Gerty," said Emily, "don't say that; you should n't hate anybody."

"Why should n't I?" said Gerty.

"Because it's wrong."

"No, it's not *wrong;* I say it *is n't!*" said Gerty; "and I do hate 'em; and I hate Nan Grant, and I always shall! Don't *you* hate anybody?"

"No," answered Emily; "I *don't.*"

"Did anybody ever drown your kitten? Did anybody ever call your father Old Smutty?" said Gerty. "If they had, I know you'd hate 'em, just as I do."

"Gerty," said Emily, solemnly, "did n't you tell me, the other day, that you were a naughty child, but that you wished to be good, and would try?"

"Yes," said Gerty.

"If you wish to become good and be forgiven, you must forgive others."

Gerty said nothing.

"Do you not wish God to forgive and love you?"

"God, that lives in heaven,—that made the stars?" said Gerty.

"Yes."

"Will he love me, and let me some time go to heaven?"

"Yes, if you try to be good, and love everybody."

"Miss Emily," said Gerty, after a moment's pause, "I can't do it,—so I s'pose I can't go."

Just at this moment a tear fell upon Gerty's forehead. She looked thoughtfully up in Emily's face, then said,

"Dear Miss Emily, are you going?"

"I am trying to."

"I should like to go with you," said Gerty, shaking her head, meditatively.

Still Emily did not speak. She left the child to the working of her own thoughts.

"Miss Emily," said Gerty, at last, in the lowest whisper, "I mean to *try,* but I don't think I *can.*"

"God bless you, and help you, my child!" said Emily, laying her hand upon Gerty's head.

For fifteen minutes or more, not a word was spoken by either. Gerty lay perfectly still in Emily's lap. By and by the latter perceived, by the child's breathing, that, worn out with the fever and excitement of all she had gone through, she had dropped into a quiet sleep. When Mrs. Ellis returned, Emily pointed to the sleeping child, and asked her to place her on the bed. She did so, wonderingly; and then, turning to Emily, exclaimed, "Upon my word Miss Emily, that's the same rude, bawling little creature, that came so near being the death of us!" Emily smiled at the idea of a child eight years old overthrowing and annihilating a woman of Mrs. Ellis's inches, but said nothing.

Why did Emily weep long that night, as she recalled the scene of the morning? Why did she, on bended knee, wrestle so vehemently with a mighty sorrow? Why did she pray so earnestly for new strength and heavenly aid? Why did she so beseechingly ask of God his blessing on the little child? Because she had felt, in many a year of darkness and bereavement, in many an hour of fearful struggle, in many a pang of despair, how a temper like that which Gerty had this day show might, in one moment of its fearful reign, cast a blight upon a lifetime, and write in fearful lines the mournful requiem of earthly joy. And so she prayed to Heaven that night for strength to keep her firm resolve, and aid in fulfilling her undying purpose, to cure that child of her dark infirmity.

CHAPTER XI

Her influence breathes, and bids the blighted heart
To life and hope from desolation start.
　　—*Hemans*

THE NEXT SABBATH afternoon found Gerty seated on a cricket, in front of a pleasant little wood-fire in Emily's own room. Her large eyes were fixed upon Emily's face, which always seemed, in some unaccountable way, to fascinate the little girl; so attentively did she watch the play of the features in a countenance the charm of which many an older person than Gerty had felt, but tried in vain to describe. It was not beauty,—at least, not brilliant beauty,—for that Emily had not possessed, even when her face was illumined, as it had once been, by beautiful hazel eyes; nor was it the effect of what is usually termed fascination of manner, for Emily's manner and voice were both so soft and unassuming that they never took the fancy by storm. It was not compassion for her blindness, though so great a misfortune might well, and always did, excite the warmest sympathy. But it was hard to realize that Emily *was* blind. It was a fact never forced upon her friends' recollection by any repining or selfish indulgence on the part of the sufferer; and, as there was nothing painful in the appearance of her closed lids, shaded and fringed as they were by her long and heavy eyelashes, it was not unusual for those immediately about her to converse upon things which could only be evident to the sense of sight, and even direct her attention to one object and another, quite forgetting, for the moment, her sad deprivation; and Emily never sighed, never seemed hurt at their want of consideration, or showed any lack of interest in objects thus shut from her gaze; but, apparently quite satisfied with the descriptions she heard, or the pictures which she formed in her imagination, would talk pleasantly and playfully upon whatever was uppermost in the minds of her companions. Some said that Emily had the sweetest mouth in the world, and they loved to watch its ever-varying expression. Some said her chief attraction lay in a small dimple in her right cheek; others (and these were young girls who wanted to be charming themselves) remarked that if they thought they could make their hair wave like Emily's, they'd braid it up every night; it was *so* becoming! But the chosen few, who were capable, through their own spirituality, of understanding and appreciating Emily's character,— the few, the very few, who had known of her struggles, and had witnessed her triumphs,—had *they* undertaken to express their belief concerning the source whence she derived that power by which her face and voice stole into the hearts of young and old, and won their love and admiration, *they* would have said, as Gerty did, when she sat gazing so earnestly at Emily on the very Sunday afternoon of which we speak, "Miss Emily, I know you've been with God."

Gerty was certainly a strange child. All untaught as she was, she had felt Emily's entire superiority to any being she had ever seen before; and, yielding to that belief in her belonging to an order above humanity, she reposed implicit confidence in what she told her, allowed herself to be guided and influenced by one whom she felt loved her and sought only her good; and, as she sat at her feet and listened to her gentle voice while she gave her her first lesson upon the distinction between right and wrong, Emily, though she could not see the little thoughtful face that was looking up at her, knew, by the earnest attention she had gained, by the child's perfect stillness, and, still more, by the little hand which had sought hers, and now held it tight, that one great point was won.

Gerty had not been to school since the day of her battle with the great girls. All True's persuasions had failed, and she would not go. But Emily understood the child's nature so much better than True did, and urged upon her so much more forcible motives than the old man had thought of employing, that *she* succeeded where *he* had failed. Gerty considered that her old friend had been insulted, and that was the chief cause of indignation with her; but Emily placed the matter in a different light, and, convincing her at last that, if she loved Uncle True, she would show it much better by obeying his wishes than by retaining her foolish anger, she finally obtained Gerty's promise that she would go to school the next morning. She also advised her how to conduct herself towards the scholars whom she so disliked, and gave her some simple directions with regard to her behavior the next day; telling her that perhaps Mr. Flint would go with her, make suitable apologies to the teacher for her absence, and that, in such case, she would have no further trouble.

The next morning True, much pleased that Gerty's repugnance to the school was at last overcome, went with her, and, inquiring for the teacher at the door, stated the case to her in his blunt, honest way, and then left Gerty in her special charge.

Miss Browne, who was a young woman of good sense and good feelings, saw the matter in the right light; and, taking an opportunity to speak privately to the girls who had excited Gerty's temper by their rudeness, made them feel so ashamed of their conduct, that they no longer molested the child; and, as Gerty soon after made friends with one or two quiet children of her own age, with whom she played in recess, she got into no more such difficulties.

The winter passed away. The pleasant, sunny spring days came, days when Gerty could sit at open windows, or on the door-step, when birds sang in the morning among the branches of an old locust-tree that grew in the narrow yard, and the sun at evening threw bright rays across True's great room, and Gerty could see to read almost until bed-time. She had been to school steadily all winter, and had moved as rapidly as most intelligent children do, who are first given the opportunity to learn at an age when, full of ambition, the mind is most fertile and capable of progress. She was looking healthy and well; her clothes were clean and neat, for her wardrobe was well stocked by Emily, and the care of it superintended by Mrs. Sullivan. She was bright and happy too, and tripped round the house so joyously and lightly, that True declared his birdie knew not what it was to touch her heel to the ground, but flew about on the tips of her toes.

The old man could not have loved the little adopted one better had she been his own child; and, as he sat by her side on the wide settle, which, when the warm weather came, was moved outside the door, and listened patiently and attentively while she read aloud to him story after story, of little girls who never told lies, boys who always obeyed their parents, or, more frequently still, of the child who knew how to keep her temper, they seemed, as indeed they were, most suitable companions for each other. The old man's interest in the story-books, which were provided by Emily, and read and re-read by Gerty, was as keen and unflagging as if he had been a child himself; and he would sit with his elbows on his knees, hearing the simple stories, laughing when Gerty laughed, sympathizing as fully and heartily as she did in the sorrows of her little heroines, and rejoicing with her in the final triumph of truth, obedience and patience.

Emily knew the weight that such tales often carried with them to the hearts of children, and most carefully and judiciously did she select books for Gerty. Gerty's life was now as happy and prosperous as it had once been wretched and miserable. Six months before, she had felt herself all alone, unloved, uncared-for. Now she had many friends, and knew what it was to be thought of, provided for, and caressed. All the days in the week were joyous; but Saturday and Sunday were marked days with her, as well as with Mrs. Sullivan; for Saturday brought Willie home to hear her recite her lessons, walk, laugh and play, with her. He had so many pleasant things to tell, he was so full of life and animation, so ready to enter into all her plans, and in every way promote her amusement, that on Monday morning she began to count the days until Saturday would come again. Then, if anything went wrong or got out of order,—if the old clock stopped, or her toys got broken, or, worse still, if her lessons troubled, or any little childish grief oppressed her,—Willie knew how to put everything right, to help her out of every difficulty. So Willie's mother looked not more anxiously for his coming than Gerty did.

Sunday afternoon Gerty always spent with Emily, in Emily's own room, listening to her sweet voice, and, half-unconsciously, imbibing a portion of her sweet spirit. Emily preached no sermons, nor did she weary the child with exhortations and precepts. Indeed, it did not occur to Gerty that she went there to be *taught* anything; but simply and gradually the blind girl imparted light to the child's dark soul, and the truths that make for virtue, the lessons that are divine, were implanted in her so naturally, and yet so forcibly, that she realized not the work that was going on; but long after,—when goodness had grown strong within her, and her first feeble resistance of evil, her first attempts to keep her childish resolves, had matured into deeply-rooted principles, and confirmed habits of right,—she felt, as she looked back into the past, that on those blessed Sabbaths, sitting on her cricket at Emily's knee, she had received into her heart the first beams of that immortal light that never could be quenched.

Thus her silent prayer was answered. God had chosen an earthly messenger to lead his child into everlasting peace; a messenger from whose closed eyes the world's paths were all shut out, but who had been so long treading the heavenly road, that it was now familiar ground. Who so fit to guide the little one as she, who with patience had learned the way? Who so well able to cast light upon the darkness of another soul as she, to whose own darkened life God had lent a torch divine?

It was a grievous trial to Gerty, about this time, to learn that the Grahams were soon going into the country for the summer. Mr. Graham owned a pleasant residence about six miles from Boston, to which he invariably resorted as soon as the planting-season commenced; for, though devoted to business during the winter, he had of late years allowed himself much relaxation from his counting-room in the summer; and legers and day-books were now soon to be supplanted, in his estimation, by the labors and delights of gardening. Emily promised Gerty, however, that she should come and pass a day with her when the weather was fine; a visit which Gerty enjoyed three months in anticipation, and more than three in retrospection.

It was some compensation for Emily's absence that, as the days became long, Willie was frequently able to leave the shop and come home for an hour or two in the evening; and Willie, as we have said, always knew how to comfort Gerty, whatever the trouble might be.

CHAPTER XII

"Let every minute, as it springs,
Convey fresh knowledge on its wings;
Let every minute, as it flies,
Record thee good, as well as wise."
——*Cotton*

IT WAS ONE pleasant evening in the latter part of April, that Gerty, who had been to see Miss Graham and bid her good-by, before her departure for the country, stood at the back part of the yard weeping bitterly. She held in her hand a book and a new slate, Emily's parting gifts; but she had not removed the wrapper from the one, and the other was quite be-smeared with tears. She was so full of grief at the parting (with her, the first of those many sad partings life is so full of), that she did not hear any one approach, and was unconscious of any one's presence, until a hand was placed upon each of her shoulders; and, as she turned round, she found herself encircled by Willie's arms, and face to face with Willie's sunny countenance.

"Why, Gerty!" said he, "this is no kind of a welcome, when I've come home on a week-night, to stay with you all the evening. Mother and grandfather are both gone out somewhere, and then, when I come to look for you, you're crying so I can't see your face through such oceans of tears. Come, come! *do* leave off; you don't know how shockingly you look!"

"Willie!" sobbed she, "do you know Miss Emily's gone?"

"Gone where?"

"Way off, six miles, to stay all summer!"

But Willie only laughed. "Six miles!" said he; "that's a terrible way, certainly!"

"But I can't see her any more!" said Gerty.

"You can see her next winter," rejoined Willie.

"O, but that's so long!" said the child.

"What makes you think so much of her?" asked Willie.

"She thinks much of me; she can't see me, and she likes me better than anybody but Uncle True."

"I don't believe it; I don't believe she likes you half as well as I do. I *know* she don't! How can she, when she's blind, and never saw you in her life, and I see you all the time, and love you better than I do anybody in the world, except my mother?"

"Do you *really*, Willie?"

"Yes, I do. I always think, when I come home, Now I'm going to see Gerty; and everything that happens all the week, I think to myself—I shall tell Gerty that."

"I should n't think you'd like me so well."

"Why not?"

"O, because you're so handsome, and I an't handsome a bit. I heard Ellen Chase tell Lucretia Davis, the other day, that she thought Gerty Flint was the worst-looking girl in school."

"Then she ought to be ashamed of herself," said Willie. "I guess she an't very good-looking. I should hate the looks of *her,* or any *other* girl that said that."

"O, Willie!" exclaimed Gerty, earnestly, "it's true; as true as can be."

"No, it an't *true,*" said Willie. "To be sure, you haven't got long curls, and a round face, and blue eyes, like Belle Clinton's, and nobody'd think of setting you up for a beauty; but when you've been running, and have rosy cheeks, and your great black eyes shine, and you laugh so heartily as you do sometimes at anything funny, I often think you're the brightest-looking girl I ever saw in my life; and I don't care what other folks think, as long as I like your looks. I feel just as bad when you cry, or anything's the matter with you, as if it were myself, and worse. George Bray struck his little sister Mary yesterday, because she tore his kite; I should have liked to give him a flogging. I wouldn't strike you, Gerty, if you tore all my playthings to pieces."

Such professions of affection on Willie's part were frequent, and always responded to by a like declaration from Gerty. Nor were they mere professions. The two children loved each other dearly. They were very differently constituted, for Willie was earnest, persevering and patient, calm in his temperament, and equal in his spirits. Gerty, on the other hand, excitable and impetuous, was constantly thrown off her guard; her temper was easily roused, her spirits variable, her whole nature sensitive to the last degree. Willie was accustomed to be loved, expected to be loved, and *was* loved by everybody. Gerty had been an outcast from all affection, looked not for it, and, except under favorable circumstances and by those who knew her well, did not readily inspire it. But that they loved *each other* there could be no doubt; and, if in the spring the bond between them was already strong, autumn found it cemented by still firmer ties; for, during

Emily's absence, Willie filled her place and his own too, and though Gerty did not forget her blind friend, she passed a most happy summer, and continued to make such progress in her studies at school, that, when Emily returned to the city in October, she could hardly understand how so much had been accomplished in what had seemed to her so short a time.

The following winter, too, was passed most profitably by Gerty. Miss Graham's kindly feeling towards her little protegée, far from having diminished, seemed to have been increased by time and absence, and Gerty's visits to Emily became more frequent than ever. The profit derived from these visits was not all on Gerty's part. Emily had been in the habit, the previous winter, of hearing her read occasionally, that she might judge of her proficiency; now, however, she discovered, on the first trial, that the little girl had attained to a greater degree of excellence in this accomplishment than is common among grown people. She read understandingly, and her accent and intonations were so admirable, that Emily found rare pleasure in listening to her.

Partly with a view to the child's benefit, and partly for her own gratification, she proposed that Gerty should come every day and read to her for an hour. Gerty was only too happy to oblige her dear Miss Emily, who, in making the proposal, represented it as a personal favor to herself, and a plan by which Gerty's eyes could serve for them both. It was agreed that when True started on his lamp-lighting expeditions he should take Gerty to Mr. Graham's, and call for her on his return. Owing to this arrangement, Gerty was constant and punctual in her attendance at the appointed time; and none but those who have tried it are aware what a large amount of reading may be accomplished in six months, if only an hour is devoted to it regularly each day. Emily, in her choice of books, did not confine herself to such as come strictly within a child's comprehension. She judged, rightly, that a girl of such keen intelligence as Gerty was naturally endowed with would suffer nothing by occasionally encountering what was beyond her comprehension; but that, on the contrary, the very effort she would be called upon to make would enlarge her capacity, and be an incentive to her genius. So history, biography, and books of travels, were perused by Gerty at an age when most children's literary pursuits are confined to stories and pictures. The child seemed, indeed, to give the preference to this comparatively solid reading; and, aided by Emily's kind explanations and encouragement, she stored up in her little brain many an important fact and much useful information. At Gerty's age the memory is strong and retentive, and things impressed on the mind then are usually better remembered than what is learned in after years, when the thoughts are more disturbed and divided.

Her especial favorite was a little work on astronomy, which puzzled her more than all the rest put together, but which delighted her in the same proportion; for it made some things clear, and all the rest, though a mystery still, was to her a beautiful mystery, and one which she fully meant some time to explore to the uttermost. And this ambition to learn more, and understand better, by and by, was, after all, the greatest good she derived. Awaken a child's ambition, and implant in her a taste for literature, and more is gained than by years of school-room drudgery, where the heart works not in unison with the head.

From the time Gerty was first admitted, until she was twelve years old, she continued to attend the public schools, and was rapidly advanced and promoted; but what she learned with Miss Graham, and acquired by study with Willie at home, formed nearly as important a part of her education. Willie, as we have said, was very fond of study, and was delighted at Gerty's warm participation in his favorite pursuit. They were a great advantage to each other, for each found encouragement in the other's sympathy and cooperation. After the first year or two of their acquaintance, Willie could not be properly called a child, for he was in his fifteenth year, and beginning to look quite manly. But Gerty's eagerness for knowledge had all the more influence upon him; for, if the little girl ten years of age was patient and willing to labor at her books until after nine o'clock, the youth of fifteen must not rub his eyes and plead weariness. It was when they had reached these respective years that they commenced studying French together. Willie's former teacher continued to feel a kindly interest in the boy, who had long been his best scholar, and who would certainly have borne away from his class the first prizes, had not a higher duty called him to inferior labors previous to the public exhibition. Whenever he met him in the street, or elsewhere, he inquired concerning his mode of life, and whether he continued his studies. Finding that Willie had considerable spare time, he earnestly advised him to learn the French language,—that being a branch of knowledge which would undoubtedly prove useful to him, whatever business he might chance to pursue in life,—and offered to lend him such books as he would need at the commencement.

Willie availed himself of his teacher's advice, and his kind offer, and began to study in good earnest. When he was at home in the evening, he was in the habit of coming into True's room, partly for the sake of quiet (for True was a quiet man, and had too great a veneration for learning to interrupt the students with his questions), and partly for the sake of being with Gerty, who was usually, at that time, occupied with her books. Gerty, as may be supposed, conceived a strong desire to learn French, too. Willie was willing she should try, but had no confidence that she would long persevere. To his surprise, however, she not only discovered a wonderful determination, but a decided talent for language; and, as Emily furnished her with books similar to Willie's, she kept pace with him, oftentimes translating more during the week than he could find time to do. On Saturday evening, when they always had a fine study time together, True would sit on his old settle by the fire, watching Willie and Gerty, side by side, at the table, with their eyes bent on the page, which to him seemed the greatest of earthly labyrinths. Gerty always looked out the words, in which employment she had great skill, her bright eyes diving, as if by magic, into the very heart of the dictionary, and transfixing the right word at a glance, while Willie's province was to make sense. Almost the only occasion when True was known to disturb them, by a word even, was when he first heard Willie talk about making sense. "Making sense, Willie?" said the old man; "is that what ye're after? Well, you couldn't do a better business. I'll warrant you a market for it; there's want enough on 't in the world!"

It was but natural that, under such favorable influences as Gerty enjoyed, with Emily to advise and direct, and Willie to aid and encourage, her intellect should rapidly expand and strengthen. But how is it with that little heart of hers, that, at once warm and affectionate, impulsive, sensitive and passionate, now throbs with love and gratitude, and now again burns as vehemently with the consuming fire that a sense of wrong, a consciousness of injury, to herself or her friends, would at any moment enkindle? Has she, in two years of happy childhood, learned self-control? Has she also attained to an enlightened sense of the distinction between right and wrong, truth and falsehood? In short, has Emily been true to her self-imposed trust, her high resolve, to soften the heart and instruct the soul of the little ignorant one? Has Gerty learned religion? Has she found out God, and begun to walk patiently in that path which is lit by a holy light, and leads to rest?

She had *begun;* and though her footsteps often falter, though she sometimes quite turns aside, and, impatient of the narrow way, gives the rein to her old irritability and ill-temper, she is yet but a child, and there is the strongest foundation for hopefulness in the sincerity of her good intentions, and the depth of her contrition when wrong has had the mastery. Emily has spared no pains in teaching her where to place her strong reliance, and Gerty has already learned to look to higher aid than Emily's and to lean on a mightier arm.

Miss Graham had appointed for herself no easy task, when she undertook to inform the mind and heart of a child utterly untaught in the ways of virtue. In some important points, however, she experienced far less difficulty than she had anticipated. For instance, after her first explanation to Gerty of the difference between honesty and dishonesty, the truth and a lie, she never had any cause to complain of the child, whose whole nature was the very reverse of deceptive, and whom nothing but extreme fear had ever driven to the meanness of falsehood. If Gerty's greatest fault lay in a proud and easily-roused temper, that very fault carried with it its usual accompaniment of frankness and sincerity. Under almost any circumstances, Gerty would have been too proud to keep back the truth, even before she became too virtuous. Emily was convinced, before she had known Gerty six months, that she could always depend upon her word; and nothing could have been a greater encouragement to Miss Graham's unselfish efforts than the knowledge that truth, the root of every holy thing, had thus easily and early been made to take up its abode in the child. But this sensitive, proud temper of Gerty's seemed an inborn thing; abuse and tyranny had not been able to crush it; on the contrary, it had flourished in the midst of the unfavorable influences amid which she had been nurtured. Kindness could accomplish almost anything with her, could convince and restrain; but restraint from any other source was unbearable, and, however proper and necessary a check it might be, she was always disposed to resent it. Emily knew that to such a spirit even parental control is seldom sufficient. She knew of but one influence that is strong enough, one power that never fails to quell and subdue earthly pride and passion; the power of Christian humility, engrafted into the heart,—the humility of *principle,* of *conscience,*—the only power to which native pride ever will pay homage.

She knew that a command, of almost any kind, laid upon Gerty by herself or Uncle True, would be promptly obeyed, for, in either case, the little girl would know that the order was given in love, and she would fulfil it in the same spirit; but, to provide for all contingencies, and to make the heart right as well as the life, it was necessary to inspire her with a higher motive than merely pleasing either of these friends; and, in teaching her the spirit of her Divine Master, Emily was making her powerful to do and to suffer, to bear and to forbear, when, depending on herself, she should be left to her own guidance alone. How much Gerty had improved in the two years that had passed since she first began to be so carefully instructed and provided for, the course of our story must develop. We cannot pause to dwell upon the trials and struggles, the failures and victories, that she experienced. It is sufficient to say that Miss Graham was satisfied and hopeful, True proud and overjoyed, while Mrs. Sullivan, and even old Mr. Cooper, declared she had improved wonderfully in her behavior and her looks, and was remarkably mannerly for such a child.

CHAPTER XIII

No caprice of mind,
No passing influence of idle time,
No popular show, no clamor from the crowd,
Can move him, erring, from the path of right.
　　　　—W. G. Simms

ONE SATURDAY EVENING in December, the third winter of Gerty's residence with True, Willie came in with his French books under his arm, and, after the first salutations were over, exclaimed, as he threw the grammar and dictionary upon the table, "O, Gerty! before we begin to study, I *must* tell you and Uncle True the funniest thing, that happened to-day; I have been laughing so at home, as I was telling mother about it!"

"I heard you laugh," said Gerty. "If I had not been so busy, I should have gone into your mother's room, to hear what it was so very droll. But come, do tell us!"

"Why, you will not think it's anything like a joke when I begin; and I should not be so much amused, if she hadn't been the very queerest old woman that ever I saw in my life."

"Old woman!—You haven't told us about any old woman!"

"But I'm going to," said Willie. "You noticed how everything was covered with ice, this morning. How splendidly it looked, didn't it? I declare, when the sun shone on that great elm-tree in front of our shop, I thought I never saw anything so handsome in my life. But, there, that's nothing to do with my old woman,—only that the side-walks were just like everything else, a perfect glare."

"I know it," interrupted Gerty; "I fell down, going to school."

"Did you?" said Willie; "didn't you get hurt?"

74

"No, indeed. But go on; I want to hear about your old woman."

"I was standing at the shop-door, about eleven o'clock, looking out, when I saw the strangest-looking figure that you ever imagined, coming down the street. I must tell you how she was dressed. She did look so ridiculous! She had on some kind of a black silk or satin gown, made very scant, and trimmed all round with some brownish-looking lace (black, I suppose it had been once, but it isn't now); then she had a gray cloak, of some sort of silk material, that you certainly would have said came out of the ark, if it hadn't been for a little cape, of a different color, that she wore outside of it, and which must have dated a generation further back. I would not undertake to describe her bonnet; only I know it was twice as big as anybody's else, and she had a figured lace veil thrown over on one side, that reached nearly to her feet. But her goggles were the crowner; such immense, horrid-looking things, I never saw! She had a work-bag, made of black silk, with pieces of cloth of all colors in the rainbow sewed on to it, zigzag; then her pocket-handkerchief was pinned to her bag, and a great feather fan (only think, at this season of the year!), that was pinned on somewhere (by a string, I suppose), and a bundle-handkerchief and a newspaper! O, gracious! I can't think of half the things; but they were all pinned together with great brass pins, and hung in a body on her left arm, all depending on the strength of the bag-string. Her dress, though, wasn't the strangest thing about her. What made it funny was to see her way of walking; she looked quite old and infirm, and it was evident she could hardly keep her footing on the ice; and yet she walked with such a smirk, such a consequential little air! O, Gerty, it's lucky you didn't see her; you'd have laughed from then till this time."

"Some poor crazy crittur', wasn't she?" asked True.

"O, no!" said Willie, "I don't think she was; queer enough, to be sure, but not crazy. Just as she got opposite the shop-door her feet slipped, and, the first thing I knew, she fell flat on the side-walk. I rushed out, for I thought the fall might have killed the poor little thing; and Mr. Bray, and a gentleman he was waiting upon, followed me. She did appear stunned, at first; but we carried her into the shop, and she came to her senses in a minute or two. Crazy, you asked if she were, Uncle True. No, not she! She's bright as a dollar. As soon as she opened her eyes, and seemed to know what she was about, she felt for her work-bag and all its appendages; counted them up, to see if the number were right, and then nodded her head very satisfactorily. Mr. Bray poured out a glass of cordial, and offered it to her. By this time she had got her airs and graces back again; so, when he recommended to her to swallow the cordial, she retreated, with a little old-fashioned curtsey, and put up both hands to express her horror at the idea of such a thing. The gentleman that was standing by smiled, and advised her to take it, telling her it would do her no harm. Upon that, she turned round, made another curtsey to him, and answered, in a little, cracked voice, 'Can you assure me, sir, as a gentleman of candor and gallantry, that it is not an exhilarating potion?' The gentleman could hardly keep from laughing; but he told her it was nothing that would hurt her. 'Then,' said she, 'I will venture to sip the beverage; it has a most aromatic fragrance.' She seemed to like the taste, as well as the smell, for she drank every drop of it; and, when she had set the glass down on the counter, she turned to me and said, 'Except upon this gentleman's assurance of the harmlessness of the liquid, I would not have swallowed it in your presence, my young master, if it were only for the *example*. I have set my seal to no temperance-pledge, but I am abstemious because it becomes a lady;—it is with me a matter of choice—a matter of *taste*.' She now seemed quite restored, and talked of starting again on her walk; but it really was not safe for her to go alone on the ice, and I rather think Mr. Bray thought so, for he asked her where she was going. She told him, in her roundabout way, that she was proceeding to pass the day with Mistress somebody, that lived in the neighborhood of the Common. I touched Mr. Bray's arm, and said, in a low voice, that, if he could spare me, I'd go with her. He said he shouldn't want me for an hour; so I offered her my arm, and told her I should be happy to wait upon her. You ought to have seen her then! If I had been a grown-up man, and she a young lady, she couldn't have tossed her head or giggled more. But she took my arm, and we started off. I knew Mr. Bray and the gentleman were laughing to see us, but I didn't care; I pitied the old lady, and I did not mean she should get another tumble.

"Every person we met stared at us; and it's no wonder they did, for we must have been a most absurd-looking couple. She not only accepted my offered crook, but clasped her hands together round it, making a complete handle of her two arms; and so she hung on with all her might.— But, there, I ought not to laugh at the poor thing; for she needed somebody to help her along, and I'm sure she wasn't heavy enough to tire me out, if she did make the most of herself. I wonder who she belongs to. I shouldn't think her friends would let her go about the streets so, especially such walking as it is to-day."

"What's her name?" inquired Gerty. "Didn't you find out?"

"No," answered Willie; "she wouldn't tell me. I asked her; but she only said, in her little, cracked voice (and here Willie began to laugh immoderately), that she was the *incognito,* and that it was the part of a true and gallant knight to discover the name of his fair lady. O, I promise you, she was a case! Why, you never heard any one talk so ridiculously as she did! I asked her how old she was.—Mother says that was very impolite, but it's the only uncivil thing I did, or said, as the only lady would testify herself, if she were here."

"How old is she?" said Gerty.

"Sixteen."

"Why, Willie, what do you mean?"

"That's what she told me," returned Willie; "and a true and gallant knight is bound to believe his fair lady."

"Poor body!" said True; "she's childish!"

"No, she isn't, Uncle True," said Willie; "you'd think so, part of the time, to hear her run on with her nonsense; and then, the next minute, she'd speak as sensibly as anybody, and say how much obliged she was to me for showing such a spirit of conformity as to be willing to put myself to so much trouble for the sake of an old woman like her. Just as we turned into Beacon-street, we met a whole school of girls, blooming beauties, handsome enough to kill, my old lady called them; and, from the instant they came in sight, she seemed to take it for granted I should try to get away from her, and run after some of them. But she held on with a vengeance! It's lucky I had no idea of forsaking her, for it would have been impossible. Some of them stopped and stared at us,—of course, I didn't care how much they stared; but she seemed to think I should be terribly mortified; and when we had passed them all, she complimented me again and again on my spirit of conformity,—her favorite expression."

Here Willie paused, quite out of breath. True clapped him upon the shoulder. "Good boy, Willie!" said he; "clever boy! You always look out for the old folks; and that's right. Respect for the aged is a good thing; though your grandfather says it's very much out of fashion."

"I don't know about fashion, Uncle True; but I should think it was a pretty mean sort of a boy that would see an old lady get one fall on the ice, and not save her from another by seeing her safe home."

"Willie's always kind to everybody," said Gerty.

"Willie's either a hero," said the boy, "or else he has got two pretty good friends,—I rather think it's the latter. But, come, Gerty; Charles the

XII is waiting for us, and we must study as much as we can to-night. We may not have another chance very soon; for Mr. Bray isn't well this evening; he seems threatened with a fever, and I promised to go back to the shop after dinner to-morrow. If he should be sick, I shall have plenty to do, without coming home at all."

"O, I hope Mr. Bray is not going to have a fever," said True and Gerty, in the same breath.

"He's such a clever man!" said True.

"He's so good to you, Willie!" added Gerty.

Willie hoped not, too; but his hopes gave place to his fears, when he found, on the following day, that his kind master was not able to leave his bed, and the doctor pronounced the symptoms alarming.

A typhoid fever set in, which in a few days terminated the life of the excellent apothecary.

The death of Mr. Bray was so sudden and dreadful a blow to Willie, that he did not at first realize the important bearing the event had upon his own fortunes. The shop was closed, the widow having determined to dispose of the stock and remove into the country as soon as possible.

Willie was thus left without employment, and deprived of Mr. Bray's valuable recommendation and assistance. His earnings during the past year had been very considerable, and had added essentially to the comfort of his mother and grandfather, who had thus been enabled to relax the severity of their own labors. The thought of being a burden to them, even for a day, was intolerable to the independent and energetic spirit of the boy; and he earnestly set himself to work to obtain another place. He commenced by applying to the different apothecaries in the city. But none of them wanted a youth of his age, and one day was spent in fruitless inquiries.

He returned home at night, disappointed, but not by any means discouraged. If he could not obtain employment with an apothecary, he would do something else.

But what should he do? That was the question. He had long talks with his mother about it. She felt that his talents and education entitled him to fill a position equal, certainly, to that he had already occupied, and could not endure the thought of his descending to more menial service. Willie, without too much self-esteem, thought so too. He knew, indeed, that he was capable of giving satisfaction in a station which required more business talent than his situation at Mr. Bray's had ever given scope to. But, if he could not obtain such a place as he desired, he would take what he could get. So he made every possible inquiry; but he had no one to speak a good word for him, and he could not expect people to feel confidence in a boy concerning whom they knew nothing.

So he met with no success, and day after day returned home silent and depressed. He dreaded to meet his mother and grandfather, after every fresh failure. The care-worn, patient face of the former turned towards him so hopefully, that he could not bear to sadden it by the recital of any new disappointment, and his grandfather's incredulity in the possibility of his ever having anything to do again was equally tantalizing, so long as he saw no hope of convincing him to the contrary. After a week or two, Mrs. Sullivan avoided asking him any questions concerning the occurrences of the day; for her watchful eye saw how much such inquiries pained him, and therefore she waited for him to make his communications, if he had any.

Sometimes nothing was said, on either side, of the manner in which Willie had passed his day. And many an application did he make for employment, many a mortifying rebuff did he receive, of which his mother never knew.

CHAPTER XIV

Yet where an equal poise of hope and fear
Does arbitrate the event, my nature is
That I incline to hope, rather than fear.
——*Comus*

THIS WAS ALTOGETHER a new experience to Willie, and one of the most trying he could have been called upon to bear. But he bore it, and bore it bravely; kept all his worst struggles from his anxious mother and desponding grandfather, and resolved manfully to hope against hope. Gerty was now his chief comforter. He told her all his troubles, and, young as she was, she was a wonderful consoler. Always looking on the bright side, always prophesying better luck to-morrow, she did much towards keeping up his hopes, and strengthening his resolutions. Gerty was so quick, sagacious and observing, that she knew more than most children of the various ways in which things are often brought about; and she sometimes made valuable suggestions to Willie, of which he gladly availed himself. Among others, she one day asked him if he had applied at the intelligence-offices.[1] He had never thought of it,—wondered he had not, but would try the plan the very next day. He did so, and for a time was buoyed up with the hopes held out to him; but they proved fleeting, and he was now almost in despair, when his eye fell upon an advertisement in a newspaper, which seemed to afford still another chance. He showed the notice to Gerty. It was just the thing. He had only to apply; he was the very boy that man wanted;—just fifteen, smart, capable and trustworthy; and would like, when he had learned the business, to go into partnership. That was what was required; and Willie was the very person, she was sure.

Gerty was so sanguine, that Willie presented himself the next day at the place specified, with a more eager countenance than he had ever yet worn. The gentleman, a sharp-looking man, with very keen eyes, talked with him some time; asked a great many questions, made the boy very uncomfortable by hinting his doubts about his capability and honesty, and, finally, wound up by declaring that, under the most favorable circumstances, and with the very best recommendations, he could not think of engaging with any young man, unless his friends were willing to take some interest in the concern, and invest a small amount on his account.

This, of course, made the place out of the question for Willie, even if he had liked the man; which he did not, for he felt in his heart that he was a knave, or not many degrees removed from one.

Until now, he had never thought of despairing; but when he went home after this last interview, it was with such a heavy heart, that it seemed to him utterly impossible to meet his mother, and so he went directly to True's room. It was the night before Christmas. True had gone out, and Gerty was alone. There was a bright fire in the stove, and the room was dimly lighted by the last rays of the winter sunset, and by the glare of the coals, seen through one of the open doors of the stove.

Gerty was engaged in stirring up an Indian cake for tea,—one of the few branches of the cooking department in which she had acquired some little skill. She was just coming from the pantry, with a scoop full of meal in her hand, when Willie entered at the opposite door. The manner in which he tossed his cap upon the settle, and, seating himself at the table, leaned his head upon both his hands, betrayed at once to Gerty the defeat the poor boy had met with in this last encounter with ill-fate. It was so unlike Willie to come in without even speaking,—it was such a strange thing to see his bright young head bowed down with care, and his elastic figure looking tired and old,—that Gerty knew at once his brave heart had given way. She laid down the scoop, and, walking softly and slowly up to him, touched his arm with her hand, and looked up anxiously into his face. Her sympathetic touch and look were more than he could bear. He laid his head on the table, and in a minute more Gerty heard great heavy sobs, each one of which sank deep into her soul. She often cried herself,—it seemed only natural; but Willie,—the laughing, happy, light-hearted Willie,— she had never seen *him* cry; she didn't know he *could*. She crept up on the rounds of his chair, and, putting her arm round his neck, whispered,

"I shouldn't mind, Willie, if I didn't get the place; I don't believe it's a *good* place."

"I don't believe it is, either," said Willie, lifting up his head; "but what shall I do? I can't get *any* place, and I can't stay here, doing nothing."

"We like to have you at home," said Gerty.

"It's pleasant enough to be at home. I was always glad enough to come when I lived at Mr. Bray's, and was earning something, and could feel as if anybody was glad to see me."

"*Everybody* is glad to see you *now.*"

"But not as they were *then,*" said Willie, rather impatiently. "Mother always looks as if she expected to hear I'd got something to do; and grand-father, I believe, never thought I should be good for much; and now, just as I was beginning to earn something, and be a help to them, I've lost my chance!"

"But that an't your fault, Willie; you couldn't help Mr. Bray's dying. I shouldn't think Mr. Cooper would blame you for not having anything to do *now.*"

"He don't *blame* me; but, if you were in my place, you'd feel just as I do, to see him sit in his arm-chair, evenings, and groan and look up at me, as much as to say, 'it's *you* I'm groaning about.' He thinks this is a dreadful world, and that he's never seen any good luck in it himself; so I suppose he thinks I never shall."

"*I* think you will," said Gerty. "I think you'll be rich, some time,— and *then* won't he be astonished?"

"O, Gerty! you're a nice child, and think I can do anything. If ever I am rich, I promise to go shares with you; but," added he, despondingly, "'t an't so easy. I used to think I could make money when I grew up; but it's pretty slow business."

Here he was on the point of leaning down upon the table again, and giving himself up to melancholy; but Gerty caught hold of his hands. "Come," said she, "Willie. Don't think any more about it. People have troubles always, but they get over 'em; perhaps next week you'll be in a better shop than Mr. Bray's, and we shall be as happy as ever. Do you know," said she, by way of changing the subject (a species of tact which children understand as well as grown people), "it's just two years to-night since I came here?"

"Is it?" said Willie. "Did Uncle True bring you home with him the night before Christmas?"

"Yes."

"Why, that was Santa Claus carrying you to good things, instead of bringing good things to you, wasn't it?"

Gerty did not know anything about Santa Claus, that special friend of children; and Willie, who had only lately read about him in some book, undertook to tell her what he knew of the veteran toy-dealer.

Finding the interest of the subject had engaged his thoughts in spite of himself, Gerty returned to her cooking, listening attentively, however, to his story, while she stirred up the corn-cake. When he had finished, she was just putting her cake in the oven; and, as she sat on her knee by the stove, swinging the handle of the oven-door in her hand, her eyes twinkled with such a merry look that Willie exclaimed, "What are you thinking of, Gerty, that makes you look so sly?"

"I was thinking that perhaps Santa Claus would come for you to-night. If he comes for folks that need something, I expect he'll come for you, and carry you to some place where you'll have a chance to grow rich."

"Very likely," said Willie, "he'll clap me into his bag, and trudge off with me as a present to somebody,—some old Crœsus, that will give me a fortune for the asking. I do hope he will; for, if I don't get something to do before New Year, I shall give up in despair."

True now came in, and interrupted the children's conversation by the display of a fine turkey, a Christmas present from Mr. Graham. He had also a book for Gerty, a gift from Emily.

"Isn't that queer?" exclaimed Gerty. "Willie was just saying you were my Santa Claus, Uncle True; and I do believe you are." As she spoke, she opened the book, and in the frontispiece was a portrait of that individual. "It looks like him, Willie! I declare it does!" shouted she; "a fur cap, a pipe, and just such a pleasant face! O! Uncle True, if you only had a sack full of toys over your shoulder, instead of your lantern and that great turkey, you would be a complete Santa Claus. Haven't you got anything for Willie, Uncle True?"

"Yes, I've got a little something; but I'm afeared he won't think much on 't. It's only a bit of a note."

"A note for me?" inquired Willie. "Who can it be from?"

"Can't say," said True, fumbling in his great pockets; "only, just round the corner, I met a man who stopped me to inquire where Miss Sullivan lived. I told him she lived jist here, and I'd show him the house. When he saw I belonged here too, he give me this little scrap o' paper, and asked me to hand it over, as it was directed to Master William Sullivan. I s'pose that's you, an't it?"

He now handed Willie the slip of paper; and the boy, taking True's lantern in his hand, and holding the note up to the light, read aloud:

"R. H. Clinton would like to see William Sullivan on Thursday morning, between ten and eleven o'clock, at No. 13 ——— Wharf."

Willie looked up in amazement. "What does it mean?" said he; "I don't know any such person."

"I know who he is," said True; "why, it's he as lives in the great stone house in ——— street. He's a rich man, and that's the number of his store—his counting-room, rather,—on ——— Wharf."

"What! father to those pretty children we used to see in the window?"

"The very same."

"What can he want of me?"

"Very like he wants your sarvices," suggested True.

"Then it's a place!" cried Gerty, "a real good one, and Santa Claus came and brought it! I said he would! O, Willie, I'm so glad!"

Willie did not know whether to be glad or not. It was such a strange message, coming too from an utter stranger. He could not but hope, as Gerty and True did, that it might prove the dawning of some good fortune; but he had reasons, of which they were not aware, for believing that no offer from this quarter could be available to him, and therefore made them both promise to give no hint of the matter to his mother or Mr. Cooper.

On Thursday, which was the next day but one, being the day after Christmas, Willie presented himself at the appointed time and place. Mr. Clinton, a gentlemanly man, with a friendly countenance, received him very kindly, asked him but a few questions, and did not even mention such a thing as a recommendation from his former employer; but, telling him that he was in want of a young man to fill the place of junior clerk in his counting-room, offered him the situation. Willie hesitated; for, though the offer was most encouraging to his future prospects, Mr. Clinton made no mention of any salary; and that was a thing the youth could not dispense with. Seeing that he was undecided, Mr. Clinton said, "Perhaps you do not like my proposal, or have already made some other engagement."

"No, indeed," answered Willie, quickly. "You are very kind to feel so much confidence in a stranger as to be willing to receive me, and your offer is a most unexpected and welcome one; but I have been in a retail store, where I obtained regular earnings, which were very important to my mother and grandfather. I had far rather be in a counting-room, like yours, sir, and I think I might learn to be of use; but I know there are numbers of boys, sons of rich men, who would be glad to be employed by you, and would ask no compensation for their services; so that I could not expect any salary, at least for some years. I should, indeed, be well repaid, at the end of that time, by the knowledge I might gain of mercantile affairs; but unfortunately, sir, I can no more afford it than I could afford to go to college."

The gentleman smiled. "How did you know so much of these matters, my young friend?"

"I have heard, sir, from boys who were at school with me, and are now clerks in mercantile houses, that they received no pay, and I always considered it a perfectly fair arrangement; but it was the reason why I felt bound to content myself with the position I held in an apothecary's shop, which, though it was not suited to my taste, enabled me to support myself, and to relieve my mother, who is a widow, and my grandfather, who is old and poor."

"Your grandfather is—"

"Mr. Cooper, sexton of Mr. Arnold's church."

"Aha!" said Mr. Clinton; "I know him."

"What you say, William," added he, after a moment's pause, "is perfectly true. We are not in the habit of paying any salary to our young clerks, and are overrun with applications at that rate; but I have heard good accounts of you, my boy (I shan't tell you where I had my information, though I see you look very curious), and, moreover, I like your countenance, and believe you will serve me faithfully. So, if you will tell me what you received from Mr. Bray, I will pay you the same next year, and, after that, increase your salary, if I find you deserve it; and, if you please, you shall commence with me the first of January."

Willie thanked Mr. Clinton in the fewest possible words, and hastened away.

The senior clerk, who, as he leaned over his accounts, listened to the conversation, thought the boy did not express much gratitude, considering the unusual generosity of the merchant's offer. But the merchant himself, who was watching the boy's countenance, while despondency gave place to surprise, and surprise again was superseded by hope, joy, and a most sincere thankfulness, saw there a gratitude too deep to express itself in words, and remembered the time when he too, the only son of his mother, and she a widow, had come alone to the city, sought long for employment, and, finding it at last, had sat down to write and tell her how he hoped soon to earn enough for himself and her.

The grass had been growing on that parent's grave, far back in the country, more than twenty years, and the merchant's face was furrowed with the lines of care; but, as he returned slowly to his desk, and unconsciously traced, on a blank sheet of paper, and with a dry pen, the words "Dear mother," she for the time became a living image; he, a boy again; and those invisible words were the commencement of the very letter that carried her the news of his good fortune.

No. The boy was not ungrateful, or the merchant would not thus have been reminded of the time when his own heart had been so deeply stirred.

And the spirits of those mothers who have wept, prayed, and thanked God over similar communications from much-loved sons, may know how to rejoice and sympathize with good little Mrs. Sullivan, when she heard from Willie the joyful tidings. Mr. Cooper and Gerty also have their prototypes in many an old man, whose dim and world-worn eye lights up occasionally with the hope that, disappointed as he has been himself, he cannot help cherishing for his grandson; and in many a proud little sister, who now sees her noble brother appreciated by others, as he has always been by her. Nor, on such an occasion, is the band of rejoicing ones complete, without some such hearty friend as True to come in unexpectedly, tap the boy on the shoulder, and exclaim, "Ah! Master Willie, they needn't have worried about you, need they? I've told your grandfather, more than once, that I was of the 'pinion 't would all come out right, at last."

The great mystery of the whole matter was Mr. Clinton's ever having heard of Willie at all. Mrs. Sullivan thought over all her small circle of acquaintances, and suggested a great many impossible ways. But as, with much conjecturing, they came no nearer to the truth, they finally concluded to do as Gerty did, set it all down to the agency of Santa Claus.

CHAPTER XV

Whether the day its wonted course renewed,
Or midnight vigils wrapt the world in shade,
Her tender task assiduous she pursued,
To soothe his anguish, or his wants to aid.
——*Blacklock*

"*I WONDER,*" *SAID* Miss Peekout, as she leaned both her hands on the sill of the front-window, and looked up and down the street,——a habit in which she indulged herself for about ten minutes, after she had washed up the breakfast things, and before she trimmed the solar-lamp,——"I wonder who that slender girl is who walks by here every morning, with that feeble-looking old man leaning on her arm! I always see them at just about this time, when the weather and walking are good. She's a nice child, I know, and seems to be very fond of the old man,——probably her grandfather. I notice she's careful to leave the best side of the walk for him, and she watches every step he takes; she needs to, indeed, for he totters sadly. Poor little thing! she looks pale and anxious; I wonder if she takes all the care of the old man!" But they are quite out of sight, and Miss Peekout turns round to *wonder* whether the solar-lamp doesn't need a new wick.

"I *wonder,*" said old Mrs. Grumble, as she sat at her window, a little further down the street, "if I should live to be old and infirm (Mrs. Grumble was over seventy, but as yet suffered from no infirmity but that of a very irritable temper),——I *wonder* if anybody would wait upon me, and take care of me, as that little girl does of her grandfather! No, I'll warrant not! Who can the patient little creature be?"

"There, look Belle!" said one young girl to another, as they walked up the shady side of the street, on their way to school; "there's the girl that we meet every day with the old man. How can you say you don't think she's pretty? I admire her looks!"

"You always do manage, Kitty, to *admire* people that everybody else thinks are horrid-looking."

"Horrid-looking!" replied Kitty, in a provoked tone; "she's anything but *horrid-looking!* Do notice, now, Belle, when we meet them, she has the *sweetest* way of looking up in the old man's face, and talking to him. I *wonder* what is the matter with him! Do see how his arm shakes,—the one that's passed through hers."

The two couples are now close to each other, and they pass in silence.

"Don't *you* think she has an interesting face?" said Kitty, eagerly, as soon as they were out of hearing.

"She's got handsome eyes," answered Belle. "I don't see anything else that looks interesting about her. I *wonder* if she don't hate to have to walk in the street with that old grandfather; trudging along so slow, with the sun shining right in her face, and he leaning on her arm, and shaking so he can hardly stand on his feet! I wouldn't do it for anything."

"Why, Belle!" exclaimed Kitty, "how can you talk so? I'm sure I pity that old man dreadfully."

"Lor!" said Belle, "what's the use of pitying? If you are going to begin to pity, you'll have to do it all the time. Look,"—and here Belle touched her companion's elbow,—"there's Willie Sullivan, father's clerk; an't he a beauty? I want to stop and speak to him."

But, before she could address a word to him, Willie, who was walking very fast, passed her with a bow, and a pleasant "Good-morning, Miss Isabel;" and, ere she had recovered from the surprise and disappointment, was some rods down the street.

"Polite!" muttered the pretty Isabel.

"Why, Belle! do see," said Kitty, who was looking back over her shoulder, "he's overtaken the old man and my interesting little girl. Look,— look! He's put the old man's other arm through his, and they are all three walking off together. Isn't that quite a coincidence?"

"Nothing very remarkable," replied Belle, who seemed a little annoyed. "I suppose they are persons he's acquainted with. Come, make haste; we shall be late at school."

Reader! Do *you wonder* who they are, the girl and the old man? or, have you already conjectured that they are no other than Gerty and Trueman Flint? True is no longer the brave, strong, sturdy protector of the feeble, lonely little child. The cases are quite reversed. True has had a paralytic stroke. His strength is gone, his power even to walk alone. He sits all day in his arm-chair, or on the old settle, when he is not out walking with Gerty. The blow came suddenly; struck down the robust man, and left him feeble as a child. And the little stranger, the orphan girl, who, in her weakness, her loneliness and her poverty, found in him a father and a mother, she now is all the world to him; his staff, his stay, his comfort and his hope. During four or five years that he has cherished the frail blossom, she has been gaining strength for the time when *he* should be the leaning, *she* the sustaining power; and when the time came,—and it came full soon,—she was ready to respond to the call. With the simplicity of a child, but a woman's firmness; with the stature of a child, but a woman's capacity; the earnestness of a child, but a woman's perseverance,—from morning till night, the faithful little nurse and housekeeper labors untiringly in the service of her first, her best friend. Ever at his side, ever attending to his wants, and yet most wonderfully accomplishing many things which he never sees her do, she seems, indeed, to the fond old man, what he once prophesied she would become,—God's embodied blessing to his latter years, making light his closing days, and cheering even the pathway to the grave.

Though disease had robbed True's limbs of all their power, the blast had happily spared his mind, which was clear and tranquil as ever; while his pious heart was fixed in humble trust on that God whose presence and love he had ever acknowledged, and on whom he so fully relied, that even in this bitter trial he was able to say, in perfect submission, "Thy will, not mine, be done!" Little did those who *wondered,* as day after day they watched the invalid and his childish guardian, at the patience and self-sacrifice of the devoted girl, little did they understand the emotions of Gerty's loving, grateful heart. Little did they realize the joy it was to her to sustain and support her beloved friend. Little did *she,* who would have been too proud to walk with the old paralytic, know what Gerty's pride was made of. She would have wondered, had she been told that the heart of the girl, whom she would have pitied, could she have spared time to pity *any one,* had never swelled with so fervent and noble a satisfaction as when, with the trembling old man leaning on her arm, she gloried in the burden.

The outward world was nothing at all to her. She cared not for the conjectures of the idle, the curious or the vain. She lived for True now; she might almost be said to live *in* him, so wholly were her thoughts bent on promoting his happiness, prolonging and blessing his days.

It had not long been thus. Only about two months previous to the morning of which we have been speaking had True been stricken down with this weighty affliction. He had been in failing health, but had still been able to attend to all his duties and labors, until one day in the month of June, when Gerty went into his room, and found, to her surprise, that he had not risen, although it was much later than his usual hour. On going to the bed-side and speaking to him, she perceived that he looked strangely, and had lost the power of replying to her questions. Bewildered and frightened, she ran to call Mrs. Sullivan. A physician was summoned, the case pronounced one of paralysis, and for a time there seemed reason to fear that it would prove fatal. He soon, however, began to amend, recovered his speech, and in a week or two was well enough to walk about, with Gerty's assistance.

The doctor had recommended as much gentle exercise as possible; and every pleasant morning, before the day grew warm, Gerty presented herself bonneted and equipped for those walks, which, unknown to her, excited so much observation. She usually took advantage of the opportunity to make such little household purchases as were necessary, that she might not be compelled to go out again and leave True alone; that being a thing she as much as possible avoided doing.

On the occasion already alluded to, Willie accompanied them as far as the provision-shop, which was their destination; and, having seen True comfortably seated, proceeded to —— Wharf, while Gerty stepped up to the counter to bargain for the dinner. She purchased a bit of veal suitable for broth, gazed wistfully at some tempting summer vegetables, turned away and sighed. She held in her hand the wallet which contained all their money; it had now been in her keeping for some weeks, and was growing light, so she knew it was no use to think about the vegetables; and she sighed, because she remembered how much Uncle True enjoyed the green peas last year.

"How much is the meat?" asked she of the rosy-cheeked butcher, who was wrapping it up in a paper.

He named the sum. It was very little; so *little* that it almost seemed to Gerty as if he had seen into her purse, and her thoughts too, and knew how glad she would be that it did not cost any more. As he handed her the change, he leaned over the counter, and asked, in an under tone, what kind of nourishment Mr. Flint was able to take.

"The doctor said any wholesome food," replied Gerty.

"Don't you think he'd relish some green peas? I've got some first-rate ones, fresh from the country; and, if you think he'd eat 'em, I should like to send you some. My boy shall take round half a peck or so, and I'll put the meat right in the same basket."

"Thank you," said Gerty; "he likes green peas."

"Very well, very well! Then I'll send him some beauties;" and he turned away to wait upon another customer, so quick that Gerty thought he did not see how the color came into her face and the tears into her eyes. But he *did* see, and that was the *reason* he turned away so quickly. He was a clever fellow, that rosy-cheeked butcher!

True had an excellent appetite, enjoyed and praised the dinner exceedingly, and, after eating heartily of it, fell asleep in his chair.

The moment he awoke, Gerty sprang to his side, exclaiming, "Uncle True, here's Miss Emily!—here's dear Miss Emily come to see you!"

"The Lord bless you, my dear, dear young lady!" said True, trying to rise from his chair and go towards her.

"Don't rise, Mr. Flint, I beg you will not," exclaimed Emily, whose quick ear perceived the motion. "From what Gerty tells me, I fear you are not able. Please give me a chair, Gerty, nearer to Mr. Flint."

She drew near, took True's hand, but looked inexpressibly shocked as she observed how tremulous it had become.

"Ah, Miss Emily!" said he; "I'm not the same man as when I saw you last; the Lord has given me a warnin', and I shan't be here long!"

"I'm so sorry I did not know of this!" said Emily. "I should have come to see you before, but I never heard of your illness until to-day. George, my father's man, saw you and Gertrude at a shop this morning, and mentioned it to me as soon as he came out of town. I have been telling this little girl that she should have sent me word."

Gerty was standing by True's chair, smoothing his gray locks with her slender fingers. As Emily mentioned her name, he turned and looked at her. O, what a look of love he gave her! Gerty never forgot it.

"Miss Emily," said he, "'t was no need for anybody to be troubled. The Lord provided for me, his own self. All the doctors and nurses in the land couldn't have done half as much for me as this little gal o' mine. It wan't at all in my mind, some four or five years gone,—when I brought the little barefoot mite of a thing to my home, and when she was sick and e'en-a-'most dyin' in this very room, and I carried her in my arms night and day,—that her turn would come so soon. Ah! I little thought then, Miss Emily, how the Lord would lay me low,—how those very same feet would run about in my service, how her bit of a hand would come in the dark nights to smooth my pillow, and I'd go about daytimes leaning on her little arm. Truly God's ways are not like our ways, nor his thoughts like our thoughts."

"O, Uncle True!" said Gerty, "I don't do much for you; I wish I could do a great deal more. I wish I could make you strong again."

"I daresay you do, my darlin', but that can't be in this world; you've given me what's far better than strength o' body. Yes, Miss Emily," added he, turning again towards the blind girl, "it's you we have to thank for all the comfort we enjoy. I loved my little birdie; but I was a foolish man, and I should ha' spiled her. You knew better what was for her good, and mine too. You made her what she is now, one of the lambs of Christ, a hand-maiden of the Lord. If anybody'd told me, six months ago, that I should become a poor cripple, and sit in my chair all day, and not know who was going to furnish a livin' for me or birdie either, I should ha' said I never could bear my lot with patience, or keep up any heart at all. But I've learned a lesson from this little one. When I first got so I could speak, after the shock, and tell what was in my mind, I was so mightily troubled a'thinkin' of my sad case, and Gerty with nobody to work or do anything for her, that I took on bad enough, and said, 'What shall we do now?—what shall we do now?' And then she whispered in my ear, 'God will take care of us, Uncle True!' And when I forgot the sayin', and asked, 'Who will feed and clothe us now?' she said again, 'The Lord will provide.' And, in my deepest distress of all, when one night I was full of anxious thoughts about my child, I said aloud, 'If I die, who will take care of Gerty?' the little thing, that I supposed was sound asleep in her bed, laid her head down beside me and said, 'Uncle True, when I was turned out into the dark street all alone, and had no friends nor any home, my Heavenly Father sent you to me; and now, if he wants you to come to him, and is not ready to take me too, he will send somebody else to take care of me the rest of the time I stay.' After that, Miss Emily, I gave up worryin' any more. Her words, and the blessed teachin's of the Holy Book that she reads me every day, have sunk deep into my heart, and I'm at peace.

"I used to think that, if I lived and had my strength spared me, Gerty would be able to go to school and get a sight o' larnin', for she has a nateral lurch for it, and it comes easy to her. She's but a slender child, and I never could bear the thought of her bein' driv to hard work for a livin'; she don't seem made for it, somehow. I hoped, when she grew up, to see her a schoolmistress, like Miss Browne, or somethin' in that line; but I've done bein' vexed about it now. I know, as she says, it's all for the best, or it wouldn't be."

When he finished speaking, Gerty, whose face had been hid against his shoulder, looked up and said, bravely, "O, Uncle True, I'm sure I can do almost any kind of work. Mrs. Sullivan says I sew very well, and I can learn to be a milliner or a dressmaker; that isn't hard work."

"Mr. Flint," said Emily, "would you be willing to trust your child with me? If you should be taken from her, would you feel as if she were safe in my charge?"

"Miss Emily," said True, "would I think her safe in angel-keepin'? I should believe her in little short o' that, if she could have you to watch over her."

"O, do not say that," said Miss Emily, "or I shall be afraid to under-take so solemn a trust. I know too well that my want of sight, my ill-health and my inexperience, almost unfit me for the care of a child like Gerty. But, since you approve of the teaching I have already given her, and are so kind as to think a great deal better of me than I deserve, I know you will at least believe in the sincerity of my wish to be of use to her; and, if it will be any comfort to you to know that in case of your death I will gladly take Gerty to my home, see that she is well educated, and, as long as I live, provide for and take care of her, you have my solemn assurance (and here she laid her hand on his), that it shall be done, and that to the best of my ability I will try to make her happy."

Gerty's first impulse was to rush towards Emily, and fling her arms around her neck; but she was arrested in the act, for she observed that True was weeping like an infant. In an instant his feeble head was resting upon her bosom; her hand was wiping away the great tears that had rushed to his eyes. It was an easy task, for they were tears of joy,—of a joy that had quite unnerved him in his present state of prostration and weakness.

The proposal was so utterly foreign to his thoughts or expectations, that it seemed to him a hope too bright to be relied upon; and, after a moment's pause, an idea occurring to him which seemed to increase his doubts, he gave utterance to it in the words, "But your father, Miss Emily!—Mr. Graham!—he's partickler, and not over-young now. I'm afeared he wouldn't like a little gal in the house."

"My father is indulgent to *me*," replied Emily; "he would not object to any plan I had at heart, and I have become so much attached to Gertrude that she would be of great use and comfort to me. I trust, Mr. Flint, that you will recover a portion at least of your health and strength, and be spared to her for many a year yet; but, in order that you may in no case feel any anxiety on her account, I take this opportunity to tell you that, if I should outlive you, she will be sure of a home with me."

"Ah, Miss Emily!" said the old man, "my time's about out, I feel right sure o' that; and, since you're willin', you'll soon be called to take charge on her. I haven't forgot how tossed I was in my mind, the day after I

brought her home with me, with thinkin' that p'raps I wasn't fit to undertake the care of such a little thing, and hadn't ways to make her comfortable; and then, Miss Emily, do you remember you said to me, 'You've done
quite right; the Lord will bless and reward you'? I've thought many a time
since that you was a true prophet, and that your words were, what I
thought 'em then, a whisper right from heaven! And now you talk o' doin'
the same thing yourself; and I, that am just goin' home to God, and feel as if
I read his ways clearer than ever afore, *I tell you,* Miss Emily, that you're
doin' right, too; and, if the Lord rewards you as he has done me, there'll
come a time when this child will pay you back in love and care all you ever
do for her.—Gerty?"

"Shes not here," said Emily; "I heard her run into her own room."

"Poor birdie!" said True, "she doesn't like to hear o' my leavin' her;
I'm sad to think how some day soon she'll almost sob her heart away over
her old uncle. Never mind now! I was goin' to bid her be a good child to
you; but I think she will, without biddin'; and I can say my say to her
another time. Good-by, my dear young lady;"—for Emily had risen to go,
and George the man-servant, was waiting at the door for her,—"if I never
see you again, remember that you've made an old man so happy that he's
nothing in this world left to wish for; and that you carry with you a dyin'
man's best blessin', and his prayer that God may grant such perfect peace
to your last days as now He does to mine."

That evening, when True had already retired to rest, and Gerty had
finished reading aloud in her little Bible, as she always did at bed-time,
True called her to him, and asked her, as he had often done of late, to
repeat his favorite prayer for the sick. She knelt at his bed-side and, with a
solemn and touching earnestness fulfilled his request.

"Now, darlin', the prayer for the dyin';—isn't there such a one in
your little book?"

Gerty trembled. There *was* such a prayer, a beautiful one; and the
thoughtful child, to whom the idea of death was familiar, knew it by
heart,—but could she repeat the words? Could she command her voice?
Her whole frame shook with agitation; but Uncle True wished to hear it, it
would be a comfort to him, and she would try. Concentrating all her
energy and self-command, she began, and, gaining strength as she proceeded, went on to the end. Once or twice her voice faltered, but with new
effort she succeeded, in spite of the great bunches in her throat; and her
voice sounded so clear and calm that Uncle True's devotional spirit was
not once disturbed by the thought of the girl's sufferings; for, fortunately,

he could not hear how her heart beat and throbbed, and threatened to burst.

She did not rise at the conclusion of the prayer,—she could not,—but remained kneeling, her head buried in the bed-clothes. For a few moments there was a solemn stillness in the room; then the old man laid his hand upon her head.

She looked up.

"You love Miss Emily, don't you, birdie?"

"Yes, indeed."

"You'll be a good child to her, when I'm gone?"

"O, Uncle True!" sobbed Gerty, "you mustn't leave me! I can't live without you, *dear* Uncle True!"

"It is God's will to take me Gerty; he has always been good to us, and we mustn't doubt him now. Miss Emily can do more for you than I could, and you'll be very happy with her."

"No, I shan't!—I shan't ever be happy again in this world! I never was happy until I came to you; and now, if you die, I wish I could die too!"

"You mustn't wish that, darlin'; you are young, and must try to do good in the world, and bide your time. I'm an old man, and only a trouble now."

"No, no, Uncle True!" said Gerty, earnestly; "you are not a trouble, you never could be a trouble! I wish *I'd* never been so much trouble to *you.*"

"So far from that, birdie, God knows you've long been my heart's delight! It only pains me now to think that you're a spendin' all your time, and slavin' here at home, instead of goin' to school, as you used to; but, O! we all depend on each other so!—first on God, and then on each other! And that 'minds me, Gerty, of what I was goin' to say. I feel as if the Lord would call me soon, sooner than you think for now; and, at first, you'll cry, and be sore vexed, no doubt; but Miss Emily will take you with her, and she'll tell you blessed things to comfort you;—how we shall all meet again and be happy in that world where there's no partin's; and Willie'll do everything he can to help you in your sorrer; and in time you'll be able to smile again. At first, and p'raps for a long time, Gerty, you'll be a care to Miss Emily, and she'll have to do a deal for you in the way o' schoolin', clothin', and so on; and what I want to tell you is, that Uncle True expects you'll be as good as can be, and do just what Miss Emily says; and, by and by, may be, when you're bigger and older, you'll be able to do somethin' for her. She's blind, you know, and you must be eyes for her; and she's not over strong, and you must lend a helpin' hand to her weakness, just as you do to mine; and, if you're good and patient, God will make your heart light at last, while you're only tryin' to make other folks happy; and when you're sad and troubled (for everybody is, sometimes), then think of old Uncle True, and how he used to say, 'Cheer up, birdie, for I'm of the 'pinion 't will all come out right, at last.' There, don't feel bad about it; go to bed, darlin', and to-morrow we'll have a nice walk,—and Willie's goin' with us, you know."

Gerty tried to cheer up, for True's sake, and went to bed. She did not sleep for some hours; but when, at last, she did fall into a quiet slumber, it continued unbroken until morning.

She dreamed that morning was already come; that she and Uncle True and Willie were taking a pleasant walk; that Uncle True was strong and well again,—his eye bright, his step firm, and Willie and herself laughing and happy.

And, while she dreamed the beautiful dream, little thinking that her first friend and she should no longer tread life's paths together, the messenger came,—a gentle, noiseless messenger,—and, in the still night, while the world was asleep, took the soul of good old True, and carried it home to God!

CHAPTER XVI

The stars are mansions built by Nature's hand;
And, haply, there the spirits of the blest
Dwell, clothed in radiance, their immortal vest.
——*Wordsworth*

TWO MONTHS HAVE passed since Trueman Flint's death, and Gertrude has for a week been domesticated in Mr. Graham's family. It was through the newspaper that Emily first heard of the little girl's sudden loss, and, immediately acquainting her father with her wishes and plans concerning the child, she found she had no opposition to fear from him. He reminded her, however, of the inconvenience that would attend Gertrude's coming to them at once, as they were soon to start on a visit to some distant relatives, from which they would not return until it was nearly time to remove to the city for the winter. Emily felt the force of this objection; for, although Mrs.

Ellis would be at home during their absence, she knew that, even were she willing to undertake the charge of Gertrude, she would be a very unfit person to console her in her time of sorrow and affliction.

This thought troubled Emily, who now considered herself the orphan girl's sole protector; and she regretted much that this unusual journey should take place so inopportunely. There was no help for it, however, for Mr. Graham's plans were arranged, and must not be interfered with, unless she would make Gertrude's coming, at the very outset, unwelcome and disagreeable. She started for town, therefore, the next morning, quite undecided what course to pursue, under the circumstances.

The day was Sunday, but Emily's errand was one of charity and love, and would not admit of delay; and, an hour before the time for morning service, Mrs. Sullivan, who stood at her open window, which looked out upon the street, saw Mr. Graham's carryall stop at the door. She ran to meet Emily, and, with the politeness and kindness always observable in her, waited upon her into her neat parlor, guided her to a comfortable seat, placed in her hand a fan (for the weather was excessively warm), and then proceeded to tell her how thankful she was to see her, and how sorry she felt that Gertrude was not at home. Emily wonderingly asked where Gertrude was, and learned that she was out walking with Willie. A succession of inquiries followed, and a long and touching story was told by Mrs. Sullivan of Gertrude's agony of grief, the impossibility of comforting her, and the fears the kind little woman had entertained lest the girl would die of sorrow.

"I couldn't do anything with her myself," said she. "There she sat, day after day, last week, on her little cricket, by Uncle True's easy-chair, with her head on the cushion, and I couldn't get her to move or eat a thing. She didn't appear to hear me when I spoke to her; and, if I tried to move her, she didn't struggle (for she was very quiet), but she seemed just like a dead weight in my hands; and I couldn't bear to make her come away into my room, though I knew it would change the scene, and be better for her. If it hadn't been for Willie, I don't know what I should have done, I was getting so worried about the poor child; but he knows how to manage her a great deal better than I do. When he is at home, we get along very well; for he takes her right up in his arms (he's very strong, and she's as light as a feather, you know), and either carries her into some other room or out into the yard; and somehow he contrives to cheer her up wonderfully. He persuades her to eat, and in the evenings, when he comes home from the store, takes long walks with her. Now, last evening they went way over Chelsea Bridge, where it was cool and pleasant, you know; and I suppose he diverted her attention and amused her, for she came home brighter than I've seen her at all, and quite tired. I got her to go to bed in my room, and she slept soundly all night, so that she really looks quite like herself to-day. They've gone out again this morning, and, being Sunday, and Willie at home all day, I've no doubt he'll keep her spirits up, if anybody can."

"Willie shows very good judgment," said Emily, "in trying to change the scene for her, and divert her thoughts. I'm thankful she has had such kind friends. I promised Mr. Flint she should have a home with me when he was taken away, and, not knowing of his death until now, I consider it a great favor to myself, as well as her, that you have taken such excellent care of her. I felt sure you had been all goodness, or it would have given me great regret that I had not heard of True's death before."

"O, Miss Emily!" said Mrs. Sullivan, "Gertrude is so dear to us, and we have suffered so much in seeing her suffer, that it was a kindness to ourselves to do all we could to comfort her. Why, I think she and Willie could not love each other better, if they were own brother and sister; and Willie and Uncle True were great friends; indeed, we shall all miss him very much. My old father doesn't say much about it, but I can see he's very down-hearted."

More conversation followed, in the course of which Mrs. Sullivan informed Emily that a cousin of hers, a farmer's wife, living in the country, about twenty miles from Boston, had invited them all to come and pass a week or two with her at the farm, and, as Willie was now to enjoy his usual summer vacation, they proposed accepting the invitation.

She spoke of Gertrude's accompanying them as a matter of course, and enlarged upon the advantage it would be to her to breathe the country air, and ramble about the fields and woods, after all the fatigue and confinement she had endured.

Emily, finding from her inquiries that Gertrude would be a welcome and expected guest, cordially approved of the visit, and also arranged with Mrs. Sullivan that she should remain under her care until Mr. Graham removed to Boston for the winter. She was then obliged to leave, without waiting for Gertrude's return, though she left many a kind message for her, and placed in Mrs. Sullivan's hands a sufficient sum of money to provide for all her wants and expenses.

Gertrude went into the country, and abundance of novelty, of country fare, healthful exercise, and heartfelt kindness and sympathy, brought the color into her cheek, and calmness and composure, if not happiness, into her heart.

Soon after the Sullivans' return from their excursion, the Grahams removed to the city, and, as we have said before, Gertrude had now been with them about a week.

"Are you still standing at the window, Gertrude? What are you doing, dear?"

"I'm watching to see the lamps lit, Miss Emily."

"But they will not be lit at all. The moon will rise at eight o'clock, and light the streets sufficiently for the rest of the night."

"I don't mean the street-lamps."

"What do you mean, my child?" said Emily, coming towards the window, and lightly resting a hand on each of Gertrude's shoulders.

"I mean the stars, dear Miss Emily. O, how I wish you could see them too!"

"Are they very bright?"

"O, they are beautiful! and there are so many! The sky is as full as it can be."

"How well I remember when I used to stand at this very window, and look at them as you are doing now! It seems to me as if I saw them this moment, I know so well how they look."

"I love the stars,—all of them," said Gertrude; "but my own star I love the best."

"Which do you call yours?"

"That splendid one, there, over the church-steeple; it shines into my room every night, and looks me in the face. Miss Emily (and here Gertrude lowered her voice to a whisper), it seems to me as if that star were lit on purpose for me. I think Uncle True lights it every night. I always feel as if he were smiling up there, saying 'See, Gerty, I'm lighting the lamp for you.' Dear Uncle True! Miss Emily, do you think he loves me now?"

"I do, indeed, Gertrude; and I think, if you make him an example, and try to live as good and patient a life as he did, that he will really be a lamp to your feet and as bright a light to your path as if his face were shining down upon you through the star."

"I was patient and good when I lived with him; at least, I almost always was; and I'm good when I'm with you; but I don't like Mrs. Ellis. She tries to plague me, and she makes me cross, and then I get angry, and don't know what I do or say. I did not mean to be impertinent to her to-day, and I wish I hadn't slammed the door; but how could I help it, Miss Emily, when she told me, right before Mr. Graham, that I tore up the last night's *Journal,* and I *know* that I did not? It was an old paper that she saw me tying your slippers up in, and I am almost sure that she lit the library fire with that very *Journal,* herself; but Mr. Graham will always think *I* did it."

"I have no doubt, Gertrude, that you had some reason to feel provoked, and I believe you when you say that you were not the person to blame for the loss of the newspaper. But you must remember, my dear, that there is no merit in being patient and good-tempered, when there is nothing to irritate you. I want you to learn to bear even injustice, without losing your self-control. You know Mrs. Ellis has been here a number of years; she has had everything her own way, and is not used to young people. She felt, when you came, that it was bringing new care and trouble upon her, and it is not strange that when things go wrong she should sometimes think you in fault. She is a very faithful woman, very kind and attentive to me, and very important to my father. It will make me unhappy if I have any reason to fear that you and she will not live pleasantly together."

"I do not want to make you unhappy; I do not want to be a trouble to anybody," said Gertrude, with some excitement; "I'll go away! I'll go off somewhere, where you will never see me again!"

"Gertrude!" said Emily, seriously and sadly. Her hands were still upon the young girl's shoulders, and, as she spoke, she turned her round, and brought her face to face with herself. "Gertrude, do you wish to leave your blind friend? Do you not love me?"

So touchingly grieved was the expression of the countenance that met her gaze, that Gertrude's proud, hasty spirit was subdued. She threw her arms round Emily's neck, and exclaimed, "No! dear Miss Emily, I would not leave you for all the world! I will do just as you wish. I will never be angry with Mrs. Ellis again, for your sake."

"Not for *my* sake, Gertrude," replied Emily,—"for your own sake; for the sake of duty and of God. A few years ago I should not have expected you to be pleasant and amiable towards any one whom you felt ill-treated you; but, now that you know so well what is right; now that you are familiar with the life of that blessed Master, who, when he was reviled, reviled not again; now that you have learned faithfully to fulfil so many important duties; I had hoped that you had learned, also, to be forbearing, under the most trying circumstances. But do not think, Gertrude, because I remind you when you have done wrong, I despair of your becoming one day all I wish to see you. What you are experiencing now being a new trial, you must bring new strength to bear upon it; and I have such confidence in you as to believe that, knowing my wishes, you will try to behave properly to Mrs. Ellis on all occasions."

"I will, Miss Emily, I will. I'll not answer her back when she's ugly to me, if I have to bite my lips to keep them together."

"O, I do not believe it will be so bad as that," said Emily, smiling. "Mrs. Ellis' manner is rather rough, but you will get used to her."

Just then a voice was heard in the entry,—"To see *Miss Flint!* Really! Well, *Miss Flint* is in Miss Emily's room. She's going to entertain company, is she?"

Gertrude colored to her temples, for it was Mrs. Ellis' voice, and the tone in which she spoke was very derisive.

Emily stepped to the door, and opened it.—"Mrs. Ellis!"

"What say, Emily?"

"Is there any one below?"

"Yes; a young man wants to see Gertrude; it's that young Sullivan, I believe."

"Willie!" exclaimed Gertrude, starting forward.

"You can go down and see him, Gertrude," said Emily. "Come back here when he's gone,—and, Mrs. Ellis, I wish you would step in and put my room a little in order. I think you will find plenty of pieces for your ragbag about the carpet,—Miss Randolph always scatters so many when she is engaged with her dress-making."

Mrs. Ellis made her collection, and then, seating herself on a couch at the side of the fireplace, with her colored rags in one hand and the white in the other, commenced speaking of Gertrude.

"What are you going to do with her, Emily?" said she; "send her to school?"

"Yes. She will go to Mr. W.'s, this winter."

"Why! Isn't that a very expensive school for a child like her?"

"It is expensive, certainly; but I wish her to be with the best teacher I know of, and father makes no objection to the terms. He thinks, as I do, that if we undertake to fit her to instruct others, she must be thoroughly taught herself. I talked with him about it the first night after we came into town for the season, and he agreed with me that we had better put her out to learn a trade at once, than half-educate, make a fine lady of her, and so unfit her for anything. He was willing I should manage the matter as I pleased, and I resolved to send her to Mr. W.'s. So she will remain with us for the present. I wish to keep her with me as long as I can, not only because I am fond of the child, but she is delicate and sensitive, and now that she is so sad about old Mr. Flint's death, I think we ought to do all we can to make her happy; don't you, Mrs. Ellis?"

"I always calculate to do my duty," said Mrs. Ellis, rather stiffly. "Where is she going to sleep when we get settled?"

"In the little room at the end of the passage."

"Then where shall I keep the linen press?"

"Can't it stand in the back entry? I should think the space between the windows would accommodate it."

"I suppose it's *got* to," said Mrs. Ellis, flouncing out of the room, and muttering to herself,—"everything turned topsy-turvy for the sake of that little upstart!"

Mrs. Ellis was vexed on more accounts than one. She had long had her own way in the management of all household matters at Mr. Graham's, and had consequently become rather tyrannical. She was capable, methodical, and neat; accustomed to a small family, and now for many years quite *unaccustomed* to children; Gertrude was in her eyes an unwarrantable intruder—one who must of necessity be continually in mischief, continually deranging her most cherished plans. Then, too, Gertrude had been reared, as Mrs. Ellis expressed it, among the lower classes; and the housekeeper, who was not in reality very hard-hearted, and quite approved of all public and private charities, had a slight prejudice in favor of high birth. Indeed, though now depressed in her circumstances, she prided herself on being of a good family, and considered it an insult to her dignity to expect that she should feel an interest in providing for the wants of one so inferior to her in point of station.

More than all this, she saw in the new inmate a formidable rival to herself in Miss Graham's affections; and Mrs. Ellis could not brook the idea of being second in the regard of Miss Emily, who, owing to her peculiar misfortune and to her delicate health, had long been her especial charge, and for whom she felt as much tenderness as it was in her nature to feel for any one.

Owing to all these circumstances, Mrs. Ellis was far from being favorably disposed towards Gertrude; and Gertrude, in her turn, was not yet prepared to love Mrs. Ellis very cordially.

CHAPTER XVII

And thou must sail upon this sea, a long,
Eventful voyage. The wise *may* suffer wreck,
The foolish *must*. O, then, be early wise.
——*Ware*

EMILY SAT ALONE in her room. Mr. Graham had gone to a meeting of bank-directors. Mrs. Ellis was stoning raisins in the dining-room. Willie still detained Gertrude in the little library below stairs, and Emily, with the moonlight now streaming across the chamber, which was none the less dark to her on that account, was indulging in a long train of meditation. Her head rested on her hand; her face, usually so placid, was sad and melancholy in its expression; and her whole appearance and attitude denoted despondency and grief. As thought pressed upon thought, and past sorrows arose in quick succession, her head gradually sunk upon the cushions of the couch where she sat, and tears slowly trickled through her fingers.

Suddenly, a hand was laid softly upon hers. She gave a quick start, as she always did when surprised, for her unusual preoccupation of mind had made Gertrude's approaching step unheard.

"Is anything the matter, Miss Emily?" said Gertrude. "Do you like best to be alone, or may I stay?"

The sympathetic tone, the delicacy of the child's question, touched Emily. She drew her towards her, saying, as she did so, "O yes, stay with me;" then observing, as she passed an arm round the little girl, that she trembled, and seemed violently agitated, she added, "but what is the matter with you, Gerty? What makes you tremble and sob so?"

At this, Gertrude broke forth with, "O, Miss Emily! I thought you were crying when I came in, and I hoped you would let me come and cry with you; for I am so miserable I can't do anything else."

Calmed herself by the more vehement agitation of the child, Emily endeavored to discover the cause of this evidently new and severe affliction. It proved to be this: Willie had been to tell her that he was going away, going out of the country; as Gertrude expressed it, to the very other end of the world—to India. Mr. Clinton was interested in a mercantile house in Calcutta, and had offered William the most favorable terms to go abroad as clerk to the establishment. The prospect thus afforded was far better than he could hope for by remaining at home; the salary was, at the very first, sufficient to defray all his own expenses, and provide for the wants of those who were now becoming every year more and more dependent upon him. The chance, too, of future advancement was great; and, though the young man's affectionate heart clung fondly to home and friends, there was no hesitation in his mind as to the course which both duty and interest prompted. He agreed to the proposal, and, whatever his own struggles were at the thought of five, or perhaps ten years' banishment, he kept them manfully to himself, and talked cheerfully about it to his mother and grandfather.

"Miss Emily," said Gertrude, when she had acquainted her with the news, and become again somewhat calm, "how can I bear to have Willie go away? How can I live without Willie? He is so kind, and loves me so much! He was always better than any brother, and, since Uncle True died, he has done everything in the world for me. I believe I could not have borne Uncle True's death if it had not been for Willie; and now how can I let him go away?"

"It is hard, Gertrude," said Emily, kindly, "but it is no doubt for his advantage; you must try and think of that."

"I know it," replied Gertrude,—"I suppose it is; but, Miss Emily, you do not know how I love Willie. We were so much together; and there were only us two, and we thought everything of each other; he was so much older than I, and always took such good care of me! O, I don't think you have any idea what friends we are!"

Gertrude had unconsciously touched a chord that vibrated through Emily's whole frame. Her voice trembled as she answered, "*I*, Gertrude! *not know,* my child! I know better than you imagine how dear he must be to you. *I,* too, had"—then checking herself, she paused abruptly, and there was a few moments silence, during which Emily got up, walked hastily to the window, pressed her aching head against the frosty glass, and then, returning to Gertrude, said, in a voice which had recovered its usual calmness, "O, Gertrude! in the grief that oppresses you now, you little realize how much you have to be thankful for. Think, my dear, what a blessing it is that Willie will be where you can often hear from him, and where he can have constant news of his friends."

"Yes," replied Gerty; "he says he shall write to his mother and me very often."

"Then too," said Emily, "you ought to rejoice at the good opinion

Mr. Clinton must have of Willie; the perfect confidence he must feel in his uprightness, to place in him so much trust. I think that is very flattering."

"So it is," said Gertrude; "I did not think of that."

"And you have lived so happily together," continued Emily, "and will part in such perfect peace. O, Gertrude! Gertrude! such a parting as that should not make you sad; there are so much worse things in the world. Be patient, my dear child, do your duty, and perhaps there will some day be a happy meeting, that will quite repay you for all you suffer in the separation."

Emily's voice trembled as she uttered the last few words. Gertrude's eyes were fixed upon her friend with a very puzzled expression. "Miss Emily," said she, "I begin to think everybody has trouble."

"Certainly, Gertrude; can you doubt it?"

"I did not use to think so. I knew *I* had, but I thought other folks were more fortunate. I fancied that rich people were all happy; and, though you are blind, and that is a dreadful thing, I supposed you were used to it; and you always looked so pleasant and quiet, I took it for granted nothing ever vexed you now. And then, Willie!—I believed once that nothing could make him look sad, he was always so gay; but when he hadn't any place, I saw him really cry; and then, when Uncle True died, and now again to-night, when he was telling me about going away, he could hardly speak, he felt so badly. And so, Miss Emily, since I see that you and Willie have troubles, and that tears will come, though you try to keep them back, I think the world is full of trials, and that everybody gets a share."

"It *is* the lot of humanity, Gertrude, and we must not expect it to be otherwise."

"Then who can be happy, Miss Emily?"

"Those only, my child, who have learned submission; those who, in the severest afflictions, see the hand of a loving Father, and, obedient to his will, kiss the chastening rod."

"It is very hard, Miss Emily."

"It is hard, my child, and therefore few in this world can rightly be called happy; but, if, even in the midst of our distress, we can look to God in faith and love, we may, when the world is dark around, experience a peace that is a foretaste of heaven."

And Emily was right. Who that is striving after the Christian life has not experienced moments when, amid unusual discouragements and disappointments, the heart, turning in love and trust to its great Source, experiences emotions of ecstatic joy and hope, that never come to the prosperous and the world-called happy? He who has had such dreams of eternal peace can form some conception of the rest which remaineth for the people of God, when, with an undivided affection, and a faith undimmed by a single doubt, the soul reposes in the bosom of its Creator.

Gertrude had often found in time and the soothing influences of religious faith some alleviation to her trials; but never until this night, did she feel a spirit not of earth, coming forth from the very chaos of sorrow into which she was plunged, and enkindling within her the flame of a higher and nobler sensation than she ever yet had cherished.

When she left Emily that night, it was with a serenity which is strength; and, if the spirit of Uncle True, looking down upon her through the bright star which she so loved, sighed to see the tears which glittered in her eyes, it was reassured by the smile of a heaven-lit light that played over her features, and when she sunk to slumber stamped them with the seal of peace.

Willie's departure was sudden, and Mrs. Sullivan had only a week in which to make those arrangements which a mother's thoughtfulness deems necessary. Her hands were therefore full of work, and Gerty, whom Emily at once relinquished for the short time previous to the vessel's sailing, was of great assistance to her. Willie was very busy daytimes, but was always with them in the evening.

On one occasion, he returned home about dusk, and, his mother and grandfather both being out, and Gertrude having just put aside her sewing, he said to her, "Come, Gerty, if you are not afraid of taking cold, come and sit on the door-step with me, as we used to in old times; there will be no more such warm days as this, and we may never have another chance to sit there, and watch the moon rise above the old house at the corner."

"O, Willie," said Gertrude, "do not speak of our never being together in this old place again! I cannot bear the thought; there is not a house in Boston I could ever love as I do this."

"Nor I," replied Willie; "but there is not one chance in a hundred, if I should be gone five years, that there would not be a block of brick stores in this spot, when I come to look for it. I wish I did not think so, for I shall have many a longing after the old home."

"But what will become of your mother and grandfather, if this house is torn down?"

"It is not easy to tell, Gerty, what will become of any of us by that time; but, if there is any necessity for their moving, I hope I shall be able to provide a better house than this for them."

"You won't be here, Willie."

"I know it, but I shall be always hearing from you, and we can talk about it by letters, and arrange everything. The idea of any such changes, after all," added he, "is what troubles me most in going away; I think they would miss me and need me so much. Gertrude, you will take care of them, won't you?"

"I!" said Gertrude, in amazement; "such a child as I!—what can I do?"

"If I am gone five or ten years, Gerty, you will not be a child all that time, and a woman is often a better dependence than a man; especially such a good, brave woman as you will be. I have not forgotten the beautiful care you took of Uncle True; and, whenever I imagine grandfather or mother old and helpless, I always think of you, and hope you will be near them; for I know, if you are, you will be a greater help than I could be. So I leave them in your care, Gerty, though you *are* only a child yet."

"Thank you, Willie," said Gertrude, "for believing I shall do everything I can for them. I certainly will, as long as I live. But, Willie, *they* may be strong and well all the time you are gone; and *I*, although I am so young, may be sick and die,—nobody knows."

"That is true enough," said Willie, sadly; "and I may die myself; but it will not do to think of that. It seems to me I never should have courage to go, if I didn't hope to find you all well and happy when I come home. You must write to me every month, for it will be a much greater task to mother, and I am sure she will want you to do nearly all the writing; and, whether my letters come directed to her or you, it will be all the same, you know. And, Gerty, you must not forget me, darling; you must love me just as much when I am gone,—won't you?"

"Forget you, Willie! I shall be always thinking of you, and loving you the same as ever. What else shall I have to do? But you will be off in a strange country, where everything will be different, and you will not think half as much of me, I know."

"If you believe that, Gertrude, it is because you do *not* know. You will have friends all around you, and I shall be alone in a foreign land; but every day of my life my heart will be with you and my mother, and I shall live here a great deal more than there."

They were now interrupted by Mr. Cooper's return, nor did they afterwards renew the conversation on the above topics; but the morning Willie left them, when Mrs. Sullivan was leaning over a neatly-packed trunk in the next room, trying to hide her tears, and Mr. Cooper's head was bowed lower than usual, while the light had gone out in the neglected pipe, which he still held in his hand, Willie whispered to Gerty, who was standing on a small chest of books, in order to force down the lid for him to lock it, "Gerty, dear, for my sake take good care of *our* mother and grandfather—they are *yours* almost as much as mine."

On Willie's thus leaving home, for the first time, to struggle and strive among men, Mr. Cooper, who could not yet believe that the boy would be successful in the war with fortune, gave him many a caution against indulging hopes which never would be realized, and reminded him again and again that he knew nothing of the world.

Mrs. Sullivan bestowed on her son but little parting counsel. Trusting to the lessons he had been learning from his childhood, she compressed her parental advice into few words, saying, "Love and fear God, Willie, and do not disappoint your mother."

We pause not to dwell upon the last night the youth spent at home, his mother's last evening prayer, her last morning benediction, the last breakfast they all took together (Gertrude among the rest), or the final farewell embrace.

And Willie went to sea. And the pious, loving, hopeful woman, who for eighteen years had cherished her boy with tenderness and pride, maintained now her wonted spirit of self-sacrifice, and gave him up without a murmur. None knew how she struggled with her aching heart, or whence came the power that sustained her. No one had given the little widow credit for such strength of mind, and the neighbors wondered much to see how quietly she went about her duties the day before her son sailed; and how, when he had gone, she still kept on with her work, and wore the same look of patient humility that ever characterized her.

At the present moment, when emigration offers rare hopes and inducements, there is scarcely to be found in New England a village so insignificant, or so secluded, that there is not there some mother's heart bleeding at the perhaps life-long separation from a darling son. Among the wanderers, we hope,—ay, we *believe* that there is many a one who is actuated, not by the love of gold, the love of change, the love of adventure, but by the love he bears his *mother,*—the earnest longing of his heart to save her from a life of toil and poverty. Blessings and prosperity to him who goes forth with such a motive! And, if he fail, he has not lived in vain; for, though stricken by disease or violence at the very threshold of his labors, he dies in attestation of the truth that there are sons worthy of a mother's love, a love which is the highest, the holiest, the purest type of God on earth.

And now, in truth, commenced Gertrude's residence at Mr. Graham's, hitherto in various ways interrupted. She at once commenced attending school, and until the spring labored diligently at her studies. Her life was varied by few incidents, for Emily never entertained much company, and in the winter scarcely any at all, and Gertrude formed no intimate acquaintances among her companions. With Emily she passed many happy hours; they took walks, read books and talked much with each other, and Miss Graham found that in Gertrude's observing eyes, and her feeling and glowing descriptions of everything that came within their gaze, she was herself renewing her acquaintance with the outside world. In errands of charity and mercy Gertrude was either her attendant or her messenger; and all the dependents of the family, from the cook to the little boy who called at the door for the fragments of broken bread, agreed in loving and praising the child, who, though neither beautiful nor elegantly dressed, had a fairy lightness of step, a grace of movement and a dignity of bearing, which impressed them all with the conviction that she was no beggar in spirit, whatever might be her birth or fortune,—and all were in the invariable habit of addressing her as *Miss* Gertrude.

Mrs. Ellis' prejudices against her were still strong; but, as Gertrude was always civil, and Emily prudently kept them much apart, no unhappy result had yet ensued.

Mr. Graham, seeing her sad and pensive, did not at first take much notice of her; but, having on several occasions found his newspaper carefully dried, and his spectacles miraculously restored, after a vain search on his part, he began to think her a smart girl; and when, a few weeks after, he took up the last number of the *Working Farmer,* and saw, to his surprise, that the leaves were cut and carefully stitched together, he, supposing she had done it for her own benefit, pronounced her decidedly an *intelligent* girl.

She went often to see Mrs. Sullivan, and, as the spring advanced they began to look for news of Willie. No tidings had come, however, when the season arrived for the Grahams to remove into the country for the summer. A letter, written by Gertrude to Willie, soon after they were established there, will give some idea of her situation and mode of life.

After dwelling at some length upon the disappointment of not having yet heard from him, and giving an account of the last visit she had made his mother before leaving the city, she went on to say: "But you made me promise, Willie, to write about myself, and said you should wish to hear everything that occurred at Mr. Graham's which concerned me in any way; so, if my letter is more tedious than usual, it is your own fault, for I have much to tell of our removal to D——, and of the way in which we live here, so different from our life in Boston. I think I hear you say, when you have read so far, 'O dear! now Gerty is going to give me a description of Mr. Graham's country-house!'—but you need not be afraid; I have not forgotten how, the last time I undertook to do so, you placed your hand over my mouth to stop me, and assured me you knew the place as well as if you had lived there all your life, for I had described it to as often as once a week ever since I was eight years old. I made you beg my pardon for being so uncivil; but I believe I talked enough about my first visit here to excuse you for being quite tired of the subject. Now, however, quite to my disappointment, everything looks smaller and less beautiful than it seemed to me then; and, though I do not mean to describe it to you again, I must just tell you that the entry and piazzas are much narrower than I expected, the rooms lower, and the garden and summer-houses not nearly so large. Miss Emily asked me, a day or two ago, how I liked the place, and if it looked as it used to. I told her the truth; and she was not at all displeased, but laughed at my old recollections of the house and grounds, and said it was always so with things we had seen when we were little children.

"I need not tell you that Miss Emily is kind and good to me as ever; for nobody who knows her as you do would suppose she could ever be anything but the best and loveliest person in the world. I can never do half enough, Willie, to repay her for all her goodness to me; and yet, she is so pleased with little gifts, and so grateful for trifling attentions, that it seems as if everybody might do something to make her happy. I found a few violets in the grass yesterday, and when I brought them to her she kissed and thanked me as if they had been so many diamonds; and little Ben Gately, who picked a hatful of dandelion-blossoms, without a single stem, and then rang at the front-door bell and asked for Miss Ga'am, so as to give them to her himself, got a sweet smile for his trouble, and a 'thank you, Bennie,' that he will not soon forget. Wasn't it pleasant in Miss Emily, Willie?

"Mr. Graham has given me a garden, and I mean to have plenty of flowers for her, by and by,—that is, if Mrs. Ellis doesn't interfere; but I expect she will, for she does in almost everything. Willie, Mrs. Ellis is my trial, my *great* trial. She is just the kind of person I cannot endure. I believe there are some people that other people *can't* like,—and she is just the sort I can't. I would not tell anybody else so, because it would not be right, and I do not know as it is right to mention it at all; but I always tell you everything. Miss Emily talks to me about her, and says I must learn to love her; and *when I do* I shall be an angel.

"There, I know you will think that is some of Gerty's old temper; and perhaps it is, but you don't know how she tries me: it is in little things that I cannot tell very easily, and I would not plague you with them if I could, so I won't write about her any more,—I will try to be perfect, and love her dearly.

"You will think that now, while I am not going to school, I shall hardly know what to do with my time; but I have plenty to do. The first week after we came here, however, I found the mornings very dull. You know I am always an early riser; but, as it does not agree with Miss Emily to keep early hours, I never see her until eight o'clock, full two hours after I am up and dressed. When we were in Boston, I always spent that time studying; but this spring, Miss Emily, who noticed that I was growing fast, and heard Mr. Arnold observe how pale I looked, fancied it would not do for me to spend so much time at my books; and so, when we came to D——, she planned my study-hours, which are very few, and arranged that they should take place after breakfast and in her own room. She also advised me, if I could, to sleep later in the morning; but I could not, and was up at my usual time, wandering around the garden. One day I was quite surprised to find Mr. Graham at work, for it was not like his winter habits; but he is a queer man. He asked me to come and help him plant onion-seeds, and I rather think I did it pretty well; for after that he let me help him plant a number of things, and label little sticks to put down by the side of them. At last, to my joy, he offered to give me a piece of ground for a garden, where I might raise flowers. He does not care for flowers, which seems *so* strange; he only raises vegetables and trees.

"And so I am to have a garden. But I am making a very long story, Willie, and have not time to say a thousand other things that I want to. O! if I could see you, I could tell you in an hour more than I can write in a week. In five minutes I expect to hear Miss Emily's bell, and then she will send for me to come and read to her.

"I long to hear from you, dear Willie, and pray to God, morning and
evening, to keep you in safety, and soon send tidings of you to your loving
Gerty

CHAPTER XVIII

Is it not lovely? Tell me, where doth dwell
The fay that wrought so beautiful a spell?—
In thine own bosom, brother, didst thou say?
Then cherish as thine own so good a fay.
—*Dana*

A FEW WEEKS after the date of this letter, Gerty learned through George,
who went daily to the city to attend to the marketing, that Mrs. Sullivan
had left word at the shop of our old acquaintance, the rosy-cheeked
butcher, that she had received a letter from Willie, and wanted Gerty to
come into town and see it. Emily was willing to let her go, but afraid it
would be impossible to arrange it, as Charlie, the only horse Mr. Graham
kept, was in use, and she saw no way of sending her.

"Why don't you let her go in the omnibus?" asked Mrs. Ellis.

Gerty looked gratefully at Mrs. Ellis; it was the first time that lady
had ever seemed anxious to promote her views.

"I don't think it's safe for her to go alone in the coach," said Emily.

"Safe!—What, for that great girl!" exclaimed Mrs. Ellis, whose position in the family was such that there were no forms of restraint in her
intercourse with Miss Graham.

"Do you think it is?" inquired Emily. "She seems a child to me, to be
sure; but, as you say, she is almost grown up, and I daresay is capable of
taking care of herself. Gertrude, are you sure you know the way from the
omnibus-office in Boston to Mrs. Sullivan's?"

"Perfectly well, Miss Emily."

Without further hesitation, two tickets for the coach were put into
Gertrude's hand, and she set forth on her expedition with beaming eyes
and a full heart. She found Mrs. Sullivan and Mr. Cooper well, and rejoicing over the happiest tidings from Willie, who, after a long but agreeable
voyage, had reached Calcutta in health and safety. A description of his new
home, his new duties and employers, filled all the rest of the letter, except-

ing what was devoted to affectionate messages and inquiries, a large share of which were for Gerty. Gertrude stayed and dined with Mrs. Sullivan, and then hastened to the omnibus. She took her seat, and, as she waited for the coach to start, amused herself with watching the passers-by. It was nearly three o'clock, and she was beginning to think she should be the only passenger, when she heard a strange voice proceeding from a person whose approach she had not perceived. She moved towards the door, and saw, standing at the back of the coach, the most singular-looking being she had ever beheld. It was an old lady, small, and considerably bent with years. Gertrude knew, at a glance, that the same original mind must have conceived and executed every article of the most remarkable toilet she had ever witnessed. But, before she could observe the details of that which was as a whole so wonderfully grotesque, her whole attention was arrested by the peculiar behavior of the old lady.

She had been vainly endeavoring to mount the inconvenient vehicle, and now, with one foot upon the lower step, was calling to the driver to come to her assistance.

"Sir," said she, in measured tones, "is this travelling equipage under your honorable charge?"

"What say, marm?—Yes, I'm the driver;" saying which, he came up to the door, opened it, and, without waiting for the polite request which was on the old lady's lips, placed his hand beneath her elbow, and before she was aware of his intention lifted her into the coach and shut the door.

"Bless me!" ejaculated she, as she seated herself opposite Gertrude, and began to arrange her veil and other draperies, "that individual is not versed in the art of assisting a lady without detriment to her habiliments. O dear, O dear!" added she, in the same breath, "I've lost my parasol!"

She rose as she spoke; but the sudden starting of the coach threw her off her balance, and she would have fallen, had it not been for Gertrude, who caught her by the arm and reseated her, saying, as she did so, "Do not be alarmed, madam; here is the parasol."

As she spoke she drew into view the missing article, which, though nearly the size of an umbrella, was fastened to the old lady's waist by a green ribbon, and, having slipped out of place, was supposed lost. And not a parasol only did she thus bring to light; numerous other articles, arranged in the same manner, and connected with the same green string, now met Gertrude's astonished eyes;—a reticule of unusual dimensions and a great variety of colors, a black lace cap, a large feather fan, a roll of fancy paper, and several other articles. They were partly hidden under a thin black silk shawl, and Gertrude began to think her companion had been on a pilfering expedition. If so, however, the culprit seemed remarkably at her ease, for before the coach had gone many steps she deliberately placed her feet on the opposite seat, and proceeded to make herself comfortable. In the first place, much to Gertrude's horror, she took out all her teeth and put them in her work-bag; then drew off a pair of black silk gloves, and replaced them by cotton ones; removed her lace veil, folded and pinned it to the green string. She next untied her bonnet, threw over it, as a protection from the dust, a large cotton handkerchief, and, with some difficulty, unloosing her fan, applied herself diligently to the use of it, closing her eyes as she did so, and evidently intending to go to sleep. She probably did fall into a doze, for she was very quiet, and Gertrude, occupied with her own thoughts, and with observing some heavy clouds that were arising from the west, forgot to observe her fellow-traveller, until she was startled by a hand suddenly laid upon her own, and an abrupt exclamation of "My dear young damsel, do not those dark shadows betoken adverse weather?"

"I think it will rain very soon," replied Gertrude.

"This morn, when I ventured forth," soliloquized the old lady, "the sun was bright, the sky serene; even the winged songsters, as they piped their hymns, proclaimed their part in the universal joy; and now, before I can regain my retirement, my delicate lace flounces (and she glanced at the skirt of her dress) will prove a sacrifice to the pitiless storm."

"Doesn't the coach pass your door?" inquired Gertrude, her compassion excited by the old lady's evident distress.

"No! O, no! not within half a mile. Does it better accommodate you, my young miss?"

"No. I have a mile to walk beyond the omnibus-office."

The old lady, moved by a deep sympathy, drew nearer to Gertrude, saying, in the most doleful accents, "Alas for the delicate whiteness of your bonnet-ribbon!"

The coach had by this time reached its destination, and the two passengers alighted. Gertrude placed her ticket in the driver's hand, and would have started at once on her walk, but was prevented by the old lady, who grasped her dress, and begged her to wait for her, as she was going the same way. And now great difficulty and delay ensued. The old lady refused to pay the amount of fare demanded by the driver; declared it was not the regular fare, and accused the man of an intention to put the surplus of two cents in his own pocket. Gertrude was impatient, for she was every moment expecting to see the rain pour in torrents; but at last, the matter being compromised between the driver and his closely-calculating passenger, she was permitted to proceed. They had walked about a quarter of a mile, and that at a very slow rate, when the rain commenced falling; and now Gertrude was called upon to unloose the huge parasol, and carry it over her companion and herself. In this way they had accomplished nearly as much more of the distance, when the water began to descend as if all the reservoirs of heaven were at once thrown open. At this moment Gertrude heard a step behind them, and, turning, she saw George, Mr. Graham's man, running in the direction of the house. He recognized her at once, and exclaimed, "Miss Gertrude, you'll be wet through; and Miss Pace too," added he, seeing Gerty's companion. "Sure and ye'd better baith hasten to her house, where ye'll be secure."

So saying, he caught Miss Pace in his arms, and signing to Gertrude to follow, rushed across the street, and hurrying on to a cottage near by, did not stop until he had placed the old lady in safety beneath her own porch; and Gerty at the same instant gained its shelter. Miss Pace—for such was the old lady's name—was so bewildered that it took her some minutes to recover her consciousness; and, in the mean time, it was arranged that Gertrude should stop where she was for an hour or two, and that George should call for her when he passed that way with the carriage, on his return from the depot, where he went regularly on three afternoons in the week for Mr. Graham.

Miss Patty Pace was not generally considered a person of much hospitality. She owned the cottage which she occupied, and lived there quite alone, keeping no servants and entertaining no visitors. She was herself a famous visitor; and, as but a small part of her life had been passed in D——, and all her friends and connections lived either in Boston or at a much greater distance, she was a constant frequenter of omnibuses and other public vehicles. But though, through her travelling propensities and her regular attendance at church, she was well known, Gertrude was, perhaps, the first visitor that had ever entered her house; and she, as we have seen, could scarcely be said to have come by invitation.

Even when she was at the very door, she found herself obliged to take the old lady's key, unlock and open it herself, and finally lead her hostess into the parlor, and help her off with her innumerable capes, shawls and veils. Once come to a distinct consciousness of her situation, however, Miss Patty Pace conducted herself with all the elegant politeness for which she was remarkable. Suffering though she evidently was with a thousand regrets at the trying experience her own clothes had sustained, she commanded herself sufficiently to express nearly as many fears lest Gertrude had ruined every article of her dress. It was only after many assurances from the latter that her boots were scarcely wet at all, her gingham dress and cape not likely to be hurt by rain, and her nice straw bonnet safe under the scarf she had thrown over it, that Miss Patty could be prevailed upon to so far forget the duties of a hostess as to retire and change her lace flounces for something more suitable for home-wear.

As soon as she left the room, Gertrude, whose curiosity was wonderfully excited, hastened to take a nearer view of numbers of articles, both of ornament and use, which had already attracted her attention from their odd and singular appearance.

Miss Pace's parlor was as remarkable as its owner. Its furniture, like her apparel, was made up of the gleanings of every age and fashion, from chairs that undoubtedly came over in the Mayflower, to feeble attempts at modern pincushions, and imitations of crystallized grass, that were a complete failure. Gertrude's quick and observing eye was revelling amid the few relics of ancient elegance, and the numerous specimens of folly and bad taste, with which the room was filled, when the old lady returned.

A neat though quaint black dress having taken the place of the much-valued flounces, she now looked far more ladylike. She held in her hand a tumbler of pepper and water, and begged her visitor to drink, assuring her it would warm her stomach and prevent her taking cold; and when Gertrude, who could only with great difficulty keep from laughing in her face, declined the beverage, Miss Patty seated herself, and, while enjoying the refreshment, carried on a conversation which at one moment satisfied her visitor she was a woman of sense, and the next persuaded her that she was either foolish or insane.

The impression which Gertrude made upon Miss Patty, however, was more decided. Miss Patty was delighted with the young miss, who, she declared, possessed an intellect that would do honor to a queen, a figure that was airy as a gazelle, and motions more graceful than those of a swan.

When George came for Gertrude, Miss Pace, who seemed really sorry to part with her, cordially invited her to come again, and Gertrude promised to do so.

The satisfactory news from Willie, and the amusing adventures of the afternoon, had given to Gertrude such a feeling of buoyancy and light-heartedness, that she bounded into the house, and up the stairs, with that fairy quickness Uncle True had so loved to see in her, and which, since his death, her subdued spirits had rarely permitted her to exercise. She hastened to her own room to remove her bonnet and change her dress before seeking Emily, to whom she longed to communicate the events of the day.

At the door of her room she met Bridget, the housemaid, with a dust-pan, hand-broom, etc. On inquiring what was going on there at this unusual hour, she learned that during her absence her room, which had since their removal been in some confusion, owing to Mrs. Ellis' not having decided what furniture should be placed there, had been subjected to a thorough and comprehensive system of spring cleaning. Alarmed, though she scarcely knew why, at the idea of Mrs. Ellis having invaded her premises, she surveyed the apartment with a slight feeling of agitation, which, as she continued her observations, swelled into a storm of angry excitement.

When Gertrude went from Mrs. Sullivan's to Mr. Graham's house in the city, she carried with her, beside a trunk containing her wardrobe, an old bandbox, which she stored away on the shelf of a closet in her chamber.

There it remained, during the winter, unpacked and unobserved by any one. When the family went into the country, however, the box went also, carefully watched and protected by its owner. As there was no closet or other hiding-place in Gertrude's new room, she placed it in a corner behind the bed, and the evening before her expedition to the city had been engaged in removing and inspecting a part of its contents. Each article was endeared to her by the charm of old association, and many a tear had the little maiden shed over her stock of valuables. There was the figure of the Samuel, Uncle True's first gift, now defaced by time and accident. As she surveyed a severe contusion on the back of the head, the effect of an inadvertent knock given it by True himself, and remembered how patiently the dear old man labored to repair the injury, she felt that she would not part with the much-valued memento for the world. There, too, were his pipes, of common clay, and dark with smoke and age; but, as she thought how much comfort they had been to him, she felt that the possession of them was a consolation to her. She had brought away too his lantern, for she had not forgotten its pleasant light, the first that ever fell upon the darkness of her life; nor could she leave behind an old fur cap, beneath which she had often sought a kindly smile, and, never having sought in vain, could hardly realize that there was not one for her still hidden beneath its crown. There were some toys too, and picture-books, gifts from Willie, a little basket he had carved for her from a nut, and a few other trifles.

All these things, excepting the lantern and cap, Gertrude had left upon the mantel-piece; and now, upon entering the room, her eye at once sought her treasures. They were gone. The mantel-piece was nicely dusted, and quite empty. She ran towards the corner, where she had left the old box. That too was gone. To rush after the retreating house-maid, call her back, and pour forth a succession of eager inquiries, was but the work of an instant.

Bridget was a new comer, a remarkably stupid specimen, but Gertrude contrived to obtain from her all the information she needed. The image, the pipes and the lantern, were thrown among a heap of broken glass and crockery, and, as Bridget declared, smashed all to nothing. The cap, pronounced moth-eaten, had been condemned to the flames; and the other articles, Bridget could not be sure, but "troth, she belaved she was just afther laving them in the fireplace." And all this in strict accordance with Mrs. Ellis' orders. Gertrude allowed Bridget to depart unaware of the greatness of her loss; then, shutting the door, she threw herself upon the bed, and gave way to a violent fit of weeping.

So this, thought she, was the reason why Mrs. Ellis was so willing to forward my plans,—and I was foolish enough to believe it was for my own sake! She wanted to come here and rob me, the thief!

She rose from the bed as suddenly as she had thrown herself down, and started for the door; then, some new thought seeming to check her, she returned again to the bed-side, and, with a loud sob, fell upon her knees, and buried her face in her hands. Once or twice she lifted her head, and seemed on the point of rising and going to face her enemy. But each time something came across her mind and detained her. It was not fear;— O, no! Gertrude was not afraid of anybody. It must have been some stronger motive than that. Whatever it might be, it was something that had, on the whole, a soothing influence; for, after every fresh struggle, she grew calmer, and presently, rising, seated herself in a chair by the window, leaned her head on her hand, and looked out. The window was open; the shower was over, and the smiles of the refreshed and beautiful earth were reflected in a glowing rainbow, that spanned the eastern horizon. A little bird came, and perched on a branch of a tree close to the window, and shouted forth a *Te Deum*. A Persian lilac-bush in full bloom sent up a delicious fragrance. A wonderful composure stole into Gertrude's heart, and, ere she had sat there many minutes, she felt "the grace that brings peace succeed to the passions that produce trouble." She had conquered; she had achieved the greatest of earth's victories, a victory over herself. The brilliant rainbow, the carol of the bird, the fragrance of the blossoms, all the bright things that gladdened the earth after the storm, were not half so beautiful as the light that overspread the face of the young girl when, the storm within her laid at rest, she looked up to heaven, and her heart sent forth its silent offering of praise.

The sound of the tea-bell startled her. She hastened to bathe her face and brush her hair, and then went down stairs. There was no one in the dining-room but Mrs. Ellis; Mr. Graham had been detained in town, and Emily was suffering with a severe headache. Consequently, Gertrude took tea alone with Mrs. Ellis. The latter, though unaware of the great value Gertrude attached to her old relics, was conscious she had done an unkind thing; and as the injured party gave no evidence of anger or ill will, not even mentioning the subject, the aggressor felt more uncomfortable and mortified than she would have been willing to allow. The matter was never recurred to, but Mrs. Ellis experienced a stinging consciousness of the fact that Gertrude had shown a superiority to herself in point of forbearance.

The next day, Mrs. Prime, the cook, came to the door of Emily's room, and obtaining a ready admittance, produced the little basket, made of a nut, saying, "I wonder now, Miss Emily, where Miss Gertrude is; for I've found her little basket in the coal-hod, and I guess she'll be right glad on 't—'t an't hurt a mite." Emily inquired "What basket?" and the cook, placing it in her hands, proceeded with eagerness to give an account of the destruction of Gertrude's property, which she had herself witnessed with great indignation. She also gave a piteous description of the distress the young girl manifested in her questioning of Bridget, which the sympathizing cook had overheard from her own not very distant chamber.

As Emily listened to the story, she well remembered having thought, the previous afternoon, that she heard Gertrude sobbing in her room, which on one side adjoined her own, but that she afterwards concluded herself to have been mistaken. "Go," said she, "and carry the basket to Gertrude; she is in the little library; but please, Mrs. Prime, don't tell her that you have mentioned the matter to me." Emily expected, for several days, to hear from Gertrude the story of her injuries; but Gertrude kept her trouble to herself, and bore it in silence.

This was the first instance of complete self-control in Gerty, and the last we shall have occasion to dwell upon. From this time she continued to experience more and more the power of governing herself; and, with each new effort gaining new strength, became at last a wonder to those who knew the temperament she had had to contend with. She was now nearly fourteen years old, and so rapid had been her recent growth that, instead of being below the usual stature, she was taller than most girls of her age. Freedom from study, and plenty of air and exercise, prevented her, however, from suffering from this circumstance.

Her garden was a source of great pleasure to her, and, flowers seeming to prosper under her careful training, she had always a bouquet ready to place by Emily's plate at breakfast-time.

Occasionally she went to see her friend Miss Patty Pace, and always met with a cordial reception. Miss Patty's attention was very much engrossed by the manufacture of paper flowers, and, as Gertrude's garden furnished the models, she seldom went empty-handed; but, the old lady's success being very ill proportioned to her efforts, it would have been a libel upon nature to pronounce even the most favorable specimens of this sort of fancy-work true copies of the original. Miss Patty was satisfied, however; and it is to be hoped that her various friends, for whom the large bunches were intended that travelled about tied to her waist by the green string, were satisfied also.

Miss Patty seemed to have a *great many* friends. Judging from the numbers of people that she talked about to Gertrude, the latter concluded she must be acquainted with everybody in Boston. And it would have been hard to find any one whose intercourse extended to a wider circle. She had, in her youth, learned an upholsterer's trade, which she had practiced for many years in the employment (as she said) of the first families in the city; and so observing was she, and so acute in her judgment, that a report at one time prevailed that Miss Pace had eyes in the back of her head, and two pairs of ears. Notwithstanding her wonderful visionary and comprehending powers, she had never been known to make mischief in families. She was prudent and conscientious, and, though always peculiar in her habits and modes of expression, and so wild in some of her fancies as to be often thought by strangers a little *out,* she had secured and continued to retain the good will of a great many kindly-disposed ladies and gentlemen, at whose houses she was always well received and politely treated. She calculated, in the course of every year, to go the rounds among all these friends, and thus kept up her intimacy with households in every member of which she felt a warm personal interest.

Miss Patty labored under one great and absorbing regret, and frequently expatiated to Gertrude on the subject; it was, that she was without a companion. "Ah, Miss Gertrude," she would sometimes exclaim, seeming for the time quite forgetful of her age and infirmities, "I should do vastly well in this world, if I only had a companion;" and here, with a slight toss of the head, and a little, smirking air, she would add, in a whisper, "and you must know, my dear, I somewhat meditate matrimony." Then, seeing Gertrude's look of surprise and amusement, she would apologize for having so long delayed fulfilling what had always been her intention; and, at the same time that she admitted not being as young as she had once been, would usually close with the remark, "It is true, time is inexorable; but I cling to life, Miss Gertrude, I cling to life, and may marry yet."

On the subject of fashion, too, she would declaim at great length, avowing, for her own part, a rigid determination to be modern, whatever the cost might be. Gertrude could not fail to observe that she had failed in this intention as signally as in that of securing a youthful swain; and she was also gradually led to conclude that Miss Pace, whatever might be her means, was a terrible miser. Emily, who knew the old lady very well, and had often employed her, did not oppose Gertrude's visits to the cottage, and sometimes accompanied her; for Emily loved to be amused, and Miss Patty's quaint conversation was as great a treat to her as to Gertrude. These calls were so promptly returned, that it was made very evident that Miss Patty preferred doing the greater part of the visiting herself; observing which, Emily gave her a general invitation to the house, of which she was not slow to avail herself.

CHAPTER XIX

More health, dear maid, thy soothing presence brings,
Than purest skies, or salutary springs.
——*Mrs. Barbauld*

PERSONS WHO OWN residences within six miles of a large city cannot be properly said to enjoy country life. They have large gardens, oftentimes extensive grounds, and raise their own fruit and vegetables; they usually keep horses, drive about and take the air. Some maintain quite a barn-yard establishment, and pride themselves upon their fat cattle and Shanghae fowls. But, after all, these suburban residents do not taste the charms of true country life. There are no pathless woods, no roaring brooks, no waving fields of grain, no wide stretches of pasture-land. Every eminence commands a view of the near metropolis, the hum of which is almost audible; and every hourly-omnibus, or train of cars, carries one's self, or one's neighbor, to or from the busy mart.

Those who seek retirement and seclusion, however, can no-where be more sure to find it than in one of these half-country, half-city homes; and many a family will, summer after summer, resort to the same quiet corner, and, undisturbed by visitors or gossip, maintain an independence of life which would be quite impossible either in the crowded streets of the town, where one's acquaintances are forever dropping in, or in the strictly country villages, where every new comer is observed, called upon and talked about.

Mr. Graham's establishment was of the medium order, and little calculated to attract notice. The garden was certainly very beautiful, abounding in rich shrubbery, summer-houses, and arbors covered with grape-vines; but a high board-fence hid it from public view, and the house, standing back from the road, was rather old-fashioned and very unobtrusive in its appearance.

Excepting his horticultural propensities, Mr. Graham's associations were all connected with the city; and Emily, being unfitted for much general intercourse with society, entertained little company, save that of the neighbors who made formal calls, and some particular friends, such as Mr. Arnold, the clergyman, and a few intimates, who often towards evening drove out of town to see Emily and eat fruit.

The summer was passing away most happily, and Gertrude, in the constant enjoyment of Emily's society, and in the consciousness that she was, in various ways, rendering herself useful and important to this excellent friend, was finding in every day new causes of contentment and rejoicing, when a seal was suddenly set to all her pleasure.

Emily was taken ill with a fever, and Gertrude, on occasion of her first undertaking to enter the sick room, and share in its duties, was rudely repulsed by Mrs. Ellis, who had constituted herself sole nurse, and who declared, when the poor girl pleaded hard to be admitted, that the fever was catching, and Miss Emily did not want her there,—that when she was sick she never wanted any one about her but herself.

For three or four days Gertrude wandered about the house, inconsolable. On the fifth morning after her banishment from the room, she saw Mrs. Prime, the cook, going up stairs with some gruel; and, thrusting into her hand some beautiful rose-buds, which she had just gathered, she begged her to give them to Emily, and ask if she might not come in and see her.

She lingered about the kitchen awaiting Mrs. Prime's return, in hopes of some message, at least, from the sufferer. But when the cook came down the flowers were still in her hand, and, as she threw them on the table, the kind-hearted woman gave vent to her feelings.

"Well! folks do say that first-rate cooks and nurses are allers as cross as bears! 'T an't for me to say whether it's so 'bout cooks, but 'bout nurses there an't no sort o' doubt! I would not want to go there, Miss Gertrude; I would n't insure you but what she'd bite your head off."

"Wouldn't Miss Emily take the flowers?" asked Gertrude, looking quite grieved.

"Well, she hadn't no word in the matter. You know she couldn't see what they were, and Miss Ellis flung 'em outside the door, vowin' I might as well bring pison into the room with a fever, as them roses. I tried to speak to Miss Emily, but Miss Ellis set up such a hush-sh-sh I s'posed she was goin' to sleep, and jest made the best o' my way out. Ugh! don't she scold when there's anybody sick?"

Gertrude sauntered out into the garden. She had nothing to do but think anxiously about Emily, who, she feared, was very ill. Her work and her books were all in Emily's room, where they were usually kept; the library might have furnished amusement, but it was locked up. So the garden was the only thing left for her, and there she spent the rest of the morning; and not that morning only, but many others; for Emily continued to grow worse, and a fortnight passed away without Gertrude's seeing her, or having any other intimation regarding her health than Mrs. Ellis' occasional report to Mr. Graham, who, however, as he saw the physician every day, and made frequent visits to his daughter himself, did not require that particular information which Gertrude was eager to obtain. Once or twice she had ventured to question Mrs. Ellis, whose only reply was, "Don't bother me with questions! what do you know about sickness?"

One afternoon, Gertrude was sitting in a large summer-house at the lower end of the garden; her own piece of ground, fragrant with mignonette and verbena, was close by, and she was busily engaged in tying up and marking some little papers of seeds, the gleanings from various seed-vessels, when she was startled by hearing a step close beside her, and, looking up, saw Dr. Jeremy, the family physician, just entering the building.

"Ah! what are you doing?" exclaimed the doctor, in a quick, abrupt manner, peculiar to him. "Sorting seeds, eh?"

"Yes, sir," replied Gerty, looking up and blushing, as she saw the doctor's keen black eyes scrutinizing her face.

"Where have I seen you before?" asked he, in the same blunt way.

"At Mr. Flint's."

"Ah! True Flint's! I remember all about it. You're his girl! Nice girl, too! And poor True, he's dead! Well, he's a loss to the community! So this is the little nurse I used to see there. Bless me! how children do grow!"

"Doctor Jeremy," asked Gertrude, in an earnest voice, "will you please to tell me how Miss Emily is?"

"Emily! she an't very well, just now."

"Do you think she'll die?"

"Die! No! What should she die for? I won't let her die, if you'll help me keep her alive. Why an't you in the house, taking care of her?"

"I wish I might!" exclaimed Gertrude, starting up; "I wish I might!"

"What's to hinder?"

"Mrs. Ellis, sir; she won't let me in, she says Miss Emily doesn't want anybody but her."

"She's nothing to say about it, or Emily either; it's my business, and I want you. I'd rather have you to take care of my patients than all the Mrs. Ellises in the world. She doesn't know anything about nursing; let her stick to her cranberry-sauce and squash-pies. So, mind, to-morrow you're to begin."

"O, thank you, doctor!"

"Don't thank me yet; wait till you've tried it,—it's hard work taking care of sick folks. Whose orchard is that?"

"Mrs. Bruce's."

"Is that her pear-tree?"

"Yes, sir."

"By George, Mrs. Bruce, I'll try your pears for you!"

As he spoke, the doctor, a man some sixty-five years of age, stout and active, sprung over a stone wall, which separated them from the orchard, and, carried along by the impetus the leap had given him, reached the foot of the tree almost at a bound.

As Gertrude, full of mirth, watched the proceeding, she observed the doctor stumble over some obstacle, and only save himself from falling by stretching forth both hands, and sustaining himself against the huge trunk of the fine old tree. At the same instant a head, adorned with a velvet smoking-cap, was slowly lifted from the long grass, and a youth, about sixteen or seventeen years of age, raised himself upon his elbow, and stared at the unlooked-for intruder.

Nothing daunted, the doctor at once took offensive ground towards the occupant of the place, saying, "Get up, lazy bones! What do you lie there for, tripping up honest folks?"

"Who do you call honest folks, sir?" inquired the youth, apparently quite undisturbed by the doctor's epithet and inquiry.

"I call myself and my little friend here remarkably honest people," replied the doctor, winking at Gertrude, who, standing behind the wall and looking over, was laughing heartily at the way in which the doctor had got caught.

The young man, observing the direction of the latter's eyes, turned and gave a broad stare at Gertrude's merry face.

"Can I do anything for you, sir?" asked he.

"Yes, certainly," replied the doctor. "I came here to help myself to pears; but you are taller than I,—perhaps, with the help of that crooked-handled cane of yours, you can reach that best branch."

"A remarkably honorable and honest errand!" muttered the young man. "I shall be happy to be engaged in so good a cause."

As he spoke, he lifted his cane, which lay by his side, and, drawing down the end of the branch, so that he could reach it with his hand, shook it vigorously. The ripe fruit fell on every side, and the doctor, having filled his pockets, and both his hands, started for the other side of the wall.

"Have you got enough?" asked the youth, in a very lazy tone of voice.

"Plenty, plenty," said the doctor.

"Glad of it," said the boy, indolently throwing himself on the grass, and still staring at Gertrude.

"You must be very tired," said the doctor, stepping back a pace or two; "I'm a physician, and should advise a nap."

"Are you, indeed!" replied the youth, in the same half-drawling, half-ironical tone of voice in which he had previously spoken; "then I think I'll take your advice;" saying which, he threw himself back upon the grass and closed his eyes.

Having emptied his pockets upon the seat of the summer-house, and invited Gertrude to partake, the doctor, still laughing so immoderately at his boyish feat that he could scarcely eat the fruit, happened to bethink himself of the lateness of the hour. He looked at his watch. "Half-past four! The cars go in ten minutes. Who's going to drive me down to the depot?"

"I don't know, sir," replied Gertrude, to whom the question seemed to be addressed.

"Where's George?"

"He's gone to the meadow to get in some hay, but he left white Charlie harnessed in the yard; I saw him fasten him to the chain, after he drove you up from the cars."

"Ah! then you can drive me down to the depot."

"I can't, sir; I don't know how."

"But you must; I'll show you how. You're not afraid!"

"O, no, sir; but Mr. Graham"—

"Never you mind Mr. Graham—do you mind me. I'll answer for your coming back safe enough."

Gertrude was naturally courageous; she had never driven before, but, having no fears, she succeeded admirably, and, being often afterwards called upon by Dr. Jeremy to perform the same service, she soon became skilful in the use of the reins,—an accomplishment not always particularly desirable in a lady, but which, in her case, proved very useful.

Dr. Jeremy was true to his promise of installing Gertrude in Emily's sick room. The very next visit he made to his patient, he spoke in terms of the highest praise of Gertrude's devotion to her old uncle, and her capability as a nurse, and asked why she had been expelled from the chamber.

"She is timid," said Emily, "and is afraid of catching the fever."

"Don't believe it," said Dr. Jeremy; "'t an't like her."

"Do you think not?" inquired Emily, earnestly. "Mrs. Ellis—"

"Told a lie," interrupted the doctor. "Gerty wants to come and take care of you, and she knows how as well as Mrs. Ellis, any day; it isn't much you need done. You want quiet, and that's what you can't have, with that great talking woman about. So I'll send her to Jericho to-day, and bring my little Gertrude up here. She's a quiet little mouse, and has got a head on her shoulders."

It is not to be supposed that Gertrude could provide for Emily's wants any better, or even as well, as Mrs. Ellis; and Emily, knowing this, took care that the housekeeper should not be sent to Jericho; for, though Dr. Jeremy, a man of strong prejudices, did not like her, she was excellent in her department, and could not be dispensed with. Had it been otherwise, Emily would not have hurt her feelings by letting her see that she was in any degree superseded.

So, though Emily, Dr. Jeremy and Gertrude, were all made happy by the free admission of the latter to the sick-room, the housekeeper, unhandsomely as she had behaved, was never conscious that any one knew the wrong she had done to Gertrude, in keeping her out of sight and giving a false reason for her continued absence.

There was a watchfulness, a care, a tenderness, in Gertrude, which only the warmest love could have dictated.

When Emily awoke at night from a troubled sleep, found a cooling draught ready at her lips, and knew from Mrs. Ellis' deep snoring that it was not her hand that held it,—when she observed that all day long no troublesome fly was ever permitted to approach her pillow, her aching head was relieved by hours of patient bathing, and the little feet that were never weary were always noiseless,—she realized the truth, that Dr. Jeremy had brought her a most excellent medicine.

A week or two passed away, and she was well enough to sit up nearly all the time, though not yet able to leave her room. A few weeks more, and the doctor began to insist upon air and exercise. "Drive out two or three times every day," said he.

"How can I?" said Emily. "George has so much to do, it will be very inconvenient."

"Let Gertrude drive you; she is a capital hand."

"Gertrude," said Emily, smiling, "I believe you are a great favorite of the doctor's; he thinks you can do anything. You never drove in your life, did you?"

"Hasn't she driven me to the depot, every day, for these six weeks?" inquired the doctor.

"Is it possible?" asked Emily, who was unaccustomed to the idea of a lady's attempting the management of a horse.

Upon her being assured that this was the case, and the doctor insisting that there was no danger, Charlie was harnessed into the carryall, and Emily and Mrs. Ellis went out to drive with Gertrude; an experiment which, being often repeated, was a source of health to the invalid, and pleasure to them all. In the early autumn, when Emily's health was quite restored, old Charlie was daily called into requisition; sometimes Mrs. Ellis accompanied them, but, as she was often engaged about household duties, they usually went by themselves, in a large, old-fashioned buggy, and Emily declared that Gertrude's learning to drive had proved one of the greatest sources of happiness she had known for years.

Once or twice, in the course of the summer and autumn, Gertrude saw again the lazy youth whom Dr. Jeremy had stumbled over when he went to steal pears.

Once he came and sat on the wall while she was at work in her garden, professed himself astonished at her activity, talked a little with her about her flowers, asked some questions concerning her friend Dr. Jeremy, and ended by requesting to know her name.

Gertrude blushed; she was a little sensitive about her name, and, though she always went by that of Flint, and did not, on ordinary occasions, think much about it, she could not fail to remember, when the question was put to her point blank, that she had, in reality, no surname of her own.

Emily had endeavored to find Nan Grant, in order to learn from her something of Gertrude's early history; but Nan had left her old habitation, and, for years, nothing had been heard of her.

Gertrude, as we have said, blushed on being asked her name, but replied, with dignity, that she would tell hers, provided her new acquaintance would return the compliment.

"Shan't do it!" said the youth, impudently, "and don't care about knowing yours, either;" saying which, he kicked an apple with his foot, and walked off, still kicking it before him, leaving Gertrude to the conclusion that he was the most ill-bred person she had ever seen.

CHAPTER XX

A perfect woman, nobly planned,
To warn, to comfort, and command,
And yet a spirit still, and bright,
With something of an angel light.
— *Wordsworth*

IT WAS THE TWILIGHT of a sultry September day, and, wearied with many hours' endurance of an excessive heat, unlooked for so late in the season, Emily Graham sat on the front piazza of her father's house, inhaling a delicious and refreshing breeze, which had just sprung up. The western sky was still streaked with brilliant lines of red, the lingering effects of a gorgeous sunset, while the moon, now nearly at the full, and triumphing in the close of day and the commencement of her nightly reign, cast her full beams upon Emily's white dress, and gave to the beautiful hand and arm, which, escaping from the draperied sleeve, rested on the side of her rustic arm-chair, the semblance of polished marble.

Ten years had passed since Emily was first introduced to the reader; and yet, so slight were the changes wrought by time upon her face and figure, that she looked scarcely any older than on the occasion of her first meeting with Gertrude in Mr. Arnold's church.

She had even then experienced much of the sorrow of life, and learned how to distil from the bitter dregs of suffering a balm for every pain. Even then, that experience, and the blessed knowledge she had gained from it, had both stamped themselves upon her countenance: the one in a sobered and subdued expression, which usually belongs to more mature years; the other, in that sweet, calm smile of trust and hope, which proclaims the votary of Heaven.

Therefore time had little power upon her, and as she was then so was she now; lovely in her outward appearance, and still more lovely in heart and life. A close observer might, however, perceive in her a greater degree of buoyancy of spirit, keenness of interest in what was going on about her, and evident enjoyment of life, than she had formerly evinced; and this was due, as Emily felt and acknowledged, to her recent close companionship with one to whom she was bound by the warmest affection, and who, by her lively sympathy, her constant devotion, her natural appreciation of the entertaining and the ludicrous, as well as the beautiful and the true, and her earnest and unsparing efforts to bring her much-loved friend into communion with everything she herself enjoyed, had called into play faculties which blindness had rendered almost dormant, and become what Uncle True bade her be, eyes to her benefactor.

On the present occasion, however, as Emily sat alone, shut out from the beautiful sunset, and unconscious of the shadows that played over her in the moonlight, her thoughts seemed to be sad. She held her head a little on one side, in a listening attitude, and, as often as she heard the sound of the gate swinging in the breeze, she would start, while a look of anxiety, and even pain, would cross her features.

At length, some one emerges from behind the high fence which screens the garden from public gaze, and approaches the gate. None but Emily's quick ear could have distinguished the light step; but she hears it at once, and, rising, goes to meet the new comer, whom we must pause to introduce, for, though an old acquaintance, time has not left *her* unchanged, and it would be hard to recognize in her our little quondam Gertrude.

The present Gertrude—for she it is—has now become a young lady. She is some inches taller than Emily, and her figure is slight and delicate. Her complexion is dark, but clear, and rendered brilliant by the rosy hue that flushes her cheeks; but that may be the effect of her rapid walk from the railroad station. She has taken off her bonnet, and is swinging it by the string,—a habit she always had as a child; so we will acquit her of any coquettish desire to display an unusually fine head of hair.

Gertrude's eyes have retained their old lustre, and do not now look too large for her face; and, if her mouth be less classically formed than the strict rule of beauty would commend, one can easily forgive that, in consideration of two rows of small pearly teeth, which are as regular and even as a string of beads. Her neat dress of spotted muslin fits close to her throat, and her simple black mantle does not conceal the roundness of her taper waist.

What then? Is Gertrude a beauty?

By no means. Hers is a face and form about which there would be a thousand different opinions, and out of the whole number few would pronounce her beautiful. But there are faces whose ever-varying expression one loves to watch,—tell-tale faces, that speak the truth and proclaim the sentiment within; faces that now light up with intelligence, now beam with mirth, now sadden at the tale of sorrow, now burn with a holy indignation for that which the soul abhors, and now, again, are sanctified by the divine presence, when the heart turns away from the world and itself, and looks upward in the spirit of devotion. Such a face was Gertrude's.

There are forms, too, which, though neither dignified, queenly or fairy-like, possess a grace, an ease, a self-possession, a power of moving lightly and airily in their sphere, and never being in any one's way,—and such a form was Gertrude's.

Whatever charm these attractions might give her,—and there were those who estimated it highly,—it was undoubtedly greatly enhanced by an utter unconsciousness, on her part, of possessing any attractions at all. The early-engrafted belief in her own personal plainness had not yet deserted her; but she no longer felt the mortification she had formerly labored under on that account.

As she perceived Miss Graham coming to meet her, she quickened her pace, and, joining her near the door-step, where a path turning to the right led into the garden, passed her arm affectionately over Emily's shoulder, in a manner which the latter's blindness, and Gertrude's superior height and ability to act as guide, had of late rendered usual, and, turning into the walk which led from the house, said, while she drew the shawl closer around her blind friend,

"Here I am again, Emily! Have you been alone ever since I went away?"

"Yes, dear, most of the time, and have been quite worried to think you were travelling about in Boston this excessively warm day."

"It has not hurt me in the least; I only enjoy this cool breeze all the more; it is such a contrast to the heat and dust of the city!"

"But, Gerty," said Emily, stopping short in their walk, "what are you coming away from the house for? You have not been to tea, my child."

"I know it, Emily, but I don't want any supper."

They walked on for some time, slowly and in perfect silence. At last Emily said,

"Well, Gertrude, have you nothing to tell me?"

"O, yes, a great deal, but—"

"But you know it will be sad news to me, and so you don't like to speak it; is it not so?"

"I ought not to have the vanity, dear Emily, to think it would trouble you very much; but, ever since last evening, when I told you what Mr. W. said, and what I had in my mind, and you seemed to feel so badly at the thought of our being separated, I have felt almost doubtful what it was right for me to do."

"And I, on the other hand, Gertrude, have been reproaching myself for allowing you to have any knowledge of my feeling in the matter, lest I should be influencing you against your duty, or, at least, making it harder for you to fulfil. I feel that you are right, Gertrude, and that, instead of opposing, I ought to do everything I can to forward your plans."

"Dear Emily!" exclaimed Gertrude, vehemently, "if you thought so from what I told you yesterday, you would be convinced, had you seen and heard all that I have to-day."

"Why? are matters any worse than they were at Mrs. Sullivan's?"

"Much worse than I described to you. I did not then know myself all that Mrs. Sullivan had to contend with; but I have been at their house nearly all the time since I left home this morning (for Mr. W. did not detain me five minutes), and it really does not seem to me safe for such a timid, delicate woman as Mrs. Sullivan to be alone with Mr. Cooper, now that his mind is in such a dreadful state."

"But, do you think you can do any good, Gertrude?"

"I know I can, dear Emily; I can manage him much better than she can, and at the same time do more for his comfort and happiness. He is like a child now, and full of whims. When he can possibly be indulged, Mrs.

Sullivan will please him at any amount of inconvenience, and even danger, to herself; not only because he is her father, and she feels it her duty, but I actually think she is afraid of him, he is so irritable and violent. She tells me he often takes it into his head to do the strangest things, such as going out late at night, when it would be perfectly unsafe; and sleeping with his window wide open, though his room is on the lower floor."

"Poor woman!" exclaimed Emily; "What does she do in such cases?"

"I can tell you, Emily, for I saw an instance of it to-day. When I first went in this morning, he was preparing to make a coal-fire in the grate, notwithstanding the heat, which was becoming intense in the city."

"And Mrs. Sullivan?" said Emily.

"Was sitting on the lower stair, in the front entry, crying."

"Poor thing!" murmured Emily.

"She could do nothing with him," continued Gertrude, "and had given up in despair."

"She ought to have a strong woman, or a man, to take care of him."

"That is what she dreads, more than anything. She says it would kill her to see him unkindly treated, as he would be sure to be by a stranger; and, besides, I can see that she shrinks from the idea of having any one in the house to whom she is unaccustomed. She is exceedingly neat and particular in all her arrangements, has always done her work herself, and declares she would sooner admit a wild beast into her family than an Irish girl." [1]

"Her new house has not been a source of much pleasure to her yet, has it?"

"O, no. She was saying, to-day, how strange it seemed, when she had been looking forward so long to the comfort of a new and well-built tenement, that, just as she had moved in and got everything furnished to her mind, she should have this great trial come upon her."

"It seems strange to me," said Emily, "that she did not sooner perceive its approach. I noticed, when I went with you to the house in E—— street, the failure in the old man's intellect."

"I had observed it for a long time," remarked Gertrude, "but never spoke of it to her; and I do not think she was in the least aware of it, until about the time of their removal, when the breaking up of old associations had a sad effect upon poor Mr. Cooper."

"Don't you think, Gertrude, that the pulling down of the church, and his consequent loss of employment, were a great injury to his mind?"

"Yes, indeed, I am sure of it; he altered very much after that, and

never seemed so happy, even while they were in the house in E——
street; and when the owners of that land concluded to take it for stores and
warehouses, and gave Mrs. Sullivan notice that she would be obliged to
leave, the old sexton's mind gave way entirely."

"Sad thing!" said Emily. "How old is he, Gertrude?"

"I don't know exactly, but I believe he is very old; I remember Mrs.
Sullivan's telling me, some time ago, that he was near eighty."

"Is he so old as that? Then I am not surprised that these changes have
made him childish."

"O, no. Melancholy as it is, it is no more than we may any of us come
to, if we live to his age; and, as he seems for the most part full as contented
and happy as I have ever seen him appear, I do not lament it so much on his
own account as on Mrs. Sullivan's. But I do, Emily, feel dreadfully anxious
about *her*."

"Does it seem to be so very hard for her to bear up under it?"

"I think it would not be, if she were well; but there is something the
matter with her, and I fear it is more serious than she allows, for she looks
very pale, and has, I know, had several alarming ill turns lately."

"Has she consulted a physician?"

"No; she doesn't wish for one, and insists upon it she shall soon be
better; but I do not feel sure that she will, especially as she takes no care of
herself; and that is one great reason for my wishing to be in town as soon as
possible. I am anxious to have Dr. Jeremy see her, and I think I can bring it
about without her knowing that he comes on her account. I'll have a severe
cold myself, if I can't manage it in any other way."

"You speak confidently of being in town, Gertrude; so I suppose it is
all arranged."

"O, I have not told you, have I, about my visit to Mr. W.? Dear, good
man, how grateful I ought to be to him! He has promised me the
situation."

"I had no doubt he would, from what you told me he said to you at
Mrs. Bruce's."

"You hadn't, really! Why, Emily, I was almost afraid to mention it to
him. I couldn't believe he would have sufficient confidence in me; but he
was so kind! I hardly dare tell you what he said about my capacity to teach,
you will think me so vain."

"You need not tell me, my darling; I know, from his own lips, how
highly he appreciates your ability; you could not tell me anything so flattering as what he told me himself."

"Dear Uncle True always wanted me to be a teacher; it was the height of his ambition. He would be pleased, wouldn't he, dear Emily?"

"He would no doubt have been proud enough to see you assistant in a school like Mr. W.'s. I am not sure, however, but he would think, as I do, that you are undertaking too much. You expect to be occupied in the school the greater part of every morning, and yet you propose to establish yourself as nurse to Mrs. Sullivan, and guardian to her poor old father. My dear child, you are not used to so much care, and I shall be constantly troubled for you, lest your own health and strength give way."

"O, dear Emily, there is no occasion for any anxiety on my account; I am well and strong, and fully capable of all that I have planned for myself. My only dread is in the thought of leaving you; and the only fear I have is, that you will miss me and perhaps feel as if—"

"I know what you would say, Gertrude. You need not fear that; I am sure of your affection. I am confident you love me next to your duty, and I would not for the world that you should give me the preference. So dismiss that thought from your mind, and do not carry with you the belief that I would be selfish enough to desire to retain you a moment. I only wish, my dear, that for the present you had not thought of entering the school. You might then have gone to Mrs. Sullivan's, staid as long as you were needed, and perhaps found, by the time we are quite ready to start on our southern tour, that your services could be quite dispensed with; in which case, you could accompany us on a journey which I am sure your health will by that time require."

"But, dear Emily, how could I do that? I could not propose myself as a visitor to Mrs. Sullivan, however useful I might intend to be to her; nor could I speak of nursing to a woman who will not acknowledge that she is ill. I thought of all that, and it seemed to me impossible, with all the delicacy and tact in the world, to bring it about; for I have been with you so long that Mrs. Sullivan, I have no doubt, thinks me entirely unfitted for her primitive way of life. It was only when Mr. W. spoke of his wanting an assistant, and, as I imagined, hinted that he should like to employ me in that capacity, that the present plan occurred to me. I knew, if I told Mrs. Sullivan that I was engaged to teach there, and that you were not coming to town at all, but were soon going south, and represented to her that I wanted a boarding-place for the winter, she would not only be loth to refuse me a home with her, but would insist that I should go nowhere else."

"And it proved as you expected?"

"Exactly; and she showed so much pleasure at the thought of my being with her, that I realized still more how much she needed some one."

"She will have a treasure in you, Gertrude; I know that, very well."

"No, indeed! I do not hope to be of much use. The feeling I have is, that, however little I may be able to accomplish, it will be more than any one else could do for Mrs. Sullivan. She has lived so retired that she has not an intimate friend in the city, and I do not really know of any one, except myself, whom she would willingly admit under her roof. She is used to me and loves me; I am no restraint upon her, and she allows me to assist in whatever she is doing, although she often says that I live a lady's life now, and am not used to work. She knows, too, that I have an influence over her father; and I *have,*—strange as it may seem to you,—I *have* more than I know how to account for myself. I think it is partly because I am not at all afraid of him, and am firm in opposing his unreasonable fancies, and partly because I am more of a stranger than Mrs. Sullivan. But there is still another thing which gives me a great control over him. He naturally associates me in his mind with Willie; for we were for some years constantly together, both left the house at the same time, and he knows, too, that it is through me that the correspondence with him is chiefly carried on. Since his mind has been so weak, he seems to think continually of Willie, and I can at any moment, however irritable or wilful he may be, make him calm and quiet by proposing to tell him the latest news from his grandson. It does not matter how often I repeat the contents of the last letter, it is always new to him; and you have no idea, Emily, what power this little circumstance gives me. Mrs. Sullivan sees how easily I can guide his thoughts, and I noticed what a load of care seemed to be taken from her mind by merely having me there to-day. She looked so happy when I came away to-night, and spoke so hopefully of the comfort it would be during the winter to have me with her, that I felt repaid for any sacrifice it has been to me. But when I came home, and saw you, and thought of your going so far away, and of the length of time it might be before I should live with you again, I felt as if—" Gertrude could say no more. She laid her head on Emily's shoulder, and wept.

Emily soothed her with the greatest tenderness. "We have been very happy together, Gerty," said she, "and I shall miss you sadly; half the enjoyment of my life has of late years been borrowed from you. But I never loved you half so well as I do now, at the very time that we must part; for I see in the sacrifice you are making of yourself one of the noblest and most important traits of character a woman can possess. I know how much you love the Sullivans, and you have certainly every reason for being attached to them, and desiring to repay your old obligations; but your leaving us at this time, and renouncing, without a murmur, the southern tour from which you expected so much pleasure, proves that my Gerty is the brave, good girl I always hoped and prayed she might become. You are in the path of duty, Gertrude, and will be rewarded by the approbation of your own conscience, if in no other way."

As Emily finished speaking, they reached a corner of the garden, and were here met by a servant-girl, who had been looking for them to announce that Mrs. Bruce and her son were in the parlor, and had asked for them both.

"Did you get her buttons in town, Gertrude?" inquired Emily.

"Yes, I found some that were an excellent match for the dress; she probably wants to know what success I had; but how can I go in?"

"I will return to the house with Katy, and you can go in at the side-door, and reach your own room without being seen. I will excuse you to Mrs. Bruce for the present; and, when you have bathed your eyes, and feel composed, you can come in and report concerning the errand she intrusted to you."

CHAPTER XXI

But had we best retire? I see a storm.
—*Milton*

ACCORDINGLY, when Gertrude entered the room half an hour afterwards, there was no evidence in her appearance of any unusual distress of mind. Mrs. Bruce nodded to her good-naturedly from a corner of the sofa. Mr. Bruce rose and offered his chair, at the same time that Mr. Graham pointed to a vacant window-seat near him, and said, kindly, "Here is a place for you, Gertrude."

Declining, however, the civilities of both gentlemen, she withdrew to an ottoman which stood near an open glass door, where she was almost immediately joined by Mr. Bruce, who, seating himself in an indolent attitude upon the upper row of a flight of steps which led from the window to the garden, commenced conversation with her.

Mr. Bruce—the same gentleman who some years before wore a

velvet smoking-cap, and took afternoon naps in the grass—had recently returned from Europe, and, glorying in the renown acquired from a moustache, a French tailor, and the possession of a handsome property in his own right, now viewed himself with more complacency than ever.

"So you've been in Boston all day, Miss Flint?"

"Yes, nearly all day."

"Didn't you find it distressingly warm?"

"Somewhat so."

"I tried to go in to attend to some business that mother was anxious about, and even went down to the depot; but I had to give it up."

"Were you overpowered by the heat?"

"I was."

"How unfortunate!" remarked Gertrude, in a half-compassionate, half-ironical tone of voice.

Mr. Bruce looked up, to judge, if possible, from her countenance, whether she were serious or not; but, there being little light in the room, on account of the warmth of the evening, he could not decide the question in his mind, and therefore replied, "I dislike the heat, Miss Gertrude, and why should I expose myself to it unnecessarily?"

"O, I beg your pardon; I thought you spoke of important business."

"Only some affair of my mother's. Nothing I felt any interest in, and she took the state of the weather for an excuse. If I had known that you were in the cars, as I have since heard, I should certainly have persevered, in order to have had the pleasure of walking down Washington-street with you."

"I did not go down Washington-street."

"But you would have done so with a suitable escort," suggested the young man.

"If I had gone out of my way for the sake of accompanying my escort, the escort would have been a very doubtful advantage," said Gertrude, laughing.

"How very practical you are, Miss Gertrude! Do you mean to say that, when you go to the city, you always have a settled plan of operations, and never swerve from your course?"

"By no means. I trust I am not difficult to influence when there is a sufficient motive."

The young man bit his lip. "Then you never act without a motive; pray, what is your motive in wearing that broad-brimmed hat when you are at work in the garden?"

"It is an old habit, adopted some years ago from motives of convenience, and still adhered to, in spite of later inventions, which would certainly be better protection from the sun. I must plead guilty, I fear, to a little obstinacy in my partiality for that old hat."

"Why not acknowledge the truth, Miss Gertrude, and confess that you wear it in order to look so very fanciful and picturesque that the neighbors' slumbers are disturbed by the very thoughts of it? My own morning dreams, for instance, as you are well aware, are so haunted by that hat, as seen in company with its owner, that I am daily drawn, as if by magnetic attraction, in the direction of the garden. You will have a heavy account to settle with Morpheus, one of these days, for defrauding him of his rights; and your conscience too will suffer for injuries to my health, sustained by continued exposure to early dews."

"It is hard to condemn me for such innocent and unintentional mischief; but, since I am to experience so much future remorse on account of your morning visits, I shall take upon myself the responsibility of forbidding them."

"O! you wouldn't be so unkind!—especially after all the pains I have taken to impart to you the little I know of horticulture."

"Very little I think it must have been; or I have but a little memory," said Gertrude, laughing.

"Now, how can you be so ungrateful? Have your forgotten the pains I took yesterday to acquaint you with the different varieties of roses? Don't you remember how much I had to say at first of damask roses and damask bloom; and how, before I had finished, I could not find words enough in praise of blushes, especially such sweet and natural ones as met my eyes while I was speaking?"

"I know you talked a great deal of nonsense. I hope you don't think I listened to it all."

"O, Miss Gertrude! It is of no use to say flattering things to you; you always look upon my compliments as so many jokes."

"I have told you, several times, that it was the most useless thing in the world to waste so much flattery upon me. I am glad you are beginning to realize it."

"Well, then, to ask a serious question, where were you this morning?"

"At what hour?"

"Half-past seven."

"On my way to Boston, in the cars."

"Is it possible?—so early! Why, I thought you went at ten. Then, all the time I was watching by the garden wall to get a chance to say good-morning, you were half a dozen miles away. I wish I had not wasted that hour so; I might have spent it in sleeping."

"Very true, it is a great pity."

"And then half an hour more here this evening! How came you to keep me waiting so long?"

"I?—When?"

"Why, now, to-night."

"I was not aware of doing so. I certainly did not take your visit to myself."

"My visit certainly was not meant for any one else."

"Ben," said Mr. Graham, approaching rather abruptly, and taking part in the conversation, "are you fond of gardening? I thought I heard you just now speaking of roses."

"Yes, sir; Miss Flint and I were having quite a discussion upon flowers,—roses especially."

Gertrude, availing herself of Mr. Graham's approach, tried to make her escape and join the ladies at the sofa; but Mr. Bruce, who had risen on Mr. Graham's addressing him, saw her intention, and frustrated it by placing himself in the way, so that she could not pass him without positive rudeness. Mr. Graham continued, "I propose placing a small fountain in the vicinity of Miss Flint's flower-garden; won't you walk down with me, and give your opinion of the plan?"

"Isn't it too dark, sir, to—"

"No, no, not at all; there is ample light for our purpose; this way, if you please;" and Mr. Bruce was compelled to follow where Mr. Graham led, though, in spite of his acquaintance with Paris manners, he made a wry face, and shook his head menacingly.

Gertrude was now permitted to relate to Mrs. Bruce the results of the shopping which she had undertaken on her account, and display the buttons, which proved very satisfactory. The gentlemen, soon after returning to the parlor, took seats near the sofa, and, the company forming one group, the conversation became general.

"Mr. Graham," said Mrs. Bruce, "I have been questioning Emily about your visit to the south; and, from the route which she tells me you propose taking, I think it will be a charming trip."

"I hope so, madam,—we have been talking of it for some time; it will be an excellent thing for Emily, and, as Gertrude has never travelled at all, I anticipate a great deal of pleasure for her."

"Ah! then you are to be of the party, Miss Flint?"

"Of course, of course," answered Mr. Graham, without giving Gertrude a chance to speak for herself; "we depend upon Gertrude,— couldn't get along at all without her."

"It will be delightful for you," continued Mrs. Bruce, her eyes still fixed on Gertrude.

"I did expect to go with Mr. and Miss Graham," answered Gertrude, "and looked forward to the journey with the greatest eagerness; but I have just decided that I must remain in Boston this winter."

"What are you talking about, Gertrude?" asked Mr. Graham. "What do you mean? This is all news to me."

"And to me, too, sir, or I should have informed you of it before. I supposed you expected me to accompany you, and there is nothing I should like so much. I should have told you before of the circumstances that now make it impossible; but they are of quite recent occurrence."

"But we can't give you up, Gertrude; I won't hear of such a thing; you must go with us, in spite of circumstances."

"I fear I shall not be able to," said Gertrude, smiling pleasantly, but still retaining her firmness of expression; "you are very kind, sir, to wish it."

"Wish it!—I tell you I insist upon it. You are under my care, child, and I have a right to say what you shall do."

Mr. Graham was beginning to get excited. Gertrude and Emily both looked troubled, but neither of them spoke.

"Give me your reasons, if you have any," added Mr. Graham, vehemently, "and let me know what has put this strange notion into your head."

"I will explain it to you to-morrow, sir."

"To-morrow! I want to know now."

Mrs. Bruce, plainly perceiving that a family storm was brewing, wisely rose to go. Mr. Graham suspended his wrath until she and her son had taken leave; but, as soon as the door was closed upon them, burst forth with real anger.

"Now tell me what all this means! Here I plan my business, and make all my arrangements, on purpose to be able to give up this winter to travelling,—and that, not so much on my own account as to give pleasure to both of you,—and, just as everything is settled, and we are almost on the point of starting, Gertrude announces that she has concluded not to go. Now, I should like to know her reasons."

Emily undertook to explain Gertrude's motives, and ended by expressing her own approbation of her course. As soon as she had finished, Mr. Graham, who had listened very impatiently, and interrupted her with many a "pish!" and "pshaw!" burst forth with redoubled indignation.

"So Gerty prefers the Sullivans to us, and you seem to encourage her in it! I should like to know what they've ever done for her, compared with what I have done!"

"They have been friends of hers for years, and, now that they are in great distress, she does not feel as if she could leave them; and I confess I do not wonder at her decision."

"I must say I do. She prefers to make a slave of herself in Mr. W.'s school, and a still greater slave in Mrs. Sullivan's family, instead of staying with us, where she has always been treated like a lady, and, more than that, like one of my own family!"

"O, Mr. Graham!" said Gertrude, earnestly, "it is not a matter of preference or choice, except as I feel it to be a duty."

"And what makes it a duty? Just because you used to live in the same house with them, and that boy out in Calcutta has sent you home a camel's-hair scarf, and a cage-full of miserable little birds, and written you a great package of letters, you think you must forfeit your own interests to take care of his sick relations! I can't say that I see how their claim compares with mine. Haven't I given you the best of educations, and spared no expense either for your improvement or your happiness?"

"I did not think, sir," answered Gertrude, humbly, and yet with quiet dignity, "of counting up the favors I had received, and measuring my conduct accordingly. In that case, my obligations to you are immense, and you would certainly have the greatest claim upon my services."

"Services! I don't want your *services,* child. Mrs. Ellis can do quite as well as you can for Emily, or me either; but I like your *company,* and think it is very ungrateful in you to leave us, as you talk of doing."

"Father," said Emily, "I thought the object, in giving Gertrude a good education, was to make her independent of all the world, and not simply dependent upon us."

"Emily," said Mr. Graham, "I tell you it is a matter of feeling,—you don't seem to look upon the thing in the light I do; but you are both against me, and I won't talk any more about it."

So saying, Mr. Graham took a lamp, went to his study, shut the door hard,—not to say slammed it,—and was seen no more that night.

Poor Gertrude! Mr. Graham, who had been so kind and generous, who had seldom before spoken harshly to her, and had always treated her with great indulgence, was now deeply offended. He had called her ungrateful; he evidently felt that she had abused his kindness, and believed that he and Emily stood in her estimation secondary to other, and, as he considered them, far less warm-hearted friends. Deeply wounded and grieved, she hastened to say good-night to the no less afflicted Emily, and, seeking her own room, gave way to feelings that exhausted her spirit, and caused her a sleepless night.

CHAPTER XXII

Virtue is bold, and goodness never fearful.
——*Shakespeare*

LEFT AT THREE YEARS of age dependent upon the mercy and charity of a world in which she was friendless and alone, Gertrude had, during the period of her residence at Nan Grant's, found little of that mercy, and still less of that charity. But, although her turbulent spirit rebelled at the treatment she received, she was then too young to reason upon the subject, or come to any philosophical conclusions upon the general hardness and cruelty of humanity; and, had she done so, such impressions could not but have been effaced amid the atmosphere of love and kindness which surrounded her during the succeeding period, when, cherished and protected in the home of her kind foster father, she enjoyed a degree of parental tenderness which rarely falls to the lot of an orphan.

And having, through a similar providence, found in Emily additional proof of the fact that the tie of kindred blood is not always needed to bind heart to heart in the closest bonds of sympathy and affection, she had hitherto, in her unusually happy experience, felt none of the evils that spring from dependence upon the bounty of strangers. The unfriendly conduct of Mrs. Ellis had, at times, been a source of irritation to her; but the housekeeper's power and influence in the family were limited by her own dependence upon the good opinion of those she served, and

Gertrude's patience and forbearance had at last nearly disarmed her enmity.

From Mr. Graham she had until now experienced only kindness. On her first coming to live with them, he had, to be sure, taken very little notice of her, and, so long as she was quiet, well-mannered, and no trouble to anybody, had been quite indifferent concerning her. He observed that Emily was fond of the girl and liked to have her with her; and, though he wondered at her taste, was glad that she should be indulged. It was not long, however, before he was led to notice in his daughter's favorite a quickness of mind and propriety of deportment which had the effect of creating an interest in her that soon increased to positive partiality, especially when he discovered her taste for gardening, and her perseverance in laboring among her flowers. He not only set off a portion of his grounds for her use, but, charmed with her success during the first summer after the appropriation was made, added to the original flower-garden, and himself assisted in laying out and ornamenting it. Emily formed no plan with regard to Gertrude's education to which she did not obtain a ready assent from her father; and Gertrude, deeply grateful for so much bounty, spared no pains to evidence her sense of obligation and regard, by treating Mr. Graham with the greatest respect and attention.

But, unfortunately for the continuance of these amicable relations, Mr. Graham possessed neither the disinterested, forbearing spirit of Uncle True, or the saintly patience and self-sacrifice of Emily. Mr. Graham was a liberal and highly respectable man; he had the reputation, as the world goes, of being a remarkably high-minded and honorable man; and not without reason, for his conduct had oftentimes justified this current report of him. But, alas! he was a *selfish* man, and often took very one-sided views. He had supported and educated Gertrude,—he liked her,—she was the person whom he preferred for a travelling companion for himself and Emily,—nobody else had any claim upon her to compare with his,—and he either *could* not or *would* not see that her duty lay in any other direction.

And yet, while he was ready to act the tyrant, he deceived himself with the idea that he was the best friend she had in the world. He was not capable of understanding that kind of regard which causes one to find gratification in whatever tends to the present or future welfare of another, without reference to himself or his own interests. Acting, therefore, under the influence of his own prejudiced and narrow sentiments, Mr. Graham gave way to his ill-temper, and distressed Gertrude by the first really harsh and severe language he had ever used towards her.

During the long hours of a wakeful and restless night, Gertrude had ample time to review and consider her own situation and circumstances. At first, her only emotion was one of grief and distress, such as a child might feel on being reproved; but that gradually subsided, as other and bitter thoughts rose up in her mind. "What right," thought she, "had Mr. Graham to treat me thus,—to tell me I *shall* go with them on this southern journey, and speak as if my other friends were ciphers in his estimation, and ought to be in my own? Does he consider that my freedom is to be the price of my education, and am I no longer to be able to say yes or no? Emily does not think so; Emily, who loves and needs me a thousand times more than Mr. Graham, thinks I have acted rightly, and assured me, only a few hours ago, that it was my duty to carry out the plans I had formed. And my solemn promise to Willie! is that to be held for nothing? No," thought she, "it would be tyranny in Mr. Graham to insist upon my remaining with them, and I am glad I have resolved to break away from such thraldom. Besides, I was educated to teach, and Mr. W. says it is important to commence at once, while my studies are fresh in my mind. Perhaps, if I yielded now, and staid here living in luxury, I should continue to do so until I lost the power of regaining my independence. It is cruel in Mr. Graham to try to deprive me of my free-will."

So much said pride; and Gertrude's heart, naturally proud, and only kept in check by strict and conscientious self-control, listened a while to such suggestions. But not long. She had accustomed herself to view the conduct of others in that spirit of charity which she desired should be exercised towards her own, and milder thoughts soon took the place of these excited and angry feelings.

"Perhaps," said she to herself, as she reviewed in her mind the conversation of the evening, "it is, after all, pure kindness to me that prompted Mr. Graham's interference. He may think, as Emily does, that I am undertaking too much. It is impossible for him to know how strong my motives are, how deep I consider my obligations to the Sullivans, and how much I am needed by them at this time. I had no idea, either, that it was such an understood thing that I was to be of the party to the south; for, though Emily talked as if she took it for granted, Mr. Graham never spoke of it, or asked me to go, and I could not suppose it would be any great disappointment to him to have me refuse; but, after his planning the journey, as he says he has done, with reference to the enjoyment of us both, I do not wonder at his being somewhat annoyed. He probably feels, too, as if I had been under his guardianship so long that he has almost a right to decide upon my conduct. And he *has* been very indulgent to me,—and I a stranger, with no claims! O! I hate to have him think me so ungrateful!

"Shall I then decide to give up my teaching, go to the south, and leave dear Mrs. Sullivan to suffer, perhaps die, while I am away? No, that is impossible. I will never be such a traitor to my own heart, and my sense of right; sorry as I shall be to offend Mr. Graham, I must not allow fear of his anger to turn me from my duty."

Having thus resolved to brave the tempest that she well knew she must encounter, and committed her cause to Him who judgeth righteously, Gertrude tried to compose herself to sleep; but found it impossible to obtain any untroubled rest. Scarcely had slumber eased her mind of the weight that pressed upon it, before dreams of an equally painful nature seized upon her, and startled her back to consciousness. In some of these visions she beheld Mr. Graham, angry and excited as on the previous evening, and threatening her with the severest marks of his displeasure if she dared to thwart his plans; and then, again, she seemed to see Willie, the same boyish youth from whom she had parted nearly five years before, beckoning her with a sad countenance to the room where his pale mother lay in a swoon, as Gertrude had a few weeks before discovered her. Exhausted by a succession of such harassing images, she at length gave up the attempt to obtain any rest through sleep, and, rising, seated herself at the window, where, watching the now descending moon, and the first approach of dawn, she found, in quiet self-communing, the strength and courage which, she felt, would be requisite to carry her calmly and firmly through the following day; a day destined to witness her sad separation from Emily, and her farewell to Mr. Graham, which would probably be of a still more distressing character. It may seem strange that anything more than ordinary mental courage and decision should be needful to sustain Gertrude under the present emergency. But, in truth, it required no small amount of both these qualities for a young girl of eighteen years, long dependent upon the liberality of an elderly man, well known as a stern dictator in his household, to suddenly break the bonds of custom and habit, and mark out a course for herself in opposition to his wishes and intentions; and nothing but an urgent motive could have led the grateful and peace-loving Gertrude to such a step. The tyrannical disposition of Mr. Graham was well understood in his family, each member of which was accustomed to respect all his wishes and whims; and though he was always indulgent, and usually kind, none ever ventured to brave a temper, which, when excited, was violent in the extreme. It cannot then be surprising that Gertrude's heart should have almost failed her, when she stood, half an hour before breakfast-time, with the handle of the dining-room door in her hand, summoning all her energies for another meeting with the formidable opposer of her plans. She paused but a moment, however, then opened the door and went in. Mr. Graham was where she expected to see him, sitting in his arm-chair, and on the breakfast-table by his side lay the morning paper. It had been Gertrude's habit, for a year or two, to read that paper aloud to the old gentleman at this same hour, and it was for that very purpose she had now come.

She advanced towards him with her usual "good-morning."

The salutation was returned in a purposely constrained voice. She seated herself, and leaned forward to take the newspaper; but he placed his hand upon it and prevented her.

"I was going to read the news to you, sir."

"And I do not wish to have you read, or do anything else for me, until I know whether you have concluded to treat me with the respect I have a right to demand from you."

"I certainly never intended to treat you otherwise than with respect, Mr. Graham."

"When girls or boys set themselves in opposition to those older and wiser than themselves, they manifest the greatest disrespect they are capable of; but I am willing to forgive the past, if you assure me, as I think you will after a night's reflection, that you have returned to a right sense of your duty."

"I cannot say, sir, that I have changed my views with regard to what that duty is."

"Do you mean to tell me," asked Mr. Graham, rising from his chair and speaking in a tone which made Gerty's heart quake, in spite of her brave resolutions, "do you mean to tell me that you have any idea of persisting in your folly?"

"Is it folly, sir, to do right?"

"Right!—There is a great difference of opinion between you and me as to what right is in this case."

"But, Mr. Graham, I think, if you knew all the circumstances, you would not blame my conduct. I have told Emily the reasons that influenced me, and she—"

"Don't quote Emily to me!" interrupted Mr. Graham, as he walked the floor rapidly. "I don't doubt she'd give her head to anybody that asked for it; but I hope I know a little better what is due to myself; and I tell you plainly, Miss Gertrude Flint, without any more words in the matter, that if you leave my house, as you propose doing, you leave it with my displeasure; and *that,* you may find one of these days, it is no light thing to have incurred,—unnecessarily, too," he muttered,—"as you are doing."

"I am very sorry to displease you, Mr. Graham, but—"

"No, you're not *sorry;* if you were, you would not walk straight in the face of my wishes," said Mr. Graham, who began to observe the expression of Gertrude's face, which, though grieved and troubled, had in the last few minutes acquired additional firmness, instead of quailing beneath his severe and cutting words;—"but, I have said enough about a matter which is not worthy of so much notice. You can go or stay, as you please. I wish you to understand, however, that, in the former case, I utterly withdraw my protection and assistance from you. You must take care of yourself, or trust to strangers. I suppose you expect your Calcutta friend will support you, perhaps come home and take you under his especial care; but, if you think so, you know little of the world. I daresay he is married to an Indian by this time, and, if not, has pretty much forgotten you."

"Mr. Graham," said Gertrude, proudly, "Mr. Sullivan will not probably return to this country for many years, and I assure I neither look to him or any one else for support; I intend to earn a maintenance for myself."

"A heroic resolve!" said Mr. Graham, contemptuously, "and pronounced with a dignity I hope you will be able to maintain. Am I to consider, then, that your mind is made up?"

"It is, sir," said Gertrude, not a little strengthened for the dreaded necessity of pronouncing her final resolution by Mr. Graham's sarcastic speeches.

"And you go?"

"I must. I believe it to be my duty, and am therefore willing to sacrifice my own comfort, and, what I assure you I value far more, your friendship."

Mr. Graham did not seem to take the least notice of the latter part of her remark, and before she had finished speaking so far forgot his usual politeness as to drown her voice in the violent ringing of the table-bell.

It was answered by Katy with the breakfast; and Emily and Mrs. Ellis coming in at the same moment, all seated themselves at table, and the meal was commenced in unusual silence and constraint,—for Emily had heard the loud tones of her father's voice, and was filled with anxiety and alarm, while Mrs. Ellis plainly saw, from the countenances of all present, that something unpleasant had occurred.

When Mr. Graham, whose appetite appeared undiminished, had finished eating a hearty breakfast, he turned to Mrs. Ellis, and deliberately and formally invited her to accompany himself and Emily on their journey to the south, mentioning the probability that they should pass some weeks in Havana.

Mrs. Ellis, who had never before heard any intimation that such a tour was contemplated, accepted the invitation with pleasure and alacrity, and proceeded to ask a number of questions concerning the proposed route and length of absence; while Emily hid her agitated face behind her tea-cup; and Gertrude, who had lately been reading "Letters from Cuba,"[1] and was aware that Mr. Graham knew the strong interest she consequently felt in the place, pondered in her mind whether it were possible that he could be guilty of the small and mean desire to vex and mortify her.

Breakfast over, Emily hastily sought her room, where she was immediately joined by Gertrude.

In answering Emily's earnest inquiries as to the scene which had taken place, Gertrude forbore to repeat Mr. Graham's most bitter and wounding remarks; for she saw, from her kind friend's pained and anxious countenance, how deeply she participated in her own sense of wrong and misapprehension. She told her, however, that it was now well understood by Mr. Graham that she was to leave, and, as his sentiments towards her were far from kindly, she thought it best to go at once, especially as she could never be more needed by Mrs. Sullivan than at present. Emily saw the reasonableness of the proposal, assented to it, and agreed to accompany her to town that very afternoon; for, deeply sensitive at any unkindness manifested towards Gertrude, she preferred to have her depart thus abruptly, rather than encounter her father's contemptuous neglect.

The remainder of the day, therefore, was spent by Gertrude in packing, and other preparations; while Emily sat by, counselling and advising the future conduct of her adopted darling, lamenting the necessity of their separation, and exchanging with her reiterated assurances of continued and undiminished affection.

"O! if you could only write to me, dear Emily, during your long absence, what a comfort it would be!" exclaimed Gertrude.

"With Mrs. Ellis' assistance, my dear," replied Emily, "I will send you such news as I can of our movements; but, though you may not be able to hear much from me, you will be ever in my thoughts, and I shall never forget to commend my beloved child to the protection and care of One who will be to her a better counsellor and friend than I can be."

In the course of the day Gertrude sought Mrs. Ellis, and astonished that lady by announcing that she had come to have a few farewell words with her. Surprise and curiosity, however, were soon superseded by the housekeeper's eagerness to expatiate upon the kindness and generosity of Mr. Graham, and the delights of the excursion in prospect. After wishing her a great deal of pleasure, Gertrude begged to hear from her by letter during her absence; to which apparently unheard request Mrs. Ellis only replied by asking if Gertrude thought a thibet dress would be uncomfortable on the journey; and, when it was repeated with still greater earnestness, she, with equal unsatisfactoriness to the suppliant for epistolary favors, begged to know how many pairs of under-sleeves she should probably require. Having responded to her questions, and at last gained her ear and attention, Gertrude obtained from her a promise to write *one* letter, which would, she declared, be more than she had done for years.

Before leaving the house, Gertrude sought Mr. Graham's study, in hopes that he would take a friendly leave of her; but, on her telling him that she had come to bid him "good-by," he indistinctly muttered the simple words of that universal formula, so deep in its meaning when it comes from the heart; so chilling when uttered, as on the present occasion, by stern and nearly closed lips; and, turning his back upon her, took up the tongs to mend his fire.

So she went away, with a tear in her eye and sadness in her heart, for until now Mr. Graham had been a good friend to her.

A far different scene awaited her in the upper kitchen, where she went to seek Mrs. Prime and Katy.

"Bless yer soul, dear Miss Gertrude!" said the former, stumbling up the staircase which led from the lower room, and wiping her hands on her apron,—"how we shall miss yer! Why, the house won't be worth livin' in when you're out of it. My gracious! if you don't come back, we shall all die out in a fort-night. Why, you're the life and soul of the place! But there, I guess you know what's right; so, if you must go, we must bear it.—though Katy and I'll cry our eyes out, for aught I know."

"Sure, Miss Gairthrude," said Irish Katy, "and it's right gude in you to be afther comin' to bid us good-by. I don't see how you gets memory to think of us all, and I'm shure yer'll never be betther off than what I wish her. I can't but think, miss, it'll go to help yer along, that everybody's gude wishes and blessin' goes with yer."

"Thank you, Katy, thank you," said Gertrude, much touched by the simple earnestness of these good friends. "You must come and see me some time in Boston; and you too, Mrs. Prime, I shall depend upon it. Good-by;" and the good-by that *now* fell upon Gertrude's ear was a hearty and a true one; it followed her through the hall, and as the carryall drove away she heard it mingling with the rattling of the vehicle.

CHAPTER XXIII

One of that stubborn sort he is,
Who, if they once grow fond of an opinion,
They call it honor, honesty and faith,
And sooner part with life than let it go.
—*Rowe*

PASSING OVER GERTRUDE'S parting with Emily, her cordial reception by Mrs. Sullivan, and her commencement of school duties, we will look in upon her and record the events of a day in November, about two months after she left Mr. Graham's.

Rising with the sun, she made her neat toilet in a room so cold that before it was completed her hands were half-benumbed; nor did she, in spite of the chilling atmosphere, omit, ere she commenced the labors of the day, to supplicate Heaven's blessing upon them. Then, noiselessly entering the adjoining apartment, where Mrs. Sullivan was still sleeping, she lit a fire, the materials for which had been carefully prepared the night before, in a small grate, and, descending the stairs with the same light footstep, performed a similar service at the cooking-stove, which stood in a comfortable room, where, now that the weather was cold, the family took their meals. The table was set, and the preparations for breakfast nearly completed, when Mrs. Sullivan entered, pale, thin and feeble in her appearance, and wrapped in a large shawl.

"Gertrude," said she, "why will you let me sleep so, mornings, while you are up and at work? I believe it has happened so every day this week."

"For the very best reason in the world, auntie; because I sleep all the early part of the night, and am wide awake at day-break, and with you it is just the reverse. Besides, I like to get the breakfast, I make such beautiful coffee. Look!" said she, pouring some into a cup, and then lifting the lid of the coffee-pot and pouring it back again; "see how clear it is! Don't you long for some of it, this cold morning?"

Mrs. Sullivan smiled, for, Uncle True having always preferred tea, Gertrude did not at first know how to make coffee, and had been obliged to come to her for instructions.

"Now," said Gertrude, playfully, as she drew a comfortable chair close to the fire, "I want you to sit down here and watch the tea-kettle boil, while I run and see if Mr. Cooper is ready to let me tie up his cue."

She went, leaving Mrs. Sullivan to think what a good girl she was; and presently returning with the old man, who was dressed with perfect neatness, she placed a chair for him, and having waited, as for a child, while he seated himself, and then pinned a napkin about his throat, she proceeded to place the breakfast on the table.

While Mrs. Sullivan poured out the coffee, Gertrude, with a quiet tact which rendered the action almost unobserved, removed the skin from a baked potato and the shell from a boiled egg, and, placing both on the plate destined for Mr. Cooper, handed him his breakfast in a state of preparation which obviated the difficulty the old man experienced performing these tasks for himself, and spared Mrs. Sullivan the anxiety she always felt at witnessing his clumsiness and sadly-increasing carelessness on those points of neatness so sacred in her eyes. Poor Mrs. Sullivan had no appetite, and it was with difficulty Gertrude persuaded her to eat anything; a few fried oysters, however, unexpectedly placed before her, proved such a temptation that she was induced to taste and finally to eat several, with a degree of relish she rarely felt, lately, for any article of food. As Gertrude gazed at her languid face, she realized, more than ever before, the change which had come over the active, energetic little woman; and, confident that nothing but positive disease could have effected such a transformation, she resolved that not another day should pass without her seeing a physician.

Breakfast over, there were dishes to wash, rooms to be put in order, dinner to be decided on and partially prepared; and all this Gertrude exerted herself and saw accomplished, chiefly through her own labor, before she went to rearrange her dress, previous to her departure for the school, where she had now been some weeks installed as assistant teacher. A quarter before nine she looked in at the kitchen door, and said, in a cheering tone, to the old man, who was cowering gloomily over the fire,

"Come, Mr. Cooper, won't you go over and superintend the new church a little while, this morning? Mr. Miller will be expecting you; he said yesterday that he depended on your company when he was at work."

The old man rose, and taking his great-coat from Gertrude, put it on with her assistance, and accompanied her in a mechanical sort of way, that seemed to imply a great degree of indifference whether he went or stayed. As they walked in silence down the street, Gertrude could not but revolve in her mind the singular coincidence which had thus made her the almost daily companion of another infirm old man; nor could she fail to draw a comparison between the genial, warm-hearted Uncle True, and the gloomy, discontented Paul Cooper, who, never, as we have said, possessing a genial temperament, now retained, in his state of mental imbecility, his old characteristics in an exaggerated form. Unfavorable as the comparison necessarily was to the latter, it did not diminish the kindness and thought-fulness of Gertrude towards her present charge, who was in her eyes an object of sincere compassion. They soon reached the new church of which Gertrude had spoken,—a handsome edifice, built on the site of the old building in which Mr. Cooper had long officiated as sexton. It was not yet finished, and a number of workmen were at this time engaged in the completion of the interior.

A man with a hod-full of mortar preceded Gertrude and her com-panion up the steps which led to the main entrance, but stopped inside the porch, on hearing himself addressed by name, and, laying down his bur-den, turned to respond to the well-known voice.

"Good-morning, Miss Flint," said he. "I hope you're very well, this fine day. Ah! Mr. Cooper, you've come to help me a little, I see;—that's right! We can't go on very well without you—you're so used to the place. Here, sir, if you'll come with me, I'll show you what has been done since you were here last; I want to know how you think we get along."

So saying, he was walking away with the old sexton; but Gertrude followed, and detained him a moment, to ask if he would do her the favor to see Mr. Cooper safe home when he passed Mrs. Sullivan's house on his way to dinner.

"Certainly, Miss Flint," replied the man, "with all the pleasure in the world; he has usually gone with me pretty readily, when you have left him in my care."

Having obtained this promise, Gertrude hastened towards the school, rejoicing in the certainty that Mr. Cooper would be safe and well and amused during the morning, and that Mrs. Sullivan, freed from all responsibility concerning him, would be left to the rest and quiet she so much needed.

This cordial coadjutor in Gertrude's plan of diverting and occupying the old man's mind was a respectable mason, who had often been in Mr. Graham's employ, and whose good-will and gratitude Gertrude had won by the kindness and attention she had shown his family during the previous winter, when they were sick and afflicted. In her daily walk past the church, she had frequently seen Mr. Miller at his work, and it occurred to her that, if she could awaken in Mr. Cooper's mind an interest in the new structure, he might find amusement in coming there and watching the workmen. She had some difficulty in persuading him to visit a building to the erection of which he had been vehemently opposed, not only because it was inimical to his interests, but on account of the strong attachment he had for the old place of worship. Once there, however, he became interested in the work, and, as Mr. Miller took pains to make him comfortable, and even awakened in him the belief that he was useful, he gradually acquired a habit of passing the greater part of every morning in watching the men engaged in their various branches of industry. Sometimes Gertrude called for him on her return from school; and sometimes, as on the present occasion, Mr. Miller undertook to accompany him home.

Since Gertrude had been at Mrs. Sullivan's there was a very perceptible alteration in Mr. Cooper. He was much more manageable, looked better contented, and manifested far less irritability than he had previously done; and this favorable change, together with the cheering influence of Gertrude's society, had for a time produced a proportionately beneficial effect upon Mrs. Sullivan; but, within the last few days, her increased debility, and one or two sudden attacks of faintness, had awakened all, and more than all, of Gertrude's former fears. She had left home with the determination, as soon as she should be released from her school duties, to seek Dr. Jeremy and request his attendance; and it was in order to secure leisure for that purpose that she had solicited Mr. Miller's superintending care for Mr. Cooper.

Of Gertrude's school-duties we shall say nothing, save that she was found by Mr. W. fully competent to the performance of them, and that she met with those trials and discouragements only to which all teachers are more or less subjected, from the idleness, obstinacy, or stupidity of their pupils. On this day, however, she was, from various causes, detained to a later hour than usual, and the clock struck two at the very moment that she was ringing Dr. Jeremy's door-bell. The girl who opened the door knew Gertrude by sight, having often seen her at her master's house; and, telling her that, though the doctor was just going to dinner, she thought he would see her, asked her into the office, where he stood, with his back to the fire, eating an apple, as it was his invariable custom to do before dinner. He laid it down, however, and advanced to meet Gertrude, holding out both his hands. "Gertrude Flint, I declare!" exclaimed he. "Why, I'm glad to see you, my girl. Why have n't you been here before, I should like to know?"

Gertrude explained that she was living with friends, one of whom was very old, the other an invalid; and that so much of her time was occupied in school that she had no opportunity for visiting.

"Poor excuse!" said the doctor; "poor excuse! But, now we've got you here, we shan't let you go very soon;" and, going to the foot of the staircase, he called, in the loudest possible tone of voice, "Mrs. Jerry! Mrs. Jerry! come!—come down to dinner as quick as you can, and put on your best cap,—we've got company.—Pour soul!" added he, in a lower tone, addressing himself to Gertrude, and smiling good-naturedly, "she can't hurry, can she, Gerty?—she's fat."

Gertrude now protested against staying to dinner, declaring she must hasten home, and announcing Mrs. Sullivan's illness and the object of her visit.

"An hour can't make much difference in such a case," insisted the doctor. "You must stay and dine with me, and then I'll go wherever you wish, and take you with me in the buggy."

Gertrude hesitated; the sky had clouded over, and a few flakes of snow were falling; she should have an uncomfortable walk; and, moreover, it would be better for her to accompany the doctor, as the street in which she lived was principally composed of new houses, not yet numbered, and he might, if he were alone, have some difficulty in finding the right tenement.

At this stage of her reflections, Mrs. Jeremy entered. Fat she certainly was, very uncommonly fat, and flushed too with her unwonted haste, and the excitement of anticipating the company of a stranger. She kissed Gertrude in the kindest manner, and then, looking round and seeing that there was no one else present, exclaimed, glancing reproachfully at the doctor,

"Why, Dr. Jerry!—an't you ashamed of yourself? I never will believe you again; you made me think there was some great stranger here."

"And, pray, Mrs. Jerry, who's a greater stranger in this house than Gerty Flint?"

"Sure enough" said Mrs. Jeremy. "Gertrude *is* a stranger, and I've got a scolding in store for her on that account; but, you know, Dr. Jerry, I should n't have put on my lilac-and-pink for Gertrude to see; she likes me just as well in my old yellow, if she did tell me, when I bought it, the saucy girl, that I'd selected the ugliest cap in Boston. Do you remember that, Gerty?"

Gerty laughed heartily at the recollection of a very amusing scene that took place at the milliner's when she went shopping with Mrs. Jeremy. "But come, Gerty," continued that lady, "dinner's ready; take off your cloak and bonnet, and come into the dining-room; the doctor has got a great deal to say, and had been wanting dreadfully to see you."

They had been sitting some minutes without a word's having been spoken, beyond the usual civilities of the table, when the doctor, suddenly laying down his knife and fork, commenced laughing, and laughed till the tears came into his eyes. Gertrude looked at him inquiringly, and Mrs. Jeremy said, "There, Gertrude!—for one whole week he had just such a laughing-fit two or three times a day. I was as much astonished at first as you are; and, I confess, I don't quite understand now what could have happened between him and Mr. Graham that was so very funny."

"Come, wife," said the doctor, checking himself in his merriment; "don't you forestall my communication. I want to tell the story myself. I don't suppose," continued he, turning towards Gertrude, "you've lived five years at Mr. Graham's, without finding out what a cantankerous, opinionative, obstinate old hulk he is?"

"Doctor!" said Mrs. Jeremy, reprovingly, and shaking her head at him.

"I don't care for winking or head-shaking, wife; I speak my mind, and that's the conclusion I've come to with regard to Mr. Graham; and Gertrude, here, has done the same, I have n't a particle of doubt, only she's a good girl, and won't say so."

"I never saw anything that looked like it," said Mrs. Jeremy, "and I've seen as much of him as most folks. I meet him in the street almost every day, and he looks as smiling as a basket of chips, and makes a beautiful bow."

"I daresay," said the doctor; "Gertrude and I know what gentlemanly manners he has when one does not walk in the very teeth of his opinions,—eh, Gertrude?—but when one does—"

"In talking politics, for instance," suggested Mrs. Jeremy. "It's your differences with him on politics that have set you against him so."

"No, it is n't," replied the doctor, "A man may get angry talking politics, and be a pretty good-natured man too, in the main. I get angry *myself* on *politics,* but that is n't the sort of thing I have reference to at all. It's Graham's wanting to lay down the law to everybody that comes within ten miles of him that I can't endure; his dictatorial way of acting, as if he were the Grand Mogul of Cochin China. I thought he'd improved of late years; he had a serious lesson enough in that sad affair of poor Philip Amory's; but, fact, I believe he's been trying the old game again. Ha! ha! ha!" shouted the good doctor, leaning forward, and giving Gertrude a light tap in the shoulder,—"was n't I glad when I found he'd met at last with a reasonable opposition?—and that, too, where he least expected it!"

Gertrude looked her astonishment at his evident knowledge of the misunderstanding between herself and Mr. Graham; and in answer to that look he continued, "You wonder where I picked up my information, and I'll tell you. It was partly from Graham himself; and what diverts me is to think how hard the old chap tried to hide his defeat, and persuade me that he'd had his own way after all, when I saw through him, and knew as well as he did that he'd found his match in you."

"Dr. Jeremy," interposed Gertrude, "I hope you don't think—"

"No, my dear, I *don't* think you a *professed pugilist;* but I consider you a girl of sense—one who knows what's right—and will do what's right, in spite of Mr. Graham, or anybody else; and when you hear my story you will know the grounds on which I formed my opinion with regard to the course things had taken, and the reasons I have for understanding the state of the case rather better than Graham meant I should. One day,—perhaps it was about two months ago—you may remember the exact time better than I do,—I was summoned to go and see one of Mr. W.'s children, who had an attack of croup. Mr. W. was talking with me, when he was called away to see a visitor; and, on his return, he mentioned that he had just secured your services in his school. I was not surprised, for I knew Emily intended you for a teacher, and I was thankful you had got so good a situation. I had hardly left Mr. W.'s, however, before I encountered Mr. Graham, and he entertained me, as we went down the street, with an account of his plans for the winter. 'But Gertrude Flint is not going with you.' said I.—'Gertrude!' said he; 'certainly she is.'—'Are you sure of that?' I asked. 'Have you invited her?'—'Invited her!—No,' was his answer; 'but, of course, I know she will go, and be glad enough of the opportunity; it is n't every girl in her situation that is so fortunate.' Now, Gerty, I felt a little provoked at his way of speaking, and I answered, in nearly as confident a tone as his own, 'I doubt, myself, whether she will accept the invitation.' Upon that, Mr. Dignity straightened up, and such a speech as he made! I never can recall it without being amused, especially when I think of the come-down that followed so soon after. I can't repeat it; but, goodness, Gertrude! one would have thought, to hear him, that it was not only impossible you should oppose his wishes, but actual treason in me to suggest such a thing. Of course, I knew better than to tell what I had just heard from Mr. W., but I never felt a greater curiosity about anything than I did to know how the matter would end. Two or three times I planned to drive out with my wife, see Emily, and hear the result; but a doctor can never call a day his own, and I got prevented. At last, one Sunday, I heard Mrs. Prime's voice in the kitchen (her niece lives here), and down I went to make my inquiries. That woman is a friend of yours, Gertrude, and pretty sharp where you are concerned. She told me the truth, I rather think; though not, perhaps, all the particulars. It was not more than a day or two after that before I saw Graham. 'Ah!' said I; 'when do you start?'—'To-morrow,' replied he,—'Really,' I exclaimed 'then I shan't see your ladies again. Will you take a little package from me to Gertrude?'—'I know nothing about Gertrude!' said he, stiffly.—'What!' rejoined I, affecting the greatest surprise, 'has Gertrude left you?'—'She has,' answered he.— 'And dared,' continued I, quoting his own words, 'to treat you with such disrespect,—to trifle so with your dignity?'—'Dr. Jeremy!' exclaimed he, 'I don't wish to hear that young person mentioned; she has behaved as ungratefully as she has unwisely.'—'Why, about the gratitude, Graham,' said I, 'I believe you said it would only be an additional favor on your part if you took her with you, and I can't say but what I think it is wisdom in her to make herself independent at home. But I really am sorry for you and Emily; you will miss her so much.'—'We can dispense with your sympathy, sir,' answered he, 'for that which is no loss.'—'Ah! really!' I replied; 'now, I was thinking Gertrude's society would be quite a loss.'—'*Mrs. Ellis* goes with us,' said he, with a marked emphasis, that seemed to say *she* was a person whose company compensated for all deficiencies.—'Ah!' said I, 'charming woman, Mrs. Ellis!' Graham looked annoyed, for he is aware that Mrs. Ellis is my antipathy."

"Well, you ought to have known better, Dr. Jerry," said his kind-hearted wife, "than to have attacked a man so on his weak point; it was only exciting his temper for nothing."

"I was taking up the cudgels for Gertrude, wife."

"And I don't believe Gertrude wants you to take up the cudgels for her. I have no manner of doubt that she has the kindest of feeling towards Mr. Graham, this blessed minute."

"I have, indeed, Mrs. Jeremy," said Gertrude; "he has been a most generous and indulgent friend to me."

"Except when you wanted to have your own way," suggested the doctor.

"Which I seldom did, when it was in opposition to his wishes."

"And what if it were?"

"I always considered it my duty to submit to him, until, at last, a higher duty compelled me to do otherwise."

"And then, my dear," said Mrs. Jeremy, "I daresay it pained you to displease him; and that is a right woman's feeling, and one that Dr. Jerry, in his own heart, can't but approve of, though one would think, to hear him talk, that he considered it pretty in a young girl to take satisfaction in browbeating an old gentleman. But, don't let us talk any more about it; he has had his say, and now it's my turn. I want to hear how you are situated, Gerty, where you live, and how you like teaching."

Gertrude answered all these questions; and the doctor who has heard Mrs. Sullivan spoken of as a friend of True's and Gerty's, at the time when he attended the former, made many inquiries concerning the state of her health. It was by this time beginning to snow fast, and Gertrude's anxiety to return home in good season being very manifest to her kind host and hostess, they urged no further delay, and, after she had given many a promise to repeat her visit on the earliest opportunity, she drove away with the doctor.

CHAPTER XXIV

No simplest duty is forgot;
Life hath no dim and lowly spot
That doth not in her sunshine share.
—*Lowell*

"*I HAVE BEEN* thinking," said Gertrude, as she drew near home, "how we shall manage, doctor, so as not to alarm Mrs. Sullivan."

"What's going to alarm her?" asked the doctor.

"You, if she knows at once that you are a physician. I think I had better introduce you as a friend, who brought me home in the storm."

"O! so we are going to act a little farce, are we? Stage-manager, Gertrude Flint—unknown stranger, Dr. Jeremy. I'm ready. What shall I say first?"

"I leave that to a wiser head than mine, doctor, and trust entirely to your own discretion to obtain some knowledge of her symptoms, and only gradually disclose to her that you are a physician."

"Ah, yes! pretend, at first, to be only a private individual of a very inquiring mind. I think I can manage it."

They went in. As they opened the door, Mrs. Sullivan rose from her chair with a troubled countenance, and hardly waited for the introduction to Gertrude's friend before she turned to her and asked, with some anxiety, if Mr. Cooper were not with them.

"No, indeed," replied Gertrude. "Has n't he come home?"

Upon Mrs. Sullivan's saying that she had not seen him since morning, Gertrude informed her, with a composure she was far from feeling, that Mr. Miller had undertaken the care of him, and could, undoubtedly, account for his absence. She would seek him at once.

"O, I'm so sorry," said Mrs. Sullivan, "that you should have to go out again in such a storm! but I feel very anxious about grandpa—don't you, Gerty?"

"Not very; I think he is safe in the church. But I'll go for him at once; you know, auntie, I never mind the weather."

"Then take my great shawl, dear." And Mrs. Sullivan went to the entry-closet for her shawl, giving Gertrude an opportunity to beg of Dr. Jeremy that he would await her return; for she knew that any unusual

158

agitation of mind would often occasion an attack of faintness in Mrs. Sullivan, and was afraid to have her left alone, to dwell with anxiety and alarm upon Mr. Cooper's prolonged absence.

It was a very disagreeable afternoon, and already growing dark. Gertrude hastened along the wet side-walks, exposed to the blinding storm (for the wind would not permit her to carry an umbrella), and, after passing through several streets, gained the church. She went into the building, now nearly deserted by the workmen, saw, at once, that Mr. Cooper was not there, and was beginning to fear that she should gain no information concerning him, when she met Mr. Miller coming from the gallery. He looked surprised at seeing her, and asked if Mr. Cooper had not returned home. She answered in the negative, and he then informed her that his utmost efforts were insufficient to persuade the old man to go home at dinner-time, and that he had therefore taken him to his own house; he had supposed, however, that long before this hour he would have been induced to allow one of the children to accompany him to Mrs. Sullivan's.

As it now seemed probable that he was still at Mr. Miller's, Gertrude took the direction (for the family had moved within a year, and she did not know where to seek them), and, declining the company of the friendly mason, whom she was unwilling to take from his work, proceeded thither at once. After another uncomfortable walk, and some difficulty in finding the right street and house, she reached her destination. She knocked at the out-side door; but there was no response, and, after waiting a moment, she opened it and went in. Through another door, at the right, there was the sound of children's voices, and so much noise that she believed it impossible to make herself heard, and, therefore, without further ceremony, entered the room. A band of startled children dispersed at the sight of a stranger, and ensconced themselves in corners; and Mrs. Miller, in dismay at the untidy appearance of her kitchen, hastily pushed back a clothes-horse against the wall, thereby disclosing to view the very person Gertrude had come to seek, who, in his usual desponding attitude, sat cowering over the fire. But, before she could advance to speak to him, her whole attention was arrested by another and most unexpected sight. Placed against the side of the room, directly opposite the door, was a narrow bed, in which some person seemed to be sleeping. Hardly, however, had Gertrude presented herself in the doorway, before the figure suddenly raised itself, gazed fixedly at her, lifted a hand as if to ward off her approach, and uttered a long piercing shriek.

The voice and countenance were not to be mistaken, and Gertrude, pale and trembling, felt something like a revival of her old dread, as she beheld the well-known features of Nan Grant.

"Go away! go *away!*" cried Nan, as Gertrude, after a moment's hesitation, advanced into the room. Again Gertrude paused, for the wildness of Nan's eyes and the excitement of her countenance were such that she feared to excite her further.

Mrs. Miller now came forward, and interfered. "Why, Aunt Nancy!" said she, "what is the matter? This is Miss Flint, one of the best young ladies in the land."

"No, 't an't!" said Nan, fiercely, "I know better!"

Mrs. Miller now drew Gertrude aside, into the shadow of the clothes-horse, and conversed with her in an under tone, while Nan, leaning on her elbow, and peering after them into the dim corner to which they had retreated, maintained a watchful, listening attitude. Gertrude was informed that Mrs. Miller was a niece of Ben Grant's, but had seen nothing of him or his wife for years, until, a few days previous, Nan had come there in a state of the greatest destitution, and threatened with the fever under which she was now laboring. "I could not refuse her a shelter," said Mrs. Miller; "but, as you see, I have no accommodation for her, and it's not only bad for me to have her sick right here in the kitchen, but, what with the noise of the children and all the other discomforts, I'm afraid the poor old thing will die."

"Have you a room that you could spare above stairs?" asked Gertrude.

"Why, there's our Jane," answered Mrs. Miller; "she's a good-hearted girl as ever lived; she said, right off, she'd give up her room to poor Aunt Nancy, and she'd sleep in with the other children; I did n't feel, though, as if we could afford to keep another fire a-going, and so I thought we'd put up a bed here for a day or two, and just see how she got along. But she's looked pretty bad to-day, and now I'm thinking, from her actions, that she's considerable out of her head."

"She ought to be kept quiet," said Gertrude; "and, if you will have a fire in Jane's room at my expense, and do what you can to make her comfortable, I'll try and send a physician here to see her." Mrs. Miller was beginning to express the warmest gratitude, but Gertrude interrupted her with saying, "Don't thank me, Mrs. Miller; Nancy is not a stranger to me; I have known her before, and, perhaps, feel more interest in her than you do yourself."

Mrs. Miller looked surprised; but Gertrude, whose time was limited, could not stop to enter into a further explanation. Anxious, however, if possible, to speak to Nan, and assure her of her friendly intentions, she went boldly up to the side of the bed, in spite of the wild and glaring eyes which were fixed steadily upon her.

"Nan," said she, "do you know me?"

"Yes! yes!" replied Nan, in a half-whisper, speaking quickly and catching her breath; "what have you come for?"

"To do you good, I hope."

But Nan still looked incredulous, and in the same undertone, and with the same nervous accent, inquired, "Have you seen Gerty? Where is she?"

"She is well," answered Gertrude, astonished, however, at the question; for she had supposed herself recognized.

"What did she say about me?"

"She said that she forgives and pities you, and is in hopes to do something to help you and make you well."

"Did she?" said the sick woman; "then you won't kill me?"

"Kill you?—No, indeed. We are in hopes to make you comfortable, and cure you."

Mrs. Miller, who had been preparing a cup of tea, now drew near, with it in her hand. Gertrude took it and offered it to Nan, who drank eagerly of it, staring at her, however, in the mean time, over the edge of the cup. When she had finished, she threw herself heavily upon the pillow, and began muttering some indistinct sentences, the only distinguishable word being the name of her son Stephen. Finding the current of her thoughts thus apparently diverted, Gertrude, now feeling in haste to return and relieve Dr. Jeremy, who had so kindly agreed to stay with Mrs. Sullivan, moved a little from the bed-side, saying, as she did so, "Good-by, I will come and see you again."

"You won't hurt me?" exclaimed Nan, starting up once more.

"O no. I will try to bring you something you will like."

"Don't bring Gerty here with you! I don't want to see her."

"I will come alone," replied Gertrude.

Nan now laid down, and did not speak again while Gertrude remained in the house, though she watched her steadily until she was outside the door. Mr. Cooper made no objection to accompanying his young guide, and, though the severity of the storm was such that they did not escape a thorough wetting, they reached home in safety, in a little more than an hour from the time she started on her expedition.

Dr. Jeremy, seated at the side of the grate, with his feet upon the fender, had the contented appearance of one who is quite at home; he seemed, indeed, unconscious that he was waiting for Gertrude's return, or anything else but his own pleasure. He had been talking with Mrs. Sullivan about the people of a country town where they had both passed some time in their childhood, and the timid, retiring woman had, in the course of conversation, come to feel so much at her ease in the society of the social and entertaining physician, that, although he had, in his unguarded discourse, accidentally disclosed his profession, she allowed him to question her upon the state of her health, without any of the alarm she had nervously fancied she should feel at the very sight of a doctor. By the time Gertrude had returned, he had made himself well acquainted with the case, and was prepared, on Mrs. Sullivan's leaving the room to provide dry clothes for her father, to report to Gertrude his opinion.

"Gertrude," said he, as soon as the door was shut, "that's a very sick woman."

"Do you think so, Dr. Jeremy?" said Gertrude, much alarmed, and sinking into the nearest chair.

"I do," replied he, thoughtfully. "I wish to mercy I had seen her six months ago!"

"Why, doctor! Do you date her illness so far back as that?"

"Yes, and much further. She has borne up under the gradual progress of a disease which is now, I fear, beyond the aid of medical treatment."

"Dr. Jeremy," said Gertrude, in tones of great distress, "you do not mean to tell me that auntie is going to die, and leave me and her poor old father, and without ever seeing Willie again, too! O, I had hoped it was not nearly so bad as that!"

"Do not be alarmed, Gertrude," said the doctor, kindly. "I did not mean to frighten you;—she may live some time, yet. I can judge better of her case in a day or two. But it is absolutely *unsafe* for you to be here alone with these two friends of yours,—to say nothing of its overtasking your strength. Has not Mrs. Sullivan the means to keep a nurse, or even a domestic? She tells me she has no one."

"Yes, indeed," answered Gerty; "her son supplies her wants most generously. I know that she never draws nearly the whole of the amount he is anxious she should expend."

"Then you must speak to her about getting some one to assist you at once; for, if you do not, *I* shall."

"I intend to," said Gertrude. "I have seen the necessity for some time past; but she has such a dread of strangers that I hated to propose it."

"Nonsense," said the doctor; "that's only imagination in her; she would soon get used to being waited upon."

Mrs. Sullivan now returned, and Gertrude, giving an account of her unexpected rencounter with Nan Grant, begged Dr. Jeremy, who knew the particulars of her own early life, and had frequently heard of Nan, to go the next day and see her. "It will be a visit of charity," said she, "for she is probably penniless, and, though staying with your old patients the Millers, she is but distantly connected, and has no claim upon them. That never makes any difference with you, however, I know very well."

"Not a bit, not a bit," answered the doctor. "I'll go and see her to-night, if the case requires it, and to-morrow I shall look in to report how she is, and hear the rest of what Mrs. Sullivan was telling me about her wakeful nights. But, Gertrude, do you go, child, and change your wet shoes and stockings. I shall have you on my hands, next."

Mrs. Sullivan was delighted with Dr. Jeremy, and when he was gone eagerly sounded his praise. "So different," said she, "from common doctors (a portion of humanity for which she seemed to have an unaccountable aversion); so sociable and friendly! Why, I felt, Gertrude, as if I could talk to him about my sickness as freely as I could to you."

Gertrude readily joined in the praises bestowed upon her much-valued friend, and it was tea-time before Mrs. Sullivan was weary of the subject. After the evening meal was over, and Mr. Cooper, much wearied with the fatigues of the day, had been persuaded to retire to rest, while Mrs. Sullivan, comfortably reclining on the sofa, was enjoying what she always termed her happiest hour, Gertrude broached the subject recommended by Dr. Jeremy. Contrary to her expectations, Mrs. Sullivan no longer objected to the proposal of introducing a domestic into the family. She was convinced of her own incompetency to perform any active labor, and was equally opposed to the exertion on Gertrude's part which had, during the last week, been requisite. Gertrude suggested Jane Miller as a girl remarkably well suited to their wants, and it was agreed that she should be applied for on the following morning.

One more glance at Gertrude, and we shall have followed her to the conclusion of the day. She is alone. It is ten o'clock, and the house is still. Mr. Cooper is sound asleep. Gertrude has just listened at his door, and heard his loud breathing. Mrs. Sullivan, under the influence of a soothing draught recommended by Dr. Jeremy, has fallen into an unusually quiet slumber. The little Calcutta birds, ten in number, that occupy a large cage in the window, are nestled, side by side, on their slender perch, in a close, unbroken row, and Gertrude had throw a warm covering over them, that they may not suffer from the cold night-air. She has locked the doors, made all things safe, fast and comfortable, and now sits down to read, to meditate, and pray. Her trials and cares are multiplying. A great grief stares her in the face, and a great responsibility; but she shrinks not from either. No! on the contrary, she thanks God that she is here; that she had the resolution to forsake pleasure and ease, and in spite of her own weakness and man's wrath, to place herself in the front of life's battle, and bravely wait its issues. She thanks God that she knows where to look for help; that the bitter sorrows of her childhood and early youth left her not without a witness of His love who can turn darkness into light, and that no weight can now overshadow her whose gloom is not illumined by rays from the throne of God. But, though her heart is brave and her faith firm, she has a woman's tender nature; and, as she sits alone, she weeps—weeps for herself, and for him who, far away in a foreign land, is counting the days, months and years, which shall restore him to a mother he is destined never to see again. With the recollection, however, that she is to stand in the place of a child to that parent, and that hers is the hand that must soothe the pillow of the invalid, and minister to all her wants, comes the stern necessity of self-control,—a necessity to which Gertrude has long since learned to submit,—and, rallying all her calmness and fortitude, she wipes away the blinding tears, commends herself to Him who is strength to the weak and comfort to the sorrowing, and, soothed by the communion of her spirit with the Father of spirits, she seeks her couch, and, worn out by the varied mental and bodily fatigues of her day's experience, follows the rest of the household to the land of dreams.

CHAPTER XXV

Some say that gleams of a remoter world
Visit the soul in sleep.
    —*Shelley*

IT WAS A FORTUNATE thing for Gertrude that Thanksgiving week was approaching, as that was a vacation time at Mr. W.'s school, and she would thus be more at leisure to attend to her multiplied cares. She considered herself favored, too, in obtaining the services of Jane, who willingly consented to come and help Miss Gertrude. She did not, she said, exactly like the idea of living out, but could n't refuse a young lady who had been so good to them in times past. Gertrude had feared that, with Nan Grant sick in the house, Mrs. Miller would not be able to give up her eldest daughter; but Mary, a second girl, having returned home unexpectedly, one of them could be very conveniently spared. Under Gertrude's tuition, Jane, who was neat and capable, was able, after a few days, to relieve Mrs. Sullivan of nearly all her household duties, and so far provide for many of her personal wants as to leave Gertrude at liberty to pay frequent visits to the sick room of Nan, whose fever, having reached its height, rendered her claim for aid at the present the most imperative.

We need hardly say that, in Gertrude's still vivid recollection of her former sufferings under the rule of Nan, there remained nothing of bitterness or a spirit of revenge. If she remembered the past, it was only to pity and forgive her persecutor; if she meditated upon the course she should herself pursue towards her once hated tyrant, it was only to revolve in her mind how she could best serve and comfort her.

Therefore, night after night found her watching by the bed-side of the sick woman, who, though still delirious, had entirely lost the fear and dread she had at first seemed to feel at her presence. Nan talked much of little Gerty,—sometimes in a way that led Gertrude to believe herself recognized, but more frequently as if the child were supposed to be absent; and it was not until a long time after that Gertrude was led to adopt the correct supposition, which was, that she had been mistaken for her mother, whom she much resembled, and whom, though tended in her last sickness by Nan herself, the fevered, diseased, and conscience-stricken sufferer believed had come back to claim the child at her hands. It was only the continued assurances of good-will on Gertrude's part, and her unwearied efforts to soothe and comfort her, that finally led Nan to the belief that the injured mother had found her child in health and safety, and was ignorant of the wrongs and unkindness she had endured.

One night—it was the last of Nan's life—Gertrude, who had scarcely left her during the previous day, and was still maintaining her watch, heard her own name mingled with those of others in a few rapid sentences. She approached the bed and listened intently, for she was always in hopes, during these partly incoherent ravings, to gain some information concerning her own early life. Her name was not repeated, however, and for some time the muttering of Nan's voice was indistinct. Then, suddenly starting up and addressing herself to some imaginary person, she shouted aloud, "Stephie! Stephie! give me back the watch, and tell me what you did with the rings!—They will ask—those folks!—and what shall I tell them?" Then, after a pause, during which her eyes were fixed steadily upon the wall, she said, in a more feeble but equally earnest voice, "No, no, Stephie, I never 'll tell.—I *never, never* will!" The moment the words had left her lips, she started, turned, saw Gertrude standing by the bed-side, and, with a frightened look, shrieked, rather than asked, "Did you hear? Did you hear?—You did," continued she, "and you 'll tell! O, if you *do!*" She was here preparing to spring from the bed, but, overcome with exhaustion, sank back on the pillow. Summoning both Mr. and Mrs. Miller, who, half expecting to be called up during the night, had lain down in the next room, the agitated Gertrude, believing that her own presence was too exciting, left the now dying woman to their care, and sought in another part of the house to calm her disturbed mind and disordered nerves. Learning, about an hour afterwards, from Mrs. Miller, that Nan had become comparatively calm, but was utterly prostrated in strength, and seemed near her end, Gertrude thought it best not to enter the room again; and, sitting down by the kitchen-stove, pondered in her mind the strange scene she had witnessed. Day was just dawning when Mrs. Miller came to tell her that Nan had breathed her last.

Gerty's work of mercy, forgiveness and Christian love, being thus finished, she hastened home to recruit her wasted strength, and fortify herself, as she best might, for the labor and suffering yet in store for her.

And it was no ordinary strength and fortitude that she needed to sustain her through a period such as persons in this world are often called upon to meet, when scenes of suffering, sickness and death, follow each other in such quick succession, that, ere one shock can be recovered from, and composure of mind restored, another blow comes to add its force to the already overwhelming torrent. In less than three weeks from the time of Nan Grant's death, Paul Cooper was smitten by the destroyer's hand, and, after a brief illness, he, too, was laid to his last rest; and though the deepest feelings of Gertrude's heart were not in either case fully awakened, it was no slight call upon the mental and physical endurance of a girl of eighteen to bear up under the self-imposed duties occasioned by each event, and that, too, at a time when her mind was racked by the apprehension of a new and far more intense grief. Emily' absence was also a sore trial to her, for she was accustomed to rely upon her for advice and counsel, and, in seasons of peculiar distress, to learn patience and submission from one who was herself a living exemplification of both virtues. Only one letter had been received from the travellers, and that, written by Mrs. Ellis, contained little that was satisfactory. It was written from Havana, where they were boarding in a house kept by an American lady, and crowded with visitors from Boston, New York, and other northern cities.

"It an't so very pleasant, after all, Gertrude," wrote Mrs. Ellis, "and I only wish we were safe home again; and not on my own account, either, so much as Emily's. She feels kind of strange here; and no wonder, for it's a dreadful uncomfortable sort of a place. The windows have no glass about them, but are grated just like a prison; and there is not a carpet in the house, nor a fireplace, though sometimes the mornings are quite cold. There's a *widder*¹ here, with a brother and some nieces. The widder is a flaunting kind of a woman, that I begin to think, if you'll believe it, is either setting her cap for Mr. Graham, or means to make an old fool of him. She is one of your loud-talking women, that dress up a good deal, and like to take the lead; and Mr. Graham is just silly enough to follow after her party, and go to all sorts of rides and excursions;—it's so *ridiculous,*—and her over sixty-five years old! Emily and I have pretty much done going into the parlor, for these gay folks don't take any sort of notice of us. Emily does n't say a word, or complain a bit, but I know she is not happy here, and would be glad to be back in Boston; and so should I, if it was n't for that horrid steamboat. I liked to have died with sea-sickness, Gertrude, coming out; and I dread going home so, that I don't know what to do."

Gertrude wrote frequently to Emily; but, as Miss Graham was dependent upon Mrs. Ellis' eye-sight, and the letters must, therefore, be subject to her scrutiny, she could not express her inner-most thoughts and feelings as she was wont to do in conversation with her sympathizing and indulgent friend.

Every India mail brought news from William Sullivan, who, prosperous in business, and rendered happy, even in his exile, by the belief that the friends he loved best were in the enjoyment of the fruits of his exertions, wrote always in his accustomed strain of cheerfulness.

One Sabbath afternoon, a few weeks after Mr. Cooper's death, found Gertrude with an open letter in her hand, the numerous postmarks on the outside of which proclaimed from whence it came. It had that day been received, and Mrs. Sullivan, as she lay stretched upon her couch, had been listening for the third time to the reading of its contents. The bright hopes expressed by her son, and the gay tone in which he wrote, all unconscious, as he yet was, of the cloud of sorrow that was gathering for him, formed so striking a contrast to her own reflections, that she lay with her eyes closed, and oppressed with an unwonted degree of sadness; while Gertrude, as she glanced at the passage in which Willie dilated upon the "joy of once more clasping in his arms the dear little mother whom he so longed to see again," and then turned her gaze upon the wasted form and faded cheek of that mother, felt an indescribable chill at her heart. Dr. Jeremy's first fears were all confirmed, and, her disease still further aggravated by the anxiety and agitation which attended her father's sickness and death, Mrs. Sullivan was rapidly passing away.

Whether she were herself aware that this was the case, Gertrude had not yet been able to determine. She had never spoken upon the subject, or intimated in any manner a conviction of her approaching end; and Gertrude, as she surveyed her placid countenance, was almost inclined to believe that she was yet deceiving herself with the expectation of recovery.

All doubt on this point was soon removed; for, after remaining a short time engaged in deep thought, or perhaps in prayer, Mrs. Sullivan opened her eyes, fixed them upon her young attendant, and said, in a calm, distinct voice,

"Gertrude, I shall never see Willie again!"

Gertrude made no reply.

"I wish to write and tell him so myself," she continued; "or, rather, if you will write for me, as you have done so many times already, I should like to tell you what to say; and I feel that no time is to be lost, for I am failing fast, and may not long have strength enough left to do it. It will devolve upon you, my child, to let him know when all is over; but you have had too many sad duties already, and it will spare you somewhat to have me prepare him to hear bad news. Will you commence a letter to-day?"

"Certainly, auntie, if you think it best."

"I do, Gerty. What you wrote by the last mail was chiefly concerning grandpa's sickness and death; and there was nothing mentioned which would be likely to alarm him on my account, was there?"

"Nothing at all."

"Then it is quite time he should be forewarned, poor boy! I do not need Dr. Jeremy to tell me that I am dying."

"Did he tell you so?" asked Gertrude, as she went to her desk and began to arrange her writing-materials.

"No, Gerty! he was too prudent for that; but *I* told *him,* and he did not contradict me. You have known it some time, have you not?" inquired she, gazing earnestly in the face of Gertrude, who had returned to the couch, and, seated upon the edge of it, was bending over the invalid, and smoothing the hair from her forehead.

"Some weeks," replied Gertrude, as she spoke imprinting a kiss upon the pale brow of the sufferer.

"Why did you not tell me?"

"Why should I, dear auntie?" said Gertrude, her voice trembling with emotion. "I knew the Lord could never call you at a time when your lamp would not be trimmed and burning."

"Feebly, it burns feebly!" said the humble Christian.

"Whose, then, is bright," responded Gertrude, "if yours be dim? Have you not, for years past, been a living lesson of piety and patience? Unless it be Emily, auntie, I know of no one who seems so fit for heaven."

"O, no, Gerty! I am a sinful creature, full of weakness; much as I desire to meet my Saviour, my earthly heart pines with the vain desire for one more sight of my boy, and all my dreams of heaven are mingled with the aching regret that the one blessing I most craved on earth had been denied me."

"O, auntie!" exclaimed Gertrude, "we are all human! Until the mortal puts on immortality, how *can* you cease to think of Willie, and long for his presence in this trying hour? It cannot be a sin,—that which is so natural!"

"I do not know, Gerty; perhaps it is not; and, if it be, I trust, before I go hence, I shall be blessed with a spirit of perfect submission, that will atone for the occasional murmuring of a mother's heart! Read to me, my dear, some holy words of comfort; you always seem to open the good book at the passage I most need. It is sinful, indeed, in me, Gertrude, to indulge the least repining, blessed as I am in the love and care of one who is dear to me as a daughter!"

Gertrude took her Bible, and, opening it at the Gospel of St. Mark, her eye fell at once upon the account of our Saviour's agony in the garden of Gethsemane.[2] She rightly believed that nothing could be more appropriate to Mrs. Sullivan's state of mind than the touching description of our Lord's humanity; nothing more likely to soothe her spirit, and reconcile her to the occasional rebellion of her own mortal nature, than the evident contest of the human with the divine so thrillingly narrated by the disciple; and that nothing could be more inspiring than the example of that holy Son of God, who ever to His thrice-repeated prayer that, if possible, the cup might pass from him, added the pious ejaculation, "Thy will, not mine, be done." Without hesitation, therefore, she read what first met her glance, and had the satisfaction of seeing that the words were not without effect; for, when she had finished, she observed that as Mrs. Sullivan lay still and calm upon her couch, her lips seemed to be repeating the Saviour's prayer. Not wishing to disturb her meditations, Gertrude made no reference to the proposed letter to Willie, but sat in perfect silence, and about half an hour afterward Mrs. Sullivan fell asleep. It was a gentle, quiet slumber, and Gertrude sat and watched with pleasure the peaceful, happy expression of her features. Darkness had come on before she awoke, and so shrouded the room that Gertrude, who still sat there, was invisible in the gloom. She started, on hearing her name, and, hastily lighting a candle, approached the couch.

"O, Gertrude!" said Mrs. Sullivan, "I have had such a beautiful dream! Sit down by me, my dear, and let me tell it to you; it could not have been more vivid, if it had all been reality. I thought I was sailing rapidly through the air, and, for some time, I seemed to float on and on, over clouds and among bright stars. The motion was so gentle that I did not grow weary, though in my journey I travelled over land and sea. At last I saw beneath me a beautiful city, with churches, towers, monuments, and throngs of gay people moving in every direction. As I drew nearer, I could distinguish the faces of these numerous men and women, and among them, in a crowded street, there was one who looked like Willie. I followed him, and soon felt sure it was he. He looked older than when we saw him last, and much as I have always imagined him, since the descriptions he has given in his letters of the change that has taken place in his appearance. I followed him through several streets, and at last he turned into a fine, large building, which stood near the centre of the city. I went in also. We passed through large halls and beautifully-furnished rooms, and at last stood in a dining-saloon, in the middle of which was a table covered with bottles, glasses, and the remains of a rich dessert, such as I never saw before. There was a group of young men round the table, all well dressed, and some of them fine-looking, so that at first I was quite charmed with their appearance. I seemed, however, to have a strange power of looking into their hearts, and detecting all the evil there was there. One had a very bright, intelligent face, and might have been thought a man of talent.— and so he was; but I could see better than people usually can, and I perceived, by a sort of instinct, that all his mind and genius were converted into a means of duping and deceiving those who were so foolish or so ignorant as to be ensnared; and, in a corner of his pocket, I knew he had a pair of loaded dice.

"Another seemed by his wit and drollery to be the charm of the company; but I could detect marks of intoxication, and felt a certainty that in less than an hour he would cease to be the master of his own actions.

"A third was making a vain attempt to look happy; but his very soul was bared to my searching gaze, and I was aware of the fact that he had the day before lost at the gaming-table all his own and a part of his employer's money, and was tortured with anxiety lest he might not this evening be fortunate enough to win it back.

"There were many others present, and all, more or less sunk in dissipation, had reached various stages on the road to ruin. Their faces, however, looked animated and gay, and, as Willie glanced from one to another, he seemed pleased and attracted.

"One of them offered him a seat at the table, and all urged him to take it. He did so, and the young man at his right filled a glass with bright wine and handed it to him. He hesitated, then took it and raised it to his lips. Just then I touched him on the shoulder. He turned, saw me, and instantly the glass fell from his hand and was broken into a thousand pieces. I beckoned, and he immediately rose and followed me. The gay circle he had left called loudly upon him to return; one of them even laid a hand on his arm, and tried to detain him; but he would not listen or stay— he shook off the hand that would have held him, and we went on. Before we had got outside the building, the man whom I had first noticed, and whom I knew to be the most artful of the company, came out from a room near the door, which he had reached by some other direction, and, approaching Willie, whispered in his ear. Willie faltered, turned, and would perhaps have gone back; but I placed myself in front of him, held up my finger menacingly, and shook my head. He hesitated no longer, but, flinging aside the tempter, rushed out of the door, and was down the long flight of steps before I could overtake him. I seemed, however, to move with great rapidity, and soon found myself taking the lead, and guiding my son through the intricate, crowded streets of the city. Many were the adventures we encountered, many the snares we found laid for the unwary in every direction. More than once my watchful eye saved the thoughtless boy by my side from some pitfall or danger, into which, without me, he would surely have fallen. Occasionally I lost sight of him, and was obliged to turn back; now he had been separated from me by the crowd, and consequently missed his way, and now he had purposely lingered to witness or join in the amusements of the gay populace. Each time, however, he listened to my warning voice, and we went on in safety.

"At last, however, in passing through a brilliantly-lighted street,—for it was now evening,—I suddenly observed that he was absent from my side. I went backwards and forwards but he was nowhere to be seen. For an hour I hunted the streets, and called him by name; but there was no answer. I then unfolded my wings, and, soaring high above the crowded town, surveyed the whole, hoping that in that one glance I might, as I had at first done, detect my boy.

"I was not disappointed. In a gorgeous hall, dazzlingly lit, and filled with gayety and fashion, I beheld Willie. A brilliant young creature was leaning on his arm, and I saw into her heart, and knew that she was not blind to his beauty nor insensible to his attractions. But, O! I trembled for him now! She was lovely and rich, and it was evident to me, from the elegance of her dress and the attention she attracted, that she was also fashionable and admired. I saw into her soul, however, and she was vain, proud, cold-hearted and worldly; and, if she loved Willie, it was his beauty, his winning manners, and his smile that pleased her—not his noble nature, which she knew not how to prize. As they promenaded through the hall, and she, whom crowds were praising, gave all her time and thoughts to him, I, descending in an invisible shape, and standing by his side, touched his shoulder, as I had done before. He looked around, but, before he could see his mother's face, the siren's voice attracted all his attention. Again and again I endeavored to win him away; but he heard me not. At length she spoke some word that betrayed to my high-minded boy the folly and selfishness of her worldly soul. I seized the moment when she had thus weakened her hold upon him, and, clasping him in my arms, spread my wings and soared far, far away, bearing with me the prize I had toiled after and won. As we rose into the air, my manly son became in my encircling arms a child again, and there rested on my bosom the same little head, with its soft, silken curls, that had nestled there in infancy. Back we flew, over sea and land, and paused not until on a soft, grassy slope, under the shade of green trees, I thought I saw my darling Gerty, and was flying to lay my precious boy at her feet, when I awoke, pronouncing your name.

"And now, Gertrude the bitterness of the cup I am called upon to drink is passed away. A blessed angel has indeed ministered unto me. I no longer wish to see my son again on earth, for I am persuaded that my departure is in perfect accordance with the schemes of a merciful Providence. I now believe that Willie's living mother might be powerless to turn him from temptation and evil; but the spirit of that mother will be mighty still, and in the thought that she, in her home beyond the skies, is ever watching around his path, and striving to lead him in the straight and narrow way, he may find a truer shield from danger, a firmer rest to his tempted soul, than she could have been while yet on earth. Now, O Father, I can say, from the depths of my heart, 'Thy will, not mine, be done!'"

From this time until her death, which took place about a month afterward, Mrs. Sullivan's mind remained in a state of perfect resignation and tranquillity. As she said, the last pang had lost its bitterness. In the letter which she dictated to Willie, she expressed her perfect trust in the goodness and wisdom of Providence, and exhorted him to cherish the same submissive love for the All-wise. She reminded him of the early lessons she had taught him, the piety and self-command which she had inculcated, and made it her dying prayer that her influence might be increased, rather than diminished, and her presence felt to be a continual reality. She gave the important caution to one who had faithfully struggled with adversity, to beware of the dangers and snares which attend prosperity, and besought him never to discredit or disgrace his childhood's training.

After Gertrude had folded the letter, which she supposed completed, and left the house to attend to those duties in school which she still continued regularly to perform, Mrs. Sullivan reöpened the nearly-covered sheet, and, with her own feeble and trembling hand, recounted the disinterested, patient, loving devotion of Gertrude. "So long," said she, "my son, as you cherish in your heart the memory of your grandfather and mother, cease not to bestow all the gratitude of which that heart is capable upon one whose praises my hand is too feeble to portray."

So slow and gradual was the decline of Mrs. Sullivan, that her death at last came as an unexpected blow to Gertrude, who, though she saw the ravages of the disease, could not realize that a termination must come to their work.

In the dead hours of the night, with no one to sustain and encourage her but the frightened and trembling Jane, did she watch the departing spirit of her much-loved friend. "Are you afraid to see me die, Gertrude?" asked Mrs. Sullivan, about an hour before her death. On Gertrude's answering that she was not,—"Then turn me a little towards you," said she, "that your face, my darling, may be the last to me of earth."

It was done, and, with her hand locked fast in Gertrude's, and a look that spoke of the deepest affection, she expired.

CHAPTER XXVI

But, whatsoe'er the weal or woe
That Heaven across her lot might throw.
Full well her Christian spirit knew
Its path of virtue, straight and true.
——*Joanna Baillie*

NOT UNTIL HER WORK of love was thus ended did Gertrude become conscious that the long continuance of her labors by night and day had worn upon her frame and utterly exhausted her strength. For a week after Mrs. Sullivan was laid in her grave, Dr. Jeremy was seriously apprehensive of a severe illness for Gertrude. But, after struggling with her dangerous symptoms for several days, she rallied, and, though still pale and worn by care and anxiety, was able to resume her classes at school, and make arrangements for providing herself with another home.

Several homes had already been offered to her, several urgent invitations given, with a warmth and cordiality which made it difficult to decline their acceptance; but Gertrude, though deeply touched by the kindness thus manifested towards her in her loneliness and desolation, preferred to abide by her previously-formed resolution to seek for herself a permanent boarding-place, and, when the grounds on which she based her decision were understood by her friends, they approved her course, ceased to importune her, and manifested a sincere wish to be of service, by lending their aid to the furtherance of her plans.

Mrs. Jeremy was at first disposed to feel hurt and wounded by Gertrude's refusal to come to them without delay, and consider herself established for any length of time that she chose to remain; and the doctor himself was so peremptory with his, "Come, Gertrude, come right home with us——don't say a word!" that she was afraid lest, in her weak state of health, she should be actually carried off, without a *chance* to remonstrate. But, after he had taken upon himself to give Jane orders about packing her clothes and sending them after her, and then locking up the house and going home himself, he gave Gertrude an opportunity to expostulate, and present her reasons for wishing to decline the generous proposal.

All her reasoning upon general principles, however, proved insufficient to convince the warm-hearted couple. "It was all nonsense about independent position. She would be perfectly independent with them, and her company would be such a pleasure that she need feel no hesitation in accepting their offer, and might be sure she would herself be conferring a favor, instead of being the party obliged." At last she was compelled to make use of an argument which had greatly influenced her own mind, and would, she felt sure, carry no little weight with it in the doctor's estimation.

"Dr. Jeremy," said she, "I hope you will not condemn in me a motive which has, I confess, strengthened my firmness in this matter. I should be unwilling to mention it, if I did not know that you are so far acquainted with the state of affairs between Mr. Graham and myself as to understand, and perhaps in some degree sympathize with, my feelings. You know that he was opposed to my leaving and remaining here this winter; and must suspect that, when we parted, there was not a perfectly good understanding between us. He hinted that I should never be able to support myself, and should be driven to a life of dependence; and, since the salary which I receive from Mr. W. is sufficient for all my wants, I am anxious to be so situated, on Mr. Graham's return, that he will perceive that my assurance, or boast (if I must call it so), that I could earn my own living, was not without foundation."

"So Graham thought that, without his sustaining power, you would soon come to beggary—did he? With your talents, too!—that's just like him!"

"O, no, no!" replied Gertrude "I did not say that; but I seemed to him a mere child, and he did not realize that, in giving me an education, he had, as it were, paid my expenses in advance. It was very natural he should distrust my capacity—he had never seen me compelled to exert myself."

"I understand—I understand," said the doctor. "He thought you would be glad enough to come back to them;—yes, yes, just like him!"

"Well, now," said Mrs. Jeremy, "I don't believe he thought any such thing. He was provoked, and did n't mind what he said. Ten to one he will never think of it again, and it seems to me it is only a kind of pride in Gertrude to care anything about it."

"I don't know that, wife," said the doctor. "If it *is* pride, it's an honorable pride, that I like; and I am not sure but, if I were in Gertrude's place, I should feel just as she does; so I shan't urge her to do any other ways than she proposes. She can have a boarding-place, and yet spend a good share of her time with us, what with running in and out, coming to spend days, and so on; and she does n't need to be told that, in case of any sickness or trouble, our doors are always open to her."

"No, indeed," said Mrs. Jeremy; "and, if you feel set about it, Gerty dear, I am sure I shall want you to do whatever pleases you best; but one thing I do insist on, and that is, that you leave this house, which must look dreary enough to you now, this very day, go home with me, and stay until you get recruited."

Gertrude, very gladly consenting to a short visit, compromised the matter by accompanying them without delay; and it was chiefly owing to the doctor's persevering skill and care bestowed upon his young guest, and the kind and motherly nursing of Mrs. Jeremy, that she escaped the illness which had so severely threatened her.

Mr. and Mrs. W., who had felt great sympathy for Gertrude, in consequence of the acquaintance they had had with the trying nature of her winter's experience, pressed her to come to their house, and remain until the return of Mr. Graham and Emily; but, on being assured by her that she was quite unaware of the period of their absence, and should not probably reside with them for the future, they were satisfied that she acted with wisdom and judgment in at once providing herself with an independent situation.

Mr. and Mrs. Arnold, who had been constant in their attentions both to Mrs. Sullivan and Gertrude, and were the only persons, except the physician, who had been admitted to the sick room of the invalid, felt that they had a peculiar claim to the guardianship and care of the doubly-orphaned girl, and were not slow to urge upon her to become a member of their household, and accept of their protection, limiting their invitation, as the W.'s had done, to the time when Emily should be back from the south. Mr. Arnold's family, however, being large, and his house and salary small in proportion, true benevolence alone prompted this proposal; and, on Gertrude's acquainting his economical and prudent wife with the ample means she enjoyed from her own exertions, and the decision she had formed of procuring an independent home, she received the warm approbation of both, and found in the latter an excellent adviser and assistant.

Mrs. Arnold had a widowed sister, who was in the habit of adding to her moderate income by receiving into her family, as boarders, a few young ladies, who came to the city for purposes of education. Gertrude did not know this lady personally, but had heard her warmly praised; and she indulged the hope that, through her friend, the clergyman's wife, she might obtain with her an agreeable and not too expensive residence. In this she was not disappointed. Mrs. Warren had fortunately vacant, at this time, a large and cheerful front chamber; and, Mrs. Arnold having recommended Gertrude in the warmest manner, suitable terms were agreed upon, and the room immediately placed at her disposal. Mrs. Sullivan had bequeathed to her all her furniture, a part of which had lately been purchased, and was, in accordance with Willie's injunctions, most excellent, both in material and workmanship; and Mrs. Arnold and her two eldest daughters insisted that, in consideration of her recent fatigue and bereavement, she should consent to attend only to her school duties, and leave to them the task of furnishing her room with such articles as she preferred to have placed there, and superintending the packing away of all other movables; for Gertrude was unwilling that anything should be sold. It was a great relief to be thus spared the cruel trial of seeing the house her lost friend had taken so much pleasure and pride in stripped and left desolate; and though, on first entering her apartment at Mrs. Warren's, a deep sadness crept into her heart at the sight of the familiar furniture, she could not but think, as she observed the neatness, care and taste, with which everything had been arranged for her reception, that it would be a sin to repine and call one's self wretched and alone in a world which contained hearts so quick to feel, and hands so ready to labor, as those that had interested themselves for her.

On entering the dining-room the first evening after she took up her residence at Mrs. Warren's, she expected to meet only strangers at the tea-table, but was agreeably disappointed at the sight of Fanny Bruce, who, left in Boston while her mother and brother were spending the winter in travelling, had now been several weeks an inmate of Mrs. Warren's house. Fanny was a school-girl, twelve or thirteen years of age; and having, for some summers past, been a near neighbor to Gertrude, had been in the habit of seeing her frequently at Mr. Graham's, had sometimes begged flowers from her, borrowed books, and obtained assistance in her fancy-work. She admired Gertrude exceedingly; had hailed with great delight the prospect of knowing her better, as she hoped to do at Mrs. Warren's; and when she met the gaze of her large, dark eyes, and saw a smile of pleasure overspread her countenance at the sight of a familiar face, she felt emboldened to come forward, shake hands, and beg that Miss Flint would sit next her at the table.

Fanny Bruce was a girl of good disposition and warm heart, but she had been much neglected by her mother, whose chief pride was in her son, the same Ben of whom we have previously spoken. She had often been left behind in some boarding-house, while her pleasure-loving mother and indolent brother passed their time in journeying; and had not always been so fortunately situated as at present. A sense of loneliness, a want of sympathy in any of her pursuits, had been a source of great unhappiness to the poor child, who labored under the painful consciousness that but little interest was felt by any one in her improvement or happiness.

Gertrude had not been long at Mrs. Warren's before she observed that Fanny occupied an isolated position in the family. She was a few years younger than her companions, three dressy misses, who could not condescend to admit her into their clique; and Mrs. Warren's time was so much engrossed by household duties that she took but little notice of her. Her apparent loneliness could not fail to excite the compassion of one who was herself suffering from recent sorrow and bereavement; and, although the quiet and privacy of her own room were, at this time, grateful to Gertrude's feelings, pity for poor Fanny induced her to invite her frequently to come and sit with her, and she often so far forgot her own griefs as to exert herself in providing entertainment for her young visitor, who, on her part, considered it privilege enough to share Gertrude's retirement, read her books, and feel confident of her friendship. During the month of March, which was unusually stormy, Fanny spent almost every evening with Gertrude; and she, who at first felt that she was making a sacrifice of her own comfort and ease by giving another such constant access to her apartment, came, at last, to realize the force of Uncle True's prophecy, that, in her efforts for the happiness of others, she would at last find her own; for Fanny's lively and often amusing conversation drew Gertrude from the contemplation of her trials, and the interest and affection she awakened saved her from painful consciousness of her solitary situation.

April arrived, and still no further news from Emily. Gertrude's heart ached with a vain longing to once more pour out her griefs on the bosom of that dear friend, and find in her consolation, encouragement, and support. She longed to tell her how many times during the winter she had sighed for the gentle touch of the soft hand which was wont to rest so lovingly on her head, the sound of that sweet voice whose very tones were comforting. For some time Gertrude wrote regularly, but of late she had not known where to direct her letters; and since Mrs. Sullivan's death there had been no communication between her and the travellers. She was sitting at her window, one evening, thinking of that group of friends whom she had loved with a daughter's and a sister's love, and who were now separated from her by distance, or that greater barrier, death, when she was summoned below stairs to see Mr. Arnold and his daughter Anne.

After the usual civilities and inquiries, Miss Arnold turned to Gertrude and said, "Of course you have heard the news, Gertrude?"

"No," replied Gertrude, "I have heard nothing special."

"What!" exclaimed Mr. Arnold, "have you not heard of Mr. Graham's marriage?"

Gertrude started up in surprise. "Do you really mean so, Mr. Arnold? Mr. Graham married! When? To whom?"

"To the widow Holbrook, a sister-in-law of Mr. Clinton's; she has been staying at Havana with a party from the north, and the Grahams met her there."

"But, Gertrude," asked Miss Arnold, "how does it happen you had not heard of it? It is in all the newspapers—'Married in New Orleans, J. H. Graham, Esq., of Boston, to Mrs. Somebody or other Holbrook.'"

"I have not seen a newspaper for a day or two," replied Gertrude.

"And Miss Graham's blindness, I suppose, prevents her writing," said Anne; "but I should have thought Mr. Graham would have sent wedding compliments."

Gertrude made no reply, and Miss Arnold continued, laughingly, "I suppose his bride engrosses all his attention."

"Do you know anything of this Mrs. Holbrook?" asked Gertrude.

"Not much," answered Mr. Arnold. "I have seen her occasionally at Mr. Clinton's. She is a handsome, showy woman, fond of society, I should think."

"I have seen her very often," said Anne. "She is a coarse, noisy, dashing person,—just the one to make Miss Emily miserable."

Gertrude looked distressed, and Mr. Arnold glanced reprovingly at his daughter.

"Anne," said he, "are you sure you speak advisedly?"

"Belle Clinton is my authority, father. I only judge from what I used to hear her say at school about her Aunt *Bella,* as she always used to call her."

"Did Isabel represent her so unfavorably?"

"Not intentionally," replied Anne; "she meant the greatest praise, but I never liked anything she told us about her."

"We will not condemn her until we can decide upon acquaintance," said Mr. Arnold, mildly; "perhaps she will prove the very reverse of what you suppose her."

"Can you tell me anything concerning Emily?" asked Gertrude, "and whether Mr. Graham is soon to return?"

"Nothing," said Miss Arnold. "I have seen only the notice in the papers. When did you hear from them yourself?"

Gertrude mentioned the date of her letter from Mrs. Ellis, the account she had given of the gay party from the north, and suggested the probability that the present Mrs. Graham was the widow she had described.

"The same, undoubtedly," said Mr. Arnold.

Their knowledge of the facts was so slight, however, that little remained to be said concerning the marriage, and other topics of conversation were introduced. But Gertrude found it impossible to give her thoughts to any other subject; the matter was one of such vital importance to Emily, that her mind constantly recurred to it, and she found it difficult to keep pace with Anne Arnold's rapidly-flowing words and ideas. The necessity which at last arose of replying to a question which she had not at all understood was fortunately obviated by the sudden entrance of Dr. and Mrs. Jeremy. The former held in his hand a sealed letter, directed to Gertrude, in the hand-writing of Mr. Graham; and, as he handed it to her, he rubbed his hands, and, looking at Anne Arnold, exclaimed, "Now, Miss Anne, we shall hear all about these famous nuptials!"

Finding her visitors thus eager to learn the contents of her letter, Gertrude dispensed with ceremony, broke the seal, and hastily perused its contents.

The envelope contained two or three pages closely written by Mrs. Ellis, and also a somewhat lengthy note from Mr. Graham. Surprised as Gertrude was at any communication from one who had parted from her in anger, her strongest desire was to hear particularly from Emily, and she therefore gave the preference to the housekeeper's document, that being most likely to contain the desired information. It ran as follows:

"*New York, March 31, 1852.*

"DEAR GERTRUDE: As there were plenty of Boston folks at the wedding, I daresay you have heard before this of Mr. Graham's marriage. He married the widder Holbrook, the same I wrote you about. She was determined to have him, and she's got him. I don't hesitate to say he's got the worst of the bargain. He likes a quiet life, and he's lost his chance of that,—poor man!—for she's the greatest hand for company that ever I saw. She followed Mr. Graham up pretty well at Havana, but I guess he thought better of it, and did n't really mean to have her. When we got to New Orleans, however, she was there; and the long and short of it is, she carried her point, and married him. Emily behaved beautifully; she never said a word against it, and always treated the widder as pleasantly as could be; but, dear me! how will our Emily get along with so many young folks as there are about all the time now, and so much noise and confusion? For my part, I an't used to it, and don't pretend that I think it's agreeable. The new lady is civil enough to me, now she's married. I daresay she thinks it stands in her hand, as long as she's one of the family, and I've been in it so long. But I suppose you've been wondering what had become of us, Gertrude, and will be surprised to find we've got so far as New York, on our way home,—*my* way home, I should say, for I'm the only one that talks of coming at present. The truth is, I kept meaning to write while we were in New Orleans, but there was so much going on I did n't get a chance; and, after that horrid steamboat from Charleston here, I was n't good for anything for a week. But Emily was so anxious to have you written to that I could n't put it off any longer than until to-day. Poor Emily is n't very well; I don't mean that she's downright sick,—it's low spirits and nervousness, I suppose, more that anything. She gets tired and worried very quick, and is easily startled and disturbed, which did n't use to be the case. I think likely it's the new wife, and all the nieces, and other disagreeable things. She never complains, and nobody would know but what she was pleased to have her father married again; but she has n't seemed quite happy all winter, and now it troubles me to see how sad she looks sometimes. She talks a sight about you, and felt dreadfully not to get any more letters. To come to the principal thing, however, they are all going to Europe,—Emily and all. I take it it's the new wife's idea; but, whoever proposed the thing, it's all settled now. Mr. Graham wanted me to go, but I would not hear of such a thing; I would as soon be hung as venture on the sea again, and I told him so, up and down. So now he has written for you to go with Emily; and, if you are not afraid of sea-sickness, I hope you won't refuse, for it would be dreadful for her to have a stranger, and you know she always needs somebody, on account of her blindness. I do not think she has the least wish to go; but she would not ask to be left behind, for fear her father should think she did not like the new wife.

"As soon as they sail,—which will be the last of April,—I shall come back to the house in D——, and see to things there while they are away. I am going to write a postscript to you from Emily, and I believe I will add nothing more myself, except that we shall be very impatient to hear your answer; and I must say once more that I hope you will not refuse to go with Emily.

"Yours, very truly,

"Sarah H. Ellis."

The postscript contained the following:

"I need not tell my darling Gertrude how much I have missed her, and longed to have her with me again; how I have thought of her by night and day, and prayed to God to strengthen and fit her for many trials and labors. The letter written soon after Mr. Cooper's death, is the last that has reached me, and I do not know whether Mrs. Sullivan is still living. Write to me at once, my dear child, if you cannot come to us. Father will tell you of our plans, and ask you to accompany us to Europe; my heart will be light if I can take my dear Gerty with me, but not if she leave any other duty behind. I trust to you, my love, to decide aright. You have heard of father's marriage. It is a great change for us all, but will, I trust, result in happiness. Mrs. Graham has two nieces who are with us at the hotel. They are to be of our party to go abroad, and are, I understand, very beautiful girls, especially Belle Clinton, whom you have seen in Boston some years ago. Mrs. Ellis is very tired of writing, and I must close with assuring my dearest Gertrude of the devoted affection of

Emily Graham."

It was with great curiosity that Gertrude unfolded Mr. Graham's epistle; she thought it would be awkward for him to address her, and wondered much whether he would maintain his severe and authoritative tone, or condescend to explain and apologize. Had she known him better, she would have been assured that nothing would ever induce him to do the latter, for he was one of those persons who never believe themselves in the wrong. The letter ran thus:

"MISS GERTRUDE FLINT: I am married, and intend to go abroad on the 28th of April; my daughter will accompany us, and, as Mrs. Ellis dreads the sea, I am induced to propose that you join us in New York, and attend the party, as a companion to Emily. I have not forgotten the ingratitude with which you once slighted a similar offer on my part, and nothing would compel me to give you another opportunity to manifest such a spirit, but a desire to promote the happiness of Emily, and a sincere wish to be of service to a young person who has been in my family so long that I feel a friendly interest in providing for her. I thus put it in your power, by complying with our wishes, to do away from my mind the recollection of your past behavior; and, if you choose to return to us, I shall enable you to maintain the place and appearance of a lady. As we sail the last of the month, it is important you should be here in the course of a fort-night; and, if you will write and name the day, I will myself meet you at the boat. Mrs. Ellis being anxious to return to Boston, I hope you will come as soon as possible. As you will be obliged to incur expenses, I enclose a sum of money sufficient to cover them. If you have contracted debts, let me know to what amount, and I will see that all is made right before you leave. Trusting to your being now come to a sense of your duty, I am ready to subscribe myself your friend,

J. H. GRAHAM."

Gertrude was sitting near a lamp whose light fell directly upon her face, which, as she glanced over Mr. Graham's note, flushed crimson with wounded pride. Dr. Jeremy, who was watching her countenance, observed that she changed color; and during the few minutes that Mr. and Miss Arnold staid to hear he news he gave an occasional glance of defiance at the letter, and as soon as they were gone begged to be made acquainted with its contents, assuring Gertrude that if she did not let him know what Graham said, he should believe it a thousand times more insulting than it really was.

"He writes," said Gertrude, "to invite me to accompany them to Europe."

"Indeed!" said Dr. Jeremy, with a low whistle, "and he thinks you'll be silly enough to pack up and start off at a minute's notice!"

"Why, Gerty," said Mrs. Jeremy, "you'll like to go, shan't you, dear? It will be delightful."

"Delightful nonsense! Mrs. Jerry," exclaimed the doctor. "What is there delightful, I want to know, in travelling about with an arrogant old tyrant, his blind daughter, upstart, dashy wife, and her two fine-lady nieces? A pretty position Gertrude would be in, a slave to the whims of all that company!"

"Why, Dr. Jerry," interrupted his wife, "you forget Emily."

"Emily,—to be sure, she's an angel, and never would impose upon anybody, least of all her own pet; but she 'll have to play second fiddle herself, and I'm mistaken if she does n't find it pretty hard to defend her rights and maintain a comfortable position in her father's enlarged family circle."

"So much the more need, then," said Gertrude, "that some one should be enlisted in her interests, to ward off the approach of every annoyance."

"Do you mean, then, to put yourself in the breach?" asked the doctor."

"I mean to accept Mr. Graham's invitation," replied Gertrude, "and join Emily at once; but I trust the harmony that seems to subsist between her and her new connections will continue undisturbed, so that I shall have no occasion to take up arms on *her* account, and on *my own* I do not entertain a single fear."

"Then you really think you shall go," said Mrs. Jeremy.

"I do," said Gertrude; "nothing but my duty to Mrs. Sullivan and her father led me to think of leaving Emily. That duty is at an end, and now that I can be of use to her, and she wishes me back, I cannot hesitate a moment. I see very plainly, from Mrs. Ellis' letter, that Emily is not happy, and nothing which I can do to make her so must be neglected. Only think, Mrs. Jeremy, what a friend she has been to me!"

"I know it," said Mrs. Jeremy, "and I dare say you will enjoy the journey, in spite of all the scare-crows the doctor sets up to frighten you; but still, I declare, it does seem a sacrifice for you to leave your beautiful room, and all your comforts, for such an uncertain life as one has travelling with a large party."

"Sacrifice!" interrupted the doctor, "it's the greatest sacrifice that ever I heard of! It is not merely giving up three hundred and fifty dollars a year [1] of her own earning, and as pleasant a home as there is in Boston; it is relinquishing all the independence that she has been striving after, and which she was so anxious to maintain that she would not accept of anybody's hospitality for more than a week or two."

"No, doctor," said Gertrude, warmly, "nothing that I do for *Emily's* sake can be called a sacrifice; it is my greatest pleasure."

"Gerty always finds her pleasure in doing what is right," remarked Mrs. Jeremy.

"O, no," said Gertrude, "my wishes would often lead me astray; but not in this case. The thought that our dear Emily was dependent upon a stranger for all those little attentions that are only acceptable from those she loves would make me miserable; our happiness has for years been almost wholly in each other, and when one has suffered the other has suffered also. I *must* go to her; I cannot think of doing otherwise."

"I wish I thought," muttered Dr. Jeremy, "that the sacrifice you make would be half appreciated. But there's Graham, I'll venture to say, thinking it will be the greatest favor in the world to take you back again. Perhaps he addresses you as a beggar; it would n't be the first time he's done such a thing. I wonder what would have induced poor Philip Amory to go back." Then, in a louder tone, he inquired, "Has he made any apology in his letter for past unkindness?"

"I do not think he considered any to be needed," replied Gertrude.

"Then he did n't make any sort of excuse for his ungentlemanly behavior! I might have known he would n't. I declare, it's a shame you should be exposed to any more such treatment; but I always *did* hear that women were self-forgetful in their friendship, and I believe it. Gertrude makes an excellent friend. Mrs. Jerry, we must cultivate her regard, and some time or other perhaps make a loud call upon her services."

"And if ever you do, sir, I shall be ready to respond to it; if there is a person in the world who owes a debt to society, it is myself. I hear the world called cold, selfish and unfeeling; but it has not been so to me. I should be ungrateful if I did not cherish a spirit of universal love; how much more so, if I did not feel bound heart and hand to those dear friends who have bestowed upon me such affection as no orphan ever found before!"

"Gertrude," said Mrs. Jeremy, "I believe that you were right in leaving Emily when you did, and that you are right in returning to her now; and, if your being such a good girl as you are is at all due to her, she certainly has a great claim upon you."

"She has a claim, indeed, Mrs. Jeremy! It was Emily who first taught me the difference between right and wrong—"

"And she is going to reap the benefit of that knowledge in you," said the doctor, in continuation of her remark. "That's fair! But, if you are resolved to take this European tour, you will be busy enough with your preparations. Do you think Mr. W. will be willing to give you up?"

"I hope so," said Gertrude; "I am sorry to be obliged to ask it of him, for he has been very indulgent to me, and I have been absent from school two weeks out of the winter already; but, as there want only a few months to the summer vacation, he will, perhaps, be able to supply my place. I shall speak to him about it to-morrow."

Mrs. Jeremy now interested herself in the details of Gertrude's arrangements, offered an attic-room for the storage of her furniture, gave up to her a dress-maker whom she had engaged for herself, and, before she had left, a plan was laid out, by following which Gertrude would be enabled to start for New York in less than a week.

Mr. W., on being applied to, relinquished Gertrude, though deeply regretting, as he told her, to lose so valuable an assistant; and, after a few days busily occupied in preparation, she bade farewell to the tearful Fanny Bruce, the bustling doctor and his kind-hearted wife, all of whom accompanied her to the railroad-station. She promised to write to the Jeremys, and they, on their part, agreed to forward to her any letters that might arrive from Willie.

In less than a fortnight from the time of her departure, Mrs. Ellis returned to Boston, and brought news of the safe conclusion of Gertrude's journey. A letter, received a week after, by Mrs. Jeremy, announced that they should sail in a few days. She was, therefore, surprised, when a second epistle was put into her hands, dated the day succeeding that on which she supposed Mr. Graham's party to have left the country. It was as follows:

"*New York, April 29th*

"MY DEAR MRS. JEREMY: As yesterday was the day on which we expected to sail for Europe, you will be somewhat astonished to hear that we are yet in New York, and still more so to learn that the foreign tour is now indefinitely postponed. Only two days since, Mr. Graham was seized with his old complaint, the gout, and the attack proved so violent as seriously to threaten his life. Although to-day somewhat relieved, and considered by his physician out of immediate danger, he remains a great sufferer, and a sea-voyage is pronounced impracticable for months to come. His great anxiety is to be at home; and, as soon as it is possible for him to bear the journey, we shall all hasten to the house in D———. I enclose a note for Mrs. Ellis. It contains various directions which Emily is desirous she should receive; and, as we did not know how to address her, I have sent it to you, trusting to your kindness to see it forwarded. Mrs. Graham and her nieces, who had been anticipating much pleasure from going abroad, are, of course, greatly disappointed at the entire change in their plans for the summer. It is particularly trying to Miss Clinton, as her father has been absent more than a year, and she was hoping to meet him in Paris.

"It is impossible that either Emily or myself should personally regret a journey of which we felt only dread, and, were it not for Mr. Graham's illness being the cause of its postponement, we should both, I think, find it hard not to realize a degree of selfish satisfaction in the prospect of returning to the dear old place in D——, where we hope to be established in the course of the next month. I say *we,* for neither Mr. Graham nor Emily will hear of my leaving them again.

"With the kindest regards to yourself, and my friend the doctor,   I am yours, very sincerely,
GERTRUDE FLINT

CHAPTER XXVII

I see her;
Her hair in ringlets fluttering free,
And her lips that move with melody.

Not she.——There's a beauty that lovelier glows,
Though her coral lip with melody flows.

I see her; 't is she of the ivory brow
And heaven-tinged orbs: I know her now.

Not she.——There's another more lovely still,
With a chastened mind, and a tempered will.
—*Caroline Gilman.*

MR. GRAHAM'S COUNTRY-HOUSE boasted a fine, old-fashioned entry, with a door at either end, both of which usually stood open during the warm weather, admitting a cool current of air, and rendering the neighborhood of the front entrance a favorite resort for the family, especially during the early hours of the day, when the warm sun had no access to the spot; and the shady yard, which sloped gradually down to the road, was refreshing and grateful to the sight. Here, on a pleasant June morning, Isabel Clinton, and her cousin Kitty Ray, had made themselves comfortable, each according to her own idea of what constituted comfort.

Isabel had drawn a large arm-chair close to the door-sill, ensconced herself in it, and, although she held in her hand a piece of worsted-work, was gazing idly down the road. She was a beautiful girl, tall and finely formed, with a delicate complexion, clear blue eyes, and rich, light, flowing curls. The same lovely child, whom Gertrude had gazed upon with rapture, as, leaning against the window of her father's house, she watched old True while he lit his lamp, had ripened into an equally lovely woman. Her uncommon beauty aided and enhanced by all the advantages of dress which skill could suggest or money provide, she was universally admired, flattered and caressed.

At an early age deprived of her mother, and left for some years almost wholly to the care of servants, she soon learned to appreciate at more than their true value the outward attractions she possessed; and her aunt, under whose tutelage she had been since she left school, was little calculated to counteract in her this undue self-admiration. An appearance of conscious superiority which distinguished her, and the independent air with which she tapped against the door-step with her little foot, might safely be attributed, then, to her conviction that Belle Clinton, the beauty and the heiress, was looking vastly well, as she sat there, attired in a blue cashmere morning-dress, richly embroidered, and flowing open in front, for the purpose of displaying an equally rich flounced cambric petticoat. It can scarcely be wondered at that she was herself pleased and satisfied with an outward appearance that could not fail to please and satisfy the most severe critic.

On a low step at her feet sat Kitty Ray, a complete contrast to her cousin in looks, manners, and many points of character. Kitty was one of those whom the world usually calls a sweet little creature, lively, playful, and affectionate. She was so small that her childish manners became her; so full of spirits that her occasional rudeness claimed pardon on that score; too thoughtless to be always amiable or always wise; and for all other faults her warm-heartedness and generous enthusiasm must plead an excuse to one who wished, or even endeavored, to love her as she wished and expected to be loved by everybody. She was a pretty girl, always bright and animated, mirthful and happy; fond of her cousin Belle, and sometimes influenced by her, though often, on the other hand, enlisting with all her force on the opposite side of some contested question. Unlike Belle, she was seldom well dressed, for, though possessed of ample means, she was very careless. On the present occasion, her dark silk wrapper was half concealed by a crimson flannel sack, which she held tightly around her, declaring it was a dreadful chilly morning, and she was half-frozen to death—she certainly would go and warm herself at the kitchen fire, if she were not afraid of encountering that *she-dragon* Mrs. Ellis; she was sure she did not see, if they must sit in the door-way, why Belle could n't come to the side-door, where the sun shone beautifully. "O, I forgot, though," added she; "complexion!"

"Complexion!" said Belle; "I'm no more afraid of hurting my complexion than you are; I'm sure I never freckle, or tan either."

"I know that; but you burn all up, and look like a fright."

"Well, if I did n't, I should n't go there to sit; I like to be at the front of the house, where I can see the passing. I wonder who those people are, coming up the road; I've been watching them for some time."

Kitty stood up, and looked in the direction to which Belle pointed. After observing the couple who were approaching for a minute or two, she exclaimed, "Why, that's Gertrude Flint! I wonder where she's been! and who can that be with her? I did n't know there was a beau to be had about here."

"Beau!" said Belle, sneeringly.

"And why not a beau, Cousin Belle! I'm sure he looks like one."

"I would n't give much for any of her beaux!" said Belle.

"Would n't you?" said Kitty. "You'd better wait until you see who they are; you near-sighted people should n't decide in such a hurry. I can tell you that he is a gentleman you would n't object to walking with, yourself; it's Mr. Bruce, the one we met in New Orleans."

"I don't believe it!" exclaimed Belle, starting up.

"You will soon have a chance to see for yourself; for he is coming home with her."

"*He is?*—What can he be walking with her for?"

"To show his taste, perhaps. I am sure he could not find more agreeable company."

"You and I don't agree about that," replied Belle. "I don't see anything very agreeable about her."

"Because you are determined not to, Belle. Everybody else thinks her charming, and Mr. Bruce is opening the gate for her as politely as if she were a queen; I like him for that."

"Do see," said Belle; "she's got on that white cape-bonnet of hers! and that checked gingham dress! I wonder what Mr. Bruce thinks of her, and he such a critic in regard to ladies' dress."

Gertrude and her companion now drew near the house; the former looked up, saw the young ladies in the door-way, and smiled pleasantly at Kitty, who was making strange grimaces, and giving significant glances, over Belle's shoulder; but Mr. Bruce, who seemed much engaged by the society he was already enjoying, did not observe either of them; and they distinctly heard him say, as he handed Gertrude a small parcel he had been carrying for her, "I believe I won't come in; it's such a bore to have to talk to strangers.—Do you work in the garden, mornings, this summer?"

"No," replied Gertrude, "there is nothing left of my garden but the memory of it."

"Why, Miss Gertrude!" said the young man, "I hope these new comers have n't interfered with—" Here, observing the direction of Gertrude's eyes, he raised his own, saw Belle and Kitty standing opposite to him, and, compelled now to recognize and speak with them, went forward to shake hands, trusting to his remarks about strangers in general, and these new comers in particular, not having been overheard.

Although overheard, the young ladies chose to take no notice of that which they supposed intended for unknown individuals.

They were mistaken, however; Mr. Bruce knew, perfectly well, that the nieces of the present Mrs. Graham were the same girls whom he had met at the south, and was, nevertheless, indifferent about renewing his acquaintance. His vanity, however, was not proof against the evident pleasure they both manifested at seeing him again, and he was in a few minutes engaged in an animated conversation with them, while Gertrude quietly entered the house, and went upstairs unnoticed. She sought Emily's room, to which she had always free access, and was giving an account of her morning's expedition to the village, and the successful manner in which she had accomplished various commissions and errands, when Mrs. Ellis put her head in at the door, and said, with a most distressed voice and countenance, "Has n't Gertrude?—O, there you are! Do tell me what Mrs. Wilkins said about the strawberries."

"I engaged three quarts; has n't she sent them?"

"No, but I'm thankful to hear they're coming; I have been so plagued about the dinner."

She now came in, shut the door, and, seating herself, exclaimed, with something like a groan, "I declare, Emily, such an ironing as our girls have got to do to-day! you never saw anything like it! There's no end to the fine clothes Mrs. Graham and those nieces of hers put into our wash. I declare, it's a shame! Rich as they are, they might put out their washing. I've been helping, *myself*, as much as I could; but, as Mrs. Prime says, one can't do everything at once; and I've had to see the butcher, make puddings and blanc-mange, and been worried to death, all the time, because I had forgotten to engage those strawberries. So Mrs. Wilkins had n't sent her fruit to the market when you got there?"

"No, but she was in a great hurry, getting it ready; it would have been gone in a very short time."

"Well, that was lucky. I don't know what I should have done without the berries, for I've no time to hunt up anything else for dessert. I've got just as much as I can do till dinner-time. Mrs. Graham never kept house before, and don't know how to make allowance for anything. She comes home from Boston, expects to find everything in apple-pie order, and never asks or cares who does the work."

Mrs. Prime's voice was now heard, calling at the back-staircase,—
"Mrs. Ellis, Miss Wilkins' boy has fetched your strawberries, and the hulls an't off o' one on'em; he said they had n't no time."

"That's too bad!" exclaimed the tired, worried housekeeper. "Who's going to take the hulls off, I should like to know? Katy is busy enough, and I'm sure I can't do it."

"I will, Mrs. Ellis,—let *me* do it," said Gertrude, following Mrs. Ellis, who was now half-way down stairs.

"No, no! don't you touch to, Miss Gertrude," said Mrs. Prime; "they'll only stain your fingers all up."

"No matter if they do; my hands are not made of white kid. They'll bear washing."

Mrs. Ellis was only too thankful for Gertrude's help, and, seating herself in the dining-room, she commenced the task. In the mean while, Belle and Kitty were doing their best to entertain Mr. Bruce, who, sitting on the door-steps, and leaning back against a pillar of the piazza, from time to time cast his eyes down the entry, and up the staircase, in hopes of Gertrude's reappearance; and, despairing of it at last, he was on the point of taking his departure, when his sister Fanny came in at the gate, and, running up the yard, was rushing past the assembled trio and into the house.

Her brother, however, stretched out his arm, caught her, and, before he let her go, whispered something in her ear.

"Who is that wild Indian?" asked Kitty Ray, as Fanny ran across the entry and disappeared.

"A sister of mine," answered Ben, in a nonchalant manner.

"Why! is she?" inquired Kitty, with interest; "I have seen her here several times, and never took any notice of her. I did n't know she was *your* sister. What a pretty girl she is!"

"Do you think so?" said Ben; "sorry I can't agree with you. I think she's a fright."

Fanny now reappeared, and, stopping a moment on her way up stairs, called out, without any ceremony, "She says she can't come; she's busy."

"Who?" asked Kitty, in her turn catching Fanny and detaining her.

"Miss Flint."

Mr. Bruce colored slightly, and Belle Clinton observed it.

"What is she doing?" inquired Kitty.

"Hulling strawberries."

"Where are you going, Fanny?" asked her brother.

"Up stairs."

"Do they let you go all over the house?"

"Miss Flint said I might go up and bring down the birds."

"What birds?"

"Her birds. I am going to hang them in the sun, and then they'll sing beautifully."

She ran off, and soon came back again with a cage in her hand, containing the little monias, sent by Willie from Calcutta.

"There, Kitty," cried Belle; "I think those are the birds that wake us up so early every morning with their noise."

"Very likely," said Kitty; "bring them here, will you, Fanny? I want to see them.—Goodness!" continued she, "what little creatures they are!—do look at them, Mr. Bruce,—they are sweet and pretty."

"Put them down on the door-step, Fanny," said Ben, "so that we can see them better."

"I'm afraid you'll frighten them," replied Fanny; "Miss Gertrude does n't like to have them frightened."

"No, we won't," said Ben; "we are disposed to be very friendly to Miss Gertrude's birds. Where did she get them,—do you know, Fanny?"

"Why, they are India birds; Mr. Sullivan sent them to her."

"Who is he?"

"O, he is a very particular friend; she has letters from him every little while."

"What Mr. Sullivan?" asked Belle. "Do you know his Christian name?"

"I suppose it's William," said Fanny. "Miss Emily always calls the birds little Willies."

"Belle!" exclaimed Kitty, "that's your William Sullivan!"

"What a favored man he seems to be!" said Mr. Bruce, in a tone of sarcasm; "the property of one beautiful lady, and the particular friend of another."

"I don't know what you mean, Kitty," said Belle, tartly. "Mr. Sullivan is a junior partner of my father's, but I have not seen him for years."

"Except in your dreams, Belle," suggested Kitty. "You forget."

Belle now looked angry.

"Do you dream about Mr. Sullivan?" asked Fanny, fixing her eyes on Belle as she spoke. "I mean to go and ask Miss Gertrude if she does."

"Do," said Kitty; "I'll go with you."

They ran across the entry, opened the door into the dining-room, and both put the question to her at the same moment.

Taken thus by surprise, Gertrude neither blushed nor looked confused, but answered, quietly, "Yes, sometimes, but what do you, either of you, know of Mr. Sullivan;—why do you ask?"

"O, nothing," answered Kitty; "only *some others do,* and we are inquiring round to see how many there are;" and she shut the door and ran back in triumph, to tell Belle she might as well be frank, like Gertrude, and plead guilty to the weakness; it looked so much better than blushing and denying it.

But it would not do to joke with Belle any longer; she was seriously offended, and took no pains to conceal the fact. Mr. Bruce felt awkward and annoyed, and soon went away, leaving the two cousins to settle their difficulty as they best could. As soon as he had gone, Belle folded up her work, and walked up stairs to her room with great dignity, while Kitty staid behind to laugh over the matter, and improve her opportunity to make friends with Fanny Bruce; for Kitty was not a little interested in the brother, and labored under the common, but often mistaken idea, that in cultivating the acquaintance of the sister she should advance her cause. Perhaps she was somewhat induced to this step by her having observed that Gertrude appeared to be an equal favorite with both.

She therefore called Fanny to sit beside her, put her arm round her waist, and commenced talking about Gertrude, and the origin and extent of the intimacy which seemed to exist between her and the Bruce family.

Fanny, who was always communicative, willingly informed her of the circumstances which had attached her so strongly to a friend who was some years her senior.

"And your brother," said Kitty; "he has known her some time, has n't he?"

"Yes, indeed, I suppose so," answered Fanny, carelessly.

"Does he like her?"

"I don't know; I should think he would; I don't see how he can help it."

"What did he whisper to you, when you came up the steps?"

Fanny could not remember at once; but, on being reminded of the answer she had given, she replied, promptly,

"O, he bade me ask Miss Gertrude if she wasn't coming back to see him again, and tell her he was tired to death waiting for her."

Kitty pouted and looked vexed. "I want to know," said she, "if Miss Flint has been in the habit of receiving company here, and being treated like an equal?"

"Of course she has," answered Fanny, with spirit; "why shouldn't she? She's the most perfect lady I ever saw, and mother says she has beautiful manners, and I must take pattern by her."

"O! Miss Gertrude," called she, as Gertrude, who had been to place the strawberries in the refrigerator, crossed the back part of the long entry, "are you ready now?"

"Yes, Fanny, I shall be in a moment," answered Gertrude.

"Ready for what?" inquired Kitty.

"To read," said Fanny. "She is going to read the rest of Hamlet to Miss Emily; she read the first three acts yesterday, and Miss Emily let me sit in her room and hear it. I can't understand it, when I read it myself; but when I listen to Miss Gertrude it seems quite plain. She's a splendid reader, and I came in to-day on purpose to hear the play finished."

Kitty's last companion having deserted her, she stretched herself on the entry sofa and fell asleep. She was wakened by her aunt, who returned from the city a short time before dinner, and, finding her asleep in her morning wrapper, shook her by the arm, and said, in a voice which the best intentions could never render otherwise than loud and coarse, "Kitty Ray, wake up and go dress for dinner! I saw Belle at the chamber-window, looking like a beauty. I wish you'd take half the pains she does to improve your appearance."

Kitty yawned, and, after delaying as long as she chose, finally followed Mrs. Graham's directions. It was Kitty's policy, after giving offence to her cousin Belle, to appear utterly unconscious of the existence of any unkind feelings; and, though Belle often manifested some degree of sulkiness, she was too dependent upon Kitty's society to retain that disposition long. They were soon, therefore, chatting together as usual.

"Belle," said Kitty, as she stood arranging her hair at the glass, "do you remember a girl we used to meet every morning, on our way to school, walking with a paralytic old man?"

"Yes."

"Do you know, I think it was Gertrude Flint. She has altered very much, to be sure; but the features are still the same, and there certainly never was but one such pair of eyes."

"I have no doubt she is the same person" said Belle, composedly.

"Did you think of it before?"

"Yes, as soon as Fanny spoke of her knowing Willie Sullivan."

"Why, Belle, did n't you speak of it?"

"Lor', Kitty, I don't feel so much interest in her as you and some others do."

"What others?"

It was now Belle's turn to be provoking.

"Why, Mr. Bruce; don't you see he is half in love with her?"

"No, I don't see any such thing; he has known her for a long time (Fanny says so), and, of course, he feels a regard and respect for a girl that the Grahams make so much account of. But I don't believe he'd think of such a thing as being in love with a poor girl like her, with no family connections to boast of."

"Perhaps he did n't *think* of being."

"Well, he *would n't* be. She is n't the sort of person that would suit him. He has been in society a great deal, not only at home, but in Paris; and he would want a wife that was very lively and fond of company, and knew how to make a show with money."

"A girl, for instance, like Kitty Ray."

"How ridiculous, Belle! just as if people could n't talk without thinking of themselves all the time! What do I care about Ben Bruce?"

"I don't know that you care anything about him; but I would n't pull all the hair out of my head about it, as you seem to be doing. There's the dinner-bell, and you'll be late, as usual."

CHAPTER XXVIII

She hath a natural, wise sincerity,
A simple truthfulness, and these have lent her
A dignity as moveless as the centre.
—*Lowell*

TWILIGHT OF THIS same day found Gertrude and Emily seated at a window which commanded a delightful western view. Gertrude had been describing to her blind friend the gorgeous picture presented to her vision by the masses of rich and brilliantly-painted cloud; and Emily, as she listened to the glowing description of nature, as she unfolded herself at an hour which they both preferred to all others, experienced a participation in Gertrude's enjoyment. The glory had now faded away, save a long strip of gold which skirted the horizon; and the stars, as they came out, one by one, seemed to look in at the chamber-window with a smile of recognition.

In the parlor below there was company from the city, and the sound of mirth and laughter came up on the evening breeze; so mellowed, however, by distance, that it contrasted with the peace of the quiet room, without disturbing it.

"You had better go down, Gertrude," said Emily; "they appear to be enjoying themselves, and I love to hear your laugh mingling with the rest."

"O, no, dear Emily!" said Gertrude; "I prefer to stay with you; they are nearly all strangers to me."

"As you please, my dear; but don't let me keep you from the young people."

"You can never keep me with you, dear Emily, longer than I wish to stay; there is no society I love so well." And so she staid, and they resumed their pleasant conversation, which, though harmonious and calm, was not without its playfulness and occasional gleams of wit.

They were interrupted by Katy, whom Mrs. Graham sent to announce a new visitor,—Mrs. Bruce,—who had inquired for Emily.

"I suppose I must go down," said Emily; "you'll come too, Gertrude?"

"No, I believe not, unless she asked for me. Did she, Katy?"

"Mrs. Graham was only afther mintioning Miss Emily," said Katy.

"Then I will stay here," said Gertrude; and Emily, finding it to be her wish, went without her.

There was soon another loud ring at the door-bell. It seemed to be a reception evening, and this time Gertrude's presence was particularly requested, to see Dr. and Mrs. Jeremy.

When she entered the parlor, she found a great number of guests assembled, and every seat in the room occupied. As she came in alone, and unexpected by the greater part of the company, all eyes were turned upon her. Contrary to the expectation of Belle and Kitty, who were watching her with curiosity, she manifested neither embarrassment nor awkwardness; but, glancing leisurely at the various groups, until she recognized Mrs. Jeremy, crossed the large saloon with characteristic grace, and as much ease and self-possession as if she were the only person present. After greeting that lady with her usual warmth and cordiality, she turned to speak to the doctor; but he was sitting next Fanny Bruce in the window-seat, and was half concealed by the curtain. Before he could rise and come forward, Mrs. Bruce nodded pleasantly from the opposite corner, and Gertrude went to shake hands with her; Mr. Bruce, who formed one in a gay circle of young ladies and gentlemen collected in that part of the room, and who had been observing Gertrude's motions so attentively as to make no reply to a question put to him by Kitty Ray, now rose and offered his chair, saying, "Miss Gertrude, do take this seat."

"Thank you," said Gertrude, "but I see my friend the doctor, on the other side of the room; he expects me to come and speak to him,—so don't let me disturb you."

Dr. Jeremy now came half-way across the room to meet her, and, taking her by both hands, led her into the recess formed by the window, and placed her in his own seat, next to Fanny Bruce. To the astonishment of all who knew him, Ben Bruce brought his own chair and placed it for the doctor opposite to Gertrude. So much respect for age had not been anticipated from the modern-bred man of fashion.

"Is that a daughter of Mr. Graham?" asked a young lady of Belle Clinton, who sat next her.

"No, indeed," replied Belle; "she is a person to whom Miss Graham gave an education, and now she lives here to read to her, and be a sort of companion; her name is Flint."

"What did you say that young lady's name was?" asked a dashing lieutenant, leaning forward and addressing Isabel.

"Miss Flint."

"Flint, ah! she's a genteel-looking girl. How peculiarly she dresses her hair!"

"Very becoming, however, to that style of face," remarked the young lady who had first spoken. "Don't you think so?"

"I don't know," replied the lieutenant; "something becomes her; she makes a fine appearance. Bruce," said he, as Mr. Bruce returned, after his unusual effort at politeness, "who is that Miss Flint?—I have been here two or three times, and I never saw her before."

"Very likely," said Mr. Bruce; "she won't always show herself. Isn't she a fine-looking girl?"

"I haven't made up my mind yet; she's got a splendid figure, but who is she?"

"She's a sort of adopted daughter of Mr. Graham's, I believe; a protegée of Miss Emily's?"

"Ah! poor thing! An orphan?"

"Yes, I suppose so," said Ben, biting his lip.

"Pity!" said the young man; "poor thing! but, as you say, Ben, she's good-looking, particularly when she smiles; there is something very attractive about her face."

There certainly was to Ben, for, a moment after, Kitty Ray missed him from the room, and immediately espied him standing on the piazza, and leaning through the open window to talk with Gertrude, Dr. Jeremy and Fanny. The conversation soon became very lively; there seemed to be a war of wits going on; the doctor, especially, laughed very loud, and Gertrude and Fanny often joined in the merry peal. Kitty endured it as long as she could, and then ran boldly across to join the party, and hear what they were having so much fun about.

But it was all an enigma to Kitty. Dr. Jeremy was talking with Mr. Bruce concerning something which had happened many years ago; there was a great deal about a fool's cap, with a long tassel, and taking afternoon naps in the grass; the doctor was making queer allusions to some old pear-tree, and traps set for thieves, and kept reminding Gertrude of circumstances which attended their first acquaintance with each other and with Mr. Bruce.

Kitty was beginning to feel that, as she was uninitiated in all they were talking about, she had placed herself in the position of an intruder, and was thereupon looking a little embarrassed and ill at ease, when Gertrude touched her arm, and, kindly making room for her next herself, motioned to her to sit down, saying, as she did so, "Dr. Jeremy is speaking of the time when he (or he and *I,* as he chooses to have it) went fruit-stealing in Mrs. Bruce's orchard, and were unexpectedly discovered by Mr. Bruce."

"You mean, my dear," interrupted the doctor, "that Mr. Bruce was discovered by us. Why, it's my opinion he would have slept until this time if I had n't given him such a thorough waking up!"

"My first acquaintance with you was certainly the greatest awakening of my life," said Ben, speaking as if to the doctor, but looking meaningly at Gertrude; "that was not the only nap it cost me. How sorry I am, Miss Gertrude, that you've given up working in the garden, as you used to! Pray, how does it happen?"

"Mrs. Graham has had it remodelled," replied Gertrude, "and the new gardener neither needs nor desires my services. He has his own plans, and it is not well to interfere with the professor of an art; I should be sure to do mischief."

"I doubt whether his success compares with yours," said Ben. "I do not see anything like the same quality of flowers in the room that *you* used to have."

"I don't think," said Gertrude, "that he is as fond of cutting them as I was. I did not care so much for the appearance of the garden as for having plenty of flowers in the house; but with him it is the reverse."

Kitty now addressed some remark to Mr. Bruce on the subject of gardening, and Gertrude, turning to Dr. Jeremy, continued in earnest conversation with him, until Mrs. Jeremy rose to go, when, approaching the window, she said, "Dr. Jerry, have you given Gertrude her letter?"

"Goodness me!" exclaimed the doctor, "I came near forgetting it." Then, feeling in his pocket, he drew forth an evidently foreign document, the envelope literally covered with various-colored post-office stamps. "See here, Gerty, genuine Calcutta; no mistake!"

Gertrude took the letter, and, as she thanked the doctor, her countenance expressed pleasure at receiving it; a pleasure, however, somewhat tempered by sadness, for she had heard from Willie but once since he learned the news of his mother's death, and that letter had been such an outpouring of his vehement grief that the sight of his hand-writing almost pained her, as she anticipated something like a repetition of the outburst.

Mr. Bruce, who kept his eyes upon her, and half expected to see her change color, and look disconcerted, on the letter being handed to her in the presence of so many witnesses, was reassured by the composure with which she took it, and held it openly in her hand while she bade the doctor and his wife good-evening. She followed them to the door, and was then retreating to her own apartment, when she was met at the foot of the stairs by Mr. Bruce, who had noticed the movement, and now entered from the piazza in time to arrest her steps, and ask if her letter was of such importance that she must deny the company the pleasure of her society in order to study its contents.

"It is from a friend of whose welfare I am anxious to hear," said Gertrude, gravely. "Please excuse me to your mother, if she inquires for me; and, as the rest of the guests are strangers, I shall not be missed by them."

"O, Miss Gertrude," said Mr. Bruce, "it's no use coming here to see you, you are so frequently invisible. What part of the day is one most likely to find you disengaged?"

"Hardly any part," said Gertrude. "I am always a very busy character; but good-night, Mr. Bruce,—don't let me detain you from the other young ladies;" and Gertrude ran up stairs, leaving Mr. Bruce uncertain whether to be vexed with himself or her.

Contrary to Gerty's expectations, her letter from William Sullivan proved very soothing to the grief she had felt on his account. His spirit had been so weighed down and crushed by the intelligence of the death of his grandfather, and finally of his second and still greater loss, that his first communication to Gertrude had alarmed her, from the discouraged, disheartened tone in which it was written; she had feared lest his Christian fortitude would give way to the force of this double affliction.

She was, therefore, much relieved to find that he now wrote in a calmer strain; that he had taken to heart his mother's last entreaty and prayer for a submissive disposition on his part; and that, although deeply afflicted, he was schooling himself to patience and resignation. But he did not, in this letter, dwell long upon his own sufferings under bereavement.

The three closely-written pages were almost wholly devoted to fervent and earnest expressions of gratitude to Gertrude for the active kindness and love which had cheered and comforted the last days of his much-regretted friends. He prayed that Heaven would bless her, and reward her disinterested and self-denying efforts, and closed with saying, "You are all there is left to me, Gertrude. If I loved you before, my heart is now bound to you by ties stronger than those of earth; my hopes, my labors, my prayers, all are for you. God grant we may some day meet again!"

For an hour after she had finished reading, Gertrude sat lost in meditation; her thoughts went back to her home at Uncle True's, and the days when she and Willie passed so many happy hours in close companionship, little dreaming of the long separation so soon to ensue. She rehearsed, in her mind, all the succeeding events which had brought her into her present position, and was only startled at last from the revery she was indulging in by the voices of Mrs. Graham's visitors, who were now taking leave.

Mrs. Bruce and her son lingered a little, until the carriages had driven off with those of the guests who were to return to the city, and, as they were making their farewells on the door-step, directly beneath Gertrude's window, she heard Mrs. Graham say, "Remember, Mr. Bruce, we dine at two; and, Miss Fanny, we shall hope to see you also. I presume you will join the walking party."

This, then, was an arrangement which was to bring Mr. Bruce there to dinner, at no very distant period; and Gertrude's reflections, forsaking the past, began to centre upon the present.

Mr. Bruce's attentions to her had that day been marked; and the professions of admiration he had contrived to whisper in her ear had been still more so. Both these attentions and this admiration were unsought and undesired; neither were they in any degree flattering to the high-minded girl, who was superior to coquetry, and whose self-respect was even wounded by the confident and assured manner in which Mr. Bruce made his advances. As a youth of seventeen, she had marked him as indolent and ill-bred. Her sense of justice, however, would have obliterated this recollection, had his character and manners appeared changed on the renewal of their acquaintance, some years after. This was not the case, however, for the outward polish, bestowed by fashion and familiarity with society, could not cloud Gertrude's discernment; and she quickly perceived that his old characteristics still remained, heightened and rendered more glaring by an ill-concealed vanity. As a boy, he had stared at Gertrude from impudence, and inquired her name out of idle curiosity; as a youthful coxcomb, he had resolved to flirt with her, because his time hung heavy on his hands, and he could think of nothing better to do. But, to his surprise, he found the country girl (for such he considered her, never having seen her elsewhere) was quite insensible to the flattery and notice which many a city belle had coveted; appeared wholly indifferent to his admiration; and that when he tried raillery he usually proved the disconcerted party. If he sought her, as he was frequently in the habit of doing, when she was at work among the flowers, he found it impossible to distract her attention from her labors, or detain her after they were completed; if he joined her in her walks, and, with his wonted self-conceit, made her aware of the honor he supposed himself conferring, she either maintained a dignity which warded off his fulsome adulation, or, if he ventured to make her the object of direct compliment, received it as a jest, and retorted with a playfulness and wit which often left the opaque wits of poor Ben in some doubt whether he had not been making himself ridiculous; and this, not because Gertrude was willing to wound the feelings of one who was disposed to admire her, but because she perceived that he was far from being sincere, and she had an honorable pride which would not endure to be trifled with.

It was something new to Mr. Bruce to find any lady thus indifferent to his merits; and proved such an awakening to his ambition, that he resolved, if possible, to recommend himself to Gertrude, and consequently improved every opportunity of gaining admittance to her society.

While laboring, however, to inspire her with a due appreciation of himself, he fell into his own snare; for, though he failed in awakening Gertrude's interest, he could not be equally insensible to her attractions. Even the comparatively dull intellect of Ben Bruce was capable of measuring her vast superiority to most girls of her age; and her vivacious originality was a contrast to the insipidity of fashionable life, which at length completely charmed him.

His earnestness and perseverance began to annoy the object of his admiration before she left Mr. Graham's in the autumn, and she was glad soon after to hear that he had accompanied his mother to Washington, as it insured her against meeting him again for months to come.

Mr. Bruce regretted losing sight of Gertrude, but amid the gayety and dissipation of southern cities contrived to waste his time with tolerable satisfaction. He was reminded of her again on meeting the Graham party at New Orleans, and it is some credit to his understanding to say, that in the comparison which he constantly drew between her and the vain daughters of fashion she stood higher than ever in his estimation. He did not hesitate to tell her so on the morning already mentioned, when, with evident satisfaction, he had recognized her and joined her; and the increased devotion of his words and manner, which now took a tone of truth in which they had before been wanting, alarmed Gertrude, and led to a serious resolve on her part to avoid him on all possible occasions. It will soon be seen how difficult she found it to carry out this resolution.

On the day succeeding the one of which we have been speaking, Mr. Graham returned from the city about noon, and, joining the young ladies in the entry, unfolded his newspaper, and, handing it to Kitty, asked her to read the news.

"What shall I read?" said Kitty, taking the paper rather unwillingly.

"The leading article, if you please."

Kitty turned the paper inside and out, looked hastily up and down its pages, and then declared her inability to find it. Mr. Graham stared at her in astonishment, then pointed in silence to the wished-for paragraph. She began, but had scarcely read a sentence before Mr. Graham stopped her, saying, impatiently, "Don't read so fast,—I can't hear a single word!" She now fell into the other extreme, and drawled so intolerably that her auditor interrupted her again, and bade her give the paper to her cousin.

Belle took it from the pouting Kitty, and finished the article,—not, however, without being once or twice compelled to go back and read more intelligibly.

"Do you wish to hear anything more, sir?" asked she.

"Yes; won't you turn to the ship-news, and read me the list by the steamer."

Belle, more fortunate than Kitty, found the place, and commenced. "'At Canton, April 30th, ship Ann Maria, Ray, d-i-s-c-g.'—What does that mean?"

"Discharging, of course; go on."

"'S-l-d—a-b-t 13th,'" spelt Belle, looking dreadfully puzzled all the while.

"Stupid!" muttered Mr. Graham, almost snatching the newspaper out of her hands; "not to know how to read ship-news! Where's Gertrude? Where's Gertrude Flint? She's the only girl I ever saw that did know anything. Won't you speak to her, Kitty?"

Kitty went, though rather reluctantly, to call Gertrude, and told her for what she was wanted. Gertrude was astonished; since the day when she had persisted in leaving his house, Mr. Graham had never asked her to read to him; but, obedient to the summons, she presented herself, and, taking the seat which Belle had vacated near the door, commenced with the ship-news, and, without asking any questions, turned to various items of intelligence, taking them in the order which she knew Mr. Graham preferred.

The old gentleman, leaning back in his easy-chair, and resting his gouty foot upon an ottoman opposite to him, looked amazingly contented and satisfied; and when Belle and Kitty had gone off to their room, he remarked, "This seems like old times, does n't it, Gertrude?" He now closed his eyes, and Gertrude was soon made aware, by his deep breathing, that he had fallen asleep.

Seeing that, as he sat, it would be impossible for her to pass without waking him, she laid down the paper, and was preparing to draw some work from her pocket (for Gertrude seldom spent her time in idleness), when she observed a shadow in the doorway, and, looking up, saw the very person whom she had yesterday resolved to avoid.

Mr. Bruce was staring her in the face, with an indolent air of ease and confidence, which she always found very offensive. He had in one hand a bunch of roses, which he held up to her admiring gaze.

"Very beautiful!" said Gertrude, as she glanced at the little branches, covered with a luxurious growth of moss-rose buds, both pink and white.

She spoke in a low voice, fearing to awaken Mr. Graham. Mr. Bruce, therefore, softening his to a whisper, remarked, as he dangled them above her head, "I thought they were pretty when I gathered them, but they suffer from the comparison, Miss Gertrude;" and he gave a meaning look at the roses in her cheeks.

Gertrude, to whom this was a stale compliment, coming from Mr. Bruce, took no notice of it, but, rising, advanced to make her exit by the front-door, saying, "I will go across the piazza, Mr. Bruce, and send the ladies word that you are here."

"O, pray, don't!" said he, putting himself in her way. "It would be cruel; I have n't the slightest wish to see them."

He so effectually prevented her, that she was unwillingly compelled to retreat from the door and resume her seat. As she did so, she took her work from her pocket, her countenance in the mean time expressing vexation.

Mr. Bruce looked his triumph, and took advantage of it.

"Miss Gertrude," said he, "will you oblige me by wearing these flowers in your hair to-day?"

"I do not wear gay flowers," replied Gertrude, without lifting her eyes from the piece of muslin on which she was employed.

Supposing this to be on account of her mourning (for she wore a plain black dress), he selected the white buds from the rest, and, presenting them to her, begged that, for his sake, she would display them in contrast with her dark silken braids.

"I am much obliged to you," said Gertrude; "I never saw more beautiful roses, but I am not accustomed to be so much dressed, and believe you must excuse me."

"Then you won't take the flowers?"

"Certainly I will, with pleasure," said she, rising, "if you will let me get a glass of water, and place them in the parlor, where we can all enjoy them."

"I did not cut my flowers, and bring them here, for the benefit of the whole household," said Ben, in a half-offended tone. "If you won't wear them, Miss Gertrude, I will offer them to somebody that will."

This, he thought, would alarm her, for his vanity was such that he attributed her behavior wholly to coquetry, and, as instances of this sort had always served to enhance his admiration, he believed that they were intended to produce that effect. "I will punish her," thought he, as he tied the roses together again, and arranged them for presentation to Kitty, whom he knew would be flattered to receive them.

"Where's Fanny to-day?" asked Gertrude, anxious to divert the conversation.

"I don't know," answered Ben, with a manner which implied that he had no idea of talking about Fanny.

A short silence ensued, during which he gazed idly at Gertrude's fingers, as she sat sewing.

"How attentive you are to your work!" said he, at last; "your eyes seem nailed to it. I wish I were as attractive as that piece of muslin!"

"I wish you were as inoffensive," thought Gertrude.

"I do not think you take much pains to entertain me," added he, "when I've come here on purpose to see you."

"I thought you came by Mrs. Graham's invitation," said Gertrude.

"And did n't I have to court Kitty for a hour in order to get it?"

"If you obtained it by artifice," said Gertrude, smiling, "you do not deserve to be entertained."

"It is much easier to please Kitty than you," remarked Ben.

"Kitty is very amiable and pleasant," said Gertrude.

"Yes, but I'd give more for one smile from you than—"

Gertrude now interrupted him with, "Ah! here is an old friend coming to see us; please let me pass, Mr. Bruce."

The gate at the end of the yard swung to as she spoke, and Ben, looking in that direction, beheld approaching the person whom Gertrude seemed desirous to go and meet.

"Don't be in such a hurry to leave me!" said Ben; "that little crone, whose coming seems to give you so much satisfaction, can't get here this half-hour, at the rate she is travelling."

"She is an old friend," replied Gertrude; "I must go and welcome her." Her countenance expressed so much earnestness that Mr. Bruce was ashamed to persist in his incivility, and, rising, permitted her to pass. Miss Patty Pace—for she it was who was toiling up the yard—seemed overjoyed at seeing Gertrude, and, the moment she recognized her, commenced waving in a theatrical manner, a huge feather fan, her favorite mode of salutation. As she drew near, Miss Patty took her by both hands, and stood talking with her some minutes before they proceeded together up the yard. They entered the house at the side-door, and Ben, being thus disappointed of Gertrude's return, sallied out into the garden, in hopes to attract the notice of Kitty.

Ben Bruce had such confidence in the power of wealth and a high station in fashionable life, that it never occurred to him to doubt that Gertrude would gladly accept his hand and fortune, if it were placed at her disposal. No degree of coldness, or even neglect, on her part, would have induced him to believe that an orphan girl, without a cent in the world, would forego such an opportunity to establish herself.

Many a prudent and worldly-wise mother had sought his acquaintance; many a young lady, even among those who possessed property and rank of their own, had received his attention with favor; and believing, as he did, that he had money enough to purchase for a wife any woman whom he chose to select, he would have laughed at the idea that Gertrude would presume to hold herself higher than the rest.

He had not made his mind up to such an important step, however, as the deliberate surrender of the many advantages of which he was the fortunate possessor. He had merely determined to win Gertrude's good opinion and affection; and, although more interested in her than he was aware of himself, he at present made that his ultimate object. He felt conscious that as yet she had given no evidence of his success; and, having resolved to resort to some new means of winning her, he, with a too common selfishness and baseness, fixed upon a method which was calculated, if successful, to end in the mortification, if not the unhappiness, of a third party. He intended, by marked devotion to Kitty Ray, to excite the jealousy of Gertrude; and it was with the view to furthering his intentions that he walked in the garden, hoping to attract her observation.

O! it was a shameful scheme! for Kitty liked him already. She was a warm-hearted girl,—a credulous one too, and likely to become a ready victim to his duplicity.

CHAPTER XXIX

Is this the world of which we want a sight?
Are these the beings who are called polite?
—*Hannah More*

A HALF-HOUR BEFORE dinner, Mrs. Graham and her nieces, Mr. Bruce, his sister Fanny, and Lieutenant Osborne, as they sat in the large parlor, had their curiosity much excited by the merriment which seemed to exist in Emily's room, directly above. It was not noisy or rude, but strikingly genuine. Gertrude's clear laugh was very distinguishable, and even Emily joined frequently in the outburst which would every now and then occur; while still another person appeared to be of the party, as a strange and most singular voice occasionally mingled with the rest.

Kitty ran to the entry two or three times, to listen, and hear, if possible, the subject of their mirth, and at last returned with the announcement that Gertrude was coming down stairs with the very queen of witches.

Presently Gertrude opened the door, which Kitty had slammed behind her, and ushered in Miss Patty Pace, who advanced with measured, mincing steps to Mrs. Graham, and, stopping in front of her, made a low curtsey.

"How do you do, ma'am?" said Mrs. Graham, half inclined to believe that Gertrude was playing off a joke upon her.

"This, I presume, is the mistress," said Miss Patty.

Mrs. Graham acknowledged her claim to that title.

"A lady of presence!" said Miss Patty to Gertrude, in an audible whisper, pronouncing each syllable with a manner and emphasis peculiar to herself. Then, turning towards Belle, who was shrinking into the shadow of a curtain, she approached her, held up both hands in astonishment, and exclaimed, "Miss Isabella, as I still enjoy existence! and radiant, too, as the morning! Bless my heart! how your youthful charms have expanded!"

Belle had recognized Miss Pace the moment she entered the room, but, with foolish pride, was ashamed to acknowledge the acquaintance of so eccentric an individual, and would have still feigned ignorance, but Kitty now came forward, exclaiming, "Why, Miss Pace, where did you come from?"

"Miss Catharina," said Miss Pace, taking her hands in an ecstasy of astonishment, "*then you knew me!* Blessings on your memory of an old friend!"

"Certainly, I knew you in a minute; you're not so easily forgotten, I assure you. Belle, don't you remember Miss Pace? It's at your house I've always seen her."

"O is it she?" said Belle, with a poor attempt to conceal the fact that she had any previous knowledge of a person who had been a frequent visitor at her father's house, and was held in esteem by both her parents.

"I apprehend," said Miss Patty to Kitty, in the same loud whisper, "that she carries a proud heart."—Then, without having appeared to notice the gentlemen, who were directly behind her, she added, "Sparks, I see, Miss Catharina, young sparks! Whose?—yours, or hers?"

Kitty laughed, for she saw that the young men heard her and were much amused, and replied, without hesitation, "O, mine, Miss Patty, mine, both of 'em!" Miss Patty now looked round the room, and, missing Mr. Graham, advanced to his wife, saying, "And where, madam, is the bridegroom?"

Mrs. Graham, a litle confused, replied that her husband would be in presently, and invited Miss Pace to be seated.

"No, mistress, I am obliged to you; I have an inquiring mind, and, with your leave, will take a survey of the apartment. I love to see everything that is modern." She then proceeded to examine the pictures upon the walls, but had not proceeded far before she turned to Gertrude and asked, still loud enough to be distinctly heard, "Gertrude, my dear, what have they done with the second wife?" Gertrude looked surprised, and Miss Pace corrected her remark, saying, "O, it is the counterfeit that I have reference to; the original, I am aware, departed long since but where is the counterfeit of the second Mistress Graham? It always hung here, if my memory serves me."

Gertrude whispered a reply to this question, and Miss Pace then

uttered the following soliloquy: "The garret! well, 't is the course of nature; what is new obliterates *the recollection, even,* of the old."

She now linked her arm in Gertrude's, and made her the companion
of her survey. When they had completed the circuit of the room, she
stopped in front of the group of young people, all of whom were eying her
with great amusement, claimed acquaintance with Mr. Bruce, and asked to
be introduced to the member of the war department, as she styled Lieutenant Osborne. Kitty introduced her with great formality, and at the same
time presented the lieutenant to Gertrude, a ceremony which she felt
indignant that her aunt had not thought proper to perform. A chair was
now brought, Miss Patty joined their circle, and entertained them until
dinner-time. Gertrude again sought Emily's room.

At the table, Gertrude, seated next to Emily, whose wants she always
made her care, and with Miss Patty on the other side, had no time or
attention to bestow on any one else; much to the chagrin of Mr. Bruce,
who was anxious she should observe his assiduous devotion to Kitty,
whose hair was adorned with moss-rose buds and her face with smiles.

Belle was also made happy by the marked admiration of her young
officer, and no one felt any disposition to interfere with either of the well-
satisfied girls. Occasionally, however, some remark made by Miss Pace
irresistibly attracted the attention of every one at the table, and extorted
either the laughter it was intended to excite, or a mirth which, though
perhaps ill-timed, it was impossible to repress.

Mr. Graham treated Miss Patty with the most marked politeness and
attention, and Mrs. Graham, who was possessed of great suavity of manners when she chose to exercise it, and who loved dearly to be amused,
spared no pains to bring out the old lady's conversational powers. She
found, too, that Miss Patty was acquainted with everybody, and made
most appropriate and amusing comments upon almost every person who
became the topic of conversation. Mr. Graham at last led her to speak of
herself and her lonely mode of life; and Fanny Bruce, who sat next, asked
her, bluntly, why she never got married.

"Ah, my young miss," she said, "we all wait our time, and I may take
a companion yet."

"You should," said Mr. Graham. "Now you have property, Miss
Pace, and ought to share it with some nice, thrifty man." Mr. Graham
knew her weak point.

"I have but an insignificant trifle of worldly wealth," said Miss Pace, "and am not as youthful as I have been; but I may suit myself with a companion, notwithstanding. I approve of matrimony, and have my eye upon a young man."

"A *young man!*" exclaimed Fanny Bruce, laughing.

"O, yes, Miss Frances," said Miss Patty; "I am an admirer of youth, and of everything that is modern. Yes, I cling to life—I cling to life."

"Certainly," remarked Mrs. Graham, "Miss Pace must marry somebody younger than herself; some one to whom she can leave all her property, if he should happen to outlive her."

"Yes," said Mr. Graham; "at present you would not know how to make a will, unless you left all your money to Gertrude, here; I rather think *she* would make a good use of it."

"That would certainly be a consideration to me," said Miss Pace; "I should dread the thought of having my little savings squandered. Now, I know there's more than a sufficiency of pauper population, and plenty that would be glad of legacies; but I have no intention of bestowing on such. Why, sir, nine-tenths of them will *always* be poor. No, no! I shouldn't give to such! No, no! I have other intentions."

"Miss Pace," asked Mr. Graham, "what has become of Gen. Pace's family?"

"*All dead!*" replied Miss Patty, promptly, "*all dead!* I made a pilgrimage to the grave of that branch of the family. It was a melancholy and touching scene," continued she, in a pathetic tone of voice. "There was a piece of grassy ground, belted about with an iron railing, and in the centre a beautiful white-marble monument, *in which* they were all buried; it was pure as alabaster, and on it was inscribed these lines:

'PACE'"[1]

"What were the lines?" inquired Mrs. Graham, who believed her ears had deceived her.

"Pace, ma'am, Pace; nothing else."

Solemn as was the subject, a universal titter pervaded the circle; and Mrs. Graham, perceiving that Kitty and Fanny would soon burst into uncontrollable fits of laughter, made the move for the company to quit the table.

The gentlemen did not care to linger, and followed the ladies into the wide entry, the refreshing coolness of which invited every one to loiter there during the heat of the day. Miss Patty and Fanny Bruce compelled the unwilling Gertrude to join the group there assembled; and Mrs.

Graham, who was never disposed to forego her afternoon nap, was the only member of the family who absented herself.

So universal was the interest Miss Patty excited, that all private dialogue was suspended, and close attention given to whatever topic the old lady was discussing.

Belle maintained a slightly scornful expression of countenance, and tried, with partial success, to divert Lieutenant Osborne's thoughts into another channel; but Kitty was so delighted with Miss Pace's originality, that she made no attempt at any exclusive conversation, and, with Mr. Bruce sitting beside her and joining in her amusement, looked more than contented.

Dress and fashion, two favorite themes with Miss Patty, were now introduced, and, after discoursing at some length upon her love of the beautiful, as witnessed in the mantua-making and millinery arts, she deliberately left her seat, and going towards Belle (the only one of the company who seemed desirous to avoid her), began to examine the material of her dress, and finally requested her to rise and permit her to further inspect the mode in which it was made, declaring the description of so modern and finished a master-piece of art would be a feast to the ears of some of her junior acquaintances.

Belle indignantly refused to comply, and shook off the hand of the old lady as if there had been contamination in her touch.

"Do stand up, Belle," said Kitty, in an under tone; "don't be so cross."

"Why don't you stand up yourself," said Belle, "and show off your own dress, for the benefit of her low associates?"

"She didn't ask me to," replied Kitty, "but I will, with the greatest pleasure, if she will condescend to look at it. Miss Pace," continued she, gayly, placing herself in front of the inquisitive Miss Patty, "do admire my gown at your leisure, and take a pattern of it, if you like; I should be proud of the honor."

For a wonder, Kitty's dress was pretty and well worthy of observation. Miss Patty made many comments, especially on the train, as she denominated its unnecessary and inconvenient length; and then, her curiosity being satisfied, commenced retreating towards the place she had left, first glancing behind her to see if it was still vacant, and then moving towards it with a backward motion, consisting of a series of curtseys.

Fanny Bruce, who stood near, observing that she had made an exact calculation how many steps would be required to reach her seat, placed her hand on the back of the chair, as if to draw it away; and, encouraged by a look and smile from Isabel, moved it, slightly, but still enough to endanger the old lady's safety.

On attempting to regain it, Miss Pace stumbled, and would have fallen, but Gertrude—who had been watching Fanny's proceedings—sprang foward in time to fling an arm around her, and place her safely in the chair, casting at the same time a reproachful look at Fanny; who, much confused, turned to avoid Gertrude's gaze, and in doing so accidentally trod on Mr. Graham's gouty toes, which drew from him an exclamation of pain.

"Fan," said Mr. Bruce, who had observed the latter accident only, "I wish you could learn politeness."

"Who am I to learn it from?" asked Fanny, pertly,—"you?"

Ben looked provoked, but forbore to reply; while Miss Pace, who had now recovered her composure, took up the word and said,

"Politeness! Ah, a lovely, but rare virtue; perceptibly developed, however, in the manners of my friend Gertrude, which I hesitate not to affirm would well become a princess."

Belle curled her lip, and smiled disdainfully. "Lieutenant Osborne," said she, "don't you think Miss Devereux has beautiful manners?"

"Very fine," replied the lieutenant; "the style in which she receives company, on her reception-day, is elegance itself."

"Who are you speaking of?" inquired Kitty; "Mrs. Harry Noble?"

"Miss Devereux, we were remarking upon," said Belle, "but Mrs. Noble is also very stylish."

"I think she is," said Mr. Bruce; "do you hear, Fanny?—we have found a model for you,—you must imitate Mrs. Noble."

"I don't know anything about Mrs. Noble," retorted Fanny; "I'd rather imitate Miss Flint. Miss Gertrude," said she, with a seriousness which Gertrude rightly believed was intended to express regret for her late rudeness, "how *shall I* learn politeness?"

"Do you remember," asked Gertrude, speaking low, and giving Fanny a look full of meaning, "what your music-master told you about learning to *play* with expression? I should give you the same rule for improvement in politeness."

Fanny blushed deeply.

"What is that?" said Mr. Graham; "let us know, Fanny, what is *Gertrude's* rule for politeness."

"She only said," answered Fanny, "that it was the same my music-master gave me last winter."

"And what did *he* say?" inquired her brother, with a tone of interest.

"I asked Mr. Hermann," said Fanny, "how I should learn to play with expression, and he said, 'You must cultivate your *heart* Miss Bruce; you must cultivate your *heart.*'"

This new direction for the attainment of a great accomplishment was received with countenances that indicated as great a variety of sentiment as there was difference of character among Fanny's audience. Mr. Graham bit his lip, and walked away, for *his* politeness was founded on no such rule, and he knew that Gertrude's *was.* Belle looked glorious disdain; Mr. Bruce and Kitty, puzzled and half amused; while Lieutenant Osborne proved himself not quite callous to a noble truth, by turning upon Gertrude a glance of admiration and interest. Emily's face evidenced how fully she coincided in the opinion thus unintentionally made public, and Miss Patty unhesitatingly expressed her approbation.

"Miss Gertrude's remark is undeniably a verity," said she. "The only politeness which is trustworthy is the spontaneous offering of the heart. Perhaps this goodly company of masters and misses would condescend to give ear to an old woman's tale of a rare instance of true politeness, and the fitting reward it met."

All professed a strong desire to hear Miss Patty's story, and she began:

"On a winter's day, some years ago, an old woman of many foibles and besetting weaknesses, but with a keen eye and her share of worldly wisdom,—Miss Patty Pace by name,—started by special invitation for the house of one worshipful Squire Clinton, the honored parent of Miss Isabella, the fair damsel yonder. Every tall tree in our good city was spangled with frost-work, more glittering far than gems that sparkle in Golconda's mine, and the side-walks were a snare to the feet of the old and the unwary.

"I lost my equilibrium, and fell. Two gallant gentlemen lifted and carried me to a neighboring apothecary's emporium, restored my scattered wits, and revived me with a fragrant cordial. I went on my way with many a misgiving, however, and scarcely should I have reached my destination with bones unbroken, had it not been for a knight with a rosy countenance, who overtook me, placed my old arm within his own more strong and youthful one, and protected my steps to the very end of my journey. No slight courage either, my young misses, did my noble escort need, to carry him through what he had undertaken. Paint to your imaginations a youth fresh and beautiful as a sunbeam, straight as an arrow,—a perfect Apollo, indeed,—linked to the little bent body of poor Miss Patty Pace. I will not spare myself, young ladies; for, had you seen me then, you would consider me now vastly ameliorated in outward presentment. My double row of teeth were stowed away in my pocket, my frisette was pushed back from my head by my recent fall, and my gogs—the same my father wore before me—covered my face, and they alone attracted attention, and created some excitement. But he went on unmoved; and, in spite of many a captivating glance and smile from long rows of beautiful young maidens whom we met, and many a sneer from the youths of his own age, he sustained my feeble form with as much care as if I had been an empress, and accommodated his buoyant step to the slow movement which my infirmities compelled. Ah! what a spirit of conformity he manifested!— my knight of the rosy countenance!—Could you have seen him, Miss Catharina, or you, Miss Frances, your palpitating hearts would have taken flight forever. He was a paragon, indeed.

"Whither his own way tended I cannot say, for he moved in conformity to mine, and left me not until I was safe at the abode of Mistress Clinton. I hardly think he coveted my old heart, but I sometimes believe it followed him; for truly he is still a frequent subject of my meditations."

"Ah! then *that* was his reward!" exclaimed Kitty.

"Not so, Miss Kitty; guess again."

"I can think of *nothing so desirable,* Miss Patty."

"His *fortune in life,* Miss Catharina,—that was his reward; it may be that he cannot yet estimate the full amount of his recompense."

"How so?" exclaimed Fanny.

"I will briefly narrate the rest. Mistress Clinton encouraged me always to converse much in her presence. She knew my taste, was disposed to humor me, and I was pleased to be indulged. I told my story, and enlarged upon the merits of my noble youth, and his wonderful spirit of conformity. The squire, a gentleman who estimates good breeding, was present, with his ears open; and when I recommended my knight with all the eloquence I could command, he was amused, interested, pleased. He promised to see the boy, and did so; the noble features spake for themselves, and gained him a situation as clerk, from which he has since advanced in the ranks, until now he occupies the position of partner and confidential agent in a creditable and wealthy house. Miss Isbella, it would rejoice my heart to hear the latest tidings from Mr. William Sullivan."

"He is well, I believe," said Isabella, sulkily. "I know nothing to the contrary."

"O, Gertrude knows," said Fanny. "Gertrude knows all about Mr. Sullivan; she will tell you."

All turned, and looked at Gertrude, who, with face flushed, and eyes glistening with the interest she felt in Miss Patty's narrative, stood leaning upon Emily's chair. Miss Patty now appealed to her, much surprised, however, at her having any knowledge of her much-admired and well-remembered young escort. Gertrude drew near, and answered all her questions without the least hesitation or embarrassment, but in a tone of voice so low that the others, most of whom felt no interest in Willie, entered into conversation, and left her and Miss Patty to discourse freely concerning a mutual friend.

Gertrude gave Miss Pace a brief account of the wonder and curiosity which Willie and his friends had felt concerning the original author of his good fortune; and the old lady was so entertained and delighted at hearing of the various conjectures and doubts which arose on the reception of Mr. Clinton's unexpected summons, and of the matter being finally attributed to the agency of Santa Claus, that her laugh was nearly as loud, and quite as heart-felt, as that of the gay party near the door-step, whom Kitty and Fanny had excited to unusual merriment. Miss Pace was just taxing Gertrude with interminable compliments and messages of remembrance to be despatched in her next letter to Willie, when Mrs. Graham presented herself, refreshed both in dress and countenance since her nap, and arrested the attention of the whole company, by exclaiming, in her abrupt manner and loud tones,

"What! are you all here still? I thought you were bound for a walk in the woods. Kitty, what has become of your cherished scheme of climbing Sunset Hill?"

"I proposed it, aunt, an hour ago, but Belle insisted it was too warm. *I* think the weather is just right for a walk."

"It will soon be growing cool," said Mrs. Graham, "and I think you had better start; it is some distance if you go round through the woods."

"Who knows the way?" asked Kitty.

No one responded to the question, and, on being individually appealed to, all professed total ignorance; much to the astonishment of Gertrude, who believed that every part of the woody ground and hill beyond were familiar to Mr. Bruce. She did not stay, however, to hear any further discussion of their plans; for Emily was beginning to suffer from headache and weariness, and Gertrude, perceiving it, insisted that she should seek the quiet of her own room, to which she herself accompanied her. She was just closing the chamber-door, when Fanny called from the staircase, "Miss Gertrude, an't you going to walk with us?"

"No," replied Gertrude, "not to-day."

"Then I won't go," said Fanny, "If you don't. Why don't you go, Miss Gertrude?"

"I shall walk with Miss Emily, by and by, if she is well enough; you can accompany us, if you like, but I think you would enjoy going to Sunset Hill much more."

Meantime a whispered consultation took place below, in which some one suggested that Gertrude was well acquainted with the path which the party wished to follow through the woods. Belle opposed her being invited to join them; Kitty hesitated between her liking for Gertrude and her fears regarding Mr. Bruce's allegiance; Lieutenant Osborne forbore to urge what Belle disapproved; and Mr. Bruce remained silent, trusting to the final necessity of her being invited to act as guide, in which capacity he had purposely concealed his own ability to serve. This necessity was so obvious, that, as he had foreseen, Kitty was at last despatched to find Gertrude and make known their request.

CHAPTER XXX

There are haughty steps that would walk the globe
O'er necks of humbler ones.
—*Miss L. P. Smith*

GERTRUDE WOULD HAVE declined, and made her attendance upon Emily an excuse for non-compliance; but Emily herself, believing that the exercise would be beneficial to Gertrude, interfered, and begged her to agree to Kitty's apparently very cordial proposal; and, on the latter's declaring that the expedition must otherwise be given up, she consented to join it. To change her slippers for thick walking-boots occupied a few minutes only; a few more were spent in a vain search for her flat hat, which was missing from the closet where it usually hung.

"What are you looking for?" said Emily, hearing Gertrude once or twice open and shut the door of the large closet at the end of the upper entry.

"My hat; but I don't see it. I believe I shall have to borrow your sun-bonnet again," and she took up a white sun-bonnet, the same she had worn in the morning, and which now lay on the bed.

"Certainly, my dear," said Emily.

"I shall begin to think it's mine, before long," said Gertrude, gayly, as she ran off; "I wear it so much more than you do." She found Fanny waiting for her; the rest of the party had started, and were some distance down the road, nearly out of sight. Emily now called from the staircase, "Gertrude, my child, have you thick shoes? It is always very wet in the meadow beyond the Thornton place." Gertrude assured her that she had; but, fearing that the others were less carefully equipped, inquired of Mrs. Graham whether Belle and Kitty were insured against the dampness, possibly the mud, they might encounter.

Mrs. Graham declared they were not, and was at a loss what to do, as they were now quite out of sight, and it would be so much trouble for them to return.

"I have some very light India-rubbers," said Gertrude, "I will take them with me, and Fanny and I shall be in time to warn them before they come to the place."

It was an easy matter to overtake Belle and the lieutenant, for they walked very slowly, and seemed not unwilling to be left in the rear. The reverse, however, was the case with Mr. Bruce and Kitty, who appeared purposely to keep in advance; Kitty hastening her steps from her reluctance to allow an agreeable tête-a-tête to be interfered with, and Ben from a desire to occupy such a position as would give Gertrude a fair opportunity to observe his devotion to Kitty, which increased the moment *she* came in sight whose jealousy he was desirous to arouse.

They had now passed the Thornton farm, and only one field separated them from the meadow, which, covered with grass, and fair to the eye, was nevertheless in the centre a complete quagmire, and only passable, even for the thickly shod, by keeping close to the wall, and thus skirting the field. Gertrude and Fanny were some distance behind, and already nearly out of breath with a pursuit in which the others had gained so great an advantage. As they were passing the farm-house, Mrs. Thornton appeared at the door and addressed Gertrude, who, foreseeing that she should be detained some minutes, bade Fanny run on, acquaint her brother and Kitty with the nature of the soil in advance, and beg them to wait at the bars until the rest of the party came up. Fanny was too late, notwithstanding the haste she made; they were half across the meadow when she reached the bars, proceeding, however, in perfect safety, for Mr. Bruce was conducting Kitty by the only practicable path, close under the wall, proving to Gertrude, who in a few moments joined Fanny, that he was no stranger to the place. When they were about half-way across, they seemed to encounter some obstacle, for Kitty stood poised on one foot and clinging to the wall, while Mr. Bruce placed a few stepping-stones across the path. He then helped her over, and they went on, their figures soon disappearing in the grove beyond.

Isabel and the lieutenant were so long making their appearance that Fanny became very impatient, and urged Gertrude to leave them to their fate. They at last turned the corner near the farm-house, and came on, Belle maintaining her leisurely pace, although it was easy to be seen that the others were waiting for her.

"Are you lame, Miss Clinton?" called out Fanny, as soon as they were within hearing.

"Lame!" said Belle; "what do you mean?"

"Why, you walk so slow," said Fanny, "I thought something must be the matter with your feet."

Belle disdained any reply to this, and, tossing her head, entered the damp meadow, in close conversation with her devoted young officer, not deigning even to look at Gertrude, who, without appearing to notice her haughtiness, took Fanny's hand, and, turning away from the direct path, to make the circuit of the field, said to Belle, with an unruffled ease and courtesy of manner, "This way, if you please, Miss Clinton; we have been waiting to guide you through this wet meadow."

"Is it wet?" asked Belle, in alarm, glancing down at her delicate slipper; she then added, in a provoked tone, "I should have thought you would have known better than to bring us this way. I shan't go across."

"Then you can go back," said the pert Fanny; "nobody cares."

"It was not my proposition," remarked Gertrude, mildly, though with a heightened color, "but I think I can help you through the difficulty. Mrs. Graham was afraid you had worn thin shoes, and I brought you a pair of India-rubbers."

Belle took them, and, without the grace to express any thanks, said, as she unfolded the paper in which they were wrapped, "Whose are they?"

"Mine," replied Gertrude.

"I don't believe I can keep them on," muttered Belle; "they'll be immense, I suppose."

"Allow me," said the lieutenant; and, taking one of the shoes, he stooped to place it on her foot, but found it difficult to do so, as it proved quite too small. Belle, perceiving this to be the case, bent down to perform the office for herself, and treated Gertrude's property with such angry violence that she snapped the slender strap which passed across the instep, and even then only succeeded in partially forcing her foot into the shoe.

Meantime, as she bent forward, Fanny's attention was attracted by a very tasteful broad-brimmed hat, which she wore jauntily set on one side of her head, and which Fanny at once recognized as Gertrude's. It was a somewhat fanciful article of dress, that Gertrude would hardly have thought of purchasing for herself, but which Mr. Graham had selected and brought home to her the previous summer, to replace a common garden hat which he had accidentally crushed and ruined. As the style of it was simple and in good taste, she had been in the habit of wearing it often in her country walks, and usually kept it hung in the entry closet, where it had been found and appropriated by Belle. It had been seen by Fanny in Gertrude's room at Mrs. Warren's; she had also been permitted to wear it on one occasion, when she took part in a charade, and could not be mistaken as to its identity. Having heard Gertrude remark to Emily upon its being missing, she was astonished to see it adorning Belle; and, as she stood behind her, deliberately pointed, made signs to Gertrude, opened her eyes, distorted her countenance, and performed a series of pantomimic gestures expressive of an intention to snatch it from Miss Clinton's head, and place it on that of its rightful owner.

Gertrude's gravity nearly gave way; she shook her head at Fanny, held up her finger, made signs for her to forbear, and, with a face whose laughter was only concealed by the deep white bonnet which she wore, took her hand, and hastened with her along the path, leaving Belle and beau to follow.

"Fanny," said she, "you must not make me laugh so; if Miss Clinton had seen us, she would have been very much hurt."

"She has no business to wear your hat," said Fanny, "and she shan't!"

"Yes, she shall," replied Gertrude; "she looks beautifully in it. I am delighted to have her wear it, and you must not intimate to her that it is mine."

Fanny would not promise, and there was a sly look in her eye which prophesied mischief.

The walk through the woods was delightful, and Gertrude and her young companion, in the quiet enjoyment of it, had almost forgotten that they were members of a gay party, when they suddenly came in sight of Kitty and Mr. Bruce. They were sitting at the foot of an old oak, Kitty earnestly engaged in the manufacture of an oak-wreath, which she was just fitting to her attendant's hat; while he himself, when Gertrude first caught sight of him, was leaning against the tree in a careless, listless attitude. As soon, however, as he perceived their approach, he bent forward, inspected Kitty's work; and, when they came within hearing, was uttering a profusion of thanks and compliments, which he took care should reach Gertrude's ears, and which the blushing, smiling Kitty received with manifest plea-sure,—a pleasure which was still further enhanced by her perceiving that Gertrude had apparently no power to withdraw his attention from her, but that, on the contrary, he permitted her rival to seat herself at a distance, and continued to pour into her own ear little confidential nothings. Poor, simple Kitty! she believed him honest, while he bought her heart with counterfeits.

"Miss Gertrude," said Fanny, "I wish we could go into some pine woods, so that I could get some cones to make baskets and frames of."

"There are plenty of pines in that direction," said Gertrude, pointing with her finger.

"Why can't we go and look for cones?" asked Fanny; "we could get back by the time Belle Clinton reaches this place."

Gertrude professed her willingness to do so, and she and Fanny started off, having first tied their bonnets to the branch of a tree. They were gone some time, for Fanny found plenty of cones, and made a large collection of them, but was then at a loss how to carry them home. "I have thought," said she, at last; "I will run back and borrow brother Ben's handkerchief or, if he won't let me have it, I'll take my own bonnet and fill it full." Gertrude promised to await her return, and she ran off. When she came near the spot where she had left Kitty and Mr. Bruce, she heard several voices and loud laughter. Belle and the lieutenant had arrived, and they were having great sport about something. Belle was standing with the white cape-bonnet in her hand. She had bent it completely out of shape, so as to give it the appearance of an old woman's cap, had adorned the front with white-weed and dandelions, and finally pinned on a handkerchief to serve as a veil. It certainly looked very ridiculous;—she was holding it up on the end of the lieutenant's cane, and endeavoring to obtain a bid for Miss Flint's bridal bonnet.

Fanny listened a moment with an indignant countenance, then advanced with a bound, as if just running from the woods. Kitty caught her frock as she passed, and exclaimed, "Why, Fanny, are you here? Where's Gertrude?"

"O, she's in the pine woods!" replied Fanny, "and I'm going right back; she only sent me to get her hat, the sun's so warm where we are."

"Ah, yes!" said Belle, "her Paris hat. Please give it to her, with our compliments."

"No, that isn't hers," said Fanny; "*that* is Miss Emily's. *This* is hers;" and she laid her hand upon the straw head-dress which the gentlemen had but a moment before been assuring Belle was vastly becoming, and, without ceremony, snatched it from her head.

Belle's eyes flashed angrily. "What do you mean?" said she, "you saucy little creature! Give me that hat," and she stretched out her hand to take it.

"I shan't do any such thing," said Fanny; "it's Gertrude's hat. She looked for it this afternoon, but concluded it was either lost or stolen, and so borrowed Miss Emily's cape-bonnet; but she'll be very glad to find it, and I'll carry it to her. I rather think," said she, looking over her shoulder, as she ran off, "I rather think Miss Emily would be willing you should wear her bonnet home, if you'll be careful and not bend it!"

A few moments of embarrassment and anger to Belle, laughter from Kitty and Mr. Bruce, and concealed amusement on Lieutenant Osborne's part, and Gertrude came hastily from the woods, with the hat in her hand, Fanny following her, and taking advantage of Belle's position, with her back towards her, to resume her pantomimic threats and insinuations. "Miss Clinton," said Gertrude, as she placed the hat in her lap, "I am afraid Fanny has been very rude in my name. I did not send her for either hat or bonnet, and shall be pleased to have you wear this as often as you like."

"I don't want it," said Belle, scornfully; "I'd no idea it belonged to you."

"Certainly not; I am aware of it," said Gertrude. "But I trust that will not prevent your making use of it for to-day, at least." Without urging the matter further, she proposed that they should hasten on to the top of the hill, which they could not otherwise reach before sundown; and set the example by moving forward in that direction, Fanny accompanying her, and busying herself as she went with stripping the decorations from Emily's despised bonnet; Belle tying an embroidered handkerchief under her chin, and Mr. Bruce swinging on his arm the otherwise neglected hat.

Belle did not recover her temper for the evening; the rest found their excursion agreeable, and it was nearly dark when they reached the Thornton farm on their return. Here Gertrude left them, telling Fanny that she had promised to stop and see Jemmy Thornton, one of her Sunday-school class, who was sick with a fever, and refusing to let her remain, as her mother might not wish her to enter the house where several of the family were sick.

About an hour after, as Gertrude was walking home in some haste, she was joined near Mr. Graham's house by Mr. Bruce, who, with her hat still hanging on his arm, seemed to have been awaiting her return. She started on his abruptly joining her, for it was so dark that she did not at once recognize him, and supposed it might be a stranger.

"Miss Gertrude," said he, "I hope I don't alarm you."

"O, no," said she, reassured by the sound of his voice, "I did not know who it was."

He offered his arm, and she took it; for his recent devotion to Kitty had served in some degree to relieve her of any fear she had felt lest his attentions carried meaning with them; and, concluding that he liked to play beau-general, she had no objection to his escorting her home.

"We had a very pleasant walk, this evening," said he; "at least, I had. Miss Kitty is a very entertaining companion."

"I think she is," replied Gertrude; "I like her frank, lively manners much."

"I am afraid you found Fanny rather poor company. I should have joined you occasionally, but I could hardly find an opportunity to quit Miss Kitty, we were so much interested in what we were saying."

"Fanny and I are accustomed to each other, and very happy together," said Gertrude.

"Do you know we have planned a delightful drive for to-morrow?"

"No, I was not aware of it."

"I suppose Miss Ray expects I shall ask her to go with me; but supposing, Miss Gertrude, I should give you the preference, and ask you,—what should you say?"

"That I was much obliged to you, but had an engagement to take a drive with Miss Emily," replied Gertrude, promptly.

"Indeed!" said he, in a surprised and provoked tone, "I thought you would like it; but Miss Kitty, I doubt not, will accept. I will go in and ask her (for they had now reached the house). Here is your hat."

"Thank you," said Gertrude, and would have taken it; but Ben still held it by one string, and said,

"Then you won't go, Miss Gertrude?"

"My engagement with Miss Emily cannot be postponed on any account," answered Gertrude, thankful that she had so excellent a reason for declining.

"Nonsense!" said Mr. Bruce; "you could go with me if you chose; and, if you don't, I shall certainly invite Miss Kitty."

The weight he seemed to attach to this threat astonished Gertrude. "Can it be possible," thought she, "that he expects thus to pique and annoy me?" and she replied to it by saying, "I shall be happy if my declining prove the means of Kitty's enjoying a pleasant drive; she is fond of variety, and has few opportunities here to indulge her taste."

They now entered the parlor. Mr. Bruce sought Kitty in the recess of the window, and Gertrude, not finding Emily present, staid but a short time in the room; long enough, however, to observe Mr. Bruce's exaggerated devotion to Kitty, which was marked by others beside herself. Kitty promised to accompany him the next day, and did so. Mrs. Graham, Mrs. Bruce, Belle and the lieutenant, went also in another vehicle; and Emily and Gertrude, according to their original intention, took a different direction, and, driving white Charlie in the old-fashioned buggy, rejoiced in their quiet independence.

CHAPTER XXXI

Sporting at will, and moulding sport to art,
With that sad holiness—the human heart.
—*New Timon*

AND NOW DAYS and even weeks passed on, and no marked event took place in Mr. Graham's household. The weather became intensely warm, and no more walks and drives were planned. The lieutenant left the neighboring city, which was at this season nearly deserted by the friends of Mrs. Graham and her nieces; and Isabel, who could neither endure with patience excessive heat or want of society, grew more irritable and fretful than ever.

To Kitty, however, these summer-days were fraught with interest. Mr. Bruce remained in the neighborhood, visited constantly at the house, and exercised a marked influence upon her outward demeanor and her inward happiness, which were changeable and fluctuating as his attentions were freely bestowed or altogether suspended. No wonder the poor girl was puzzled to understand one whose conduct was certainly inexplicable to any but those initiated into his motives. Believing, as he did, that Gertrude would in time show a disposition to win him back, he was anxious only to carry his addresses to Kitty to such a point as would excite a serious alarm in the mind of the poor protegée of the Grahams, who dared to slight his proffered advances. Acting then as he did almost wholly with reference to Gertrude, it was only in her presence, or under such circumstances that he was sure it would reach her ears, that he manifested a marked interest in Kitty; and his behavior was, therefore, in the highest degree unequal, leading the warm-hearted Kitty to believe one moment that he felt for her almost the tenderness of a lover, and the next to suffer under the apprehension of having unconsciously wounded or offended him by her careless gayety or conversation. Unfortunately, too, Mrs. Graham took every opportunity to tease and congratulate her upon her conquest, thereby increasing the simple girl's confidence in the sincerity of Mr. Bruce's admiration.

Nor were Mr. Bruce and Kitty the only persons who found occasion for vexation and anxiety in this matter. Gertrude, whose eyes were soon opened to the existing state of things, was filled with regret and apprehension on account of Kitty, for whose peace and welfare she felt a tender and affectionate concern. The suspicions to which Mr. Bruce's conduct gave rise, during the scenes which have been detailed, were soon strengthened into convictions; for, on several occasions, after he had been offering Kitty ostentatious proofs of devotion, he thought proper to test their effect upon Gertrude by the tender of some attention to herself; more than intimating, at the same time, that she had it in her power to rob Kitty of all claim upon his favor.

Gertrude availed herself of every opportunity to acquaint him with the truth, that he could not possibly render himself more odious in her eyes than by the use of such mean attempts to mortify her; but, attributing her warmth to the very feeling of jealousy which he desired to excite, the selfish young man persevered in his course of folly and wickedness. As he only proffered his attentions, and made no offer of his heart and hand, Gertrude did not in the least trust his professions towards *herself,* considering them merely as intended, if possible, to move her from her firm and consistent course of behavior, in order to gratify his self-love. But she saw plainly that, however light and vain his motives might be in her own case, they were still more so with reference to Kitty; and she was deeply grieved at the evident unconsciousness of this fact which the simple girl constantly exhibited.

For, strangely enough, Kitty, having quite forgotten that she had a few weeks back looked upon Gertrude as a rival, now chose her for her bosom friend and confidant. Her aunt was too coarse and rough, Belle too selfish and vain, to be intrusted with little matters of the heart; and, though Kitty had no idea of confessing her partiality for Mr. Bruce, the transparency of her character was such, that she betrayed her secret to Gertrude without being in the least aware that she had done so. Though no one but Gertrude appeared to observe it, Kitty was wonderfully changed;—the gay, laughing, careless Kitty had now her fits of musing,— her sunny face was subject to clouds, that flitted across it, and robbed it of all its brightness. Now, her spirits were unnaturally free and lively; and now, she wore a pensive expression, and, stealthily lifting her eyes, fixed them anxiously on the face of Mr. Bruce, as if studying his temper or his sentiments. If she saw Gertrude walking in the garden, or sitting alone in her room, she would approach, throw her arm around her, lean against her shoulder, and talk on her favorite topic. She would relate, with a mixture of simplicity and folly, the complimentary speeches and polite attentions of Mr. Bruce; talk about him for an hour, and question Gertrude as to her opinion of his merits, and the sincerity of his avowed admiration for herself. She would intimate her perception of some fault possessed by him, who was in her eyes almost perfection; and when Gertrude coincided with her, and expressed regret at the evident failing, she would exhaust a great amount of strength and ingenuity in her efforts to prove that they were both mistaken in attributing it to him, and that, if he had a fault, it was in reality quite the reverse. She would ask if Gertrude really supposed he meant all he said, and add that of course *she* didn't believe he did,—it was all nonsense. And if Gertrude embraced the opportunity to avow the same opinion, and declare that it was not best to trust all his high-flown flatteries, poor Kitty's face would fall, and she would proceed to give her reasons for *sometimes* thinking he was sincere, he had such a *truthful, earnest* way of speaking.

It was no use to throw out hints, or try to establish safeguards. Kitty was completely infatuated. At last Mr. Bruce thought proper to try

Gertrude's firmness by offering to her acceptance a rich ring. Not a little surprised at his presumption, she declined it without hesitation or ceremony, and the next day saw it on the finger of Kitty, who was eager to give an account of its presentation.

"And did you *accept* it?" asked Gertrude, with such a look of astonishment, that Kitty observed it, and evaded an acknowledgment of having done so, by saying, with a blushing countenance, that she agreed to wear it a little while.

"I wouldn't," said Gertrude.

"Why not?"

"Because, in the first place, I do not think it is in good taste to receive rich gifts from gentlemen; and then, again, if strangers notice it, you may be subjected to unpleasant, significant remarks."

"What would you do with it:" asked Kitty.

"I should give it back."

Kitty looked very undecided; but, on reflection, concluded to offer it to Mr. Bruce, and tell him what Gertrude said. She did so, and that gentleman, little appreciating Gertrude's motives, and believing her only desirous of making difficulty between him and Kitty, jumped at the conclusion that her heart was won at last, and that his triumph would now be complete. He was disappointed, therefore, when, on his next meeting with her, she treated him, as she had invariably done of late, with cool civility; indeed, it seemed to him that she was more insensible than ever to his attractions; and, hastily quitting the house, much to the distress of Kitty (who spent the rest of the day in thinking over everything she had done and said which could by any possibility have given offence), he sought his old haunt under the pear-tree, and gave himself up to the consideration of a weighty question.

Seldom did Ben Bruce feel called upon to take serious views of any subject; seldom was he accustomed to rally and marshal the powers of his mind, and deliberately weigh the two sides of an argument. Living, as he did, with no higher aim than the promoting of his own selfish gratification, he had been wont to avail himself of every opportunity for amusement and indulgence, and even to bring mean and petty artifice to the furtherance of his plans. Possessed, as he was, notwithstanding his narrow mind, with what is often called "a good look-out," he was rarely cheated or defrauded of his rights. He knew the value of his money and position in life, and never suffered himself to be sacrificed to the designs of those who hoped to reap a benefit from his companionship. *Self-sacrifice,* too, was a thing of which he had no experience, and with which, as seen in others, he felt no sympathy. Now, however, a crisis had arrived when his own interests and wishes clashed; when necessity demanded that one should be immolated at the shrine of the other, and a choice must be made between the two. It was certainly a matter which claimed deep deliberation; and if Ben Bruce, for the first time in his life, devoted a whole afternoon to careful thought, and an accurate measurement of opposing forces, the occurrence must be attributed to the fact that he was making up his mind on the most important question that ever yet had agitated it.

"Shall I," thought he, "conclude to marry this poor girl? Shall I, who am master of a handsome fortune, and have additional expectations, forego the prospect they afford me of making a brilliant alliance, and condescend to share my wealth and station in society with this adopted child of the Grahams; who, in spite of her poverty, will not grant me a smile even, except at the price of all my possessions? If she were one atom less charming, I would disappoint her, after all! I wonder how she'd feel if I should marry Kitty! I daresay I never should have the satisfaction of knowing; for she's so proud that she would come to my wedding, for aught I know, bend her slender neck as gracefully as ever, and say, '*Good-evening, Mr. Bruce,*' as politely and calmly as she does now, every time I go to the house! It provokes me to see how a poor girl like that carries herself. But, as *Mrs. Bruce,* I should be proud of that manner, certainly. I wonder how I ever got in love with her;—I'm sure I don't know. She isn't handsome; at least, mother thinks she isn't, and so does Belle Clinton. But, then again, Lieutenant Osborne noticed her the minute she came into the room; and there's Fan raves about her beauty. I don't know what I think myself; I believe she's bewitched me, so that I'm not capable of judging; but, if it isn't beauty, it is because it's something more than mere good looks."

Thus he soliloquized; and as, every time he revolved the subject, he commenced by dwelling upon the immense sacrifice he was making, and ended with reflections upon Gertrude's charms, it may well be supposed that he ultimately came to the conclusion that he should suffer less by laying his fortune at her feet than by the endeavor to enjoy that fortune without her. For a few days after he arrived at a resolve on this point, he had no opportunity to address a word to Gertrude, who was now doubly anxious to avoid him, and spent nearly the whole day above stairs, except when, at Emily's request, she accompanied her for a short time into the parlor; and even then she took pains, under some pretext or other, to remain close by the side of her blind friend.

About this time, Mrs. Graham and Mrs. Bruce, with their families, received cards for a levee to be held at the house of an acquaintance nearly five miles distant. It was on the occasion of the marriage of a schoolmate of Isabel's, and both she and Kitty were desirous to be present. Mrs. Bruce, who had a close carriage, invited both the cousins to accompany her; and, as Mr. Graham's carryall, when closed, would only accommodate himself and lady, the proposal was gladly acceded to.

The prospect of a gay assembly and an opportunity for display revived Isabel's drooping spirits and energy. Her rich evening dresses were brought out for the selection of the most suitable and becoming; and as she stood before her mirror, and tried on first one wreath and then another, and looked so beautiful in each that it was difficult to make a choice, Kitty, who stood by, eagerly endeavoring to win her attention, and obtain her advice concerning the style and color most desirable for herself, gave up in despair, and ran off to consult Gertrude.

She found her reading in her own room; but, on Kitty's abrupt entrance, she laid down her book, and gave her undivided attention to the subject which was under discussion.

"Gertrude," said Kitty, "what shall I wear this evening? I've been trying to get Belle to tell me, but she never will speak a word, or hear what I ask her, when she's thinking about her own dress!—I declare, she's dreadfully selfish!"

"Who advises *her?*" asked Gertrude.

"O, nobody; she always decides for herself; but then she has so much taste, and I haven't the least in the world!—So, do tell me, Gertrude, what had I better wear to-night."

"I'm the last person you should ask, Kitty; I never went to a fashionable party in my life."

"That doesn't make any difference. I'm sure, if you did go, you'd look better than any of us; and I'm not afraid to trust to your opinion, for I never in my life saw you wear anything that didn't look genteel;—even your gingham morning-gown has a sort of stylish air."

"Stop, stop, Kitty! you are going too far; you must keep within bounds, if you want me to believe you."

"Well, then," said Kitty, "to say nothing of yourself (for I know you 're superior to flattery, Gertrude,—*somebody* told me so), who furnishes Miss Emily's wardrobe? Who selects her dresses?"

"I have done so, lately, but—"

"I thought so! I thought so!" interrupted Kitty. "I knew poor Miss Emily was indebted to you for always looking so nice and so beautiful."

"No, indeed, Kitty, you are mistaken; I have never seen Emily better dressed than she was the first time I met her; and her beauty is not borrowed from art—it is all her own."

"O, I know she is lovely, and everybody admires her; but no one can suppose she would take pains to wear such pretty things, and put them on so gracefully, just to please herself."

"It is not done merely to please herself; it was to please her father that Emily first made the exertion to dress with taste as well as neatness. I have heard that, for some time after she lost her eye-sight, she was disposed to be very careless; but, having accidentally discovered that it was an additional cause of sorrow to him she roused herself at once, and, with Mrs. Ellis' assistance, contrived always afterwards to please him in that particular. But you observe, Kitty, she never wears anything showy or conspicuous."

"No, indeed,—that is what I like; but, Gertrude, hasn't she always been blind?"

"No; until she was sixteen she had beautiful eyes, and could see as well as you can."

"What happened to her? how did she lose them?"

"I don't know."

"Didn't you ever ask?"

"No."

"Why not?—how queer!"

"I heard that she didn't like to speak of it."

"But she would have told you; she half worships you."

"If she had wished me to know, she would have told without my asking."

Kitty stared at Gertrude, wondering much at such unusual delicacy and consideration, and instinctively admiring a forbearance of which she was conscious she should herself have been incapable.

"But, your dress!" said Gertrude, smiling at Kitty's abstraction.

"O, yes! I had almost forgotten what I came here for," said Kitty. "What shall it be, then,—thick or thin; pink, blue, or white?"

"What has Isabel decided upon?"

"Blue,—a rich blue silk; that is her favorite color, always; but it doesn't become me."

"No, I should think not," said Gertrude; "but come, Kitty, we will go to your room and see the dresses, and I will give my opinion."

Kitty's wardrobe having been inspected, and Gertrude having expressed her preference for a thin and flowing material, especially in the summer season, a delicate white crape was fixed upon. And now there was a new difficulty; among all her head-dresses, none proved satisfactory,—all were more or less defaced, and none of them to be compared with a new and exquisite wreath which Isabel was arranging among her curls.

"I cannot wear any of them," said Kitty, "they look so mean by the side of Isabel's; but O!" exclaimed she, glancing at a box which lay on the dressing-table, "these are just what I should like! O, Isabel, where did you get these beautiful carnations?" and she took up some flowers, which were, indeed, a rare imitation of nature, and, displaying them to Gertrude, added that they were just what she wanted.

"O, Kitty," said Isabel, angrily, turning away from the glass, and observing what her cousin had in her hand, "don't touch my flowers! you will spoil them!" and, snatching them from her, she replaced them in the box, opened a drawer in her bureau, and, having deposited them there, took the precaution to lock them up and put the key in her pocket,—an action which Gertrude witnessed with astonishment, not unmingled with indignation.

"Kitty," said she, "I will arrange a wreath of natural flowers for you, if you wish."

"Will you, Gertrude?" said the disappointed and provoked Kitty. "O, that will be delightful! I should like it, of all things! And, Isabel, you cross old miser, you can keep all your wreaths to yourself! It is a pity you can't wear two at a time!"

True to her promise, Gertrude prepared a head-dress for Kitty; and so tastefully did she mingle the choicest productions of the garden, that, when Isabel saw her cousin arrayed under a more careful and affectionate superintendence than she often enjoyed, she felt, notwithstanding her own proud consciousness of superior beauty, a sharp pang of jealousy of Kitty, and dislike to Gertrude.

It had been no small source of annoyance to Isabel, who could not endure to be outshone, that Kitty had of late been the object of marked attention to Mr. Bruce, while she herself had been entirely overlooked. Not that she felt any partiality for the gentleman whom Kitty was so anxious to please; but the dignity conferred on her cousin by his admiration, the interest the affair awakened in her aunt, and the meaning looks of

Mrs. Bruce, all made her feel herself of second-rate importance, and rendered her more eager than ever to supplant, in general society, the comparatively unpretending Kitty. Therefore, when Mrs. Graham complimented the latter on her unusually attractive appearance, and declared that *somebody* would this night be more charmed than ever, Isabel curled her lip with mingled disdain and defiance, while the blushing Kitty turned to Gertrude and whispered in her ear, "Mr. Bruce likes white; he said so, the other day, when you passed through the room dressed in your mulled muslin."

CHAPTER XXXII

Know, then, that I have supported my pretensions to your hand in the way that best suited my character.
——*Ivanhoe*

EMILY WAS NOT WELL this evening. It was often the case, lately, that headache, unwonted weariness, or a nervous shrinking from noise and excitement, sent her to her own room, and sometimes led her to seek her couch at an early hour. After Mrs. Graham and her nieces had gone down stairs to await Mr. Graham's pleasure and Mrs. Bruce's arrival, Gertrude returned to Emily, whom she had left only a short time before, and found her suffering more than usual from what she termed her troublesome head. She was easily induced to seek the only infallible cure—sleep; and Gertrude, seating herself on the bed-side, as she was frequently in the habit of doing, bathed her temples until she fell into a quiet slumber. The noise of Mrs. Bruce's carriage, coming and going, seemed to disturb her a little; but in a few moments more she was so sound asleep that, when Mr. and Mrs. Graham departed, the loud voice of the latter, giving her orders to one of the servants, did not startle her in the least. Gertrude sat some time longer without changing her position; then, quietly rising and arranging everything for the night, according to Emily's well-known wishes, she closed the door gently behind her, sought a book in her own room, and, entering the cool and vacant parlor, seated herself at a table, to enjoy the now rare opportunity for perfect stillness and repose.

Either her own thoughts, however, proved more interesting than the volume she held, or, it may be, the insects, attracted by the bright lamp, annoyed her; or, the beauty of the evening won her observation; for she soon forsook her seat at the table, and, going towards the open glass-doors, placed herself near them, and, leaning her head upon her hand, became absorbed in meditation.

She had not long sat thus when she heard a foot-step in the room, and, turning, saw Mr. Bruce beside her. She started, and exclaimed, "Mr. Bruce! is it possible? I thought you had gone to the wedding."

"No, there were greater attractions for me at home. Could you believe, Miss Gertrude, I should find any pleasure in a party which did not include yourself?"

"I certainly should not have the vanity to suppose the reverse," replied Gertrude.

"I wish you had a little more vanity, Miss Gertrude. Perhaps then you would sometimes believe what I say."

"I am glad you have the candor to acknowledge, Mr. Bruce, that, without that requisite, one would find it impossible to put faith in your fair speeches."

"I acknowledge no such thing. I only say to you what any other girl but yourself would be willing enough to believe; but how shall I convince you that I am serious, and wish to be so understood? How shall I persuade you to converse freely with me, and no longer shun my society?"

"By addressing me with simple truthfulness, and sparing me those words and attentions which I have endeavored to convince you are unacceptable to me and unworthy of yourself."

"But I have a meaning, Gertrude, a *deep* meaning. I have been trying for several days to find an opportunity to tell you of my resolve, and you *must* listen to me now;" for he saw her change color and look anxious and uneasy. "You must give me an answer at once, and one that will, I trust, be favorable to my wishes. You like plain speaking; and I will be plain enough, now that my mind is made up. My relatives and friends may talk and wonder as much as they please at my choosing a wife who has neither money nor family to boast of; but I have determined to defy them all, and offer, without hesitation, to share my prospects with you. After all, what is money good for, if it doesn't make a man independent to do as he pleases? And, as to the world, I don't see but you can hold your head as high as anybody, Gertrude; so, if you 've no objection to make, we'll play at cross purposes no longer, and consider the thing settled;" and he endeavored to take her hand.

But Gertrude drew back; the color flushed her cheeks, and her eyes glistened as she fixed them upon his face with an expression of astonishment and pride that could not be mistaken.

The calm, penetrating look of those dark eyes spoke volumes, and Mr. Bruce replied to their inquiring gaze in these words: "I hope you are not displeased at my frankness."

"With your frankness," said Gertrude, calmly; "no, that is a thing that never displeases me. But what have I unconsciously done to inspire you with so much confidence that, while you defend yourself for defying the wishes of your friends, you hardly give me a voice in the matter?"

"Nothing," said Bruce, in an apologizing tone; "but I thought you had labored under the impression that I was disposed to trifle with your affections, and had therefore kept aloof and maintained a distance towards me which you would not have done had you known how much I was in earnest; but, believe me, I only admired you the more for behaving with so much dignity, and if I have presumed upon your favor, you must forgive me. I shall be only too happy to receive a favorable answer from you."

The expression of wounded pride vanished from Gertrude's face. "He knows no better," thought she; "I should pity his vanity and ignorance, and sympathize in his disappointment;" and, in disclaiming, with a positiveness which left no room for further self-deception, any interest in Mr. Bruce beyond that of an old acquaintance and sincere well-wisher, she nevertheless softened her refusal by the choice of the mildest language, and terms the least likely to grieve or mortify him. She felt, as every true woman must under similar circumstances, that her gratitude and consideration were due to the man who, however little she might esteem *him*, had paid *her* the highest honor; and, though her regret in the matter was somewhat tempered by the thought of Kitty, and the strangeness of Mr. Bruce's conduct towards her, now rendered doubly inexplicable, she did not permit *that* reflection, even, to prevent her from maintaining the demeanor, not only of a perfect lady, but of one who, in giving pain to another, laments the necessity of so doing.

She almost felt, however, as if her thoughtfulness for his feelings had been thrown away, when she perceived the spirit in which he received her refusal.

"Gertrude," said he, "you are either trifling with me or yourself. If you are still disposed to coquet with me, I desire to have it understood that I shall not humble myself to urge you further; but if, on the other hand, you are so far forgetful of your own interests as deliberately to refuse such a fortune as mine, I think it's a pity you have n't got some friend to advise you. Such a chance doesn't occur every day, especially to poor school-mistresses; and if you are so foolish as to overlook it, I'll venture to say you'll never have another."

Gertrude's *old temper* rose at this insulting language, beat and throbbed in her chafed spirit, and even betrayed itself in the tips of her fingers, which trembled as they rested on the table near which she stood (having risen as Mr. Bruce spoke); but, though this was an unlooked-for and unwonted rebellion of an old enemy, her feelings had too long been under strict regulation to yield to the blast, however sudden, and she replied in a tone which, though slightly agitated, was far from being angry, "Allowing I could so far forget *myself,* Mr. Bruce, I would not do *you* such an injustice as to marry you for your fortune. I do not despise wealth, for I know the blessing it may often be; but my affections cannot be bought with gold;" and as she spoke she moved towards the door.

"Stay!" said Mr. Bruce, catching her hand; "listen to me one moment; let me ask you one question. Are you jealous of my late attentions to another?"

"No," answered Gertrude; "but I confess I have not understood your motives."

"Did you think," asked he, eagerly, "that I cared for that silly Kitty? Did you believe, for a moment, that I had any other desire than to show you that my devotion was acceptable elsewhere? No, upon my word, I never had the least particle of regard for her; my heart has been yours all the time, and I only danced attendance upon *her* in hopes to win a glance from *you,*—an *anxious* glance, if might be. O, how often I have wished that you would show one quarter of the pleasure that she did in my society; would blush and smile as she did; would look sad when I was dull, and laugh when I was merry; so that I might flatter myself, as I could in her case, that your heart was won! But, as to *loving* her,—pooh! Mrs. Graham's poodle-dog might as well try to rival you as that soft—"

"Stop! stop!" exclaimed Gertrude; "for *my* sake, if not for your *own!* O, how—" She could say no more, but, sinking into the nearest seat, burst into tears, and hiding her face in her hands, as had been her habit in childhood, wept without restraint.

Mr. Bruce stood by in utter amazement; at last he approached her, and asked, in a low voice, "What is the matter? what have I done?"

It was some minutes before she could reply to the question; then, lifting her head, and tossing the hair from her forehead, she displayed features expressive only of the deepest grief, and said, in broken accents, "What have you done? O, how can you ask? She is gentle, and amiable, and affectionate. She loves everybody, and trusts everybody. You have *deceived* her, and *I* was the cause of it! O, how, how could you do it!"

A most disconcerted appearance did Ben present at her words, and hesitating was the tone in which he muttered, "She will get over it."

"Get over *what?*" said Gertrude; "her love for you? Perhaps so; I know not how deep it is. But, think of her happy, trusting nature, and how it has been betrayed! Think how she believed your flattering words, and how hollow they were, all the while! Think how her confidence has been abused! how that fatherless and motherless girl, who had a claim to the sympathy of all the world, has been taught a lesson of distrust!"

"I didn't think you would take it so," said Ben.

"How else could I view it?" asked Gertrude. "Could you expect that such a course would win my respect?"

"You take it very seriously, Gertrude; such flirtations are common."

"I am sorry to hear it," said Gertrude. "To my mind, unversed in the ways of society, it is a dreadful thing to trifle thus with a human heart. Whether Kitty loves you, is not for me to say; but what opinion—alas!— will she have of your sincerity?"

"I think you're rather hard, Miss Gertrude, when it was my love for you that prompted my conduct."

"Perhaps I am," said Gertrude. "It is not my place to censure; I speak only from the impulse of my heart. One orphan girl's warm defence of another is but natural. Perhaps she views the thing lightly, and does not *need* an advocate; but, O, Mr. Bruce, do not think so meanly of my sex as to believe that one woman's heart can be won to love and reverence by the author of another's betrayal! She were less than woman who could be so false to her sense of right and honor."

"Betrayal!—Nonsense! you are very high-flown."

"So much so, Mr. Bruce, that half an hour ago I could have wept that you should have bestowed your affection where it met with no requital; and if now I weep for the sake of her whose ears have listened to false professions, and whose peace has, to say the least, been *threatened* on my account, you should attribute it to the fact that my sympathies have not been exhausted by contact with the world."

A short silence ensued. Ben went a step or two towards the door, then stopped, came back, and said, "After all, Gertrude Flint, I believe the time will come when your notions will grow less romantic, and you will look back to this night and wish you had acted differently. You will find out, in time, that this is a world where people must look out for themselves."

Immediately upon this remark he left the room, and Gertrude heard him shut the hall-door with a loud bang as he went out.

A moment after, the silence that ensued was disturbed by a slight sound, which seemed to proceed from the deep recess in the window. Gertrude started, and, as she went towards the spot, heard distinctly a smothered sob. She lifted a draperied curtain, and there, upon the wide window-seat, her head bent over and buried in the cushions, and her little slender form distorted into a strange and forlorn attitude,—such as might be seen in a grieved child,—sat, or rather crouched, poor Kitty Ray. The crumpled folds of her white crape dress, her withered wreath,—which had half fallen from her head, and hung drooping on her shoulders,—her disordered hair, and her little hand clinging to a thick cord connected with the window-curtain, all added to the appearance of extreme distress.

"Kitty!" cried Gertrude, at once recognizing her, although her face was hid.

At the sound of her voice, Kitty sprung suddenly from her recumbent posture, threw herself into Gertrude's arms, laid her head upon her shoulder, and, though she did not, *could* not weep, shook and trembled with an agitation which was perfectly uncontrollable. Her hand, which grasped Gertrude's, was fearfully cold; her eyes seemed fixed; and occasionally, at intervals, the same hysterical sound which had at first betrayed her in her hiding-place alarmed her young protector, to whom she clung as if seized with sudden fear. Gertrude supported her to a seat, and then, folding the slight form to her bosom, chafed the cold hands, and again and again kissing the rigid lips, succeeded at last in restoring her to something like composure. For an hour she lay thus, receiving Gertrude's caresses with evident pleasure, and now and then returning them convulsively, but speaking no word, and making no noise. Gertrude, with the truest judgment and delicacy, refrained from asking questions, or recurring to a conversation the whole of which had been thus overheard and comprehended; but, patiently waiting until Kitty grew more quiet and calm, prepared for her a soothing draught; and then, finding her completely prostrated, both in mind and body, passed her arm around her waist, guided her up stairs, and, without the ceremony of an invitation, took her into her own room, where, if she proved wakeful, she would be spared the wonder and scrutiny of Isabel. Still clinging to Gertrude, the poor girl, to whose relief tears came at last, sobbed herself to sleep; and all her sufferings were for a time forgotten in that oblivion in which childhood and youth find a temporary rest, and often a healing balm to pain.

It was otherwise, however, with Gertrude, who, though of nearly the same age as Kitty, had seen too much trouble, experienced too much care, to enjoy, in times of disquiet, the privilege of sinking easily to repose. She felt under the necessity, too, of remaining awake until Isabel's return, that she might inform her what had become of Kitty, whom she would be sure to miss from the room which they occupied in common. She seated herself, therefore, at the window, to watch for her return; and was pained to observe that Kitty tossed restlessly on her pillows, and occasionally muttered in her sleep, as if distressed by uneasy dreams. It was past midnight when Mrs. Graham and her niece returned home, and Gertrude went immediately to inform the latter that her cousin was asleep in her room. The noise of the carriages, however, had awakened the sleeper, and when Gertrude returned she was rubbing her eyes, and trying to collect her thoughts.

Suddenly the recollection of the scene of the evening flashed upon her, and, with a deep sigh, she exclaimed, "O, Gertrude! I have been dreaming of Mr. Bruce! Should you have thought he would have treated me so?"

"No, I should not," said Gertrude; "but I wouldn't dream about him, Kitty, nor think of him any more; we will both go to sleep and forget him."

"It is different with you," said Kitty, with simplicity. "He loves you, and you do not care for him; but I—I—" Here her feelings overpowered her, and she buried her face in the pillow.

Gertrude approached, laid her hand kindly upon the head of the poor girl, and finished the sentence for her. "You have such a large heart, Kitty, that he found some place there, perhaps; but it is too good a heart to be shared by the mean and base. You must think no more of him—he is not worthy of your regard."

"I can't help it," said Kitty; "I am silly, just as he said."

"No, you are not," said Gertrude, encouragingly; "and you must prove it to him."

"How?"

"Let him see that, with all her softness, Kitty Ray is strong and brave; that she has ceased to believe his flattery, and values his professions at just what they are worth."

"Will you help me, Gertrude? You are my best friend; you took my part, and told him how wicked he had been to me. May I come to you for comfort when I can't make believe happy any longer to him, and my aunt, and Isabel?"

Gertrude's fervent embrace was assurance enough of her cooperation and sympathy.

"You will be as bright and happy as ever in a few weeks," said she; "you will soon cease to care for a person whom you no longer respect."

Kitty disclaimed the possibility of ever being happy again; but Gertrude, though herself a novice in the ways of the human heart, was much more sanguine and hopeful. She saw that Kitty's violent outburst of sobs and tears was like a child's impetuous grief, and suspected that the deepest recesses of her nature were safe, and unendangered by the storm.

She felt a deep compassion for her, however, and many fears lest she would be wanting in sufficient strength of mind to behave with dignity and womanly pride in her future intercourse with Mr. Bruce, and would also expose herself to the ridicule of Isabel, and the contempt of her aunt, by betraying in her looks and behavior her recent trying and mortifying experience.

Fortunately, the first-mentioned trial was spared her, by Mr. Bruce's immediately absenting himself from the house, and in the course of a few days leaving home for the remainder of the summer; and, as this circumstance involved both his own and Mrs. Graham's family in doubt and wonder as to the cause of his sudden departure, Kitty's outward trials consisted chiefly in the continued and repeated questionings from her aunt and cousin, to which she was incessantly exposed, as to her share in this sudden and unlooked-for occurrence. Had she refused him? Had she quarrelled with him?—and why?

Kitty denied that she had done either; but she was not believed, and the affair remained a strange and interesting mystery.

Both Mrs. Graham and Isabel were aware that Kitty's refusing at the last moment to attend the wedding levee was owing to her having accidentally learned, just before the carriage drove to the door, that Mr. Bruce was not to be of the party; and, as they wrung from her the confession that he had passed a part of the evening at the house, they came to the very natural conclusion that some misunderstanding had arisen between the supposed lovers.

Isabel was too well acquainted with Kitty's sentiments to believe she had voluntarily relinquished an admirer who had evidently been highly prized; and she also saw that the sensitive girl winced under every allusion to the deserter. One would have thought, then, that comon affection and delicacy would have taught her to forbear any reference to the painful subject. But this was not the case. She made Mr. Bruce and his strange disappearance her almost constant topic; and, on occasion of the slightest difference or disagreement arising between herself and Kitty, she silenced and distressed the latter by some pointed and cutting sarcasm relative to her late love affair. Kitty would then seek refuge with Gertrude, relate her trials, and claim her sympathy; and she not only found in her a friendly listener to her woes, but invariably acquired in her society greater strength and cheerfulness than she could elsewhere rally to her aid, so that she became gradually dependent upon her for the only peace she enjoyed; and Gertrude, who felt a sincere interest in the girl who had been on her account subjected to such cruel deception, and whose drooping spirits and pensive countenance spoke touchingly of her inner sorrow, spared no pains to enliven her sadness, divert her thoughts, and win her to those occupations and amusements in which she herself had often found a relief from preying care and vexation.

A large proportion of her time was necessarily devoted to her dearest and best friend, Emily; but there was nothing exclusive in Emily's nature; when not suffering from those bodily afflictions to which she was subject, she was ever ready to extend a cordial welcome to all visitors who could find pleasure or benefit from her society; and even the wild and thoughtless Fanny never felt herself an intruder in Emily's premises, so sweet was the smile with which she was greeted, so forbearing the indulgence which was awarded to her waywardness. It can hardly be supposed, then, that Kitty would be excluded from her hospitality, especially after Emily, with a truly wonderful perception, became aware that she was less gay and happy than formerly, and had therefore an additional claim upon her kindness.

Many a time, when Isabel had been tantalizing and wounding Kitty beyond what her patience could endure, and Gertrude had been vainly sought elsewhere, a little figure would present itself at the half-open door of Miss Graham's room, and was sure to hear the sweetest of voices saying from within, "I hear you, Kitty; come in, my dear; we shall be glad of your pleasant company;" and once there, seated by the side of Gertrude, learning from her some little art in needle-work, listening to an agreeable book, or Emily's more agreeable conversation, Kitty passed hours which were never forgotten, so peaceful were they, so serene, so totally unlike any she had ever spent before. Nor did they fail to leave a lasting impression upon her, for the benefit of her mind and heart.

None could live in familiar intercourse with Emily, listen to her words, observe the radiance of her heavenly smile, and breathe in the pure atmosphere that environed her very being, and not carry away with them the *love* of virtue and holiness, if not something of their *essence*. She was so unselfish, so patient, notwithstanding her privations, that Kitty would have been ashamed to repine in her presence; and there was a contagious cheerfulness ever pervading her apartment, which, in spite of Kitty's recent cause of unhappiness, often led her to forget herself, and break into her natural tone of buoyancy and glee. As week after week passed away, and her sufferings and regrets, which at first were so vehement and severe, began to wear off as rapidly as such hurricane sorrows are apt to do, and the process of cure went on silently and unconsciously, another work at the same time progressed, to her equally salutary and important. In her constant intercourse with the pure heart and superior mind of Emily, and her still more familiar intimacy with one who had sat at her feet and learned of her, Kitty imbibed an elevation of thought and worthiness of aim quite foreign to her quondam character.

The foolish child, whose heart was ensnared by the flatteries of Mr. Bruce, learned—partly through the example and precepts of her new counsellors and friends, and partly through her own bitter experience—the vanity and emptiness of the food thus administered to her mind; and resolving, for the first time in her life, to cultivate and cherish her immortal powers, she now developed the first germs of her better nature; which, expanding in later years, and through other influences, transformed the gay, fluttering, vain child of fashion, into the useful, estimable and lovely woman.

CHAPTER XXXIII

Small slights, neglect, unmixed perhaps with hate,
Make up in number what they want in weight.
These, and a thousand griefs minute as these,
Corrode our comfort and destroy our ease.
                                        —*Hannah More*

LITTLE DID GERTRUDE imagine, while she was striving most disinterestedly to promote the welfare and happiness of Kitty, who had thrown herself upon her love and care, the jealousy and ill-will she was exciting in others. Isabel, who had never liked one whose whole tone of action and life was a continual reproach to her own vanity and selfishness, and who saw in her the additional crime of being the favored friend of a youth of whose interesting boyhood she herself retained a sentimental recollection, was ready and eager to seize the earliest opportunity of rendering her odious in the eyes of Mrs. Graham. She was not slow to observe the remarkable degree of confidence that seemed to exist between Kitty and Gertrude; she remembered that her cousin had forsaken her own room for that of the latter the very night after her probable quarrel and parting with Bruce; and, her resentment and anger excited still further by the growing friendship which her own coldness and unkindness to Kitty served only to strengthen and confirm, she hastened to communicate to Mrs. Graham her suspicion that Gertrude had, for purposes of her own, made a difficulty between Bruce and Kitty, fostered and widened the breach, and succeeded at last in breaking off the match.

Mrs. Graham readily adopted Belle's opinion. "Kitty," said she, "is weak-minded, and evidently very much under Miss Flint's influence. I shouldn't be surprised if you were right, Belle!"

Thus leagued together, they endeavored to surprise or entrap Kitty into a confession of the means which had been taken by Gertrude to drive away her lover, and out-wit herself. But Kitty, while she indignantly denied Gertrude's having thus injured her, persisted obstinately in refusing to reveal the occurrences of the eventful evening of the wedding levee. It was the first secret Kitty ever did keep; but her woman's pride was involved in the affair, and she preserved it with a care which both honor and wisdom prompted.

Mrs. Graham and Belle were now truly angry, and many were the private discussions held by them on the subject, many the vain conjectures which they conjured up; and as, day after day, they became more and more incensed against Gertrude, so they gradually began to manifest it in their demeanor.

Gertrude soon perceived the incivility to which she was constantly subjected; for, though in a great degree independent of their friendship, she could not live under the same roof without their having frequent opportunities to wound her by their rudeness, which soon became marked, and would have been unendurable to one whose disposition was less thoroughly schooled than Gertrude's.

With wonderful patience, however, did she preserve her equanimity. She had never looked for kindness and attention from Mrs. Graham and Isabel. She had seen from the first that between herself and them there could be little sympathy, and now that they manifested open dislike she struggled hard to maintain, on her part, not only self-command and composure, but a constant spirit of charity. It was well that she did not yield to this comparatively light trial of her forbearance, for a new, unexpected, and far more intense provocation was in store for her. Her malicious persecutors, incensed and irritated by an unlooked-for calmness and patience, which gave them no advantage in their one-sided warfare, now made their attack in another quarter; and Emily, the sweet, lovely, unoffending Emily, became the object against whom they aimed many of their shafts of unkindness and ill-will.

Gertrude could bear injury, injustice, and even hard and cruel language, when exercised towards herself only; but her blood boiled in her veins when she began to perceive that her cherished Emily was becoming the victim of mean and petty neglect and ill usage. To address the gentle Emily in other words than those of courtesy was next to impossible; it was equally hard to find fault with the actions of one whose life was so good and beautiful; and the somewhat isolated position which she occupied on account of her blindness seemed to render her secure from interference; but Mrs. Graham was coarse and blunt, Isabel selfish and unfeeling, and long before the blind girl was herself aware of any unkind intention on their part, Gertrude's spirit had chafed and rebelled at the sight and knowledge of many a word and act, well calculated, if perceived, to annoy and distress a sensitive and delicate spirit. Many a stroke ws warded off by Gertrude; many a neglect atoned for, before it could be felt; many a nearly defeated plan, which Emily was known to have had at heart, carried through and accomplished by Gertrude's perseverance and energy; and for some weeks Emily was kept ignorant of the fact that many a little office formerly performed for her by a servant was now fulfilled by Gertrude, who would not let her know that Bridget had received from her mistress orders which were quite inconsistent with her usual attendance upon Miss Graham's wants.

Mr. Graham was, at this time, absent from home; some difficulty and anxiety in business matters having called him to New York, at a season when he usually enjoyed his leisure, free from all such cares. His presence would have been a great restraint upon his wife, who was well aware of his devoted affection for his daughter, and his wish that her comfort and ease should always be considered of first-rate importance. Indeed, his love and thoughtfulness for Emily, and the enthusiastic devotion manifested towards her by every member of the household, had early rendered her an object of jealousy to Mrs. Graham, who was therefore very willing to find ground of offence against her; and, in her case, as in Isabel's, Kitty's desertion to what her aunt and cousin considered the unfriendly party was only a secondary cause of distrust and dislike.

The misunderstanding with Mr. Bruce, and their unworthy suspicions of its having been fostered by Gertrude, aided and abetted by Emily, furnished, however, an ostensible motive for the indulgence of their animosity, and one of which they resolved to avail themselves to the utmost.

Shortly before Mr. Graham's return home, Mrs. Graham and Isabel were sitting together, endeavoring to while away the tedious hours of a sultry August afternoon by indulging themselves in an unlimited abuse of the rest of the household, when a letter was brought to Mrs. Graham, which proved to be from her husband. After glancing over its contents, she remarked, with an air of satisfaction, "Here is good news for us, Isabel, and a prospect of some pleasure in the world;" and she read aloud the following passage: "The troublesome affair which called me here is nearly settled, and the result is exceedingly favorable to my wishes and plans. I now see nothing to prevent our starting for Europe the latter part of next month, and the girls must make their arrangements accordingly. Tell Emily to spare nothing towards a full and complete equipment for herself and Gertrude."

"He speaks of Gertrude," said Isabel, sneeringly, "as if she were one of the family. I'm sure I don't see any very great prospect of pleasure in travelling all through Europe with a blind woman and her disagreeable appendages; I can't think what Mr. Graham wants to take them for."

"I wish he would leave them at home," said Mrs. Graham; "it would be a good punishment for Gertrude. But, mercy! he would as soon think of going without his right hand as without Emily."

"I hope, if ever I am married," exclaimed Isabel, "it won't be to a man that's got a blind daughter!—Such a dreadful good person, too, whom everybody has got to worship, and admire, and wait upon!"

"*I* don't have to wait upon her," said Mrs. Graham; "that's Gertrude's business—it's what she's going for."

"That's the worst of it; blind girl has to have a waiting-maid, and waiting-maid is a great lady, who doesn't mind cheating your nieces out of their lovers, and even robbing them of each other's affection."

"Well, what can I do, Belle? I'm sure I don't want Gertrude's company any more than you do; but I don't see how I can get rid of her."

"I should think you'd tell Mr. Graham some of the harm she's done already. If you have any influence over him, you might prevent her going."

"It would be no more than she deserves," said Mrs. Graham, thoughtfully, "and I am not sure but I shall give him a hint of her behavior; he'll be surprised enough when he hears of Bruce's sudden flight. I know he thought it would be a match between him and Kitty."

At this point in the conversation, Isabel was summoned to see visitors, and left her aunt in a mood pregnant with consequences.

As Isabel descended the front staircase, to meet with smiles and compliments the guests whom in her heart she wished a thousand miles away on this intensely hot afternoon, Gertrude came up by the back way from the kitchen, and passed along a passage leading to her own room. She carried, over one arm, a dress of delicate white muslin, and a number of embroidered collars, sleeves and ruffles, together with other articles evidently fresh from the ironing-board. Her face was flushed and heated; she looked tired, and, as she reached her room, and carefully deposited her burden upon the bed, she drew a long breath, as if much fatigued, seated herself by a window, brushed the hair back from her face, and threw open a blind, to feel, if possible, a breath of cool air. Just at this moment, Mrs. Prime put her head in at the half-open door, and, seeing Gertrude alone, entered the room, but stood fixed with astonishment on observing the evidences of her recent laborious employment; then, glancing directly opposite at the fruits of her diligence, she burst forth, indignantly, "My sakes alive! Miss Gertrude, I do believe you've been doin' up them muslins yourself, after all!"

Gertrude smiled, but did not reply.

"Now, if that an't too bad!" said the friendly and kind-hearted woman, "to think you should ha' been at work down in that 'ere hot kitchen, and all the rest on us takin' a spell o' rest in the heat of the day! I'll warrant, if Miss Emily knew it, she'd never put on that white gown in this 'ere world!"

"It hardly looks *fit* for her to wear," said Gertrude. "I'm not much used to ironing, and have had a great deal of trouble with it; one side got dry before I could smooth out the other."

"It looks elegant, Miss Getrude; but what should you be doin' Bridget's work for, I want to know?"

"Bridget always has enough to do," said Gertrude, evading a direct answer, "and it's very well for me to have some practice; knowledge never comes amiss, you know, Mrs. Prime."

" 'Tan't no kind of an afternoon for 'speriments o' that sort; and you would n't ha' done it, I'll venture to say, if you hadn't been afeard Miss Emily would want her things, and find out they wan't done. Times is changed in this house, when Mr. Graham's own daughter, that was once to the head of everything, has to have her clothes laid by to make room for other folks. Bridget ought to know better than to mind these upstarters, when they tell her, as I heard Miss Graham yesterday, to let alone that heap o' muslins, and attend to something that was o' more consequence. Our Katy would ha' known better; but Bridget's a new comer, like all the rest. Thinks I to myself then, what would Miss Gertrude say, if she suspected as how Miss Emily was bein' neglected! But I'll *tell* Miss Emily, as sure as my name's Prime, just how things go;—you shan't get so red in the face with ironing agin, Miss Gertrude. If the kind o' frocks she likes to wear can't be done up at home,—and yourn too, what's more,—the washin' ought to be put out. There's money enough, and some of it ought to be spent for the use o' the ladies as is ladies! I wish to heart *that* Isabella could have to start round a little lively; 't would do her good; but, Lor', Miss Gertrude, it goes right to my heart to see all the vexatious things as is happenin' now-a-days! I'll go right to Miss Emily, this minute, and blow my blast!"

"No, you won't, Mrs. Prime," said Gertrude, persuasively, "when I ask you not to. You forget how unhappy it would make her if she knew that Mrs. Graham was so wanting in consideration. I would rather iron dresses every day, or do anything else for our dear Miss Emily, than to let her *suspect* even that anybody could willingly be unkind to her."

Mrs. Prime hesitated. "Miss Gertrude," said she, "I thought I loved our dear young lady as well as anybody could, but I believe you love her better still, to be so thoughtful and wise-like all for her sake; and I wouldn't say nothin' about it, only I think a sight o' *you,* too; you've been here ever since you was a little gal, and we all set lots by you, and I can't see them folks ride over your head, as I know they mean to."

"I know you love me, Mrs. Prime, and Emily too; so, for the sake of us both, you mustn't say a word to anybody about the change in the family arrangements. We'll all do what we can to keep Emily from pain, and, as to the rest, we won't care for ourselves; if they don't pet and indulge me as much as I've been accustomed to, the easiest way is not to notice it; and you mustn't put on your spectacles to see trouble."

"Lord bless yer heart, Miss Gertrude, them folks is lucky to have you to deal with; it isn't everybody as would put up with 'em. They don't come much in my way, thank fortin'! I let Miss Graham see, right off, that I wouldn't put up with interference; cooks is privileged to set up for their rights, and I scared her out o' my premises pretty quick, I tell yer! It's mighty hard for me to see our own ladies imposed upon; but since you say 'mum,' Miss Gertrude, I'll try and hold my tongue as long as I can. It's a shame though, I do declare!"—and Mrs. Prime walked off, muttering to herself.

An hour after, Gertrude was at the glass, braiding up the bands of her long hair, when Mrs. Ellis, after a slight knock at the door, entered.

"Well, Gertrude," said she "I didn't think it would come to this!"

"Why, what is the matter?" inquired Gertrude, anxiously.

"It seems we are going to be turned out of our rooms!"

"Who?"

"You, and I next, for aught I know."

Gertrude colored, but did not speak, and Mrs. Ellis went on to relate that she had just received orders to fit up Gertrude's room for some visitors who were expected the next day. She was astonished to hear that Gertrude had not been consulted on the subject. Mrs. Graham had spoken so carelessly of her removal, and seemed to think it so mutually agreeable for Emily to share her apartment with her young friend, that Mrs. Ellis concluded the matter had been prearranged.

Deeply wounded and vexed, both on her own and Emily's account, Gertrude stood for a moment silent and irresolute. She then asked if Mrs. Ellis had spoken to Emily on the subject. She had not. Gertrude begged her to say nothing about it.

"I cannot bear," said she, "to let her know that the little sanctum she fitted up so carefully has been unceremoniously taken from me. I sleep in her room more than half the time, as you know; but she always likes to have me call this chamber mine, that I may be sure of a place where I can read and study by myself. If you will let me remove my bureau into your room, Mrs. Ellis, and sleep on a couch there occasionally, we need not say anything about it to Emily."

Mrs. Ellis assented. She had grown strangely humble and compliant within a few months, and Gertrude had completely won her good-will; first by forbearance, and latterly by the frequent favors and assistance she had found it in her power to render the overburdened housekeeper. So she made no objection to receive her into her room as an inmate, and even offered to assist in the removal of her wardrobe, work-table and books.

But, though yielding and considerate towards Gertrude, whom, with Emily and Mrs. Prime, she now considered members of the oppressed and injured party to which she herself belonged, no words could express her indignation with regard to the late behavior of Mrs. Graham and Isabel. "It is all of a piece," said she, "with the rest of their conduct! Sometimes I almost feel thankful that Emily is blind, it would grieve her so to see the goings on. I should have liked to box Isabella's ears for taking your seat at the table so impudently as she did yesterday, and then neglecting to help Emily to anything at all; and there sat dear Emily, angel as she is, all unconscious of her shameful behavior, and asking her for butter as sweetly as if it were by mere accident that you had been driven from the table, and she left to provide for herself. And all those strangers there, too! I saw it all from the china-closet! And then Emily's dresses and muslins!—there they laid in the press-drawer, till I thought they would mildew. I'm glad to see Bridget has been allowed to do them at last, for I began to think Emily would one of these warm days be without a clean gown in the world. But, there, it's no use talking about it; all I wish is, that they'd all go off to Europe, and leave us here to ourselves. You don't want to go, do you, Gertrude?"

"Yes, if Emily goes."

"Well, you're better than I am; I couldn't make such a martyr of myself, even for her sake."

It is needless to detail the many petty annoyances to which Gertrude was daily subjected; especially after the arrival of the expected visitors, a gay and thoughtless party of fashionables, who were taught to look upon her as an unwarrantable intruder, and upon Emily as a troublesome incumbrance. Nor, with all the pains taken to prevent it, could Emily be long kept in ignorance of the light estimation in which both herself and

Gertrude were regarded. Kitty, incensed at the incivility of her aunt and Isabel, and indifferent towards the visitors, to whose folly and levity of character her eyes were now partially opened, hesitated not to express both to Emily and Gertrude her sense of the injuries they sustained, and her own desire to act in their defence. But Kitty was no formidable antagonist to Mrs. Graham and Belle, for, her spirits greatly subdued, and her fears constantly excited by her cousin's sarcastic looks and speeches, she had become a sad coward, and no longer dared, as she would once have done, to thwart their schemes, and stand between her friends and the indignities to which they were exposed.

But Mrs. Graham, thoughtless woman, went too far, and became at last entangled in difficulties of her own weaving. Her husband returned, and it now became necessary to set bounds to her own insolence, and, what was far more difficult, to that of Isabel. Mrs. Graham was a woman of tact; she knew just how far her husband's forbearance would extend,— just the point to which his perceptions might be blinded; and had also sufficient self-control to check herself in any course which would be likely to prove obnoxious to his imperious will. In his absence, however, she acted without restraint, permitted Belle to fill the house with her lively young acquaintances, and winked at the many open and flagrant violations of the law of politeness, manifested by the young people towards the daughter of their absent host, and her youthful friend and attendant. Now, however, a check must be put to all indecorous proceedings; and, unfortunately for the execution of the wife's wise precautions, the head of the family returned unexpectedly, and under circumstances which forestalled any preparation or warning. He arrived just at dusk, having come from town in an omnibus, which was quite contrary to his usual custom.

It was a cool evening; the windows and doors of the house were closed, and the parlor was so brilliantly lighted that he at once suspected the truth that a large company was being entertained there. He felt vexed, for it was Saturday night, and, in accordance with old New England customs, Mr. Graham loved to see his household quiet on that evening. He was, moreover, suffering from a violent headache, and, avoiding the parlor, he passed on to the library, and then to the dining-room; both were chilly and deserted. He then made his way up stairs, walked through several rooms, glanced indignantly at their disordered and slovenly appearance,— for he was excessively neat,—and finally gained Emily's chamber. He opened the door noiselessly, and looked in.

A bright wood-fire burned upon the hearth; a couch was drawn up beside it, on which Emily was sitting; and Gertrude's little rocking-chair occupied the opposite corner: The fire-light reflected upon the white curtains, the fragrant perfume which proceeded from a basket of flowers upon the table, the perfect neatness and order of the apartment, the placid, peaceful face of Emily, and the radiant expression of Gertrude's countenance, as she looked up and saw the father and protector of her blind friend looking pleasantly in upon them, proved such a charming contrast to the scenes presented in other parts of the house, that the old gentleman, warmed to more than usual satisfaction with both of the inmates, greeted his surprised daughter with a hearty paternal embrace, and, bestowing upon Gertrude an equally affectionate greeting, exclaimed, as he took the arm-chair which the latter wheeled in front of the fire for his accommodation, "Now, girls, this looks pleasant and homelike! What in the world is going on down stairs? What is everything up in arms about?"

Emily explained that there was company staying in the house.

"Ugh! company!" grunted Mr. Graham, in a dissatisfied tone. "I should think so! Been emptying rag-bags about the chambers, I should say, from the looks!"

Gertrude asked if he had been to tea.

He had not, and should be thankful for some;—he was tired. So she went down stairs to see about it.

"Don't tell anybody that I've got home, Gerty," called he, as she left the room; "I want to be left in peace to-night, at least."

While Gertrude was gone, Mr. Graham questioned Emily as to her preparations for the European tour; to his surprise, he learned that she had never received his message communicated in the letter to Mrs. Graham, and knew nothing of his plans. Equally astonished and angry, he nevertheless restrained his temper for the present;—he did not like to acknowledge to himself, far less to his daughter, that his commands had been disregarded by his wife. It put him upon thinking, however.

After he had enjoyed a comfortable repast, at which Gertrude presided, they both returned to Emily's room; and now Mr. Graham's first inquiry was for the *Evening Transcript.*

"I will go for it," said Gertrude, rising.

"Ring!" said Mr. Graham, imperatively. He had observed at the tea-table that Gertrude's ring was disregarded, and wished to know the cause of so strange a piece of neglect. Gertrude rang several times, but obtained no answer to the bell. At last she heard Bridget's step in the entry, and, opening the door, said to her, "Bridget, won't you find the *Transcript,* and bring it to Miss Emily's room." Bridget soon returned, with the announcement that Miss Isabella was reading it, and declined to give it up.

A storm gathered on Mr. Graham's brow. "Such a message to *my daughter!*" he exclaimed. "Gertrude, go yourself, and tell the impertinent girl that *I* want the paper! What sort of behavior is this?" muttered he.

Gertrude entered the parlor with great composure, and, amid the stares and wonder of the company, spoke in a low tone to Belle, who immediately yielded up the paper, blushing and looking much confused as she did so. Belle was afraid of Mr. Graham; and, on her informing her aunt of his return, it was that lady's turn, also, to look disconcerted. She had fully calculated upon seeing her husband before he had access to Emily; she knew the importance of giving the desired bias to a man of his strong prejudices.

But it was too late now. She would not go to *seek* him; she must take her chance, and trust to fortune to befriend her. She used all her tact, however, to disperse her friends at an early hour, and then found Mr. Graham smoking in the dining-room.

He was in an unpleasant mood (as she told her niece afterwards, cross as a bear); but she contrived to conciliate rather than irritate him, avoided all discordant subjects, and was able the next morning to introduce to her friends an apparently affable and obliging host.

This serenity was disturbed, however, long before the Sabbath drew to a close. As he walked up the church-aisle, before morning service, with Emily, according to invariable custom, leaning upon his arm, his brow darkened at seeing Isabel complacently seated in that corner of the old-fashioned square pew which all the family were well aware had for years been sacred to his blind daughter. Mrs. Graham, who accompanied them, winked at her niece; but Isabel was mentally rather obtuse, and was, consequently, subjected to the mortification of having Mr. Graham deliberately take her hand and remove her from the seat, in which he immediately placed Emily, while the displaced occupant, who had been so mean as for the last three Sundays to purposely deprive Miss Graham of this old established right, was compelled to sit during the service in the only vacant place, beside Mr. Graham, with her back to the pulpit. And very angry was she at observing the smiles visible upon many countenances in the neighboring pews; and especially chagrined when Fanny Bruce, who was close to her in the next pew, giggled outright.

Emily would have been grieved if she had been in the least aware of the triumph she had unconsciously achieved. But her heart and thoughts were turned upward, and, as she had felt no pang of provocation at Isabel's past encroachment, so had she no consciousness of present satisfaction, except as the force of habit made her feel more at ease in her old seat.

Mr. Graham had not been at home a week before he understood plainly the existing state of feeling in the mind of his wife and Isabel, and the manner in which it was likely to act upon the happiness of the household. He saw that Emily was superior to complaint; he knew that she had never in her life complained; he observed, too, Gertrude's devotion to his much-loved child, and it stamped her in his mind as one who had a claim to his regard which should never be disputed. It is not, then, to be wondered at, that when, with much art and many plausible words, Mrs. Graham made her intended insinuations against his youthful protegée, Mr. Graham treated them with indifference and contempt.

He had known Gertrude from a child. She was high-spirited,—he had sometimes thought her wilful,—but *never* mean or false. It was no use to tell him all that nonsense;—he was glad, for his part, that it was all off between Kitty and Bruce; for Ben was an idle fellow, and would never make a good husband; and, as to Kitty, he thought her much improved of late, and if it were owing to Gertrude's influence, the more they saw of each other the better.

Mrs. Graham was in despair. "It is all settled," said she to Isabel. "It is no use to contest the point; Mr. Graham is firm as a rock, and as sure as *we* go to Europe, Emily and Gertrude will go *too.*"

She was almost startled, therefore, by what she considered an excess of good luck, when informed, a few days afterwards, that the couple she had so dreaded to have of the party were in reality to be left behind, and that, too, at Miss Graham's special request. Emily's scruples with regard to mentioning to her father the little prospect of pleasure the tour was likely to afford her all vanished when she found that Gertrude, whose interest she ever had at heart, would be likely to prove a still greater sufferer from the society to which she would be subjected.

Blind as she was, Emily understood and perceived almost everything that was passing around her. Quick of perception, and with a hearing rendered doubly intense by her want of sight, the events of the summer were, perhaps, more familiar to her than to any other member of the family. She more than suspected the exact state of matters betwixt Mr. Bruce and Gertrude, though the latter had never spoken to her on the subject. She imagined the manner in which Kitty was involved in the affair (no very difficult thing to be conceived by one who enjoyed the confidences which the simple-hearted girl unconsciously, but continually, made during her late intercourse with her).

As Mrs. Graham's and Isabel's abuse of power became more open and decided, Mrs. Ellis and Mrs. Prime both considered the embargo upon free speech in Miss Graham's presence wholly removed; and any pain which the knowledge of their neglect might have caused her was more than compensated to Emily by the proofs it had called forth of devoted attachment and willing service on the part of her adopted child, as she loved to consider Gertrude.

Calmly, and without hesitation, as without excitement, did she resolve to adopt a course which should at once free Gertrude from her self-sacrificing service. That she encountered much opposition from her father may well be imagined; but he knew too well the impossibility of any pleasure to be derived to herself from a tour in which mental pain was added to outward deprivation, to persist in urging her to accompany the party; and, concluding at last that it was, after all, the only way to reconcile opposing interests, and that Emily's plan was, perhaps, the best that could be adopted under the circumstances, decided to resign himself to the long separation from his daughter, and permit her to be happy in her own way. He had seen, during the previous winter at the south, how entirely Emily's infirmity unfitted her for travelling, especially when deprived of Gertrude's attendant eyes; he now realized how totally contrary to her tastes and habits were the tastes and habits of his new wife and her nieces; and, unwilling to be convinced of the folly of his sudden choice, and the probable chance of unhappiness arising from it, he appreciated the wisdom of Emily's proposal, and felt a sense of relief in the adoption of a course which would satisfy all parties.

CHAPTER XXXIV

A course of days, composing happy months.
—*Wordsworth*

MRS. WARREN'S PLEASANT boarding-house was the place chosen by Emily for her own and Gertrude's winter home; and one month from the time of

Mr. Graham's return from New York his country-house was closed, he, with his wife, Isabel and Kitty, were on their way to Havre; Mrs. Ellis gone to enjoy a little rest from care with some cousins at the eastward; and Mrs. Prime established as cook in Mrs. Warren's household, where all the morning she grumbled at the increase of duty she was here called upon to perform, and all the evening blessed her stars that she was still under the same roof with her dear young ladies.

Although ample arrangements were made by Mr. Graham, and all-sufficient means provided for the support of both Emily and Gertrude, the latter was anxious to be once more usefully employed, and, therefore, resumed a portion of her school duties at Mr. W.'s. Much as Emily loved Gertrude's constant presence, she gladly resigned her for a few hours every day, rejoiced in the spirit which prompted her exertions, and rewarded her with her encouragement and praise. In the undisturbed enjoyment of each other's sociey, and in their intercourse with a small but intelligent circle of friends, they passed a season of sweet tranquillity. They read, walked and communed, as in times long past. Together they attended lectures, concerts, and galleries of art. As they stood before the works of a master's hand, whether in the sculptured marble or the painted canvas, and Emily listened while Gertrude, with glowing eyes and a face radiant with enthusiasm, described with minuteness and accuracy the subject of the pieces, the manner in which the artist had expressed in his work the original conception of his mind,—the attitudes of figures, the expression of faces, the coloring of landscapes, and the effect produced upon her mind and heart by the thoughts which the work conveyed,—such was the eloquence of the one, and the sympathizing attention of the other, that, as they stood there in striking contrast, forgetful of all around, they were themselves a study, if not for the artist, for the observer of human nature, as manifested in novel forms and free from affectation and worldliness.

Then, too, in their daily walks, or gazing upon the glories of a brilliant winter's night, Gertrude, enraptured at the work of the great Master of the universe, poured out without reserve her soul's deep and earnet admiration, dilated upon the gorgeousness of a clear sunset, or in the sweet hour of twilight sat watching the coming on of beautiful night, and lighting of Heaven's lamps, then would Emily, from the secret fountains of her largely-illumined nature, speak out such truths of the inner life as made it seem that she alone were blessed with the true light, and all the seeing world sat in comparative darkness.

It was a blissful and an improving winter which they thus passed together. They lived not for themselves alone; the poor blessed them, the sorrowful came to them for sympathy, and the affection which they both inspired in the family circle was boundless. Gertrude often recurred to it, in her after life, as the time when she and Emily lived in a beautiful world of their own. Spring came, and passed, and still they lingered there, loth to leave a place where they had been so happy; and nothing at last drove them from the city, but a sudden failure in Emily's health, and Dr. Jeremy's peremptory command that they should at once seek the country air, as the best restorative.

Added to her anxiety about Emily, Gertrude began to feel much troubled at Willie Sullivan's long silence; no word from him for two or three months. Willie could not have forgotten or meant to neglect her. That was impossible. But why this strange suspension to their correspondence? She tried, however, not to feel disturbed about it, and gave all her care to Emily, who now began indeed to require it.

They went to the sea-side for a few weeks; but the clear and bracing atmosphere brought no strength to the blind girl's feeble frame. She was obliged to give up her daily walks; a continued weariness robbed her step of its elasticity, and her usually equal spirits were subject to an unwonted depression, while her nervous temperament became so susceptible that the utmost care was requisite to preserve her from all excitement.

The good doctor came frequently to see his favorite patient, but, finding on every visit that she seemed worse instead of better, he at last ordered her back to the city, declaring that Mrs. Jerry's front chamber was as cool and comfortable as the little stived-up apartments of the crowded boarding-house at Nahant, and there he should insist upon both her and Gertrude's taking up their quarters, at least for a week or two; at the end of which time, if Emily had not found her health, he hoped to have leisure to start off with them in search of it.

Emily thought she was doing very well where she was; was afraid she should be troublesome to Mrs. Jeremy.

"Don't talk about trouble, Emily. You ought to know Mrs. Jerry and me better, by this time. Come up to-morrow; I'll meet you at the cars! Good-by!" and he took his hat and was off.

Gertrude followed him. "I see, doctor, you think Emily is not so well."

"No; how should she be? What with the sea roaring on one side, and Mrs. Fellows' babies on the other, it's enough to wear away her strength. I won't have it so! This isn't the place for her, and do you bring her up to my house to-morrow."

"The babies don't usually cry as much as they have to-day," said Gertrude, smiling; "and as to the ocean, Emily loves dearly to hear the waves rolling in. She sits and listens to them by the hour together."

"Knew she did!" said the doctor. "Shan't do it; bad for her; it makes her sad, without her knowing why. Bring her up to Boston, as I tell you."

It was full three weeks after the arrival of his visitors before the popular physician could steal away from his patients to enjoy a few weeks' recreation in travelling. For his own sake he would hardly have thought of attempting so unusual a thing as a journey; and his wife, too, loved home so much better than any other place, that she was loth to start for parts unknown; but both were willing, and even anxious, to sacrifice their long-indulged habits for what they considered the advantage of their young friends.

Emily was decidedly better; so much so as to view with pleasure the prospect of visiting West Point, Catskill and Saratoga, even on her own account; and when she reflected upon the probable enjoyment the trip would afford Gertrude, she felt herself endowed with new strength for the undertaking. Gertrude needed change of scene and diversion of mind almost as much as Emily. The excessive heat of the last few weeks, and her constant attendance in the invalid's room, had paled the roses in her cheeks, while care and anxiety had weighed upon her mind. The late improvement in Emily, however, and the alacrity with which she entered into the doctor's plans, relieved Gertrude of her fears, and, as she moved actively about to complete the few preparations which were needed in her own and her friend's wardrobe, her step was as light, and her voice as gladsome, as her fingers were busy and skilful.

New York was their first destination; but the heat and dust of the city were almost insufferable, and during the one day which they passed there Dr. Jeremy was the only member of the party who ventured out of the hotel, except on occasion of a short expedition which Mrs. Jeremy and Gertrude made in search of dress-caps, the former lady's stock being still limited to the old yellow and lilac-and-pink, neither of which, she feared, would be just the thing for Saratoga.

The doctor, however, seemed quite insensible to the state of the weather, so much was he occupied with visits to some of his Æsculapian brethren, several of whom were college class-mates whom he had not seen for years. He passed the whole day in the revival of old acquaintances and associations; and, a number of these newly-found but warm-hearted friends having presented themselves at the hotel in the evening, to be introduced to Mrs. Jeremy and her travelling companions, their parlor was enlivened until a late hour by the happy and cheerful conversation of a group of elderly men, who, as they recalled the past and dwelt upon the scenes and incidents of their youthful days, seemed to renew their boyish spirits, so joyous was the laughter and excitement with which each anecdote of former times received as it fell from the lips of the spokesman,—an office which each filled by turns. Dr. Jeremy had been a great favorite among his circle, and almost every narrative of college days (save those which he himself detailed) bore reference to some exploit in which he had borne a spirited and honorable part; and the three female auditors, especially Gertrude, who was enthusiastic in her own appreciation of the doctor's merits, listened triumphantly to this corroborative testimony of his worth.

The conversation, however, was not of a character to exclude the ladies from participating in as well as enjoying it; and Gertrude, who always got on famously with elderly men, and whom the doctor loved dearly to draw out, contributed not a little to the mirth and good-humor of the company by her playful and amusing sallies, and the quickness of repartee with which she responded to the adroit, puzzling, and sometimes ironical questions and jokes of an old-bachelor physician, who, from the first, took a wonderful fancy to her.

Emily listened with delighted interest to a conversation which had for her such varied charms, and shared with Gertrude the admiration of the doctor's friends, who were all excited to the warmest sympathy for her misfortune; while Mrs. Jeremy, proud, smiling and happy, looked so complacent as she sat ensconced in an arm-chair, listening to the encomiums pronounced on her husband's boyhood, that Gertrude declared, as they separated for the night, that she had almost come to the conclusion that the old yellow was becoming to her, and her new caps altogether superfluous.

Upon hearing that Dr. Jeremy's party were going to the Hudson the next morning, Dr. Gryseworth, of Philadelphia, who had many years before been a student of our good doctor's, expressed his satisfaction in the prospect of meeting them on board the boat, and introducing to Gertrude his two daughters, whom he was about to accompany to Saratoga to meet their grandmother, already established at Congress Hall[1] for the summer.

It was midnight before Gertrude could compose her mind, and so far quiet her imagination (which, always lively, was now keenly excited by the next day's promise of pleasure) as to think of the necessity of fortifying herself by sleep; and Emily was finally obliged to check her gayety and loquacity by positively refusing to join in another laugh, or listen to another word that night. Thus condemned to silence, she sunk at once to slumber, unconscious that Emily, usually an excellent sleeper, had, in this instance, acted solely for her benefit, being herself so strangely wakeful that morning found her unrefreshed, and uncertain whether she had once during the night been lulled into a perfect state of repose.

Gertrude, who slept soundly until wakened by Miss Graham, started up in astonishment on seeing her dressed and standing by the bed-side,—a most unusual circumstance, and one which reversed the customary order of things, as Gertrude's morning kiss was wont to be Emily's first intimation of daylight.

"Six o'clock, Gerty, and the boat starts at seven! The doctor has already been knocking at our door."

"How soundly I have slept!" exclaimed Gertrude. "I wonder if it's a pleasant day."

"Beautiful," replied Emily, "but very warm. The sun was shining in so brightly, that I had to close the blinds on account of the heat."

Gertrude made haste to repair for lost time, but was not quite dressed when they were summoned to the early breakfast prepared for travellers. She had, also, her own and Emily's trunks to lock, and therefore insisted upon the others preceding her to the breakfast-hall, where she promised to join them in a few moments.

The company assembled at this early hour was small, consisting only of two parties beside Dr. Jeremy's, and a few gentlemen, most of them business men, who, having partaken of their food in a business-like manner, started off in haste for their different destinations. Of those who still lingered at the table when Gerty made her appearance, there was only one whom she particularly observed, during the few moments allowed her by Dr. Jeremy for the enjoyment of her breakfast.

This was a gentleman who sat at some distance from her, idly balancing his tea-spoon on the edge of his cup. He had concluded his own repast, but seemed quite at his leisure, and previous to Gertrude's entrance had won Mrs. Jeremy's animadversions by a slight propensity he had manifested to make a more critical survey of her party than she found wholly agreeable. "Do, pray," said she to the doctor, "send the waiter to ask that man to take something himself: I can't bear to have anybody looking at me so when I'm eating!"

"He isn't looking at you, wife; it's Emily that has taken his fancy. Emily, my dear, there's a gentleman, over opposite, who admires you exceedingly."

"Is there?" said Emily, smiling. "I am very much obliged to him. May I venture to return the compliment?"

"Yes. He's a fine-looking fellow, though wife, here, doesn't seem to like him very well."

At this moment Gertrude joined them, and, as she made her morning salutation to the doctor and his wife, and gayly apologized to the former for her tardiness, the fine color which mantled her countenance, and the deep brilliancy of her large dark eyes, drew glances of affectionate admiration from the kind old couple, and were, perhaps, the cause of the stranger's attention being at once transferred from the lovely and interesting face of Emily to the more youthful, beaming and eloquent features of Gertrude.

She had hardly taken her seat before she became aware of the notice she was attracting. It embarrassed her, and she was glad when, after a moment or two, the gentleman hastily dropped his tea-spoon, rose and left the room. As he passed out, she had an opportunity of observing him, which she had not ventured to do while he sat opposite to her.

He was a man considerably above the middle height, slender, but finely formed, and of a graceful and dignified bearing. His features were rather sharp, but expressive, and even handsome; his eyes, dark, keen and piercing, had a most penetrating look, while his firmly-compressed lips spoke of resolution and strength of will.

But the chief peculiarity of his appearance was his hair, which was deeply tinged with gray, and in the vicinity of his temples almost snowy-white. This was so strikingly in contrast with the youthful fire of his eye, and the easy lightness of his step, that, instead of seeming the effect of age, and giving him a title to veneration, it rather enhanced the contradictory claims of his otherwise apparent youth and vigor.

"What a queer-looking man!" exclaimed Mrs. Jeremy, when he had passed out.

"An elegant-looking man, isn't he?" said Gertrude.

"Elegant?" rejoined Mrs. Jeremy. "What! with that gray head?"

"I think it's beautiful," said Gertrude; "but I wish he didn't look so melancholy; it makes me quite sad to see him."

"How old should you think he was?" asked Dr. Jeremy.

"About fifty," said Mrs. Jeremy.

"About thirty," said Gertrude, and both in the same breath.

"A wide difference," remarked Emily. "Doctor, you must decide the point."

"Impossible! I wouldn't venture to tell that man's age within ten years, at least. Wife has got him old enough, certainly: I'm not sure but I should set him as low even as Gertrude's mark. Age never turned *his* hair gray—that is certain."

Intimation was now given that passengers for the boat must be on the alert; and all speculation upon the probable age of the stranger (a fruitless kind of speculation, often indulged in, and, sometimes a source of vain and endless discussion) was suddenly and peremptorily suspended.

CHAPTER XXXV

His mien is lofty, but his gaze
Too well a wandering soul betrays:
His full, dark eye at times is bright
With strange and momentary light,
And oft his features and his air
A shade of troubled mystery wear,—
A glance of hurried wildness, fraught
With some unfathomable thought.
—*Mrs. Hemans*

TO MOST OF OUR travelling public a little trip from Boston into New York State seems an every-day affair, scarce worth calling a journey; but to Dr. Jeremy it was a momentous event, calling the good physician out of a routine of daily professional visits, which, during a period of twenty years, had not been interrupted by a week's absence from home, and plunging him at once into that whirl of hurry, tumult and excitement, which exists on all our great routes, especially in the summer season, the time when the American populace takes its yearly pleasure excursion.

The doctor was by nature and habit a social being; never shrinking from intercourse with his fellow-men, but rather seeking and enjoying

259

their companionship on all occasions. He knew how to adapt himself to the taste of young and old, rich and poor, and was well acquainted with city life in all its forms. In the art of travelling, however,—an art to be acquired by practice only,—he was totally unversed. He had yet to learn the adroit use of those many springs, which, touched at the right moment, and by a skilful hand, soften the obdurate hearts of landlords, win the devoted attendance of waiters, inspire railroad conductors and steamboat officials with a spirit of accommodation, and convert the clamorous, noisy hackmen into quiet, obedient and humble servants at command. In Dr. Jeremy's travelling days the stage-coach was the chief vehicle of convenience and speed; the driver was a civil fellow, each passenger a person of consequence, and each passenger's baggage a thing not to be despised. Now, on the contrary, people moved in masses; a single individual was a man of no influence, a mere unit in the great whole, and his much-valued luggage that which seemed in his eyes a mark for the heaviest knocks and bruises. Dr. Jeremy was appalled at this new state of things, and quite unable to reconcile to it either his taste or temper. To him the modern landlord resembled the keeper of an intelligence-office, who condescendingly glances at his books to see if he can furnish the humble suppliant with a situation, and often turns him away mortified and disappointed; the waiters, whom the honest and unsophisticated doctor scorned to bribe, were an impudent, lazy set of varlets; conductors and steamboat masters, lordly tyrants; and the hackmen, a swarm of hungry, buzzing, stinging wasps, let loose on wharves and in depots for the torment of their victims.

Thus were these important members of society stigmatized, and loudly were they railed at by our traveller, who invariably, at the commencement and close of every trip, got wrought up to a high pitch of excitement at the wrongs and indignities to which he was subjected. It was astonishing, however, to see how quickly he cooled down, and grew comfortable and contented, when he was once established in car or steamboat, or had succeeded in obtaining suitable quarters at a hotel. He would then immediately subside into the obliging, friendly and sociable man of the world; would make acquaintance with everybody about him, and talk and behave with such careless unconcern, that one would have supposed he considered himself fixed for life, and was moreover perfectly satisfied with the fate that destiny had assigned to him.

Thankful, therefore, were the ladies of his party when they were safe on board the steamboat; a circumstance upon which they were still congratulating themselves and each other, while they piled up their heavy shawls and other extra garments in an out-of-the-way corner of the cabin, when the doctor's voice was again heard calling to them from the other end of the long saloon: "Come, come, wife,—Gertrude,—Emily! what are you staying down in this stived-up place for? you'll lose the best part of the view;" and, coming towards them, he took Gertrude's arm, and would have hurried her away; leaving Mrs. Jeremy and Emily to follow when they were ready; but Gertrude would not trust Emily to ascend the cabin-stairs under any guardianship but her own, and Mrs. Jeremy immediately engaged the doctor in an animated discussion as to the advisability of his adopting a straw hat, which the thoughtful wife had brought from home in her hand, and which she was eager to see enjoyed. By the time the question was settled, and Emily, at Gertrude's persuasion, had been induced to exchange her thin mantilla for a light travelling-cloak, which the latter was sure she would require, as there was a fresh breeze stirring on the river, the boat had proceeded some distance; and when our party finally gained the head of the stairs, and looked about them for seats on deck, not a single vacant bench or accommodation of any sort was to be seen. There was an unusually large number of passengers, nearly all of whom were collected at the stern of the boat. Dr. Jeremy was obliged to leave his ladies, and go off in search of chairs.

"Don't let us stay here!" whispered Mrs. Jeremy to Gertrude and Emily. "Let's go right back, before the doctor comes! There are beautiful great rocking-chairs down in the cabin, without a soul to sit in them, and I'm sure we an't wanted here to make up a company. I hate to stand with all these people staring at us, and crowing to think they've got such nice places; don't you, Emily?"

Mrs. Jeremy was one of the people who were constantly forgetting that Emily could not see.

But Gertrude was not—she never forgot it; and, as she stood with her arm lightly passed around her friend's waist, to prevent the motion of the boat from throwing her off her balance, it was no wonder they attracted attention; the one so bright, erect, and strong with youth and health, that she seemed a fit protector for the other, who, in her sweet and gentle helplessness, leaned upon her so trustingly.

"I think, when we get seated in the shade, we shall find it cooler here than it is below," said Emily, in reply to Mrs. Jeremy's urgent proposition that they should make their escape in the doctor's absence. "You always prefer the coolest place, I believe."

"So I do; but I noticed there was a good draught of air in the ladies' saloon, and——" Here the good woman's argument was interrupted by the cordial salutation of Dr. Gryseworth, who, previously seated with his back towards them, had turned at the sound of Emily's flute-like voice, which, once heard, invariably left an impression upon the memory. When he had finished shaking hands, he insisted upon giving up his seat to Mrs. Jeremy; and, at the same instant, another gentleman, who, owing to the throng of passengers, had hitherto been unnoticed by our party, rose, and bowing politely, placed his own chair for the accommodation of Emily, and then walked quickly away. It was the stranger whom they had seen at breakfast. Gertrude recognized his keen, dark eye, even before she perceived his singular hair; and, as she thanked him, and placed Emily in the offered seat, she felt herself color under his earnest glance. But Dr. Gryseworth immediately claimed her attention for the introduction to his daughters, and all thought of the retreating stranger was banished for the present.

The Miss Grysworths were intelligent-looking girls; the eldest, lately returned from Europe, where she had been travelling with her father, was considered a very elegant and superior person, and Gertrude was charmed with the lady-like cordiality with which they both made her acquaintance, and still more with the amiable and sympathizing attentions which they paid to Emily.

By the time that Dr. Jeremy returned with the solitary chair which he had been able to obtain, he found Gertrude and Dr. Gryseworth comfortably accommodated, through the skilful agency of the latter, and was thus enabled to sink at once into his seat, and subside into that state of easy unconcern which admirably became his pleasant, genial temperament.

Long before the boat reached West Point, where the Jeremys were to go on shore, it was plain to be seen that an excellent understanding subsisted between Gertrude and the Miss Gryseworths, and that time only was wanting to ripen their acquaintance into friendship.

Gertrude was not one of those young persons who consider every girl of their own age entitled to their immediate intimacy and confidence. She had her decided preferences, and, though invariably civil and obliging, was rarely disposed to admit new members into her sacred circle of friends. She was quick, however, to recognize a congenial spirit; and such an one, once found, was claimed by her enthusiastic nature, and engrafted into her affections as something of kindred birth. Nor was the readily adopted tie easily loosened or broken. Whom Gertrude once loved, she loved long and well; faithful was she in her efforts to serve, and prompt in her sympathy to feel for those whose interest and happiness friendship made dear to her as her own.

Perhaps Ellen Gryseworth divined this trait of her character, and appreciated the value of so steady and truthful a regard; for she certainly tried hard to win it; and her father, who had heard Gertrude's history from Dr. Jeremy, smiled approvingly, as he witnessed the pains which his high-bred and somewhat aristocratic daughter was taking to render herself agreeable to one whose social position had in it nothing to excite her ambition, and whose person, mind and manners, constituted her sole recommendation.

They had been for about an hour engaged in the enjoyment of each other's society, and in the view of some of the most charming scenery in the world, when Netta Gryseworth touched her sister's arm, and, glancing towards another part of the boat, said, in an under tone, "Ellen, do invite Mr. Phillips to come back and be introduced to Miss Flint!—see how lonesome the poor man looks."

Gertrude followed the direction of Netta's eye, and saw the stranger of the morning at some distance from them, slowly pacing up and down, with a serious and abstracted air.

"He has not been near us for an hour," said Netta. "I am afraid he has got the blues."

"I hope we have not frightened your friend away," said Gertrude.

"O, no, indeed!" replied Ellen. "Although Mr. Phillips is but a recent acquaintance, we have found him so independent, and sometimes so whimsical, that I am never astonished at his proceedings, or mortified at being suddenly forsaken by him. There are some people, you know, for whom it is always sufficient excuse to say, *It is their way.* I wish he would condescend to join us again, however; I should like to introduce him to you, Miss Flint."

"You would n't like him," said Netta.

"Now, that is not fair, Netta!" exclaimed her sister; "to try and prejudice Miss Flint against my friend. You must n't let her influence you," added she, addressing Gertrude. "She has n't known him half as long as I have; and I do not dislike him, by any means. My little, straight-forward sister never likes odd people, and I must confess that Mr. Phillips is somewhat eccentric; but he interests me all the more on that account, and I feel positive he and you would have many ideas and sentiments in common."

"How can you say so, Ellen?" said Netta. "I think they are totally different."

"You must consider Netta's remark very complimentary, Miss Flint," said Ellen, good-naturedly; "it would not be quite so much so, if it had come from me."

"But you wished me to become acquainted with your oddity," remarked Gertrude, addressing herself to Netta. "I suspect you act on the principle that one's misfortunes should be shared by one's friends."

Netta laughed. "Not exactly," said she; "it was compassion *for him* that moved me. I can't help pitying him when he looks so homesick, and I thought your society would brighten him up and do him good."

"Ah, Netta! Netta!" cried her sister; "he has excited your sympathy, I see. A few days more, and I should n't be surprised if you went beyond me in your admiration of him. If so, take care, you transparent creature, not to betray your inconsistency." Then, turning to Gertrude, she said, "Netta met Mr. Phillips yesterday for the first time, and has not seemed very favorably impressed. Father and I were passengers in the same steamer in which he came from Liverpool, a few weeks ago. He had an ill turn in the early part of the voyage, and it was in a professional way that father first made his acquaintance. I was surprised at seeing him on board the boat to-day, for he mentioned no such intention yesterday."

Gertrude suspected that the agreeable young lady might herself be the cause of his journey; but she did not say so,—her native delicacy and the slight knowledge she had of the parties forbade such an allusion,— and the conversation soon taking another turn, Mr. Phillips was not again adverted to, though Gertrude observed, just before the boat stopped at West Point, that Dr. Jeremy and Dr. Gryseworth, having left their party, had joined him, and that the trio were engaged in a colloquy which seemed to possess equal interest to them all.

At West Point Gertrude parted from her new friends, who expressed an earnest hope that they should again meet in Saratoga; and before the bustle of going on shore had subsided, and she had found on the narrow pier a safe place of refuge for Emily and herself, the boat was far up the river, and the Miss Gryseworths quite undistinguishable among the crowd that swarmed the deck.

Our travellers passed one night only at West Point. The weather continued extremely hot, and Dr. Jeremy, perceiving that Emily drooped under the oppressive atmosphere, was desirous to reach the summit of Catskill Mountain before the Sabbath, which was now near at hand.

One solitary moonlight evening, however, sufficed to give Gertrude some idea of the beauties of the place. She had no opportunity to observe it in detail; she saw it only as a whole; but, thus presented to her vision in all the dreamy loveliness of a summer's night, it left on her fresh and impressive mind a vague sentiment of wonder and delight at the surpassing sweetness of what seemed rather a glimpse of Paradise than an actual show of earth, so harmonious was the scene, so calm, so still, so peaceful. "Emily, darling," said she, as they stood together in a rustic arbor, commanding the most striking prospect both of the river and the shore, "it looks like you; you ought to live here, and be the priestess of such a temple!" and, locking her hand in that of Emily, she poured into her attentive ear the holy and elevated sentiments to which the time and the place gave birth. To pour out her thoughts to Emily was like whispering to her own heart, and the response to those thoughts was as sure and certain.

So passed the evening away, and an early hour in the morning found them again steaming up the river. Their first day's experience having convinced them of the danger of delay, they lost no time in securing places on deck, for the boat was as crowded as on the previous morning; but the shores of West Point were hardly passed from their view before Gertrude's watchful eye detected in Emily's countenance the well-known signs of weariness and debility. Sacrificing, without hesitation, the intense pleasure she was herself deriving from the beautiful scenes through which the boat was at the moment passing, she at once proposed that they should seek the cabin, where Miss Graham might rest in greater stillness and comfort.

Emily, however, would not listen to the proposal; would not think of depriving Gertrude of the rare pleasure she knew she must be experiencing.

"The prospect is all lost upon me now, Emily," said Gertrude. "I see only your tired face. Do go and lie down, if it be only to please me; you hardly slept at all, last night."

"Are you talking of going below?" exclaimed Mrs. Jeremy. "I, for one, shall be thankful to; it's as comfortable again, and we can see all we want to from the cabin-windows; can't we, Emily?"

"Should you really prefer it?" inquired Emily.

"Indeed, I should!" said Mrs. Jeremy, with such emphasis that her sincerity could not be doubted.

"Then, if you will promise to stay here, Gertrude," said Emily, "I will go with Mrs. Jeremy."

Gertrude assented to the plan; but insisted upon first accompanying them, to find a vacant berth for Emily, and see her under circumstances which would promise repose.

Dr. Jeremy having, in the mean time, gone to inquire about dinner, they at once carried their plan into effect. Emily was really too weak to endure the noise and confusion on deck, and, after she had lain down in the quiet and nearly deserted saloon, Gertrude stood smoothing back her hair, and watching her pale countenance, until she was accused of violating the conditions of their agreement, and was at last driven away by the lively and good-natured doctor's lady, who declared herself perfectly well able to take care of Emily.

"You'd better make haste back," said she, "before you lose your seat; and mind, Gerty, don't let the doctor come near us; he 'll be teasing us to go back again, and we 've no idea of doing any such thing." Saying which, Mrs. Jeremy untied her bonnet-strings, put her feet up in the opposite chair, clapped her hands at Gertrude, and bade her be gone.

Gertrude ran off laughing, and a smile was still on her face when she reached the staircase. As she came up with her usual quick and light step, a tall figure moved aside to let her pass. It was Mr. Phillips. He bowed, and Gertrude, returning the salutation, passed on to the place she had left, wondering how he came to be again their travelling companion. He could not have been on board previously to her going below with Emily; she was sure she should have seen him; she should have known him among a thousand. He must have taken the boat at Newburgh; it stopped there while she was in the cabin.

As these reflections passed through her mind, she resumed her seat, which was placed at the very stern of the boat, and, with her back to most of the company, gazed out upon the river. She had sat thus for about five minutes, her thoughts divided between the scenery and the interesting countenance of the stranger, when a shadow passed before her, and, looking up, prepared to see and address Dr. Jeremy, she betrayed a little confusion at again encountering a pair of eyes whose earnest, magnetic gaze had the power to disconcert and bewilder her. She was turning away, somewhat abruptly, when the stranger spoke.

"Good-morning, young lady! our paths still lie in the same direction, I see. Will you honor me by making use of my guide-book?"

As he spoke, he offered her a little book containing a map of the river, and the shores on either side. Gertrude took it, and thanked him. As she unfolded the map, he stationed himself a few steps distant, and leaned over the railing, in an apparently absent state of mind; nor did he speak to her again for some minutes. Then, suddenly turning towards her, he said, "You like all this very much."

"Very much," said Gertrude.

"You have never seen anything so beautiful before in your life." He did not seem to question her; he spoke as if he knew.

"It is an old story to you, I suppose," said Gertrude.

"What makes you think so?" asked he, smiling.

Gertrude was disconcerted by his look, and still more by his smile; it changed his whole face so,—it made him look so handsome, and yet so melancholy. She blushed, and could not reply; he saved her the trouble.—"That is hardly a fair question, is it? You probably think you have as much reason for your opinion as I had for mine. You are wrong, however; I never was here before; but I am too old a traveller to carry my enthusiasm in my eyes—as you do," added he, after a moment's pause, during which he looked her full in the face. Then, seeming, for the first time, to perceive the embarrassment which his scrutiny of her features occasioned, he turned away, and a shadow passed over his fine countenance, lending it for a moment an expression of mingled bitterness and pathos, which served at once to disarm Gertrude's confusion at his self-introduction and subsequent remarks, and render her forgetful of everything but the strange interest with which this singular man inspired her.

Presently, taking a vacant chair next hers, he directed her attention to a beautiful country residence on their right, spoke of its former owner, whom he had met in a foreign land, and related some interesting anecdotes concerning an adventurous journey which they had taken together. This again introduced other topics, chiefly connected with wanderings in countries almost unknown, even in this exploring age; and so rich and varied was the stranger's conversation, so graphic were his descriptions, so exuberant and glowing his imagination, and so powerful his command of words and his gift at expressing and giving force to his thoughts, that his young and enthusiastic listener sat entranced with admiration and delight.

Her highly-wrought and intellectual nature sympathized fully with the fervor and poetry of a mind as sensitive as her own to the great and wonderful, whether in nature or art; and, her fancy and interest thus taken by storm, her calm and observant entertainer had soon the satisfaction of perceiving that he had succeeded in disarming her diffidence and embarrassment; for, as she listened to his words, and even met the occasional glance of his dark eyes, her animated and beaming countenance no longer showed signs of fear or distrust.

He took no advantage, however, of the apparent self-forgetfulness with which she enjoyed his society, but continued to enlarge upon such subjects as naturally presented themselves, and was careful not to disturb her equanimity by again bestowing upon her the keen and scrutinizing gaze which had proved so disconcerting. By the time, therefore, that Dr. Jeremy came in search of his young charge, conversation between her and the stranger had assumed so much ease and freedom from restraint that the doctor opened his eyes in astonishment, shrugged his shoulders, and exclaimed, "This is pretty well, I declare!"

Gertrude did not see the doctor approach, but looked up at the sound of his voice. Conscious of the surprise it must be to him to find her talking so familiarly with a complete stranger, she colored slightly at his abrupt remark; but, observing that her companion was quite unconcerned, and even received it with a smile, she felt herself rather amused than embarrassed; for, strangely enough, the latter feeling had almost entirely vanished, and she had come to feel confidence in her fellow-traveller, who rose, shook hands with Dr. Jeremy, to whom he had, the previous day, been introduced, and said, with perfect composure, "Will you have the kindness, sir, to present me to this young lady? We have already had some conversation together, but do not yet know by what name we may address each other."

Dr. Jeremy having performed the ceremony of introduction, Mr. Phillips bowed gracefully, and looked at Gertrude in such a benignant, fatherly way that she hesitated not to take his offered hand. He detained hers a moment while he said. "Do not be afraid of me when we meet again;" and then walked away, and paced slowly up and down the deck until passengers for Catskill were summoned to dinner, when he, as well as Dr. Jeremy and Gertrude, went below.

The doctor tried to rally Gertrude a little about her gray-headed beau, declaring that he was yet young and handsome, and that she could have his hair dyed any color she pleased. But he could not succeed in annoying her in that way, for her interest in him, which she did not deny, was quite independent of his personal appearance.

The bustle, however, of dinner, and going on shore at Catskill, banished from the good doctor's head all thought of everything except the safety of himself, his ladies, and their baggage; fit cause, indeed, for anxiety to a more experienced traveller than he. For, so short was the time allotted for the boat to stop at the landing and deposit the passengers, and such was the confusion attending the operation of pushing them on shore and flinging their baggage after them, that when the panting engine was again set in motion the little crowd collected on the wharf resembled rather a flock of frightened sheep than human beings with a free will of their own.

Emily, whose nervous system was somewhat disordered, clung trem- blingly to Gertrude; and Gertrude found herself, she knew not how, lean- ign on the arm of Mr. Phillips, to whose silent exertions they were both indebted for their safety in disembarking. Mrs. Jeremy, in the mean time, was counting up the trunks, while her husband, with his foot upon one of them, and a carpet-bag in his left hand, was loudly denouncing the steam- boat, its conductors, and the whole hurrying, skurrying Yankee nation.

Two stage-coaches were waiting at the wharf to take passengers up the mountain, and before Dr. Jeremy had turned his back upon the river Emily and Gertrude were placed in one of them by Mr. Phillips, who, without asking questions, or even speaking at all, took this office upon himself, and then went to inform the doctor of their whereabouts. The doctor and his wife soon joined them; a party of strangers occupied the other seats in the coach, and, after some delay, they commenced the after- noon's drive.

CHAPTER XXXVI

Believe in God as in the sun,—and, lo!
Along thy soul morn's youth restored shall glow;
As rests the earth, so rest, O, troubled heart,
Rest, till the burden of the cloud depart!
—*New Timon*

BEFORE THEY HAD passed through the dusty village, and gained the road leading in the direction of the Mountain House, they became painfully conscious of the vast difference between the temperature of the river and that of the inland country, and, in being suddenly deprived of the refresh- ing breeze they had enjoyed on board the boat, they fully realized the extreme heat of the weather. For the first few miles Gertrude's whole attention was required to shield Emily and herself from the rays of a burning sun which shone into the coach full upon their faces, and it was a great relief when they at last reached the steep but smooth and beautifully- shaded road which led up the side of the mountain.

The atmosphere being perfectly clear, the gradually widening prospect was most beautiful, and Gertrude's delight and rapture were such that the restraint imposed by stage-coach decorum was almost insupportable. When, therefore, the ascent became so laborious that the gentlemen were invited to alight, and relieve the weary horses of a part of their burden, Gertrude gladly accepted Dr. Jeremy's proposal that she should accompany him on a walk of a mile or two.

Gertrude was an excellent walker, and she and the still active doctor soon left the coaches far behind them. At a sudden turn in the road they stopped to view the scene below, and, lost in silent admiration, stood enjoying the stillness and beauty of the spot, when they were startled by a voice close beside them saying, "A fine landscape, certainly!"

They looked around, and saw Mr. Phillips seated upon a moss-grown rock, against which Gertrude was at the moment leaning. His attitude was easy and careless, his broad-brimmed straw hat lay on the ground, where it had fallen, and his snow-besprinkled but wavy and still beautiful hair was tossed back from his high and expanded forehead. One would have thought, to look at him, leaning so idly and even boyishly upon his hand, that he had been sitting there for hours at least, and felt quite at home in the place. He rose to his feet, however, immediately upon being perceived, and joined Dr. Jeremy and Gertrude.

"You have got the start of us, sir," said the former.

"Yes; I have walked from the village,—my practice always when the roads are such that no time can be gained by riding."

As he spoke, he placed in Gertrude's hand, without looking at her, or seeming conscious what he was doing, a bouquet of rich laurel-blossoms, which he had probably gathered during his walk. She would have thanked him, but his absent manner was such that it afforded her no opportunity, especially as he went on talking with the doctor, as if she had not been present.

All three resumed their walk. Mr. Phillips and Dr. Jeremy conversed in an animated manner, and Gertrude, content to be a listener, soon perceived that she was not the only person to whom the stranger had power to render himself agreeable. Dr. Jeremy engaged him upon a variety of subjects, upon all of which he appeared equally well-informed; and Gertrude smiled to see her old friend more than once rub his hands together, according to his well-known manner of expressing boundless satisfaction.

Now, Gertrude thought their new acquaintance must be a botanist by profession, so versed was he in everything relating to that department of science. Then, again, she was equally sure that geology must have been with him an absorbing study, so intimate seemed his acquaintaince with mother earth; and both of these impressions were in turn dispelled, when he talked of the ocean like a sailor, of the counting-room like a merchant, of Paris like a man of fashion and the world.

In the mean time, she walked beside him, silent but not forgotten or unnoticed; for, as they approached a rough and steep ascent, he offered his arm, and expressed a fear lest she should become fatigued. She assured him there was no danger of that. Dr. Jeremy declared it his belief that Gerty could out-walk them both; and, thus satisfied, Mr. Phillips resumed the broken thread of their discourse, into which, before long, Gertrude was drawn, almost unawares.

Mr. Phillips was a man who knew how to inspire awe, and even fear, when such was his pleasure. The reverse being the case, however, he had equal ability to dispel such sentiments, awaken confidence, and bid character unfold itself at his bidding. He no longer seemed in Gertrude's eyes a stranger;—he was a mystery, certainly, but not a forbidding one. She longed to know more of him; to learn the history of a life which many an incident of his own narrating proved to have been made up of strange and mingled experience; especially did her sympathetic nature desire to fathom the cause of that deep-seated melancholy which shadowed and darkened his noble countenance, and made his very smile a sorrowful thing.

Dr. Jeremy, who, in a degree, shared her curiosity, asked a few leading questions, in hopes to obtain some clue to his new friend's personal history; but in vain. Mr. Phillips' lips were either sealed on the subject, or opened only to baffle the curiosity of his interrogator.

At length the doctor was compelled to give way to a weariness which he could no longer disguise from himself or his companions, much as he disliked to acknowledge the fact; and, seating themselves by the road-side, they awaited the arrival of the coach.

There had been a short silence, when the doctor, looking at Gertrude, remarked, "There will be no church for us to-morow, Gerty."

"No church!" exclaimed Gertrude, gazing about her with a look of reverence; "how *can* you say so?"

Mr. Phillips bestowed upon her a smile of interest and inquiry, and said, in a peculiar tone, "There is no Sunday here, Miss Flint; it does n't come up so high."

He spoke lightly,—too lightly, Gertrude thought,—and she replied with some seriousness, and much sweetness, "I have often rejoiced that the Sabbath had been sent *down* into the *lower* earth; the higher we go, the nearer we come, I trust, to the eternal Sabbath."

Mr. Phillips bit his lip, and turned away without replying. There was an expression about his mouth which Gertrude did not exactly like; but she could not find it in her heart to reproach him for the slight sneer which his manner, rather than his look, implied, for, as he gazed a moment or two into vacancy, there was in his wild and absent countenance such a look of sorrow, that she could only pity and wonder. The coaches now came up, and, as he placed her in her former seat, he resumed his wonted serene and kindly expression, and she felt convinced that it was only doing justice to his frank and open face to believe that nothing was hid behind it that would not do honor to the man.

An hour more brought them to the Mountain House, and, greatly to their joy, they were at once shown to some of the most excellent rooms the hotel afforded. As Gertrude stood at the window of the chamber allotted to herself and Emily, and heard the loud murmurs of some of her fellow-travellers who were denied any tolerable accommodations, she could not but be astonished at Dr. Jeremy's unusual good fortune in being treated with such marked partiality.

Emily, being greatly fatigued with the toilsome journey, had supper brought to her own room, and Gertrude partaking of it with her, neither of them sought other society that night, but at an early hour betook themselves to rest.

The last thing that Getrude heard, before falling asleep, was the voice of Dr. Jeremy, saying, as he passed their door, "Take care, Gerty, and be up in time to see the sun rise."

She was not up in time, however, nor was the doctor, himself; neither of them had calculated upon the sun's being such an early riser; and though Gertrude, mindful of the caution, sprung up almost before her eyes were open, a flood of daylight was pouring in at the window, and a scene met her gaze which at once put to flight every regret at having overslept herself, since nothing, she thought, could be more solemnly glorious than that which now lay outspread before her.

From the surface of the rocky platform upon which the house was built, far out to the horizon, nothing was to be seen but a sea of snowy clouds, which wholly overshadowed the lower earth, and hid it from view. Vast, solid, and of the most perfect whiteness, they stretched on every side, forming, as they lay in thick masses, between which not a crevice was discernible, an unbroken curtain, dividing the heavens from the earth.

While most of the world, however, was thus shut out from the clear light of morning, the mountain-top was rejoicing in an unusually brilliant and glorious dawn, the beauty of which was greatly enhanced by those very clouds which were obscuring and shadowing the dwellings of men below. A fairy bark might have floated upon the undulating waves which glistened in the sunshine like new-fallen snow, and which contrasted with the clear blue sky above, formed a picture of singular grandeur. The foliage of the oaks, the pines and the maples, which had found root in this lofty region, was rich, clear and polished, and tame and fearless birds of various note were singing in the branches. Gertrude gave one long look, then hastened to dress herself and go out upon the platform. The house was perfectly still; no one seemed yet to be stirring, and she stood for some time entranced, almost breathless, with awe and admiration.

At length she heard footsteps, and, looking up, saw Dr. and Mrs. Jeremy approaching; the former, as usual, full of life, and dragging forward his reluctant, sleepy partner, whose countenance proclaimed how unwillingly she had forgone her morning nap. The doctor rubbed his hands as they joined Gertrude. "Very fine this, Gerty! A touch beyond anything I had calculated upon."

Gertrude turned upon him or her beaming eyes, but did not speak. Satisfied, however, with the expression of her face, which was sufficient, without words, to indicate her appreciation of the scene, the doctor stepped to the edge of the flat rock upon which they stood, placed his hands beneath his coat-tails, and indulged in a soliloquy, made up of short exclamations and interjectional phrases, expressive of his approbation, still further confirmed and emphasized by a quick, regular nodding of his head.

"Why, this looks queer, does n't it?" said Mrs. Jeremy, rubbing her eyes, and gazing about her; "but I dare say it would be just so an hour or two hence. I don't see what the doctor would make me get up so early for." Then, catching sight of her husband's position, she darted forward, exclaiming, "Dr. Jerry, for mercy's sake, don't stand so near the edge of that precipice! Why, are you crazy, man? You frighten me to death! you'll fall over and break your neck, as sure as the world!"

Finding the doctor deaf to her entreaties, she caught hold of his coat, and tried to drag him backwards; upon which he turned about, inquired what was the matter, and, perceiving her anxiety, considerably retreated a few paces; the next moment, however, he was once more in the same precarious spot. The same scene was reenacted, and finally, after the poor woman's fears had been excited and relieved half a dozen times in succession, she grew so disturbed, that, looking most imploringly at Gertrude, she begged her to get the doctor away from that dangerous place, for the poor man was so venturesome he would surely be killed.

"Suppose we explore that little path at the right of the house," suggested Gertrude; "it looks attractive."

"So it does," said Mrs. Jeremy; "beautiful little shady path! Come, doctor, Gerty and I are going to walk up here,—come."

The doctor looked in the direction in which she pointed. "Ah!" said he, "that is the path the man at the office spoke about; it leads up to the pine gardens. We'll climb up, by all means, and see what sort of a place it is."

Gertrude led the way, Mrs. Jeremy followed, and the doctor brought up the rear,—all walking in single file, for the path was a mere foot-track. The ascent was very steep, and they had not proceeded far before Mrs. Jeremy, panting with heat and fatigue, stopped short, and declared her inability to reach the top; she would not have thought of coming, if she had known what a horrid hard hill she had got to climb. Encouraged and assisted, however, by her husband and Gertrude, she was induced to make a further attempt; and they had gone on some distance, when Gertrude, who happened for a moment to be some steps in advance, heard Mrs. Jeremy give a slight scream. She looked back; the doctor was laughing heartily, but his wife, who was the picture of consternation, was endeavoring to pass him, and retrace her steps down the hill, at the same time calling upon her to follow.

"What is the matter?" asked Gertrude.

"Matter!" cried Mrs. Jeremy; "why, this hill is covered with rattlesnakes, and here we are all going up to be bitten to death!"

"No such thing, Gerty!" said the doctor, still laughing. "I only told her there had been one killed here this summer, and now she's making it an excuse for turning back."

"I don't care!" said the good-natured lady, half-laughing herself, in spite of her fears; "if there's been one, there may be another, and I won't stay here a minute longer! I thought it was a bad enough place before, and now I'm going down faster than I came up."

Finding her determined, the doctor hastened to accompany her, calling to Gertrude as he went, however, assuring her there was no danger, and begging her to keep on and wait for him at the top of the hill, where he would join her after he had left his wife in safety at the hotel. Gertrude, therefore, went on alone. For the first few rods she looked carefully about her, and thought of rattlesnakes; but the path was so well worn that she felt sure it must be often trod and was probably safe, and the beauty of the place soon engrossed all her attention. After a few moments spent in active climbing, she reached the highest point of ground, and found herself once more on an elevated woody platform, from which she could look forth as before upon the unbroken sea of clouds.

She seated herself at the root of an immense pine-tree, removed her bonnet, for she was warm from recent exercise, and, as she inhaled the refreshing mountain breeze, gave herself up to the train of reflection which she had been indulging when disturbed by Dr. and Mrs. Jeremy.

She had sat thus but a moment when a slight rustling noise startled her; she remembered the rattlsnakes, and was springing to her feet, but, hearing a low sound, as of some one breathing, turned her eyes in the direction from which it came, and saw, only a few yards from her, the figure of a man stretched upon the ground, apparently asleep. She went towards it with a careful step, and before she could see the face the large straw hat, and the long, blanched, wavy hair, betrayed the identity of the individual. Mr. Phillips was, or appeared to be, sleeping; his head was pillowed upon his arm, his eyes were closed, and his attitude denoted perfect repose. Gertrude stood still and looked at him. As she did so, his countenance suddenly changed; the peaceful expression gave place to the same unhappy look which had at first excited her sympathy. His lips moved, and in his dreams he spoke, or rather shouted, "No! no! no!" each time that he repeated the word pronouncing it with more vehemence and emphasis; then, wildly throwing one arm above his head, he let it fall gradually and heavily upon the ground, and, the excitement subsiding from his face, he uttered the simple words, "*O dear!*" much as a grieved and tired child might do, as he leans his head upon his mother's knee.

Gertrude was deeply touched. She forgot that he was a stranger; she saw only a sufferer. An insect lit upon his fair, open forehead; she leaned over him, brushed away the greedy creature, and, as she did so, one of the many tears that filled her eyes fell upon his cheek.

Quietly, then, without motion or warning, he awoke, and looked full in the face of the embarrassed girl, who started, and would have hastened away, but, leaning on his elbow, he caught her hand and detained her. He gazed at her for a moment without speaking; then said, in a grave voice, "My child, did you shed that tear for me?"

She did not reply, except by her eyes, which were still glistening with the dew of sympathy.

"I believe you *did,*" said he, "and from my heart I bless you! But never again weep for a stranger; you will have woes enough of your own, if you live to be of my age."

"If I had not had sorrows already," said Gerturde, "I should not know how to feel for others; if I had not often wept for myself, I should not weep now for you."

"But you are happy?"

"Yes."

"Some find it easy to forget the past."

"*I* have not forgotten it."

"Children's griefs are trifles, and you are still scarce more than a child."

"I *never* was a child," said Gertrude.

"Strange girl!" soliloquized her companion. "Will you sit down and talk with me a few minutes?"

Gertrude hesitated.

"Do not refuse; I am an old man, and very harmless. Take a seat here under this tree, and tell me what you think of the prospect."

Gertrude smiled inwardly at the idea of his being such an old man, and calling her a child; but, old or young, she had it not in her heart to fear him, or refuse his request. She sat down, and he seated himself beside her, but did not speak of the prospect, or of anything, for a moment or two; then turning to her abruptly, he said, "So you never were unhappy in your life?"

"Never!" exclaimed Gertrude. "O, yes; often."

"But never long?"

"Yes, I can remember whole years when happiness was a thing I had never even dreamed of."

"But comfort came at last. What do you think of those to whom it never comes?"

"I know enough of sorrow to pity and wish to help them."

"What can you do for them?"

"*Hope* for them, *pray* for them!" said Gertrude, with a voice full of feeling.

"What if they be past hope?—beyond the influence of prayer?"

"There are no such," said Gertrude, with decision.

"Do you see," said Mr. Phillips, "this curtain of thick clouds, now overshadowing the world? Even so many a heart is weighed down and overshadowed by thick and impenetrable darkness."

"But the light shines brightly above the clouds," said Gertrude.

"Above! well, that may be; but what avails it to those who see it not?"

"It is sometimes a weary and toilsome road that leads to the mountain-top; but the pilgrim is well repaid for the trouble which brings him *above the clouds,*" replied Gertrude, with enthusiasm.

"Few ever find the road that leads so high," reponded her melancholy companion; "and those who do cannot live long in so elevated an atmosphere. They must come down from their height, and again dwell among the common herd; again mingle in the warfare with the mean, the base and the cruel; thicker clouds will gather over their heads, and they will be buried in redoubled darkness."

"But they have seen the glory; they know that the light is ever burning on high, and will have faith to believe it will pierce the gloom at last. See, see!" said she, her eyes glowing with the fervor with which she spoke,—"even now the heaviest clouds are parting; the sun will soon light up the valley!"

She pointed, as she spoke, to a wide fissure which was gradually disclosing itself, as the hitherto solid mass of clouds separated on either side, and then turned to the stranger to see if he observed the change; but, with the same smile upon his unmoved countenance, he was watching, not the display of nature in the distance, but that close at his side. He was gazing with intense interest upon the young and ardent worshipper of the beautiful and the true; and, in studying her features and observing the play of her countenance, he seemed so wholly absorbed, that Gertrude—believing he was not listening to her words, but had fallen into one of his absent moods—ceased speaking, rather abruptly, and was turning away, when he said,

"Go on, happy child! Teach *me,* if you can, to see the world tinged with the rosy coloring it wears for *you;* teach me to love and pity, as you do, that miserable thing called *man.* I warn you that you have a difficult task, but you seem to be very hopeful."

"Do you hate the world?" asked Gertrude, with straight-forward simplicity.

"Almost," was Mr. Phillips' answer.

"*I* did *once,*" said Gertrude, musingly.

"And will again, perhaps."

"No, that would be impossible; it has been a good foster-mother to its orphan child, and now I love it dearly."

"Have they been kind to you?" asked he, with eagerness. "Have heartless strangers deserved the love you seem to feel for them?"

"Heartless strangers!" exclaimed Gertrude, the tears rushing to her eyes. "O, sir, I wish you could have known my Uncle True, and Emily, dear, blind Emily! You would think better of the world, for their sakes."

"Tell me about them," said he, in a low, unsteady voice, and looking fixedly down into the precipice which yawned at his feet.

"There is not much to tell, only that one was old and poor, and the other wholly blind; and yet they made everything rich, and bright, and beautiful, to me, a poor, desolate, injured child."

"Injured! Then you acknowledge that you had previously met with wrong and injustice?"

"I!" exclaimed Gertrude; "my earliest recollections are only of want, suffering, and much unkindness."

"And these friends took pity on you?"

"Yes. One became an earthly father to me, and the other taught me where to find a heavenly one."

"And ever since then you have been free and light as air, without a wish or care in the world?"

"No, indeed, I did not say so,—I do not mean so," said Gertrude. "I have had to part from Uncle True, and to give up other dear friends, some for years and some forever; I have had many trials, many lonely, solitary hours, and even now am oppressed by more than one subject of anxiety and dread."

"How, then, so cheerful and happy?" asked Mr. Phillips.

Gertrude had risen, for she saw Dr. Jeremy approaching, and stood with one hand resting upon a solid mass of stone, under whose protecting shadow she had been seated. She smiled a thoughtful smile at Mr. Phillips' question; and after casting her eyes a moment into the deep valley beneath her, turned them upon him with a look of holy faith, and said, in a low but fervent tone, "I see the gulf yawning beneath me, but I lean upon the Rock of ages."

Gertrude had spoken truly when she said that more than one anxiety and dread oppressed her; for, mingled with a daily increasing fear lest the time was fast approaching when Emily would be taken from her, she had of late been harassed and grieved by the thought that Willie Sullivan, towards whom her heart yearned with more than a sister's love, was fast forgetting the friend of his childhood, or, at least, ceasing to regard her with the love and tenderness of former years. It was now some months since she had received a letter from India; the last was short, and written in a haste which Willie apologized for on the score of business cares and duties, and Gertrude was compelled unwillingly to admit the chilling presentiment that now that his mother and grandfather were no more the ties which bound the exile to his native home were sensibly weakened.

Nothing would have induced her to hint, even to Emily, a suspicion of neglect on Willie's part; nothing would have shocked her more than hearing such neglect imputed to him by another; but still, in the depths of her own heart, she sometimes mused with wonder upon his long silence, and the strange diminution of intercourse between herself and him. During several weeks in which she had received no tidings she had still continued to write as usual, and felt sure that such reminders must have reached him by every mail. What, then, but illness or indifference could excuse his never replying to her faithfully despatched missives? She often tried to banish from her mind any self-questioning upon a subject so involved in uncertainty; but at times a sadness came over her which could only be dispersed by turning her thoughts upward with that trusting faith and hope which had so often sustained her drooping spirits, and it was from one of these soaring reveries that she had turned with pitying looks and words to the fellow-sufferer whose moans had escaped him even in his dreams.

Dr. Jeremy's approach was the signal for hearty congratulations and good-mornings between himself and Mr. Phillips; the doctor began to converse in his animated manner, spoke with hearty delight of the beauty and peacefulness of that bright Sabbath morning in the mountains; and Mr. Phillips, compelled to exert himself, and conceal, if he could not dispel, the gloom which weighed upon his mind, talked with an ease, and even playfulness, which astonished Gertrude, who walked back to the house silently wondering at this strange and inconsistent man. She did not see him at breakfast, and at dinner he took a seat at some distance from Dr. Jeremy's party, and merely acknowledged their acquaintance by a graceful salutation to Gertrude as she left the dining-hall.

Still later in the day, he suddenly made his appearance upon the broad piazza where Emily and Gertrude were seated, one pair of eyes serving, as usual, to paint pictures for the minds of both. There had been a thunder-shower, but, as the sun went down, and the storm passed away, a brilliant bow, and its almost equally brilliant reflection, spanned the horizon, seemingly far beneath the height of the moutain-top, and the lights and shadows which were playing upon the valley and its shining river were brilliant and beautiful in the extreme. Gertrude hoped Mr. Phillips would join them; she knew that Emily would be charmed with his rich and varied conversation, and felt an instinctive hope that the sweet tones of the comfort-carrying voice which so many loved and blessed would speak to his heart a lesson of peace. But she hoped in vain; he started on seeing them, walked hastily away, and Gertrude soon after espied him toiling up the same steep path which had attracted them both in the morning,—nor did he make his appearance at the hotel again that night.

The Jeremys stayed two days longer at the Mountain House; the invigorating air benefited Emily, who appeared stronger than she had done for weeks past, and was able to take many a little stroll in the neighborhood of the house.

Gertrude was never weary of the glorious prospect, upon which she gazed with ever increasing delight; and an excursion which she and the doctor made on foot to the cleft in the heart of the mountain, where a narrow stream leaps a distance of two hundred feet into the valley below, furnished the theme for many a descriptive revery, of which Emily reaped a part of the enjoyment. They saw no more of their new acquaintance, who had disappeared without their knowledge. Dr. Jeremy inquired of their host concerning him, and learned that he left at an early hour on Monday, and took up a pedestrian course down the mountain.

The doctor was surprised and disappointed, for he liked Mr. Phillips exceedingly, and had flattered himself, from some particular inquiries he had made concerning their proposed route, that he had an idea of attaching himself to their party.

"Never mind, Gerty," said he, in a tone of mock condolence. "I daresay we shall come across him yet, some time when we least expect it."

CHAPTER XXXVII

Led by simplicity divine,
She pleased, and never tried to shine.
—*Hannah More*

FROM CATSKILL Dr. Jeremy proceeded directly to Saratoga. The place was crowded with visitors, for the season was at its height, and the improvident traveller having neglected to secure rooms, they had no right to expect any accommodation.

"Where do you propose stopping?" inquired an acquaintance of the doctor's, whom they accidentally encountered in the cars.

"At Congress Hall," was the reply. "It will be a quiet place for us old folks, and more agreeable than any other house to Miss Graham, who is an invalid."

"You are expected, I conclude?"

"Expected?—No; who should be expecting us?"

"Your landlord. If you have not engaged rooms you will fare badly, for every hotel is crowded to overflowing."

"We must take our chance, then," said the doctor, with an indifference of manner which wholly forsook him upon his fairly arriving at his destination, and learning that his friend's words were true.

"I don't know what we are going to do," said he, as he joined the ladies, whom he had left for a few moments while he made inquiries; "they say every house is full; and, if so, we'd better take the next train of cars and be off, for we can't sleep in the street."

"Carriage, sir?" shouted a hackman, leaning over a railing a few steps distant, and beckoning to the doctor with all his might, while another and still bolder aspirant for employment tapped his shoulder, and made a similar suggestion, in a most insinuating tone of voice.

"Carriage!" repeated the doctor, angrily. "What for? where would you carry us, for mercy's sake? There is n't a garret to be had in your town, for love or money."

"Well, sir," said the last-mentioned petitioner (a sort of omnibus attaché, taking off his cap as he spoke, and wiping his forehead with a torn and soiled pocket-handkerchief), "the houses is pretty considerable full just now, to be sure, but may-be you can get colonized out."

"*Colonized out?*" said the doctor, still in a tone of extreme vexation. "That's what I think we are already; what I want is to get *in* somewhere. Where do you usually drive your coach?"

"To Congress Hall."

"Drive up, then, and let us get in; and, mind, if they don't take us at Congress Hall, we shall expect you to keep us until we find better accommodations."

Mrs. Jeremy, Emily and Gertrude, were consequently assisted into a small omnibus, and closely packed away among half a dozen ladies and children, who, tired, and anxious, were schooling themselves to patience, or encouraging themselves with hope. The doctor took a seat upon the outside, and the moment the vehicle stopped hastened to present himself to the landlord. As he had anticipated, there was not a vacant corner in the house. Wishing to accommodate him, however, the office-keeper announced the possibility that he might be able before night to furnish him with one room in a house in the next street.

"One room! in the next street!" cried the doctor. "Ah, that's being colonized out, is it? Well, sir, it won't do for me; I must have a place to put my ladies in at once. Why in conscience don't you have hotels enough for your visitors?"

"It is the height of the season, sir, and—"

"Why, Dr. Jeremy!" exclaimed the youthful voice of Netta Gryseworth, who was passing through the hall with her grandmother, "how do you do, sir? Are Miss Graham and Miss Flint with you? Have you come to stay?"

Before the doctor could answer her questions, and pay his respects to Madam Gryseworth, a venerable old lady, whom he had known thirty years before, the landlord of the hotel accosted him.

"Dr. Jeremy?" said he. "Excuse me, I did not know you. Dr. Jeremy, of Boston?"

"The same," said the doctor, bowing.

"Ah! we are all right, then. Your rooms are reserved, and will be made ready in a few minutes; they were vacated two days ago, and have not been occupied since."

"What is all this?" exclaimed the honest doctor. "I engaged no rooms."

"A friend did it for you, then, sir; a fortunate circumstance, especially as you have ladies with you. Saratoga is very crowded at this season; there were seven thousand strangers in the town yesterday."

The doctor thanked his stars and his unknown friend, and summoned the ladies to enjoy their good fortune.

"Why, now, an't we lucky?" said Mrs. Jeremy, as she glanced round the comfortable room allotted to herself, and then, crossing the narrow entry, took a similar survey of Emily's and Gertrude's apartment. "After all the talk everybody made, too, about the crowd of folks there were here scrambling for places!"

The doctor, who had just come up stairs, having waited to give directions concerning his baggage, approached the door in time to hear his wife's last remark, and entering with his finger upon his lip, and a mock air of mystery, exclaimed, in a low voice, "Hush! hush! don't say too much about it! We are profiting by a glorious mistake on the part of our good landlord. These rooms were engaged for somebody, that's certain, but not for us. However, they can't do more than turn us out when the right folks come, and until then we have a prospect, I see, of very good lodgings."

But, if the Jeremys were not the right folks, the right folks never came, and, in the course of a week, our party not only ceased to be conscious of their precarious footing in the house, but even had the presumption to propose, and the good fortune to obtain, a favorable exchange for Emily to a bed-room upon the first floor, which opened directly into the drawing-room, and saved her the necessity of passing up and down the often crowded staircases.

It was nearly tea-time on the day of their arrival, and Emily and Gertrude had just completed their toilet, when there was a light rap upon their door. Gertrude hastened to open it, and to admit Ellen Gryseworth, who, while she saluted her with southern warmth of manner, hesitated at the threshold, saying, "I am afraid you will think me an intruder, but Netta told me you had arrived, and hearing accidentally from the chambermaid that you had the next room to mine, I could not forbear stopping a moment as I passed to tell you how very glad I am to see you again."

Gertrude and Emily expressed their pleasure at the meeting, thanked her for her want of ceremony, and urged her to come in and remain with them until the gong sounded for tea. She availed herself of the invitation, and taking a seat upon the nearest trunk, proceeded to inquire concerning their travels and Emily's health since they parted at West Point.

Among other adventures, Gertrude mentioned their having again encountered Mr. Phillips. "Indeed!" said Miss Gryseworth, "he seems to be a ubiquitous individual. He was in Saratoga a day or two ago, and sat opposite to me at our dinnertable, but I have not seen him since. Did you become acquainted with him, Miss Graham?"

"I am sorry to say, I did not," replied Emily; then, looking smilingly at Gertrude, she added, "Gerty was so anxious for an opportunity to introduce me, that I was quite grieved for her disappointment."

"Then you liked him!" said Miss Gryseworth, addressing herself to Gertrude, and speaking with great earnestness. "I knew you would."

"He interested me much," replied Gertrude. "He is very agreeable, very peculiar, and to me rather incomprehensible."

"Non-committal, I see," said Miss Gryseworth, archly. "I hope you will have a chance to make up your mind; it is more than I can do, I confess; for, every time I am in his company, I recognize some new and unexpected trait of character. He got so angry with one of the waiters, the day he dined with us in New York, that I was actually frightened. However, I believe my fears were groundless, for he is too much of a gentleman to bandy words with an inferior, and though his eyes flashed like coals of fire, he kept his temper from blazing forth. I will do him the justice to say that this great indignation did not spring from any neglect he had himself received, but from the man's gross inattention to two dowdy-looking women from the country, who had never thought of such a thing as feeing him, and therefore got nothing to eat until everybody else had finished, and looked all the time as disappointed and ashamed as if they were just out of the State Prison."

"Too bad!" exclaimed Gertrude, energetically. "I don't wonder Mr. Phillips felt provoked with the mercenary fellow. I like him for that."

"It *was* too bad," said Miss Gryseworth. "I could n't help pitying them, myself. One of them—a young girl, fresh from the churn, who had worn her best white gown on purpose to make a figure in the city—looked just ready to burst out crying."

"I hope such instances of neglect are not very common," said Gertrude. "I am afraid, if they are, Emily and I shall be on the crying list, for Dr. Jeremy never will fee the waiters before-hand; he says it is a mean thing, and he should scorn to command attention in that way."

"O, you need have no such fear," said Miss Gryseworth. "Persons in the least accustomed to hotel life can always command a moderate share of attention, especially in so well-regulated an establishment as this. Grandmamma shares the doctor's views with regard to bargaining for it beforehand, but no one ever sees her neglected here. The case which occurred in New York was a gross instance of that partiality for which the public are partly to blame. The waiters can tell easily enough who will endure to be imposed upon, and the embarrassed faces of the two country ladies, who found so fierce an advocate in Mr. Phillips, were alone sufficient to lay them open to any degree of neglect."

Another light tap at the door, and this time it was Netta Gryseworth, who entered, exclaiming, "I hear Ellen's voice, so I suppose I may come in. I am provoked," added she, as she kissed Emily's hand, and shook Gertrude's with a freedom and vivacity which seemed to spring partly from girlish hoydenism and partly from high-bred independence of manner, "to think that while I have been watching about the drawing-room-doors for this half-hour, so as to see you the first minute you came in, Ellen has been sitting here on a trunk, as sociable as all the world, enjoying your society, and telling you every bit of the news."

"Not every bit, Netta," said Ellen; "I have left several choice little morsels for you."

"Have you told Miss Flint about the Foxes and the Coxes that were here yesterday?—Has she, Miss Flint?"

"Not a word about them," said Gertrude.

"Nor about the fright we had on board the steamboat?"

"No."

"Nor about Mr Phillips' being here?"

"O, yes! she told us that."

"Ah, she did!" exclaimed Netta, with an arch look, which called up her sister's blushes. "And did she tell you how he occupied this room, and how we heard him through the thin partition pacing up and down all night, and how it kept me from sleeping, and gave me a terrrible headache all the next day?"

"No, she did not tell me that," said Getrude.

"You don't either of you walk all night, do you?" asked Netta.

"Not often."

"O, how thankful we ought to be to have you for neighbors!" replied Netta. "If that horrible man had staid here and kept up that measured tread, there would have been a suicide either in his room or ours before many nights."

"Do you think he was ill?" inquired Gertrude.

"No, indeed," said Ellen; "it was nothing very remarkable,—not for him, at least,—all his habits are peculiar; but it kept Netta awake an hour or two, and made her fidgetty."

"An hour or two, Ellen?" cried Netta. "It was the whole night."

"My dear sis," said Ellen, "you don't know what a whole night is. You never saw one."

A little sisterly discussion might have ensued about the length of Mr. Phillips' walk and Netta's consequent wakefulness, but, fortunately, the gong sounded, and Netta flew off to her own room to brush out her puffs before tea.

Saratoga is a queer place. One sees congregated there, at the height of the season, delegates from every part of our own and from many foreign countries. Fashion's ladder is transplanted thither, and all its rounds are filled. Beauty, wealth, pride and folly, are well represented; and so too are wit, genius and learning. Idleness reigns supreme, and no one, not even the most active, busy and industrious citizen of our working land, dares, in this her legitimate province, to dispute her temporary sway. Every rank of society, every profession, and almost every trade, meet each other on an easy and friendly footing. The acknowledged belle, the bearer of an aristocratic name, the owner of a well-filled purse, the renowned scholar, artist or poet, have all a conspicuous sphere to shine in. There are many counterfeits, too. The nobodies at home stand a chance to be considered somebodies here; and the *first people* of a distant city, accustomed to consider themselves somebodies, sit in corners and pout at suddenly finding themselves nobodies. All come, however, from a common motive; all are in pursuit of amusement, recreation and rest from labor; and, in this search after pleasure, a friendly and benevolent sentiment for the most part prevails. All are in motion, and the throngs of well-dressed people moving to and fro, on foot, on horseback, and in carriages, together with the gay assemblages crowded upon the piazzas of the hotels, constitute a lively and festive scene; and he who loves to observe human nature may study it here in its most animated form.

It was a wholly new experience to Gertrude; and although, in the comparative retirement and privacy of Congress Hall, she saw only the reflection of Saratoga gayety, and heard only the echo of its distant hum, there was enough of novelty and excitement to entertain, amuse and surprise one who was a complete novice in the ways of fashionable life. In the circle of high-bred, polished, literary and talented persons whom Madam Gryseworth drew about her, and into which Dr. Jeremy's party were at once admitted as honored members, Gertrude found much that was congenial to her cultivated and superior taste, and she herself soon came to be appreciated and admired as she deserved. Madam Gryseworth was a lady of the old school,—one who had all her life been accustomed to the best society, and who continued, in spite of her advanced years, to enjoy and to adorn it. She was still an elegant-looking woman, tall and stately; and, though a little proud, and to strangers a little reserved, she soon proved herself an agreeable companion to people of all ages. For the first day or two of their acquaintance, poor Mrs. Jeremy stood much in awe of her, and could not feel quite at ease in her presence; but this feeling wore off wonderfully quick, and the stout little doctor's lady soon became exceedingly confiding and chatty towards the august dame.

One evening, when the Jeremys had now been a week at Saratoga, as Emily and Gertrude were leaving the tea-table, they were joined by Netta Gryseworth, who, linking her arm in Gertrude's, exclaimed, in her usual gay manner, "Gertrude, I shall quarrel with you soon!"

"Indeed!" said Gertrude, "on what ground?"

"Jealousy."

Gertrude blushed slightly.

"O! you need n't turn so red; it is not on account of any gray-headed gentleman's staring at you all dinner-time, from the other end of the table. No; I'm indifferent on that score. Ellen and you may disagree about Mr. Phillips' attentions, but I'm jealous of those of another person."

"I hope Gertrude is n't interfering with your happiness in any way," said Emily, smiling.

"She is, though," replied Netta, "my happiness, my pride, my comfort. She is undermining them all; she would not dare to conduct so, Miss Graham, if you could see her behavior."

"Tell me all about it," said Emily, coaxingly, "and I will promise to interest myself for you."

"I doubt that," answered Netta; "I am not sure but you are a coadjutor with her. However, I will state my grievance. Do you not see how entirely she engrosses the attention of an important personage? Are you not aware that Peter has ceased to have eyes for any one else? For my own part, I can get nothing to eat or drink until Miss Flint is served, and I'm determined to ask papa to change our seats at the table. It is n't that I care about my food; but I feel insulted,—my pride is essentially wounded. A few days ago, I was a great favorite with Peter, and all my pet dishes were sure to be placed directly in front of me; but now the tune is changed, and, this very evening, I saw him pass Gertrude the blackberries, which the creature knows I delight in, while he pushed a dish of blues towards me in a contemptuous manner, which seemed to imply, 'Blueberries are good enough for *you,* miss!'"

"I have noticed that the waiters are very attentive to us," said Emily; "do you suppose Gertrude has been secretly bribing them?"

"She says not," replied Netta. "Did n't you tell me so yesterday, Gertrude, when I was drawing a similar comparison between their devotion to you and to our party? Did n't you tell me that neither the doctor nor any of you ever gave Peter a cent?"

"Certainly," answered Gertrude; "his attentions are all voluntary; but I attribute them entirely to Emily's influence, and his desire to serve her."

"It 's no such thing!" said Netta, emphasizing her remark by a mysterious little shake of the head;—"it 's sorcery, I 'm sure of it; you 've been practising the black art, Gertrude, and I 'll warn Peter this very day."

As she spoke, they reached a corner of the drawing-room where the old ladies Gryseworth and Jeremy were sitting upon a sofa, engaged in earnest conversation, while Ellen, who had just returned from a drive with her father, stood talking with him and a Mr. Petrancourt, who had that evening arrived from New York.

The ladies on the sofa made room for Emily, and Netta and Gertrude seated themselves near by. Occasionally, Madam Gryseworth cast glances of annoyance at a group of children on the other side of the room, who by their noisy shouts continually interrupted her remarks, and prevented her understanding those of her neighbor. Gertrude's attention soon became attracted by them also to such a degree that she did not hear more than half of the lively and gay sallies of wit and nonsense which Netta continued to pour forth.

"Do go and play with those children, Gertrude," said Netta, at last; I know you 're longing to."

"I'm longing to stop their play!" exclaimed Gertrude; an apparently ill-natured remark, which we are bound to explain. Some half-dozen gayly and fancifully-dressed children, whose mothers were scattered about on the piazzas, and whose nurses were at supper, had collected around a strange little new-comer, whom they were subjecting to every species of persecution. Her clothes, though of rich material, were most untidily arranged, and appeared somewhat soiled by travelling. Her little black silk frock (for the child was clad in mourning) seemed to be quite outgrown, being much shorter than some of her other garments, and her whole appearance denoted great negligence on the part of her parents or guardian. When Madam Gryseworth's evident disturbance first led Gertrude to

288

notice the youthful group, this little girl was standing in their midst, looking wildly about her for a chance to escape; but this the children prevented, and continued to ply her with questions, each of which called forth
a derisive shout from all but the poor little object of attack, who, on her
part, looked ready to burst into tears. Whether the scene reminded
Gertrude of some of her own experiences, or merely touched the chord of
a universal spirit of sympathy for the injured, she could not keep her eyes
from the little party; and, just as Netta was fairly launched upon one of her
favorite topics,—namely, Mr. Phillips and his unaccountable conduct,—
she sprung from her seat, exclaiming, "They shan't torment that child so!"
and hastily crossed the room to the rescue.

Netta burst into a hearty laugh at Gertrude's excited and enthusiastic
manner of starting on her benevolent errand; and this, together with the
unusual circumstance of her crossing the large and crowded room hastily
and alone, drew the inquiries of all the circle whom she had left, and
during her absence she unconsciously became the subject of discussion and
remark.

"What is the matter, Netta?" asked Madam Gryseworth "Where has
Gertrude gone?"

"To offer herself, as a champion, grandmamma, for that little rowdy-
dowdy looking child."

"Is she the one who has been making all this noise?"

"No, indeed, but I believe she is the cause of it."

"It is n't every girl," remarked Ellen, "who could cross a great room
like this so gracefully as Gertrude can."

"She has a remarkably good figure," said Madam Gryseworth, "and
knows how to walk; a very rare accomplishment, now-a-days."

"She is a very well-formed girl," remarked Dr. Gryseworth, who had
observed Gertrude attentively as she crossed the room, and now, hearing
her commented upon, turned to take his part in the criticism; "but the
true secret of her looking so completely the lady lies in her having uncommon dignity of character, being wholly unconscious of observation and
independent of the wish to attract it, and therefore simply acting herself.
She dresses well, too;—Ellen, I wish you would imitate Miss Flint's style of
dress; nothing could be in better taste."

"Or a greater saving to your purse, papa," whispered Netta, "Gertrude dresses very simply."

"Miss Flint's style of dress would not become Miss Gryseworth," said the fashionable Mrs. Petrancourt, who approached in time to hear the doctor's remark. "Your daughter, sir, is a noble, showy-looking girl, and can carry off a great deal of dress."

'So can a milliner's doll, Mrs. Petrancourt. However, I suppose, in a certain sense, you are right. The two girls are not sufficiently alike to resemble each other, if their dresses were matched with Chinese exactness."

"Resemble each other!—You surely would not wish to see your beautiful daughter the counterpart of one who has not half her attractions."

"Are you much acquainted with Miss Flint?"

"Not at all; but Netta pointed her out to me at the tea-table as being a particular friend."

"Then you must excuse me, ma'am, if I remark that it is impossible you should have any idea of her attractions, as they certainly do not lie on the surface."

"You confess, then, that you do not think her handsome, sir?"

"To tell the truth, I never thought anything about it. Ask Petrancourt; he is an acknowledged judge;" and the doctor bowed in a flattering manner to the lady, who had been the belle of the season at the time her husband paid his addresses to her.

"I will, when I can get a chance; but he is standing too near the blind lady,—Miss Flint's aunt, is she not?"

"Particular friend; not her aunt."

This conversation had been carried on in a low voice, that Emily might not hear it. Others, however, were either more careless or more indifferent to her presence; for Madam Gryseworth began to speak of Gertrude without restraint, and she was at this moment saying, "One must see her under peculiar circumstances to be struck with her beauty at once;— for instance, as I did yesterday, when she had just returned from horseback-riding, and her face was in a glow from exercise and excitement; or as she looks when animated by her intense interest in some glowing and eloquent speaker, or when her feelings are suddenly touched, and the tears start into her eyes, and her whole soul shines out through them!"

"Why, grandmamma!" cried Netta, "you are really eloquent!"

"So is Gertrude, at such times as those I speak of. O! she is a girl after my own heart."

"She must be a very agreeable young lady, from your account," said Mr. Petrancourt. "We must know her."

"You will not find her at all the same stamp as most of the agreeable young ladies whom you meet in the gay circles. I must tell you what Horace Willard said of her. He is an accomplished man and a scholar,—his opinion is worth something. He had been staying a fortnight at the United States Hotel, and used to call here occasionally, to see us. The day he left, he came to me and said, 'Where is Miss Flint? I must have one more refreshing conversation with her before I go. It is a perfect *rest* to be in that young lady's society, for she never seems to be making the least effort to talk with me, or to expect any attempt on my part; she is one of the few girls who never speak unless they have something to say.'—How she has contrived to quiet those children!"

Mr. Petrancourt followed the direction of Madam Gryseworth's eyes. "Is that the young lady you are speaking of?" asked he. "The one with great, dark eyes, and such a splendid head of hair? I have been noticing her for some time."

"Yes, that is she, talking to the little girl in black."

"Madam Gryseworth," said Dr. Jeremy, through the long, open window, and stepping inside as he spoke, "I see you appreciate our Gerty; I did not say too much in praise of her good sense, did I?"

"Not half enough, doctor; she is a very bright girl, and a very good one, I believe."

"Good!" exclaimed the doctor; "I did n't know that goodness counted in these places; but, if goodness is worth speaking of, I should like to tell you a little of what I know of that girl;"—and, without going closely into particulars, he commenced dilating enthusiastically upon Gertrude's noble and disinterested conduct under trying circumstances, and, warming with his subject, had recounted, in a touching manner, her devotion to one old paralytic,—to another infirm, imbecile and ill-tempered old man and his slowly-declining daughter,—and would have proceeded, perhaps, to speak of her recent self-sacrificing labors in Emily's service; but Miss Graham touched his arm, spoke in a low voice, and interrupted him.

He stopped abruptly. "Emily, my dear," said he, "I beg your pardon; I did n't know you were here; but what you say is very true. Gertrude is a private character, and I have no right to bring her before the public. I am an old fool, certainly; but there, we are all friends." And he looked around the circle a little anxiously, cast a slightly suspicious glance at the Petrancourts, and finally rested his gaze upon a figure directly behind Ellen Gryseworth. the latter turned, not having been previously aware that any stranger was in the neighborhood, and, to her surprise, found herself face to face with Mr. Phillips!

"Good-evening, sir," said she, on recognizing him; but he did not seem to hear her. Madam Gryseworth, who had never seen him before, looked up inquiringly.

"Mr. Phillips," said Ellen, "shall I make you acquainted with Mrs. Gryseworth, my—" But, before she could complete the introduction, he had darted quickly through the window, and was walking across the piazza with hasty strides. He drew forth his handkerchief, wiped the moisture from his brow, and unseen and unsuspected, brushed away a tear.

CHAPTER XXXVIII

It was not thus in other days we met:
Hath time, hath absence, taught thee to forget?
——*Mrs. Hemans*

LATER IN THE EVENING, when Gertrude, having resigned her little charge to the nurse who came to seek her, had again joined her party, the attention of every one assembled in the drawing-room was attracted by the entrance of a beautiful and showily-dressed young lady, attended by two or three gentlemen. After glancing round the room for the person whom she came to seek, she advanced towards Mrs. Petrancourt, who, on her part, rose to receive her young visitor. Unexpected as the meeting was to Gertrude, she at once recognized Isabel Clinton, who, however, passed both her and Emily without observing them, and, there being no vacant chair near at hand, seated herself with Mrs. Petrancourt on a couch a little further up the room, and entered into earnest and familiar conversation; nor did she change her position or look in the direction of Dr. Jeremy's party, until just as she was taking her leave. She would have passed them then without noticing their presence, but accidentally hearing Dr. Gryseworth address Miss Flint by name, she half turned, caught Gertrude's eye, spoke a careless "How do you do," with that sort of indifference with which one salutes a very slight acquaintance, cast a look back at Emily, surveyed with an impertinent air of curiosity the rest of the circle to which they belonged, and, without stopping to exchange words or inquiries, walked off whispering to her companions some satirical comments both upon the place and the company.

"O, what a beauty!" exclaimed Netta to Mrs. Petrancourt. "Who is she?"

Mrs. Petrancourt related what she knew of Miss Clinton; told how she had travelled with her in Switzerland, and met her afterwards in Paris, where she was universally admired; then, turning to Gertrude, she remarked, "You are acquainted with her, I see, Miss Flint."

Gertrude replied that she knew her before she went abroad, but had seen nothing of her since her return.

"She has but just arrived," said Mrs. Petrancourt; "she came with her father in the last steamer, and has been in Saratoga but a day or two. She is making a great sensation at the United States, I hear, and has troops of beaux."

"Most of whom are probably aware," remarked Mr. Petrancourt, "that she will have plenty of money one of these days."

Emily's attention was by this time attracted. She had been conversing with Ellen Gryseworth, but now turned to ask Gertrude if they were speaking of Isabel Clinton.

"Yes," said Dr. Jeremy, taking upon himself to reply, "and if she were not the rudest girl in the world, my dear, you would not have remained so long in ignorance of her having been here."

Emily forbore to make any comment. It did not surprise her to hear that the Clintons had returned home, as they had separated from the Grahams soon after the latter went abroad, and she had since heard nothing of their movements; nor was she astonished at any degree of incivility from one who sometimes seemed ignorant of the most common rules of politeness. Gertrude was silent also; but she burned inwardly, as she always did, at any slights being offered to the gentle Emily.

Gertrude and Dr. Jeremy were always among the earliest morning visitors at the spring. The doctor enjoyed drinking the water at this hour; and, as Gertrude was an early riser and fond of walking before breakfast, he made it a point that she should accompany him, partake of the beverage of which he was himself so fond, and afterwards join him in brisk pedestrian exercise until near the hour of the morning meal, which was as early as Mrs. Jeremy or Emily cared to have their slumbers disturbed.

On the morning succeeding the evening of which we have been speaking they had as usual presented themselves at the spring. Gertrude had gratified the doctor, and made a martyr of herself, by imbibing a tumbler-full of a water which she found very unpalatable; and he having quaffed his seventh glass, they had both proceeded some distance on one more walk around the grounds, when he suddenly missed his cane, and, believing that he had left it at the spring, declared his intention to return and look for it.

Gertrude would have gone back also, but, as there might be some difficulty and delay in recovering it, he insisted upon her continuing her walk in the direction of the circular railway, promising to come round the other way and meet her. She had proceeded some little distance, and was walking thoughtfully along, when, at an abrupt winding in the path, she observed a couple approaching her,—a young lady leaning on the arm of a gentleman. A straw hat partly concealed the face of the latter, but in the former she at once recognized Belle Clinton. It was equally evident, too, that Belle saw Gertrude, and knew her, but did not mean to acknowledge her acquaintance; for, after the first glance, she kept her eyes obstinately fixed either upon her companion or the ground. This conduct did not disturb Gertrude in the least; Belle could not feel more indifferent about the acquaintance than she did; but, being thus saved the necessity of awaiting and returning any salutation from that quarter, she naturally bestowed her passing glance upon the gentleman who accompanied Miss Clinton. He looked up at the same instant, fixed his full gray eyes upon her, with merely that careless look, however, with which one stranger regards another, then, turning as carelessly away, made some slight remark to his companion.

They pass on. They have gone some steps,—but Gertrude stands fixed to the spot. She feels a great throbbing at her heart. She knows that look, that voice, as well as if she had seen and heard them yesterday. Could Gertrude forget Willie Sullivan?

But he has forgotten her. Shall she run after him, and stop him, and catch both his hands in hers, and compel him to see, and know, and speak to her? She started one step forward in the direction he had taken, then suddenly paused and hesitated. A crowd of emotions choked, blinded, suffocated her, and while she wrestled with them and they with her, he turned the corner and passed out of sight. She covered her face with her hands (always her first impulse in moments of distress), and leaned against a tree.

It was Willie. There was no doubt of that; but not her Willie,—the *boy* Willie. It was true, time had added but little to his height or breadth of figure, for he was a well-grown youth when he went away. But six years of Eastern life, including no small amount of travel, care, exposure and suffering, had done the work that twice that time would ordinarily have accomplished.

The fresh complexion of the boy had given place to the paler, beard-darkened and somewhat sun-browned tints that mark a ripened manhood; the joyous eye had a deeper cast of thought, the elastic step a more firm and measured tread; while the beaming, sunny expression of countenance had given place to a certain grave and composed look, which marked his features when in repose.

The winning attractiveness of the boy, however, had but given place to equal, if not superior qualities in the man, who was still eminently handsome, and gifted with that inborn and natural grace and ease of deportment which win universal remark and commendation. The broad, open forehead, the lines of mild but firm decision about the mouth, the frank, fearless manner, were as marked as ever, and were alone sufficient to betray his identity to one upon whose memory these, and all his other characteristics, were indelibly stamped; and Gertrude needed not the sound of his well-known voice, though that, too, at the same moment fell upon her ear, to proclaim at once to her beating heart that Willie Sullivan had met her face to face, had passed on, and that she was left alone, unrecognized, unknown, and, to all appearance, unthought of and uncared for!

For a time, this bitter thought, "He does not know me," was alone present to her mind; it filled and engrossed her entire imagination, and sent a thrill of surprise and agony through her whole frame. She did not stop to reflect upon the fact that she was but a child when she parted from him, and that the change in her appearance must be immense. Far less did it occur to her to congratulate herself upon a transformation every shade of which had been to her a proportionate improvement and advantage. The one painful idea, that she was forgotten and lost, as it were, to the dear friend of her childhood, obliterated every other recollection. Had they both been children, as in the earlier days of their brother and sister hood, it would have been easy, and but natural, to dart forward, overtake, and claim him. But time, in the changes it had wrought, had built up a huge barrier between them. Gertrude was a woman now, with all a woman's pride; and delicacy and maiden modesty deterred her from the course which impulse and old affection prompted. Other feelings, too, soon crowded into her mind, in confused and mingled array. Why was Willie here, and with Isabel Clinton leaning on his arm? How came he on this side the ocean? and how happened it that he had not immediately sought herself, the earliest, and, as she had supposed, almost the only friend he had left to welcome him back to his native land? Why had he not written and warned her of his coming? How should she account for his strange silence, and the still stranger circumstance of his hurrying at once to the haunts of fashion, without once visiting the city of his birth, and the sister of his adoption?

Question after question, and doubt following doubt, rushed into her mind so confusedly, that she could not reflect, could not come to any conclusion in the matter. She could only feel and weep; and, giving way to her overpowering emotion, she burst into a flood of tears.

Poor child! It was so different a meeting from what she had imagined and expected! For the six years that she had been growing into woman-hood, it had been the dream of her waking hours, and had come as a beautiful though transient reality to her happy sleep. He could hardly have presented himself at any hour of the day or night, scarcely in any disguise, that would not have been foreseen and anticipated. He could have used no form of greeting that had not already rung in the ears of her fancy; he could bestow upon her no look that would not be familiar. What Willie would say when he first saw her, what he would do to express his delight, the questions he would ask, the exclamations he would utter and the corre-sponding replies on her part, the happiness of them both (lately sobered and subdued to her imagination by the thought of the dear departed ones they had both loved so well),—all this had been rehearsed by Gertrude again and again, in every new instance taking some new form, or varied by some additional circumstance.

But, among all her visions, there had been none which in the least approached the reality of this painful experience that had suddenly plunged her into disappointment and sorrow. Her darkest dreams had never pictured a meeting so chilling; her most fearful forebodings (and she had of late had many) had never prefigured anything so heart-rending as this seemingly total annihilation of all the sweet and cherished relations that had subsisted between herself and the long-absent and exiled wanderer.

No wonder, then, that she forgot the place, the time, everything but her own overwhelming grief; and that, as she stood leaning against the old tree, her chest heaved with sobs too deep for utterance, and great tears trickled from her eyes, and between the little taper fingers that vainly sought to hide her disturbed countenance.

She was startled from her position by the sound of an approaching footstep. Hastily starting forward, without looking in the direction from which it came, and throwing a lace veil (which, as the day was warm, was the only protection she wore upon her head) in such a manner as to hide her face, she wiped away her fast-flowing tears, and hastened on, to avoid being overtaken and observed by any of the numerous strangers who frequented the grounds at this hour.

Half-blinded, however, by the thick folds of the veil, and her sight rendered still dimmer by the tears which continued to fill her eyes, she was scarcely conscious of the unsteady course she was pursuing, when suddenly a loud, whizzing noise, close to her ears, frightened and confused her so that she knew not which way to turn; nor had she time to take a single step; for, at the same instant, an arm was suddenly flung round her waist, she was forcibly lifted from her feet with as much ease and lightness as if she had been a little child, and, before she was conscious what was taking place, found herself detained and supported by the same strong arm, while just in front of her a little hand-car containing two persons was whirling by at full speed. One step more, and she would have reached the track of the miniature railway, and been exposed to serious, perhaps fatal injury, from the rapidly-moving vehicle. Flinging back her veil, she at once perceived her fortunate escape; and, being at the same moment released from the firm grasp of her rescuer, she turned upon him a half-confused, half-grateful face, whose disturbed expression was much enhanced by her previous excitement and tears.

Mr. Phillips—for it was he—looked upon her in the most tender and pitying manner. "Poor child!" said he, soothingly, at the same time drawing her arm through his, "you were very much frightened. Here, sit down upon this bench;" and he would have drawn her towards a seat, but she shook her head, and signified by a movement her wish to proceed towards the hotel. She could not speak; the kindness of his look and voice only served to increase her trouble, and rob her of the power to articulate.

So he walked on in perfect silence, supporting her, however, with the greatest care, and bestowing upon her many an anxious glance. At last, making a great effort to recover her calmness, she partially succeeded,—so much so that he ventured to speak again, and asked, "Did *I* frighten you?"

"You?" replied she, in a low, and somewhat unsteady voice. "O, no! you are very kind."

"I am sorry you are so disturbed," said he; "those little cars are troublesome things; I wish they'd put a stop to them."

"The car?" said Gertrude, in an absent way. "O, yes I forgot."

"You are a little nervous, I fear; can't you get Dr. Jeremy to prescribe for you?"

"The doctor! He went back for his cane, I believe."

Mr. Phillips saw that she was bewildered, obtuse he knew she never was; for, within the last few days, his acquaintance with her had grown and ripened by frequent intercourse. He forbore any attempt at conversation, and they continued their walk to the hotel without another word. Just before leaving her, however, he said, in a tone of the deepest interest, as he held her hand for a moment at parting, "Can I do anything for you? Can I help you?"

Gertrude looked up at him. She saw at once, from his countenance, that he understood and realized that she was unhappy, not nervous. Her eyes thanked him as they again glistened behind a shower of tears. "No, no," gasped she, "but you are very good;" and she hastened into the house, leaving him standing for more than a minute in the spot where she had left him, gazing at the door by which she had disappeared, as if she were still in sight, and he were watching her.

Gertrude's first thought, after parting from Mr. Phillips and gaining the shelter of the hotel, was, how she might best conceal from all her friends, and especially from Miss Graham, any knowledge of the load of grief she was sustaining. That she would receive sympathy and comfort from Emily there could be no doubt; but, in proportion as she loved and respected her benefactress, did she shrink, with jealous sensitiveness, from any disclosure which was calculated to lessen Willie Sullivan in the estimation of one in whose opinion she was anxious that he should sustain the high place to which her own praises had exalted him.

The chief knowledge that Emily had of Willie was derived from Gertrude, and with a mingled feeling of tenderness for him and pride on her own account did the latter dread to disclose the fact that he had returned after so many years of absence, that she had met him in the public walks of Saratoga, and that he had passed her carelessly by.

The possibility naturally presented itself to her mind that he had indeed visited Boston, sought her, and, learning where she might be found, had come hither purposely to see her; nor, on calm reflection, did this supposition seem contradicted by his failing, on a mere casual glance, to recognize her; for she could not be ignorant or insensible of the vast change which had taken place both in her face and figure. But the ray of hope which this thought called up was quickly dissipated by the recollection of a letter received the previous evening from Mrs. Ellis (now acting as house-keeper at Dr. Jeremy's), which would certainly have mentioned the arrival of so important a visitor. There was, however, the still further possibility that this arrival might have taken place since the date of Mrs. Ellis' concise epistle, and that Willie might have but just reached his destination, and not yet had time to discover her temporary place of abode. Though the lei-surely manner in which he was escorting Miss Clinton on her morning walk seemed to contradict the supposition, Gertrude, clinging fondly to this frail hope, and believing that the rest of the day would not pass with-out his presenting himself at the hotel, determined to concentrate all her energies in the effort to maintian her usual composure, at least until her fears should become certainties.

It was very hard for her to appear as usual, and elude the vigilance of the affectionate and careful Emily, who, always deeply conscious of her responsibility towards her young charge, and fearful lest, owing to her blindness, she might often be an insufficient protection to one of so ardent and excitable a temperament, was keenly alive to every sensation and emotion experienced by Gertrude, especially to any fluctuation in her usually cheerful spirits.

And Gertrude's spirits, even when she had armed herself with confi-dence and hope by the encouraging thought that Willie would yet prove faithful to his old friendship, could not but be sorely depressed by the consciousness now forced upon her that he could no longer be to her as he had once been; that they could never meet on the same footing on which they had parted; that he was a man of the world now, with new relations, new cares, new interests; and that she had been deceiving herself, and laboring under a fond delusion, in cherishing the belief that in their case the laws of nature would be suspended, and time have no power to alter or modify the nature and extent of their mutual affection. There was something in the very circumstance of her first meeting him in company with Isabel Clinton which tended to impress her with this conviction. Isabel, of all people, one so essentially worldly, and with whom she had so little sympathy or congeniality! True, she was the daughter of Willie's early and generous employer, now the senior partner in the mercantile house to which he belonged, and would not only be likely to form his acquaintance, but would have an undoubtd claim to every polite attention he might have it in his power to pay her; but still Gertrude could not but feel a greater sense of estrangement, a chilling presentiment of sorrow, from seeing him thus familiarly associated with one who had invariably treated her with scorn and incivility.

There was but one thing for her to do, however; to call up all her self-command, bring pride even to her aid, and endeavor, in any event, to behave with serenity and composure. The very fear that one keen and searching pair of eyes had already penetrated her secret so far as to discover that she was afflicted in some form or other served to put her still more upon her guard; and she therefore compelled herself to enter the room where Emily was awaiting her, bid her a cheerful "good-morning," and assist, as usual, in the completion of her toilet. Her face still bore indications of recent tears; but that Emily could not see, and by breakfast-time even they were effectually removed.

Now, again, new trials awaited her; for Dr. Jeremy, according to his promise, had, after recovering the missing cane, gone to meet her in the direction agreed upon, and, finding her false to her appointment, and nowhere to be found among the grounds, was full of inquiries as to the path she had taken, and her reasons for giving him the slip.

Now, for the first time, she recollected the doctor's promise to rejoin her, and the stipulation that she should proceed in the path she was then following; but, having, until these questions were put to her, quite forgotten the old gentleman, she was unprepared for a reply, blushed, and became very much confused. The truth was that when Gertrude heard Mr. Phillips approaching in the direction she should have taken, she, in her eagerness to avoid meeting any one, took the contrary path to that she had been pursuing, and, after he joined her, retraced her steps to the hotel in the same way she had come, consequently eluding the search of the doctor.

But, before she could plead any excuse, Netta Gryseworth came running up, evidently full of pleasantry and fun, and leaning over Gertrude's shoulder, said, in a whisper loud enough to be heard by all the little circle, who were being delayed on their way to breakfast by the doctor's demand for an explanation, "Gertrude, my dear, such affecting partings ought to be private; I wonder you allow them to take place directly at the door-step."

This remark did not lessen Gertrude's discomfiture, which became extreme on Dr. Jeremy's catching Netta by the arm, as she was about to run off, and insisting upon knowing her meaning, declaring that he already had suspicions of Gertrude, and wanted to know who she had been walking with.

"O, a certain tall young beau of hers, who stood gazing after her when she left him, until I began to fear the cruel creature had turned him into stone. What did you do to the poor man, Gertrude?"

"Nothing," replied Gertrude. "He saved me from being thrown down by the little rail-car, and afterwards walked home with me."

Gertrude answered seriously; she could have laughed and joked with Netta at any other time, but now her heart was too heavy. The doctor did not perceive her growing agitation, however, and pushed the matter still further.

"Quite romantic! imminent danger! providential rescue! tête-a–tête walk home, carefully avoiding the old doctor, who might prove an interruption!—I understand!"

Poor Gertrude, blushing scarlet and pitiably distressed, tried to offer some explanation, and stammered out, with a faltering voice, that she did not notice—she did n't remember.

Ellen Gryseworth gave her a scrutinizing glance,—Emily, an anxious one,—and Netta, half-pitying, half-enjoying her confusion, dragged her off towards the breakfast-hall saying, "Never mind, Gertrude; it 's no such dreadful thing, after all."

She made a pretence of eating breakfast, but could not conceal her want of appetite, and was glad, when Emily had finished her light repast, to accompany her to their own room, where, after relating circumstantially her escape from accident, and Mr. Phillips' agency in that escape, she was permitted by her apparently satisfied hearer to sit down quietly and read aloud to her in a book lent them by that gentleman, to whom, however, owing to unfriendly fortune, no opportunity had ever yet occurred of introducing Emily.

The whole morning passed away, and nothing was heard from Willie. Every time a servant passed through the entry, Gertrude was on the tiptoe of expectation; and on occasion of a tap at the door, such as occurred several times before dinner, she trembled so that she could hardly lift the latch. There was no summons to the parlor, however, and by noon the feverish excitement of alternate expectation and disappointment had brought a deep flush into her face, and she experienced, what was very unusual, symptoms of a severe headache. Conscious, however, of the wrong construction which would be sure to be put upon her conduct, if, upon any plea whatever, she on this day absented herself from the dinner-table, she made the effort to dress with as much care as usual; and, as she passed up the hall to her seat, it was not strange that, though suffering herself, the rich glow that mantled her cheeks, and the brilliancy which excitement had given to her dark eyes, attracted the notice of others beside Mr. Phillips, who, seated at some distance, continued, during the short time that he remained at the table, to observe her attentively.

CHAPTER XXXIX

O'er the wrung heart, from midnight's breathless sky,
Lone looks the pity of the Eternal Eye.
——New Timon

WHEN GERTRUDE WENT to her room after dinner, which she did as soon as she had seen Emily comfortably established in the drawing-room in conversation with Madam Gryseworth, she found there a beautiful bouquet of the choicest flowers, which the chamber-maid assured her she had been commissioned to deliver to herself. She rightly imagined the source from whence they came, divined at once the motives of kindness and sympathy which had prompted the donor of so sweet and acceptable a gift, and felt that, if she must accept pity from any quarter, Mr. Phillips was one from whom she could more easily bear to receive it than from almost any other.

Notwithstanding Netta's intimations, she did not for a moment suspect that any other motives than those of kindness and compassion had instigated the offering of the beautiful flowers. Nor had she reason to do so; Mr. Phillips' manner towards her was rather fatherly than lover-like, and though she began to look upon him as a valuable friend, that was the only light in which she had ever thought of viewing him, or believed that he ever regarded her. She placed the flowers in water, returned to the parlor, and constrained herself to talk on indifferent subjects, until she was happily relieved by the breaking up of their circle, part to ride on horseback, part to take a drive, and the rest a nap. Among these last was Gertrude, who availed herself of her headache as an excuse to Emily for this unwonted indulgence. But she could not sleep, and the day wore wearily on.

Evening came at last, and with it an urgent invitation to Gertrude to accompany Dr. Gryseworth, his daughters, and the Petrancourts, to a concert to be given at the United States Hotel. This she declined doing, and persisted in her refusal, in spite of every endeavor to shake her resolution. She felt that it would be impossible for her to undergo another such encounter as that of the morning,—she should be sure to betray herself; and now that the whole day had passed, and Willie had made no attempt to see her, she felt that she would not, for the world, put herself in his way, and run the risk of being discovered and recognized by him in a crowded concert-room. No,—she would wait; she should see him soon, at the latest, and under the present circumstances she should not know how to meet him; she would preserve her incognito a little longer.

So they all went without her, and many others from their hotel; and the parlor, being half-deserted, was very quiet,—a great relief to Gertrude's aching head and troubled mind. Later in the evening, an elderly man, a clergyman, had been introduced to Emily, and was talking with her; Madam Gryseworth and Dr. Jeremy were entertaining each other, Mrs. Jeremy was nodding, and Gertrude, believing that she should not be missed, was gliding out of the room to go and sit a while by herself in the moonlight, when she met Mr. Phillips in the hall.

"What are you here all alone for?" asked he. "Why did n't you go to the concert?"

"I have a headache."

"I saw you had, at dinner. Is it no better?"

"No. I believe not."

"Come and walk with me on the piazza a little while. It will do you good."

She went; and he talked very entertainingly to her, told her a great many amusing anecdotes, succeeded in making her smile, and even laugh, and seemed very much pleased at having done so. He related many amusing things he had seen and heard since he had been staying at Saratoga in the character of a spectator, and ended by asking her if she did n't think it was a heartless show.

The question took Gertrude by surprise. She asked his meaning.

"Don't you think there is something very ridiculous in so many thousand people coming here to enjoy themselves?"

"I don't know," answered Gertrude; "but it has not seemed so to me. I think it's an excellent thing for those who *do* enjoy themselves."

"And how many do?"

"The greater part, I suppose."

"Pshaw! no, they don't. More than half go away miserable, and nearly all the rest dissatisfied."

"Do you think so? Now, I thought the charm of the place was seeing so many happy faces; they have nearly all looked happy to me."

"O, that's all on the surface, and, if you 'll notice, those who look happy one day are wretched enough the next. Yours was one of the happy faces yesterday, but it is n't to-day, my poor child."

Then, perceiving that his remark caused the hand which rested on his arm to tremble, while the eyes which had been attentively raised to his suddenly fell, and hid themselves under their long lashes, he continued. "However, we will trust soon to see it as bright as ever. But they should not have brought you here. Catskill Mountain was a fitter place for your lively imagination and reflecting mind; a sensitive nature should not be exposed to all the shafts of malice, envy and ill-will, it is sure to encounter in one of these crowded resorts of selfish, base and cruel humanity."

"O!" exclaimed Gertrude, at once comprehending that Mr. Phillips suspected her to be smarting under some neglect, feeling of wounded pride, or, perhaps, serious injury; "you speak harshly; all are not selfish, all are not unkind."

"Ah! you are young, and full of faith; trust whom you can, and as long as you can. *I* trust *no one.*"

"No one! Is there none, then, in the whole world, whom you love and confide in?"

"Scarcely; certainly not more than one. Whom should I trust?"

"The good, the pure, the truly great."

"And who are they? How shall we distinguish them? I tell you, my young friend, that in my experience—and it has been rich, ay, very rich,"—and he set his teeth and spoke with bitterness,—"the so-called good, the honorable, the upright man, has proved but the varnished hypocrite, the highly-finished and polished sinner. Yes," continued he, his voice growing deeper, his manner more excited as he spoke, "I can think of one, a respectable man, one of your *first* men, yes, and a church-member, whose hardness, injustice and cruelty, made my life what it has been—a desert, a blank, or worse than that; and I can think of another, an old, rough, intemperate sailor, over whose head a day never passed that he did not take the name of his God in vain, who had, nevertheless, at the bottom of his heart, a drop of such pure, unsullied essence of virtue as could not be distilled from the souls of ten thousand of your polished rogues. Which, then, shall I trust,—the good, religious men, or the low, profane and abject ones?"

"Trust in *goodness,* wherever it be found," answered Gertrude. "But, O, trust *all,* rather than *none.*"

"Your world, your religion, draws a closer line."

"Call it not *my* world, or *my* religion," said Gertrude. "I know of no such line. I know of no religion but that of the heart. Christ died for us all alike, and, since few souls are so sunk in sin that they do not retain some spark of virtue and truth, who shall say in how many a light will at last spring up, by aid of which they may find their way to God?"

"You are a good child, and full of hope and charity," said Mr. Phillips, pressing her arm closely to his side. "I will try and have faith in *you.* But, see! our friends have returned from the concert. Let us go and meet them."

They had had a delightful time; Alboni had excelled herself, and they were *so* sorry Gertrude did not go. "But perhaps," whispered Netta, "you have enjoyed yourself more at home." She half repented of the sly intimation, even before the words had escaped her; for Gertrude, as she stood leaning unconcernedly upon Mr. Phillips' arm, looked so innocent of confusion or embarrassment, that her very manner refuted Netta's suspicions.

"Miss Clinton was there," continued Netta, "and looked beautifully. She had a crowd of gentlemen about her; but did n't you notice (and she turned to Mrs. Petrancourt) that one seemed to meet with such marked favor that I wonder the rest were not discouraged. I mean that tall, handsome young man, who waited upon her into the hall, and went out soon after. She devoted herself to him while he stayed."

"It was the same one, was it not," asked Ellen, "who afterwards, towards the close of the concert, came in and stood leaning against the wall for some minutes?"

"Yes," answered Netta; "but he only waited for Alboni to finish singing, and then, approaching Miss Clinton, leaned over and whispered a word or two in her ear. After that she got up, left her seat, and they both went off, rather to the mortification of the other gentlemen. I noticed them pass by the window where we sat, and walk across the grounds together."

"Yes, just in the midst of that beautiful piece from Lucia," said Ellen. "How could they go away?"

"O, it is not strange, under the circumstances," said Mr. Petrancourt, "that Miss Clinton should prefer a walk with Mr. Sullivan to the best music in the world."

"Why?" asked Netta. "Is he very agreeable? Is he supposed to be the favored one?"

"I should think there was no doubt of it," answered Mr. Petrancourt. "I believe it is generally thought to be an engagement. He was in Paris with them during the spring, and they all came home in the same steamer. Everybody knows it is the wish of Mr. Clinton's heart, and Miss Isabel makes no secret of her preference."

"O, certainly," interposed Mrs. Petrancourt; "it is an understood thing. I heard it spoken of by two or three persons this evening."

What became of Gertrude, all this time? Could she, who for six years had nursed the fond idea that to Willie she was and should still continue to be, all in all,—could she stand patiently by, and hear him thus disposed of and given to another?

She did do it; not consciously, however, for her head swam round, and she would have fallen but for the firm support of Mr. Phillips, who held her arm so tightly that though he felt, the rest could not see, how she trembled. Fortunately, too, none but he thought of noticing her blanched face; and, as she stood somewhat in the shadow, he alone, fully aware of her agitation, was watching the strained and eager eyes, the parted and rigid lips, the death-like pallor of her countenance.

Standing there with her heart beating like a heavy drum, and almost believing herself in a horrid dream, she listened attentively, heard and comprehended every word. She could not, however, have spoken or moved for her life, and in an instant more accident might have betrayed her excited and almost alarming condition. But Mr. Phillips acted, spoke and moved *for* her, and she was spared an exposure from which her delicate and sensitive spirit would have shrunk indeed.

"Mr. Sullivan!" said he. "Ah! a fine fellow I know him. Miss Gertrude, I must tell you an anecdote about that young man;" and, moving forward in the direction in which they had been walking when they met the party from the concert, he made as if they were still intending to prolong their promenade,—a promenade, however, in which he was the only walker, for Gertrude was literally borne upon his arm, until the rest of the company, who started at the same moment for the parlor, were hid within its shelter, and he and his companion were left the sole occupants of that portion of the piazza.

Until then he proceeded with his story, and went so far as to relate that he and Mr. Sullivan were, a few years previous, travelling together across an Arabian desert, when the latter proved of signal service in saving him from a sudden attack by a wandering tribe of Bedouins. By the time he had thus opened his narration, her perceived that all danger of observations was passed, and hesitated not to stop abruptly, and, without ceremony or apology, place her in an arm-chair which stood conveniently near. "Sit here," said he, "while I go and bring you a glass of water." He then wrapped her mantle tightly about her, and walked quickly away.

O, how Gertrude thanked him in her heart for thus considerately leaving her, and giving her time to recover herself! It was the most judicious thing he could have done, and the kindest. He saw that she would not faint, and knew that left alone she would soon rally her powers; perhaps be deceived by the idea that even he was only half aware of her agitation, and wholly ignorant of its cause.

He was gone some minutes, and when he returned she was perfectly calm. She tasted the water, but he did not urge her to drink it; he knew she did not require it. "I have kept you out too long," said he; "come, you had better go in now."

She rose; he put her arm once more through his, guided her feeble steps to a window which opened into hers and Emily's room, and then, pausing a moment, said, in a meaning tone, at the same time enforcing his words by the fixed glance of his piercing eye, "You exhort me, Miss Gertrude, to have faith in everybody; but I bid you, all inexperienced as you are, to beware lest you believe too much. Where you have good foundation for confidence, abide by it, if you can, firmly and bravely; but trust nothing which you have not fairly tested, and, especially, rest assured that the idle gossip of a place like this is utterly unworthy of credit. Good-night."

What an utter revulsion of feeling these words occasioned Gertrude! They came to her with all the force of a prophecy, and struck deep into her heart. Was there not wisdom in the stranger's counsel? It was true, she thought, that he spoke merely such simple axioms as a long experience of the world might dictate; but how forcible, in her case, was their application! Had not she, blindly yielding to her gloomy presentiments and fears, been willing to lend a too ready ear to the whisperings of her own jealous imagination, and a too credulous one to the idle reports of others, while in reality she had proved a traitor to a more noble trust? Who, during the many years she had known him, could have proved himself more worthy of confidence than Willie? Had he not, from his boyhood, been exemplary in every virtue, superior to every meanness and every form of vice? Had he not in his early youth forsaken all that he held most dear, to toil and labor beneath an Indian sun, that he might provide comforts and luxuries for those whose support he eagerly took upon himself? Had he not ever proved honorable, high-minded, sincere and warm of heart? Above all, had he not been imbued from his infancy with the highest and purest of Christian principles?

He had, indeed been all this; and while Gertrude called it to mind, and dwelt upon each phase of his consistent course, she could not fail to remember, too, that Willie, whether as the generous, kind-hearted boy, the adventurous, energetic youth, the successful, respected, yet sorrow-tried man, had ever manifested towards herself the same deep, ardent, enthusiastic attachment. The love which he had shown for her in her childhood, and during that period when, though still a child, she labored under the full-grown care and sorrow entailed upon her by Uncle True's sickness and death, had seemed to grow and deepen in every successive day, month and year, of their separation.

During their long and regular correspondence, no letter had come from Willie that did not breathe the same spirit of devoted affection for Gertrude,—an exclusive affection, in which there could be no rivalship. All his thoughts of home and future happy days were inseparably associated with her; and although Mrs. Sullivan, with that instinctive reserve which was one of her characteristics, never broached the subject to Gertrude, her whole treatment of the latter sufficiently evinced that to her mind the event of her future union with her son was a thing certain. The bold declaration on Willie's part, conveyed in the letter received by Gertrude soon after his mother's death, that his hopes, his prayers, his labors, were now all for her, was not a more convincing proof of the tender light in which he regarded her than all their previous intercourse had been.

Should Gertrude, then, distrust him? Should she at once set aside all past evidences of his worth, and give ready credence to his prompt desertion of his early friend? No! she resolved immediately to banish the unworthy thought; to cherish still the firm belief that some explanation would shortly offer itself, which would yet satisfy her aching heart. Until then, she would trust him; bravely and firmly too would she trust, for her confidence was not without foundation.

As she made this heroic resolve, she lifted up her drooping head and gazed out into the night. The moon had gone down, and the sky was studded with stars, bright, clear and beautiful. Gertrude loved a starry night. It invigorated and strengthened her; and now, as she looked up, directly above her head stood the star she so much loved,—the star which she had once fondly fancied it was Uncle True's blessed privilege to light for her. And, as in times long past these heavenly lights had spoken of comfort to her soul, she seemed now to hear ringing in her ears the familiar saying of the dear old man, "Cheer up, birdie, for I 'm of the 'pinion 't will all come out right at last."

Gertrude continued through the short remainder of the evening in an elevated frame of mind, which might almost be termed joyful; and, thus sustained, she was able to go back to the drawing-room for Emily, say good-night to her friends with a cheerful voice, and before midnight she sought her pillow and went quietly to sleep.

This composed state of mind, however, was partly the result of strong excitement, and therefore could not last. The next morning found her once more yielding to depressed spirits, and the effort which she made to rise, dress and go to breakfast, was almost mechanical. She excused herself from her customary walk with the doctor, for to that she felt quite unequal. Her first wish was to leave Saratoga; she longed to go home, to be in a quiet place, where so many eyes would not be upon her; and when the doctor came in with the letters which had arrived by the early mail, she looked at them so eagerly that he observed it, and said, smilingly, "None for you, Gerty; but one for Emily, which is the next best thing, I suppose."

To Gertrude this was the *very* best thing, for it was a long-expected letter from Mr. Graham, which would probably mention the time of his return from abroad, and consequently determine the continuance of her own and Emily's visit at Saratoga.

To their astonishment, he had already arrived in New York, and desired them to join him there the following day. Gertrude could hardly conceal her satisfaction, which was, however, if noticed by her friends, merely attributed to the pleasure she probably felt at the return of Mr. and Mrs. Graham; and Emily, really delighted at the prospect of so soon meeting her father, to whom she was fondly attached, was eager to commence preparations for leaving.

They therefore retired to their own room, and Gertrude's time until dinner was fully occupied in the business of packing. Throughout the whole of the previous day she had been anxiously hoping that Willie would make his appearance at their hotel; now, on the contrary, she as earnestly dreaded such an event. To meet him in so public a manner too as must here be inevitable, would, under her present state of feelings, be insupportable; she would infinitely prefer to be in Boston when he should first see and recognize her; and, if she tormented herself yesterday with the fear that he would not come, the dread that he might do so was a still greater cause of distress to her to-day.

She was therefore relieved when, after dinner, Mr. Phillips kindly proposed a drive to the lake. Dr. Gryseworth and one of his daughters had, he assured Gertrude, agreed to take seats in a carriage which he had provided, and he hoped she would not refuse to occupy the fourth. As it was an hour when Emily would not require her presence, and she would thus be sure to avoid Willie, she gladly consented to the arrangement.

They had been at the lake nearly an hour. Dr. Gryseworth and his daughter Ellen had been persuaded by a party whom they met there to engage in bowling. Mr. Phillips and Gertrude had declined taking part, but stood for some time looking on. The day, however, being warm, and the air in the building uncomfortably close, they had gone outside and seated themselves on a bench at a little distance, to wait until the game was concluded. As they sat thus, surveying the beautiful sheet of water, now rosy red with the rays of the descending sun, a couple approached and took up a position near them. Mr. Phillips was quite screened from their observation by the trunk of a huge tree, and Gertrude sufficiently so to be unnoticed, though the sudden paleness which overspread her face as they drew near was so marked as clearly to indicate that she saw and recognized William Sullivan and Isabel Clinton. The words which they spoke, also, fell distinctly upon her ear.

"Shall I, then, be so much missed?" asked Isabel, looking earnestly in the face of her companion, who, with a serious air, was gazing out upon the water.

"Missed!" replied he, turning towards her, and speaking in a slightly-reproachful voice. "How can it be otherwise? Who can supply your place?"

"But it will be only two days."

"A short time, under ordinary circumstances," said Willie, "but an eternity—" He here checked himself, and made a sudden motion to proceed on their walk.

Isabel followed him, saying, "But you will wait here until my return?"

He again turned to reply, and this time the reproachful look which overspread his features was visible to Gertrude, as he said, with great earnestness, "Certainly; can you doubt it?"

The strange, fixed, unnatural expression which took possession of Gertrude's countenance as she listened to this conversation, to her so deeply fraught with meaning, was fearful to witness.

"Gertrude!" exclaimed Mr. Phillips, after watching her for a moment. "Gertrude, for heaven's sake do not look so! Speak, Gertrude! What is the matter?"

But she did not turn her eyes, did not move a feature of that stony face; she evidently did not hear him. He took her hand. It was cold as marble. His face now wore an appearance of distress almost equal to her own;—great tears rushed to his eyes, and rolled down his cheeks. Once he stretched forth his arms, as if he would gladly clasp her to his bosom and soothe her like a little child, but with evident effort he repressed the emotion. "Gertrude," said he, at length, leaning forward and fixing his eyes full upon hers, "what have these people done to you? Why do you care for them? If that young man has injured you,—the rascal!—he shall answer for it;" and he sprung to his feet.

The words and the action brought Gertrude to herself. "No, no!" said she, "he is not that. I am better now. Do not speak of it; don't tell," and she looked anxiously in the direction of the bowling-alley. "I am a great deal better." And, to his astonishment,—for the fearful, rigid look upon her face had frightened him,—she rose with perfect composure, and proposed going home.

He accompanied her silently, and before they were half-way up the hill where they had left the carriage, they were overtaken by the rest of their party, and, in a few moments, were driving towards Saratoga.

During the whole drive and the evening which followed Gertrude preserved this same rigid, unnatural composure. Once or twice before they reached the hotel Dr. Gryseworth asked her if she felt ill, and Mr. Phillips turned many an anxious glance towards her. The very tones of her voice were constrained,—so much so that Emily, on her reaching the house, inquired, at once, "What is the matter, my dear child?"

But she declared herself quite well, and went through all the duties and proprieties of the evening, bidding farewell to many of her friends, and when she parted from the Gryseworths arranging to see them again in the morning.

To the careless eye, Emily was the more troubled of the two; for Emily could not be deceived, and reflected back, in her whole demeanor, the better-concealed sufferings of Gertrude. Gertrude neither knew at the time, nor could afterwards recall, one-half of the occurrences of that evening. She never could understand what it was that sustained her, and enabled her, half unconsciously, to perform her part in them. How she so successfully concealed the misery she was enduring she never could comprehend or explain. She remembered it only as if it had all been a dream.

Not until the still hours of the night, when Emily appeared to be soundly sleeping by her side, did she venture for an instant to loosen the iron bands of restraint which she had imposed upon herself; but then, the barrier removed, the pent-up torrent of her grief burst forth without check or hindrance. She rose from her bed, and, burying her face in the cushions of a low couch which stood near the window, gave herself up to blessed tears, every drop of which was a relief to her aching soul. Since her early childhood she had never indulged so long and unrestrained a fit of weeping; and, the heaving of her chest, and the deep sobs she uttered, proved the depth of her agony. All other sorrows had found her in a great degree fortified and prepared, armed with religious trust and encouraged by a holy hope; but beneath this sudden and unlooked-for blow she bent, staggered and shrunk, as the sapling of a summer's growth heaves and trembles beneath the wintry blast.

That Willie was faithless to his first love she could not now feel a shadow of doubt; and with this conviction she realized that the prop and stay of her life had fallen. Uncle True and Mrs. Sullivan were both her benefactors, and Emily was still a dear and steadfast friend; but all of these had been more or less dependent upon Gertrude, and, although she could ever repose in the assurance of their love, two had long before they passed away come to lean wholly upon her youthful arm, and the other, the last one left, not only trusted to her to guide her uncertain steps, but those steps were evidently now tending downwards to the grave.

Upon whom, then, should Gertrude lean? To whom should she look as the staff of her young and inexperienced life? To whom could she, with confidence, turn for counsel, protection, support and love? To whom but Willie? And Willie had given his heart to another,—and Gertrude would soon be left alone!

No wonder, then, that she wept as the broken-hearted weep; wept until the fountain of her tears was dry, and she felt herself sick, faint and exhausted. And now she rose, approached the window, flung back from her forehead the heavy folds of her long hair, leaned out, and from the breath of the cool night-breeze drank in a refreshing influence. Her soul grew calmer, as, with her eyes fixed upon the bright lights which shone so sweetly and calmly down, she seemed to commune with holy things. Once more they seemed to compassionate her, and, as in the days of her lonely childhood, to whisper, "Gerty!—Gerty!—poor little Gerty!"

Softened and touched by their pitying glance, she gradually sunk upon her knees; her uplifted face, her clasped hands, the sweet expression of resignation now gradually creeping over her countenance, all gave evidence that, as on the occasion of her first silent prayer to the then unknown God, her now enlightened soul was holding deep communion with its Maker, and once more her spirit was uttering the simple words, "Here am I, Lord!"

O, blessed religion which can sustain the heart in such an hour as this! O, blessed faith and trust, which, when earthly support fails us, and our strongest earthly stay proves but a rope of sand, lifts the soul above all other need, and clasps it to the bosom of its God!

And now a gentle hand is laid upon her head. She turns and sees Emily, whom she had believed to be asleep, but from whom anxiety had effectually banished slumber, and who, with fears redoubled by the sobs which Gertrude could not wholly repress, is standing by her side.

"Gertrude," said she, in a grieved tone, "are you in trouble, and did you seek to hide it from me? Do not turn from me, Gertrude!" and, throwing her arms around her, she drew her head close to her bosom, and whispered, "Tell me all, my darling! What is the matter with my poor child?"

And Gertrude unburdened her heart to Emily, disclosing to her attentive ear the confession of the only secret she had ever kept from her; and Emily wept as she listened, and when Gertrude had finished she pressed her again and again to her heart, exclaiming, as she did so, with an excitement of tone and manner which Gertrude had never before witnessed in the usually calm and placid blind girl, "Strange, strange, that you, too, should be thus doomed! O, Gertrude, my darling, we may well weep together; but still, believe me, your sorrow is far less bitter than mine!"

And then, in the darkness of that midnight hour, was Gertrude's confidence rewarded by the revelation of that tale of grief and woe which twenty years before had blighted Emily's youth, and which, notwithstand-

ing the flight of time, was still vivid to her recollection, casting over her life
a dark shadow, of which her blindness was but a single feature.

CHAPTER XL

When, lo! arrayed in robes of light,
   A nymph celestial came;
She cleared the mists that dimmed my sight—
   Religion was her name.
She proved the chastisement divine,
   And bade me kiss the rod;
She taught this rebel heart of mine
   Submission to its God.
     —*Hannah More*

"*I WAS YOUNGER* than you, Gertrude," said she, "when my trial came,
and hardly the same person in any respect that I have been since you first
knew me. You are aware, perhaps, that my mother died when I was too
young to retain any recollection of her; but my father soon married again,
and in this step-parent, whom I remember with as much tenderness as if
she had been my own mother, I found a love and care which fully compensated for my loss. I can recall her now as she looked towards the latter part
of her life,—a tall, delicate, feeble woman, with a very sweet, but rather
sad face. She was a widow when my father married her, and had one son,
who became at once my sole companion, the partner of all my youthful
pleasures. You told me, many years ago, that I could not imagine how
much you loved Willie, and I was then on the point of confiding to you a
part of my early history, and convincing you that my own experience
might well have taught me how to understand such a love; but I checked
myself, for you were too young then to be burdened with the knowledge of
so sad a story as mine, and I kept silent. How dear my young playmate
became to me, no words can express. The office which each filled, the
influence which each of us exerted upon the other, was such as to create
mutual dependence; for, though his was the leading spirit, the strong and
determined will, and I was ever submissive to a rule which to my easily-
influenced nature was never irksome, there was one respect in which my

bold young protector and ruler ever looked to me for aid and support. It was to act as mediator between him and my father; for, while the boy was almost an idol to his mother, he was ever treated with coldness and distrust by my father, who never understood or appreciated his many noble qualities, but seemed always to regard him with an eye of suspicion and dislike. To my supplicating looks and entreating words, however, he ever lent a willing ear, and all my eloquence was sure to be at the service of my companion when he had a favor to obtain or an excuse to plead.

"That my father's sternness towards her son was a great cause of unhappiness to our mother, I can have no doubt; for I well remember the anxiety with which she strove to conceal his faults and misdemeanors, and the frequent occasions on which she herself instructed me how to propitiate the parent, who, for my sake, would often forgive the boy, whose bold, adventurous, independent disposition, was continually bringing him into collision with one of whose severity, when displeased, you have yourself had some opportunity to judge. My step-mother had been extremely poor in her widowhood, and her child, having inherited nothing which he could call his own, was wholly dependent upon my father's bounty. This was a stinging cause of mortification and trial to the pride of which even as a boy he had an unusual share; and often have I seen him chafed and irritated at the reception of favors which he well understood were far from being awarded by a paternal hand; my father, in the mean time, who did not understand this feeling, mentally accusing him of gross ingratitude.

"As long as our mother was spared to us we lived in comparative harmony; but at last, when I was just sixteen years old, she was stricken with sudden illness, and died. Well do I remember, the last night of her life, her calling me to the bedside, and saying, in a solemn voice, 'Emily, my dying prayer is that you will be a guardian-angel to my boy!' God forgive me," ejaculated the now tearful blind girl, "if I have been faithless to the trust!

"He of whom I am telling you (for Emily carefully forbore to mention his name) was then about eighteen. He had lately become a clerk in my father's counting-room, much against his will, for he earnestly desired a collegiate education; but my father was determined, and, at his mother's and my persuasion, he was induced to submit. My step-mother's death knit the tie between her son and myself more closely than ever. He still continued an inmate of our house, and we passed all the time that he could be spared from the office in the enjoyment of each other's society; for my father was much from home, and, when there, usually shut himself up in his library, leaving us to entertain each other. I was then a school-girl, fond of books, and an excellent student. How often, when you have spoken of the assistance Willie was to you in your studies, have I been reminded of the time when I, too, received similar encouragement and aid from my own youthful companion and friend, who was ever ready to exert hand and brain in my behalf! We were not invariably happy, however. Often did my father's face wear that stern expression which I most dreaded to see; while the excited, disturbed and occasionally angry countenance of his step-son, denoted plainly that some storm had occurred, probably at the counting-room, of which I had no knowledge, except from its after effects. My office of mediator, too, was suspended, from the fact that the difficulties which arose were usually concerning some real or supposed neglect or mismanagement of business matters on the part of the young and inexperienced clerk; a species of faults with which my father, a most thorough merchant and exact accountant, had very little patience, and to which the careless and unbusiness-like delinquent was exceedingly prone. Matters went on thus for about six months, when it suddenly became evident that my father had either been powerfully influenced by insinuations from some foreign quarter, or had himself suddenly conceived a new and alarming idea. He is, as you are aware, a plain man, honest and straight-forward in his purposes, whatever they may be; and, even if it occurred to him to manœuvre, incapable of carrying out successfully, or with tact, any species of artifice. Our eyes could not, therefore, long be closed to the fact that he was resolved to put an immediate check upon the freedom of intercourse which had hitherto subsisted between the two youthful inmates of his house; to forward which purpose he immediately introduced into the family, in the position of housekeeper, Mrs. Ellis, who has continued with us ever since. The almost constant presence of this stranger, together with the sudden interference of my father with such of our long-established customs as favored his step-son's familiar intimacy with me, sufficiently proved his intention to uproot and destroy, if possible, the closeness of our friendship. Nor was it surprising, considering the circumstance that I had already reached the period of womanhood, and the attachment between us could no longer be considered a childish one, while any other might be expected to draw forth my father's disapproval, since his wife's idolized son was as far as ever from being a favorite with him.

"My distress at these proceedings was only equalled by the indignation of my companion in suffering, whom no previous conduct on my father's part had ever angered as this did; nor did the scheme succeed in separating him from me; for, while he on every possible occasion avoided the presence of that spy (as he termed Mrs. Ellis), his inventive genius continually contrived opportunities of seeing and conversing with me in her absence,—a course of behavior calculated to give still greater coloring to my father's suspicions.

"I am convinced that he was mainly actuated to this course by a deep sense of unkindness and injustice, and a desire to manifest his independence of what he considered unwarrantable tyranny; nor have I reason to believe that the idea of romance, or even future marriage with myself, entered at all into his calculations; and I, who at that time knew, or, at least, was influenced by no higher law than his will, lent myself unhesitatingly to a species of petty deception, to elude the vigilance which would have kept us apart. My father, however, as is frequently the case with people of his unsocial temperament and apparent obtuseness of observation, saw more of our manœuvring than we were aware of, and imagined far more than ever in reality existed. He watched us carefully, and, contrary to his usual course of proceeding, forbore for a time any interference. I have since been led to think that he designed to wean us from each other in a less unnatural manner than that which he had at first attempted, by availing himself of the earliest opportunity to transfer his step-son to a situation connected with his own mercantile establishment, either in a foreign country, or a distant part of our own; and forbore, until his plans were ripe, to distress and grieve me by giving way to the feelings of annoyance and displeasure which were burning within him,—for he was, and had ever been, as kind and indulgent toward his undeserving child as was consistent with a due maintenance of his authority.

"Before such a course could be carried out, however, circumstances occurred, and suspicions became aroused, which destroyed one of their victims, and plunged the other—"

Here Emily's voice failed her. She laid her head upon Gertrude's shoulder, and sobbed bitterly.

"Do not try to tell me the rest, dear Emily," said Gertrude. "It is enough for me to know that you are so unhappy. Do not make yourself wretched by dwelling, for my sake, upon sorrows that are past."

"Past!" replied Emily, recovering her voice, and wiping away her tears; "no, they are never past; it is only because I am so little wont to speak of them that they overcome me now. Nor am I unhappy, Gertrude. It is but rarely that my peace is shaken; nor would I now allow my weak nerves to be unstrung by imparting to another the secrets of that never-to-be-forgotten time of trial, were it not that, since you know so well how harmoniously and sweetly my life is passing on to its great and eternal awakening, I desire to prove to my darling child the power of that heavenly faith which has turned my darkness into marvellous light, and made afflictions such as mine the blessed harbingers of final joy.

"But I have not much more to tell, and that shall be in as few words as possible."

She then went on, in a firm though low and suppressed voice.

"I was suddenly taken ill with a fever. Mrs. Ellis, whom I had always treated with coldness, and often with disdain (for you must remember I was a spoiled child), nursed me by night and day with a care and devotion which I had no right to expect at her hands; and, under her watchful attendance, and the skilful treatment of our good Dr. Jeremy (even then the family physician), I began, after some weeks, to recover. One day, when I was sufficiently well to be up and dressed for several hours at a time, I went, for change of air and scene, into my father's library, the room next my own, and there quite alone lay half reclining upon the sofa. Mrs. Ellis had gone to attend to household duties, but, before she left me, she brought from the adjoining chamber and placed within my reach a small table, upon which were arranged various phials, glasses, etc., and among them everything which I could possibly require before her return. It was towards the latter part of an afternoon in June, and I lay watching the approach of sunset from an opposite window. I was oppressed with a sad sense of loneliness, for during the past six weeks I had enjoyed no society but that of my nurse, together with periodical visits from my father; and felt therefore no common satisfaction and pleasure when my most congenial but now nearly forbidden associate unexpectedly entered the room. He had not seen me since my illness, and after this unusually protracted and painful separation our meeting was proportionately tender and affectionate. He had, with all the fire of a hot and ungoverned temper, a woman's depth of feeling, warmth of heart, and sympathizing sweetness of manner. Well do I remember the expression of his noble face, the manly tones of his voice, as, seated beside me on the wide couch, he bathed the temples of my aching head with cologne, which he took from the table near by, at the same time expressing again and again his joy at once more seeing me.

"How long we had sat thus I cannot tell, but the twilight was deepening in the room, when we were suddenly interrupted by my father, who entered abruptly, came towards us with hasty steps, but, stopping short when within a yard or two, folded his arms and confronted his step-son with such a look of angry contempt as I had never before seen upon his face. The latter rose and stood before him with a glance of proud defiance, and then ensued a scene which I have neither the wish nor the power to describe.

"It is sufficient to say that in the double accusation which my excited parent now brought against the object of his wrath he urged the fact of his seeking (as he expressed it) by mean, base, and contemptible artifice to win the affections, and with them the expected fortune, of his only child, as a secondary and pardonable crime, compared with his deeper, darker, and but just detected guilt of forgery,—forgery of a large amount, and upon his benefactor's name.

"To this day, so far as I know," said Emily, with feeling, "that charge remains uncontradicted; but I did not then, I do not now, and I never *can* believe it. Whatever were his faults (and his impetuous temper betrayed him into many), of this dark crime (though I have not even his own word in attestation) I dare pronounce him innocent.

"You cannot wonder, Gertrude, that in my feeble and invalid condition I was hardly capable of realizing at the time, far less of retaining any distinct recollection of the circumstances that followed my father's words. A few dim pictures, however, the last my poor eyes ever beheld, are still engraved upon my memory, and visible to my imagination. My father stood with his back to the light, and from the first moment of his entering the room I never saw his face again; but the countenance of the other, the object of his accusation, illumined as it was by the last rays of the golden sunset, stands ever in the foreground of my recollection. His head was thrown proudly back; conscious but injured innocence proclaimed itself in his clear, calm eye, which shrunk not from the closest scrutiny; his hand was clenched, as if he were vainly striving to repress the passion which proclaimed itself in the compressed lips, the set teeth, the deep and angry indignation which overspread his face. He did not speak,—apparently he could not command voice to do so; but my father continued to upbraid him, in language, no doubt, cutting and severe, though I remember not a word of it. It was fearful to watch the working of the young man's face, while he stood there listening to taunts and enduring reproaches which were no doubt believed by him who uttered them to be just and merited, but which wrought the youth to a degree of frenzy which it was terrible indeed to witness. Suddenly he took one step forward, slowly lifting the clenched hand which had hitherto hung at his side. I know not whether he might then have intended to call Heaven to witness his innocence of the crime with which he was charged, or whether he might have designed to strike my father; for I sprang from my seat, prepared to rush between them, and implore them, for my sake, to desist; but my strength failed me, and with a shriek I sunk back in a fainting fit.

"O, the horror of my awakening! How shall I find words to tell it?—and yet I must! Listen, Gertrude. He—the poor, ruined boy—sprung to help me; and, maddened by injustice, he knew not what he did. Heaven is my witness, I never blamed him; and if, in my agony, I uttered words that seemed like a reproach, it was because I too was frantic, and knew not what I said!"

"What!" exclaimed Gertrude; "he did not—"

"No, no! he did not—he *did not* put out my eyes!" exclaimed Emily; "it was an accident. He reached forward for the cologne which he had just had in his hand. There were several bottles, and, in his haste, he seized one containing a powerful acid which Mrs. Ellis had found occasion to use in my sick room. It had a heavy glass stopper,—and he—his hand was unsteady, and he spilt it all—"

"On your eyes?" shrieked Gertrude.

Emily bowed her head.

"O, poor Emily!" cried Gertrude, "and wretched, wretched young man!"

"Wretched indeed!" ejaculated Emily. "Bestow all your pity on him, Gertrude, for his was the harder fate of the two."

"O, Emily! how intense must have been the pain you endured! How could you suffer so, and live?"

"Do you mean the pain from my eyes? That was severe indeed, but the mental agony was worse!"

"What became of him?" said Gertrude. "What did Mr. Graham do?"

"I cannot give you any exact account of what followed. I was in no state to know anything of my father's treatment of his step-son. You can imagine it, however. He banished him from his sight and knowledge forever; and it is easy to believe it was with no added gentleness, since he had now, beside the other crimes imputed to him, been the unhappy cause of his daughter's blindness."

"And did you never hear from him again?"

"Yes. Through the good doctor, who alone knew all the circumstances, I learned—after a long interval of suspense—that he had sailed for South America; and, in the hope of once more communicating with the poor exile, and assuring him of my continued love, I rallied from the wretched state of sickness, fever and blindness, into which I had fallen; the doctor had even some expectation of restoring sight to my eyes, which were in a much more hopeful condition. Several months passed away, and my kind friend, who was most diligent and persevering in his inquiries, having at length learned the actual residence and address of the ill-fated youth, I was commencing, through the aid of Mrs. Ellis (whom pity had now wholly won to my service), a letter of love, and an entreaty for his return, when a fatal seal was put to all my earthly hopes. He died, in a foreign land, alone, unnursed, untended, and uncared for; he died of that inhospitable southern disease,[1] which takes the stranger for its victim; and I, on hearing the news of it, sunk back into a more pitiable malady; and— alas for the encouragement the good doctor had held out of my gradual restoration to sight!—I wept all his hopes away!"

Emily paused. Gertrude put her arms around her, and they clung closely to each other; grief and sorrow made the union between them dearer than ever.

"I was then, Gertrude," continued Emily, "a child of the world, eager for worldly pleasures, and ignorant of any other. For a time, therefore, I dwelt in utter darkness,—the darkness of despair. I began too again to feel my bodily strength restored, and to look forward to a useless and miserable life. You can form no idea of the utter wretchedness in which my days were passed. Often have I since reproached myself for the misery I must have caused my poor father, who, though he never spoke of it, was, I am sure, deeply pained by the recollection of the terrible scenes we had lately gone through, and who would, I am convinced, have given worlds to restore the past.

"But at last there came a dawn to my seemingly everlasting night. It came in the shape of a minister of Christ, our own dear Mr. Arnold; who opened the eyes of my understanding, lit the lamp of religion in my now softened soul, taught me the way to peace, and led my feeble steps into that blessed rest which even on earth remaineth to the people of God.

"In the eyes of the world, I am still the unfortunate blind girl; one who, by her sad fate, is cut off from every enjoyment; but so great is the awakening I have experienced, that to me it is far otherwise,—and I am ready to exclaim, like him who in old time experienced his Saviour's healing power, 'Once I was blind, but now I see!'"

Gertrude half forgot her own troubles while listening to Emily's sad story; and when the latter laid her hand upon her head, and prayed that she too might be fitted for a patient endurance of trial, and be made stronger and better thereby, she felt her heart penetrated with that deep love and trust which seldom come to us except in the hour of sorrow, and prove that it is through suffering only we are made perfect.

CHAPTER XLI

But in that hour of agony the maid
Deserted not herself; her very dread
Had calmed her; and her heart
Knew the whole horror, and its only part.
  —*Southey*

AS MR. GRAHAM had expressed in his letter the intention of being at the steamboat wharf in New York to meet his daughter and Gertrude on their arrival, Dr. Jeremy thought it unnecessary for him to accompany his charges further than Albany, where he could see them safely on their way, and then proceed to Boston with his wife over the Western Railroad; Mrs. Jeremy being now impatient to return home, and having, moreover, no disposition to revisit the great metropolis of New York during the warm weather.

"Good-by, Gerty," said the doctor, as he bade them farewell on the deck of one of the Hudson-river boats. "I 'm afraid you 've lost your heart in Saratoga; you don't look quite so bright as you did when we first arrived there. It can't have strayed far, however, I think, in such a place as that; so be sure and find it before I see you in Boston."

He had hardly gone, and it wanted a few minutes only of the time for the boat to start, when a gay group of fashionables made their appearance, talking and laughing too loud, as it seemed to Gertrude, to be well-bred; and conspicuous among them was Miss Clinton, whose companions were evidently making her the subject of a great deal of wit and pleasantry, by which, although she feigned to be teased and half-offended, her smiling, blushing face gave evidence that she felt flattered and pleased. At length, the significant gestures of some of the party, and a half-smothered hush-h! gave intimation of the approach of some one who must not overhear their remarks; and presently William Sullivan, with a travelling-bag in his hand, a heavy shawl thrown over one arm, and his countenance grave, as if he had not quite recovered from the chagrin of the previous evening, appeared in sight, passed Gertrude, whose veil was drawn over her face, and joined Isabel, placing his burden on a chair which stood near.

He had hardly commenced speaking to Miss Clinton, however, before the violent ringing of the bell gave notice to all but the passengers to quit the boat, and he was compelled to make a hasty movement to depart. As he did so, he drew a step nearer Gertrude, a step further from her whom he was addressing, and the former plainly distinguished the closing words of his remark: "Then, if you will do your best to return on Thursday, I will try not to be impatient in the mean time."

A moment more, and the boat was on its way; not, however, until a tall figure, who reached the landing just as she started had, to the horror of the spectators, daringly leaped the gap that already divided her from the shore; after which, he sought the gentleman's saloon, threw himself upon a couch, drew a book from his pocket, and commenced reading.

As soon as the boat was fairly under way, and quite prevailed in their neighborhood, Emily spoke softly to Gertrude, and said,

"Did n't I just now hear Isabel Clinton's voice?"

"She is here," replied Gertrude, "on the opposite side of the deck, but sitting with her back towards us."

"Did n't she see us?"

"I believe she did," answered Gertrude, "She stood looking this way while her party were arranging their seats."

"And then chose one which commanded a *different* view?"

"Yes."

"Perhaps she is going to New York to meet Mrs. Graham."

"Very possible," replied Gertrude. "I did n't think of it before."

There was then quite a pause. Emily appeared to be engaged in thought. Presently she asked, in the softest of whispers, "Who was the gentleman who came and spoke to her just before the boat started?"

"Willie," was the tremulous response.

Emily pressed Gertrude's hand, and was silent. She, too, had overheard his farewell remark, and felt its significance.

Several hours passed away, and they had proceeded some distance down the river; for the motion of the boat was rapid—too rapid, as it seemed to Gertrude, for safety. At first occupied by her own thoughts, and unable to enjoy the beautiful scenery, which a few weeks previously had caused her such keen delight, she had sat, inattentive to all around, gazing down into the deep blue water, and communing with her own heart. Gradually, however, she was led to observe several circumstances, which excited so much curiosity, and finally so much alarm, that, effectually aroused from the train of reflections she had been indulging, she had leisure only to take into view her own and Emily's present situation, and its probable consequences.

Several times, since they left Albany, had the boat in which they were passengers passed and repassed another of similar size, construction and speed, likewise responsibly charged with busy, living freight, and bound in the same direction. Occasionally, during their headlong and reckless course, the contiguity of the two boats was such as to excite the serious alarm of one sex, and the unmeasured censure of the other. The rumor began to be circulated that they were racing, and racing desperately. Some few, regardless of danger, and entering upon the interest of the chase with an insane and foolish excitement, watched with pleased eagerness the mad career of rival ambition; but by far the majority of the company, including all persons of reason and sense, looked on in indignation and fear. The usual stopping-places on the river were either recklessly passed by, or only paused at, while, with indecent haste, passengers were shuffled backwards and forwards, at the risk of life and limb, their baggage (or somebody's else) unceremoniously flung after them, the panting, snorting engine in the mean time bellowing with rage at the check thus unwillingly imposed upon its freedom. Towards noon the fever of agitation had reached its height, and could not be wholly quieted even by the assurance from head-quarters that there was no danger.

Gertrude sat with her hand locked in Emily's, anxiously watching every indication of terror, and endeavoring to judge from the countenances and words of her most intelligent-looking fellow-travellers the actual degree of their insecurity. Emily, shut out from the sight of all that was going on, but rendered, through her acute hearing, vividly conscious of the prevailing alarm, was perfectly calm, though very pale; and, from time to time, questioned Gertrude concerning the vicinity of the other boat, a collision with which was the principal cause of fear.

At length their boat for a few moments distanced its competitor; the assurance of perfect safety was impressively asserted, anxiety began to be relieved, and, most of the passengers being restored to their wonted composure, the various parties scattered about the deck resumed their newspapers or their conversation. The gay group to which Isabel Clinton belonged, several of whom had been the victims of nervous agitation and trembling, seemed reassured, and began once more to talk and laugh merrily. Emily, however, still looked pallid, and, as Gertrude fancied, a little faint. "Let us go below, Emily," said she; "it appears now to be very quiet and safe. There are sofas in the ladies' cabin, where you can lie down; and we can both get a glass of water."

Emily assented, and in a few minutes was comfortably reclining in a corner of the saloon, where she and Gertrude remained undisturbed until dinner-time. They did not go to the dinner-table; it was not their intention from the first, and, after the agitation of the morning, was far from being desirable. So they stayed quietly where they were, while the greater part of the passengers crowded from every part of the boat, to invigorate themselves, after their fright, by the enjoyment of a comfortable meal; which they had reason to expect, as the racing appeared to have ceased, and everything was orderly and peaceable.

Gertrude opened her travelling-basket, and took out the package which contained their luncheon. It was not one of those luncheons which careful mothers provide for their travelling families, choice in its material, and tempting in its arrangement; but consisted merely of such dry morsels as had been hastily collected and put up at their hotel, in Albany, by Dr. Jeremy's direction. Gertrude looked from the little withered slices of tongue and stale bread to the veteran sponge-cakes which completed the assortment, and was hesitating which she could most conscientiously recommend to Emily, when a civil-looking waiter appeared, bearing a huge tray of refreshments, which he placed upon a table close by, at the same time turning to Gertrude, and asking if there was anything else he could serve her with.

"This is not for us," said Gertrude. "You have made a mistake."

"No mistake," replied the man. "Orders was for de blind lady and hansum young miss. I only 'beys orders. Anyting furder, miss?"

Gertrude dismissed the man with the assurance that they wanted nothing more, and then, turning to Emily, asked, with an attempt at cheerfulness, what they should do with this Aladdin-like repast.

"Eat it, my dear, if you can," said Emily. "It is no doubt meant for us."

"But to whom are we indebted for it?"

"To my blindness and your beauty, I suppose," said Emily, smiling. She then continued with wonderful simplicity, "Perhaps the chief steward, or master of ceremonies, took pity on our inability to come to dinner, and so sent the dinner to us. At any rate, my child, you must eat it before it is cold."

"I!" said Gertrude, conscious of her utter want of appetite; "I am not hungry; but I will select a nice bit for you."

The sable waiter, when he came to remove the dishes, really looked sad to see how little they had eaten. Gertrude drew out her purse, and, after bestowing a fee upon the man, inquired whom she should pay for the meal.

"Pay, miss!" said the man, grinning. "Bless my stars! de gentleman pays for all!"

"Who? What gentleman?" asked Gertrude, in surprise.

But before the man could give her any reply, another white-aproned individual appeared, and beckoned to his fellow-waiter, who, thereupon, snatched up his tray and trotted off, bending beneath its weight, and leaving Gertrude and Emily to wonder who the benevolent gentleman might be.

They finally came to the conclusion that this unexpected attention was due to the thoughtfulness of Dr. Jeremy, who must have given orders to that effect before he left the boat; and great was the unmerited praise and the undeserved gratitude which the doctor received that day, for an act of considerate politeness of which the old gentleman, with all his kindness of heart, would never have dreamed.

Dinner concluded, Emily again laid down, advised Gertrude to do the same, and, supposing that her advice was being followed, slept for an hour; while her companion sat by, watching the peaceful slumber of her friend, and carefully and noiselessly brushing away every fly that threatened to disturb a repose much needed by Miss Graham, who could, in her feeble state of health, ill afford to spare the rest she had been deprived of for one or two previous nights.

"What time is it?" asked she, on awaking.

"Nearly a quarter past three," replied Gertrude, glancing at her watch (a beautiful gift from a class of her former pupils).

Emily started up. "We can't be far from New York," said she; "where are we now?"

"I don't know exactly," replied Gertrude; "I think we must be near the Palisades; if you will stay here, I will go and see." She passed across the saloon, and was about ascending the staircase, when she was startled and alarmed by a rushing sound, mingled with the hurried tread of feet. She kept on, however, though once or twice jostled by persons with frightened faces, who crowded past and pressed forward to learn the cause of the commotion. She had just gained the head of the stairway, and was looking fearfully round her, when a man rushed past, gasping for breath, his face of an ashen paleness, and shrieking the horrid word of alarm—fire—fire!

A second more, and a scene of dismay and confusion ensued too terrible for description. Shrieks rose upon the air, groans and cries of despair burst forth from hearts that were breaking with fear for others, or maddened at the certainty of their own destruction. Each called upon each for help, when all were alike helples. Those who had never prayed before poured out their souls in the fervent ejaculation. "O, my God!" Many a brain reeled in that time of darkness and peril. Many a brave spirit sickened and sunk under the fearfulness of the hour.

Gertrude straightened her slight figure, and, with her dark eyes almost starting from their sockets, gazed around her upon every side. All was alike tumult; but the destroyer was as yet discernible in one direction only. Towards the centre of the boat, where the machinery, heated to the last degree, had fired the parched and inflammable vessel, a huge volume of flame was already visible, darting out its fiery fangs, and causing the stoutest hearts to shrink and crouch in horror. She gave but one glance; then bounded down the stairs, bent solely on rejoining Emily. But she was arrested at the very onset. One step only had she taken when she felt herself encircled by a pair of powerful arms, and a movement made to again rush with her upon deck; while a familiar voice gasped forth the words, "Gertrude, my child! my own darling! Be quiet—be quiet!—I will save you!"

Well might he urge her to be quiet,—for she was struggling madly. "No, no!" shouted she; "Emily! Emily! Let me die! let me die! but I must find Emily!"

"Where is she?" asked Mr. Phillips; for it was he.

"There, there," pointed Gertrude,—"in the cabin. Let me go! let me go!"

He cast one look around him; then said, in a firm tone, "Be calm, my child! I can save you both; follow me closely!"

With a leap he cleared the staircase, and rushed into the cabin. In the farthest corner knelt Emily, her head thrown back, her hands clasped, and her face like the face of an angel.

Gertrude and Mr. Phillips were by her side in an instant. He stooped to lift her in his arms, Gertrude at the same time exclaiming, "Come, Emily, come! He will save us!"

But Emily resisted. "Leave me, Gertrude—leave me, and save your-selves! O!" said she, looking imploringly in the face of the stranger,— "leave me, and save my child." Ere the words had left her lips, however, she was borne half-way across the saloon, Gertrude following closely.

"If we can cross to the bows of the boat, we are safe!" said Mr. Phillips, in a husky voice.

To do so, however, proved impossible. The whole centre of the boat was now one sheet of flame. "Good Heavens!" exclaimed he, "we are too late! we must go back!"

A moment more, and they had with much difficulty regained the long saloon. And now the boat, which, as soon as the fire was discovered, had been turned towards the shore, struck upon the rocks, and parted in the middle. Her bows were consequently brought near to the land; near enough to almost insure the safety of such persons as were at that part of the vessel. But, alas for those near the stern! which was far out in the river, while the breeze which blew fresh from the shore fostered and spread the devouring flame in the very direction to place those who yet clung to the broken fragment between two equally fatal elements.

Mr. Phillips' first thought, on gaining the saloon, was to beat down a window-sash, spring upon the guards, and drag Emily and Gertrude after him. Some ropes hung upon the guards; he seized one, and, with the ease and skill of an old sailor, made it fast to the boat; then turned to Gertrude, who stood firm and unwavering by his side.

"Gertrude," said he, speaking distinctly and steadily, "I shall swim to the shore with Emily. If the fire comes too near, cling to the guards; as a last chance, hold on to the rope. Keep your veil flying; I shall return."

"No, no!" cried Emily. "Gertrude, go first!"

"Hush, Emily!" exclaimed Gertrude; "we shall both be saved."

"Cling to my shoulder in the water, Emily," said Mr. Phillips, utterly regardless of her protestations. He took her once more in his arms; there was a splash, and they were gone. At the same instant Gertrude was seized from behind. She turned, and found herself grasped by Isabel Clinton, who, kneeling upon the platform, and frantic with terror, was clinging so closely to her as utterly to disable them both; at the same time shrieking, in pitiable tones, "O, Gertrude! Gertrude! save me!"

Gertrude tried to lift her up, but she was immovable; and, without making the slightest effort to help herself, was madly winding Gertrude's thick travelling-dress around her person, as if for a protection from the flames; while ever, as they darted forth new and nearer lightnings, the frightened girl would cling more wildly to her companion in danger, at the same time praying, with piercing shrieks, that she would help and save her.

But so long as Gertrude stood thus imprisoned and restrained by the arms which were clasped entirely around her she was powerless to do anything for her own or Isabel's salvation. She looked forth in the direction Mr. Phillips had taken, and, to her joy, she saw him returning. He had deposited Emily on board a boat, which was fortunately at hand, and was now approaching to claim another burden. At the same instant, a volume of flame swept so near the spot where the two girls were stationed, that Gertrude, who was standing upright, felt the scorching heat, and both were almost suffocated with smoke.

And now a new and heroic resolution took possession of the mind of Gertrude. One of them could be saved; for Mr. Phillips was within a few rods of the wreck. It should be Isabel! She had called on her for protection, and it should not be denied her! Moreover, Willie loved Isabel. Willie would weep for her loss, and that must not be. He would not weep for Gertrude—at least not much; and, if one must die, it should be she.

With Gertrude, to resolve was to do. "Isabel," said she, in a tone of such severity as one might employ towards a refractory child, with whom, as in this instance, milder remonstrances had failed— "Isabel, do you hear me? Stand up on your feet; do as I tell you, and you shall be saved. Do you hear me, Isabel?"

She heard, shuddered, but did not move.

Gertrude stooped down, and, forcibly wrenching apart the hands which were convulsively clenched, said, with a sternness which necessity alone extorted from her, "Isabel, if you do as I tell you, you will be on shore in five minutes, safe and well; but, if you stay there behaving like a foolish child, we shall both be burnt to death. For mercy's sake, get up quickly and listen to me!"

Isabel rose, fixed her eyes upon Gertrude's calm, steadfast face, and said, in a moaning tone, "What must I do? I will try."

"Do you see that person swimming this way?"

"Yes."

"He will come to this spot. Hold fast to that piece of rope, and I will let you gradually down to the water. But, stay!"—and, snatching the deep blue veil from her own head, she tied it round the neck and flung it over the fair hair of Isabel. Mr. Phillips was within a rod or two. "Now, Isabel, now!" exclaimed Gertrude, "or you will be too late!" Isabel took the rope between her hands, but shrunk back, appalled at the sight of the water. One more hot-burst of fire, however which issued forth through the window, gave her renewed courage to brave a mere seeming danger; and, aided by Gertrude, who helped her over the guards, she allowed herself to be let down to the water's edge. Mr. Phillips was fortunately just in time to receive her, for she was so utterly exhausted with fear that she could not have clung long to the rope. Gertrude had no opportunity to follow them with her eye; her own situation, it may well be believed, was now all-engrossing. The flames had reached her. She could hardly breathe, so enveloped was she in clouds of dark smoke, which had more than once been relieved by streaks of fire, which had darted, out within a foot of her. She could hesitate no longer. She seized the piece of rope, now left vacant by Isabel, who was rapidly approaching a place of safety, and, grasping it with all her might, leaped over the side of the fast-consuming vessel. How long her strength would have enabled her thus to cling,—how long the guards, as yet unapproached by the fire, would have continued a sure support for the cable,—there was no opportunity to test; for, just as her feet touched the cold surface of the river, the huge wheel, which was but a little distance from where she hung, gave one sudden, expiring revolution, sounding like a death-dirge through the water, which came foaming and dashing up against the side of the boat, and, as it swept away again, bore with it the light form of Gertrude!

CHAPTER XLII

🐛🐛🐛🐛🐛

> 'T is Reason's part
> To govern and to guard the heart;
> To lull the wayward soul to rest,
> When hopes and fears distract the breast.
> —*Cotton*

LET US NOW revisit calmer scenes, and turn our eyes toward the quiet, familiar country-seat of Mr. Graham.

The old gentleman himself, wearied with travels, and society but little congenial to his years, is pacing up and down his garden-walks, stopping now and then to observe the growth of some favorite tree, or the over-growth of some petted shrub, whose neglected, drooping twigs call for the master's pruning hand; his contented, satisfied countenance denoting plainly enough how rejoiced he is to find himself once more in his cherished homestead. Perhaps he would not like to acknowledge it, but it is nevertheless a fact, that no small part of his satisfaction arises from the circumstance that the repose and seclusion of his household is rendered complete and secure by the temporary absence of its bustling, excitable mistress, whom he has left behind him in New York. There is something pleasant, too, in being able to indulge his imagination so far as almost to deceive himself into the belief that the good old times have come back again when he was his own master; for, to tell the truth, Mrs. Graham takes advantage of his years and growing infirmities, and rules him with wonderful tact.

Emily and Gertrude, too, are closely associated with those good old times; and it adds greatly to the delusion of his fancy to dwell upon the certainty that they are both in the house, and that he shall see them at dinner; a cosey, comfortable dinner, at which Mrs. Ellis will preside with her wonted formality and precision, and which no noisy, intruding up-starts will venture to interrupt or disturb.

Yes, Gertrude is there, as well as the rest, saved (she hardly knew how) from the watery grave that threatened and almost engulfed her, and established once more in the peaceful, venerable spot, now the dearest to her on earth.

When, with some difficulty, restored to the consciousness which had utterly forsaken her in the protracted struggle between death and life, she was informed that she had been found and picked up by some humane individuals, who had hastily pushed a boat from the shore, and aided in the rescue of the sufferers; that she was clinging to a chair, which she had probably grasped when washed away by the sudden rushing of the water, and that her situation was such that, a moment more, and it would have been impossible to save her from the flames, close to which she was drifting.

But of all this she had herself no recollection. From the moment when she committed her light weight to the frail tenure of the rope, until she opened her eyes in a quiet spot, and saw Emily leaning anxiously over the bed upon which she lay, all had been a blank to her senses. A few hours from the time of the terrible catastrophe brought Mr. Graham to the scene, and the next day restored all three in safety to the long-deserted old mansion-house in D————.

This respectable, venerable habitation, and its adjoining grounds, wore nearly the same aspect as when they met the admiring eyes of Gerty on the first visit that she made Miss Graham in her early childhood,—that long-expected and keenly-enjoyed visit, which proved a lasting topic for her youthful enthusiasm to dwell upon.

The great elm-trees, casting their deep shade upon the green and velvety lawn in front; the neat, smooth gravel-walk, which led to the door-step, and then wound off in separate directions, into the mass of embowered shrubbery on the right, and the peach-orchard on the left; the old arbor, with its luxuriant growth of woodbine; the large summer-house, with its knotted, untrimmed, rustic pillars; the little fish-pond and fountain; and especially the flower-garden, during the last season nearly restored, by Gertrude's true friend George, to its original appearance when under her superintendence; all had the same friendly, familiar look as during the first happy summers, when Emily, sitting in her garden-chair beneath the wide-spreading tulip-tree, listened with delight to the cheerful voice, the merry laugh, and the light step of the joyous little gardener, who, as she moved about in her favorite element among the flowers, seemed to her affectionate, loving blind friend the sweetest Flora of them all.

Now and then, a stray robin, the last of the numerous throng that had flocked to the cherry-feast and departed long ago, came hopping across the paths, and over the neatly-trimmed box, lifting his head, and looking about him with an air that seemed to say, "It is time for me, too, to be off." A family of squirrels, on the other hand, old pets of Gertrude's, whom she loved to watch as they played in the willow-tree opposite her window, were just gathering in their harvest, and were busily journeying up and down, each with a nut in its mouth (for there were nut-trees in that garden, and quiet corners, such as squirrels love). Last year they did not come,—at least, they did not *stay*—for Mrs. Graham and her new gardener voted them a nuisance; but this year they had had it all their own way, and were laying up rich stores for the coming winter.

The old house itself had a look of contentment and repose. The hall-door stood wide open. Mr. Graham's arm-chair was in its usual place; Gertrude's birds, of which Mrs. Ellis had taken excellent care, were hopping about on the slender perches of the great Indian cage which hung on the wide piazza. The old house-dog lay stretched in the sun, sure that nobody would molest him. Plenty of flowers once more graced the parlor, and all was very still, very quiet, and very comfortable; and Mr. Graham thought so, as he came up the steps, patted the dog, whistled to the birds, sat down in the arm-chair, and took the morning paper from the hand of the neat housemaid, who came bringing it across the hall.

The dear old place was the dear old place still. Time seemed only to lend it additional grace, to give it an air of greater peace, seclusion and repose.

But how is it with the inmates?

Mr. Graham, as we have already hinted, has been having new experiences; and although some features of his character are too closely inwrought to be ever wholly eradicated, he is, in many respects, a changed man. The time had once been when he would have resisted courageously every innovation upon his domestic prejudices and comforts; but old age and ill-health had somewhat broken his spirit, and subdued his hitherto invincible will. Just at this crisis, too, he united his fortunes with one who had sufficient energy of purpose, combined with just enough good-nature and tact, to gain her point on every occasion when she thought it material to do so. She indulged him, to be sure, in his favorite hobbies, allowed him to continue in the fond belief that his sway (when he chose to exercise it) was indisputable, and yet contrived to decide herself in all important matters, and had, at last, driven him to such extremity, that he had taken it for his maxim to get what comfort he could, and let things take their course.

No wonder, therefore, that he looked forward to a few weeks of old-fashioned enjoyment much as a school-boy does to his vacation.

Emily is sitting in her own room, carelessly clad in a loose wrapper. She is paler than ever, and her face has an anxious, troubled expression. Every time the door opens, she starts, trembles, a sudden flush overspreads her face, and twice already during the morning she has suddenly burst into tears. Every exertion, even that of dressing, seems a labor to her; she cannot listen to Gertrude's reading, but will constantly interrupt her, to ask questions concerning the burning boat, her own and others' rescue, and every circumstance connected with the terrible scene of agony and death. Her nervous system is evidently fearfully shattered, and Gertrude looks at her and weeps, and wonders to see how her wonted calmness and composure have forsaken her.

They have been together since breakfast, but Emily will not allow Gertrude to stay with her any longer. She must go away and walk, or, at least, change the scene. She may come back in an hour and help her dress for dinner,—a ceremony which Miss Graham will by no means omit, her chief desire seeming to be to maintain the appearance of health and happiness in the presence of her father. Gertrude feels that Emily is in earnest,—that she really wishes to be left alone; and, believing that, for the first time, *her* presence even is burdensome, she retires to her own room, leaving Emily to bow her head upon her hands, and, for the third time, utter a few hysterical sobs.

Gertrude is immediately followed by Mrs. Ellis, who shuts the door, seats herself, and, with a manner of her own, alone sufficient to excite alarm, adds to the poor girl's fear and distress by declaiming at length upon the dreadful effect the recollection of that shocking accident is having upon poor Emily. "She's completely upset," is the housekeeper's closing remark, "and if she don't begin to get better in a day or two, I don't hesitate to say there's no knowing what the consequences may be. Emily is feeble, and not fit to travel; I wish, for my part, she had staid at home. I don't approve of travelling, especially in these shocking dangerous times."

Fortunately for poor Gertrude, Mrs. Ellis is at length summoned to the kitchen, and she is left to reflect upon the strange circumstances of the last few days,—days fraught to her with matter of thought for years, if so long a time had been allowed her. A moment, however, and she is again interrupted. The housemaid who carried Mr. Graham his paper has something for her, too. A letter! With a trembling hand she receives it, scarcely daring to look at the writing or post-mark. Her first thought is of Willie; but before she could indulge either a hope or a fear on that score the illusion is dispelled, for, though the post-mark is New York, and he might be there, the hand-writing is wholly strange. Another idea, of scarcely less moment, flashes into her mind, and, hardly able to breathe from the violence of the emotions by which she is oppressed, she breaks the seal and reads:

"MY DARLING GERTRUDE: My much-loved child,—for such you indeed are, though a father's agony of fear and despair alone wrung from me the words that claimed you. It was no madness that, in the dark hour of danger, compelled me to clasp you to my heart and call you mine. A dozen times before had I been seized by the same emotion, and as often had it been subdued and smothered. And even now I would crush the promptings of nature, and depart and weep my poor life away alone; but the voice within me has spoken once, and cannot again be silenced. Had I seen you happy, gay and light-hearted, I would not have asked to share your joy, far less would I have cast a shadow on your path; but you are sad and troubled, my poor child, and your grief unites the tie between us closer than that of kindred, and makes you a thousand times my daughter; for I am a wretched, weary man, and know how to feel for others' woe.

"You have a kind and a gentle heart, my child. You have wept once for the stranger's sorrows,—will you now refuse to pity, if you cannot love, the solitary parent, who, with a breaking heart and a trembling hand, writes the ill-fated word that dooms him, perhaps, to the hatred and contempt of the only being on earth with whom he can claim the fellowship of a natural tie? Twice before have I striven to utter it, and, laying down my pen, have shrunk from the cruel task. But, hard as it is to speak, I find it harder to still the beating of my restless heart; therefore listen to me, though it may be for the last time. Is there one being on earth whom you shudder to think of? Is there one associated only in your mind with deeds of darkness and of shame? Is there one name which you have from your childhood learned to abhor and hate; and, in proportion as you love your best friend, have you been taught to shrink from and despise her worst enemy? It cannot be otherwise. Ah! I tremble to think how my child will recoil from her father when she learns the secret, so long pre-served, so sorrowfully revealed, that he is

"PHILIP AMORY!"

As Gertrude looked up when she had finished reading this strange and unintelligible letter, her countenance expressed only complete be-wilderment,—her eyes glistened with great tears, her face was flushed with wonder and excitement; but she was evidently at a total loss to account for the meaning of the stranger's words.

She sat for an instant wildly gazing into vacancy, then, springing suddenly up, with the letter grasped in one hand, ran across the entry towards Emily's room, to share with her the wonderful contents, and eagerly ask her opinion of their hidden meaning. She stopped, however, when her hand was on the door-lock. Emily was already ill,—the victim of agitation and excitement,—it would not do to distress or even disturb her; and, retreating to her own room as hastily as she had come, Gertrude once more sat down, to reperuse the singular words, and endeavor to find some clue to the mystery.

That Mr. Phillips and the letter-writer were identical she at once perceived. It was no slight impression that his exclamation and conduct during the time of their imminent danger on board the boat had left upon the mind of Gertrude. During the three days that had succeeded the accident, the words "My child! my own darling!" had been continually ringing in her ears and haunting her imagination. Now the blissful idea would flash upon her that the noble, disinterested stranger, who had risked his life so daringly in her own and Emily's cause, might indeed be her father; and every fibre of her being had thrilled at the thought, while her head grew dizzy and confused with the strong sensation of hope that agitated and almost overwhelmed her brain. Then, again, she had repulsed the idea, as suggesting only the height of impossibility and folly, and had compelled herself to take a more rational and probable view of the matter, and believe that the stranger's words and conduct were merely the result of powerful and overwhelming excitement, or possibly the indications of a somewhat disordered and unsettled imagination,—a supposition which much of his previous behavior seemed to warrant.

Her first inquiries, on recovering consciousness, had been for the preserver of Emily and Isabel, but he had disappeared; no trace of him could be obtained, and Mr. Graham soon arriving and hurrying them from the neighborhood, she had been reluctantly compelled to abandon the hope of seeing him again, and was consequently left entirely to her own vague and unsatisfactory conjectures.

The same motives which now induced her to forbear consulting Emily concerning the mysterious epistle had hitherto prevented her from imparting the secret of Mr. Phillips' inexplicable languge and manner; but she had dwelt upon them none the less, and day and night had silently pondered, not only upon recent events, but on the entire demeanor of this strange man towards her, ever since the earliest moment of their acquaintance.

The first perusal of the letter served only to excite and alarm her. It neither, called forth distinct ideas and impressions, nor added life and coloring to those she had already formed.

But, as she sat for more than an hour gazing upon the page, which she read and re-read until it was blistered and blotted with the great tears that fell upon it, the varying expression of her face denoted the emotions that, one after another, possessed her; and which, at last, snatching a sheet of paper, she committed to writing with a feverish rapidity, that betrayed how deeply, almost fearfully, her whole being, heart, mind and body, bent and staggered beneath the weight of contending hopes, anxieties, warmly-enkindled affections, and gloomy upstarting fears.

"MY DEAR, DEAR FATHER,—If I may dare to believe that you are so, and, if not that, my best of friends,—how shall I write to you, and what shall I say, since all your words are a mystery! Father! blessed word! O, that my noble friend were indeed my father! Yet tell me, tell me, how can this be? Alas! I feel a sad presentiment that the bright dream is all an illusion, an error. I never before remember to have heard the name of Philip Amory. My sweet, pure and gentle Emily has taught me to love all the world; and hatred and contempt are foreign to her nature, and, I trust, to my own. Moreover, she has not an enemy in the wide world; never had, or could have. One might as well war with an angel of Heaven as with a creature so holy and lovely as she.

"Nor bid me think of yourself as a man of sin and crime. It cannot be. It would be wronging a noble nature to believe it, and I say again it cannot be. Gladly would I trust myself to repose on the bosom of such a parent; gladly would I hail the sweet duty of consoling the sorrows of one so self-sacrificing, so kind, so generous; whose life has been so freely offered for me, and for others whose existence was dearer to me than my own. When you took me in your arms and called me your child, your darling child, I fancied that the excitement of that dreadful scene had for the moment disturbed your mind and brain so far as to invest me with a false identity,—perhaps confound my image with that of some loved and absent one. I now believe that it was no sudden madness, but rather that I have been all along mistaken for another, whose glad office it may perhaps be to cheer a father's saddened life, while I remain unrecognized, unsought,—the fatherless, motherless one I am accustomed to consider myself. If you have lost a daughter, God grant she may be restored to you, to love you as I would do, were I so blessed as to be that daughter! And I,—consider me not a stranger; let me be your child in heart; let me love, pray and weep for you; let me pour out my soul in thankfulness for the kind care and sympathy you have already given me. And yet, though I disclaim it all, and dare not, yes, dare not dwell for a moment on the thought that you are otherwise than deceived in believing me your child, my heart leaps up in spite of me, and I tremble and almost cease to breathe as there flashes upon me the possibility, the blissful, God-given hope! No, no! I will not think it, lest I could not bear to have it crushed! O, what am I writing? I know not. I cannot endure the suspense long; write quickly, or come to me, my father,—for I will call you so once, though perhaps never again.

"GERTRUDE."

Mr. Phillips—or rather Mr. Amory, for we will call him by his true name—had either forgotten or neglected to mention his address. Gertrude did not observe this circumstance until she had folded and was preparing to direct her letter. She then recollected the unfortunate omission, and for a moment experienced a severe pang in the thought that her communication would never reach him. She was reassured, however, on examining the post-mark, which was evidently New York, to which place she unhesitatingly addressed her missive; and then, unwilling to trust it to other hands, tied on her bonnet, caught up a veil with which to protect and conceal her agitated face, and hastened to deposit the letter herself in the village post-office.

To persons of an excitable and imaginative temperament there is, perhaps, no greater or more painful state of trial than that occasioned by severe and long-continued suspense. When we know precisely what we have to bear, we can usually call to our aid the needed strength and submission; but a more than ordinary patience and forbearance is necessary to enable us calmly and tranquilly to await the approach of an important crisis, big with events the nature of which we can have no means of foreseeing, but which will inevitably exercise an all-controlling influence upon the life. One moment hope usurps the mastery, and promises a happy issue; we smile, breathe freely, and banish care and anxiety; but an instant more, and some word, look, or even thought, changes the whole current of our feelings, clouds take the place of smiles, the chest heaves with a sudden oppression, fear starts up like a nightmare, and in proportion as we have cherished a confident joy are we plunged into the torture of doubt or the agony of despair.

Gertrude's case seemed a peculiarly trying one. She had been, already, for a week past, struggling with a degree of suspense and anxiety which agitated her almost beyond endurance; and now a new occasion of uncertainty and mystery had arisen, involving in its issues an almost equal amount of self-questioning and torture. It seemed almost beyond the power of so young, so sensitive, and so inexperienced a girl, to rally such self-command as would enable her to control her emotions, disguise them from observation, and compel herself to endure alone and in silence this cruel dispensation of her destiny.

But she did do it, and bravely, too. Whether the greatness of the emergency called forth, as it ever does in a true-hearted woman, a proportionate greatness of spirit; whether the complication of her web of destiny compelled her, with closed hands and a submissive will, to cease all efforts for its disentanglement; or, whether, with the humble trust, which ever grew more deep and ardent as the sense of her own helplessness pressed upon her, she turned for help to Him whose strength is made perfect in weakness,—it is certain that, as she took her way towards home after depositing the letter in the post-master's hand, the firmness of her step, the calm uplifting of her eye, gave token that she that moment conceived a brave resolve,—a resolve which, during the two days that intervened ere she received the expected reply, never for one moment deserted her.

And it was this. She would endeavor to suspend for the present those vain conjectures, that fruitless weighing of probabilities, which served only to harass her mind, puzzle her understanding, and destroy her peace; she would ponder no more on matters which concerned herself, but with a desperate effort turn all her mental and all her physical energy into some other and more disinterested channel, and patiently wait until the cloud which hung over her fate should be dissipated by the light of truth, and explanation triumph over mystery.

She was herself surprised, afterwards, when she called to mind and brought up in long array the numerous household, domestic and friendly duties which she almost unconsciously accomplished in those few days during which she was wrestling with thoughts that were ever struggling to be uppermost, and were only kept down by a force of will that was almost exhausting.

She dusted and rearranged every book in Mr. Graham's extensive library; unpacked and put in their appropriate places every article of her own and Emily's long-scattered wardrobe; aided Mrs. Ellis in her labors to restore order to the china-closet and the linen-press; and many other neglected or long-postponed duties now found a time for their fulfillment.

In these praiseworthy efforts to drive away such reflections as were fatal to her peace, and employ her hands, at least, if not her heart, in such services as might promote the comfort and well-being of others, let us leave her for the present.

CHAPTER XLIII

Thou neither dost persuade me to seek wealth
For empire's sake, nor empire to affect
For glory's sake, by all thy argument.
——*Milton*

IN A WELL-FURNISHED private parlor of one of those first-class hotels in which New York city abounds, Philip Amory sat alone. It was evening. The window-curtains were drawn, the gas-lamps burning brightly, bringing out the gorgeous colors of the gayly-tinted carpet and draperies, and giving a cheerful glow to the room, the comfortable appearance of which contrasted strongly with the pale countenance and desponding attitude of its solitary inmate, who, with his head bowed upon his hands, leaned upon a table in the centre of the apartment.

He had sat for nearly an hour in precisely the same position, without once moving or looking up. With his left hand, upon which his forehead rested, he had thrust back the wavy masses of his silvered hair, as if their light weight were too oppressive for his heated brow; and the occasional movement of his fingers, as they were slowly passed to and fro beneath the graceful curls, alone gave evidence that he had not fallen asleep.

Suddenly he started up, straightened his commanding figure to its full height, and slowly commenced pacing the room. A light knock at the door arrested his measured steps; a look of nervous agitation and annoyance overspread his countenance; he again flung himself into his chair, and, in reply to the servant's announcing "a gentleman, sir," was preparing to say, "I cannot be interrupted,"——but it was too late; the visitor had already advanced within the door, which the waiter quietly closed and retreated.

The new comer——a young man——stepped quickly and eagerly forward, but checked himself, somewhat abashed at the unexpected coldness of the reception he met from his host, who rose slowly and deliberately to meet his guest, while the cloud upon his countenance and the frigid manner in which he touched the young man's cordially-offered hand seemed to imply that the latter's presence was unwelcome.

"Excuse me, Mr. Phillips," said William Sullivan, for it was he who had thus unintentionally forced an entrance to the secluded man. "I am afraid my visit is an intrusion."

"Do not speak of it," replied Mr. Amory. "I beg you will be seated;" and he politely handed a chair.

Willie availed himself of the offered seat no further than to lean lightly upon it with one hand, while he still remained standing. "You are changed, sir," continued he, "since I last saw you."

"Changed! Yes, I am," returned the other, absently.

"Your health, I fear, is not—"

"My health is excellent," said Mr. Amory, interrupting his unfinished remark. Then seeming for the first time to realize the necessity of exerting himself, in order to sustain the conversation, he added, "It is a long time, sir, since we met. I have not yet forgotten the debt I owe you for your timely interference between me and Ali, that Arab traitor, with his rascally army of Bedouin rogues."

"Do not name it, sir," replied Willie. "Our meeting was fortunate indeed; but the benefit was as mutual as the danger to which we were alike exposed."

"I cannot think so. You seemed to have a most excellent understanding with your own party of guides and attendants, Arabs though they were."

"True; I have had some experience in Eastern travel, and usually know how to manage these inflammable spirits of the desert. But at the time I joined you I was myself entering the neighborhood of hostile tribes, and might soon have found our party overawed, but for the advantage of having joined forces with yourself."

"You set but a modest value upon your conciliatory powers, my young man. To you, who are so well acquainted with the facts in the case, I can hardly claim the merit of frankness for the acknowledgment that it was only my own hot temper and stubborn will which exposed us both to the imminent danger which you were fortunately able to avert. No, no! you must not deprive me of the satisfaction of once more expressing my gratitude for your invaluable aid."

"You are making my visit, sir," said Willie, smiling, "the very reverse of what it was intended to be. I did not come here this evening to receive, but, to the best of my ability, to render thanks."

"For what, sir?" asked Mr. Amory, abruptly, almost roughly. "You owe me nothing!"

"The friends of Isabella Clinton, sir, owe you a debt of gratitude which it will be impossible for them ever to repay."

"You are mistaken, Mr. Sullivan; I have done nothing which places that young lady's friends under a particle of obligation to me."

"Did you not save her life?"

"Yes; but nothing was further from my intention."

Willie smiled; "It could have been no accident, I think, which led you to risk your own life to rescue a fellow-passenger."

"It was no accident, indeed, which led to Miss Clinton's safety from destruction. I am convinced of that. But you must not thank *me:* it is due to another than myself that she does not now sleep in death."

"May I ask to whom you refer? Your words are mysterious."

"I refer to a dear and noble girl whom I swam to that burning wreck to save. Her veil had been agreed upon as a signal between us. That veil, carefully thrown over the head of Miss Clinton, whom I found clinging to the spot assigned to—to her whom I was seeking, deceived me, and I bore in safety to the shore the burden which I had ignorantly seized from the gaping waters, leaving my own darling, who had offered her life as a sacrifice, to—"

"O, not to die!" exclaimed Willie.

"No; to be saved by a miracle. Go thank her for Miss Clinton's life."

"I thank God," said Willie, with fervor, "that the horrors of such scenes of destruction are half redeemed by heroism like that."

The hitherto stern countenance of Mr. Amory softened as he listened to the young man's enthusiastic outburst of admiration at Gertrude's noble self-devotion.

"Who is she? Where is she?" continued Willie.

"Ask me not!" replied Mr. Amory, with a gesture of impatience; "I cannot tell you, if I would. I have not seen her since that ill-fated day."

His manner, even more than his words, seemed to intimate an unwillingness to enter into any further explanation regarding Isabel's rescue, and Willie, perceiving it, stood for a moment silent and irresolute. Then, advancing a step nearer, he said,

"Though you so utterly disclaim, Mr. Phillips, any participation in Miss Clinton's happy escape, I feel that my errand here would be but imperfectly fulfilled if I should fail to deliver the message which I bring to one who was, at least, the final means, if not the original cause, of her safety. Mr. Clinton, the young lady's father, desired me to tell you that, in saving the life of his only surviving child, the last of seven, all of whom but herself were doomed to an early death, you have prolonged his own days, and rendered him grateful to that degree which words on his part are powerless to express; but that, as long as his feeble life is spared, he shall never cease to bless your name, and pray to Heaven for its choicest gifts upon you and those who dwell next your heart."

There was a slight moisture in the clear, penetrating eye of Mr. Amory, but a bland and courteous smile upon his lip, as he said, in reply to Willie's words:

"All this from Mr. Clinton! Very gentlemanly, and equally sincere, I doubt not; but you surely do not mean to thank me wholly in his name, my young friend. Have you nothing to say for your own sake?"

Willie looked surprised at the question, but replied, unhesitatingly, "Certainly, sir; as one of a large circle of acquaintances and friends, whom Miss Clinton honors with her regard, you may rest assured that my admiration and gratitude for your disinterested exertions are unbounded; and, not only on her account, but on that of every other whom you had the noble satisfaction of rescuing from a most terrific form of death and destruction."

"Am I to understand, by your words, that you speak only as a friend of humanity, and that you felt no personal interest in any of my fellow-passengers?"

"I was unacquainted with nearly all of them. Miss Clinton was the only one whom I had known for any greater length of time than during two or three days of Saratoga intercourse; but I should certainly have felt deeply grieved at her death, since I was in the habit of meeting her familiarly in her childhood, have lately been continually in her society, and am aware that her father, my respected partner, an old and invaluable friend, who is now much enfeebled in health, could hardly have survived so severe a shock as the loss, under such harrowing circumstances, of an only child, whom he almost idolizes."

"You speak very coolly, Mr. Sullivan. Are you aware that the prevailing belief gives you credit for feeling more than a mere friendly interest in Miss Clinton?"

The gradual dilating of Willie's large gray eyes, as he fixed them inquiringly upon Mr. Amory,—the half-scrutinizing, half-astonished expression which crept over his face, as he deliberately seated himself in the chair, which, until then, he had not occupied,—were sufficient evidence of the effect of the question so unexpectedly put to him.

"Sir," said he, "I either misunderstood you, or the prevailing belief is a most mistaken one."

"Then you never before heard of your own engagement?"

"Never, I assure you. Is it possible that so idle a report has obtained an extensive circulation among Miss Clinton's friends?"

"Sufficiently extensive for me, a mere spectator of Saratoga life, to hear it not only whispered from ear to ear, but openly proclaimed as a fact worthy of credit."

"I am exceedingly surprised and vexed at what you tell me," said Willie, looking really disturbed and chagrined. "Nonsensical and false as such a rumor is, it will very naturally, if it should reach Miss Clinton, be a source of indignation and annoyance to her; and it is on that account, far more than my own, that I regret the circumstances which have probably given rise to it."

"Do you refer to considerations of delicacy on the lady's part, or have you the modesty to believe that her pride would be wounded by having her name thus coupled with that of her father's junior partner, a young man hitherto unknown to fashionable circles? But, excuse me; perhaps I am stepping on dangerous ground, and your own pride may shrink from the frankness of my speech."

"By no means, sir; you wrong me if you believe my pride to be of such a nature. But, in answer to your question, I have not only reference to both the motives you name, but to many others, when I assert my opinion of the resentment Miss Clinton would probably cherish, if the foolish and unwarranted remarks you mention should chance to reach her ears."

"Mr. Sullivan," said Mr. Amory, drawing his chair nearer to Willie's, and speaking in a tone of great interest, "are you sure you are not standing in your own light? Are you aware that undue modesty, coupled with false and overstrained notions of refinement, has before now stood in the way of many a man's good fortune, and is likely to interfere largely with your own?"

"How so, sir? You speak in riddles, and I am ignorant of your meaning."

"Handsome young fellows, like you," continued Mr. Amory, "can, I know, often command almost any amount of property for the asking; but many such chances rarely occur to one individual; and the world will laugh at you, if you waste so fair an opportunity as that which you now enjoy."

"Opportunity for what? You surely do not mean to advise me—"

"I do, though. I am older than you are, and I know something of the world. A fortune is not made in a day, nor is money a thing to be despised. Mr. Clinton's life is, I dare say, enfeebled and almost worn out in toiling after that wealth which will soon be the inheritance of his daughter. She is young, beautiful, and the pride of that high circle in which she moves. Both father and daughter smile upon you;—you need not look disconcerted,—I speak as between friends, and you know the truth of that which strangers have observed, and which I have frequently heard mentioned as beyond doubt. Why, then, do you hesitate? I trust you are not deterred from taking advantage of your position by any romantic and chivalrous sense of inferiority on your part, or unworthiness to obtain so fair a prize."

"Mr. Phillips," said Willie, with hesitation, and evident embarrassment, "the comments of mere casual acquaintances, such as the greater part of those with whom Miss Clinton associated in Saratoga, are not in the least to be depended upon. The peculiar relations in which I stand towards Mr. Clinton have been such as of late to draw me into constant intercourse both with himself and his daughter. He is almost entirely without relatives, has scarcely any trustworthy friend at command, and therefore appears, perhaps, to the world more favorably disposed towards me than would be found to be the case should I aspire to his daughter's hand. The lady herself, too, has so many admirers, that it would be the height of vanity in me to believe—"

"Pooh, pooh!" exclaimed Mr. Phillips, springing from his chair, and, as he commenced pacing the room, clapping the young man heartily upon the shoulder, "tell that, Sullivan, to a greater novice, a more unsophisticated individual, than I am! It is very becoming in you to say so; but (though I hate to flatter) a few slight reminders will hardly harm a youth who has such a very low opinion of his own merits. Pray, who was the gentleman for whose society Miss Clinton was a few nights since, so ready to forego the music of Alboni, the brilliancy of the well-lighted and crowded hall, and the smiles and compliments of a whole train of adorers? With whom, I say, did she, in comparison with all this, prefer a quiet moonlight walk in the garden of the United States Hotel?"

Willie hesitated a moment, while endeavoring to rally his recollection; then, as if the circumstance and its consequences had just flashed upon him, he exclaimed, "I remember!—That, then, was one of the causes of suspicion. I was, on that occasion, a messenger merely, to summon Miss Isabel to the bed-side of her father, by whom I had been anxiously watching for hours, and who, on awakening from a long-protracted and almost lethargic sleep, which had excited the alarm of the physician, inquired for his daughter with such eagerness, that I did not hesitate to interrupt the

The Lamplighter

pleasure of the evening, and call her to the post of duty, which awaited her in the cottage occupied by Mr. Clinton, at the further extremity of the grounds, to which I accompanied her by moonlight."

Mr. Amory almost laughed outright, cast upon Willie, for the first time, that look of sweet benignity which, though rare, well became his fine countenance, and exclaimed, "So much for watering-place gossip! I believe I must forbear speaking of any further evidences of a tender interest manifested by either of you. But, these things apart, and there is every reason to believe, my dear Sullivan, that though the young lady's heart be still, like her fortune, in the united keeping of herself and her father, there is nothing easier than for you to win and claim them both. You are a rising young man, and possess business talent indispensable, I hear, to the elder party; if, with your handsome face, figure and accomplishments, you cannot render yourself equally so to the younger, there is no one to blame but yourself."

Willie laughed. "If I had that object in view, I know of no one to whom I would so soon come for encouragement as to you, sir; but the flattering prospect you hold out is quite wasted upon me."

"Not if you are the man I think you," replied Mr. Amory. "I cannot believe you will be such a fool (I beg your pardon for using so strong a term) as to allow yourself to be blinded to the opportunity you see held out before you of making that appearance in society, and taking that stand in life, to which your birth, your education and your personal qualities, entitle you. Your father was a respectable clergyman (always an honorable profession); you enjoyed and profited by every advantage in your youth, and have done yourself such credit in India as would enable you, with plenty of capital at command, to take the lead in a few years among mercantile men. All this, indeed, might not, probably would not, give you an opportunity to mingle freely and at once in the highest ranks of our aristocracy; but a union with Miss Clinton would entitle you immediately to such a position as years of assiduous effort could hardly win, and you would find yourself at twenty-five at the highest point in every respect to which you could possibly aspire; nor have you, I will venture to say, lived for six years utterly deprived of female society, without becoming proportionatley susceptible to such uncommon grace and beauty as Miss Clinton's.

"A man just returned from a long residence abroad is usually thought to be an easy prey to the charms of the first of his fair countrywomen into

346

whose society he may chance to be thrown; and it can scarcely then be wondered at, if you are subdued by such winning attractions as are rarely to be met with in this land of beautiful women. Nor can it be possible that you have for six years toiled beneath an Indian sun without learning to appreciate as it deserves the unlooked-for but happy and honorable termination of your toils, the easily-attained rest from labor, whose crowning blessing will be the possession of your beautiful bride."

A moment's pause ensued, during which Mr. Amory sat watching the countenance of Willie, while he awaited his reply. He was not kept long in ignorance of the effect his glowing picture had produced.

"Mr. Phillips," said Willie, speaking with prompt decision, and a nervous energy which proved how heart-felt were the words he uttered, "I have not, indeed, spent many of the best years of my life toiling beneath a burning sun, and in a protracted exile from all that I held most dear, without being sustained and encouraged by high hopes, aims and aspirations. But you misjudge me greatly, if you believe that the ambition that has hitherto spurred me on can find its gratification in those rewards which you have so vividly presented to my imagination. No, sir! believe me, though these advantages may seem beyond the grasp of most men, I aspire to something higher yet, and should think my best endeavors wasted indeed, if my hopes and wishes tended not to a still more glorious good."

"And to what quarter do you look for the fulfillment of such flattering prospects?" asked Mr. Amory, in an ironical tone of voice.

"Not to the gay circles of fashion," replied Willie, "nor yet to that moneyed aristocracy which awards to each man his position in life. I do not depreciate an honorable standing in the eyes of my fellow-men; I am not blind to the advantages of wealth, or insensible to the claims of grace and beauty; but these were not the things for which I left my home, and it is not to claim them that I have now returned. Young as I am, I have lived long enough, and seen enough of trial, to lay to heart the belief that the only blessings worth striving for are something more enduring, more satisfying, than doubtful honors, precarious wealth, or fleeting smiles."

"To what, then, may I ask, do you look forward?"

"To a *home,* and that, not so much for myself—though I have long pined for such a rest—as for another, with whom I hope to share it. A year since,"—and Willie's lip trembled, his voice shook with emotion, as he spoke,—"and there were others, beside that dear one whose image now entirely fills my heart, whom I had fondly hoped, and should deeply have

347

rejoiced, to see reaping the fruits of my exertions. But we were not permitted to meet again; and now,—but pardon me, sir; I did not mean to intrude upon you my private affairs."

"Go on," said Mr. Amory; "go on; I deserve some degree of confidence, in return for the disinterested advice I have been giving you. Speak to me as to an old friend; I am much interested in what you say."

"It is long since I have spoken freely of myself," said Willie; "but frankness is natural to me, and, since you profess a desire to learn something of my aim in life, I know of no motive I have for reserve or concealment. But my position, sir, even as a child, was singular; and you must excuse me if I refer to it for a moment. I could not have been more than twelve or fourteen years of age when I began to realize the necessity which rested upon me. My widowed mother and her aged father were the only relatives, almost the only friends, I knew. One was feeble, delicate, and quite unequal to active exertion; the other was old and poor, being wholly dependent upon the small salary he received for officiating as sexton of a neighboring church. You are aware, for I have mentioned it in our earlier acquaintance abroad, that, in spite of these circumstances, they maintained me for several years in comfort and decency, and gave me an excellent education.

"At an age when kites and marbles are wont to be all-engrossing I became possessed with an earnest desire to relieve my mother and grandfather of a part of their burden of care and labor; and, with this purpose in view, sought and obtained a situation, in which I was well treated and well paid, and which I retained until the death of my excellent master. Then, for a time, I felt bitterly the want of employment, became desponding and unhappy; a state of mind which was fostered by constant association with one of so melancholy and despairing a temperament as my grandfather, who, having met with great disappointment in life, held out no encouragement to me, but was forever hinting at the probability of my utterly failing in every scheme for success and advancement.

"I bitterly regretted, at the time, the depressing influence of the old man's innuendoes; but I have since thought they answered a good purpose; for nothing so urged me on to ever-increasing efforts as the indomitable desire to prove the mistaken nature of his gloomy predictions, and few things have given me more satisfaction than the assurances I have frequently received during the few past years that he came at last to a full conviction that my prosperity was established beyond a doubt, and that one of his ill-fated family was destined to escape the trials and evils of poverty.

"My mother was a quiet, gentle woman, small in person, with great simplicity and some reserve of manner. She loved me like her own soul; she taught me everything I know of goodness; there is no sacrifice I would not have made for her happiness. I would have died to save her life; but we shall never meet again in this world, and I—I—am learning to be resigned!

"For these two, and one other, whom I shall speak of presently, I was ready to go away, and strive, and suffer, and be patient. The opportunity came, and I embraced it. And soon one great object of my ambition was won. I was able to earn a competency for myself and for them. In the course of time, luxuries even were within my means, and I had begun to look forward to a not very distant day, when my long-looked-for return should render our happiness perfect and complete. I little thought, then, that the sad tidings of my grandfather's death were on their way, and the news of my mother's slow but equally sure decline so soon to follow.

"It is true, however, they are both gone; and I should now be so solitary as almost to long to follow them, but for one other, whose love will bind me to earth so long as she is spared."

"And she?" exclaimed Mr. Amory, with an eagerness which Willie, engrossed with his own thoughts, did not observe.

"Is a young girl," continued Willie, "without family, wealth or beauty; but with a spirit so elevated as to make her great, a heart so noble as to make her rich, a soul so pure as to make her beautiful."

Mr. Amory's attitude of fixed attention, his evident waiting to hear more, emboldened Willie to speak still further.

"There lived in the same house which my grandfather occupied an old man, a city lamplighter. He was poor, poorer even than we were, but, I will venture to say, there never was a better or a kinder-hearted person in the world. One evening, when engaged in his round of duty, he picked up and brought home a little ragged child, whom a cruel woman had just thrust into the street to perish with cold, or die a more lingering death in the alms-house; for nothing but such devoted care as she received from my mother and Uncle True (so we always called our old friend) could have saved the feeble, half-starved creature from the consequences of long-continued exposure and ill-treatment. Through their unwearied watching and efforts she was spared, to repay in after years all, and more than all, the love bestowed upon her. She was at that time miserably thin and attenuated, sallow, and extremely plain in her appearance, besides being possessed of a violent temper, which she had never been taught to restrain, and a stubbornness of will, which undoubtedly resulted from her having long lived in opposition to all the world.

"All this, however, did not repel Uncle True, under whose loving influence new and hitherto undeveloped virtues and capacities soon began to manifest themselves. In the atmosphere of love in which she now lived, she soon became a changed being; and when, in addition to the example and precepts taught her at home, a divine light was shed upon her life by one who, herself sitting in darkness, casts a halo forth from her own spirit to illumine those of all who are blessed with her presence, she became, what she has ever since been, a being to love and trust for a lifetime. For myself, there were no bounds to the affection I soon came to cherish for the little girl, to whom I was first attracted by compassion merely.

"We were constantly together; we had no thoughts, no studies, no pleasures, sorrows or interests, that were not shared. I was her teacher, her protector, the partner of all her childish amusements; and she, on her part, was by turns an advising, consoling, sympathizing and encouraging friend. In this latter character she was indispensable to me, for she had a hopeful nature, and a buoyancy of spirit which often imparted itself to me. I well remember, when my kind employer died, and I was plunged in boyish grief and despair, the confidence and energy with which she, then very young, inspired me. The relation between her and Uncle True was beautiful. Boy as I was, I could not but view with admiration the old man's devoted love for the adopted darling of his latter years (his birdie, as he always called her), and the deep and grateful affection which she bore him in return.

"During the first few years she was wholly dependent upon him, and seemed only a fond, affectionate child; but a time came, at last, when the case was reversed, and the old man, stricken with disease, became infirm and helpless. It was then that the beauty of her woman's nature shone forth triumphant; and, O! how gently, child as she was, she guided his steps as he descended to the grave! Often have I gone to his room at midnight, fearing lest he might be in need of care which she, in her youth and inexperience, would be unable to render, and never shall I forget the little figure, seated calmly by his bed-side, at an hour when many of her years would be shrinking from fears conjured up by the night and the darkness, with a lamp dimly burning on a table before her, and she herself, with his hand in hers, sweetly soothing his wakefulness by her loving words, or with her eyes bent upon her little Bible, reading to him holy lessons.

"But all her care could not prolong his life; and, shortly before I went to India, he died, blessing God for the peace imparted to him through his gentle nurse.

"It was my task to soothe our little Gerty's sorrows, and do what I could to comfort her; an office which, before I left the country, I was rejoiced to transfer to the willing hands of the excellent blind lady who had long befriended both her and Uncle True. Before I went away, I solemnly committed to Gerty, who had in one instance proved herself both willing and able, the care of my mother and grandfather. She promised to be faithful to the trust; and nobly was that promise kept. In spite of the unkindness and deep displeasure of Mr. Graham (the blind lady's father), upon whose bounty she had for a long time been dependent, she devoted herself heart and hand to the fulfilment of duties which in her eyes were sacred and holy. In spite of suffering, labor, watching and privation, she voluntarily forsook ease and pleasure, and spent day and night in the patient service of friends whom she loved with a greater love than a daughter's, for it was that of a saint.

"With all my earnestness of purpose, I could never have done half that she did; I might have loved as much, but none but a woman's heart could have conceived and planned, none but a woman's hand could have patiently executed, the deeds that Gertrude wrought. She was more than a sister to me before; she was my constant correspondent, my dearest friend: now she is bound to me by ties that are not of earth nor of time."

CHAPTER XLIV

And opportunity I here have had
To try thee, sift thee, and confess have found thee
Proof against all temptation.
—*Milton*

"CERTAINLY," SAID MR. AMORY, who had waited patiently for the conclusion of Willie's story, "I can well understand that. A man of a generous spirit could hardly fail to cherish a deep and lasting gratitude for one who devoted herself so disinterestedly to a trying and toilsome attendance upon the fast hours of beloved friends, to whose wants he himself was prevented from ministering; and the warmth with which you eulogize this girl does you credit, Sullivan. She must, too, be a young person of great excellence, to have fulfilled so faithfully and well a promise of such remote date that it would probably have been ignored by a less disinterested friend. But do not let any enthusiastic sense of honor induce you to sacrifice yourself on the shrine of gratitude.

"I shall find it hard to believe that a young man who has had the ambition to mark out, and the energy to pursue, such a course on the road to fortune as you have thus far successfully followed, can, in his sober senses, have made a serious resolve to unite himself and his prospects with an insignificant little playmate, of unacknowledged birth, without beauty or fortune, unless there is already a standing engagement, by which he is unwillingly bound, or he allows himself to be drawn on to matrimony by the belief that the highest compliment he can pay (namely, the offer of himself) will alone cancel the immense obligations under which he labors. May I ask if you are already shackled by promises?"

"I am not," replied Willie.

"Then listen to me a moment. My motives are friendly when I beg you not to act rashly in a matter which will affect the happiness of your whole life; and to hear,—with patience, too, if you can," for Willie already gave symptoms of restlessness,—"the few words which I have to say on the subject.

"You are much mistaken, my young friend, if you believe that the happiness of Gerty, as you call her (a very ugly name, by the way), can be insured, any more than your own, by an ill-assorted union, of which you will both find occasion to repent. You have not seen her for six years; think, then, of all that has happened in the mean time, and beware how you act with precipitation.

"You have all this time been living abroad, engaged in active life, growing in knowledge of the world, and its various phases of society. In India, to be sure, you witnessed a mode of life wholly different from that which prevails with us, or in European cities; but the independence, both of character and manner, which you there acquired, fitted you admirably for the polished sphere of Parisian life, to which you were so suddenly introduced, and in which, I may say without flattery, you met with such marked success.

"Notwithstanding the privilege you enjoyed of being presented in polite circles as the friend of a man so well known and so much respected as Mr. Clinton, you cannot have been insensible to the marked attentions bestowed upon you by American residents abroad, or unaware of the

352

advantage you enjoyed, on your return home, from having been known as the object of such favor. Though not so fortunate as to meet you in Paris, I was there at the same time with yourself, and had some opportunity of being acquainted with facts which I am sure you would have too much modesty to acknowledge.

"That you were not wholly devoid of taste for choice society it is easy to infer; since, otherwise, you would never have been able to render yourself an ornament to it, or even maintain, a place within its precincts. It is also equally evident that your pride must have been flattered, and your views in life somewhat biased, by the favorable reception you have met, both abroad and at home, not only from your own sex, but especially from the young, fair, and beautiful women who have honored you with their smiles, and among whom she whose name the crowd already associates with your own stands preeminent.

"When I think of all this, and of those pecuniary hopes you may so reasonably indulge, and on which I have already dilated, and then imagine you suddenly flinging all these aside, to chivalrously throw yourself at the feet of your mother's little nurse, I confess I find it impossible to keep silent, and avoid reminding you of the reaction that must come, the disapointment that must ensue, on finding yourself at once and forever shut out from participation in pleasures which have been within your reach, and voluntarily discarded.

"You must remember that much of the consideration which is paid to a young bachelor of growing prospects ceases to be awarded to him after marriage, and is never extended to his bride, unless she be chosen from the select circles to which he aspires. This unportioned orphan, with whom you propose to share your fate,—this little patient school-mistress—"

"I did not tell you she had ever been a teacher!" exclaimed Willie, stopping short in his walk up and down the room, which latterly he had been, in his turn, pacing impatiently, while he listened to Mr. Amory's words,—"I did not tell you anything of the sort! How did you know it?"

Mr. Amory, who by his negligence had thus betrayed more knowledge than he had been supposed to possess, hesitated a moment, but, quickly recovering himself, answered, with apparent frankness,

"To tell the truth, Sullivan, I have seen the girl, in company with an old doctor."

"Dr. Jeremy?" asked Willie, quickly.

"The same."

"When did you see her? How did it happen?"

"Do not question me!" said Mr. Amory, petulantly, as if the matter were of little consequence, and he did not choose to be interrogated. "I happened to see the old gentleman in the course of my travels, and this Gertrude Flint was with him. He told me a few facts concerning her;— nothing to her disadvantage, however; in warning you against a mis-alliance, I speak only in general terms."

Willie looked at Mr. Amory in a half-scrutinizing, half-wondering manner, and appeared on the point of persisting in his attempt to learn further particulars; but Mr. Amory, taking up the thread of his previous conversation, went on, without giving him a chance to speak.

"This Gerty, as I was saying, Sullivan, will be a dead weight upon your hands; a constant drawback to all your efforts for the attainment of fashionable society, in which it is hardly to be expected she can be exactly fitted to shine. You yourself pronounce her to be without wealth or beauty; of her family you know nothing, and have certainly little reason to expect that, if discovered; it would do her any credit. I believe, then, that I only speak from the dictates of common sense, when I bid you beware how you make, in the disposal of yourself, such a very unequal bargain."

"I am very willing to believe, sir," said Willie, resuming his seat and settling himself into a composed attitude, "that the arguments you have so powerfully brought to bear upon a question most important to my welfare are grounded upon calm reasoning, and a disinterested desire to promote my prosperity. I confess you are the last man, judging from our short, but, for the length of time, intimate acquaintance, from whom I should have expected such advice; for I had believed you so independent of the opinion and so indifferent to the applause of the world that they would weigh but little with you in forming estimates for the guidance of others.

"Still, though your suggestions have failed to influence or in the least degree change my sentiments or intentions, I fully appreciate and thank you for the sincerity and earnestness with which you have sought to mould my judgment by your own; and will reply to your arguments with such frankness as will, I think, persuade you that, so far from following the impulses of a blind enthusiasm, to plunge with haste and precipitation into a course of action hereafter to be deplored, I am actuated by feelings which reason approves, and which have already stood the test of experience.

"You speak truly when you impute to me a natural taste for good society; a taste which poverty, and the retirement in which my boyhood was passed, gave me little opportunity to manifest, but which had, never-theless, no small influence in determining my aims and ambition in life.

The fine houses, equipages, and clothes of the rich, had far less charm to my fancy than the high-bred ease, refinement, and elegance of manner, which distinguished some few of their owners who chanced to come under my observation; and, much as I desired the attainment of wealth for the sake of its own intrinsic advantages, and the means it would afford of contributing to the comfort and happiness of others, it would have seemed to me divested of half its value, should it fail to secure to its possessor a free admittance to the polite and polished circles upon which I looked with admiring eyes.

"I needed not, therefore, the social deprivations I experienced in India to prepare me to enter with eager zest into the excitement and pleasure of Parisian life, to which, through the kindness and partiality of Mr. Clinton, I obtained, as you are, it seems, aware, a free and immediate introduction.

"It is true I was summoned thither at a time when my spirits had been for months struggling with the depression occasioned by sad news from home, and had not, therefore, the least disposition to avail myself of Mr. Clinton's politeness; but the feebleness of his health, and his inability to enter largely into the gayeties of the place, compelled me continually to offer myself as an escort to his daughter, who, fond of society, and reluctant to submit to any exclusion from it, invariably accepted my services, thus drawing me into the very whirl and vortex of fashionable life; in which, I confess, I soon found much to flatter, bewilder, and intoxicate. I could not be insensible to the privileges so unexpectedly accorded to me; nor could my vanity be wholly proof against the assaults made upon it. Nor was my manliness of character alone at stake. My position in fashionable circles threw other and more serious temptations in my way. The soundness of principle and simplicity of habit implanted in me from childhood, and hitherto preserved intact, soon found themselves at stake. I had withstood every kind of gross temptation, but my new and refined associates now presented it to me in that more subtle form which often proves a snare to those over whom, had it come without disguise, it would have no power. The wine-cup could never have enticed me to the coarse and disgusting scenes of drunken revelry; but, held in the hands of the polished gentlemen, who had, but a moment before, been the recipients of popular favor and women's smiles, it sparkled with a richer lustre, and its bitter dregs were forgotten. The professed gamester, the well-known rogue, would in vain have sought me for an accomplice; but I was not equally on my guard against the danger which awaited me from other and unexpected quarters; for how could I believe that my friends, Mr. Clinton's friends, the ornaments of the sphere in which they moved, would unfairly win my money, involve me in entanglements, and lead me on to ruin? I almost wonder, as I look back upon the few first weeks of my residence in Paris, that I did not finally fall a victim to some one of the numerous snares that were, on every side, spread for my destruction, and into which my social disposition, my fearless, and, at the same time, unsophisticated nature rendered me especially prone to fall. Nothing, I am persuaded, but the recollection of my pure-minded and watchful mother, whose recent death had given new freshness and life to the memory of her many warning counsels,—at the time they were bestowed demed by me unnecessary, but now, in the moment of danger, springing up and arming themselves with a solemn meaning,—nothing but the consciousness of her gentle spirit, ever hovering around my path, saddened by my conflicts, rejoicing in my triumphs, could ever have given me courage and perseverance to resist, shun, and finally escape altogether, the pitfalls into which my unwary steps would have plunged me.

"These darker evils, however, successfully combated and subdued, there were others of scarcely less magnitude awaiting me, and in which much of my future well-being and usefulness were involved. In the unvaried round of pleasure in which my days, and nights even, were frequently passed, there was much to gratify my self-love, foster my ambition, and annihilate every worthier emotion. And here, believe me, my safety lay in my success. Had I approached the outskirts of fashionable life, and been compelled to linger, with longing eyes, at the threshold, I might, even now, be loitering there, a deceived spectator of joys which it was not permitted to me to enter and share, or, having gained a partial entrance, be eagerly employed in pushing my way onward.

"Admitted, however, at once, into the very arena of a sphere I was eager to penetrate, my eyes were soon opened to the vain, hollow and worthless nature of the bauble Fashion. Not that I did not meet within its courts the grace, wit, talent and refinement, which I had hoped to find there, or that these were invariably accompanied by other and less attractive qualities. No; I truly believe there is no class which cannot boast of its heroes and heroines, and that there are within the walks of fashionable life men and women who would grace a wilderness. Nor do I despise forms and ceremonies which are becoming in themselves, and conducive to elegance and good-breeding. As long as one class is distinguished by education and refined manners, and another is marked by ignorance and vulgarity, there should, and there must, in the nature of things, be a dividing line between the two, which neither, perhaps, would desire to overstep.

"But this barrier is not *Fashion,* which, both abroad and at home, oftentimes excludes the former, and gives free admittance to the latter; and, if I presume to adopt a higher standard, it is because I have had so close an acquaintance with that already set up, that I can judge how little it is to be trusted."

"You are young," said Mr. Amory, "to be such a philosopher. Many a man has turned away with disgust from an aristocracy into which he could himself gain no admittance; but few renounce it voluntarily."

"Few, perhaps," replied Willie, "few *young* men, at least, have such opportunities as I have had to penetrate its secrets. I trust I may say without treachery, since I speak in general terms only, that I have seen more ignorance, more ill-breeding, more meanness, and more immorality, in the so-called aristocracy of our country, than I should have believed it possible would be tolerated there. I have frequently known instances in which the most accomplished gentleman, or the most beautiful lady, of a gay circle, has given evidence of unpardonable want of information on the most common topics. I have seen elegant evening assemblies disgraced by a degree of rudeness and incivility which reflected as little credit on the taste as on the feelings. I have seen the profuse and lavish expenditure of to-day atoned for by a selfish and despicable parsimony on the morrow; and I have seen a want of principle exhibited by persons of both sexes, which proves that a high position on earth is no security against such contamination of the soul as must wholly unfit it for an exalted place hereafter."

"I have witnessed no less myself," said Mr. Amory; "but my experiences have not been like those of other men, and my sight has been sharpened by circumstances. I am still astonished that you should have been awake to those facts."

"I was not, at first," answered Willie. "It was only gradually that I recovered from the dazzling, blinding effect which the glitter and show of Fashion imposed upon the clearness of my perceptions. My suspicions of its falsehood and vanity were based upon instances of selfishness, folly and cold-heartedness, which, one after another, came to my knowledge. I could relate to you the thousand mean deceits, the contemptible rivalries, the gross neglect of sacred duties, which came under my immediate observation; but I will not betray the secrets of individuals, or weary you with their recital.

"Especially was I astonished at the effect of an uninterrupted pursuit of pleasure upon the sensibilities, the tempers, and the domestic affections, of women. Though bearing within my heart an image of female goodness and purity, this sweet remembrance, this living ideal, might possibly have been driven from its throne, and supplanted by some one of the lovely faces which, at first, bewildered me by their beauty, had these last been the index to souls of equal perfection. There may be——I have no doubt that there are——noble and excellent women, moving in the highest walks of life, whose beauty, grace and other outward adornments, are less admirable than their own high natures; but among those with whom I became familiarly acquainted there was not one who could in the least compare with her who was continually present to my memory, who is still, and ever must be, a model to her sex.

"It is no wonder that others failed to come up to my conception of all that is lovely in woman, since the character of Gertrude Flint was the standard by which each in my mind was measured. How could I help contrasting the folly, the worldliness, and the cold-heartedness around me, with the cultivated mind, the self-sacrificing and affectionate dispositon, of one who possesses every quality that can adorn life, whether at home or abroad? You have indeed failed to convince me that Gertrude can in any way be a drawback or disadvantage to the man who shall be so fortunate as to call her his. For my own part, I desire no better, no more truly aristocratic position in life, than that to which she is so well entitled, and to which she would be one of the brightest ornaments,——the aristocracy of true refinement, knowledge, grace and beauty. You talk to me of wealth. Gertrude has no money in her purse, but her soul is the pure gold, tried in the furnace of sorrow and affliction, and thence come forth bright and unalloyed. You speak of family, and an honorable birth. She has no family, and her birth is shrouded in mystery; but the blood that courses in her veins would never disgrace the race from which she sprung, and every throb of her unselfish heart allies her to all that is noble.

"You are eloquent on the subject of beauty. When I parted from Gertrude, she was, in all but character, a mere child, being only twelve or thirteen years of age. Though much altered and improved since the time when she first came among us, I scarcely think she could have been said to possess much of what the world calls beauty. For myself, it was a matter of which I seldom thought or cared; and, had I been less indifferent on the subject she was so dear to me that I should have been utterly unable to form an impartial judgment of her claims in this respect.

"I well remember, however, the indignation I once felt at hearing a fellow-clerk, who had accidentally met her in one of our walks, sneeringly contrast her personal appearance with that of our mutual employer's handsome daughter, the same Miss Clinton of whom we have been speaking; and the proportionate rapture with which I listened to the excellent teacher, Miss Browne, when on a certain occasion, being present at a school-examination, I overheard her commenting to a lady upon Gertrude's wonderful promise in person as well as in mind. Whether the first part of this promise has been fulfilled, I have no means of judging; but, as I recall her dignified and graceful little figure, her large, intelligent, sparkling eyes, the glow of feeling that lit up her whole countenance, and the peaceful, almost majestic expression which purity of soul imparted to her yet childish features, she stands forth to my remembrance the embodiment of all that I hold most dear.

"Six years may have outwardly changed her much; but they cannot have robbed her of what I prize the most. She has charms over which time can have no power, a grace that is a gift of Heaven, a beauty that is eternal. Could I ask for more?

"Do not believe, then," continued he, after a short pause, "that my fidelity to my early playmate is an emotion of gratitude merely. It is true I owe her much,—far more than I can ever repay; but the honest warmth of my affection for the noble girl springs from the truest love of a purity of character and singleness of heart which I have never seen equalled.

"What is there in the wearisome and foolish walks of Fashion, the glitter and show of wealth, the homage of an idle crowd, that could so fill my heart, elevate my spirit, and inspire my exertions, as the thought of a peaceful, happy home, blessed by a presiding spirit so formed for confidence, love, and a communion that time can never dissolve, and eternity will but render more secure and unbroken?"

"And she whom you love so well?—are you sure—" asked Mr. Phillips, speaking with visible effort, and faltering ere he had completed his sentence.

"No," answered Willie, anticipating the question. "I know what you would ask.—I am *not* sure. I have no reason to indulge the hopes I have been dwelling upon so fondly; but I do not regret having spoken with such openness and candor; for, should she grieve my heart by her coldness, I should still be proud to have loved her. Until this time, ever since I gained my native land, I have been shackled with duties, which, sacred as they were, have chafed a spirit longing for freedom to follow its own impulses. In this visit to you, sir (and, as he spoke, he rose to depart), I have fulfilled the last obligation imposed upon me by my excellent friend, and to-morrow I shall be at liberty to go where duty alone prevented me from at once hastening."

He offered his hand to Mr. Amory, who grasped it with a cordiality very different from the feeble greeting he had given him on his entrance. "Good-by," said he. "You carry with you my best wishes for a success which you seem to have so much at heart; but some day or other I feel sure you will be reminded of all I have said to you this evening."

"Strange man!" thought Willie, as he walked towards his own hotel. "How warmly he shook my hand at parting! and with what a friendly manner he bade me farewell, notwithstanding the coldness of the reception he gave me, and the pertinacity with which, throughout my whole visit, I rejected his opinions and repelled his advice!"

CHAPTER XLV

Yet 't is a weary task to school the heart,
Ere years of griefs have tamed its fiery spirit
Into that still and passive fortitude
Which is but learned from suffering.
—*Hemans*

"MISS GERTRUDE," SAID Mrs. Prime, opening the parlor-door, putting her head cautiously in, looking round, and then advancing with a stealthy pace, like that of a favorite family cat which is venturing to step a little beyond its usual limits,—"my! how busy you are! Lor's sakes alive, if you an't rippin' up them great curtains of Miss Graham's for the wash! I would n't be botherin' with 'em, Miss Gertrude; she won't be here for this fortnight, and Miss Ellis will have time enough."

"O, I have nothing else to do, Mrs. Prime; it 's no trouble." Then, looking up pleasantly at the old cook, she added, "It seems very cosey for us all to be at home again; does n't it?"

"It seems beautiful!" answered Mrs. Prime, with emphasis; "and—I hope there 's no harm in sayin' it—I can't help thinkin' how nice it would be, if we could all live on jist as we are now, without no more intrusions."

Gertrude smiled, and said, "Everything looks as it used to in old times, when I first came here. I was quite a child then," continued she, with a sigh.

"Gracious me! What are you now?" said Mrs. Prime. "For mercy's sake, Miss Gertrude, don't you begin to think about growin' old! There's nothin' like feelin' young, to keep young. There's Miss Patty Pace, now—"

"I have been meaning to ask after her," exclaimed Gertrude, resuming her scissors, and commencing to rip another window-curtain. "Is she alive and well yet?"

"She!" replied Mrs. Prime. "Lor, she won't never die! Old women like her, that feels themselves young gals, allers live forever; but I came a purpose to speak to you about her. The baker's boy that fetched the loaves, this mornin', brought an arrant from her, and she wants to see you the first chance she can get; but I would n't hurry, either, about goin' there, or anywhere, Miss Gertrude, till I got rested; for I believe you an't well, you look so spent and kind o' tired out."

"Did she wish to see me?" asked Gertrude. "Poor old thing! I 'll go and see her, this very afternoon; and you need n't feel anxious about me, Mrs. Prime,—I am quite well."

And Gertrude went. It was now her second day of suspense; and this, like every other motive for action, was eagerly hailed.

She found Miss Patty nearly bent double with rheumatism, dressed with less than her usual care, and crouching over a miserable fire, built of a few chips and shavings. She appeared, however, to be in tolerable spirits, and hailed Gertrude's entrance by a cordial greeting.

The curiosity for which she was always remarkable seemed to have increased, rather than diminished, with the infirmities of age. Innumerable were the questions she put to Gertrude regarding her own personal experiences during the past year, and the movements of the circles in which she had been living. She showed a special interest in Saratoga life, the latest fashions exhibited there, and the opportunities which the place afforded for forming advantageous matrimonial connections.

"So you have not yet chosen a companion," said she, after Gertrude had patiently and good-naturedly responded to all her queries. "That is a circumstance to be regretted. Not," continued she, with a little smirk, and a slight wave of the hand, "that it is ever too late in life for one to meditate the conjugal tie, which is often assumed with advantage by persons of fifty or more; and certainly you, who are still in the bloom of your days, need not despair of a youthful swain. However, existence, I may say, is two-fold when it is shared with a congenial partner; and I had hoped that before now, Miss Gertrude, both you and myself would have formed such an alliance. Experience prompts me, when I declare the protection of the matrimonial union one of its greatest advantages."

"I hope you have not suffered from the want of it" said Gertrude.

"I have, Miss Gertrude, suffered incalculably. Let me impress upon you, however, that the keenest pangs have been those of the sensibilities; yes, the sensibilities,—the finest part of our nature, and that which will least bear wounding."

"I am sorry to hear that you have been thus grieved," said Gertrude. "I should have supposed that, living quite alone, you might have been spared this trial."

"O, Miss Gertrude!" exclaimed the old lady, lifting up both hands, and speaking in such a pitiable tone as would have excited the compassion of her listener, if it had been one grain less ridiculous,—"O, that I had the wings of a dove, wherewith to flee away from my kindred! I fondly thought to have distanced them, but within the last revolving year they have discovered my retreat, and I can no longer elude their vigilance. Hardly can I recover from the shock of one visitation,—made, as I am convinced, for the sole purpose of taking an inventory of my possessions, and measuring the length of my days,—before the vultures are again seen hovering round my dwelling. But," exclaimed the old lady, raising her voice and inwardly chuckling as she spoke, "they shall fall into their own snare; for I will dupe every one of them, yet!"

"I was not aware that you had any relations," said Gertrude; "and it seems they are such only in name."

"Name!" said Miss Pace, emphatically. "I am animated with gladness at the thought that they are not honored with a cognomen which not one of them is worthy to hear. No, they pass by a different name; a name as plebeian as their own coarse souls. There are three of them, who stand to each other in a fraternal relation, and all are alike hateful to me. One, a contemptible coxcomb, comes here to overawe me with his presence, which he conceives to be imposing; calls me aunt—aunt; thus testifying by his speech to a consanguinity which he blindly fancies makes him nearer akin to my property!" The old lady, excited to wrath, almost shrieked the last word. "And the other two," continued she, with equal heat, "are beggars! always were,—always will be,—let 'em be,—I'm glad of it!

"You hear me, Miss Gertrude; you are a young lady of quick comprehension, and I avail myself of your contiguity; which, although you deny the charge, may shortly be interrupted by some eager lover, to request at your hands a favor, such as I little thought once I should ever feel compelled to seek. I want you—I sent for you to write (Miss Patty lowered her voice to a whisper) the last will and testament of Miss Patty Pace."

The poor woman's trembling voice evidenced a deep compassion for herself, which Gertrude could not help sharing; and she expressed a willingness to comply with her wishes as far as was in her power, at the same time declaring her utter ignorance of all the forms of law.

To Gertrude's astonishment, Miss Patty announced her own perfect acquaintaince with all the legal knowledge which the case demanded; and in so complete and faultless a manner did she dictate the words of the important instrument, that, being afterwards properly witnessed, signed and sealed, it was found at the end of a few months,—at which time Miss Patty was called upon to give up her earthly trust,—free from imperfection and flaw, and proved a satisfactory direction for the disposal of the inheritance.

It may be as well to state here, however, that he who was pronounced sole heir to her really valuable property never availed himself of the bequest, otherwise than to make a careful bestowal of it among the most needy and worthy of her relatives. Notwithstanding the protestations of several respectable individuals who were present at the attestation of the document, all of whom pronounced Miss Patty sane and collected to her last moments, he never would believe that a sound mind could have made so wild and erratic a disposal of the hardly-earned and carefully-preserved savings of years.

This sole inheritor of her estates was William Sullivan, the knight of the rosy countenance; and the same chivalrous spirit which won Miss Patty's virgin heart, and gained for him her lasting favor, prompted him to disclaim and utterly refuse the acceptance of a reward so wholly disproportioned to the slight service he had rendered the old lady.

Though he could not fail to be amused, he was nevertheless deeply touched, by the preamble to the will, in which Miss Patty set forth in a most charcteristic manner the feelings and motives which had influenced her in the choice of an heir to her possessions.

"A gentlewoman, of advanced years, who has clung to life and its hopes, and, in spite of many vexatious vicissitudes, feels something loth to depart, has been forcibly reminded by her relations that ere another smiling spring-time she may have a call to join the deceased line of Paces,—a family which will, on her departure, here become extinct. With the most polite of courtesies, and a passing wave of the hand, Miss Patty acknowledges the forethought of her relations of the other branch, in reminding her, before it be too late, of the propriety of naming the individual for whose benefit it is her desire to make a testamentary provision.

"She has looked about the world, viewed all her fellows in the glass of memory, and made her final election. The youth himself—the most gallant young gentleman of his day—will open his eyes in astonishment, and declare, 'Madam, I know you not!' But, sir, Miss Patty, old, ugly and infirm, has a heart which feels as keenly as it did in youth. She has not forgotten—she means now to signify, by her last deeds, how vividly she remembers—the rosy-cheeked youth who once raised her from the frosty earth, took her withered hand, placed it within his vigorous young arm, and, with sunny smiles and cheering words, escorted the rheumatic old woman to a refuge from the wintry elements. Miss Patty has a natural love of courtesy and the deference offered by gay and beautiful youth to helpless and despised old age has touched a sensitive chord. Miss Patty—it is no secret—has some little hoarded treasures; and, since she cannot be on the spot to superintend their expenditure, she has, after some struggles, resolved to secure them from pollution by awarding these savings of years to one possessed of such true gentility as Master William Sullivan, confidently assured that he will never disgrace the former owner of the property, or permit her wealth to flow into vulgar channels."

Then followed an inventory of the estate,—a most remarkable estate, consisting of odds and ends of everything; and finally a carefully and legally worded document, assigning the whole of the strange medley, without legacies or encumbrances, to the sole use and disposal of the appointed heir.

Gertrude found it no easy task to gather and transfix in writing the exact idea which the old woman's rambling dictation was intended to convey; and it was two or three hours before the manuscript was completed, and the patient and diligent scribe permitted to depart.

The sky was overcast, and a drizzling rain beginning to fall, as she commenced walking towards home; but the distance was not great, and the only damage she sustained was a slight dampness to her garments. Emily perceived it at once, however. "Your dress is quite wet," said she. "You must go and sit by the parlor-fire. I shall not go down until tea-time, but father is there, and will be glad of your company; he has been alone all the afternoon."

Gertrude found Mr. Graham sitting in front of a pleasant wood-fire, half dozing, half reading. She took a book and a low chair, and joined him. Finding the heat too great, however, she soon retreated to a sofa, at the opposite side of the room.

Hardly had she done so when there was a ring at the front-door bell. The housemaid, who was passing by the door, opened it, and immediately ushered in a visitor.

It was Willie!

Gertrude rose, but trembling form head to foot, so that she dared not trust herself to take a step forward. Willie advanced into the centre of the room, then looked at Gertrude, bowed, hesitated, and said, "Miss Flint!— is she here?"

The color rushed into Gertrude's face. She attempted to speak, but failed.

It was not necessary. The blush was enough. Willie recognized her, and, starting forward, eagerly seized her hand.

"Gerty! Is it possible?"

The perfect naturalness and ease of his manner, the warmth and earnestness with which he took and retained her hand, reassured the agitated girl. The spell seemed partially removed. For a moment he became in her eyes the Willie of old, her dear friend and playmate, and, she found voice to exclaim, "O, Willie! you have come at last! I am so glad to see you!"

The sound of their voices disturbed Mr. Graham, who had fallen into a nap, from which the ringing of the door-bell and the entrance of a strange step had failed to arouse him. He turned round in his easy-chair, then rose. Willie dropped Gertrude's hand, and stepped towards him. "Mr. Sullivan," said Gertrude, with a feeble attempt at a suitable introduction.

They shook hands, and then all three sat down.

And now all Gertrude's embarrassment returned. It is not unfrequently the case that when the best of friends meet after a long separation they salute or embrace each other, and then, not-withstanding the weight of matter pressing on the mind of each,—sufficient, perhaps, to furnish subjects of conversation for weeks to come,—nothing of importance presents itself at once, and a pause ensues, which is finally filled up by some most trivial and unimportant question concerning the journey of the newly-arrived party, or the safety of his baggage. But to these latter questions, or any of a similar nature, Gertrude required no answer. She had seen Willie before; she was aware of his arrival; knew even the steamer in which he had come; but was anxious to conceal from him this knowledge. She could not tell him, since he seemed so ignorant of the fact himself, that they had met before; and it may well be imagined that she was at an utter loss what to do or say, under the circumstances. Her embarrassment soon communicated itself to Willie; and Mr. Graham's presence, which was a restraint to both, made matters worse.

Willie, however, first broke the momentary silence. "I should hardly have known you, Gertrude. I did not know you. How——"

"How did you come?" asked Mr. Graham, abruptly, apparently unconscious that he was interrupting Willie's remark.

"In the Europa," replied Willie. "She got into New York about a week ago."

"Out here, I meant," said Mr. Graham, rather stiffly. "Did you come out in the coach?"

"O, excuse me, sir," rejoined Willie; "I misunderstood you. No, I drove out from Boston in a chaise."

"Did any one take your horse?"

"I fastened him in front of the house."

Willie glanced out of the window (it was now nearly dusk) to see that the animal was still where he had left him. Mr. Graham settled himself in his easy-chair, and looked into the fire. There was another pause, more painful than the first.

"You are changed, too," said Gertrude, at last, in reply to Willie's unfinished comment. Then, fearing he might feel hurt at what he must know to be true in more ways than one, the color, which had retreated, mounted once more to her cheeks.

He did not seem to feel hurt, however, but replied, "Yes, an Eastern climate makes great changes; but I think I can hardly have altered more than you have. Why, only think, Gerty, you were a child when I went away! I suppose I must have known I should have found you a young lady, but I begin to think I never fully realized it."

"When did you leave Calcutta?"

"The latter part of February. I passed the spring months in Paris."

"You did not write," said Gertrude, in a faltering voice.

"No, I was expecting to come across by every steamer, and wanted to surprise you."

Conscious that she had probably seemed far less surprised than he expected, she looked confused, but replied, "I was disappointed about the letters, but I am very glad to see you again, Willie."

"You can't be so glad as I am," said he, lowering his voice, and looking at her with great tenderness. "You seem more and more like yourself to me every minute that I see you. I begin to think, however, that I ought to have written, and told you I was coming."

Gertrude smiled. Willie's manner was so unchanged, his words so affectionate, that it seemed unkind to doubt his friendliness, although to his undivided love she felt she could have no claim.

"No," said she, "I like surprises. Don't you remember, I always did?"

"Remember?—Certainly," replied he; "I have never forgotten anything that you liked."

Just at this moment, Gertrude's birds, whose cage hung in the window at which Willie sat, commenced a little twittering noise, which they always made just at night. He looked up. "Your birds," said Gertrude; "the birds you sent me."

"Are they all alive, and well?" asked he.

"Yes, all of them."

"You have been a kind mistress to the little things. They are very tender."

"I am very fond of them."

"You take such care of those you love, dear Gerty, that you are sure to preserve their lives as long as may be."

His tone, still more than his words, betrayed the deep meaning with which he spoke. Gertrude was silent.

"Is Miss Graham well?" asked Willie.

Gertrude related, in reply, that her nerves had been recently much disturbed by the terrible experiences through which she had passed; and this led to the subject of the recent disaster, at which Gertrude forbore to mention her having been herself present.

Willie spoke with feeling of the sad catastrophe, and with severity of the reckless carelessness which had been the cause of it; and ended by remarking that he had valued friends on board the boat, but was unaware that Miss Graham, whom he loved for Gertrude's sake, was among them.

Conversation between Gertrude and Willie had by this time assumed a footing of ease, and something of their former familiarity. The latter had taken a seat near her, on the sofa, that they might talk more unrestrainedly; for, although Mr. Graham might have dropped asleep again, for anything they knew to the contrary, it was not easy wholly to forget his presence.

There were many subjects, however, on which it would have seemed natural for them to speak, had not Gertrude purposely avoided them. The causes of Willie's sudden return, his probable stay, his future plans in life, and especially his reasons for having postponed his visit to herself until he had been in the country more than a week;—all these were inquiries which even ordinary interest and curiosity would have suggested; but to Gertrude they all lay under embargo. She neither felt prepared to receive nor willing to force his confidence on matters which must inevitably be influenced by his engagement with Miss Clinton; and therefore preserved utter silence on these topics, even taking pains to avoid them. And Willie, deeply grieved at this strange want of sympathy on her part, forbore to thrust upon her notice these seemingly forgotten or neglected circumstances.

They talked of Calcutta life, of Parisian novelties, of Gertrude's school-keeping, and many other things, but spoke not a word of matters which lay nearest to the hearts of both. At length a servant appeared at the door, and, not observing that there was company, announced tea. Mr. Graham rose, and stood with his back to the fire. Willie rose also, and prepared to take leave. Mr. Graham, with frigid civility, invited him to remain, and Gertrude hesitated not to urge him to do so; but he declined with such decision that the latter understood plainly that he perceived and felt the neglect with which Mr. Graham had treated him and his visit. In addition to the fact that the old gentleman disliked young men as a class, and that Willie had intruded upon the rare and sacred privacy in which he was indulging, there was the bitter and still rankling recollection that Gertrude had once forsaken himself and Emily (for so he, in his own mind, styled her conscientious choice between conflicting duties) for the very family of which their visitor was the only remaining member; a recollection which did not tend to soften or conciliate the easily-prejudiced and obstinate-minded man.

Gertrude accompanied Willie to the door. The rain had ceased, but the wind whistled across the piazza. It seemed to be growing cold. Willie buttoned his coat, while he promised to see Gertrude on the following day.

"You have no overcoat," said she; "the night is chilly, and you are accustomed to a hot climate. You had better take this shawl;" and she took from the hat-tree a heavy scotch plaid, which always hung there to be used on occasions like the present.

He thanked her, and threw it over his arm; then, taking both her hands in his, looked her steadily in the face for a moment, as if he would fain have spoken. Seeing, however, that she shrank from his mild and affectionate gaze, he dropped her hands, and, with a troubled expression, bade her good-night, and ran down the door-steps.

Gertrude stood with the handle of the door in her hand until she heard the sound of his horse's hoofs as he drove down the road; then, hastily shutting it, ran and hid herself in her own room. Well as she had borne up during the longed-for and yet much-dreaded meeting, calmly and naturally as she had sustained her part, her courage all forsook her now, and in looking forward to days, weeks and months, of frequent intercourse, she felt that the most trying part of the struggle was yet to come.

Had Willie been wholly changed,—had he seemed the thoughtless worldling, the fashionable man of society, the cold-hearted devotee of business or of gain,—in one of which characters she had lately half-fancied he would appear,—had he greeted her with chilling formality, with heartless indifference, or with awkward restraint, she might, while she despised, pitied or blamed, have learned to love him less. But he had come back as he went, open-hearted, generous, manly and affectionate. He had manifested the same unaffected warmth of feeling, the same thoughtful tenderness, he had ever shown. In short, he was the Willie she had thought of, dreamed of, imagined and loved. It was evident that in giving his heart to another he had never wholly forgotten her; while he loved Isabel, he would still feel a friendly, almost a brotherly regard for Gertrude. More than that it had never occurred to him to bestow.

And she must school herself to the cruel task of seeing him day by day, hearing the story of his love for another, and wishing him all joy, as a sister might do a kind and affectionate brother. She must learn to subdue the love whose depth and intensity she had scarcely known until now, and mould it into friendship. As she thought of all this, she found it impossible to still the wildly-beating waves that swelled against her aching, throbbing heart. She threw herself upon the bed, buried her face in pillows, and wept.

Presently there was a light tap at her door. Believing it to be a summons to the tea-table, she said, without rising, "Jane, is that you? I do not wish for any supper."

"It is n't that, miss," said the girl; "but I have brought you a letter."

Gertrude sprung up, and opened the door.

"A little boy handed it to me, and then ran off as fast as he could," said the girl, placing a package in her hand. "He told me to give it to you straight away."

"Bring me a light," said Gertrude.

The girl went for a lamp, Gertrude, in the mean time, endeavoring to judge what a package of such unusual size and thickness could contain. She thought it impossible that any letter could so soon arrive from Mr. Amory. The next morning was the earliest time at which she had expected one. Who, then, could it be from? And, while she was wondering, Jane brought a lamp, by the light of which she at once detected his hand-writing; and, breaking the seal, she drew from the envelope several closely-written pages, whose contents she perused with all the eagerness and excitement which the weight, import, and intense interest of the subject, might well demand.

CHAPTER XLVI

There are swift hours in life,—strong, rushing hours,
that do the work of tempests in their might!
      —*Hemans*

IT RAN as follows:

"MY DAUGHTER,—My loving, tender-hearted girl. Now that your own words encourage me with the assurance that my worst fear was unfounded (the fear that my name was already blasted to your young ears, and your father doomed by your young heart to infamy),—now that I can appeal to you as to an impartial witness, I will disclose the story of my life, and, while I prove to you your parentage, will hope that my unprejudiced child, at least, will believe, love and trust her father, in spite of a world's injustice.

"I will conceal nothing. I will plunge at once into those disclosures which I most dread to utter, and trust to after explanation to palliate the darkness of my tale.

"Mr. Graham is my step-father, and my blessed mother, long since dead, was, in all but the tie of nature, a true mother to Emily. Thus allied, however, to those whom you love best, I am parted from them by a heavy curse; for, not only was mine the ill-fated hand (O, hate me not yet, Gertrude!) which locked poor Emily up in darkness, but, in addition to that horrid deed, I stand accused in the eyes of my fellow-men of another crime, deep, dark and disgraceful. And yet, though living under a ban, wandering up and down the world a doomed and a broken-hearted man, I am innocent as a child of intentional wrong, as you will learn, if you can trust to the truth of the tale I am about to tell.

"Nature gave and education fostered in me a rebellious spirit. I was the idol of my invalid mother, who, though she loved me with a love for which I bless her memory, had not the energy to tame and subdue the passionate and wilful nature of her boy. Though ungoverned, however, I was neither cruelly nor viciously disposed, and though my sway at home and among my school-fellows was alike indisputable, I made many friends, and not a single enemy. But a sudden check was at length put to my freedom. My mother married, and I soon came to feel, and feel bitterly, the check which her husband, Mr. Graham, was likely to impose upon my boyish independence. Had he treated me with kindness, had he won my affection (which he might easily have done, for my sensitive and impas-sioned nature disposed me to every tender and grateful emotion), it is impossible to measure the influence he might have had in moulding my yet unformed character.

"But the reverse was the case. His behavior towards me was that of chilling coldness and reserve. He repelled with scorn the first advance on my part, which led me, at my mother's instigation, to address him by the paternal title,—an offense of which I never again was guilty. And yet, while he seemed to ignore the relationship, he assumed its privileges and authority, thus wounding my feelings and my pride, and exciting a spirit of rebellious opposition to his commands.

"Two things served to embitter my sentiments and strengthen my growing dislike for my overbearing step-father. One was the consciousness of my utter dependence upon his bounty; the other, a hint, which I re-ceived through the mistaken kindness of a domestic who had always known the family, that Mr. Graham's dislike to me had its origin in an old enmity between himself and my own father,—an honorable and high-minded man, whom it was ever my greatest pride to be told that I resembled.

"Great, however, as was the warfare in my heart, power rested with Mr. Graham; for I was yet but a child, and necessarily subject to govern-ment. Nor could I be deaf to my mother's entreaties that, for her sake, I would learn submission. It was only occasionally, therefore, when I had been, as I considered, most unjustly thwarted, that I broke forth into direct rebellion; and even then there were influences ever at work to preserve at least outward harmony in our household. Thus years passed on, and, though I did not learn to love Mr. Graham more, the force of habit, the intense interest afforded by my studies, and a growing capability of self-control, rendered my mode of life far less obnoxious to me than it had once been.

"There was one great compensation for my trials, and that was the love I cherished for Emily, who responded to it with equal warmth on her part. It was not because she stood between me and her father, a mediator and a friend; it was not because she submitted patiently to my dictation, and aided me in all my plans. It was because our natures were made for each other, and, as they grew and expanded, were bound together by ties which a rude hand only could snap and rend asunder. I pause not to dwell upon the tenderness and depth of this affection; it is enough to say that it became the life of my life.

"At length my mother died. I was at that time—sorely against my will—employed in Mr. Graham's counting-house; and still continued an inmate of his family. And now, without excuse or even warning, my step-father commenced a course of policy as unwise as it was cruel; and so irritating to my pride, so torturing to my feelings, and so maddening to my hot nature, that it excited and angered me almost to frenzy. He tried to rob me of the only thing that sweetened and blessed my existence—the love of Emily. I will not here recount the motives I imputed to him, nor the means he employed. It is sufficient to say that they were such as to change my former dislike into bitter hatred,—my unwilling obedience to his will into open and deliberate opposition.

"Instead of submitting to what I considered his tyrannical inter-ference, I sought Emily's society on all occasions, and persuaded the gentle girl to lend herself to my schemes for thwarting her father's purposes. I did not speak to her of love; I did not seek to bind her to me by promises; I hinted not at marriage; a sense of honor forbade it. But, with a boyish independence, which I have since feared was the height of folly and impru-dence, I sought every occasion, even in her father's presence, to manifest my determination to maintain that constant freedom and familiarity of intercourse which had been the growth of circumstances, and could not, without force, be restrained.

"At length Emily was taken ill, and for six weeks I was debarred her presence. As soon as she was sufficiently recovered to leave her room, I constantly sought and at last obtained an opportunity to see and speak with her. We had been together in the library more than an hour when Mr. Graham suddenly entered, and came towards us with a face whose harshness and severity I shall not soon forget. I did not heed an interruption, for the probable consequences of which I believed myself prepared. I was little prepared, however, for the nature of the attack actually made upon me.

"That he would accuse me of disobedience to wishes which he had hinted in every possible way, and even intimate more plainly than before his resolve to place barriers between Emily and myself, I fully expected, and was ready with my replies; but when he burst forth with a torrent of unqualified and ungentlemanly abuse,—when he stormed and raved, imputing to me mean, selfish and contemptible motives, which had never for a moment influenced me, or even occurred to my mind,—I was struck dumb with surprise, and impatience and anger.

"But this was not all. It was then, in the presence of the pure-minded girl whom I worshipped, that he charged me with a dark and horrid crime,—the crime of forgery,—asserting my guilt as recently discovered, but positive and undoubted. My spirit had raged before,—now it was on fire. I lifted my hand, and clenched my fist. What I would have done I know not. Whether I should have found words to assert my innocence, fling back the lie, and refute a charge as unexpected as it was false,—or whether, my voice failing me from passion, I should have swept Mr. Graham from my path, perhaps felled him to the floor, while I strode away to rally my calmness in the open air,—I cannot now conjecture; for a wild shriek from Emily recalled me to myself, and, turning, I saw her fall fainting upon the sofa.

Forgetting everything then but the apparently dying condition into which the horror of the scene had thrown her, I sprung forward to her relief. There was a table beside her, and some bottles upon it. I hastily snatched what I believed to be a simple restorative, and, in my agitation, emptied the contents of the phial in her face. I know not what the exact character of the mixture could have been; but it matters not,—its effect was too awfully evident. The deed was done,—the fatal deed,—and mine was the hand that did it!

"Brought suddenly to consciousness by the intolerable torture that succeeded, the poor girl sprung screaming from the sofa, flung her arms wildly above her head, rushed in a frantic manner through the room, and finally crouched in a corner. I followed, in an agony scarce less than her own; but she repelled me with her hands, at the same time uttering piercing shrieks. Mr. Graham, who for an instant had looked like one paralyzed by the scene, now rushed forward like a madman. Instead of aiding me in my efforts to lift poor Emily from the floor, and so far from compassionating my situation, which was only less pitiable than hers, he, with a fierceness redoubled at my being, as he considered, the sole cause of the disaster, attacked me with a storm of jeering taunts and cruel reproaches, declaring that I had killed his child. With words like these, which are still ringing in my ears, he drove me from the room and the house; a repulsion which I, overpowered by the misery of contrition and remorse, had neither the wish nor the strength to resist.

"O! the terrible night and day that succeeded! I can give you no idea how they were passed. I wandered out into the country, spent the whole night walking beneath the open sky, endeavoring to collect my thoughts and compose my mind, and still morning found me with a fevered pulse and excited brain. With the returning light, however, I began to realize the necessity of forming some future plan of action.

"Emily's sad situation, and my intense anxiety to learn the worst effects of the fatal accident, gave me the strongest motives for hastening, with the earliest morning, either openly or by stealth, to Mr. Graham's house. Everything also which I possessed,—all my money, consisting merely of the residue of my last quarter's allowance, my clothing, and a few valuable gifts from my mother,—were in the chamber which I had there occupied. There seemed, therefore, to be no other course for me than to return thither once more, at least; and having thus resolved, I retraced my steps to the city, determined, if it were necessary in order to gain the desired particulars concerning Emily, to meet her father face to face. As I drew near the house, however, I hesitated, and dared not proceed. Mr. Graham had exhausted upon me already every angry word, had threatened even deeds of violence, should I ever again cross his threshold; and I feared to trust my own fiery spirit to a collision in which I might be led on to an open resistance of the man whom I had already sufficiently injured.

"In the terrible work I had but yesterday done,—a work of whose fatal effect I had even then a gloomy foreshadowing,—I had blighted the existence of his worshipped child, and drawn a dark pall over his dearest hopes. It was enough. I would not, for worlds, be guilty of the added sin of lifting my hand against the man who, unjust as he had been towards an innocent youth, had met a retaliation far, far too severe.

"Still, I knew his wrath to be unmitigated, was well aware of his power to excite my hot nature to frenzy, and resolved to beware how I crossed his path. Meet him I must, to refute the false charges he had brought against me; but not within the walls of his dwelling, the home of his suffering daughter. In the counting-house, where the crime of forgery was said to have been committed, and in the presence of my fellow-clerks, I would publicly deny the deed, and dare him to its proof. But first I must either see or hear from Emily; before I met the father at all, I must learn the exact nature and extent of the wrong I had done him in the person of his child. For this, however, I must wait, until, under cover of the next night's darkness, I could enter the house unperceived.

"So I wandered about all day in torment, without tasting or even desiring food or rest, the thought of my poor, darling, tortured Emily ever present to my wretched thoughts. The hours seemed interminable. I remember that day of suspense as if it had been a whole year of misery. But night came at last, cloudy, and the air thickened with a heavy fog, which, as I approached the street where Mr. Graham lived, enveloped the neighborhood, and concealed the house until I was directly opposite to it. I shuddered at the sight of the physician's chaise standing before the door; for I knew that Dr. Jeremy had closed his visits to Emily more than a week previously, and must have been summoned to attend her since the accident. Finding him there, and thinking it probable Mr. Graham was also in the house at this hour, I forbore to enter, but stood effectually concealed by the cloud of mist, and watching my opportunity.

"Once or twice Mrs. Ellis, the housekeeper, passed up and down the staircase, as I could distinctly see through the sidelights of the door, which afforded me a full view of the entryway; and presently Dr. Jeremy descended slowly, followed by Mr. Graham. The doctor would have passed hastily out; but Mr. Graham detained him, to question him regarding his patient, as I judged from the deep anxiety depicted on my step-father's countenance, while, with one hand resting on the shoulder of this old friend of the family, he sought to read his opinion in his face. The doctor's back was towards me, and I could only judge of his replies by the effect they produced on the questioner, whose haggard, worn appearance became more fearfully distressed at every syllable that fell from the honest and truthful lips of medical man, whose words were oracles to all who knew his skill.

"I needed, therefore, no further testimony to force upon me the conviction that Emily's fate was sealed; and, as I looked with pity upon the afflicted parent, and shudderingly thought how immediate had been my agency in the work of destruction, I felt that the unhappy father could not curse me more bitterly than I cursed myself. Deeply, however, as I mourned, and have never ceased to repent, my share in the exciting of that storm wherein the poor girl had been so cruelly shipwrecked, I could not forget the part that Mr. Graham had borne in the transaction, or forgive the wicked injustice and insults which had so unnerved and unmanned me as to render my hand a fit instrument only of ruin; and as, immediately after the doctor's departure, I watched my step-father also come down the steps and walk away, and saw, by a street-lamp, that the look of pain had passed from his face, giving place to his usual composed, self-complacent and arrogant expression, and understood, by the loud and measured manner in which he struck his cane upon the pavement, that he was far from sharing my humble, penitent mood, I ceased to waste upon him a compassion which he seemed so little to require or deserve; and, pitying myself only, I looked upon his stern face with a soul which cherished for him no other sentiment than that of unmitigated hatred.

"Do not shrink from me, Gertrude, as you read this frank confession of my passionate, and, at that moment, deeply-stirred nature. You know not, perhaps, what it is to hate; but have you ever been tried as I was?

"As Mr. Graham turned the corner of the street, I approached his house, drew forth a pass-key of my own, by means of which I opened the door, and went in. It was perfectly quiet within, and no person was to be seen in any of the lower rooms. I then passed noiselessly up stairs, and entered a little chamber at the head of the passage which communicated with Emily's room. I waited here a long time, hearing no sound and seeing no one. At length, fearing that Mr. Graham would shortly return, I determined to ascend to my own room, which was in the next story, collect my money, and a few articles of value, which I was unwilling to leave behind, and then make my way to the kitchen, and gain what news I could of Emily from Mrs. Prime, the cook, a kindhearted woman, who would, I felt sure, befriend me.

"The first pat of my object was accomplished, and I had descended the back staircase to gain Mrs. Prime's premises, when I suddenly encountered Mrs. Ellis coming from the kitchen, with a bowl of gruel in her hand. This woman was a recent addition to the household, introduced there a few weeks before as a spy upon my actions, and intolerable to me on that account. She was well acquainted with all the particulars of the accident, and had been a witness to my expulsion from the house. She stopped short on seeing me, gave a slight scream, dropped the bowl of gruel, and prepared to make her escape, as if from a wild beast, which I doubt not that I resembled; since wretchedness, fasting, suffering and desperation, must all have been depicted in my features.

"I placed myself in her path, and compelled her to stop and listen to me. But before my eager questions could find utterance, an outburst from her confirmed my worst fears.

"'Let me go!' she exclaimed. 'You villain! you will be putting my eyes out, next!'

"'Where is Emily?' I cried. 'Let me see her!'

"'See her!' replied she. 'You horrid wretch! No! she has suffered enough from you. She is satisfied herself now; so let her alone.'

"'What do you mean?' shouted I, shaking the housekeeper violently by the shoulder, for her words seared my very soul, and I was frantic.

"'Mean?' continued she. 'I mean that Emily will never see anybody again; and, if she had a thousand eyes, you are the last person upon whom she would wish to look!'

"'Does Emily hate me, too?' burst from me then, in the form of a soliloquy rather than a question.

"The reply was ready, however. 'Hate you? Yes,—more than that; she cannot find words that are bad enough for you! She mutters, even in her pain, "cruel!—wicked!" and so on. She even shudders at the sound of your name; and we are all forbidden to speak it in her presence.'

"I waited to hear no more, but, turning, rushed out of the house.

"That moment was the crisis of my life. The thunderbolt had fallen upon and crushed me. My hopes, my happiness, my fortune, my good name, had gone before; but one solitary light had, until now, glimmered in the darkness. It was Emily's love. I had trusted in that,—that only. It had passed away, and with it my youth, my faith, my hope of heaven. I was a blank on the earth, and cared not whither I went, or what became of me.

"From that moment I ceased to be myself. Then fell upon me the cloud in which I have ever since been shrouded; and under the shadow of which you have seen and known me. In that instant the blight had come, under the gnawing influence of which my happy laugh changed to the bitter smile; my frank and pleasant speech to tones of ill-concealed irony and sarcasm; my hair became prematurely gray, my features sharp, and oftentimes severe; my fellow-men, to whom it had been my noblest hope to prove some day a benefactor, were henceforth the armed hosts of antagonists, with whom I would wage endless war; and the God whom I had worshipped,—whom I had believed in, as a just and faithful friend and avenger,—who was He?—where was He?—and why did He not right my cause? What direful and premeditated deed of darkness had I been guilty of, that He should thus desert me? Alas!—greatest of all misfortunes,—I lost my faith in Heaven!

"I know not what direction I took on leaving Mr. Graham's house. I have no recollection of any of the streets through which I passed, though doubtless they were all familiar; but I paused not, until, haing reached the end of a wharf, I found myself gazing down into the deep water, longing to take one mad leap, and lose myself in everlasting oblivion!

"But for this final blow, beneath which my manhood had fallen, I would have cherished my life, at least until I could vindicate its fair fame; I would never have left a blackened memory for men to dwell upon, and for Emily to weep over. But now what cared I for my fellow-men? And Emily!—she had ceased to love, and would not mourn; and I longed for nothingness and the grave.

"There are moments in human life when a word, a look, or a thought, may weigh down the balance in the scales of fate, and decide a destiny.

"So was it with me now. I was incapable of forming any plan for myself; but accident, as it were, decided for me. I was startled from the apathy into which I had fallen by the sudden splashing of oars in the water beneath, and in a moment a little boat was moored to a pier within a rod of the spot where I stood. At the same instant I heard quick footsteps on the wharf, and, turning, saw by the light of the moon, which was just appearing from behind a heavy cloud, a stout, sea-faring man, with a heavy pea-jacket under one arm, and an old-fashioned carpet-bag in his left hand. He had a ruddy, good-humored face, and as he approached, and was about to pass me and leap into the boat, where two sailors, with their oars dipped and ready for motion, were awaiting him, he slapped me heartily on the shoulder, and exclaimed, 'Well, my fine fellow, will you ship with us?'

"I answered as readily in the affirmative; and, with one look in my face, and a glance at my dress, which seemed to assure him of my station in life, and probable ability to make compensation for the passage, he said, in a laughing tone, 'In with you, then!'

"To his astonishment,—for he had scarcely believed me in earnest,—I sprang into the boat, and in a few moments was on board of a fine bark, bound I knew not whither.

"The vessel's destination proved to be Rio de Janeiro; a fact which I did not learn, however, till we had been two or three days at sea, and to

378

which, even then, I felt wholly indifferent. There was one other passenger beside myself,—the captain's daughter, Lucy Grey, whom, during the first week, I scarcely noticed, but who appeared to be as much at home, whether in the cabin or on deck, as if she had passed her whole life at sea. I might, perhaps, have made the entire passage without giving another thought to this young girl,—half child, half woman,—had not my strange and mysterious behavior led her to conduct in a manner which at first surprised, and finally interested me. My wild and excited countenance, my constant restlessness, avoidance of food, and apparent indifference to everything that went on about me, excited her wonder and sympathy to the utmost. She at first believed me partially deranged, and treated me accordingly. She would take a seat on deck directly opposite mine, look in my face for an hour, either ignorant or regardless of my observing her, and then walk away with a heavy sigh. Occasionally she would come and offer me some little delicacy, begging that I would try and eat; and as, touched by her kindness, I took food more readily from her hand than any other, these little attentions became at last habitual. As my manners and looks grew calmer, however, and I settled into a melancholy, which, though equally deep, was less fearful than the feverish torment under which I had labored, she became proportionately reserved; and when, at last, I began to appear somewhat like my fellow-men, went regularly to the table, and, instead of pacing the deck all night, spent a part of it, at least, quietly in my state-room, Lucy absented herself wholly from that part of the vessel where I passed the greater portion of the day, and I seldom exchanged a word with her, unless I purposely sought her society.

"We experienced much stormy weather, however, which drove me to the cabin, where she usually sat on the transom, reading, or watching the troubled waes; and, as the voyage was very long, we were necessarily thrown much in each other's way, especially as Captain Grey, the same individual who had invited me to ship with him, and who seemed still to take an interest in my welfare, good-naturedly encouraged an intercourse by which he probably hoped I might be won from a state of melancholy that seemed to astonish and grieve the jolly ship-master almost as much as it did his kind-hearted, sensitive child.

"Lucy's shyness, therefore, wore gradually away, and before our tedious passage was completed I ceased to be a restraint upon her. She talked freely with, or rather to me; for while, notwithstanding her occasional intimations of curiosity, I maintained a rigid silence concerning my own past experiences, of which I could scarcely endure to *think,* much less to *speak,* she exerted herself freely for my entertainment, and related, with simple frankness, almost every circumstance of her past life. Sometimes I listened attentively; sometimes, absorbed in my own painful reflections, I would be deaf to her voice, and forgetful of her presence. In the latter case, I would often observe, however, that she had suddenly ceased speaking, and, starting from my revery, and looking quickly up, would find her eyes fixed upon me so reproachfully that, rallying my self-command, I would endeavor to appear, and not unfrequently really became, seriously interested in the artless narratives of my little entertainer. She told me that until she was fourteen years old she lived with her mother in a little cottage on Cape Cod, their home being only occasionally enlivened by the return of her father from his long absences at sea. They would then usually make a visit to the city where his vessel lay, pass a few weeks in uninterrupted enjoyment, and at length return home to mourn the departure of the cheerful, light-hearted sea-captain, and patiently count the weeks and months until he would come back again.

"She told me how her mother died at last; how bitterly she mourned her loss; and how her father wept when he came home and heard the news; how she had lived on ship-board ever since, and how sad and lonely she felt in time of storms, when, the master at his post of duty, she sat alone in the cabin, listening to the roar of the winds and waves.

"Tears would could into her eyes when she spoke of these things, and I would look upon her with pity, as one whom sorrow made my sister. Trial, however, had not yet robbed her of an elastic, buoyant spirit; and when, five minutes after the completion of some eloquent little tale of early grief, the captain would approach unseen, and surprise her by a sudden joke, exclamation, or sly piece of mischief, thus provoking her to retaliate, she was always ready and alert for a war of wits, a laughing frolic, or even a game of romps. Her sorrow forgotten, and her tears dried up, her merry voice and her playful words would delight her father, and the cabin or the deck would ring with his joyous peals of laughter; while I, shrinking from a mirth and gayety sadly at variance with my own unhappiness, and the sound of which was discordant to my sensitive nerves, would retire to brood over miseries for which it was hopeless to expect sympthy, which could not be shared, and with which I must dwell alone.

"Such a misanthrope had my misfortunes made me that the sportive raillery between the captain and his merry daughter, and the musical laugh with which she would respond to the occasional witticisms of one or two old and privileged sailors, grated upon my ears like something scarce less than personal injuries; nor could I have believed it possible that one so little able as Lucy to comprehend the depth of my sufferings could feel any sincere compassion for them, had I not once or twice been touched to see how her innocent mirth would give place to sudden gravity and sadness of countenance, if she chanced unexpectedly to encounter my woe-begone face, rendered doubly gloomy when contrasted with the gayety of herself and her companions.

"But I must not linger too long upon the details of our life on shipboard; for I have to relate events which occupied many years, and must confine myself, as far as possible, to a concise statement of facts. I must forbear giving any account of a terrific gale that we encountered, during which, for two days and a night, poor Lucy was half-frantic with fear, while I, careless of outward discomforts, and indifferent to personal danger, was afforded an opportunity to requite her kindness by such protection and encouragement as I was able to render. But this, and various other incidents of the voyage, all bore a part in inspiring her with a degree of confidence in me, which, by the time we arrived in port, was put to a severe and somewhat embarrassing test.

CHAPTER XLVII

Do not spurn me
In my prayer!
For this wandering, ever longer, evermore,
Hath overworn me,
I know not on what shore
I may rest from my despair.
——*E. B. Browning*

"*CAPTAIN GREY DIED.* We were within a week's sail of our destination when he was taken ill, and three days before we were safely anchored in the harbor of Rio he breathed his last. I shared with Lucy the office of ministering to the suffering man, closed his eyes at last, and carried the fainting girl in my arms to another part of the vessel. With kind words and persuasions I restored her to her senses; and then, as the full consciousness of her desolation rushed upon her, she sunk at once into a state of hopeless despondency, more painful to witness than her previous condition of utter insensibility. Captain Grey had made no provision for his daughter; indeed, it would have been impossible for him to do so, as the state of his affairs afterwards proved. Well might the poor girl lament her sad fate! for she was without a relative in the world, penniless, and approaching a strange shore, which afforded no refuge to the orphan. We buried her father in the sea; and, that sad office fulfilled, I sought Lucy, and endeavored, as I had several times tried to do without success, to arouse her to a sense of her situation, and advise with her concerning the future; for we were now so near our port that in a few hours we might be compelled to leave the vessel and seek quarters in the city. She listened to me without replying.

"At length I hinted at the necessity of my leaving her, and begged to know if she had any plans for the future. She answered me only by a burst of tears.

"I expressed the deepest sympathy for her grief, and begged her not to weep.

"And then, with many sobs, and interrupting herself by frequent outbreaks and exclamations of vehement sorrow, she threw herself upon my compassion, and, with unaffected simplicity and child-like artlessness, entreated me not to leave, or, as she termed it, to desert her. She reminded me that she was all alone in the world; that the moment she stepped foot on shore she should be in a land of strangers; and, appealing to my mercy, besought me not to forsake and leave her to die alone.

"What could I do? I had nothing on earth to live for. We were both alike orphaned and desolate. There was but one point of difference. I could work and protect her; she could do neither for herself. It would be something for *me* to live for; and for *her,* though but a refuge of poverty and want, it was better than the exposure and suffering that must otherwise await her. I told her plainly how little I had to offer; that my heart even was crushed and broken; but that I was ready to labor in her behalf, to guard her from danger, to pity, and, perhaps, in time, learn to love her.

"The unsophisticated girl had never thought of marriage; she had sought the protection of a friend, not a husband; but I explained to her that the latter tie only would obviate the necessity of our parting; and, in the humility of sorrow, she finally accepted my unflattering offer.

"The only confidant to our sudden engagement, the only witness of the marriage, which, within a few hours, ensued, was a veteran mariner, an old, weather-beaten sailor, who had known and loved Lucy from her childhood, and whose name will be, perhaps, familiar to you,—Ben Grant. He accompanied us on shore, and to the church, which was our first destination. He followed us to the humble lodgings with which we contrived for the present to be contented, and devoted himself to Lucy with self-sacrificing, but in one instance, alas! (as you will soon learn) with mistaken and fatal zeal.

"After much difficulty, I obtained employment from a man in whom I accidentally recognized an old and valued friend of my father. He had been in Rio several years, was actively engaged in trade, and willingly employed me as clerk, occasionally despatching me from home to transact business at a distance. My duties being regular and profitable, we were soon not only raised above want, but I was enabled to place my young wife in a situation that insured comfort, if not luxury.

"The sweetness of her disposition, the cheerfulness with which she endured privation, the earnestness with which she strove to make me happy, were not without effect. I perseveringly rallied from my gloom; I succeeded in banishing the frown from my brow; and the premature wrinkles, which her little hand would softly sweep away, finally ceased to return. The few months that I passed with your mother, Gertrude, form a sweet episode in the memory of my stormy life. I came to love her much,—not as I loved Emily; that could not be expected,—but, as the solitary flower that bloomed on the grave of all my early hopes, she cast a fragrance round my path; and her child is not more dear to me because a part of myself than as the memento of the cherished blossom, snatched hastily from my hand, and rudely crushed.

"About two months after your birth, my child, and before your eyes had ever learned to brighten at the sight of your father, who was necessarily much from home, the business in which I was engaged called me, in the capacity of an agent, to a station at some distance from Rio. I had been absent nearly a month, had extended my journey beyond my original intentions, and had written regularly to Lucy informing her of all my movements (though I have since believed that the letters never reached her), when the neighborhood in which I was stationed became infected with a fatal malaria. For the sake of my family, I took every measure to ward off contagion, but failed. I was seized with the terrible fever, and lay for weeks at the point of death. I was cruelly neglected during my illness; for I had no friends near me, and my slender purse held out little inducement for mercenary service; but my sufferings and forebodings on account of Lucy and yourself were far greater, than any which I endured from my bodily torments, although the latter were great indeed. I conjured up every fear that the imagination could conceive; but nothing, alas! which could compare with the reality that awaited me, when, after an almost interminable illness, I made my way, destitute, ragged and emaciated, back to Rio. I sought my former home. It was deserted, and I was warned to flee from its vicinity, as the fearful disease of which I had already been the prey had nearly depopulated that and the neighboring streets. I made every inquiry, but could obtain no intelligence of my wife and child. I hastened to the horrible charnel-house where, during the raging of the pestilence, the unrecognized dead were exposed; but, among the disfigured and mouldering remains, it was impossible to distinguish friends from strangers. I lingered about the city for weeks, in hopes to gain some information concerning Lucy; but could find no one who had ever heard of her. All day I wandered about the streets and on the wharves,—the latter being places which Ben Grant (in whose faithful charge I had left your mother and yourself) was in the habit of frequenting—but not a syllable could I learn of any persons that answered my description.

"My first thought had been that they would naturally seek my employer, to learn, if possible, the cause of my prolonged absence; and, on finding my home empty, I had hastened in search of him. But he too had, within a recent period, fallen a victim to the prevailing distemper. His place of business was closed, and the establishment broken up. I prolonged my search and continued my inquiries until hope died within me. I was assured that scarce an inmate of the fatal neighborhood where I had left my family had escaped the withering blast; and convinced, finally, that my fate was still pursuing me with an unmitigated wrath, of which this last blow was but a single expression, that I might have foreseen and expected, I madly agreed to work my passage in the first vessel which promised me an escape from scenes so fraught with harrowing recollections.

"And now commenced in truth that course of wretched wandering, which, knowing neither pause nor cessation, has made up the sum of my existence. With varied ends in view, following strongly-contrasted employments, and with fluctuating fortune, I have travelled over the world. My feet have trodden almost every land; I have sailed upon every sea, and breathed the air of every clime. I am familiar with the city and the wilderness, the civilized man and the savage. I have learned the sad lesson that peace is nowhere, and friendship, for the most part, but a name. If I have taught myself to hate, shun, and despise humanity, it is because I know it well.

"Once, during my wanderings, I visited the home of my boyhood. Unseen and unknown I trod familiar ground, and gazed on familiar, though

time-worn faces. I stood at the window of Mr. Graham's library; saw the
contented, happy countenance of Emily,—happy in her blindness and her
forgetfulness of the past. A young girl sat near the fire, endeavouring to
read by its flickering light. I knew not then what gave such a charm to her
thoughtful features, nor why my eyes dwelt upon them with a rare pleasure; for there was no voice to proclaim to the father's heart that he looked
on the face of his child. I am not sure that the strong impulse which
prompted me then to enter, acknowledge my indentity, and beg Emily to
speak to me a word of forgiveness, might not have prevailed over the dread
of her displeasure; but Mr. Graham at the moment made his appearance,
cold and implacable as ever; I looked upon him an instant then fled from
the house, and the next day departed for other lands.

"Although in the various labours which I was compelled to undertake to earn for myself a decent maintenance, I had more than once met
with such success as to give me temporary independence, and to enable me
to indulge myself in expensive travelling, I had never amassed a fortune;
indeed I had not cared to do so, since I had no use for money, except to
employ it in the gratification of my immediate wants. Accident, however,
at last thrust upon me a wealth which I could scarcely be said to have
sought.

"After a year spent in the wilderness of the west, amid adventures
the relation of which would seem to you almost incredible, I gradually
continued my retreat across the country, and, after encountering innumerable hardships in a solitary journey, which had in it no other object than
the indulgence of my vagrant habits, I found myself in that land which has
recently been termed the land of promise, but which has proved to many a
greedy emigrant a land of falsehood and deceit. For me, however, who
sought it not, it showered gold. I was among the earliest discoverers of its
treasure-vaults,—one of the most successful, though the least laborious of
the seekers after gain. Nor was it merely, or indeed chiefly, at the mines
that fortune favored me. With the first results of my labors I chanced to
purchase an immense tract of land, little dreaming at the time that those
desert acres were destined to become the streets and squares of a great and
prosperous city.

"So it was, however; and without effort, almost without my own
knowledge, I achieved the greatness which springs from untold wealth.

"But this was not all. The blessed accident which led me to this
golden land was the means of disclosing a pearl of price—a treasure in
comparison with which California and all its mines shrink to my mind into

insignificance. You know how the war-cry went forth to all lands, and men of every name and nation brought their arms to the field of fortune. Famine came next, with disease and death in its train; and many a man, hurrying on to reap the golden harvest, fell by the way-side, without once seeing the waving of the yellow grain.

"Half scorning the greedy rabble, I could not refuse, in this, my time of prosperity, to minister to the wants of such as fell in my way; and now, for once, my humanity found its own reward.

"A miserable, ragged, half-starved, and apparently dying man, crept to the door of my tent (for these were the primitive days, when that land afforded no better habitation), and asked in a feeble voice for charity. I did not refuse to admit him into my narrow domicile, and to the extent of my ability relieved his suffering condition. He proved to be the victim of want rather than disease, and, his hunger appeased, the savage brutality of his coarse nature soon manifested itself in the dogged indifference with which he abused my hospitality. A few days served to restore him to his strength; and then, anxious to dismiss my visitor, whose conduct had already excited suspicions of his good faith, I gave him warning that he must depart; at the same time placing in his hands a sufficient amount of gold to insure his support until he could reach the mines, which were his professed destination.

"He appeared dissatisfied, and begged permission to remain until the next morning, as the night was near, and he had no shelter provided. To this I made no objection, little imagining how base a serpent I was harboring. At midnight I was awakened from my light and easily-disturbed sleep, to find my lodger busily engaged in rifling my property, and preparing to take an unceremonious leave of my dwelling. Nor did his villany end here. Upon my seizing and charging him with the theft, he snatched a weapon which lay near at hand, and attempted the life of his benefactor. I was prepared, however, to ward off the stroke, and by means of my superior strength succeeded in a few moments in subduing and mastering my desperate antagonist. He now crouched at my feet in such abject and mean submission as might have been expected from so contemptible a knave. Well might he tremble with fear; for the lynch-law was then in full force, and summary in its execution of justice upon criminals like him. I should probably have handed the traitor over to his fate, but, ere I had time to do so, he by chance held out to my cupidity a bribe so tempting, that I forgot the deservings of my knavish guest in the eagerness with which I bartered his freedom as the price of its possession.

"He freely emptied his pockets at my bidding, and restored to me the gold, for the loss of which I never should have repined. As the base metal rolled at my feet, however, there glittered among the coins a jewel as truly *mine* as any of the rest, but which, as it met my sight, filled me with greater surprise and rapture than if it had been a new-fallen star.

"It was a ring of peculiar design and workmanship, which had once been the property of my father, and after his death, had been worn by my mother until the time of her marriage with Mr. Graham, when it was transferred to myself. I had ever prized it as a precious heirloom, and it was one of the few valuables which I took with me when I fled from my stepfather's house. This ring, with a watch and some other trinkets, had been left in the possession of Lucy when I parted with her at Rio, and the sight of it once more seemed to me like a voice from the grave. I eagerly sought to learn from my prisoner the source whence it had been obtained, but he maintained an obstinate silence. It was now my turn to plead, and at length the promise of instant permission to depart, 'unwhipped by justice,' at the conclusion of his tale, wrung from him a secret fraught to me with vital interest. What I learned from him, in disjointed and often incoherent phrases, I will relate to you in few words.

"This man was Stephen Grant, the son of my old friend Ben. He had heard from his father's lips the story of your mother's misfortunes; and the circumstance of a violent quarrel, which arose between Ben and his vixen wife, at the young stranger's introduction to their household, impressed the tale upon his recollection.

From his account, it appeared that my long-continued absence from Lucy, during the time of my illness, was construed by her honest but distrustful counsellor and friend into voluntary and cruel desertion. The poor girl, to whom my early life was all a mystery which she had never shared, and to whom much of my character and conduct was consequently inexplicable, began soon to feel convinced of the correctness of the old sailor's suspicions and fears. She had already applied to my employer for information concerning me; but he, who had heard of the pestilence to which I was exposed, and fully believed me to be among the dead, forbore to distress her by a communication of his belief, and replied to her questionings with an obscurity which served to give new force to her hitherto vague and uncertain surmises. She positively refused, however, to leave our home; and, clinging to the hope of my final return thither, remained where I had left her until the terrible fever began its ravages. Her small stock of money was by this time consumed; her strength both of mind and body gave way; and Ben, becoming every day more confident that the simple-hearted Lucy had been betrayed and forsaken, persuaded her at last to sell her furniture, and with the sum thus raised flee the infected country before it should be too late. She sailed for Boston in the same vessel in which Ben shipped before the mast; and on reaching that port her humble protector took her immediately to the only home he had to offer.

"There your mother's sad fate found a mournful termination, and you, her infant child, were left to the mercy of the cruel woman, who, but for her consciousness of guilt and her fear of its betrayal, would doubtless have thrust you at once from the miserable shelter her dwelling afforded. This guilt consisted in a foul robbery committed by Nan and her already infamous son upon your innocent and hapless mother, now rendered, through her feebleness, an easy prey to their rapacity. The fruits of this vile theft, however, were never participated in by Nan, whose promising son so far exceeded her in duplicity and craft that, having obtained possession of the jewels for the alleged purpose of bartering them away, he reserved such as he thought proper, and appropriated to his own use the proceeds of the remainder.

"The antique ring which I now hold in my possession, the priceless relic of a mournful tragedy, would have shared the fate of the rest, but for its apparent worthlessness. To the luckless Stephen, however, it proved at last a temporary salvation from the felon's doom which must finally await that hardened sinner; and to me——ah! to *me*——it remains to be proved whether the knowledge of the secrets to which it has been the key will bless my future life, or darken it with a heavier curse! Notwithstanding the information thus gained, and the exciting idea to which it gave rise, that my child might be still living and finally restored to me, I could not yet feel any security that these daring hopes were not destined to be crushed in their infancy, and that my newly-found treasure might not again elude my eager search. To my inquiries concerning you, Gertrude, Stephen, who had no longer any motives for concealing the truth, declared his inability to acquaint me with any particulars of a later period than the time of your residence with Trueman Flint. He knew that the lamplighter had taken you to his home, and was accidentally made aware, a few months later, of your continuance in that place of refuge, from the old man's being (to use my informant's expression) such a confounded fool as to call upon his mother and voluntarily make compensation for injury done to her win-dows in your outburst of childish revenge.

"Further than this I could learn nothing; but it was enough to inspire all my energies, and fill me with one desire only,—the recovery of my child. I hastened to Boston, had no difficulty in tracing your benefactor, and, though he had been long since dead, found many a truthful witness to his well-known virtues. Nor, when I asked for his adopted child, did I find her forgotten in the quarter of the city where she had passed her childhood. More than one grateful voice was ready to respond to my questioning, and to proclaim the cause they had to remember the girl who, having experienced the trials of poverty, made it both the duty and the pleasure of her prosperity to administer to the wants of a neighborhood whose sufferings she had aforetime both witnessed and shared.

"But, alas! to complete the sum of sad vicissitude with which my unhappy destiny was already crowded, at the very moment when I was assured of my daughter's safety, and my ears were drinking in the sweet praises that accompanied the mention of her name, there fell upon me like a thunder-bolt the startling words, 'She is now the adopted child of sweet Emily Graham, the blind girl.'

"O, strange coincidence! O, righteous retribution! which, at the very moment when I was picturing to myself the consummation of my cherished hopes, crushed me once more beneath the iron hand of a destiny that would not be cheated of its victim!

"My child, my only child, bound by the gratitude and love of years to one in whose face I scarcely dared to look, lest my soul should be withered by the expression of condemnation which the consciousness of my presence would inspire!

"The seas and lands, which had hitherto divided us, seemed not to my tortured fancy so insurmountable a barrier between myself and my long-lost daughter, as the dreadful reflection that the only earthly being whose love I had hoped in time to win had been reared from her infancy in a household where my very name was a thing abhorred.

"Stung to the quick by the harrowing thought that all my prayers, entreaties and explanations, could never undo her early impressions, and that all my labors and all my love could never call forth other than a cold and formal recognition of my claims, or, worse still, a feigned and hypocritical pretence of filial affection, I half resolved to leave my child in ignorance of her birth, and never seek to look upon her face, rather than subject her to the terrible necessity of choosing between the friend whom she loved and the father from whose crimes she had learned to shrink with horror and dread.

"After wrestling and struggling long with contending and warring emotions, I resolved to make one endeavor to see and recognize you, Gertrude, and at the same time guard myself from discovery. I trusted (and, as it proved, not without reason) to the immense change which time had wrought in my appearance, to conceal me effectually from all eyes but those which had known me intimately; and therefore approached Mr. Graham's house without the slightest fear of betrayal. I found it empty, and apparently deserted.

"I now directed my steps to the well-remembered counting-room, and here learned, from a clerk (who was, as it proved, but ill-informed concerning the movements of his master's family), that the whole household, including yourself, had been passing the winter in Paris, and were at present at a German watering-place. Without hesitation, or further inquiry, I took the steamer to Liverpool, and from thence hastened to Baden-Baden,—a trifling excursion in the eyes of a traveller of my experience.

"Without risking myself in the presence of my step-father, I took an early opportunity to obtain an introduction to Mrs. Graham, and, thanks to her unreserved conversation, made myself master of the fact that Emily and yourself were left in Boston, and were, at that time, under the care of Dr. Jeremy.

"It was on my return voyage, which was immediatley undertaken, that I made the acquaintaince of Dr. Gryseworth and his daughter,—an acquaintaince which accidentally proved of great value in facilitating my intercourse with yourself.

"Once more arrived in Boston, Dr. Jeremy's house also wore a desolate appearance, and looked as if closed for the season. There was a man, however, making some repairs about the door-steps, who informed me that the family were absent from town. He was not himself aware of the direction they had taken; but the servants were at home, and could, no doubt, acquaint me with their route. Upon this, I boldly rung the door-bell. It was answered by Mrs. Ellis, the woman who, nearly twenty years before, had cruelly and unpityingly sounded in my ears the death-knell of all my hopes in life. I saw at once that my incognito was secure, as she met my keen and piercing glance without quailing, shrinking or taking flight, as I fully expected she would do at sight of the ghost of my former self.

"She replied to my queries as coolly and collectedly as she had probably done during the day to some dozen of the doctor's disappointed patients,—telling me that he had left that very morning for New York, an would not be back for two or three weeks.

"Nothing could have been more favorable to my wishes than the chance thus afforded of overtaking your party, and, in the character of a travelling companion, introducing myself gradually to your notice.

"You know how this purpose was effected; how, now in the rear and now in advance, I nevertheless maintained a constant proximity to your footsteps. To add one particle to the comfort of yourself and Emily,—to learn your plans, forestall your wishes, secure to your use the best of rooms, and bribe to your service the most devoted of attendants,—I spared myself neither pains, fatigue, trouble, nor expense.

"For much of the freedom with which I approached you, and made myself an occasional member of your circle, I was indebted to Emily's blindness; for I could not doubt that otherwise time and its changes would fail to conceal from her my identity, and I should meet with a premature recognition. Nor, until the final act of the drama, when death stared us all in the face, and concealment became impossible, did I once trust my voice to her hearing.

"How closely, during those few weeks, I watched and weighed your every word and action, seeking even to read your thoughts in your face, none can tell whose acuteness is not sharpened and vivified by motives so all-engrossing as mine, and who can measure the anguish of the fond father, who, day by day, learned to worship his child with a more absorbing idolatry, and yet dared not clasp her to his heart!

"Especially when I saw you the victim of grief and trouble did I long to assert a claim to your confidence; and more than once my self-control would have given way, but for the dread inspired by the gentle Emily— gentle to all but me. I could not brook the thought that with my confession I should cease to be the trusted friend, and become the abhorred parent. I preferred to maintain my distant and unacknowledged guardianship of my child, rather than she should behold in me the dreaded tyrant who might tear her from the home from which he had himself been driven, and the hearts which, though warm with love for *her,* were ice and stone to *him.*

"And so I kept silent; and, sometimes present to your sight, but still oftener hid from view, I hovered around your path, until that dreadful day, which you will long remember, when, everything forgotten but the safety of yourself and Emily, my heart spoke out, and betrayed my secret.

"And now you know all,—my follies, misfortunes, sufferings and sins!

"Can you love me, Gertrude? It is all I ask. I seek not to steal you from your present home—to rob poor Emily of a child whom she values perhaps as much as I. The only balm my wounded spirit seeks is the simple, guileless confession that you will at least *try* to love your father.

"I have no hope in this world, and none, alas! beyond, but in yourself. Could you feel my heart now beating against its prison-bars, you would realize, as I do, that unless soothed it will burst ere long. Will you soothe it by your pity, my sweet, my darling child? Will you bless it by your love? If so, come, clasp your arms around me, and whisper to me words of peace. Within sight of your window, in the old summer-house at the end of the garden, with straining ear, I wait listening for your footsteps."

CHAPTER XLVIII

Around her path a vision's glow is cast,
Back, back her lost one comes in hues of morn!
For her the gulf is filled, the dark night fled,
Whose mystery parts the living in the dead.
    —*Hemans*

AS GERTRUDE'S EYES, after greedily devouring the manuscript, fell upon its closing words, she sprung to her feet, and the next instant her little room (the floor strewed with the scattered sheets, which had dropped from her lap as she rose) is left vacant. She has flown down the staircase, escaped through the hall-door, and, bounding over a lawn at the back of the house, now wet with the evening dew, she approaches the summer-house from the opposite entrance to that at which Mr. Amory, with folded arms and a fixed countenance, is watching for her coming.

So noiseless is her light step, that, before he is conscious of her presence, she has thrown herself upon his bosom, and, her whole frame trembling with the vehemence of long-suppressed and now uncontrolled agitation, she bursts into a torrent of passionate tears, interrupted only by frequent sobs, so deep and so exhausting that her father, with his arms folded tightly around her, and clasping her so closely to his heart that she feels its irregular beating, endeavors to still the tempest of her grief, whispering softly, as to an infant, "Hush! hush, my child! you frighten me!"

And, gradually soothed by his gentle caresses, her excitement subsides, and she is able to lift her face to his, and smile upon him through her tears. They stand thus for many minutes, in a silence that speaks far more than words. Wrapped in the folds of his heavy cloak to preserve her from the evening air, and still encircled in his strong embrace, Gertrude feels that their union of spirit is not less complete; while the long-banished man, who for years has never felt the sweet influence of a kindly smile, glows with a melting tenderness which hardening solitude has not had the power to subdue.

Again and again the moon retires behind a cloud, and peeps out to find them still in the attitude in which she saw them last. At length, as she gains a broad and open expanse, and looks clearly down, Mr. Amory, lifting his daughter's face, and gazing into her glistening eyes, while he gently strokes the disordered hair from her forehead, asks, in an accent of touching appeal, "You will love me, then?"

"O, I do! I do!" exclaimed Gertrude, sealing his lips with kisses.

His hitherto unmoved countenance relaxes at this fervent assurance. He bows his head upon her shoulder, and the strong man weeps.

Not long, however. Her self-possession all restored at seeing him thus overcome, Gertrude places her hand in his, and startles him from his position by the firm and decided tone with which she whispers, "Come!"

"Whither?" exclaims he, looking up in surprise.

"To Emily."

With a half shudder, and a mournful shake of the head, he retreats, instead of advancing in the direction in which she would lead him.— "I cannot."

"But she waits for you. She, too, weeps and longs and prays for your coming."

"Emily!—you know not what you are saying, my child!"

"Indeed, indeed, my father, it is you who are deceived. Emily does not hate you; she never did. She believed you dead long ago; but your voice, though heard but once, has half robbed her of her reason, so wholly, so entirely does she love you still. Come, and she will tell you, better than I can, what a wretched mistake has made martyrs of you both."

Emily, who had heard the voice of Willie Sullivan, as he bade Gertrude farewell on the door-step, and rightly conjectured that it was he, forbore making any inquiries for the absent girl at the tea-table, and, thinking it probable that she preferred to remain undisturbed, retired to the sitting-room at the conclusion of the meal, where (as Mr. Graham sought the library) she remained alone for more than an hour.

It was a delightful, social-looking room. The fire still burned brightly, sending forth a ruddy glow, and (as the evening was unusually chilly for the season) rendering the temperature of the great old-fashioned parlor highly agreeable. There were candles under the mirror, but they did not give light enough to destroy the pleasant effect of the shadows which the fire-light made upon the wall and about the couch where Emily was reclining.

The invalid girl, if we may call her such (for, in spite of ill health, she still retained much of the freshness and all the loveliness of her girlhood), had, by chance, chosen such a position, opposite to the cheerful blaze, that its flickering light played about her face, and brought to view the rich and unwonted bloom which inward excitement had called up in her usually pale countenance. The exquisite and refined taste which always made Emily's dress an index to the soft purity of her character was never more strikingly developed than when she wore, as on the present occasion, a flowing robe of white cashmere, fastened at the waist with a silken girdle, and with full, drapery sleeves, whose lining and border of snowy silk could have only been rivalled by the delicate hand and wrist which had escaped from beneath thier folds, and somewhat nervously played with the heavy crimson fringe of a shawl, worn in the chilly dining-room, and now thrown carelessly over the arm of the sofa.

Supporting herself upon her elbow, she sat with her head bent forward, and, as she watched the images reflected in the glass of memory, one who knew her not, and was unaware of her want of sight, might have believed that, looking forth from her long, drooping eyelashes, she were tracing imaginary forms among the shining embers, so intently was her face bent in that direction.

Occasionally, as the summer wind sighed among the branches of the trees, causing them to beat lightly against the window-pane, she would lift her head from the hand on which it rested, and, gracefully arching her slender throat, incline in a listening attitude: and then, as the trifling nature of the sound betrayed itself, she would sink, with a low sigh, into her former somewhat listless position. Once Mrs. Prime opened the door, looked around the room in search of the housekeeper, and, not finding her, retreated across the passage, saying to herself, as she did so, "Law! dear sakes alive! I wish she only had eyes now, to see how like a pieter she looks!"

At length a low, quick bark from the house-dog once more attracted her attention, and in a moment steps were heard crossing the piazza.

Before they had gained the door, Emily was standing upright, straining her ear to catch the sound of every foot-fall; and, when Gertrude and

Mr. Amory entered, she looked more like a statue than a living figure, as, with clasped hands, parted lips, and one foot slightly advanced, she silently awaited their approach.

One glance at Emily's face, another at that of her agitated father, and Gertrude was gone. She saw the completeness of their mutual recognition, and, with instinctive delicacy, forbore to mar by her presence the sacredness of so holy an interview.

As the door closed upon her retreating figure, Emily parted her clasped hands, stretched them forth into the dim vacancy, and murmured, "Philip!"

He seized them between both of his, and, with one step forward, fell upon his knees. As he did so, the half-fainting girl dropped upon the seat behind her. Mr. Amory bowed his head upon the hands, which, still held tightly between his own, now rested on her lap; and, hiding his face upon her slender fingers, tremblingly uttered her name.

"The grave has given up its dead!" exclaimed Emily. "My God, I thank thee!" and, extricating her hands from his convulsive grasp, she flung her arms around his neck, rested her head upon his bosom, and whispered, in a voice half choked with emotion, "Philip!—dear, dear Philip! am I dreaming, or have you come back again?"

The conventional rules, the enforced restrictions, which often set limits to the outbursts of natural feeling, had no existence for one so wholly the child of nature as Emily. She and Philip had loved each other in their childhood; before that childhood was fully past, they had parted; and as children they met again. During the lapse of many years, in which, shut out from the world, she had lived among the cherished memories of the past, she had been safe from worldly contagion, and had retained all the guileless simplicity of girlhood,—all the freshness of her spring-time; and Philip, who had never willingly bound himself by any ties save those imposed upon him by circumstance and necessity, felt his boyhood come rushing upon him once more, as, with Emily's soft hand resting on his head, she blessed Heaven for his safe return. She could not see how time had silvered his hair, and sobered and shaded the face that she loved. Whether he came in the shape of the fiery-eyed youth that she saw him last, the middle-aged man, with hoary hair, whose years the curious found it hard to determine, or the glorified angel which she had pictured to herself in every dream of heaven, it was all alike to one whose world was a world of spirits.

And to him, as he beheld the face he had half dreaded to encounter beaming with the holy light of sympathy and love, the blind girl's countenance seemed encircled with a halo not of earth. And, therefore, this union had in it less of earth than heaven. Had they wakened on the other side of the grave, and soul met soul in that happy land where the long-parted meet, their rapture could scarcely have been more pure, their happiness more unalloyed.

Not until, seated beside each other, with their hands still fondly clasped, Philip had heard from Emily's lips the history of her hopes, her fears, her prayers and her despair, and she, while listening to the sad incidents of his life, had dropped upon the hand she held many a kiss and tear of sympathy, did either fully realize the mercy, so long delayed, so fully accorded now, which promised even on earth to crown their days.

Emily wept at the tale of Lucy's trials and her early death; and when she learned that it was hers and Philip's child whom she had taken to her heart, and fostered with the truest affection, she sent up a silent prayer of gratitude that it had been allotted to her apparently bereaved and darkened destiny to fulfil so blest a mission.

"If I could love her more, dear Philip," exclaimed she, while the tears trickled down her cheeks, "I would do so, for your sake, and that of her sweet, innocent, suffering mother."

"And you forgive me, then, Emily?" said Philip, as, both having finished their sad recitals of the past, they gave themselves up to the sweet reflection of their present joy.

"Forgive?—O, Philip! what have I to forgive?"

"The deed that locked you in prison darkness," he mournfully replied.

"Philip!" exclaimed Emily, in a reproachful tone, "could you for one moment believe that I attributed that to you?—that I blamed you, for an instant, even in my secret thought?"

"Not willingly, I am sure, dear Emily. But, O, you have forgotten what *I* can never forget,—that in your time of anguish, not only the obtruding thought, but the lip that gave utterance to it, proclaimed how your soul refused to pity and forgive the cruel hand that wrought you so much woe!"

"You cruel, Philip! Never, even in my wild frenzy, did I so abuse and wrong you. If my unfilial heart sinfully railed 'gainst the cruel injustice of my father, it was never guilty of such treachery towards you."

"That fiendish woman lied, then, when she told me that you shuddered at my very name?"

"If I shuddered, Philip, it was because my whole nature recoiled at the thought of the wrong that you had sustained; and O, believe me, if she gave you any other assurance than of my continued love, it was because she labored under a sad and unhappy error."

"Good heavens!" ejaculated Philip. "How wickedly have I been deceived!"

"Not wickedly," replied Emily. "Mrs. Ellis, with all her stern formality, was, in that instance, the victim of circumstances. She was a stranger among us, and believed you other than you were; but, had you seen her a few weeks later, sobbing over her share in the unhappy transaction which drove you to desperation, and, as we then supposed, to death, you would have felt, as I did, that we had greatly misjudged her in return, and that she carried a heart of flesh beneath a stony disguise. The bitterness of her grief astonished me at the time; for I never until now had reason to suspect that it was mingled with remorse at the recollection of her own harshness. Let us forget, however, the sad events of the past, and trust that the loving hand which has thus far shaped our course has but afflicted us in mercy."

"In mercy?" exclaimed Philip. "What mercy does my past experience give evidence of, or your life of everlasting darkness? Can you believe it a loving hand which made me the ill-fated instrument, and you the life-long sufferer, from one of the dreariest misfortunes that can afflict humanity?"

"Speak not of my blindness as a misfortune," answered Emily; "I have long ceased to think it such. It is only through the darkness of the night that we discern the lights of heaven, and only when shut out from earth that we enter the gates of Paradise. With eyes to see the wonderful working of nature and nature's God, I nevertheless closed them to the evidences of almighty love that were around me on every side. While enjoying the beautiful and glorious gifts that were showered on my pathway, I forgot to thank and praise the Giver; but, with an ungrateful heart, walked sinfully and selfishly on, little dreaming of the beginning and deceitful snares which entangle the footsteps of youth.

"And therefore did He, who is ever over us for good, arrest with fatherly hand the child who was wandering from the only road that leads to peace; and, though the discipline of his chastening rod was sudden and severe, mercy still tempered justice. From the tomb of my buried joys sprang hopes that will bloom in immortality. From the clouds and the darkness broke forth a glorious light. What was hidden from my outer sight became manifest to my awakened soul, and even on earth my troubled spirit gained its eternal rest. Then grieve not, dear Philip, over the fate that, in reality, is far from sad; but rejoice with me in the thought of that blessed and not far distant awakening, when, with restored and beatified vision, I shall stand before God's throne, in full view of that glorious Presence, from which, but for the guiding light which has burst upon my spirit through the veil of earthly darkness, I might have been eternally shut out."

As Emily finished speaking, and Philip, gazing with awe upon the rapt expression of her soul-illumined face, beheld the triumph of an immortal mind, and pondered on the might, the majesty and power, of the influence wrought by simple piety, the door of the room opened abruptly, and Mr. Graham entered.

The sound of the well-known footstep disturbed the soaring thoughts of both, and the flush of excitement which had mounted into Emily's cheeks subsided into more than her wonted paleness, as Philip, rising slowly and deliberately from his seat at her side, stood face to face with her father.

Mr. Graham approached with the puzzled and scrutinizing air of one who finds himself called upon in the chamber of a host to greet a visitor who, though an apparent stranger, may possibly have claims to recognition, and glanced at his daughter as if hoping she would relieve the awkwardness by an introduction. But the agitated Emily maintained perfect silence, and every feature of Philip's countenance remained immovable as Mr. Graham slowly came forward.

He had advanced within one step of the spot where Philip stood waiting to receive him, when, struck by the stern look and attitude of the latter, he stopped short, gazed one moment into the eagle eyes of his stepson, then staggered, grasped at the mantel-piece, and would have fallen; but Philip, starting forward, helped him to his arm-chair, which stood opposite to the sofa.

And yet no word was spoken. At length Mr. Graham, who, having fallen into the seat, sat still gazing into the face of Mr. Amory, ejaculated, in a tone of wondering excitement, "Philip Amory! O, my God!"

"Yes, father," exclaimed Emily, suddenly rising and grasping her father's arm. "It is Philip; he, whom we have so long believed among the dead, restored to us in health and safety!"

Mr. Graham rose from his chair, and, leaning heavily on Emily's shoulder, again approached Mr. Amory, who, with folded arms, stood fixed as marble. His step tottered with a feebleness never before observable in the sturdy frame of the old man, and the hand which he extended to Philip was marked by an unusual tremulousness.

But Philip did not offer to receive the proffered hand, or reply by word to the rejected salutation.

Mr. Graham turned towards Emily, and, forgetting that this neglect was shut from her sight, exclaimed, half-bitterly, half-sadly, "I cannot blame him! God knows I wronged the boy!"

"Wronged him!" cried Philip, in a voice so deep as to be almost fearful. "Yes, wronged him, indeed! Blighted his life, crushed his youth, half-broke his heart, and wholly blasted his reputation!"

"No," exclaimed Mr. Graham, who had quailed beneath these accusations, until he reached the final one. "Not that, Philip! not that! I never harmed you there. I discovered my error before I had doomed you to infamy in the eyes of one of your fellow-men."

"You acknowledge, then, the error?"

"I do, I do! I imputed to you the deed which proved to have been accomplished through the agency of my most confidential clerk. I learned the truth almost immediately; but too late, alas! to recall you. Then came the news of your death, and I felt that the injury had been irreparable. But it was not strange, Philip; you must allow that. Archer had been in my employment more than twenty years. I had a right to believe him trustworthy."

"No! O, no!" replied Philip. "It was nothing strange that, a crime committed, you should have readily ascribed it to me. You thought me capable only of evil."

"I was unjust, Philip," answered Mr. Graham, with an attempt to rally his dignity, "but I had some cause,—I had some cause."

"Perhaps so," responded Philip; "I am willing to grant that."

"Let us shake hands upon it, then," said Mr. Graham, "and endeavor to forget the past."

Philip did not again refuse to accede to this request, though there was but little warmth or eagerness in the manner of his compliance.

Mr. Graham, seeming now to think the matter quite ended, looked relieved, and as if he had shaken off a burden which had been weighing upon his conscience for years (for he had a conscience, though not a very tender one); and, subsiding into his armchair, begged to learn the particulars of Philip's experience during the last twenty years.

The outline of the story was soon told; Mr. Graham listening to it with attention, and inquiring into its particulars with an interest which proved that, during a lengthened period of regret and remorse, his feelings had sensibly softened towards the step-son with every memory of whom there had come to his heart a pang of self-reproach.

Mr. Amory was unable to afford any satisfactory explanation of the report of his own death, which had been confidently affirmed by Dr. Jeremy's correspondent at Rio. Upon a comparison of dates, however, it seemed probable that the doctor's agent had obtained this information from Philip's employer, who, for some weeks previous to his own death, had every reason to believe that the young man had perished of the infection prevailing in the low and unhealthy region to which he had been despatched.

To Philip himself it was an almost equal matter of wonder that his friends should ever have obtained knowledge of his flight and destination. But this was more easily accounted for, since the vessel in which he had embarked returned directly to Boston, and there were among her crew and officers those who had ample means of replying to the inquiries which the benevolent doctor had set on foot some months before, and which, being accompanied by the offer of a liberal reward, had not yet ceased to attract the attention of the public.

Notwithstanding the many strange and romantic incidents which were unfolding themselves, none seemed to produce so great an impression upon Mr. Graham's mind as the singular circumstance that the child who had been reared under his roof, and endeared herself to him, in spite of some clashing of interests and opinions, should prove to be Philip's daughter. As he left the room, at the conclusion of the tale, and again sought the solitude of his library, he muttered to himself more than once, "Singular coincidence! Very singular! Very!"

Hardly had he departed, before another door was timidly opened, and Gertrude looked cautiously in.

Her father went quickly towards her, and, passing his arm around her waist, drew her towards Emily, and clasped them both in a long and silent embrace.

"Philip," exclaimed Emily, "can you still doubt the mercy and love which have spared us for such a meeting?"

"O, Emily!" replied he, "I am deeply grateful. Teach me how and where to bestow my tribute of praise."

On the hour of sweet communion which succeeded we forbear to dwell;—the silent rapture of Emily, the passionately-expressed joy of Philip, or the trusting, loving glances which Gertrude cast upon both.

It was nearly midnight when Mr. Amory rose, and announced his intention to depart. Emily, who had not thought of his leaving the spot which she hoped he would now consider his home, entreated him to remain; and Gertrude, with her eyes, joined in the eager petition. But he persisted in his resolution with a firmness and seriousness which proved how vain would be the attempt to shake it.

"Philip," said Emily, at length, laying her hand upon his arm, "you have not yet forgiven my father."

She had divined his thoughts. He shrank under her reproachful tones, and made no answer.

"But you *will,* dear Philip,—you *will,*" continued she, in a pleading voice.

He hesitated, then glanced at her once more, and replied, "I will, dearest Emily, I will—in time."

When he had gone, Gertrude lingered a moment at the door, to watch his retreating figure, just visible in the light of the waning moon; then returned to the parlor, drawing a long breath and saying, "O, what a day this has been!" but checked herself, at the sight of Emily, who, kneeling by the sofa, with clasped hands, uplifted face, and with her white garments sweeping the floor, looked the very impersonation of purity and prayer.

Throwing one arm around her neck, Gertrude knelt on the floor beside her, and together they sent up to the throne of God the incense of thanksgiving and praise!

CHAPTER XLIX

Thee have I loved, thou gentlest, from a child,
And borne thine image with me o'er the sea,—
Thy soft voice in my soul,—speak! O, yet live for me!
　　—*Hemans*

WHEN UNCLE TRUE DIED, Mr. Cooper reverently buried his old friend in the ancient grave-yard which adjoined the church where he had long officiated as sexton. It was a dilapidated-looking place, whose half-fallen and moss-grown stones proclaimed its recent neglect and disuse. But long before the adjacent and time-worn building gave place to a modern and more imposing structure the hallowed remains of Uncle True had found a quieter resting-place.

With that good taste and good feeling which, in latter days, has dedicated to the sacred dead some of the fairest spots on earth, a beautiful piece of undulating woodland in the neighborhood of Mr. Graham's country residence had been consecrated as a rural cemetery, and in the loveliest nook of this sweet and venerated spot the ashes of the good old lamplighter found their final repose.

This lot of land, which had been purchased through Willie's thoughtful liberality, selected by Gertrude, and by her made fragrant and beautiful with summer rose and winter ivy, now enclosed also the forms of Mr. Cooper and Mrs. Sullivan; and over these three graves Gertrude had planted many a flower, and watered it with her tears. Especially did she view it as a sacred duty and privilege to mark the anniversary of the death of each by a tribute of fresh garlands; and, with this pious purpose in view, she left Mr. Graham's house one beautiful afternoon, about a week after the events took place which are narrated in the previous chapter.

She carried on her arm a basket, which contained her offering of flowers; and, as she had a long walk before her, started at a rapid pace. Let us follow her, and briefly pursue the train of thought which accompanied her on her way.

She had left her father with Emily. She would not ask him to join her in her walk, though he had once expressed a desire to visit the grave of Uncle True; for he and Emily were talking together so contentedly, it would have been a pity to disturb them; and for a few moments Gertrude's reflections were engrossed by the thought of their calm and tranquil happiness. She thought of herself, too, as associated with them both; of the deep and long-tried love of Emily, and of the fond outpourings of affection daily and hourly lavished upon her by her newly-found parent, and felt that she could scarcely repay their kindness by the devotion of a lifetime.

Now and then, as she dwelt in her musings upon the sweet tie between herself and Emily, which had gained strength with every succeeding year, and the equally close and kindred union between father and child, which, though recent in its origin, was scarcely capable of being more firmly cemented by time, her thoughts would, in spite of herself, wander to that earlier-formed and not less tender friendship, now, alas! sadly ruptured and wounded, if not wholly uprooted and destroyed. She tried to banish the remembrance of Willie's faithlessness and desertion, deeming it the part of an ungrateful spirit to mourn over past hopes, regardless of the blessings that yet remained. She tried to keep in mind the resolutions lately formed to forget the most painful feature in her past life, and consecrate the remainder of her days to the happiness of her father and Emily.

But it would not do. The obtruding and painful recollection presented itself continually, notwithstanding her utmost efforts to repress it, and at last, ceasing the struggle, she gave herself up for the time to a deep and saddening revery.

She had received two visits from Willie since the one already mentioned; but the second meeting had been in its character very similar to the first, and on the succeeding occasion the constraint had increased, instead of diminishing. Several times Willie had made an apparent effort to break through this unnatural barrier, and speak and act with the freedom of former days; but a sudden blush, or sign of confusion and distress, on Gertrude's part, deterred him from any further attempt to put to flight the reserve and want of confidence which subsisted in their intercourse. Again, Gertrude, who had resolved, previous to his last visit, to meet him with the frankness and cordiality which he might reasonably expect, smiled upon him affectionately at his coming, and offered her hand with such sisterly freedom, that he was emboldened to take and retain it in his grasp, and was evidently on the point of unburdening his mind of some weighty secret, when she turned abruptly away, took up some trivial piece of work, and, while she seemed wholly absorbed in it, addressed to him an unimportant question;—a course of conduct which put to flight all his ideas, and disconcerted him for the remainder of his stay.

As Gertrude pondered the awkward and distressing results of every visit he had made her, she half hoped he would discontinue them altogether; believing that the feelings of both would be less wounded by a total separation than by interviews which must leave on the mind of each a still greater sense of estrangement.

Strange as it may seem, she had not yet acquainted him with the event so deep in its interest to herself,—the discovery of her dearly-loved father. Once she tried to speak of it, but found herself so overcome, at the very idea of imparting to the confidant of her childhood an experience of which she could scarcely yet think without emotion, that she paused in the attempt, fearing that, should she, on any topic, give way to her sensibilities, she should lose all restraint over her feelings, and lay open her whole heart to Willie.

But there was one thing that distressed her more than all others. In his first vain attempt to throw off all disguise, Willie had more than intimated to her his own unhappiness; and, ere she could find an opportunity to change the subject, and repel a confidence for which she still felt herself unprepared, he had gone so far as to speak mournfully of his future prospects in life.

The only construction which Gertrude could give to this confession was that it had reference to his engagement with Isabel; and it gave rise at once to the suspicion that, infatuated by her beauty, he had impulsively and heedlessly bound himself to one who could never make him wholly happy. The little scenes to which she had herself been a witness corroborated this idea, as, on both occasions of her seeing the lovers and overhearing their words, some cause of vexation seemed to exist on Willie's part.

"He loves her," thought Gertrude, "and is also bound to her in honor; but he sees already the want of harmony in their natures. Poor Willie! It is impossible he should ever be happy with Isabel."

And Gertrude's sympathizing heart mourned not more deeply over her own grief than over the disappointment that Willie must be experiencing, if he had ever hoped to find peace in a union with so overbearing, ill-humored and unreasonable a girl.

Wholly occupied with these and similar musings, she walked on with a pace of whose quickness she was scarcely herself aware, and soon gained the shelter of the heavy pines which bordered the entrance to the cemetery. Here she paused for a moment to enjoy the refreshing breeze that played beneath the branches; and then, passing through the gateway, entered a carriage-road at the right, and proceeded slowly up the gradual ascent. The place, always quiet and peaceful, seemed unusually still and secluded, and, save the occasional carol of a bird, there was no sound to disturb the perfect silence and repose. As Gertrude gazed upon the familiar beauties of those sacred grounds, which had been her frequent resort during several years,—as she walked between beds of flowers, inhaled the fragrant and balmy air, and felt the solemn appeal, the spiritual breathings, that haunted the holy place,—every emotion that was not in harmony with the scene gradually took its flight, and she experienced only that sensation of sweet and half-joyful melancholy which was awakened by the thought of the happy dead.

After a while, she left the broad road which she had been following, and turned into a little by-path. This she pursued for some distance; and then, again diverging through another and still narrower foot-track, gained the shady and retired spot which, partly from its remoteness to the public walks, and partly from its own natural beauty, had attracted her attention and recommended itself to her choice. It was situated on the slope of a little hill; a huge rock protected it on one side from the observation of the passer-by, and a fine old oak overshadowed it upon the other. The iron enclosure, of simple workmanship, was nearly overgrown by the green ivy, which had been planted there by Gertrude's hand, and the moss-grown rock also was festooned by its graceful and clinging tendrils. Upon a jutting piece of stone, directly beside the grave of Uncle True, Gertrude seated herself, as was her wont, and after a few moments of contemplation, during which she sat with her elbow upon her knee and her head resting upon her hand, she straightened her slight figure, sighed heavily, and then, lifting the cover of her basket, emptied her flowers upon the grass, and with skillful fingers commenced weaving a graceful chaplet, which, when completed, she placed upon the grave at her feet. With the remainder of the blossoms she strewed the other mounds; and then, drawing forth a pair of gardening-gloves and a little trowel, she employed herself for nearly an hour among the flowers and vines with which she had embowered the spot.

Her work at last being finished, she again placed herself at the foot of the old rock, removed her gloves, pushed back from her forehead the simple but heavy braids of her hair, and appeared to be resting from her labors.

It was seven years that day since Uncle True died, but the time had not yet come for Gertrude to forget the simple, kind old man. Often did his pleasant smile and cheering words come to her in her dreams; and both by day and night did the image of him who had gladdened and blessed her childhood encourage her to the imitation of his humble and patient virtue. As she gazed upon the grassy mound that covered him, and scene after scene rose up before her in which that earliest friend and herself had whiled away the happy hours, there came, to embitter the otherwise cherished remembrance, the recollection of that third and seldom absent one, who completed and made perfect the memory of their fireside joys; and Gertrude, while yielding to the inward reflection, unconsciously exclaimed aloud, "O, Uncle True! you and I are not parted yet; but Willie is not of us!"

"O, Gertrude," said a reproachful voice close at her side; "is Willie to blame for that?"

She started, turned, saw the object of her thoughts with his mild sad eyes fixed inquiringly upon her, and without replying to his question, buried her face in her hands.

He threw himself upon the ground at her feet, and, as on the occasion of their first childish interview, gently lifted her bowed head from the hands upon which it had fallen, and compelled her to look him in the face, saying, at the same time, in the most imploring accents, "Tell me, Gerty, in pity tell me why am I excluded from your sympathy?"

But still she made no reply, except by the tears that coursed down her checks.

"You make me miserable," continued he, vehemently. "What have I done that you have so shut me out from your affection? Why do you look so coldly upon me,—and even shrink from my sight?" added he, as Gertrude, unable to endure his steadfast, searching look, turned her eyes in another direction, and strove to free her hands from his grasp.

"I am not cold,—I do not mean to be," said she, her voice half-choked with emotion.

"O, Gertrude," replied he, relinquishing her hands, and turning away, "I see you have wholly ceased to love me. I trembled when I first beheld you, so lovely, so beautiful, and so beloved by all, and feared lest some fortunate rival had stolen your heart from its boyish keeper. But even then I did not dream that you would refuse me, at least, a *brother's* claim to your affection."

"I will not," exclaimed Gertrude eagerly. "O, Willie, you must not be angry with me! Let me be your sister!"

He smiled a most mournful smile. "I was right, then," continued he; "you feared lest I should claim too much, and discouraged my presumption by awarding me nothing. Be it so. Perhaps your prudence was for the best; but O, Gertrude, it has made me heart-broken!"

"Willie," exclaimed Gertrude, with excitement, "do you know how strangely you are speaking?"

"Strangely?" responded Willie, in a half-offended tone. "Is it so strange that I should love you? Have I not for years cherished the remembrance of our past affection, and looked forward to our reunion as my only hope of happiness? Has not this fond expectation inspired my labors, and cheered my toils, and endeared to me my life, in spite of its bereavements?

And can you, in the very sight of these cold mounds, beneath which lie buried all else that I held dear on earth, crush and destroy, without compassion, this solitary but all engrossing—"

"Willie," interrupted Gertrude, her calmness suddenly restored, and speaking in a kind but serious tone, "is it honorable for you to address me thus? Have you forgotten—"

"No, I have *not* forgotten," exclaimed he, vehemently. "I have not forgotten that I have no right to distress or annoy you, and I will do so no more. But, O, Gerty! my sister Gerty (since all hope of a nearer tie is at an end), blame me not, and wonder not, if I fail at present to perform a brother's part. I cannot stay in this neighborhood. I cannot be the patient witness of another's happiness. My services, my time, my life, you may command, and in my far-distant home I will never cease to pray that the husband you have chosen, whoever he be, may prove himself worthy of my noble Gertrude, and love her one-half as well as I do!"

"Willie," said Gertrude, "what madness is this? I am bound by no such tie as you describe; but what shall I think of your treachery to Isabel?"

"To Isabel?" cried Willie, starting up, as if seized with a new idea. "And has that silly rumor reached *you* too? and did you put faith in the falsehood?"

"Falsehood!" exclaimed Gertrude, lifting her hitherto drooping eyelids, and casting upon him, through their wet lashes, a look of earnest scrutiny.

Calmly returning a glance which he had neither avoided nor quailed under, Willie responded, unhesitatingly, and with a tone of astonishment not unmingled with reproach, "Falsehood?—Yes. With the knowledge you have both of her and myself, could you doubt its being such for a moment?"

"O, Willie!" cried Gertrude, "could I doubt the evidence of my own eyes and ears? Had I trusted to less faithful witnesses, I might have been deceived. Do not attempt to conceal from me the truth to which my own observation can testify. Treat me with frankness, Willie!—Indeed, indeed, I deserve it at your hands!"

"Frankness, Gertrude! It is you only who are mysterious. Could I lay my whole soul bare ot your gaze, you would be convinced of its truth, its perfect truth, to its first affection. And as to Isabel Clinton, if it is to her that you have reference, your eyes and your ears have both played you false, if—"

"O, Willie! Willie!" exclaimed Gertrude, interrupting him, "have you so soon forgotten your devotion to the belle of Saratoga; your unwillingness to sanction her temporary absence from your sight; the pain which the mere suggestion of the journey caused you, and the fond impatience which threatened to render those few days an eternity?"

"Stop! stop!" cried Willie, a new light breaking in upon him, "and tell me where you learned all this."

"In the very spot where you spoke and acted. Mr. Graham's parlor did not witness our first meeting. In the public promenade-ground, on the shore of Saratoga lake, and on board the steamboat at Albany, did I both see and recognize you—myself unknown. There too did your own words serve to convince me of the truth of that which from other lips I had refused to believe."

The sunshine which gilds the morning is scarcely more bright and gladsome than the glow of rekindled hope which now animated the face of Willie.

"Listen to me, Gertrude," said he, in a fervent and almost solemn tone, "and believe that in sight of my mother's grave, and in the presence of that pure spirit (and he looked reverently upward) who taught me the love of truth, I speak with such sincerity and candor as are fitting for the ears of angels. I do not question the accuracy with which you overheard my expostulations and entreaties on the subject of Miss Clinton's proposed journey, or the impatience I expressed at parting for her speedy return. I will not pause, either, to inquire where the object of all my thoughts could have been at the time, that, notwithstanding the changes of years, she escaped my eager eyes. Let me first clear myself of the imputation under which I labor, and then there will be room for all further explanations.

"I did, indeed, feel deep pain at Miss Clinton's sudden departure for New York, under a pretext which ought not to have weighed with her for a moment. I did indeed employ every argument to dissuade her from her purpose; and when my eloquence had failed to induce the abandonment of the scheme, I availed myself of every suggestion and motive which might possibly influence her to shorten her absence. Not because the society of the selfish girl was essential, or even conducive, to my own happiness,— far from it,—but because her excellent father, who so worshipped and idolized his only child that he would have thought no sacrifice too great by means of which he could add one particle to her enjoyment, was, at that very time, amid all the noise and discomfort of a crowded watering-place, hovering between life and death, and I was disgusted at the heartlessness which voluntarily left the fondest of parents deprived of all female tending, to the charge of a hired nurse, and an unskillful though willing youth like myself. That eternity might, in Miss Clinton's absence, set a seal to the life of her father, was a thought which, in my indignation, I was on the point of uttering; but I checked myself, unwilling to interfere too far in a matter which came not within my rightful province, and perhaps excite unnecessary alarm in Isabel. If selfishness mingled at all in my views, dear Gerty, and made me over-impatient for the return of the daughter to her post of duty, it was that I might be released from almost constant attendance upon my invalid friend, and hasten to her from whom I hoped such warmth of greeting as I was only too eager to bestow. Can you wonder, then, that your reception struck cold upon my throbbing heart?"

"But you understand the cause of that coldness now," said Gertrude, looking up at him through a rain of tears, which, like a summer sun-shower, reflected itself in rainbow smiles upon her happy countenance. "You know now why I dared not let my heart speak out."

"And this was all, then?" cried Willie; "and you are free, and I may love you still?"

"Free from all bonds, dear Willie, but those which you yourself clasped around me, and which have encircled me from my childhood."

And now, with heart pressed to heart, they pour in each other's ear the tale of a mutual affection, planted in infancy, nourished in youth, fostered and strengthened amid separation and absence, and perfected through trial, to bless and sanctify every year of their after life.

"But, Gerty," exclaimed Willie, as, confidence restored, they sat side by side, conversing freely of the past, "how could you think, for an instant, that Isabel Clinton would have power to displace you in my regard? I was not guilty of so great an injustice towards you; for, even when I believed myself supplanted by another, I fancied that other some hero of such shining qualities as could scarcely be surpassed."

"And who could surpass Isabel?" inquired Gerty. "Can you wonder that I trembled for your allegiance, when I thought of her beauty, her fashion, her family and her wealth, and remembered the forcible manner in which all these were presented to your sight and knowledge?"

"But what are all these, Gerty, to one who knows her as we do? Do not a proud eye and a scornful lip destroy the effect of beauty? Can fashion excuse rudeness, or noble birth cover natural deficiencies? And, as to money, what did I ever want of that, except to employ it for the happiness of yourself—and them?"—and he glanced at the graves of his mother and grandfather.

"O, Willie! You are so disinterested!"

"Not in this case. Had Isabel possessed the beauty of a Venus and the wisdom of a Minerva, I could not have forgotten how little happiness there could be with one who, while devoting herself to the pursuit of pleasure, had become dead to natural affections, and indifferent to the holiest of duties. Could I see her flee from the bed-side of her father to engage in the frivolities and drink in the flatteries of an idle crowd,—or, when un-willingly summoned thither, shrink from the toils and the watchings im-posed by his feebleness,—and still imagine that such a woman could bless and adorn a fireside? Could I fail to contrast her unfeeling neglect, ill-concealed petulance, flagrant levity and irreverence of spirit, with the sweet and loving devotion, the saintly patience, and the deep and fervent piety of my own Gertrude? I should have been false to myself, as well as to you, dearest, if such traits of character as Miss Clinton constantly evinced could have weakened my love and admiration for yourself. And now, to see the little playmate whose image I cherished so fondly matured into the lovely and graceful woman, her sweet attractions crowned by so much beauty as almost to place her beyond recognition, and still her heart as much my own as ever!—O, Gerty, it is too much happiness! Would that I could impart a share of it to those who loved us both so well!"

And who can say that they did not share it?—that the spirit of Uncle True was not there, to witness the completion of his many hopeful prophe-cies? that the old grandfather was not there, to see all his doubts and fears giving place to joyful certainties? and that the soul of the gentle mother, whose rapt slumbers had, even in life, foreshadowed such a meeting, and who, by the lessons she had given her child in his boyhood, the warnings spoken to his later years, and the ministering guidance of her disembodied spirit, had fitted him for the struggle with temptation, sustained him through its trials, and restored him triumphant to the sweet friend of his infancy,—who shall say that, even now, she hovered not over them with parted wings, realizing the joy prefigured in that dreamy vision which pictured to her sight the union between the son and daughter of her love, when the one, shielded by her fond care from every danger, and snatched from the power of temptation, should be restored to the arms of the other, who, by long and patient continuance in well-doing, had earned so full a recompense, so all-sufficient a reward?

CHAPTER L

🐦🐦🐦🐦🐦🐦

> "Through night to light—in every stage,
> From childhood's morn to hoary age,
> What shall illume the pilgrimage
> By mortals trod?
>
> "There is a pure and heavenly ray,
> That brightest shines in darkest day,
> When earthly beams are quenched for aye;
> 'T is lit by God."

THE SUN WAS CASTING long shadows, and the sunset hour was near, when Gertrude and Willie rose to depart. They left the cemetery by a different gateway, and in the opposite direction to that by which Gertrude had entered. Here Willie found the chaise in which he had come, though the horse had contrived to loosen the bridle by which he was fastened; had strayed to the side of the road, eaten as much grass as he wished, or the place afforded, and was now sniffing the air, looking up and down the road, and, despairing of his master's return, seemed on the point of taking his departure.

He was reclaimed, however, without difficulty, and, as if glad after his long rest to be again in motion, brought them in half an hour to Mr. Graham's door.

As soon as they came in sight of the house, Gertrude, familiar with the customary ways of the family, perceived that something unusual was going forward. Lamps were moving about in every direction; the front-door stood wide open; there was, what she had never seen before, the blaze of a bright fire discernible through the windows of the best chamber; and, as they drew still nearer, she observed that the piazza was half covered with trunks.

All these appearances, as she rightly conjectured, betokened the arrival of Mrs. Graham, and possibly of other company. She might, perhaps, have regretted the ill-timed coming of this bustling lady, at the very moment when she was eager for a quiet opportunity to present Willie to Emily and her father, and communicate to them her own happiness; but, if such a thought presented itself, it vanished in a moment. Her joy was too complete to be marred by so trifling a disappointment.

"Let us drive up the avenue, Willie," said she, "to the side-door, so that George may see us, and take your horse to the stable."

"No," said Willie, as he stopped opposite the front gate; "I can't come in now—there seems to be a house full of company; and, besides, I have an appointment in town at eight o'clock, and promised to be punctual;"—he glanced at his watch as he spoke, and added, "it is near that already. I did not think of its being so late; but I shall see you to-morrow morning, may I not?" She looked her assent, and, with a warm grasp of the hand, as he helped her from the chaise, and a mutual smile of confidence and love, they separated.

He drove rapidly towards Boston, and she, opening the gate, found herself in the arms of Fanny Bruce, who had been impatiently awaiting the departure of Willie to seize her dear Miss Gertrude, and, between tears and kisses, pour out her congratulations and thanks for her happy escape from that horrid steam-boat; for this was the first time they had met since the accident.

"Has Mrs. Graham come, Fanny?" asked Gertrude, as, the first excitement of the meeting over; they walked up to the house together.

"Yes, indeed, Mrs. Graham, and Kitty, and Isabel, and a little girl, and a sick gentleman,—Mr. Clinton, I believe; and another gentleman,—but *he's* gone."

"Who has gone?"

"O, a tall, dignified-looking man, with black eyes, and a beautiful face, and hair as white as if he were old,—and he is n't old, either."

"And do you say he has gone?"

"Yes; he did n't come with the rest. He was here when I came, and he went away about an hour ago. I heard him tell Miss Emily that he had agreed to meet a friend in Boston, but perhaps he 'd come back this evening. I hope he will, Miss Gertrude; you ought to see him."

They had now reached the house, and, through the open door, Gertrude could plainly distinguish the loud tones of Mrs. Graham's voice, proceeding from the parlor on the right. She was talking to her husband and Emily, and was just saying, as Gertrude entered, "O, it was the most *awful* thing I ever heard of in my life! and to think, Emily, of your being on

board, and our Isabel! Poor child! she has n't got her color back yet, after
her fright. And Gertrude Flint, too! By the way, they say Gertrude behaved
very well. Where is the child?"

Turning round, she now saw Gertrude, who was just entering the
room, and, going towards her, she kissed her with considerable heartiness
and sincerity; for Mrs. Graham, though somewhat coarse and blunt, was
not without good feelings when the occasion was such as to awaken them.

Gertrude's entrance having served to interrupt the stream of ex-
clamatory remarks in which the excitable lady had been indulging for ten
minutes or more, she now bethought herself of the necessity of removing
her bonnet and outside garments, a part of which, being loosed from their
fastenings, she had been dragging after her about the floor.

"Well!" exclaimed she, "I suppose I had better follow the girls' example, and go and get some of the dust off from me! I 'm half buried, I
believe! But, there, that 's better than coming on in the horrid steamboat,
last night, as my brother Clinton was so crazy as to propose. Where 's
Bridget? I want her to take up some of my things."

"I will assist you," said Gertrude, taking up a little carpet-bag,
throwing a scarf which had been stretching across the room over her arm,
and then following Mrs. Graham closely, in order to support the heavy
travelling-shawl which was hanging half off that lady's shoulders. At the
first landing-place, however, she found herself suddenly encircled in
Kitty's warm embrace, and, laying down her burdens, gave herself up for a
few moments to the hugging and kissing that succeeded.

At the head of the staircase she met Isabel, wrapped in a dressing-
gown, with a large pitcher in her hand, and a most discontented and
dissatisfied expression of countenance. She set the pitcher on the floor,
however, and saluted Gertrude with a good grace. "I'm glad to see you
alive," said she, "though I can't look at you without shuddering; it reminds
me so of that dreadful day when we were in such frightful danger. How
lucky we were to be saved, when there were so many drowned! I 've
wondered, ever since, Gertrude, how you could be so calm; I 'm sure I
should n't have known what to do, if you had n't been there to suggest.
But, O, dear! don't let us speak of it; it 's a thing I can't bear to think of!"
and, with a shudder and shrug of the shoulders, Isabel dismissed the subject, and called somewhat pettishly to Kitty,—"Kitty, I thought you went
to get our pitcher filled!"

Kitty, who, in obedience to a loud call and demand from her aunt,
had hastily run to her room with the little travelling-bag which Gertrude

had dropped on the staircase, now came back quite out of breath, saying, "I did ring the bell, twice. Has n't anybody come?"

"No!" replied Belle; "and I should like to wash my face and curl my hair before tea, if I could."

"Let me take the pitcher," said Gertrude; "I am going down stairs, and will send Jane up with the water."

"Thank you," said Belle, rather feebly; while Kitty exclaimed, "No, no, Gertrude; I 'll go myself."

But it was too late; Gertrude had gone.

Gertrude found Mrs. Ellis full of troubles and perplexities, "Only think," said the astonished housekeeper, "of their coming, five of them, without the least warning in the world; and here I 've nothing in the house fit for tea;—not a bit of rich cake, not a scrap of cold ham! And, of course, they 're hungry after their long journey, and will want something nice!"

'O, if they are very hungry, Mrs. Ellis, they can eat dried beef, and fresh biscuit, and plain cake; and, if you will give me the keys, I will get out the preserves, and the best silver, and see that the table is set properly."

Nothing was a trouble to Gertrude, that night. Everything that she touched went right. Jane caught her spirit, and became astonishingly active; and when the really bountiful table was spread, and Mrs. Ellis, after glancing around, and seeing that all was as it should be, looked into the beaming eyes and observed the glowing cheek and sunny smile of the happy girl, she exclaimed, in her ignorance, "Good gracious, Gertrude! anybody would think you were overjoyed to see all these folks back again!"

It wanted but a few moments to tea-time, and Gertrude was selecting fresh napkins from a drawer in the china-closet, when Kitty Ray peeped in at the door, and finally entered, leading by the hand a little girl, neatly dressed in black. Her face was, at first, full of smiles; but, the moment she attempted to speak, she burst into tears, and, throwing her arms round Gertrude's neck, whispered in her ear, "O, Gertrude, I 'm so happy! I came to tell you!"

"Happy?" replied Gertrude; "then you must n't cry."

Upon this, Kitty laughed, and then cried again, and then laughed once more, and, in the intervals, explained to Gertrude that she was engaged,—had been engaged a week, to the best man in the world,—and that the child she held by the hand was his orphan niece, and just like a daughter to him. "And, only think," continued she, "it 's all owing to you!"

"To me?" said the astonished Gertrude.

"Yes; because I was so vain and silly, you know, and liked folks that were not worth liking, and did n't care much for anybody's comfort but my own; and, if you had n't taught me to be something better than that, and set me a good example, which I 've tried to follow ever since, he never would have thought of looking at me, much less loving me, and believing I should be a fit mother for little Gracie, here," and she looked down affectionately at the child, who was clinging fondly to her. "He is a minister, Gertrude, and very good. Only think of such a childish creature as I am being a minister's wife!"

The sympathy which Kitty came to claim was not denied her, and Gertrude, with her own eyes brimming with tears, assured her of her full participation in her joy.

In the mean time, little Grace, who still clung to Kitty with one hand, had gently inserted the other within that of Gertrude, who, looking down upon her for the first time, recognized the child whom she had rescued from persecution in the drawing-room at Saratoga.

Kitty was charmed with the coincidence, and Gertrude, as she remarked the happy transformation which had already been effected in the countenance and dress of the little girl who had been so sadly in want of female superintendence, felt an added conviction of the wisdom of the young clergyman's choice.

Kitty was eager to give Gertrude a description of her lover, but a summons to the tea-table compelled her to postpone all further communications.

Mr. Graham's cheerful parlor had never looked so cheerful as on that evening. The weather was mild, but a light fire, which had been kindled on Mr. Clinton's account, did not render the room too warm. It had, however, driven the young people into a remote corner, leaving the neighborhood of the fireplace to Mrs. Graham and Emily, who occupied the sofa, and Mr. Clinton and Mr. Graham, whose arm-chairs were placed on the opposite side.

This arrangement enabled Mr. Graham to converse freely and uninterruptedly with his guest upon some grave topic of interest, while his talkative wife entertained herself and Emily by a recapitulation of her travels and adventures. On a table, at the further extremity of the room, was placed a huge portfolio of beautiful engravings, recently purchaed and brought home by Mr. Graham, and representing a series of European views. Gertrude and Kity were turning them carefully over; and little Grace, who was sitting in Kitty's lap, and Fanny, who was leaning over Gertrude's shoulder, were listening eagerly to the young ladies' explanations and comments.

Occasionally Isabel, the only restless or unoccupied person present, would lean over the table to glance at the likeness of some familiar spot, and exclaim, "Kitty, there 's the shop where I bought my blue silk!" or, "Kitty, there 's the waterfall that we visited in company with the Russian officers!"

While the assembled company were thus occupied, the door opened, and, without any announcement, Mr. Amory and William Sullivan entered.

Had either made his appearance singly, he would have been looked upon with astonishment by the majority of the company; but coming, as they did, together, and with an apparently good understanding existing between them, there was no countenance present (save the children's) which expressed any emotion but that of utter surprise.

Mr. and Mrs. Graham, however, were too much accustomed to society to betray any further evidence of that sentiment than was contained in a momentary glance, and, rising, received their visitors with due politeness and propriety. The former nodded carelessly to Mr. Amory, whom he had seen in the morning, presented him to Mr. Clinton (without, however, mentioning the existing connection with himself), and was preparing to go through the same ceremony to Mrs. Graham, but was saved the trouble, as she had not forgotten the acquaintance formed at Baden-Baden.

Willie's knowledge of the company also spared the necessity of introduction to all but Emily; and that being accidentally omitted, he gave an arch glance at Gertrude, and, taking an offered seat near Isabel, entered into conversation with her; Mr. Amory being in like manner engrossed by Mrs. Graham.

"Miss Gertrude," whispered Fanny, as soon as the interrupted composure of the party was once more restored, and glancing at Willie, as she spoke, "that's the gentleman you were out driving with, this afternoon. I know it is," continued she, as she observed Gertrude change color, and endeavor to hush her, while she looked anxiously round, as if fearful the remark had been overheard; "is it Willie, Gertrude?—is it Mr. Sullivan?"

Gertrude became more and more embarrassed, while the mischievous Fanny continued to ply her with questions; and Isabel, who had jealously noticed that Willie's eyes wandered more than once to the table, turned on her such a scrutinizing look as rendered her confusion distressing.

Accident came to her relief, however. The housemaid, with the evening paper, endeavored to open the door, against which her chair was placed; thus giving her an opportunity to rise, receive the paper, and, at the same time, an unimportant message. While she was thus engaged, Mr.

Clinton left his chair, with the feeble step of an invalid, crossed the room, addressed a question in a low voice to Willie, and, receiving an affirmatory reply, took Isabel by the hand, and, approaching Mr. Amory, exclaimed with deep emotion, "Sir, Mr. Sullivan tells me that you are the person who saved the life of my daughter; and here she is to thank you."

Mr. Amory rose and flung his arm over the shoulder and around the waist of Gertrude, who was passing on her way to hand the newspaper to Mr. Graham, and who, not having heard the remark of Mr. Clinton, received the caress with a sweet smile and an upturned face. "Here," said he, "Mr. Clinton, is the person who saved the life of your daughter. It is true that I swam with her to the shore; but it was under the mistaken impression that I was bearing to a place of safety my own darling child, whom I little suspected then of having voluntarily relinquished to another her only apparent chance of rescue."

"Just like you, Gertrude! Just like you!" shouted Kitty and Fanny in a breath, each struggling to obtain a foremost place in the little circle that had gathered round her.

"My own noble Gertrude!" whispered Emily, as, leaning on Mr. Amory's arm, she pressed Gertrude's hand to her lips.

"O, Gertrude!" exclaimed Isabel, with tears in her eyes, "I did n't know. I never thought——"

"Your child?" cried Mrs. Graham's loud voice, interrupting Isabel's unfinished exclamation.

"Yes, my child, thank God!" said Mr. Amory, reverently; "restored, at last, to her unworthy father, and—you have no secrets here, my darling?"—Gertrude shook her head, and glanced at Willie, who now stood at her side,—"and gladly bestowed by him upon her faithful and far more deserving lover." And he placed her hand in Willie's.

There was a moment's pause. All were impressed with the solemnity of the action. Then Mr. Graham came forward, shook each of the young couple heartily by the hand, and, passing his sleeve hastily across his eyes, sought his customary refuge in the library.

"Gertrude," said Fanny, pulling Gertrude's dress to attract her attention, and speaking in a loud whisper, "are you engaged?—are you engaged to him?"

"Yes," whispered Gertrude, anxious, if possible, to gratify Fanny's curiosity, and silence her questioning.

"O! I 'm so glad! I 'm so glad!" shouted Fanny, dancing round the room, and flinging up her arms.

"And I 'm glad, too!" said Gracie, catching the tone of the congratulation, and putting her mouth up to Gertrude for a kiss.

"And *I* am glad," said Mr. Clinton, placing his hands upon those of Willie and Gertrude, which were still clasped together, "that the noble and self-sacrificing girl, whom I have no words to thank, and no power to repay, has reaped a worthy reward in the love of one of the few men with whom a fond father may venture wholly to trust the happiness of his child."

Exhausted by so much excitement, Mr. Clinton now complained of sudden faintness, and was assisted to his room by Willie, who, after waiting to see him fully restored, returned to receive the blessing of Emily upon his new hopes, and hear with wonder and delight the circumstances which attended the discovery of Gertrude's parentage.

For, although it was an appointment to meet Mr. Amory which had summoned him back to Boston, and he had in the course of their interview acquainted him with the happy termination of a lover's doubts, he had not, until the disclosure took place in Mr. Graham's parlor, received in return the slightest hint of the great surprise which awaited him. He had felt a little astonishment at his friend's expressed desire to join him at once in a visit to Mr. Graham's; but, on being informed that he had made the acquaintance of Mrs. Graham in Germany, he concluded that a desire to renew his intercourse with the family, and possibly a slight curiosity to see the lady of his own choice, were the only motives which had influenced him.

And now, amid retrospections of the past, thanksgiving for the present, and hopes and aspirations for the future, the evening passed rapidly away.

"*COME HERE,* Gerty!" said Willie; "come to the window, and see what a beautiful night it is."

It was indeed a glorious night. Snow lay on the ground. The air was intensely cold without, as might be judged from the quick movements of pedestrians, and the brilliant icicles with which everything that had an edge was fringed. The stars were glittering, too, as they never glitter, except on the most intense of winter nights. The moon was just peeping above an old brown building,—the same old corner building which had been visible from the door-step where Willie and Gerty were wont to sit in their childhood, and from behind which they had often watched the coming of that same round moon.

Leaning on Willie's shoulder, Gertrude stood gazing until the full

418

circle was visible in a space of clear and cloudless ether. Neither of them spoke, but their hearts throbbed with the same emotion, as they thought of the days that were past.

Just then, the gas-man came quickly up the street, lit, as by an electric touch, the bright burners that in close ranks lined either side-walk, and in a moment more was out of sight.

Gertrude sighed. "It was no such easy task for poor old Uncle True," said she; "there have been great improvements since his time."

"There have, indeed!" said Willie, glancing round the well-lit, warm and pleasantly-furnished parlor of his own and Gertrude's home, and resting his eyes, at last, upon the beloved one by his side, whose beaming face but reflected back his own happiness,—"such improvements, Gerty, as we only dreamt of once! I wish the dear old man could be here to see and share them!"

A tear started to Gertrude's eye; but, pressing Willie's arm, she pointed reverently upward to a beautiful, bright star, just breaking forth from a silvery film, which had hitherto half-over-shadowed it; the star through which Gertrude had ever fancied she could discern the smile of the kind old man.

"Dear Uncle True!" said she; "his lamp still burns brightly in heaven, Willie; and its light is not yet gone out on earth!"

IN A BEAUTIFUL TOWN about thirty miles from Boston, and on the shore of one of those hill-embosomed ponds which would be immortalized by the poet in a country less rich than ours with such sheets of blue, transparent water, there stood a mansion-house of solid though ancient architecture. It had been the property of Philip Amory's paternal grandparents, and the early home and sole inheritance of his father, who so cherished the spot that it was only with great reluctance, and when driven to the act by the spur of poverty, that he was induced to part with the much-valued estate.

To reclaim the venerable homestead, repair and judiciously modernize the house, and fertilize and adorn the grounds, was a favorite scheme with Philip. His ample means now rendering it practicable, he lost no time in putting it into execution, and, the spring after he returned from his wanderings, saw the work in a fair way to be speedily completed.

In the mean time, Gertrude's marriage had taken place, the Grahams had removed to their house in town (which, out of compliment to Isabel, who was passing the winter with her aunt, was more than ever crowded with gay company), and the bustling mistress was already projecting changes in her husband's country-seat.

And Emily, who had parted with her greatest treasure, and found herself in an atmosphere which was little in harmony with her spirit, murmured not; but, contented with her lot, neither dreamed of nor asked for outward change, until Philip came to her one day, and, taking her hand, said, gently,

"This is no home for you, Emily. You are as much alone as I in my solitary farm-house. We loved each other in childhood, our hearts became one in youth, and have continued so until now. Why should we be longer parted? Your father will not oppose our wishes; and will you, dearest, refuse to bless and gladden the lonely life of your gray-haired lover?"

But Emily shook her head, while she answered, with her smile of ineffable sweetness,

"O, no, Philip! do not speak of it! Think of my frail health and my helplessness!"

"Your health, dear Emily, is improving. The roses are already coming back to your cheeks; and, for your helplessness, what task can be so sweet to me as teaching you, through my devotion, to forget it? O, do not send me away disappointed, Emily! A cruel fate divided us for years; do not by your own act prolong the separation! Believe me, a union with my early love is my brightest, my only hope of happiness!"

And she did not withdraw the hand which he held, but yielded the other also to his fervent clasp.

"My only thought had been, dear Philip," said she, "that ere this I should have been called to my Father's home; and even now I feel many a warning that I cannot be very long for earth; but while I stay, be it longer or shorter, it shall be as you wish. No word of mind shall part hearts so truly one, and your home shall be mine."

And when the grass turned green, and the flowers sent up their fragrance, and the birds sang in the branches, and the spring gales blew soft and made a gentle ripple on the water, Emily came to live on the hill-side with Philip. And Mrs. Ellis came too, to superintend all things, and especially the dairy, which became henceforth her pride. She had long since tearfully implored, and easily obtained, the forgiveness of the much-wronged Philip; and proved, by the humility of her voluntary confession, that she was not without a woman's heart.

Mrs. Prime pleaded hard for the cook's situation at the farm; but Emily kindly expostulated with her, saying,

The Lamplighter

"We cannot all leave my father, Mrs. Prime. Who would see to his hot toast, and the fire in the library?" and the good old woman saw the matter in the right light, and submitted.

And is the long-wandering, much-suffering, and deeply-sorrowing exile happy now? He is; but his peace springs not from his beautiful home, his wide possessions, an honorable repute among his fellow-men, or even the love of the gentle Emily.

All these are blessings that he well knows how to prize; but his world-tried soul has found a deeper anchor yet,—a surer refuge from the tempest and the storm; for, through the power of a living faith, he has laid hold on eternal life. The blind girl's prayers are answered; her last, best work is done; she has cast a ray from her blessed spirit into his darkened soul; and, should her call to depart soon come, she will leave behind one to follow in her footsteps, fulfill her charities, and do good on earth, until such time as he be summoned to join her again in heaven.

As they go forth in the summer evening, to breathe the balmy air, listen to the winged songster of the grove, and drink in the refreshing influences of a summer sunset, all things speak a holy peace to the new-born heart of him who has so long been a man of sorrow.

As the sun sinks among gorgeous clouds, as the western light grows dim, and the moon and the stars come forth in their solemn beauty, they utter a lesson to his awakened soul; and the voice of nature around, and the still, small voice within, whisper, in gentlest, holiest accents,

"The sun shall be no more thy light by day, neither for brightness shall the moon give light unto thee; but the Lord shall be unto thee an everlasting light, and thy God thy glory."

"Thy sun shall no more go down, neither shall thy moon withdraw itself; for the Lord shall be thine everlasting light, and the days of thy mourning shall be ended."

THE END.

APPENDIX

THE EPIGRAPHS

EPIGRAPHS ARE QUOTATIONS at the beginning of a literary work or its divisions. The use of epigraphs in novels was widespread in England and America in the eighteenth and nineteenth centuries, although the custom declined after the mid-century. Epigraphs provided a thematic or interpretive gloss on the chapter, and by situating the work in a larger literary context, imparted a kind of literariness to it. Authors drew epigraphs from their general reading (including magazine reading), from their commonplace books (journals in which they jotted down particularly apt statements), and from published dictionaries of quotations. Most epigraphs were poetry, mainly because the language of poetry is more concise than prose but also because poetry was then thought to be more literary than prose. In *The Lamplighter* only the quotation from *Ivanhoe* is not poetry. The field of possible quotations was huge, and particular epigraphs vary widely from author to author, and from work to work. Epigraphs often contain minor errors in wording or punctuation, suggesting careless transcription or perhaps citation from memory.

Cummins cites thirty authors in her fifty-chapter work, of whom seven are Americans, nine are women. Fourteen of these writers were born in the eighteenth century and had careers extending well into the nineteenth century. Another seven were born in the nineteenth century, five before 1810, the other two before 1820. Overall, then, two-thirds of the authors cited were active in the first half of the nineteenth century. Ten were still writing at the time that *The Lamplighter* appeared. Almost all the writers cited were popular in their own time and still widely read in Cummins's day. Since Shakespeare is represented only once, and by a play that would at the time have been thought of as minor (*Measure for Measure*), John Milton virtually stands alone for "great literature." The most frequently cited author is Felicia Hemans (7), followed by Milton (6), William Wordsworth (5), Hannah More (4), and Edward Bulwer-Lytton (3)—all English writers. The Americans cited are Richard Henry Dana, Sr., Caroline Gilman, James Russell Lowell, William Gilmore Simms, Louisa Smith, Henry Ware, Sr., and Nathaniel Parker Willis. Lowell is cited twice, and the others once.

As a means of comparison we may look at two contemporaneous novels by American women, *The Wide, Wide World* by Susan Warner and *The Barclays of Boston*, an 1854 novel by Mrs. Harrison Gray Otis. In *The Wide, Wide World*, with fifty-two chapters, Warner cites twenty-two authors, of whom two—Longfellow and her own sister—are American; two epigraphs come from women writers (in addition to her sister she cites Mary Howitt). Shakespeare appears sixteen times; next in frequency are Longfellow and Burns (5 each); also cited are Cowper, Chaucer, Dryden, George Herbert, Milton, Spenser, along with "old songs" and "old ballads." The women didactic writers favored by Cummins—Felicia Hemans, Hannah More, Joanna Baillie, Anna Laetitia Barbauld—are absent. We could call Warner's list a conventional, although streamlined, use of literary "greats," with the old songs standing for primitive bardic literary origins.

In *The Barclays of Boston*, thirty-five writers, of whom five are American, are cited in a fifty-chapter work. Shakespeare leads with five citations; the list includes Joanna Baillie (the only woman), Bryant, Burns, Byron, Dryden, James T. Fields (her publisher), Goldsmith, Halleck, Dr. Johnson, Keats, Longfellow, Mandeville, Marvell, Milton, Moore, Poe, Pope, Shirley, Raleigh, Watts, Willis. Like Cummins and Warner, Otis uses mainly English writers; unlike them she is clearly striving to represent the whole tradition. Like Warner, she virtually omits the women poets whom Cummins cites so extensively. Therefore, with an eye to what Cummins did that was "unique" to this admittedly limited sample, we may suggest that Cummins was attempting through her epigraphs to situate *The Lamplighter* in the field of well-known recent nineteenth-century Anglo-American literature rather than in the great tradition, *and* more specifically in a transatlantic mode of women's writing.

Appendix: The Epigraphs

CHAPTER I

"The Factory" ll. 73–76 by Letitia Elizabeth Landon (English 1802–38). Landon wrote poetry and fiction and published between 1824 and 1838. Two of her novels are *Romance and Reality* (1831) and *Ethel Churchill* (1837).

CHAPTER II

The quotation is unidentified; the writer is Emily Taylor (English 1795–1872), author of historical tales, children's guidance books, biographies, and hymns.

CHAPTER III

Sonnet 4, "Druidical Excommunication" ll. 1–2 from *Ecclesiastical Sonnets* by William Wordsworth. Wordsworth (English 1770–1850) became one of the best-known and most influential of the Romantic poets, but his greatest reputation and influence came after the middle of the nineteenth century.

CHAPTER IV

"A Complaint; or Night Thoughts on Life, Death, and Immortality" l. 297–99 by Edward Young (English 1683–1765). The 10,000-line blank verse poem, in nine books, was originally published between 1742 and 1745; it was very popular and had considerable influence, containing lines that were repeated so often as to become proverbial.

CHAPTER V

Rienzi: A Tragedy III. ii. 54–56, a historical drama by Mary Russell Mitford (English 1787–1855), author of poems, plays, and fiction. Her most famous work was *Our Village,* a series of sketches and stories published between 1824 and 1832.

Appendix: The Epigraphs

CHAPTER VI

"The Progress of Error" ll. 598–99, a satiric poem by William Cowper (English 1731–1800); his best-known poem was "The Task."

CHAPTER VII

"What is Prayer?" Stanza 2 by James Montgomery (Scottish 1771–1854).

CHAPTER VIII

Paradise Lost 9. 171–72 by John Milton (English 1608–74). In the nineteenth century Milton was considered the greatest of the English poets, and *Paradise Lost,* an epic retelling of the story of "man's first disobedience" and the expulsion from the Garden of Eden, was thought to be the greatest English poem.

CHAPTER IX

Samson Agonistes ll. 60–62, verse tragedy by John Milton, telling the story of Samson and Delilah.

CHAPTER X

"To Laura W——, Two Years of Age" ll. 25–28 by Nathaniel Parker Willis (American 1806–67), magazine editor and highly popular writer of poetry, sketches, and travel pieces.

CHAPTER XI

"Dartmoor" ll. 231–32 by Felicia Dorothea Browne Hemans (English 1793–1835), very popular poet usually called Mrs. Hemans. She published her first book of poetry at age fifteen and put out another volume virtually every year thereafter until her death. She was more popular in the United States than in England. "Her" in the citation refers to Peace.

CHAPTER XII

"Death. The Vision Last" ll. 395–98 in *Visions in Verse for the Entertainment and Instruction of Younger Minds* (1751) by Nathaniel Cotton (English 1707–88), a doctor specializing in mental illness who wrote occasional verse.

CHAPTER XIII

"Albert and Rosalie" ll. 52–55, poem in *Southern Passages and Pictures* (1839), by William Gilmore Simms (American 1806–70). Simms, a South Carolina native, began his career as a poet but became much better known in his own time as a prolific writer of historical fiction.

CHAPTER XIV

"Comus" ll. 410–12, a pastoral drama (1637) by John Milton.

CHAPTER XV

"Philanthes: A Monody" 10.15–18 by Thomas Blacklock (Scottish 1721–91).

CHAPTER XVI

"The stars are mansions built by Nature's hand" ll. 1–3, 1820 poem by William Wordsworth.

Appendix: The Epigraphs

CHAPTER XVII

"Lines to a child on his Voyage to France, to meet his Father" ll. 36–38 by Henry Ware (American 1764–1845) a liberal Congregationalist minister who became instrumental in establishing Unitarianism in the United States. He was a founder of Harvard's Divinity School in 1819. A son of the same name was a Unitarian clergyman; another son, William, was a clergyman and novelist.

CHAPTER XVIII

"The Life of God in the Soul of Man" ll. 19–22 by Richard Henry Dana (American 1787–1879), Massachusetts publisher and journalist, a founder of the prestigious quarterly, *North American Review,* in 1815. His son, Richard Henry Dana, Jr., became famous for his sea narrative, *Two Years before the Mast* (1840).

CHAPTER XIX

"To Miss R——, On Her Attendance upon Her Mother at Buxton" ll. 17–18 by Anna Laetitia Aiken Barbauld (English 1743–1824), a widely published poet also known for volumes of prose for children written with her brother John Aiken.

CHAPTER XX

"She Was a Phantom of Delight" ll. 27–30 by William Wordsworth, published in *Poems* (1807).

CHAPTER XXI

Samson Agonistes l. 1061 by John Milton.

Appendix: The Epigraphs

CHAPTER XXII

Measure for Measure II.i.182 by William Shakespeare (English 1564–1616). Homer, Virgil, Milton, and Shakespeare were the four great writers to nineteenth-century Americans.

CHAPTER XXIII

The Tragedy of Jane Shore, I.i.47–50, 1714 play by Nicholas Rowe (English 1674–1718). His best-known play was *The Fair Penitent* (1703).

CHAPTER XXIV

"My Love" 3 : 3–5 by James Russell Lowell (American 1819–91), influential Massachusetts critic, editor, and poet.

CHAPTER XXV

"Mont Blanc" ll. 49–50, philosophic poem of 1816 by Percy Bysshe Shelley (English 1792–1822), Romantic poet and radical reformer.

CHAPTER XXVI

Lady Griseld Baillie Sect. 53 by Joanna Baillie (Scottish 1762–1851), playwright and poet. Her most successful drama, *The Family Legend,* was produced in 1810.

CHAPTER XXVII

The quotation is unidentified; the author is Caroline Howard Gilman (American 1794–1888), editor of children's magazines and writer of prose and poetry.

Appendix: The Epigraphs

CHAPTER XXVIII

"Irene" ll. 13–15 by James Russell Lowell.

CHAPTER XXIX

"The Grove" ii: 264–65 from *The Search after Happiness: A Pastoral Drama for Young Ladies* by Hannah More (English 1745–1833), who (along with her sisters) ran a girls' boarding school. She wrote a great many didactic works for her students. The novel *Coelebs in Search of a Wife* (1809) was particularly well known, along with *Thoughts on the Importance of Manners of the Great* (1788).

CHAPTER XXX

"I Would Never Kneel" ll. 5–6 by Sarah Louisa P. Smith (American 1811–32).

CHAPTER XXXI

The New Timon: A Romance of London 3.3.155–56, long satirical poem published anonymously in 1846, by the prolific, popular, and controversial author, Edward George Earle Bulwer-Lytton (English 1803–73). His best-known works were two novels, *Pelham: or the Adventures of a Gentleman* (1828), and *The Last Days of Pompeii* (1834).

CHAPTER XXXII

Ivanhoe by Sir Walter Scott (Scottish 1771–1832), poet and antiquarian whose 1814 novel *Waverley* and its successors made the novel the most popular literary genre in English. As one American reviewer wrote in 1823, "A Waverley novel once or twice a year has grown into such a second nature of our intellectual constitutions, that the rising generation must be at a loss to know what their elder brothers and sisters talked about, before such things existed."

Appendix: The Epigraphs

CHAPTER XXXIII

"Sensibility: An Epistle to the Honourable Mrs. Boscawen" by Hannah More.

CHAPTER XXXIV

"The Excursion" 3.453, long poem of 1814 by William Wordsworth.

CHAPTER XXXV

"The Widow of Crescentius" 2.155–58, 161–64 from *Tales and Historic Scenes* by Felicia Hemans.

CHAPTER XXXVI

The New Timon 4.2.255–58.

CHAPTER XXXVII

"Florio: A Tale for Fine Gentlemen and Fine Ladies" 1.382–83 by Hannah More.

CHAPTER XXXVIII

"The Abencerrage" 2.241–42 from *Tales and Historic Scenes* by Felicia Hemans.

CHAPTER XXXIX

The New Timon 3.3.328–29.

Appendix: The Epigraphs

CHAPTER XL

"Sir Eldred of the Bower. A Legendary Tale" 2.101–08 by Hannah More.

CHAPTER XLI

The Curse of Kehama 14.13.4–8, long poem (1810), by Robert Southey (English 1774–1843), prolific poet and essayist associated with William Wordsworth and Samuel Taylor Coleridge, and in his own day more popular than they were.

CHAPTER XLII

"Death. The Vision Last" ll. 431–44 from *Visions in Verse* by Nathaniel Cotton.

CHAPTER XLIII

Paradise Regained 3.44–46, epic sequel to *Paradise Lost* by John Milton. (See note for Chapter 8.)

CHAPTER XLIV

Paradise Regained 4.531–33.

CHAPTER XLV

The Vespers of Palermo v.iii.53–56 by Felicia Hemans.

CHAPTER XLVI

The Forest Sanctuary 1.64.1–2 by Felicia Hemans.

Appendix: The Epigraphs

CHAPTER XLVII

Prometheus Bound, Translated from the Greek of Aeschylus ll. 681–86, 1833 work of Elizabeth Barrett Browning (English 1806–61), the most important woman poet of her day; her major poem, *Aurora Leigh,* was not published until 1857.

CHAPTER XLVIII

"O'Connor's Child" ll. 27–30 by Felicia Hemans.

CHAPTER XLIX

The Forest Sanctuary 1.60.7–9.

CHAPTER L

Anonymous and unidentified.

433

EXPLANATORY NOTES

CHAPTER I

1. Street lights at this time were oil lamps, lit with a torch. By the end of *The Lamplighter,* oil lamps have been replaced by gaslight. There are other references to urban change in the novel; the multi-apartment tenement in which Trueman Flint lives at the novel's opening, for example, originally the home of well-to-do people, is later torn down to make way for offices and warehouses.

CHAPTER V

1. An apartment in nineteenth-century parlance could be synonymous with a room; it is defined as any living space with its own outdoor entrance or with a door leading to an outside hallway. Later in the novel, Gertrude's boardinghouse room is also called an apartment, as is Emily's room in the Grahams' suburban home.

CHAPTER VI

1. Trueman brings Gerty a small plaster statue of a praying child. Samuel, whose story is told in books of the Old Testament (1 and 2 Samuel), was dedicated in childhood by his mother to God's service. He became a popular symbol for a devout child. When God called him, he answered "Here am I" (1 Sam. 3), words that are echoed in the chapter.

2. *Furren* is dialect for foreign. In only a few places in *The Lamplighter* is the presence of an immigrant population in Boston noted.

CHAPTER XIV

1. An employment agency.

Explanatory Notes

CHAPTER XX

1. Until well into the twentieth century, all but the poorest people employed domestic servants. Immigrant populations provided much of the pool for this kind of work, despite the potential for cultural conflict. A massive immigration of Irish people into the United States—Catholic Irish, as opposed to the long-settled Protestant Scotch-Irish—began during the 1840s.

CHAPTER XXII

1. *Letters Written in the Interior of Cuba* by Abiel Abbot (1770–1828) published in Boston the year after Abbot's death by Bowles and Dearborn (1829), and re-issued in 1850 by a New York publisher. The Harvard-educated Abbot was active in the establishment of the Unitarian Church in Massachusetts.

A typical southern tour at this time would have meant visiting New Orleans, parts of Florida, and Cuba.

CHAPTER XXV

1. Dialect for widow.
2. Gethsemane, near the foot of the Mount of Olives, is the scene of the agony and betrayal of Jesus. In the New Testament (Mark 14:36) knowing that he will be betrayed, Jesus prays to God: "not what I will, but what thou wilt."

CHAPTER XXVI

1. This would have been a good salary for the time, especially for a woman, and is specified as evidence of Gertrude's success in achieving independence and respectability.

Explanatory Notes

CHAPTER XXIX

1. Since the Latin word for peace is *pace,* it is inscribed on many tombstones. Miss Pace's mistakenly thinking that the reference is to her own name is the source of the joke.

CHAPTER XXXIV

1. A first-class, well-established (and hence relatively old-fashioned) hotel at Saratoga Springs, which was the most fashionable resort in New York State at the time (in fact, of the entire northeastern region of the country). It is still an important vacation spot. Located a few miles inland west of the Hudson River about 150 miles north of New York City, Saratoga achieved its status on account of its mineral springs with supposed curative powers.

The journey taken by Gertrude, Emily, and the Jeremys begins and ends with a boat trip from New York City up the Hudson River, through Catskill Mountain scenery. On the way north, they stop at various major scenic views. The Hudson River School of painting, which focused on this scenery and attached ideal and spiritual meanings to it, was at its height in the 1850s. Gertrude's susceptibility to the influence of landscape is a part of her character which, previously, has been demonstrated only by her appreciation for sunsets and night skies; here Cummins can show it more fully. It was a romantic convention to situate important emotional events in spectacular natural settings.

CHAPTER XL

1. Malaria.